WRISTWATCH A

2016

THE CATALOG

of

PRODUCERS, PRICES, MODELS,

and

SPECIFICATIONS

BY PETER BRAUN

WITH MARTON RADKAI

ABBEVILLE PRESS PUBLISHERS

New York London

Our quest for perfection.

Senator Chronograph

www.glashuette-original.com

Glashütte
ORIGINAL

German Watchmaking Art since *1845*.

Letter to the Readers

Dear Reader, one of the great fascinations—or ironies—of mechanical watches is the fact that they are instruments rooted in a solidly Newtonian paradigm, yet continue to thrive in a frenzied, globalized, quantum world dominated by seemingly haphazard forces pulling and pushing in all directions. Unlike many other products or natural resources, like oil or steel, watches are luxury items. As such, they are subject to the whims of consumers who need to be able to pay at times considerable sums for some very fine examples of micromechanical engineering. Those consumers, from the UHNWI to the average hardworking Jane or Joe, are often like high-powered antennae picking up the mood of the markets: A few clouds, a passing storm, a clap of thunder, or the squeak of a floorboard in the neighboring room, and attention may shift to safer investments. And the industry acts and reacts accordingly.

Consider the economic uncertainty of recent years. China continues to offer opportunity, but the slowdown in the economy there and the ongoing struggle against corruption, with bribes often paid in luxury watches, put a damper on that market. Latin America hasn't been performing as well as some hoped for either. On the upside is the continuing economic recovery of the United States and the concomitant firming up of the dollar, which has invigorated the American consumers' appetites for fine watches and ensured that components from Switzerland are not overpriced. The UK market, too, has become bullish, though the uptick is fairly limited and whether it will last is anyone's guess.

In the face of these unpredictable signs, many companies have sought refuge in groups that have the wherewithal to support development and where synergies and economies of scale are also possible. A sign of the times, no doubt, is Ulysse Nardin joining Kering, and Richemont building a giant campus in Meyrin next to Geneva where it can indulge in all the grand strategies latter-day business gurus like to apply.

Jean-Daniel Pasche, president of the Federation of the Swiss Watch Industry, says the Swiss industry is confident about 2015, even in the face of an unpredictable economy and the notoriously strong Swiss franc, which remains a haven currency for those with cash to park. But he points out a few uncomfortable details in the latest figures (March 2015): "There are differences among the companies. We note that the smaller brands and the suppliers are most affected, some are even struggling."

The reason does not lie in poor quality. What they often lack is sufficient funding for advertising and spectacular public events or major sponsorships, and hence the attention of the blogosphere. And that is one of the editorial goals of *Wristwatch Annual*: namely, to offer a bird's-eye view of the industry as a whole and give space

Slim d'Hermès
watch in
rose gold,
Manufacture
H1950
ultra-thin
movement.

SLIM D'HERMÈS, PURITY IN MOTION.

HERMÈS
PARIS

1-800-441-4488
Hermes.com

to some of those smaller brands. On page 12, for instance, Elizabeth Doerr casts her fine-mesh net into the pool of independents, a segment that does enormous creative work and literally drives the industry into the future. On page 24, I investigate some of the masters and mavericks of the business, this year including crazy clocks, a brand revival, and a few solo artists who do outstanding work . . .

For this edition's technical insight, watchmaker Bill Yao (Mk II) looks at shock absorbers in watches and the ingenious way in which some brands have solved the problem of protecting movements from impact on page 44. *Wristwatch Annual* is looking deeper into watchmaking as well this year with the launch of a new series on outstanding personalities to highlight insights into the almost spiritual depth of watchmaking. The 2016 spotlight is on Jean-Marc Wiederrecht, founder of Agenhor and the man behind many iconic pieces. Read more about him on page 32.

As for our A to Z section, it features a number of new members including several smaller, independent brands, like C. H. Wolf from Glashütte, Manufacture Royale and Pierre DeRoche from Switzerland, Konstantin Chaykin from Russia. Two well-worn names have made it to these pages as well, both on the merit of outstanding collections: Van Cleef & Arpels and Fabergé, which joined brands such as Hermès, having quite cleverly combined technique with the notion of poetry and design artistry.

Before closing, a word about the iWatch, which has been causing headaches in some circles and giving journalists and bloggers a good reason to post and publish many column inches. Several brands, such as Alpina, Frédérique Constant, Montblanc, and even in a minor way Bulgari, have come up with "smart" solutions of their own. Maybe next year I will eat these words, but the iWatch is, for some, cool, geeky, funny, fun—and disposable; it's a bit of a gimmick

and a consumer item that will be wiped away by the next generation or a fried chip. A well-made mechanical watch, however, is beautiful over and over again, plus it will survive most cars, or the owner for that matter. We are talking about apples and oranges.

Thanks go to Peter Braun, for his preparation of the German edition, and the intrepid Ashley Benning, for proofing the copy quickly and expertly, catching errors and tightening rambling thoughts. And my deepest gratitude goes to all the people at the brands who take the time to check prices and information while respecting our editorial independence. Any comments or suggestions are welcome, as they will help us improve the book next year.

As always, bear in mind that the prices given in these pages are subject to change.

Enjoy reading.

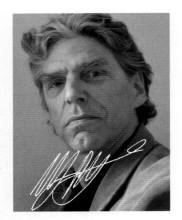

Marton Radkai

Bell & Ross
TIME INSTRUMENTS

BR-X1 THE HYPERSONIC CHRONOGRAPH

The BR-X1 is the perfect synthesis of Bell & Ross's expertise in the world of aviation watches and master watchmaking: an instrument with an innovative design, produced in a limited edition of only 250 pieces. Lightweight and resistant, the grade 5 titanium case of the BR-X1 is protected by a high-tech ceramic bezel with a rubber strap. Ergonomic and innovative, the push buttons allow the chronograph functions to be used easily and efficiently. Sophisticated and reliable, the skeleton chronograph movement of the BR-X1 is truly exceptional and combines haute horlogerie finishes with extreme lightness.

Bell & Ross Inc. +1.888.307.7887 | www.bellross.com | Download the BR SCAN app to reveal exclusive content ⊛

Father and son Preziuso: three resonating tourbillons.

The Independent Scene 2015

Elizabeth Doerr

The world of independent watchmakers continued to be a hotbed of activity in 2015. But it was probably busiest within the AHCI, which turned thirty last year. The celebrations kicked off at Baselworld with a gala dinner and the group's inaugural Young Watchmakers competition sponsored by F.P. Journe, which rewards the efforts of upcoming watchmakers.

AHCI member **Antoine Preziuso** had gone quiet of late, and now we know why: He spent the last three years hunkering down with his son Florian to develop a movement. The duo has christened their triple tourbillon timepiece housed in a two-tone red gold and titanium case **The Tourbillon of Tourbillons**. This is not just another triple-axis tourbillon, but rather three separate tourbillons connected by a triple planetary differential placed on a revolving plate embedded within the manually wound movement that beats at a frequency of 21,600 vph (3 Hz). Named Caliber AFP-TTR-3X, this double-barreled movement boasting a generous power reserve of forty-eight hours was the subject of three international patents. The object of three tourbillons connected by a differential, of course, is greater precision.

The design of the 45 x 14 mm case is very masculine with its forty-five individual components, including twenty-four "power screws" holding the titanium bezel, red gold columns on the side of the case, movable red gold lugs, and an intriguing two-tone crown engraved with the initials "AFP" (for "Antoine Florian Preziuso"). Despite the sheer magnitude of the visuals of this timepiece, it is still the choreography of three tourbillons performing their mechanical ballet in perfect sync on the dial that is the most compelling element.

WORLDLY TIME

Another anniversary of sorts was celebrated by **Svend Andersen**. He paid homage to twenty-five years of the world timer he created in commemoration of Louis Cottier's original 1950s patent with his new **Tempus Terrae**, the fifth edition of his world time watch.

Though every Svend Andersen watch can be personalized, the Danish watchmaker living in Geneva is planning seventy-five pieces: twenty-five each in yellow, red, and white gold cases. One element that collectors appreciate in Andersen's arsenal of specialties is the hand-guilloché Blue-Gold he uses on the dial and rotor. This comprises 21-karat gold with added iron elements. Once heated, it turns blue, with the hue depending on the duration of the heating. Every BlueGold dial and rotor thus has a unique color. The Tempus Terrae is powered by a historical automatic AS movement modified by Andersen Genève with an added world time module.

MAGICAL MOMENTS

All the numerals on **Ludovic Ballouard**'s second timepiece, **Half Time**, are in fact illegible, because they are cut in half—except the one showing the current hour. The illusion is seamless as the numerals appear to be on one solid plane with the rest of the dial, and thus immobile. In reality—and visible only with very close inspection—they are painted across two black disks which rotate forward when the retrograde minute hand has reached the numeral 60 and makes its lightning-quick leap back to the beginning. At which point, one disk rotates forward and the other backward, and the two puzzle halves fit together at 12 o'clock to provide one solid, full Roman numeral depicting the current hour.

Housed in a 41 mm case of platinum or 18-karat red gold, the playful Half Time is available only in a 300-piece limited edition which was conceived, designed, and completely produced by the watchmaker, who at times seems to double as a magician. The unconventional, gold-plated, brass, manually wound movement boasts thirty hours of power reserve. It is a simple device in its essence, yet complex, as necessitated by the illusion it has to drive.

Ballouard, a tall man with large hands that belie his chosen craft, moved to Geneva in 1998 to work with Franck Muller. He makes no more than fifty watches per year in his workshop just outside the city. He is also a fan of model airplanes.

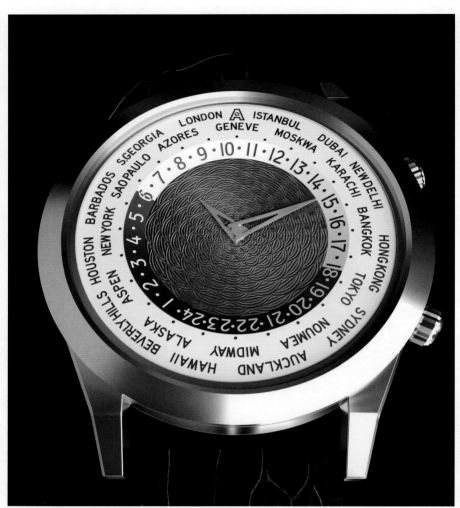

BlueGold for the blue planet, by Svend Andersen.

Ballouard halves time and puts it back together when needed.

[PRIMED]

Built in the USA

Mk II FULCRUM

In our continuing pursuit of perfection we are pleased to offer the Mk II Fulcrum. The successor to the Mk II LRRP, the Fulcrum features a new case with vintage-styled high-domed sapphire crystal and our new Lume-brik dial markers. Each timepiece is driven by a high-grade Swiss Made automatic movement and hand assembled and tested in the USA.

IRISH EYES

The soul of the 43 mm white or rose gold **Tuscar** resides within the **McGonigle** brothers and their hometown of Athlone, Ireland. The design and feel of this piece are entirely Emerald Isle: The asymmetrical crown is marked by characters from the early medieval Ogham alphabet which formed the basis of the early Irish language, and the quasi-three-quarter plate that serves as the base plate for the manual winding Caliber McG01 features hand-engraved, hand-inked details stating the name of the piece and where it was made. The McG01 is the debut movement for the McGonigle brothers. They collaborated with technical designer Alberto Papi to produce it. Watch for a new introduction from this watchmaker duo some time in the next twelve months.

SPANISH EYES

Pita Barcelona introduced the new **Steam** wristwatch in a sleek bronze aluminum case. "We have designed and manufactured every element of the watch," self-taught AHCI member Anecito Pita and his son Daniel explain. "We acquired a new CNC machine to be able to create all the parts in hard metals; this bronze aluminum is 60 percent more scratch-resistant than standard bronze alloys." The two Spanish wizards went on to explain that they also chose a special oleophobic treatment for the strap, which makes the crocodile leather repel sweat or water. Not a bad idea for a watch that is meant to be worn in water.

This watch, water-resistant to 2,000 meters (200 atm), naturally includes Pita's two patents: the TSM (time setting mechanism) and RT (remote transmission), which allow the time to be set in a watertight case, meaning no holes, gaskets, or helium valves are needed. Since the introduction of the two systems in 2009 with the Oceana, there have been no returns or servicing needed for water entry issues.

John and Stephen McGonigle tap their Irish roots for inspiration.

Father and son team Anecito and Daniel continue manufacturing crownless watches that can go anywhere.

Andreas Strehler's Papillon d'Or and the mysterious hands.

THE ESOTERICIST

Andreas Strehler's 2015 introduction is a redux of the watchmaker's recent past. The **Papillon d'Or** picks up where Strehler's original Papillon left off—but with mysterious hands driven by gear wheels made of sapphire crystal. Viewed from the front of the watch, the wheels are hardly noticeable; only upon rotation of the case do their reflections become discernible. This watch is characterized by its large 18-karat gold bridge shaped like a butterfly. A power reserve indication is visible on the back upon the balance cock.

On another note, Strehler has come out with a book to commemorate his twenty years in business called *20 Years of Independence*. The tome traces Strehler's life, right from his tender beginnings as a child growing up near Winterthur, Switzerland (where he declared that he wanted to become a baker) all the way to the very finely finished and cleverly engineered timepieces his workshop produces today.

EXTRAMURAL ACTIVITIES

Looking outside the AHCI, the outstanding engraver **Kees Engelbarts** loves his skeletonized watches, as they do a great deal to showcase his art form. "I wanted to make another kind of skeleton watch," he says about his latest creation called **Tourbillon Organic Skeleton**. "Most skeleton watches are, as you know, very symmetrical. My plan was to make a skeleton watch without a drawing or a plan before starting by just taking away material that's not needed from the base plate and bridges."

Like a sculpture, it starts out very roughly; only little by little does he get to the final shapes in a long and delicate process, as the last thing he wants is to bend or deform any of the bridges of the movement that starts out as a Technotime 791. The result is a weird and wonderful contrast between the technical elements (wheels, pinions, tourbillon, barrels, steel parts) and the imaginatively shaped base plate and bridges, which he terms "organic."

A watch by Engelbarts would hardly be a watch by Engelbarts without his signature *mokumé gane* elements. Here the etched red gold crown is crafted from *shakudo mokumé gane*, while the hands were hand-

ALTHOUGH HE HAS REACHED SUMMIT AFTER SUMMIT, HE'S STILL CHASING HIS PEAK.

When standing at its base, the rock looms large. The world's premier free-solo climber shows respect by studying its curves and crevices, its sediment and smoothness. It's the only way to create new routes to the top. Without ropes or aids, he proves that perseverance and confidence are the drivers to break records. To gain new perspectives. To set one's sights on future summits. To be Alex Honnold.

TO BE YOURSELF

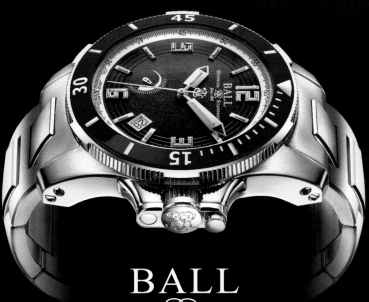

BALL
OFFICIAL ℞℞ STANDARD
Since 1891
Accuracy under adverse conditions

ENGINEER HYDROCARBON HUNLEY

Revolutionary micro gas lights
Amortiser® patented anti-shock system
7,500 Gs shock resistance
4,800 A/m anti-magnetic
200 m / 650 ft water resistance

www.ballwatch.com

Tel. 727-896-4278

Kees Engelbarts skeletonizes his Tourbillon Organic Skeleton spontaneously as he goes along.

Franc Vila's chemistry background produced the very complex platinum Inaccessible Tourbillon Répétition Minute.

made from twisted and etched *mokumé gane* of red gold and *shakudo*.

In 2015 **Laurent Ferrier** celebrated its fifth year of existence by releasing a full set of the boutique brand's timepieces to date in rose gold cases combined with chocolate dials whose markers are painted in "white chocolate" (white gold). This naturally includes the 41 mm **Galet Micro-Rotor**, which debuted in 2011. The harmonious construction and technical performance of its Caliber FBN 229.01 stem from a global approach to each of the movement parts in order to optimize energy management, which ultimately improves user-friendliness thanks to more efficient winding. Since it was founded, Laurent Ferrier has been developing movements endowed with a range of atypical and visually pleasing technical attributes. This microrotor caliber continues to cultivate this concept.

Like the design of Ferrier's whole watch, the composition of the movement is a subtle homage to observatory chronometers of the nineteenth century. Eminently observable to the trained eye is the incredible perfection in finishing: meticulously hand-applied *côtes de Genève* and beveling of the German silver plate and bridge edges. The arrangement of the bridges allows the observer to clearly see the very classically designed winding system, for example. The anniversary set also includes the Galet Traveller (originally introduced in 2013), the Lady F (from 2014), and the Galet Classic Tourbillon.

PRECIOUS VOICE

Franc Vila's complicated **Inaccessible Tourbillon Répétition Minute** is housed in a heavy platinum version of this uniquely spirited case—which is extremely unusual because repeating wristwatches are rarely, if ever, encased in platinum as the dense precious metal tends to dampen the sound of the gongs. However, Spanish-born Vila has a trick up his sleeve: In addition to a degree in arts (useful for designing watches and cases), he also boasts training in chemistry, which has provided him with a thorough knowledge of materials. Many years' experience in the watch industry have solidified his knowledge, enabling Vila to solve the "platinum-repeating problem" by combining alloys of varying density, both in the case and the components that relate to the sound diffusion of the gongs.

But that's not what most observers will focus on; it is, of course, the cutaway in the dial at 6 o'clock providing an unimpeded view of the flying tourbillon that primarily attracts the eye. Another original element of this timepiece is that the minute repeater is not wound by a traditional slide on the side of the case, but instead by rotating the platinum alloy bezel. Each one of these unique timepieces is powered by hand-wound Caliber FV No.3 comprising 315 components and boasting a ninety-hour power reserve.

Elizabeth Doerr is a freelance journalist specializing in watches and was senior editor of Wristwatch Annual *until the 2010 edition. She is now the editor in chief of Quill & Pad, an online magazine that "keeps a watch on time" (http://quillandpad.com).*

TAKE OFF!

AIRMAN BASE 22 BI-COLOR - A new look for the iconic Airman.
Displays 3 time zones and date in a 42mm stainless steel case
powered by the GL 293 automatic movement. Also vailable in a
Purist 24H display version.
GLYCINE-WATCH.CH

Cellini Jewelers

Why do we love watches?

With two locations in the heart of New York City, Cellini continues to build upon its reputation by offering an unparalleled collection of the world's best timepieces, rare and exotic jewelry, and unsurpassed personal service.

Whether you're a seasoned collector or thinking about purchasing your first fine timepiece, Cellini Jewelers will tempt you with a carefully curated collection of watches from the world's finest brands.

Widely regarded as an horological tastemaker for nearly 40 years, Cellini's flair for breaking brands in America is legendary. Both of its Manhattan boutiques were early champions of firms like A. Lange & Söhne, Greubel Forsey,

Franck Muller, and Hublot long before their popularity soared among collectors. Today the independent jeweler continues to be an influential launching pad for brands like De Bethune, HYT, and Ludovic Ballouard.

Last year, Cellini added no less than four brands: Arnold & Son, Clerc, Urwerk, and Waltham. The latter is the extraordinary American brand that helped revolutionize the watch industry in the nineteenth century. Re-launched in 2014, Waltham's Swiss-made timepieces are sporty interpretations of the brand's historic aeronautical clocks, including the cockpit timekeeper that accompanied Charles Lindbergh as he completed the first non-stop transatlantic flight in 1927.

For its modern re-launch, Waltham unveiled the Aeronaval collection, which consists of three models: Waltham XA, Waltham CDI, and Waltham ETC. "The history of Waltham is truly incredible and not really well known. I was blown away when I started learning more about what they've done and where they've been—from its precise railroad pocket watches to its expeditions to the poles," says Cellini President Leon Adams.

The Waltham XA takes it design cues from the clock Charles Lindbergh used in the Spirit of St. Louis.

Blackened 18-karat gold provides contrast for the brilliant white diamonds in this bracelet.

Whether the brand is just starting out like Waltham, or an instantly recognizable icon like Jaeger-LeCoultre, Adams considers it a point of pride to carry a company's entire collection. That incredible depth creates an unparalleled experience that resonates deeply with people who are passionate about watches. What Cellini does best, Adams says, is use that range to help someone find the *right* watch. He explains, "If you like a particular complication or style, we line up models from several brands so you can weigh your options and judge for yourself what looks and feels right. You can't find that anywhere else, especially at a mono-brand boutique."

SPARKLING PERSONALITY

But Cellini is known for more than just watches. Its boutiques are also ranked among Manhattan's finest jewelers. The company's impeccably high standards are reflected in everything from unrivaled selection and superior quality to the attentive experts who are ready to guide you through Cellini's glamorous universe.

From classic to contemporary, and subtle to stunning, the jewelry at Cellini encompasses a wide range of styles. Within this exquisite exhibition of glittering luxury, you'll find diamonds in every hue and impressive strands of pearls, as well as magnificent emeralds, rubies, and sapphires in one-of-a-kind, handmade settings. "We strive to create a world where the only limit is your imagination," Adams says.

To stay ahead of changing tastes, the collection evolves constantly, adding rare and unique pieces from around the world. For instance, as the popularity of black gold has skyrocketed, Cellini has stayed at the forefront by seeking out the most innovative designs. The wide cuff bracelet featured here underscores black gold's inexhaustible versatility.

Cellini also introduced a range of jewelry creations that provide a colorful counterpoint to black gold's dark beauty. Each piece plays with perception by using transparent gemstones to add striking depth to the intricate patterns below. Built from the bottom up, most of the elaborate metalwork and gem setting is topped by faceted quartz, amethyst, or topaz for a look that is guaranteed to spark its share of conversations.

Whether it's fine jewelry or collectible timepieces, Cellini is the place to see what's next.

Cellini is an authorized retailer for A. Lange & Söhne, Arnold & Son, Audemars Piguet, Bell & Ross, Bulgari, Cartier, Chopard, Clerc, De Bethune, Franck Muller, Girard-Perregaux, Giuliano Mazzuoli, Greubel Forsey, H. Moser & Cie, Hublot, HYT, IWC, Jaeger-LeCoultre, Ludovic Ballouard, Maîtres du Temps, Parmigiani Fleurier, Piaget, Richard Mille, Roger Dubuis, Ulysse Nardin, Urwerk, Vacheron Constantin, Waltham, and Zenith.

Faceted blue topaz earring accompanied by aquamarines and blue and black sapphires, set in 18-karat white and black gold.

Cellini's boutique on Madison Avenue was established in 1987 at the epicenter of the world's most elite shopping district.

STORE LOCATIONS

Hotel Waldorf-Astoria
301 Park Avenue at 50th Street
New York, NY 10022
212-751-9824

509 Madison Avenue at 53rd Street
New York, NY 10022
212-888-0505

800-CELLINI
CelliniJewelers.com

Storytellers

Marton Radkai

Some of the finest spices grow in the wild. And some of the most unusual watches are created by amateurs, genius hermits, or seasoned veterans slipping outside their traditional box. And their products, for lack of a better word, often show that there is no end to creativity.

Jean-Claude Biver, that indomitable booster of high-end watchmaking, former CEO of Hublot, and now at TAG Heuer, never tires of explaining that his love of fine watches originated in his boyish fascination with steam engines. The extraordinarily precise ballet of the pistons, levers, and cams, the strange motion of the eccentric, the multidimensional world of gears and pivots all conspiring to channel raw power into orderly motion does have a hypnotic effect on many people, in the same way the workings of the universe or a superb poem can transfix the mind.

MACHINES AND TIME

Miki Eleta and **Marc Jenni** have shortened the path between majestic contraptions and the watch. Eleta, born in 1950 in Višegrad (Bosnia & Herzegovina) but now at home in Switzerland, is a kinetic artist who specializes in extraordinary large clocks. The **Time Burner** represents his first foray into wristwatches while also serving as a nostalgic tribute to his childhood. While the visuals of the Timeburner are inspired in general by Eleta's love for mechanics, forces, and motion, the specific elements originate in recreating the soul—not the actual features—of a 1950 BMW motorcycle.

Eleta's sense of design together with Jenni's watchmaking expertise is simply irresistible for fans of big and small mechanics alike: Like an engine converting the chemical energy of gas into the mechanical energy

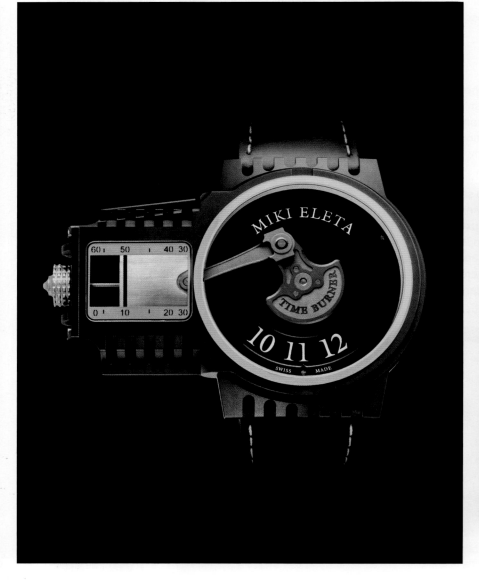

Miki Eleta and his old BMW (above) that inspired the Time Burner (left), a collaboration with watchmaker Marc Jenni.

Gas exploration on the dial of the Louis Moinet Derrick Gaz.

Seventies codes, timeless machine: the Angelus U10 Tourbillon Lumière.

of motion, this cool watch transforms spark plug energy (winding the crown) into motion along a nonlinear time scale. The piston's trajectory up and down the cylinder indicates the minutes on two scales: 0 to 30 minutes one way, and 30 to 60 the other. The piston ring is the reference point.

In some ways, **Louis Moinet** did the same when it released its very high-end **Derrick Tourbillon** a few years back (limited edition). The dial features, rather incongruously, an oil pump and a derrick (as an aside, Ulysse Nardin came up with a similar image recently). The clash of such large, industrial mechanics on a delicate watch dial in a case of precious metal was both blatant yet attractive in a Beauty and the Beast sort of way. In fact, what the creators at Moinet had done was build a classic automaton, a steampunk-inspired jacquemart perfectly in tune with watchmaking traditions. In 2015, they continued down the path of energy exploration with the **Derrick Gaz**, which, as the name suggests, shows a gas-drilling scene with an endless screw exploring the earth under a derrick, guiding the gas through piping, which is the bridge holding the tourbillon in place, to a valve that turns when the watch is wound. A manometer dis-

plays the power reserve, and finally, at the right side of the dial stands the gas tank of stainless steel.

ASCETO-PUNK

While the watches above celebrate their kinship with mechanics in general, other watches tell a story about themselves and their native industry. The Angelus **U10 Tourbillon Lumière** is just such a timepiece. It boasts complications, but without visible complexity. Instead, it imposes order on the mechanics so as to exhibit them better.

Angelus? The name will be familiar to buffs of classic wristwatches, because it was one of those grand old brands scuttled by the quartz crisis and the collapse of the dollar in the 1970s. Its last hurrah was a costly minute repeater built in partnership with Dubois Dépraz, now a much coveted collector's item.

The money behind the Angelus revival appears to come from movement maker La Joux-Perret and Arnold & Son, whose designer Sebastien Chaulmontet authored the Lumière. This good name, meaning light, is what the watch strives for. Its most visible element is a perfect, 16.25 mm tourbillon spinning in a separate window where

it can be seen from all sides, including laterally. The watch itself runs on an in-house manually wound movement with a dignified 18,000 vph rhythm and a double spring barrel delivering about ninety hours of power reserve. It features deadbeat seconds—a nod to the quartz watches that spelled the end of the original Angelus or to an Arnold specialty?—and a linear power reserve indicator in the side of the case. This new Angelus was inspired by travel alarm clocks the brand made in its heyday, and indeed, the rectangular format, the line markers, the slightly forced elements of modernism do recall the 1970s.

MANIACAL MECHANICS

Many watchmakers, especially the passionate ones without shareholders, have the liberty to tread a fine line between engineering art and artistic engineering. They do not need to represent anything as such; the beauty of the mechanics suffices on its own, and the practical use comes as a byproduct. So here is a hypothetical: What if M. C. Escher had been a watchmaker? The creator of "impossible realities," who came from an engineering family and was fond of mathematics, has a horological twin in Dan-

ESSENTIAL GEAR.

P-38 Lightning™ Valjoux Chronograph No. 9461: 44 mm, brushed stainless steel case, screw down crown & case back, antireflective sapphire crystal, fixed stainless steel bezel with an aluminum tachymeter top ring, water resistant to 200 meters, black leather strap with steel signature buckle, and Luminox self-powered illumination. Swiss Made.

A tribute to Lockheed Martin's legendary twin-boomed WWII Fighter Plane.

The Luminox P-38 Lightning™ Series is part of the **LOCKHEED MARTIN** Collection.

www.luminox.com

facebook.com/Luminox f

Constant Glow for up to 25 Years.

iel Nebel, a solo watchmaker from northern Switzerland, hence his watches named **Nord Zeitmaschinen**, meaning north time machines.

Nebel, a certified engineer, has achieved a modicum of success, but his output is limited by necessity. He has a day job to finance his passion for watchmaking. He is also a bit of a recluse, but what can one expect from a watchmaker who creates very complex systems (not just complications) and does everything by himself, except producing the base movement, the sapphire crystal, and the straps. Apparently, he even manufactured the CNC machines he works with.

The Zeitmaschine collections do not indicate time in a circular, linear, or retrograde manner. The bold minute hands travel along arcs, which in turn creates very special engineering challenges. His earlier watch, the **Variocurve**, for instance, shows the minutes on two parallel arcs stretching over the dial. The long skeletonized hand is controlled by two meshed gearwheels that share the task of driving the hand, alternately raising or lowering it. But here is the punch line: As the hand changes levels at the dial's edge, it describes a very tight angle and travels a shorter distance. So the 10-20 and 40-50 segments were put on discs that move

along with the minute hand. This ingenious mechanism creates an outstanding visual ballet. As for the hours, they emerge discreetly on another wheel that peers from beneath the minute plate at about 7 o'clock on a normal watch. Same approach for the date, at 5 o'clock.

The latest Nebel production is called the **Quickindicator**. The construction appears simpler at first glance. The hour disc has moved up to 9 o'clock, the date to 3 o'clock. The minute arcs are in fact circles that spiral psychedelically into one another, so they do not require any assistance from discs in the corner. The minute hand travels on a swirling path that is dizzying to watch when sped up. It is a touch maniacal, but then again, genuine creativity sometimes resides on the border with madness. "If possible, you should use time in a sensible way," Nebel wrote me. "But since that is relative and not always possible, then you should just take time as it comes." In this case, in crazy circles . . .

DREAMS COME TRUE

Art often results when a watchmaker or designer decides to escape from the constraints of his or her trade without losing touch with the craft, as people like Jean-Marc Wiederrecht prove (see page 34).

Long a part of *Wristwatch Annual*'s A-to-Z section, **MB&F** continues to fascinate the watch world with mind-boggling creations by top-drawer watchmakers. The energy behind them is Max Büsser, a man with an unfaltering sense of style and the courage to take a few risks. His **M.A.D. Gallery** in the rue Verdaine in Geneva, with a subsidiary in Taiwan, contains kinetic or static sculptures oftentimes unrelated or only indirectly related to timekeeping: light installations by Frank Buchwald, hair-raising motorcycles by Chicara Nagata, or the "retro-futuristic robots" by Bruno Lefèvre-Brauer, known as +Brauer, whose exhibition in June 2015 was titled "Viva la Robolución!"

Büsser, of course, is a fan of sci-fi, so the two table clocks he presented at Baselworld in 2014 and 2015 are no real surprise. They were designed in-house and executed by L'Epée 1839, a specialist clockmaker in Delémont, Switzerland. The first is the **Starfleet Machine**, an intergalactic spacecraft with a clock under the dome presumably housing the bridge for Captain Kirk or some other hero. Beneath it, two red-tipped cannons move about for a double retrograde seconds display. Another dome with strange markings turns out to be the power reserve: forty days, in fact—enough for some space travel.

Time marches to a different tune on Daniel Nebel's Variocurve.

Horological fantasy turns into an intergalactic table clock, by MB&F.

Max Büsser's Melchior—protector, timekeeper, talking piece.

The 2015 creation is deeply personal, especially, perhaps, because it celebrates the company's tenth anniversary: **Melchior**, a commando robot of sorts, is the friend that Büsser dreamt of having as an only child. The name goes back to a family tradition: The eldest sons of Büssers were called either Melchior or Balthazar for nearly 500 years. Max Büsser's grandfather, however, disliked the tradition and broke with it.

Shiny Melchior, a distant cousin of R2D2, has a face you'll want to have on your side in the battle of life. He is heavily armed, but his heart is in the right place, behind an edgy breastplate made of a jumping hour and a sweep minute wheel. His eyes are the seconds in a double retrograde system that makes them "blink" every 20 seconds. Five serially connected spring barrels deliver

forty days' power reserve indicated on his belly. The clock is run by a classic movement; the escapement is located in his head under a sapphire dome for all to see.

These clocks are stunningly creative and wild, yet ultimately classic timekeepers, no different from any Empire object that might have adorned a mantelpiece in the salon of a *grand bourgeois* in Paris. Only the source of inspiration is different. Because Büsser is not a follower, he is, in his discreet and almost humble way, a leader. His ideas are ingenious and sustainable because they open the future to all sorts of possibilities, even imaginative plagiarism. Not surprisingly, whenever Büsser speaks of creativity, he—a father himself—always comes back to the importance of childhood as the wellspring of all creativity. And creativity, in turn,

is why the independents, the mavericks, and the dissenters of all stripes are so crucial in an industry increasingly governed by brand managers. Melchior is the defender of such children, and he carries on his back his own motto, a quote from author Ursula K. LeGuin: "The creative adult is the child who has survived."

BACK TO EARTH

The gift of childhood is "un*adult*erated" enthusiasm, pun intended. Büsser has shielded his inside the industry with his ability to shape-shift into a serious person. He knows his stuff, he knows how to avoid reefs and where to pick up the next lighthouse signal. Others skim closer to shore with their ideas but still create a small niche for themselves. Take the young gemologist and designer **Thomas Quattrocchi**, the descendant of Italian immigrants to Australia after World War II. His first success was a ring for the Lamborghini Club of Australia, which allowed him then to finance his dream: **Boat Australia**, a collection of hexagonal watches representing Australia that pay homage to his grandparents and all the others who have settled the continent. The dials are always of mother-of-pearl, a Pacific specialty, and their curious geometrical pattern reveals itself on closer inspection to be large interconnected Roman numerals.

Another such character is **Kun-Chi Wu**, the man behind **Sablier**. He dreamed up a watch with a concave crystal and turned it into the "Grand Cru" (Great Vintage). The harmony of the piece lies in the concave crown, the smooth case shaped like a wineglass, the corkscrew seconds hand. Whether it is practical or reasonable is not the foremost idea. Neither is putting peas in your nose or taking apart your dad's Patek Philippe—no fun for dad, but kids find that stuff really exciting.

Kun-Chi Wu's Grand Cru, a watch connected to great wine.

Patriotic duty: Thomas Quattrocchi's Boat Australia.

Advanced winding technology, for your fine watches.

AVANTI Series:
3 | 4 | 6 | 9 | 12 | 24 | 36 | 48

The Master of Time: Jean-Marc Wiederrecht

Marton Radkai

Behind every great watch stands a great watchmaker, a personality who understands watchmaking in four dimensions. Jean-Marc Wiederrecht is one such individual.

In late 2013, Aurélie Picaud, the freshly nominated timepiece manager at Fabergé, received a tough briefing from her boss Robert Benvenuto: The venerable brand, known for its stunning eggs made for the Russian House of Romanov and for lots of *haute joaillerie* since, was going to rebuild and relaunch a watch portfolio. This was not to be a timorous try, but rather a bold push to vie with the big players in the ionosphere of high-end mechanical watches. It was to include high-end women's watches as well. "We wanted a watch that would express the brand's DNA—that is, surprise, discovery," says Picaud. To add pizzazz to the task, she received a fierce deadline: Baselworld 2015, i.e., about fifteen months.

Picaud hit the ground running. Victor Mayer, a former licensee, took on the enamel guilloche dials of the Lady Fabergé core collection, which were given a trusty Vaucher movement. The eye-catching **Summer in the Provence** went to Art&D, an exclusive company located in Geneva. For the women's collection she turned to Jean-Marc Wiederrecht: "I knew Jean-Marc only by reputation, but I was convinced that he was the right guy for our product. In my opinion he is the only watchmaker able to translate emotion and surprise in a technical movement of the highest level."

HALLOWED HALLS

She couldn't have made a better choice. In the pantheon of great watchmaking figures, Wiederrecht occupies one of the highest pedestals. Over the decades, he has collaborated on the creation of numerous icons, including MB&F's mind-boggling **Horological Machines No. 2 and 3**, Harry Winston's **Opus 9**, the **Temps Suspendu** of La Montre Hermès, and a whole series for Van Cleef & Arpels that quickly leavened public and media esteem for the brand. Even the

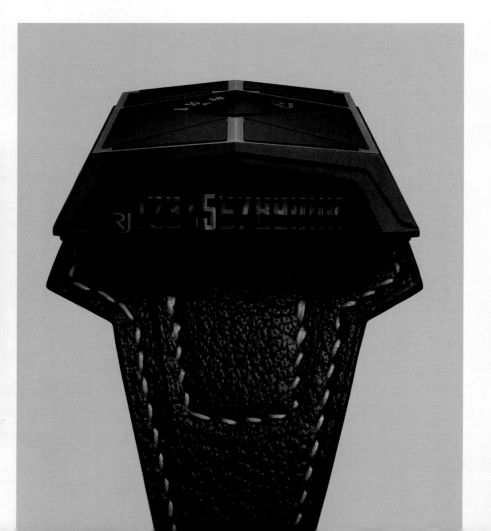

Jean-Marc Wiederrecht, author of many an icon, like Romain Jerome's edgy Spacecraft (r.).

Part Time
2015 Collection

ITAY NOY   Independent Timepiece Maker | www.itay-noy.com | studio@itay-noy.com

Milus flagship triretrograde module was his brainchild, as was the recent Skylab from Romain Jerome. Agenhor, his company, is in fact something of a Santa's workshop for many big brands.

Picaud traveled to Geneva in December 2013 and invited Wiederrecht to a presentation. But like many people devoted to their work and successful to boot, he was busy with other projects. Plus, as a hands-on dyed-in-the-wool watchmaker, he also has a latent aversion to all the bells and whistles produced by an industry dedicated to selling a very emotional product. "My initial feeling was negative," says Wiederrecht with characteristic honesty. "Fabergé had tried to rebuild their watch department several times; now they wanted to become the kings of the industry." Nevertheless, he decided to give the pitch a fair hearing.

However, loath to struggle through Geneva's egregious traffic, he invited her to come to Meyrin, where Agenhor has its facilities. Picaud, armed with her presentation and convictions, went to the master. Within an hour, she had pressed the right buttons, and Wiederrecht was on board. "She understood today's watchmaking; she understood the need to emphasize skill and creativity and get all the way to the top of the horological pyramid in order to be at the height of the brand's name. After all, we still remember the eggs, which were made with the best craftspeople." These are matters that mean a lot to Wiederrecht, who peppers our conversation with critical remarks about brands that fail to focus on the product itself and treat their watchmakers as if they were rowers on a Roman galley.

CREATOR AT WORK

With the preliminaries out of the way, the first task was to determine the design of the new watch, an area that requires the know-how and experience of a consummate watchmaker able to grasp the mechanical and design intricacies in a single thought process. Wiederrecht proposed an idea he had kicked around with journalist and friend Louis Nardin: a watch featuring a silk fan that would display retrograde minutes with the hours situated on a crown moving in the opposite direction to the opening blades. Silk, however, is too thick for a watch, so the idea remained unrealized. Fabergé returned with two ideas: the **Lady Compliquée Winter,** where the fan motif remained quasi untouched, and the stunning **Lady Compliquée Peacock,** with the bird's tail opening to indicate the minutes. The hours would be the same.

Van Cleef & Arpels' Poetic Wishes, complication by Agenhor.

The module that opens the peacock's tail on the Lady Compliquée Peacock by Fabergé.

Task number two was designing the perfect movement to drive the ribbing behind the "feathers." Modifying an existing movement was out of the question for Wiederrecht: "If you want to be right at the top, you need your own movement." It also needed to be integrated, rather than employing a module to drive the peacock's tail. Three feathers would be immobile, while four would open on the quarter-hours. The idea of one blade pulling the other three had to be discarded because it would make the whole unit shaky. "We built a kind of gear-box that ensured that each blade would go at the exact same speed." A clutch mechanism smoothly connects the blades to the four gear wheels superimposed on an arbor. A key component in the mechanism is the play-free engagement gearing, a Wiederrecht patent that has pride of place. The slit teeth offer some elasticity to ensure that they mesh without the slightest play.

The Lady Compliquée models were not only finished on time, but they rapidly became the buzz of Baselworld 2015—in particular the Peacock: a glorious watch,

Agenhor's own play-free gearing for tight meshing.

with a dial inside a 38 mm platinum case set with brilliant-cut diamonds that spill onto the bezel, tsavorites, and greenish Paraiba tourmalines.

PORTRAIT OF THE ARTIST

Authentic artists tend not to brag about it. They see themselves rather as actors in a permanent process of creation. Wiederrecht lives and breathes his craft, and has done so ever since he fell in love with watchmaking as a teenager (see the box). "I spent a lot of time at the workbench and have an intimate relationship with watches," he recalls. "I have made components, sawn, filed, and assembled things. Skeletonizing taught me a great deal about the behavior of materials, and then I started drawing things."

Like many outstanding creators, too, his work is always imbued by a core idea that changes only in form as he has gathered experience. One of his passions is the retrograde function. In 1988, he developed a stunning biretrograde perpetual calendar for Harry Winston, and one of the charming aspects of the Van Cleef & Arpels Heure d'ici & Heure d'ailleurs is undoubtedly the retrograde minute hand that shuttles in a 150° arc between the two hour openings. "Time is cyclical, yes, but it always starts and stops," he points out, "be that by the hour, the day, or the week, which starts on Monday and ends of Sunday. The retrograde function allows for better visualization."

In the wrong hands, this could become just a gimmick repeated ad infinitum to thrill an already captive audience. Wiederrecht always manages to push it a little further: **The Pont des Amoureux** from Van Cleef & Arpels, which was the talk of the SIHH when it was released in 2010, shows a woman (hour retrograde) meeting a man (minute retrograde) on a bridge at noon and midnight. They embrace. On a normal retrograde, that embrace would be very short, but Wiederrecht thought this through and added a hooking system that gives these

Fabergé's finished "Peacock," a complicated ladies' watch to wow the connoisseurs.

Inside Agenhor, assembly of special modules.

Orville Wright taking first flight with brother Wilbur running alongside at Kitty Hawk, North Carolina, 17 December 1903.

Image credit: WSU/planepix.com

A FEW SELECT PEOPLE HAVE BEEN GIVEN PART OF THE WORLD'S FIRST AIRCRAFT. PRESIDENTS, ASTRONAUTS AND ANYONE WITH A BREMONT WRIGHT FLYER.

The Bremont Wright Flyer is a tribute to the Wright Brothers' famous aircraft. It's remarkable to look at. But what makes it even more remarkable is that it features actual material from that very first aircraft. The watch also features another first: our first proprietary movement, the BWC/01. The Wright Flyer is available now in a limited edition. But it's unlikely to be available for long.

Exquisite Timepieces · 4380 Gulfshore Boulevard North, Suite 800, Naples, FL 34103 · T: +1 800 595 5300 · exquisitetimepieces.com

The final romantic story on the Pont des Amoureux (left) and a diagram of the module driving the two lovers (right).

two figures a little time with each other when they do finally meet. After all, the man has to climb the bridge eleven times before reaching his beloved, and the woman has to wait eleven hours before meeting him.

THE KISS PRINCIPLE

Retrogrades and a sense of poetry are not all that distinguishes Wiederrecht's developments. Behind the complex mechanics, the strangely shaped levers that switch functions on and off or control retrogrades, the crown gears that run the retrogrades, there is a purpose, and that is to simplify the user experience: "We are not making watches for watchmakers, we are making them for the end customer," he says, crediting colleague Carole Forestier-Kasapi from Cartier for this realization. "The customers don't really care whether the movement inside is almost impossible to build, they want a beautiful object that will correspond to their wishes."

Thus, the **Heure d'ici & Heure d'ailleurs** looks simple on the outside. Even the name is removed from any reference to mechanics or the science of horology. The dial is pure minimalism: two jumping hours, one retrograde minute track covering a 150° arc. The problem: the inertia of the hour disks would normally make them jump a little farther, so Wiederrecht had to place a braking component behind the disk. This, in turn, meant having to create a special mechanism to ensure smooth functioning. Furthermore, the second time zone can be

adjusted using the crown to avoid crowding the case barrel. Agenhor developed a special clutch that prevents the user from accidentally destroying the movement when setting the second time zone. These are the details that not only make a great watch, but also distinguish a mechanical timepiece from a garden-variety time dispenser.

Another example is the **Opus 9** from the Harry Winston series, which he worked on with Eric Giroux. Here, red garnets on a chain of contrasting white diamonds offer a new type of retrograde hours and minutes. The basic idea is no more complicated than installing a bicycle chain; the devil, however, was in the details—namely ensuring precision and a chain of a very exact length that moves without the slightest shake.

Jean-Marc Wiederrecht and Eric Giroud created the Opus 9 for Harry Winston.

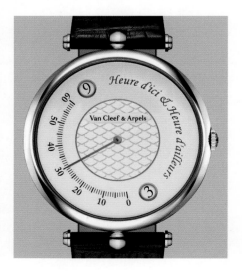

Two jumping hours and a retrograde minute hand: simplicity with complex mechanics inside.

CALLING ON THE MUSE

Inspiration in the frenetic, globalized, electronified, kerosene-driven mind-set of the early twenty-first century has become a rare commodity. For Wiederrecht, however, finding some mental and emotional space is crucial. "All the things I have done have come to me at night, in the dark, or on vacation, by the water or skiing," he says.

When starting a project, he does not take wads of notes; rather, he waits. For the stunning **Le Temps Suspendu** by La Montre Hermès, he spent half a year thinking of a solution. Wanting to "stop time" is essentially a bit platitudinous, he notes, any run-of-the-mill flyback system would do the trick. "I realized that if you stopped the hands and nothing happened, Hermès wouldn't sell a single watch." Then, after a long bull session at a restaurant with then CEO of La Montre Hermès Luc Perramond, he went skiing.

And then there was light, as it were. Maybe it was the subliminal impact of seeing the tips of his skis in the snow that inspired the resulting solution? A pusher would not only *stop* time, but it would place the hour hand at 11:30 and the minute hand just after twelve, *an impossible time on a watch.* Time is parked out of sight and resumes when the user wants it to. Finding this solution required also imagining in that same flash the faint possibility of a technical solution, a meandering lever that could switch the functions behind the dial, without the user having to think too much.

As a result, Wiederrecht's horological solutions are holistic. They break down the barrier between design and execution, between form and function, between complexity and simplicity, even between the masculine and the feminine, if one is to believe Forestier-Kasapi, who described a "female" movement as one that tells a story. "A complex watch has to be at the service of the story the watch is telling," Wiederrecht points out.

LOVING CHRONOS

That the complexities of watchmaking hold fast within the simple, wonderfully integrated designs is in some way a reflection of Wiederrecht himself. He is a calm person, with clear blue eyes, a slightly unruly shock of curly hair, cheeks that show signs of laughter. A month into retirement—or so he says with a knowing grin—he is still youthful, quick-minded, curious, and, of course, immensely knowledgeable about all aspects of his industry. He is also quite critical of a lot of newfangled ideas, like the use of silicium, which means that watches can barely be repaired, and the whole watch business with its noisiness.

Watchmakers need to be perfectionists. No play is allowed. To achieve the finest precision both in mechanics and in that frustratingly asymptotic relationship with the ideal of beauty, a watchmaker has to be self-critical. Wiederrecht often mentions "not being finished"; he speaks of "knowing better the next time." His sense of perfection extends to the Agenhor building, which was completed in 2009 and sits close to Geneva's airport, stranded in an industrial zone like a beautiful yacht relegated to the

Hermès's Le Temps Suspendu stops time in an impossible position.

The complex module behind the simple façade.

RITUALS
OF TIME

Salthora Meta

The new jumping hour
from MeisterSinger

—

www.meistersinger.net

MeisterSinger

cargo port. One of the neighbors will be the huge Richemont campus, once that multi-million-dollar project is complete. As with everything in Wiederrecht's world, the building was conceived down to the last detail for space, light, and a low carbon footprint.

In front is an idyllic garden with a pond populated by fish and a couple of ducks. One warm days, staff members gather there to take a break, chat, and have lunch or snacks. They do not look like Santa's helpers—or even watchmakers in fact. That's because Wiederrecht does not believe in all the white smocks, which make the workers look like lab assistants. "Come on, there's no dust in our cases!" he exclaims, while showing me around. Sauntering through various rooms and workshops, we pass by a few of the prizes he has won or contributed to winning. He barely mentions them. On another wall, however, is a large replica of his play-free gearing.

He does not like to sell himself, obviously. And that is perhaps why there is no Wiederrecht or Agenhor brand. The public relations alone would be too time-consuming. This is a man dedicated to that singular craft of making works of art that pay homage to the passage of time and remind us all how valuable each minute of our existence really is. Among the papers and notes pinned with magnets to a metal board is a Chinese proverb that reads: "The person who says it cannot be done should not interrupt the person doing it." That says it all.

Agenhor's building, conceived down to the last peg for a low carbon footprint.

Running through time at the Agenhor pond.

The spirit of Wiederrecht's perfection in the Slim by Hermès.

JEAN-MARC WIEDERRECHT: ENGINEERING TO TELL A STORY

Jean-Marc Wiederrecht was born in Geneva in 1950. His family came from Neuchâtel and, further back, from the Black Forest in Germany (where cuckoo clocks are made). His father would have preferred if his son did the Swiss "maturité" and went off to study, but Jean-Marc was adamant: He left college, breezed through Geneva's watchmaking school, and ended up working with the same watchmaker, Châtelain, where he had already worked, assembling movements and learning all the techniques of the trade, notably how to skeletonize.

In 1978 he went freelance. Agenhor, which stands for Atelier Genevois d'Horlogerie, opened in 1996. Today at the dawn of its twentieth anniversary, it employs thirty people in all, mostly watchmakers and designers. As many a passionate man, Wiederrecht has managed to convince his family to embark in the adventure with him. His wife Catherine does much of the administration, while his two sons Laurent and Nicolas have found their respective niches in the technical and administrative sides. Retirement for Wiederrecht is just another jumping hour.

States of Shock

Bill Yao

What makes a mechanical watch so valuable is the detail work that goes into creating stable mechanics. In past issues, *Wristwatch Annual* explored water resistance and antimagnetism. This year, watchmaker and brand owner Bill Yao takes a look at another threat to watches: shocks.

The Longines "tuna can," big enough to suspend the movement. Courtesy of E. F. Frederick.

Baselworld 2015, at the booth of a very exclusive brand: a watch journalist is *awesomely* manipulating a large watch bristling with complications. The brand rep quickly runs over, cups her hands under his, and says—with a slight tremolo in her voice—"Please, keep it over the table!" The retail price of this watch is over $700,000, but dropping it is out of the question, even if only onto the man's lap or the booth's soft carpeting. Some watches, like babies, cannot be shaken.

Shocks are one of the three most common threats to a watch's accuracy and functioning, along with water and magnetism. Dropping a watch on the floor or hitting it against a hard object is all it takes. Even playing golf or tennis is not recommended if you wear your watch on your active arm. Bones pick up the shocks from the club or racket and pass it on to the watch. This can affect the accuracy or, more seriously, damage parts of the movement.

Managing shocks has been a part of watchmaking since timekeeping became mobile with the popularization of the pocket watch in the eighteenth and nineteenth centuries. Watchmakers have approached shock protection along two basic avenues, occasionally combined: protection via case design or by working with the movement components themselves.

A FEW CASE SCENARIOS

One of the earliest known examples of a wristwatch employing shock protection in its case construction was a Longines known to collectors as the "C.O.S.D." (stamped on the back and standing for Company Ordnance Supply Depot), or better yet, the "tuna can" for its somewhat clumsy look. It was designed during World War II for Allied paratroopers to use during combat jumps. The Longines 12.68N caliber did not feature any shock protection so it was essentially suspended inside a 36 millimeter case, which, it was assumed, could somehow cushion any external shocks. The watch was not manufactured in significant numbers before the end of the war so it is unclear whether this system was more effective than the standard-issue watches. Longines recycled the movement into other watches later on, but the "tuna can" is a valuable collector's item today.

Modern-day incarnations of the COSD idea abound. One of the most memorable was the discontinued Glashütte Original Sport Evolution Impact series that featured four bright red bumpers to suspend the movement in the case. These elastomer bumpers could reduce impact forces by up to 60 percent. The system worked so well that the sales staff of Glashütte demonstrated its toughness by banging the watch against a tabletop during its debut.

One of the more dramatic incarnations to date has to be the Bremont MB series of watches. Developed in conjunction with Martin-Baker, a leading supplier of ejection seats, the MB series has been tested in some of the same protocols as the seats themselves. According to Martin-Baker the MB1 and MB2 watches survived accelerations of 12–30 G during live ejection seat testing and vibration testing designed to mimic thirty years of aircraft service. One of the main mechanisms employed to protect the movement from these stresses is a rubberized ring seated between the movement and outer wall of the case body. This allows the movement to float inside the case, thus absorbing the shocks.

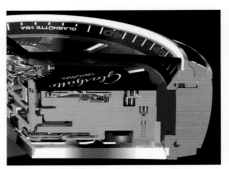

Glashütte Original: padding around the movement.

Case design beats G forces for the Bremont MB series.

Six screws to hold the Jaermann & Stübi golf caliber in place.

Inside the Richard Mille RM 27-01: cables and pulleys hold the movement steady for tennis star Rafael Nadal.

Detail of the RM 27-01 shock absorption system.

SPORTS WATCHES

One of the more surprising applications of shock absorption is for timepieces worn during sports which often require the performer to hit a ball with some form of stick or racket. Two kinds of force can impact a watch: the connection between the ball and the stick and the lateral forces generated by the swing. Jaermann & Stübi developed its brand with watches that keep score for the player and are also protected against the unique rigors of golf. Its recently reconceived ShockGuard system is especially designed to protect a movement from the shock of a golf swing by utilizing six strategically placed rubber dampers. The system also features a flexible stem crucial to allow the movement enough play as it responds to the shocks.

Tennis is another such sport. One of the most extreme examples of shock absorption in case construction is the Richard Mille RM 27-01, which combines extreme lightness with a specially conceived cable system that suspends the movement in the case. The minimal weight of the case actually minimizes its inertial mass, while the flexibility of the case materials provides shock resistance. The cable system serves to further reduce the transmission of external shocks to the movement. The result is a watch that can withstand accelerations over 5,000 G. This particular model was designed in conjunction with tennis champion Rafael Nadal, and he has worn one during his matches.

PROTECTING THE HEART OF THE MATTER

The main focus of movement protection is on the most sensitive parts of the mechanism, namely the pivots of the balance wheel. When a watch is dropped, the most common result is broken balance wheel pivots. These particular pivots tend to be the thinnest in a watch movement and have to support the largest of the wheels. This issue was first addressed in the late eighteenth century by none other than Abraham-Louis Breguet, who came up with his *pare-chute* system, from which most modern shock protection systems have evolved. According to legend—or could it be true?—Breguet presented his system to a gathering at the home of the famous Marquis de

Talleyrand by dropping his pocket watch to the floor. The marquis, never at a loss for words, remarked: "That devil Breguet always wants to improve on better." The *pare-chute* was originally developed for use in pocket watches. The idea was to keep the pivot in place using a cap jewel and a blade spring that allowed for a little bounce.

Despite their effectiveness, however, shock absorbers did not become standard features in watches until the mass adoption of the wristwatch and the development of the Incabloc system by Porte-Echappement Universel SA (aka Portescap SA, and finally Incabloc SA). The various systems essentially take up the idea of springs and cap stones to allow the balance wheel to move horizontally and vertically in response to an

Lasting values crafted by masters.

JUNGHANS
GERMANY. SINCE 1861

JUNGHANS – THE GERMAN WATCH

The name "Meister" has stood for classic watchmaking at Junghans since 1936. The Meister watches of today follow in this tradition, for they are a result of both passion for precision and close attention to quality. Choosing a **Junghans Meister** demonstrates appreciation for these values and for beautiful watchmaking — like our classic Meister, the Meister Calendar.

MADE IN GERMANY

Bella Design Jewelers: Chagrin Falls, OH – **Campanelli & Pear:** Troy, MI – **Golden Time Jewelers:** Redwood City, CA
La Garconne: New York, NY – **Legend of Time:** Chicago, IL – **Pacheco's Jewelry:** Taunton, MA – **Partita Jewelry:** San Francisco, CA
Rudi Peet Goldsmith: Canmore, Alberta – **Sid Mashburn:** Atlanta, GA – **Steven Allen:** New York, NY; San Francisco, CA & Portland, OR

For more information call 1-855-828-1969 Junghans Watches USA
Email: sales@junghanswatchesusa.net · www.junghanswatchesusa.net

An exploded view of the Incabloc system showing the famous lyre clip.

external shock. The movement not only survives the shock but continues to function because the balance wheel can return to its original position through the use of springs and cleverly shaped mountings.

In the modern shock dampening system developed by Incabloc SA there is a set of assemblies at the end of each pivot that protects it. The conical shape of the setting allows the chaton to move laterally and travel up and down along the balance wheel's vertical axis. The antishock springs apply inward pressure that keeps the system together and repositions the balance wheel into its original position after a shock.

At one time there were dozens of companies that produced competing shock protection devices for balance wheel pivots. Today the two dominant companies are Incabloc SA (Swatch Group Ltd) and Kif Parechoc SA (Rolex SA). In fact, the lyre shape of the Incabloc spring has become a symbol of superior shock protection as well as for the company itself. Generally speaking, the inclusion of shock dampeners from one of these companies is a mark of a well-constructed watch.

THE STATE OF THE ART

The standard Incabloc system features two springs that center the balance wheel by applying force along the balance wheel's vertical axis. The UlyChoc, developed for the FreakLab at Ulysse-Nardin and presented at Baselworld 2015, incorporates a significant improvement in the shock protection of the balance wheel pivots by utilizing a silicon spring to hold the chaton in its horizontal plane in combination with a spring above each pivot. This not only means fewer parts than a classic shock absorber, but also less friction, hence greater precision. There is a patent pending, of course.

What would watchmaking be without the name Breguet? The most classic of brands decided to introduce magnetism into its

watches to create the patented Magnetic Pivot system, which also improves chronometric performance by reducing friction and gravity's influence on the balance wheel. The system uses two powerful micro magnets, one positioned at each balance wheel pivot, that serve double duty as a shock protection system. The force of the magnets holds the balance wheel in place and keeps the balance wheel properly poised even in the event of a shock to the watch. Since the balance wheel only makes contact with the movement at literally one point, the pivots can no longer break due to lateral forces.

Ball Watch is another company that continues to work on practical watches for practical people. And that means producing a system the brand calls SpringLOCK®. Ball is not only addressing the survival of the movement but also the fact that external shocks can cause the timekeeping to vary by around 60 seconds per day according to watchmaking standards. The system consists of a metal cage that is placed around the balance spring. The cage protects the balance spring from the effects of shock by preserving its geometry and attachment to the balance wheel itself. The final effect of the system is to dampen shocks by up to 66 percent and minimize variation in the accuracy of the movement due to impacts.

There are many different systems designed to protect watches from sudden impacts. But in the end, even the best ones can only do so much. As with all valuable object, it is wise to simply be careful with your watch, and do not try to test its limits. Every object has them.

Bill Yao is president of Mk II in Wayne, Pennsylvania. His company specializes in customizing and modernizing retired watch designs (www.mkiiwatches.com).

Ulysse Nardin's newly developed UlyChoc with a spring on each pivot.

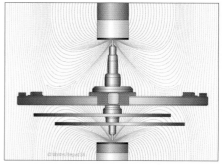

The magnetic pivot by Breguet to stabilize pivots and reduce friction.

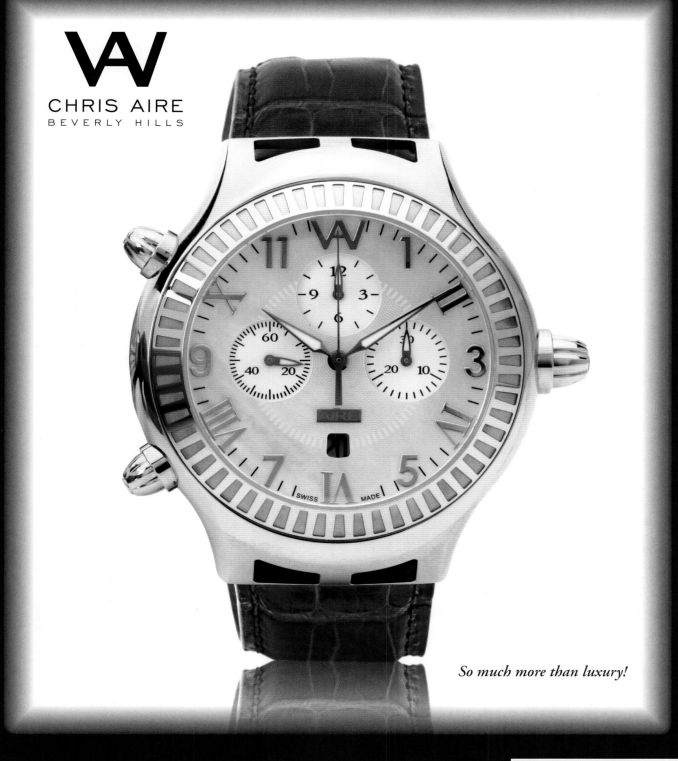

So much more than luxury!

Chris Aire is an iconic internationally acclaimed brand, sought after by the most discerning watch collectors around the world. Each design showcases true luxury, combining impeccable design, high luxury Swiss movements and technology. Designed exclusively by Chris Aire in Beverly Hills California and made by the most prestigious watch houses in Switzerland. The Chris Aire Parlay Ambidextrous model is produced in limited edition. It encases a Soprod base movement with customized modification split crown and pushers that is ideal for both right and left-handed users. Each watch is offered exclusively in the Chris Aire signature Red Gold collection. From $54.500.00

Chris Aire Beverly Hills
9619 Brighton Way • Beverly Hills, CA 90210
Tel: 310-888-4094

chrisaire.com

Lange Uhren GmbH

Ferdinand-A.-Lange-Platz 1
D-01768 Glashütte
Germany

Tel.:
+49-35053-44-0

Fax:
+49-35053-44-5999

E-Mail:
info@lange-soehne.com

Website:
www.lange-soehne.com

Founded:
1990

Number of employees:
500 employees, almost half of whom are
watchmakers

U.S. distributor:
A. Lange & Söhne
645 Fifth Avenue
New York, NY 10022
800-408-8147

Most important collections/price range:
Lange 1 / $34,700 to $332,500; Saxonia /
$14,800 to $62,100; 1815 / $24,800 to
$234,600; Richard Lange / $32,500 to
$230,400; Zeitwerk / $76,200 to $118,700

A. Lange & Söhne

On December 7, 1990, on the exact day 145 years after the firm was founded by his great-grandfather Ferdinand Adolph Lange, Walter Lange re-registered the brand A. Lange & Söhne in its old hometown of Glashütte. Ferdinand Adolph had originally launched the company as a way to provide work to the local population. And shortly after German reunification in 1990, that is exactly what Glashütte needed as well.

The company quickly regained its outstanding reputation as a robust innovator and manufacturer of classically beautiful watches. A. Lange & Söhne uses only mechanical, manually wound *manufacture* calibers or automatic winders finished according to the highest Glashütte standards. The movements are decorated and assembled by hand with the fine adjustment done in five positions. The typical three-quarter plate and all the structural parts of the movement are made of undecorated German silver; the balance cock is engraved freehand. The movements combine equal parts traditional elements and patented innovations, like the Lange large date, the SAX-O-MAT with an automatic "zero reset" for the seconds hand, or the patented constant force escapement (Lange 31, Lange Zeitwerk). Of the company's fifty calibers, thirty are currently in production, and two-thirds of those have their own balance spring.

The highlight of the new models is the Richard Lange Terraluna, whose most interesting display is on the back. It features the synodic moon cycle of the Northern Hemisphere. The moon travels around the earth—which is actually flat here—and is illuminated by the sun—the balance. On the dial side the perpetual calendar features the characteristic large date, weekday, and month, as well as a small leap year display. The time is indicated with three scales, because the hours, minutes, and seconds each have their own individual sector.

Lange 1

Reference number: 191.032
Movement: manually wound, Lange Caliber L121.1; ø 30.6 mm, height 5.7 mm; 43 jewels; 21,600 vph; swan-neck fine adjustment, hand-engraved balance cock, 8 screw-mounted gold chatons, parts finished and assembled by hand; 72-hour power reserve
Functions: hours, minutes, subsidiary seconds; power reserve indicator; large date
Case: pink gold, ø 38.5 mm, height 9.8 mm; sapphire crystal; transparent case back; water-resistant to 3 atm
Band: reptile skin, buckle
Price: $34,700
Variations: yellow gold ($34,700); platinum ($49,500)

Grand Lange 1 Moon Phase

Reference number: 139.032
Movement: manually wound, Lange Caliber L095.3; ø 34.1 mm, height 4.7 mm; 45 jewels; 21,600 vph; three-quarter, hand-engraved balance cocks, 7 screw-mounted gold chatons, screw balance, swan-neck fine adjustment; 72-hour power reserve
Functions: hours, minutes, subsidiary seconds; power reserve indicator; large date; moon phase
Case: pink gold, ø 41 mm, height 9.2 mm; sapphire crystal; transparent case back; water-resistant to 3 atm
Band: reptile skin, buckle
Price: $48,200
Variations: platinum ($63,000)

Lange 1 Timezone

Reference number: 116.039
Movement: manually wound, Lange Caliber L031.1; ø 34.1 mm, height 6.65 mm; 54 jewels; 21,600 vph; hand-engraved balance cock, 4 screw-mounted gold chatons; 72-hour power reserve; home time/ zone time with day/night indicator, city names on pusher-driven bezel
Functions: hours, minutes, subsidiary seconds; 2nd time zone; large date; power reserve indicator; day/ night indicator for both time zones
Case: white gold, ø 41.9 mm, height 11 mm; sapphire crystal; transparent case back
Band: reptile skin, buckle
Price: $51,800
Variations: pink gold ($49,400); platinum ($64,300)

Lange 1 Daymatic

Reference number: 320.032
Movement: automatic, Lange Caliber L021.1;
ø 31.6 mm; height 6.1 mm; 67 jewels; 21,600 vph;
hand-engraved balance cock, 7 screwed-mounted
gold chatons, central rotor with platinum weight;
50-hour power reserve
Functions: hours, minutes, subsidiary seconds;
large date; weekday (retrograde)
Case: pink gold, ø 39.5 mm, height 10.4 mm;
sapphire crystal; transparent case back; water-
resistant to 3 atm
Band: reptile skin, buckle
Price: $43,200
Variations: platinum ($58,100)

Lange 1 Tourbillon Perpetual Calendar

Reference number: 720.032
Movement: automatic, Lange Caliber L082.1;
ø 34.1 mm, height 7.8 mm; 68 jewels; 21,600 vph;
1-minute tourbillon on back; 4 gold chatons,
1 diamond endstone, hand-engraved cocks, rotor
with gold weight; 50-hour power reserve
Functions: hours, minutes, subsidiary seconds;
day/night indicator; perpetual calendar with large
date, weekday, month, moon phase, leap year
Case: pink gold, ø 41.9 mm, height 12.2 mm;
sapphire crystal; exhibition case; water-resistant to
3 atm
Band: reptile skin, buckle
Price: $332,500

Langematik Perpetual

Reference number: 310.026
Movement: automatic, Lange Caliber L922.1; SAX-
O-MAT; ø 30.4 mm, height 5.7 mm; 43 jewels;
21,600 vph; hand-engraved balance cock; rotor
with gold/platinum oscillating weight; hand-
setting mechanism with zero reset; main pusher for
synchronous correction of all calendar functions,
plus 3 individual pushers; 46-hour power reserve
Functions: hours, minutes, subsidiary seconds;
added 24-hour display; perpetual calendar with
large date, weekday, month, moon phase, leap year
Case: white gold, ø 38.5 mm, height 10.2 mm;
sapphire crystal; transparent back; water-resistant
to 3 atm
Band: reptile skin, buckle
Price: $84,200

Saxonia

Reference number: 219.032
Movement: manually wound, Lange Caliber L941.1;
ø 25.6 mm, height 3.2 mm; 21 jewels; 21,600 vph;
hand-engraved balance cock, 4 screw-mounted
gold chatons, screw balance, swan-neck fine
adjustment, parts finished and assembled by hand;
45-hour power reserve
Functions: hours, minutes, subsidiary seconds
Case: pink gold, ø 35 mm, height 7.3 mm; sapphire
crystal; transparent case back; water-resistant to
3 atm
Band: reptile skin, buckle
Price: $14,800
Variations: white gold ($16,000)

Saxonia Dual Time

Reference number: 386.026
Movement: automatic, Lange Caliber L086.2;
ø 30.4 mm, height 4.6 mm; 31 jewels; 21,600 vph;
hand-engraved balance cock, screw balance, swan-
neck fine adjustment; 72-hour power reserve
Functions: hours, minutes, subsidiary seconds;
additional 12-hour display (2nd time zone), day/
night indication (24-hour display)
Case: white gold, ø 38.5 mm, height 9.1 mm;
sapphire crystal; transparent case back; water-
resistant to 3 atm
Band: reptile skin, buckle
Price: $32,000
Variations: pink gold ($30,800)

Saxonia Annual Calendar

Reference number: 330.026
Movement: automatic, Lange Caliber L085.1; SAX-
O-MAT; ø 30.4 mm, height 5.4 mm; 43 jewels;
21,600 vph; hand-engraved balance cock; integrated
three-quarter rotor with gold/platinum oscillating
weight, reversing/reduction gears with 4 ball
bearings; hand-setting with zero reset; 46-hour power
reserve
Functions: hours, minutes, subsidiary seconds; full
calendar with large date, weekday, month, moon phase
Case: white gold, ø 38.5 mm, height 9.8 mm;
sapphire crystal, transparent case back; water-
resistant to 3 atm
Band: reptile skin, buckle
Price: $49,600
Variations: pink gold ($48,400); platinum ($62,100)

1815

Reference number: 235.026
Movement: manually wound, Lange Caliber L051.1; ø 30.6 mm, height 4.6 mm; 23 jewels; 21,600 vph; 5 screwed-down gold chatons, hand-engraved balance cock, finished and assembled by hand; 55-hour power reserve
Functions: hours, minutes, subsidiary seconds
Case: white gold, ø 38.5 mm, height 8.8 mm; sapphire crystal; transparent case back; water-resistant to 3 atm
Band: reptile skin, buckle
Price: $21,600
Variations: pink gold ($22,800)

1815 Tourbillon

Reference number: 730.025
Movement: manually wound, Lange Caliber L102.1; ø 32.6 mm, height 6.6 mm; 20 jewels; 21,600 vph; 1-minute tourbillon, 3 screw-mounted gold chatons, 1 diamond endstone, hand-setting mechanism with zero reset, hand-engraved seconds bridge; 72-hour power reserve
Functions: hours, minutes, subsidiary seconds
Case: platinum, ø 39.5 mm, height 11.1 mm; sapphire crystal; transparent case back
Band: reptile skin, folding clasp
Price: $201,300; limited to 100 pieces
Variations: pink gold ($164,100)

1815 Rattrapante Perpetual Calendar

Reference number: 421.032
Movement: manually wound, Lange Caliber L101.1; ø 32.6 mm, height 9.1 mm; 43 jewels; 21,600 vph; 4 screw-mounted gold chatons, hand-engraved balance cock, screw balance, swan-neck fine adjustment; 42-hour power reserve
Functions: hours, minutes, subsidiary seconds; power reserve; split-seconds chronograph; perpetual calendar with date, weekday, month, moon phase, leap year
Case: pink gold, ø 41.9 mm, height 14.7 mm; sapphire crystal, transparent case back; water-resistant to 3 atm
Band: reptile skin, folding clasp
Price: $208,600
Variations: platinum ($234,600)

Richard Lange

Reference number: 232.032
Movement: manually wound, Lange Caliber L041.2; ø 30.6 mm, height 6 mm; 26 jewels; 21,600 vph; hand-engraved balance cock, 2 screw-mounted gold chatons, finished and assembled by hand; in-house balance spring with patent-pending anchoring clip; 38-hour power reserve
Functions: hours, minutes, sweep seconds
Case: pink gold, ø 40.5 mm, height 10.5 mm; sapphire crystal; transparent case back; water-resistant to 3 atm
Band: reptile skin, buckle
Price: $32,500
Variations: platinum ($47,300)

Richard Lange Tourbillon "Pour le Mérite"

Reference number: 760.032
Movement: manually wound, Lange Caliber L072.1; ø 33.6 mm, height 7.6 mm; 32 jewels including diamond endstone; 21,600 vph; chain and fusée drive; 1-minute tourbillon; hand-engraved balance cock
Functions: hours (off-center), minutes, subsidiary seconds (on tourbillon cage)
Case: pink gold, ø 41.9 mm, height 12.2 mm; sapphire crystal; transparent case back; water-resistant to 3 atm
Band: reptile skin, buckle
Remarks: hour dial retracts to show full tourbillon
Price: $211,700

Richard Lange Perpetual Calendar "Terraluna"

Reference number: 180.032
Movement: manually wound, Lange Caliber L096.1; ø 37.3 mm, height 11.1 mm; 80 jewels; 21,600 vph; three-quarter plate, double spring barrel, constant force escapement, screw balance, 1 screwed-down gold chaton; 336-hour power reserve
Functions: hours (off-center), minutes, subsidiary seconds; power reserve indicator; perpetual calendar with large date, weekday, month, leap year, orbital moon phase with day/night display on case back
Case: pink gold, ø 45.5 mm, height 16.5 mm; sapphire crystal; transparent back; water-resistant to 3 atm
Band: reptile skin, folding clasp
Price: $229,200

1815 Chronograph

Reference number: 402.032
Movement: manually wound, Lange Caliber L951.5; ø 30.6 mm, height 6.1 mm; 34 jewels; 18,000 vph; hand-engraved balance cock, 4 screw-mounted gold chatons; 60-hour power reserve
Functions: hours, minutes, subsidiary seconds; flyback chronograph
Case: pink gold, ø 39.5 mm, height 10.8 mm; sapphire crystal; transparent case back; water-resistant to 3 atm
Band: reptile skin, buckle
Price: $50,300
Variations: white gold ($51,500)

Datograph UP/DOWN

Reference number: 405.035
Movement: manually wound, Lange Caliber L951.6; ø 30.6 mm, height 7.9 mm; 46 jewels; 18,000 vph; 4 screwed-down gold chatons; 60-hour power reserve
Functions: hours, minutes, subsidiary seconds; flyback chronograph with precisely jumping minute counter; large date; power reserve indicator
Case: pink gold, ø 41 mm, height 13.1 mm; sapphire crystal; transparent case back; water-resistant to 3 atm
Band: reptile skin, buckle
Price: $90,700
Variations: platinum

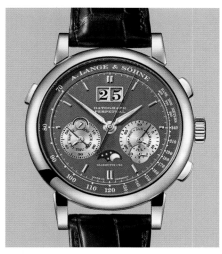

Datograph Perpetual

Reference number: 410.038
Movement: manually wound, Lange Caliber L952.1; ø 32 mm, height 8 mm; 45 jewels; 18,000 vph; column wheel control of chronograph functions; 4 screw-mounted gold chatons
Functions: hours, minutes, subsidiary seconds; additional 24-hour display; day/night indicator; flyback chronograph; perpetual calendar with month, weekday, month, moon phase, leap year
Case: white gold, ø 41 mm, height 13.5 mm; sapphire crystal; transparent case back; water-resistant to 3 atm
Band: reptile skin, buckle
Price: $137,800
Variations: pink gold ($136,600)

Zeitwerk Minute Repeater

Reference number: 147.025
Movement: manually wound, Lange Caliber L043.5; ø 37.7 mm, height 10.9 mm; 93 jewels; 18,000 vph; three-quarter, hand-engraved balance cocks, 3 screwed-in gold chatons; continuous drive through constant force escapement; 36-hour power reserve
Functions: hours and minutes (digital, jumping), subsidiary seconds; power reserve display, minute repeater
Case: platinum, ø 44.2 mm, height 14.1 mm; sapphire crystal; transparent case back; water-resistant to 3 atm
Band: reptile skin, folding clasp
Price: $467,700

Zeitwerk

Reference number: 140.029
Movement: manually wound, Lange Caliber L043.1; ø 33.6 mm, height 9.3 mm; 66 jewels; 18,000 vph; hand-engraved balance cock; 2 screw-mounted gold chatons; continuous drive through constant force escapement; 36-hour power reserve
Functions: hours and minutes (digital, jumping), subsidiary seconds; power reserve indicator
Case: white gold, ø 41.9 mm, height 12.6 mm; sapphire crystal; transparent case back; water-resistant to 3 atm
Band: reptile skin, buckle
Price: $77,400
Variations: pink gold ($76,200)

Zeitwerk Striking Time

Reference number: 145.032
Movement: manually wound, Lange Caliber L043.2; ø 36 mm, height 10 mm; 78 jewels; 18,000 vph; hand-engraved balance cock; 3 screw-mounted gold chatons; continuous drive through constant force escapement (remontoir), acoustic signal on hour/quarter hour; 36-hour power reserve
Functions: hours and minutes (digital, jumping), subsidiary seconds; power reserve indicator
Case: pink gold, ø 44.2 mm, height 13.1 mm; sapphire crystal; transparent case back; water-resistant to 3 atm
Band: reptile skin, buckle
Price: $117,500

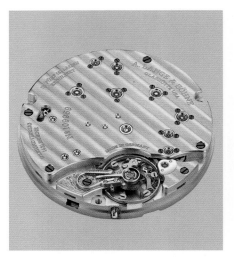

Caliber L121.1

Manually wound; stop-seconds mechanism, 8 screw-mounted gold chatons, swan-neck fine adjustment; double spring barrel, 72-hour power reserve
Functions: hours, minutes, subsidiary seconds; power reserve indicator; large date
Diameter: 30.6 mm
Height: 5.7 mm
Jewels: 43
Balance: glucydur with eccentric regulating cams
Frequency: 21,600 vph
Balance spring: in-house manufacture
Shock protection: Kif
Remarks: plates and bridges of untreated German silver, manufactured according to highest quality criteria and chiefly decorated and assembled by hand, hand-engraved balance cock

Caliber L095.3

Manually wound; stop-seconds mechanism; single spring barrel, 72-hour power reserve
Functions: hours, minutes, subsidiary seconds; power reserve display, large date, moon phase
Diameter: 34.1 mm
Height: 4.7 mm
Jewels: 45, including 7 screw-mounted gold chatons
Balance: glucydur with weighted screws
Frequency: 21,600 vph
Shock protection: Kif
Remarks: three-quarter plate of untreated German silver, manufactured according to highest quality criteria and chiefly decorated and assembled by hand, hand-engraved balance cock

Caliber L082.1

Automatic; 1-minute tourbillon with stop-second; 1-way gold rotor with platinum mass; single barrel, 50-hour power reserve
Functions: hours, minutes, subsidiary seconds; day/night; perpetual calendar, large date, weekday, month, moon phase, leap year
Diameter: 34.1 mm; **Height:** 7.8 mm
Jewels: 76, including 6 screwed golden chatons and 1 diamond counter-bearing
Balance: glucydur, eccentric regulating cams
Frequency: 21,600 vph
Balance spring: in-house manufacture
Shock protection: Incabloc
Remarks: three-quarter plate with untreated German silver mostly hand-assembled, decorated; hand-engraved balance, wheel cock, and tourbillon cock

Caliber L922.1 SAX-O-MAT

Automatic; bidirectional, finely embossed 21-karat gold and platinum three-quarter rotor, zero reset hand adjustment, stop-seconds mechanism; single spring barrel, 46-hour power reserve
Functions: hours, minutes, subsidiary seconds; additional 24-hour display; day/night indicator; perpetual calendar with large date, weekday, month, moon phase, leap year
Diameter: 30.4 mm; **Height:** 5.7 mm
Jewels: 43; **Frequency:** 21,600 vph
Balance: glucydur with weighted screws
Balance spring: Nivarox 1 with special terminal curve and swan-neck fine adjustment
Shock protection: Kif
Remarks: calendar mechanism with 48-step program disc and precisely computed moon phase transmission

Caliber L085.1 SAX-O-MAT

Automatic; bidirectional, finely embossed 21-karat gold and platinum three-quarter rotor, zero reset hand adjustment, stop-seconds mechanism; complete or individual calendar correction; single spring barrel, 46-hour power reserve
Functions: hours, minutes, subsidiary seconds; full calendar with large date, weekday, month, moon phase
Diameter: 30.4 mm; **Height:** 5.4 mm
Jewels: 43; **Balance:** glucydur with weighted screws
Frequency: 21,600 vph
Balance spring: Nivarox 1 with special terminal curve and swan-neck fine adjustment
Shock protection: Kif
Remarks: three-quarter plate of untreated German silver; chiefly decorated and assembled by hand; hand-engraved balance cock

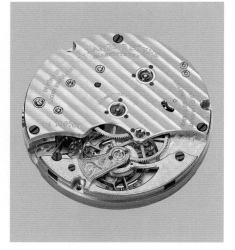

Caliber L102.1

Manually wound; 1-minute tourbillon with balance stop with zero reset hand adjustment, single spring barrel; 72-hour power reserve
Functions: hours, minutes, subsidiary seconds
Diameter: 32.6 mm
Height: 6.6 mm
Jewels: 20, including 3 screwed-mounted gold chatons
Balance: glucydur with weighted screws
Frequency: 21,600 vph
Balance spring: in-house manufacture
Shock protection: Kif
Remarks: three-quarter plate of untreated German silver, manufactured according to highest quality criteria and chiefly decorated and assembled by hand, hand-engraved balance bridge

Caliber L101.1

Manually wound; swan-neck fine adjustment; single spring barrel; 42-hour power reserve
Functions: hours, minutes, subsidiary seconds; power reserve indicator; rattrapante chronograph; perpetual calendar with date, weekday, month, moon phase, leap year
Diameter: 32.6 mm
Height: 9.1 mm
Jewels: 43, including 4 screw-mounted gold chatons
Balance: glucydur with weighted screws
Frequency: 21,600 vph
Shock protection: Kif
Remarks: manufactured according to highest quality criteria and chiefly decorated and assembled by hand

Caliber L072.1

Manually wound; chain and fusée transmission; 1-minute tourbillon with patented stop-seconds mechanism; single spring barrel, 36-hour power reserve
Functions: hours, minutes, subsidiary seconds; pivoting dial
Diameter: 33.6 mm; **Height:** 7.6 mm
Jewels: 32
Balance: glucydur with weighted screws
Frequency: 21,600 vph
Balance spring: in-house manufacture
Shock protection: Kif
Remarks: three-quarter plate of untreated German silver; chiefly decorated and assembled by hand; balance and second bridges engraved by hand; chain made of 636 individual parts, worked by hand

Caliber L096.1

Manually wound; constant force escapement with intermediate winding spring, stop-seconds; twin spring barrels, 336-hour power reserve
Functions: hours, minutes, subsidiary seconds; power reserve indicator; perpetual calendar with month, large date, weekday, month, leap year; orbital moon phase with day/night display on case back
Diameter: 37.3 mm; **Height:** 11.1 mm
Jewels: 80; **Balance:** glucydur with weighted screws
Frequency: 21,600 vph
Balance spring: in-house manufacture
Shock protection: Kif
Remarks: three-quarter plate with integrated moon phase display, manufactured according to highest quality criteria and chiefly decorated and assembled by hand, hand-engraved balance bridge

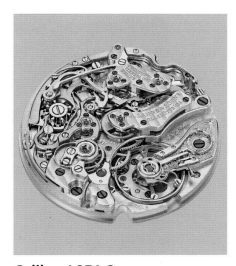

Caliber L951.6

Manually wound; stop-seconds mechanism, jumping minute counter; single spring barrel, 60-hour power reserve
Functions: hours, minutes, subsidiary seconds; power reserve indicator; flyback chronograph; large date
Diameter: 30.6 mm
Height: 7.9 mm
Jewels: 46
Balance: glucydur with weighted screws
Frequency: 18,000 vph
Balance spring: in-house manufacture
Shock protection: Kif
Remarks: three-quarter plate of untreated German silver, chiefly decorated and assembled by hand; hand-engraved balance cock

Caliber L043.5

Manually wound; 3 screwed-in gold chatons; continuous drive through constant force escapement (remontoir); stop-seconds mechanism, chiming mechanism; single spring barrel, 36-hour power reserve
Functions: hours and minutes (digital, jumping), subsidiary seconds; power reserve display; minute repeater
Diameter: 37.7 mm; **Height:** 10.9 mm
Jewels: 93; **Frequency:** 18,000 vph
Balance: glucydur with eccentric regulating cams
Balance spring: in-house manufacture
Shock protection: Incabloc
Remarks: three-quarter plate of natural German silver, hand-engraved balance cock, decorated and assembled by hand according to highest quality criteria

Caliber L043.2

Manually wound; jumping minute, continuous drive through constant force escapement (remontoir), spring barrel mechanism (patent pending); stop-seconds mechanism; chiming mechanism; single spring barrel, 36-hour power reserve
Functions: hours and minutes (digital, jumping), subsidiary seconds; acoustic signal on quarter and full hour; power reserve indicator
Diameter: 36 mm; **Height:** 10 mm; **Jewels:** 78
Balance: glucydur; **Frequency:** 18,000 vph
Balance spring: in-house spring clamp (patent pending)
Shock protection: Incabloc
Remarks: three-quarter natural German silver plate, with Glashütte ribbing, manufactured according to highest quality criteria, chiefly decorated and assembled by hand; hand-engraved balance and escape wheel cock

Alpina Watch International
Chemin de la Galaise, 8
CH-1228 Plan-les-Ouates (Geneva)
Switzerland

Tel.:
+41-22-860-87-40

Fax:
+41-22-860-04-64

E-Mail:
info@alpina-watches.com

Website:
www.alpina-watches.com

Founded:
1883

Number of employees:
100

Annual production:
10,000 watches

U.S. distributor:
Alpina Watches USA
877-61-WATCH; info@usa.alpina-watches.com

Most important collections/price range:
Extreme / from approx. $1,200; Startimer
Pilot / from approx. $2,300; Sailing / from
approx. $1,500; Tourbillon / from approx.
$50,000; Smartwatch / from approx. $1,050
to $2,595

Alpina

The brand Alpina essentially grew out of a confederation of watchmakers known as the Alpina Union Horlogère, founded by Gottlieb Hauser. The group expanded quickly to reach beyond Swiss borders into Germany, where it opened a factory in Glashütte. For a while in the 1930s, it even merged with Gruen, one of the most important watch companies in the United States. The collaboration fell apart in 1937.

After World War II, the Allied Forces decreed that the name Alpina could no longer be used in Germany, and so that branch was renamed "Dugena" for Deutsche Uhrmacher-Genossenschaft Alpina, or the German Watchmaker Cooperative Alpina.

Today, Geneva-based Alpina is no longer associated with that watchmaker cooperative of yore. Now a sister brand of Frédérique Constant, it has a decidedly modern collection enhanced with its own automatic movement—based, of course, on the caliber of its co-headquartered manufacturer. Owners Peter and Aletta Stas have built an impressive watch *manufacture* in Geneva's industrial district, Plan-les-Ouates. There, they produce about 8,000 of their own watches each year as well as reassembling other timepieces with externally manufactured movements.

Alpina likes to call itself the inventor of the modern sports watch. Its iconic Block-Uhr of 1933 and the Alpina 4 of 1938, with an in-house automatic movement, set the pace of all sports watches, with a waterproof stainless steel case, an antimagnetic system, and shock absorbers. But beyond a target group engaged in water and air sports, the brand is now looking at the twenty-first-century hipsters whose life is electronic. The Horological Smartwatch, equipped with a quartz movement, connects with mobile phones and other electronic devices and can display the data on an analog dial.

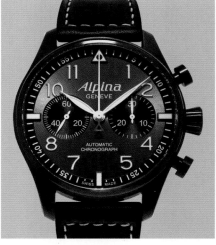

Startimer Pilot Automatic Chronograph

Reference number: AL-860GB4FBS6
Movement: automatic, Sellita Caliber SW 500; 30 jewels; 28,800 vph; 46-hour power reserve
Functions: hours, minutes, subsidiary seconds
Case: stainless steel with black PVD coating, ø 44 mm, height 14.6 mm; sapphire crystal; screw-in crown, water-resistant to 10 atm
Band: calf leather, buckle
Price: $3,395

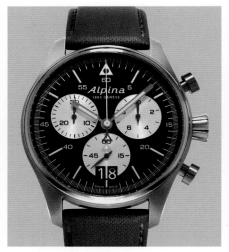

Startimer Pilot Big Date Chronograph

Reference number: AL-372BS4S6
Movement: quartz
Functions: hours, minutes, subsidiary seconds; chronograph; large date
Case: stainless steel, ø 44 mm, height 12.4 mm; sapphire crystal; screw-in crown; water-resistant to 10 atm
Band: calf leather, buckle
Price: $1,150

Startimer Pilot Manufacture

Reference number: AL-950BGR4S6
Movement: automatic, Caliber AL-950; ø 25.6 mm, 26 jewels; 28,800 vph; 42-hour power reserve
Functions: hours (off-center), minutes; date
Case: stainless steel, ø 44 mm, height 13.64 mm; sapphire crystal; screw-in crown; water-resistant to 10 atm
Band: calf leather, folding clasp
Price: $3,050

Alpiner 4 Manufacture Direct Flyback Chronograph

Reference number: AL-760SB5AQ6B
Movement: automatic, Caliber AL-760; ø 28.6 mm, height 6.1 mm; 37 jewels; 28,800 vph; 42-hour power reserve
Functions: hours, minutes, subsidiary seconds; flyback chronograph
Case: stainless steel, ø 44 mm, height 14.9 mm; sapphire crystal; screw-in crown; water-resistant to 10 atm
Band: reptile skin, folding clasp
Price: $4,750
Variations: stainless steel bracelet

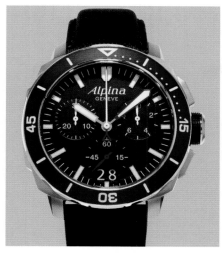

Seastrong Diver 300

Reference number: AL-372LBBRG4V6
Movement: quartz
Functions: hours, minutes, sweep seconds; chronograph; large date
Case: stainless steel, ø 44 mm, height 14.35 mm; unidirectional bezel with 60-minute divisions; sapphire crystal; screw-in crown; water-resistant to 30 atm
Band: calf leather, buckle
Price: $1,295

Alpiner Chronograph

Reference number: AL-750N4E6
Movement: automatic, Caliber AL-750 (base ETA 7750); ø 30 mm, height 7.9 mm; 25 jewels; 28,800 vph; 46-hour power reserve
Functions: hours, minutes, subsidiary seconds; date
Case: stainless steel, ø 41.5 mm, height 14 mm; sapphire crystal; water-resistant to 5 atm
Band: calf leather, folding clasp
Price: $2,695

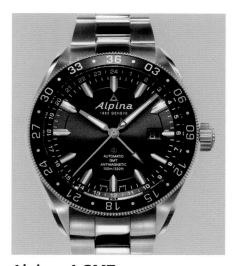

Alpiner 4 GMT

Reference number: AL.550G5AQ6B
Movement: automatic, Caliber AL-550 (base Sellita SW 200); ø 25.6 mm, height 4.6 mm; 26 jewels; 28,800 vph; 38-hour power reserve
Functions: hours, minutes, sweep seconds; additional 24-hour display (2nd time zone); date
Case: stainless steel, ø 44 mm, height 14.2 mm; bidirectional bezel with 360 divisions (compass function); sapphire crystal; water-resistant to 10 atm
Band: stainless steel, folding clasp
Price: $2,495

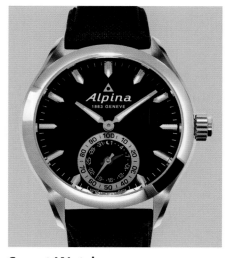

Smart Watch

Reference number: AL-285BS5AQ6
Movement: quartz
Functions: hours, minutes; electronic motion detector, sleep monitoring, alarm function (crown-controlled); date
Case: stainless steel, ø 44 mm, height 13.95 mm; sapphire crystal; water-resistant to 10 atm
Band: calf leather, buckle
Price: $1,050

Horological Smartwatch

Reference number: AL-285STD3CD6B
Movement: quartz
Functions: hours, minutes; electronic motion detector, sleep monitoring, alarm function (crown-controlled); date
Case: stainless steel, ø 39 mm, height 13.42 mm; 60 diamonds on bezel; sapphire crystal; water-resistant to 10 atm
Band: stainless steel, buckle
Remarks: dial set with 9 diamonds
Price: $2,595

Anonimo SA
Chemin des Chalets 9
CH-1279 Chavannes-de-Bogis
Switzerland

Tel.:
+41-22-566-06-06

E-Mail:
info@anonimo.com

Website:
www.anonimo.com

Founded:
1997; relaunched 2013

Distributor:
Network in construction; for inquiries contact
the brand directly.

Most important collections/price range:
Militare / $2,100 to $5,200

Anonimo

The brand Anonimo was launched on the banks of the Arno, in Florence. Watchmaking has a long history in the capital of Tuscany, going back to one Giovanni de Dondi (1318–1389) who built his first planetarium around 1368. Then came the Renaissance man Lorenzo della Volpaia (1446–1512), an architect and goldsmith, who also worked with calendars and astronomical instruments. And finally, there were the likes of the mathematician Galileo and the incomparable Leonardo da Vinci.

In more recent times, the Italian watchmaking industry was busy equipping submarine crews and frogmen with timepieces. The key technology came from Switzerland, but the specialized know-how for making robust, water-resistant watches sprang from small enterprises with competencies in building cases. The founders of Anonimo understood this strength and decided to put it in the service of their "anonymous" brand—a name chosen to "hide" the fact that many small, discreet companies are involved in their superbly finished watches.

In 2013, armed with some fresh capital and a new management team, Anonimo came out with three watch families running on Swiss technology: The mechanical movements are partially complemented with Dubois Dépraz modules or ETA and Sellita calibers. On the whole, though, the collections reflect exquisite conception and manufacturing, and the quality of the materials is unimpeachable: corrosion-resistant stainless steel, fine bronze, and titanium, appreciated for its durability and hypoallergenic properties. As for design, the cases come with some special features. On the military models, the crown has been placed in a protected area between the two upper lugs. Thanks to a clever hinge system, that crown can be pressed onto the case for an impermeable fit or released for time-setting.

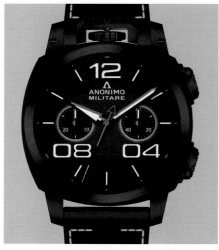

Militare Classic Chrono DLC

Reference number: AM-1120.02.003.A03
Movement: automatic, Sellita Caliber SW300 with Dubois Dépraz module 2035M; ø 26.2 mm, height 6.5 mm; 26 jewels; 28,800 vph; 42-hour power reserve
Functions: hours, minutes, subsidiary seconds; chronograph
Case: stainless steel with black DLC coating, ø 43.4 mm, height 14 mm; sapphire crystal; screw-in crown; water-resistant to 12 atm
Band: calf leather, buckle
Remarks: crown pressed onto case by upper lug for impermeable seal
Price: $4,000

Militare Classic Automatic

Reference number: AM-1020.01.002.A02
Movement: automatic, Sellita Caliber SW260; ø 25.6 mm, height 5.6 mm; 31 jewels; 28,800 vph; 42-hour power reserve
Functions: hours, minutes, subsidiary seconds; date
Case: stainless steel, ø 43.4 mm, height 14.5 mm; sapphire crystal; screw-in crown; water-resistant to 12 atm
Band: calf leather, buckle
Remarks: crown pressed onto case by upper lug for impermeable seal
Price: $2,700

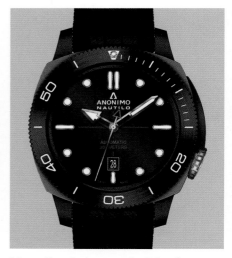

Nautilo Automatic Bicolor

Reference number: AM-1001.05.001.A11
Movement: automatic, Sellita Caliber SW200; ø 25.6 mm, height 4.6 mm; 26 jewels; 28,800 vph; 42-hour power reserve
Functions: hours, minutes, sweep seconds; date
Case: bronze, ø 45.5 mm, height 12.45 mm; stainless steel bezel with black DLC coating, unidirectional with 60-minute divisions; sapphire crystal; screw-in crown; water-resistant to 20 atm
Band: rubber, buckle
Price: $2,700

Our watches are made for moments like this.

Aquadive USA
1950 Oleander Street
Baton Rouge, LA 70806

Tel.:
888-397-9363

E-Mail:
info@aquadive.com

Website:
www.aquadive.com

Founded:
1962

Number of employees:
18

Distribution:
direct online sales

Most important collections/price range:
NOS Diver, Bathyscaphe / $1,290 to $4,490
(prices plus shipping)

Aquadive

According to Laver's Law, a style that shows up again at the fifty-year mark is "quaint." So much for the outward impact, maybe. But what about the intrinsic long-term personal and ephemeral value, the sometimes collective memories associated with a particular moment in our lives? Today, the very sight of a watch from times past might bring forth images of a different era, much like hearing the songs of Procol Harum or touching Naugahyde in an old Dodge Dart. Nostalgia is a powerful impulse, especially in an era like ours, which appears enamored by its own frenetic pace and refuses categorically to stop and reflect.

So when a group of watch experts decided to revive an iconic watch of the sixties and seventies, they were bound to strike a positive note. In its day, the Aquadive was considered a solidly built and reliable piece of equipment seriously coveted by professional divers. It might still be around had it not been put out to pasture during the quartz revolution.

In its twenty-first century incarnation, the Aquadive bears many hallmarks of the original. The look is unmistakable: the charmingly awkward hands, the puffy cushion case, the sheer stability it exudes. In fact, some of the components, like the 200 NOS case and sapphire crystal, are leftovers from the old stock. The Swiss-made automatic movements and the gaskets, of course, are new.

Modern technologies, like DLC, and advances in CNC machining have transformed the older concepts. And to ensure reliability, the watches are assembled in Switzerland. The top of the current line is the Bathyscaphe series, machined from a block of stainless steel, and featuring new shock absorbers and an automatic helium release valve.

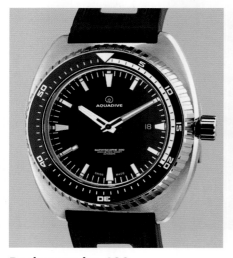

Bathyscaphe 100

Reference number: 1002.11.36211
Movement: automatic, ETA Caliber 2836-2; ø 25.6 mm, height 4.6 mm; 25 jewels; 28,800 vph; 42-hour power reserve; regulated in 5 positions
Functions: hours, minutes, sweep seconds; date
Case: stainless steel, ø 43 mm, height 14 mm; unidirectional bezel with 60-minute divisions; antimagnetic soft iron inner case; sapphire crystal; screw-in crown; automatic helium release valve; water-resistant to 100 atm
Band: Isofrane, buckle
Price: $1,690; limited to 500 pieces
Variations: mesh bracelet ($1,890); gun metal DLC-coated version ($1,890)

Bathyscaphe 300

Reference number: 3002.11.36211
Movement: automatic, ETA Caliber 2824-2; ø 25.6 mm, height 4.6 mm; 25 jewels; 28,800 vph; 42-hour power reserve; regulated in 5 positions
Functions: hours, minutes, sweep seconds; date
Case: stainless steel, ø 47 mm, height 14 mm; unidirectional bezel with 60-minute divisions; sapphire crystal; screw-in crown; automatic helium release valve; water-resistant to 300 atm
Band: Isofrane rubber, buckle
Price: $2,490

Aquadive 200

Reference number: 200NOS.11.36211
Movement: automatic, ETA Caliber 2824-2; ø 25.6 mm, height 4.6 mm; 25 jewels; 28,800 vph; 42-hour power reserve; regulated in 5 positions
Functions: hours, minutes, sweep seconds; date
Case: stainless steel, ø 37 mm, height 11 mm; bidirectional bezel; NOS fiberglass crystal; screw-in crown; water-resistant to 20 atm
Band: Isofrane, buckle
Remarks: case made from original 1962 stock
Price: $1,290
Variations: NATO strap

Aquadive Model 77

Reference number: 771.12.365112
Movement: automatic, ETA Caliber 2836-2;
ø 25.6 mm, height 4.6 mm; 25 jewels; 28,800 vph;
42-hour power reserve; regulated in 5 positions
Functions: hours, minutes, sweep seconds; date
Case: stainless steel, 41 x 51 mm, height 16 mm;
unidirectional bezel with 60-minute divisions;
sapphire crystal; screw-in crown; automatic helium
release valve; water-resistant to 100 atm
Band: rubber, buckle
Price: $1,290; limited to supply of old stock parts
Variations: with mesh bracelet ($1,390);
overhauled NOS Anton Schild movement ($1,390)

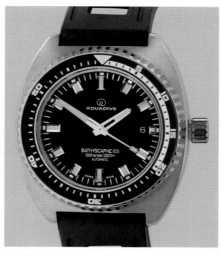

Bathyscaphe 100 Bronze

Reference number: 1006.13.365311
Movement: automatic, ETA Caliber 2836-2;
ø 25.6 mm, height 4.6 mm; 25 jewels; 28,800 vph;
42-hour power reserve; regulated in 5 positions
Functions: hours, minutes, sweep seconds; date
Case: German bronze alloy, ø 43 mm, height
15 mm; unidirectional bezel with 60-minute
divisions; sapphire crystal; screw-in crown;
automatic helium release valve; water-resistant to
100 atm
Band: Isofrane, buckle
Price: $1,690; limited to 100 pieces

Bathysphere 100 GMT

Reference number: 1001.13.935113
Movement: automatic, ETA Caliber 2893-2;
ø 25.6 mm, height 4.2 mm; 21 jewels; 28,800 vph;
42-hour power reserve; regulated in 5 positions
Functions: hours, minutes, sweep seconds; date;
GMT hand for 24-hour indication
Case: stainless steel case, ø 43 mm, height 15 mm;
unidirectional bezel with 60-minute divisions;
sapphire crystal; screw-in crown; automatic helium
release valve; water-resistant to 100 atm
Band: Isofrane, buckle
Price: $1,990; limited to 300 pieces
Variations: with mesh bracelet ($2,150); DLC-
coated gun metal ($2,090); 2 additional dial colors

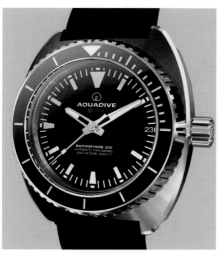

Bathysphere 500

Reference number: 5001.14.VMF.5112
Movement: automatic, decorated In House Caliber,
Geneva stripes, VMF; ø 25.6 mm, height 3.7 mm;
28 jewels; 28,800 vph; 50-hour power reserve;
regulated in 5 positions
Functions: hours, minutes, sweep seconds; date
Case: stainless steel, ø 42 mm, height 11 mm;
unidirectional bezel with 60-minute divisions;
sapphire crystal; transparent case back, screw-in
crown; water-resistant to 500 atm
Band: Isofrane, buckle
Price: $2,990
Variations: stainless steel link bracelet or mesh
bracelet

Bathyscaphe 300 DLC

Reference number: 3002.11.36211
Movement: automatic, ETA Caliber 2824-2;
ø 25.6 mm, height 4.6 mm; 25 jewels; 28,800 vph;
42-hour power reserve; regulated in 5 positions
Functions: hours, minutes, sweep seconds; date
Case: DLC steel, ø 47 mm, height 14 mm;
unidirectional bezel with 60-minute divisions;
sapphire crystal; screw-in crown; automatic helium
release valve; water-resistant to 300 atm
Band: Isofrane rubber, buckle
Price: $2,490

Model 50 Depth Gauge
New Old Stock

Reference number: 1976.50
Movement: quartz, depth gauge
Functions: hours, minutes, seconds; depth gauge
Case: stainless steel, ø 47 mm, height 17 mm;
unidirectional bezel with 60-minute divisions;
mineral crystal; screw-in crown; water-resistant to
20 atm.
Band: Isofrane rubber, buckle
Price: $4,490

Armin Strom AG
Bözingenstrasse 46
CH-2502 Biel/Bienne
Switzerland

Tel.:
+41-32-343-3344

Fax:
+41-32-343-3340

E-Mail:
info@arminstrom.com

Website:
www.arminstrom.com

Founded:
1967

Number of employees:
20

Annual production:
approx. 1,000 watches

U.S. distributor:
Contact Armin Strom headquarters.

Most important collections/price range:
Gravity, One Week, Tourbillon, Racing,
Regulator, Skeleton / $10,100 to $131,600

Armin Strom

For more than thirty years, Armin Strom's name was associated mainly with the art of skeletonizing. But this "grandmaster of skeletonizers" then decided to entrust his life's work to the next generation, which turned out to be the Swiss industrialist and art patron Willy Michel.

Michel had the wherewithal to expand the one-man show into a full-blown *manufacture* able to conceive, design, and produce its own mechanical movements. The endeavor attracted Claude Geisler, a very skilled designer, and Michel's own son, Serge, who became business manager. When this triumvirate joined forces, it was able to come up with a technically fascinating movement at the quaint little *manufacture* in the Biel suburb of Bözingen within a brief period of time.

The new movement went on to grow into a family of eight, which forms the backbone of a new collection, including a tourbillon with microrotor—no mean feat for a small firm. The acronym ARM stands for "Armin reserve de marche" (a seven-day power reserve), and AMW means "Armin manual winding" (a trimmed down manually wound movement with a single spring barrel). These base functions have given the *manufacture* the industrial autonomy to realize complete and rapid product development cycles. In sum, over the past few years, the brand has managed to gradually modernize its range of models and take on a more contemporary profile without losing touch with its origins. The in-house movements are showing off their abilities on new, at times daring, dials.

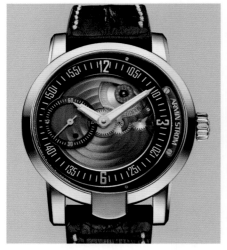

Manual Fire

Reference number: RG11-MF.90
Movement: manually wound, Caliber AMW11; ø 36.6 mm, height 6 mm; 20 jewels; 18,000 vph; Breguet spring, screw balance with gold weight screws; 120-hour power reserve
Functions: hours, minutes, subsidiary seconds
Case: rose gold, ø 43.4 mm, height 13 mm; sapphire crystal; transparent case back; water-resistant to 5 atm
Band: reptile skin, buckle
Remarks: additional rubber bracelet
Price: $21,200; limited to 100 pieces
Variations: Air ($12,000); Water ($9,200); Earth ($9,200)

Gravity Water

Reference number: ST13-GW.50
Movement: automatic, Caliber AMR13; ø 36.6 mm, height 6 mm; 32 jewels; 18,000 vph; screw balance with gold weight screws, Breguet spring; microrotor visible on dial side; 120-hour power reserve
Functions: hours, minutes, subsidiary seconds
Case: stainless steel, ø 43.4 mm, height 13 mm; sapphire crystal; transparent case back; water-resistant to 5 atm
Band: reptile skin, buckle
Remarks: additional rubber bracelet
Price: $12,900; limited to 100 pieces
Variations: Air ($15,700); Fire ($24,900); Earth ($12,900)

Gravity Date Air

Reference number: TI14-DA.50
Movement: automatic, Caliber ADD14; ø 36.6 mm, height 6 mm; 30 jewels; 18,000 vph; screw balance with 18 gold weight screws; Breguet spring; microrotor; 120-hour power reserve
Functions: hours, minutes, subsidiary seconds; additional 24-hour display with day/night indicator; date
Case: titanium, ø 43.4 mm, height 13 mm; sapphire crystal; transparent case back; water-resistant to 5 atm
Band: reptile skin, buckle
Remarks: additional rubber bracelet
Price: $19,400; limited to 100 pieces
Variations: Earth ($16,600); Water ($16,600); Fire ($28,600)

Skeleton Pure Water

Reference number: ST14-PW.05
Movement: manually wound, Caliber ARM09-S; ø 36.6 mm, height 6.2 mm; 34 jewels; 18,000 vph; 2 spring barrels, screw balance with gold weight screws, Breguet spring, crown wheels visible on dial side; skeletonized wheels and spring barrel bridges, base plate with blue PVD coating; 168-hour power reserve
Functions: hours, minutes, subsidiary seconds; power reserve indicator
Case: stainless steel, ø 43.4 mm, height 13 mm; sapphire crystal; transparent back; water-resistant to 5 atm
Band: reptile skin, buckle
Price: $30,000; limited to 100 pieces
Variations: Fire ($42,100); Air ($32,800)

Skeleton Pure Earth

Reference number: ST14-PE.40
Movement: manually wound, Caliber ARM09-S; ø 36.6 mm, height 6.2 mm; 34 jewels; 18,000 vph; 2 spring barrels, screw balance with gold weight screws, Breguet spring, crown wheels visible on dial side; skeletonized wheels and spring barrel bridges, base plate with blue PVD coating; 168-hour power reserve
Functions: hours, minutes, subsidiary seconds; power reserve indicator
Case: stainless steel with black PVD coating, ø 43.4 mm, height 13 mm; sapphire crystal; transparent back; water-resistant to 5 atm
Band: reptile skin, buckle
Price: $30,000; limited to 100 pieces
Variations: Fire ($42,100); Air ($32,800)

Tourbillon Gumball 3000

Reference number: RG15-GB.90
Movement: manually wound, Caliber ATC11-GB; ø 36.6 mm, height 6.2 mm; 24 jewels; 18,000 vph; 1-minute tourbillon, 2 spring barrels, Breguet spring, screw balance with gold weight screws, crown wheels visible on dial side, skeletonized bridges and spring barrels; 240-hour power reserve
Functions: hours, minutes, subsidiary seconds
Case: rose gold, ø 43.4 mm, height 13 mm; sapphire crystal; transparent case back; water-resistant to 5 atm
Band: reptile skin, double folding clasp
Remarks: additional rubber bracelet
Price: $138,400; limited to 5 pieces

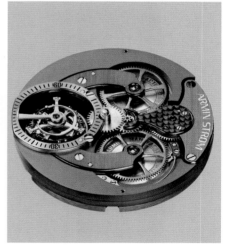

Caliber ARM09-S

Manually wound; crown wheels visible on dial side; platinum gearwheels and spring barrel bridges hand-skeletonized and engraved; double spring barrel; 168-hour power reserve
Functions: hours, minutes, subsidiary seconds
Diameter: 36.6 mm
Height: 6.2 mm
Jewels: 34
Balance: screw balance with gold weight screws
Frequency: 18,000 vph
Balance spring: Breguet spring
Shock protection: Incabloc

Caliber ADD14

Automatic; microrotor; single spring barrel; 120-hour power reserve
Functions: hours, minutes, subsidiary seconds; additional 24-hour display with day/night indicator
Diameter: 36.6 mm
Height: 6 mm
Jewels: 30
Balance: screw balance with gold weight screws
Frequency: 18,000 vph
Balance spring: Breguet spring
Shock protection: Incabloc
Remarks: fine finishing on movement

Caliber ATC11

Manually wound; 1-minute tourbillon, escapement wheel and pallet fork of massive gold with hardened functional surfaces; double spring barrel, 240-hour power reserve
Functions: hours, minutes, subsidiary seconds
Diameter: 36.6 mm
Height: 6.2 mm
Jewels: 24
Balance: screw balance with variable inertia
Frequency: 18,000 vph
Balance spring: Breguet spring
Shock protection: Incabloc
Remarks: fine finishing on movement, hand-engraved bridge

Arnold & Son
38, boulevard des Eplatures
CH-2300 La Chaux-de-Fonds
Switzerland

Tel.:
+41-32-967-9797

Fax:
+41-32-968-0755

E-Mail:
info@arnoldandson.com

Website:
www.arnoldandson.com

Founded:
1995

Number of employees:
approx. 30

U.S. distributor:
Arnold & Son USA
Time Art Distribution
550 Fifth Avenue, Suite 501
New York, NY 10036
212-221-8041

Most important collections/price range:
DBG, DBS, Golden Wheel, HMS, TB88, TBR,
TE8 (Tourbillon), Time Pyramid, UTTE / from
approx. $10,000 to $325,000

Arnold & Son

John Arnold holds a special place among the British watchmakers of the eighteenth and nineteenth centuries because he was the first to literally organize the production of his chronometers along industrial lines. He developed his own standards and employed numerous watchmakers. During his lifetime, he is said to have manufactured around 5,000 marine chronometers which he sold at reasonable prices to the Royal Navy and the West Indies merchant fleet. Arnold chronometers were packed in the trunks of some of the greatest explorers, from John Franklin and Ernest Shackleton to Captain Cook and Dr. Livingstone.

As Arnold & Son was once synonymous with precision timekeeping on the high seas, it stands to reason, then, that the modern brand should also focus its design policies on the interplay of time and geography as well as the basic functions of navigation. Independence from The British Masters Group has meant that the venerable English chronometer brand has been reorienting itself, setting its sights on classic, elegant watchmaking. With the expertise of watch manufacturer La Joux-Perret behind it (and the expertise housed in the building behind the complex on the main road between La Chaux-de-Fonds and Le Locle), it has been able to implement a number of new ideas.

There are two main lines: The Royal Collection celebrates John Arnold's art, with luxuriously designed models inspired from past creations with delicate complications, tourbillons or world-time displays, or unadorned manual windings featuring the new Caliber A&S 1001 by La Joux-Perret. The Instrument Collection is dedicated to exploring the seven seas and offers a sober look reflecting old-fashioned meters. Typically, these timepieces combine two displays on a single dial: a chronograph with jumping seconds, for example, between the off-center displays of time and the date hand or separate escapements driving a dual time display—left the sidereal time, right the solar time, and between the two, the difference. Perhaps the most remarkable timepiece in the collection is the skeletonized Time Pyramid with a dual power reserve, a crown between the lugs, and an overall modern look.

Constant Force Tourbillon

Reference number: 1FCAR.B01A.C112C
Movement: manually wound, Arnold & Son Caliber A&S5119; ø 36.8 mm, height 6 mm; 39 jewels; 21,600 vph; 1-minute tourbillon, patented constant force regulator system; double spring barrel; finely finished; 90-hour power reserve
Functions: hours, minutes, subsidiary seconds (jumping)
Case: red gold, ø 46 mm, height 12.25 mm; sapphire crystal; transparent case back; water-resistant to 3 atm
Band: reptile skin, buckle
Remarks: limited to 28 pieces
Price: $197,500

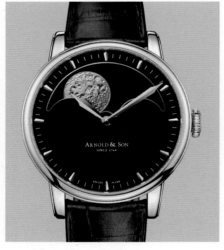

HM Perpetual Moon

Reference number: 1GLAS.B01A.C122S
Movement: manually wound, Arnold & Son Caliber A&S1512; ø 34 mm, height 5.35 mm; 27 jewels; 21,600 vph; astronomically accurate moon phase display over 122 years; 90-hour power reserve
Functions: hours, minutes, moon phase
Case: stainless steel, ø 42 mm, height 11.43 mm; sapphire crystal; transparent case back; water-resistant to 3 atm
Band: reptile skin, buckle
Remarks: sculptural moon
Price: $16,300
Variations: red gold with guillochéed blue dial ($29,950) or crème-colored dial ($29,950)

TEC1

Reference number: 1CTAG.U02A.C113G
Movement: automatic, Arnold & Son Caliber A&S8305; ø 35 mm, height 8.15 mm; 30 jewels; 28,800 vph; 1-minute tourbillon, red gold rotor; finely finished; 55-hour power reserve (w/o chronograph)
Functions: hours, minutes; chronograph
Case: palladium, ø 45 mm, height 16.5 mm; sapphire crystal; transparent case back; water-resistant to 3 atm
Band: reptile skin, buckle
Price: $86,150 (with black dial)
Variations: pink gold with anthracite dial ($99,900); red gold with blue dial ($106,400; limited to 28 pieces)

Golden Wheel

Reference number: 1HVAR.M01A.C120A
Movement: automatic, Arnold & Son Caliber A&S6018; ø 37.2 mm, height 8 mm; 29 jewels; 28,800 vph; finely finished; 50-hour power reserve
Functions: wandering hour numerals on 3 sapphire discs each covering 120° arc and serving as minute hands; deadbeat sweep seconds
Case: red gold, ø 44 mm, height 12.65 mm; sapphire crystal; transparent case back; water-resistant to 3 atm
Band: reptile skin, buckle
Remarks: limited to 125 pieces
Price: $49,950

HMS1

Reference number: 1LCAS.S02A.C111S
Movement: manually wound, Arnold & Son Caliber A&S1001; ø 30 mm, height 2.7 mm; 21 jewels; 21,600 vph; double spring barrel; finely finished; 90-hour power reserve
Functions: hours, minutes, subsidiary seconds
Case: stainless steel, ø 39.5 mm, height 7.68 mm; sapphire crystal; transparent case back; water-resistant to 3 atm
Band: reptile skin, buckle
Remarks: limited to 250 pieces
Price: $9,900
Variations: various dials; rose gold ($16,200); white gold ($17,800)

DSTB

Reference number: 1ATAS.S02A.C121S
Movement: automatic, Arnold & Son Caliber A&S6003; ø 38 mm, height 7.39 mm; 32 jewels; 28,800 vph; escapement visible on dial side; finely finished; 50-hour power reserve
Functions: hours and minutes (off-center), subsidiary seconds (retrograde)
Case: stainless steel, ø 43.5 mm, height 13 mm; sapphire crystal; transparent case back; water-resistant to 3 atm
Band: reptile skin, buckle
Remarks: limited to 250 pieces
Price: $32,555

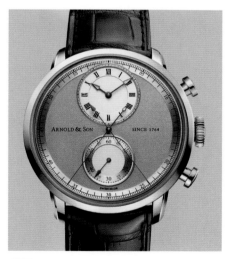

CTB

Reference number: 1CHAS.S02A.C121S
Movement: automatic, Arnold & Son Caliber A&S7103; ø 30.4 mm, height 8.2 mm; 31 jewels; 28,800 vph; finely finished; 50-hour power reserve
Functions: hours and minutes (off-center), sweep seconds (jumping); chronograph
Case: stainless steel, ø 44 mm, height 14 mm; sapphire crystal; transparent case back; water-resistant to 3 atm
Band: reptile skin, buckle
Price: $27,750
Variations: red gold ($44,350)

DBG

Reference number: 1DGAS.S01A.C121S
Movement: manually wound, Arnold & Son Caliber A&S1209; ø 35 mm, height 3.9 mm; 42 jewels; 21,600 vph; double spring barrel, 2 independent gear trains/escapement systems; 40-hour power reserve
Functions: hours and minutes (2 time zones), sweep seconds; day/night indication (per time zone)
Case: stainless steel, ø 44 mm, height 9.89 mm; sapphire crystal; transparent case back; water-resistant to 3 atm
Band: reptile skin, buckle
Remarks: precise display of any 2nd time zone, even Nepal at GMT +5:45
Price: $27,900
Variations: rose gold ($42,600)

Time Pyramid

Reference number: 1TPAS.S01A.C124S
Movement: manually wound, Arnold & Son Caliber A&S1615; ø 37 mm, height 4.4 mm; 27 jewels; 21,600 vph; skeletonized; double spring barrel; 90-hour power reserve
Functions: hours, minutes, subsidiary seconds; double power reserve indicator
Case: stainless steel, ø 44.6 mm, height 10 mm; sapphire crystal; transparent case back; water-resistant to 3 atm
Band: reptile skin, buckle
Remarks: inspired by clocks of John and Roger Arnold
Price: $31,900
Variations: red gold ($43,200)

Luxury Artpieces SA
Route de Thonon 146
CH-1222 Vésenaz
Switzerland

Tel.:
+41-22-752-4940

Website:
www.artya.com

Founded:
2010

Number of employees:
12

Annual production:
at least 365 (one a day)

U.S. distributor:
Contact headquarters for all enquiries.

Most important collections/price range:
Son of a Gun / $8,800 to $167,000; Son of Art / $3,800 to $21,000; Son of Earth / $4,300 to $183,000; Son of Love / $4,300 to $54,500; Son of Sound / $4,300 to $22,110; Son of Gears / $6,550 to $16,550

ArtyA

Shaking up the staid atmosphere of watchmaking can be achieved many ways. The conservative approach is to make some small engineering advance and then talk loudly of tradition and innovation. Yvan Arpa, founder of ArtyA watches, takes another route and enjoys "putting his boot in the anthill," in his own words.

This refreshingly candid personality arrived at watchmaking because, after spending his *Wanderjahre* crossing Papua New Guinea on foot and practicing Thai boxing in its native land, any corporate mugginess back home did not quite cut it for him. Instead he turned the obscure brand Romain Jerome into the talk of the industry with novel material choices: "I looked for antimatter to gentrify common matter," he reflects, "like the rust: proof of the passage of time and the sworn enemy of watchmaking."

After leaving Romain Jerome, he founded his own company, ArtyA, where he could get his "monster" off the slab as it were, with a divine spark. "I had worked with water, rust, dust, and other elements, so then I took fire," says Arpa. Each new ArtyA case was hit with an electrical arc, resulting in something different each time. Inside the cases, besides a solid Swiss-made mechanism, are interesting bits and pieces—from butterfly wings and cut up euros (Bye Bye Euro) to bullets (Son of a Gun). As the brand progresses, the zapped cases are giving way to new and bold shapes in more traditional materials, as in the Son of Sound series with a guitar-shaped case and chrono pushers designed like guitar pegs—Alice Cooper owns one, obviously.

Arpa wants us not only to wear a watch, but to reflect on aspects of our world and society, the meaning of money, bullets, skulls, our love-hate relationship with electronics, the passage of time, love and violence, and the significance of music. His provocations do not arise from a sophomoric need to be contrarian, but rather from his long and rich experience of an industry that tends to play it safe.

Son of Sound Guitar "Race"

Movement: automatic, Artya-Woodstock by Concepto; 27 jewels; 28,800 vph; 48-hour power reserve
Functions: hours, minutes, subsidiary seconds; date; patented active "tuning pegs" system for chronograph functions/date setting; 30-minute counter
Case: stainless steel, 36.62 x 52.3 mm, height 15 mm; water-resistant to 50 atm
Band: reptile skin, buckle
Price: $19,700; limited to 99 pieces

Son of a Gun Russian Roulette "Chocolate"

Movement: manually wound, ArtyA patent; ø 32.6 mm, height 5.7 mm; 19 jewels
Functions: hours, minutes
Case: stainless steel with PVD treatment, ø 44 mm, height 6.2 mm; "ArtyOr" inserts on case; sapphire crystal; transparent back; water-resistant to 5 atm
Band: calf leather strap buckle
Remarks: single lucky bullet spins rapidly around dial with every move
Price: $10,900; limited to 99 pieces

Son of Earth Classic Butterfly "Farfalla"

Movement: automatic Swiss-made; ø 25.6 mm, height 4.4 mm; 25 jewels; 42-hour power reserve
Functions: hours, minutes
Case: stainless steel; ø 42 mm, height 5.7 mm; sapphire crystal; transparent case back; water-resistant to 5 atm
Band: reptile skin, buckle
Remarks: dial decorated with genuine iridescent butterfly wings and gold leaf
Price: $6,500; unique piece

Son of Gears Dark Shams

Movement: manually wound, ArtyA Rising Sun exclusive; skeletonized in steel or different PVD treatment; 52-hour power reserve
Functions: hours, minutes
Case: steel with black PVD treatment, ø 44 mm, height 6.2 mm; ArtyOr or black PVD lateral inserts; screwed-down transparent case back
Band: leather, buckle
Price: $5,950

Son of a Gun Russian Roulette "Glasnost"

Movement: manually wound, ArtyA patent; ø 32.6 mm, height 5.7 mm; 19 jewels; skeletonized spinning dial with real hand-set bullet; 52-hour power reserve
Functions: hours, minutes
Case: ultralight ITR2 (Innovative, Technical, Resin and Revolutionary), 48 mm, height 12 mm; screwed-down engraved case back; water-resistant to 3 atm
Band: reptile skin, buckle
Price: $19,700; limited to 9 pieces

Son of Sound Skull "Catacomb"

Movement: automatic, Soprod A17 modified by ArtyA; 17.6 mm, height 4.8 mm; 19 jewels; rotor with cut-off rounds; 52-hour power reserve
Functions: hours, minutes, seconds
Case: stainless steel with PVD, 48 mm, height 18 mm; target engraved on bezel; screwed-down transparent engraved back; water-resistant to 3 atm
Band: reptile skin, buckle
Remarks: skulls on dial hand engraved
Price: $23,000; unique piece

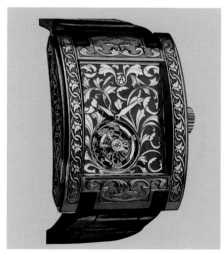

Son of Gears Tourbillon Arabesque

Movement: manual winding; exclusive for ArtyA; height 4.5 mm; flying tourbillon; arabesques on carbon plates on movement and dial side; 96-hour power reserve
Functions: hours, minutes
Case: titanium and carbon composite, 52.5 x 40 mm, height 14 mm; engraved arabesque decoration on bezel; sapphire crystal; water-resistant to 3 atm
Band: reptile skin, folding clasp
Price: $190,500

Son of a Gun Tradition "Riot"

Movement: automatic, Soprod A17 modified by ArtyA; 17.6 mm, height 4.8 mm; 19 jewels; rotor with cut-off rounds; 52-hour power reserve
Functions: hours, minutes
Case: stainless steel with PVD treatment, 48 mm, height 12 mm; target engraved on bezel; screwed-down transparent engraved case back; water-resistant to 3 atm
Band: reptile skin, buckle
Remarks: dial with real hand-set bullet
Price: $14,100; unique piece

Son of a Gun "Target"

Movement: automatic, Soprod A17 modified by ArtyA; 17.6 mm, height 4.8 mm; 19 jewels; rotor with cut-off rounds; 52-hour power reserve
Functions: hours, minutes, seconds
Case: stainless steel with PVD treatment, 47 mm, height 12 mm; target engraved on bezel; screwed-down transparent engraved case back; water-resistant to 3 atm
Band: reptile skin, buckle
Remarks: dial with real hand-set bullet
Price: $8,600

Manufacture d'Horlogerie
Audemars Piguet
Route de France 16
CH-1348 Le Brassus
Switzerland

Tel.:
+41-21-642-3900

E-Mail:
info@audemarspiguet.com

Website:
www.audemarspiguet.com

Founded:
1875

Number of employees:
approx. 1,300

Annual production:
37,000 watches

U.S. distributor:
Audemars Piguet (North America) Inc.
Service Center of the Americas
3040 Gulf to Bay Boulevard
Clearwater, FL 33759

Most important collection/price range:
Royal Oak / from approx. $17,800

Audemars Piguet

The history of Audemars Piguet is one of the most engaging stories of Swiss watchmaking folklore: Ever since their school days together in the Vallée de Joux, Jules-Louis Audemars (b. 1851) and Edward-Auguste Piguet (b. 1853) knew they would follow in the footsteps of their fathers and grandfathers and become watchmakers. They were members of the same sports association, sang in the same choir, attended the same vocational school—and both became outstandingly talented watchmakers.

The *manufacture* that was founded over 140 years ago by these two is still in family hands. The company was able to make extensive investments in production facilities and new movements thanks to the ongoing success of the sporty Royal Oak collection (launched in 1972) and the profits made from selling off shares in Jaeger-LeCoultre in 2000. The Manufacture des Forges, designed according to the latest ecological and economical standards, opened in August 2009 in Le Brassus and is a key to the future of the traditional brand. The second key is no doubt the atelier Renaud et Papi, which has belonged to AP since 1992 and specializes in the most complex complications.

Something must have clicked, because general manager Philippe C. Merk steered the brand through the recession well, even crossing the CHF 550 million mark. Merk and AP parted ways in May 2012, and the company was taken in charge by François-Henry Bennahmias, who previously handled the key Asian market. The new CEO has kept the brand on track, exploring new complications and new crafts and materials with care.

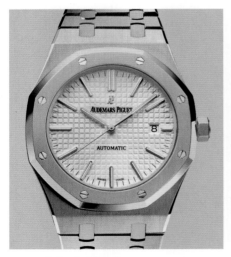

Royal Oak Bicolor

Reference number: 15400SR.00.1220SR.01
Movement: automatic, AP Caliber 3120; ø 26.6 mm, height 4.26 mm; 40 jewels; 21,600 vph; entirely hand-decorated; 60-hour power reserve
Functions: hours, minutes, sweep seconds; date
Case: stainless steel, ø 41 mm, height 9.8 mm; rose gold bezel screwed to case with 8 white gold screws; sapphire crystal; transparent case back; screw-in rose gold crown; water-resistant to 5 atm
Band: stainless steel with rose gold elements, folding clasp
Price: $25,600
Variations: various bands and dials

Royal Oak

Reference number: 15400ST.00.1220ST.01
Movement: automatic, AP Caliber 3120; ø 26.6 mm, height 4.25 mm; 40 jewels; 21,600 vph; entirely hand-decorated
Functions: hours, minutes, sweep seconds; date
Case: stainless steel, ø 41 mm, height 9.8 mm; bezel attached with 8 white gold screws; sapphire crystal; transparent case back; screw-in crown; water-resistant to 30 atm
Band: stainless steel, folding clasp
Price: $17,800
Variations: various dial colors; rose gold/leather band; rose gold/rose gold bracelet

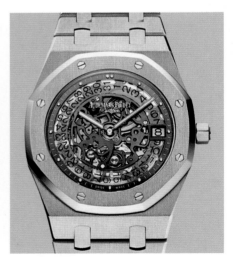

Royal Oak
Extra-Thin Squelette

Reference number: 15204OR.00.1240OR.01
Movement: automatic, AP Caliber 5122; ø 28.4 mm, height 3.05 mm; 36 jewels; 19,800 vph; bridges/rotor hand-skeletonized; entirely hand-decorated; 40-hour power reserve
Functions: hours, minutes; date
Case: rose gold, ø 39 mm, height 8.04 mm; bezel screwed to case with 8 white gold screws; sapphire crystal; transparent case back; water-resistant to 5 atm
Band: rose gold, folding clasp
Price: $85,800

Lady Royal Oak
Reference number: 15451OR.ZZ.1256OR.01
Movement: automatic, AP Caliber 3120; ø 26.6 mm, height 4.26 mm; 40 jewels; 21,600 vph; entirely hand-decorated; 60-hour power reserve
Functions: hours, minutes, sweep seconds; date
Case: rose gold, ø 37 mm, height 9.8 mm; bezel screwed to case with 8 white gold screws and set with 40 brilliants; sapphire crystal; transparent case back; water-resistant to 5 atm
Band: red gold, folding clasp
Price: $48,800

Royal Oak Offshore Diver
Reference number: 15710ST.OO.A002CA.01
Movement: automatic, AP Caliber 3120; ø 26.6 mm, height 4.26 mm; 40 jewels; 21,600 vph; entirely hand-decorated; 60-hour power reserve
Functions: hours, minutes, sweep seconds; date
Case: stainless steel, ø 42 mm, height 14.1 mm; bezel screwed to case with 8 screws; crown adjustable scale ring with 60-minute division; sapphire crystal; screw-in crown; water-resistant to 30 atm
Band: rubber, buckle
Price: $19,000

Royal Oak Offshore Diver
Reference number: 15710ST.OO.A002CA.02
Movement: automatic, AP Caliber 3120; ø 26.6 mm, height 4.26 mm; 40 jewels; 21,600 vph; entirely hand-decorated; 60-hour power reserve
Functions: hours, minutes, sweep seconds; date
Case: stainless steel, ø 42 mm, height 14.1 mm; bezel screwed to case with 8 screws; crown adjustable scale ring with 60-minute division; sapphire crystal; screw-in crown; water-resistant to 30 atm
Band: rubber, buckle
Price: $19,000

Royal Oak Offshore Chronograph
Reference number: 26402CB.OO.A010CA.01
Movement: automatic, AP Caliber 3126/3840; ø 29.92 mm, height 7.16 mm; 59 jewels; 21,600 vph; 55-hour power reserve
Functions: hours, minutes, subsidiary seconds; chronograph; date
Case: ceramic, ø 44 mm, height 14.45 mm; bezel screwed to case with 8 white gold screws; sapphire crystal; ceramic crown, pusher; water-resistant to 10 atm
Band: rubber, buckle
Price: $41,800

Royal Oak Offshore Chronograph
Reference number: 26470OR.OO.1000OR.01
Movement: automatic, AP Caliber 3126/3840; ø 29.92 mm, height 7.16 mm; 59 jewels; 21,600 vph; 55-hour power reserve
Functions: hours, minutes, subsidiary seconds; chronograph; date
Case: rose gold, ø 42 mm, height 14.54 mm; bezel screwed to case with 8 screws; sapphire crystal; transparent case back; screw-in crown; water-resistant to 10 atm
Band: rose gold, folding clasp
Price: $69,200

Royal Oak Offshore Chronograph
Reference number: 26470ST.OO.A801CR.01
Movement: automatic, AP Caliber 3126/3840; ø 29.92 mm, height 7.16 mm; 59 jewels; 21,600 vph; 55-hour power reserve
Functions: hours, minutes, subsidiary seconds; chronograph; date
Case: stainless steel, ø 42 mm, height 14.54 mm; bezel screwed to case with 8 screws; sapphire crystal; transparent case back; screw-in crown; water-resistant to 10 atm
Band: reptile skin, buckle
Price: $26,000

Royal Oak Offshore Tourbillon Chronograph Automatic

Reference number: 26550AU.OO.A002CA.01
Movement: automatic, AP Caliber 2897; ø 35 mm, height 8.32 mm; 34 jewels; 21,600 vph; 1-minute tourbillon, column wheel control of chronograph functions, rotor with platinum oscillating weight; 65-hour power reserve
Functions: hours, minutes, subsidiary seconds; chronograph
Case: carbon fiber, ø 44 mm, height 14 mm; ceramic bezel with 8 titanium screws; sapphire crystal; transparent back; water-resistant to 10 atm
Band: rubber, buckle
Price: $273,200; limited to 50 pieces

Royal Oak Offshore Grande Complication

Reference number: 26571R0.00.A010CA.01
Movement: automatic, AP Caliber 2885; ø 31.6 mm, height 8.95 mm; 52 jewels; 19,800 vph; skeletonized; 45-hour power reserve
Functions: hours, minutes, subsidiary seconds; minute repeater; split-second chronograph; perpetual calendar with date, weekday, month, moon phase
Case: rose gold, ø 44 mm, height 15.7 mm; black ceramic bezel with 8 white gold screws; sapphire crystal; transparent back; ceramic crown, pusher; water-resistant to 2 atm
Band: rubber, buckle
Price: upon request; limited to 3 pieces
Variations: titanium

Lady Royal Oak Offshore

Reference number: 67540SK.ZZ.A010CA.01
Movement: quartz
Functions: hours, minutes; date
Case: stainless steel, ø 37 mm, height 11.1 mm; bezel set with 32 diamonds, screwed to case with 8 screws; sapphire crystal; screw-in crown; water-resistant to 5 atm
Band: rubber, buckle
Price: $16,100

Royal Oak Tourbillon Concept GMT

Reference number: 26580IO.00.D010CA.01
Movement: manually wound, AP Caliber 2930; ø 35.6 mm, height 9.9 mm; 29 jewels; 21,600 vph; 1-minute tourbillon; fine hand-finishing; 237-hour power reserve
Functions: hours, minutes; additional 24-hour display (2nd time zone) with day/night indicator, crown positions shown for changing functions
Case: titanium, ø 44 mm; ceramic bezel; sapphire crystal; ceramic crown, pushers; water-resistant to 2 atm
Band: rubber, folding clasp
Price: $214,200

Royal Oak Tourbillon

Reference number: 26510OR.00.1220OR.01
Movement: manually wound, AP Caliber 2924; ø 31.5 mm, height 4.46 mm; 25 jewels; 21,600 vph; 1-minute tourbillon; 70-hour power reserve
Functions: hours, minutes; power reserve indicator (on case back)
Case: rose gold, ø 41 mm, height 8.85 mm; bezel screwed to case with 8 white gold screws; sapphire crystal; transparent case back; screw-in crown; water-resistant to 5 atm
Band: rose gold, folding clasp
Price: $165,800
Variations: stainless steel case/bracelet ($135,800)

Millenary Quadriennium

Reference number: 26149OR.00.D803CR.01
Movement: manually wound, AP Caliber 2905/B01; 37.9 x 32.9 mm, height 10.05 mm; 38 jewels; 21,600 vph; inverted design with balance and escapement on dial side; 168-hour power reserve
Functions: hours, minutes, subsidiary seconds; 4-year calendar with date, weekday, month
Case: rose gold, 47 x 42 mm, height 15.05 mm; sapphire crystal; transparent case back
Band: reptile skin, folding clasp
Price: $106,800

Millenary Minute Repeater

Reference number: 26371OR.OO.D803CR.01
Movement: manually wound, Audemars Piguet Caliber 2928; 37.9 x 32.9 mm, height 10.05 mm; 40 jewels; 21,600 vph; 165-hour power reserve
Functions: hours, minutes, subsidiary seconds; minute repeater
Case: rose gold, 47 x 42 mm, height 15.79 mm; sapphire crystal; transparent case back
Band: reptile skin, folding clasp
Remarks: enamel dial
Price: $495,700

Millenary 4101

Reference number: 15350ST.OO.D002CR.01
Movement: automatic, AP Caliber 4101; ø 37.25 mm, height 7.46 mm; 34 jewels; 28,800 vph; inverted design with balance and escapement on dial side
Functions: hours, minutes, subsidiary seconds
Case: stainless steel, ø 47 mm, height 13 mm; sapphire crystal; transparent case back
Band: reptile skin, folding clasp
Price: $24,500
Variations: pink gold ($40,300)

Ladies Millenary

Reference number: 77247OR.ZZ.A812CR.01
Movement: manually wound, AP Caliber 5201; 32.74 x 28.59 mm, height 4.16 mm; 19 jewels; 21,600 vph; inverted design with balance and escapement on dial side; 54-hour power reserve
Functions: hours, minutes, subsidiary seconds
Case: white gold, 39.5 x 35.4 mm; sapphire crystal; transparent case back
Band: reptile skin, buckle
Remarks: mother-of-pearl dials, 116 diamonds on case
Price: $28,400

Jules Audemars Chronograph

Reference number: 26153OR.OO.D088CR.01
Movement: manually wound, AP Caliber 2908; ø 37.2 mm; 33 jewels; 43,200 vph; 2 spring barrels; balance with variable inertia; inverted design with balance and escapement on dial side; fine hand-finishing; 90-hour power reserve; COSC-tested chronometer
Functions: hours, minutes, subsidiary seconds; power reserve indicator
Case: pink gold, ø 46 mm, height 12.7 mm; sapphire crystal; transparent case back
Band: reptile skin, folding clasp
Price: $212,500

Jules Audemars Extra-Thin

Reference number: 15180OR.OO.A102CR.01
Movement: automatic, AP Caliber 2120; ø 28.4 mm, height 2.45 mm; 36 jewels; 19,800 vph; 40-hour power reserve
Functions: hours, minutes
Case: rose gold, ø 41 mm, height 6.7 mm; sapphire crystal; transparent case back
Band: reptile skin, buckle
Price: $27,100
Variations: white gold

Jules Audemars Openworked Minute Repeater with Jumping Hours and Small Seconds

Reference number: 26356PT.OO.D028CR.01
Movement: manually wound, AP Caliber 2907; ø 37 mm, height 7.6 mm; 35 jewels; 21,600 vph; Breguet spring; hand-skeletonized; 72-hour power reserve
Functions: hours (jumping), minutes, subsidiary seconds; minute repeater
Case: platinum, ø 43 mm, height 12 mm; sapphire crystal; transparent case back
Band: reptile skin, buckle
Remarks: skeletonized dial
Price: $448,600

Caliber 2120

Automatic; bidirectional winding rotor; extra-flat design, lateral studs and running ring for stability; single spring barrel, 40-hour power reserve
Functions: hours, minutes
Diameter: 28 mm
Height: 2.45 mm
Jewels: 36
Balance: with variable inertia
Frequency: 19,800 vph
Shock protection: Kif Elastor
Remarks: beveled and polished steel parts, perlage on plate, bridges with côtes de Genève

Caliber 2928

Manually wound; inverted design with AP direct impulse balance; single spring barrel; 165-hour power reserve
Functions: hours, minutes, subsidiary seconds; minute repeater
Measurements: 37.9 x 32.9 mm
Height: 10.05 mm
Jewels: 40
Balance: with variable inertia
Frequency: 21,600 vph
Balance spring: double spring (counterwound)
Remarks: all components decorated by hand, 443 components

Caliber 2121

Automatic; bidirectional winding rotor; extra-flat design, lateral studs and running ring for stability; single spring barrel, 40-hour power reserve
Functions: hours, minutes; date
Diameter: 28 mm
Height: 3.05 mm
Jewels: 36
Balance: with variable inertia
Frequency: 19,800 vph
Shock protection: Kif Elastor
Remarks: beveled and polished steel parts, perlage on plate, bridges with côtes de Genève

Caliber 2324-2825

Automatic; rotor with gold weight segment; single spring barrel, 40-hour power reserve
Functions: hours, minutes; date, weekday, moon phase
Diameter: 26.6 mm
Height: 4.6 mm
Jewels: 45
Balance: with variable inertia
Frequency: 28,800 vph
Shock protection: Kif Elastor
Remarks: beveled and polished steel parts, perlage on plate, bridges with côtes de Genève

Caliber 2329-2846

Automatic; rotor with gold weight segment; single spring barrel, 40-hour power reserve
Functions: hours, minutes; 24-hour display; date; power reserve indicator; day/night indicator
Diameter: 26.6 mm
Height: 4.9 mm
Jewels: 33
Balance: with adjustable inertia
Frequency: 28,800 vph
Shock protection: Kif Elastor
Remarks: beveled and polished steel parts, perlage on plate, bridges with côtes de Genève

Caliber 2930

Manually wound; 1-minute tourbillon; central front movement bridge of white ceramic; switch for hand setting and winding; single spring barrel, 237-hour power reserve
Functions: hours, minutes; additional 12-hour indicator (2nd time zone)
Diameter: 35.6 mm
Height: 9.9 mm
Jewels: 29
Balance: screw balance
Frequency: 21,600 vph
Remarks: movement of the Royal Oak concept watch of 2014; beveled and polished steel parts, matte mainplate, straight-grain polished bridges

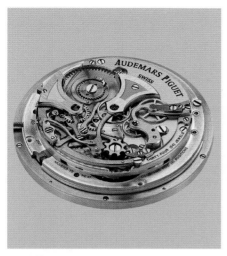

Caliber 2897

Automatic; hubless peripheral rotor with platinum weight turning on edge; column wheel control of chronograph functions; 1-minute tourbillon; simple spring barrel, 65-hour power reserve
Functions: hours, minutes, subsidiary seconds; chronograph
Diameter: 35 mm
Height: 7.75 mm
Jewels: 34
Balance: with variable inertia
Frequency: 21,600 vph
Shock protection: Kif Elastor
Remarks: beveled and guilloché steel parts, perlage on plate

Caliber 2924

Manually wound; 1-minute tourbillon; single spring barrel, 70-hour power reserve
Functions: hours, minutes; power reserve indicator (on movement side)
Diameter: 31.5 mm
Height: 4.46 mm
Jewels: 25
Balance: screw balance
Frequency: 21,600 vph
Shock protection: Kif Elastor
Remarks: beveled and polished steel parts, perlage on plate, bridges with côtes de Genève

Caliber 3120

Automatic; bidirectional winding gold rotor; single spring barrel, 60-hour power reserve
Functions: hours, minutes, sweep seconds; date
Diameter: 26.6 mm
Height: 4.25 mm
Jewels: 40
Balance: with adjustable inertia
Frequency: 21,600 vph
Shock protection: Kif Elastor
Remarks: beveled and polished steel parts, perlage on plate, bridges with côtes de Genève

Caliber 3124-3841

Automatic; bidirectional winding gold rotor; single spring barrel, 60-hour power reserve
Functions: hours, minutes, subsidiary seconds; chronograph
Diameter: 29.94 mm
Height: 7.16 mm
Jewels: 59
Balance: with adjustable inertia
Frequency: 21,600 vph
Shock protection: Kif Elastor
Remarks: beveled and polished steel parts, perlage on plate, bridges with côtes de Genève

Caliber 3126-3840

Base caliber: 3120
Automatic; bidirectional winding gold rotor; single spring barrel, 60-hour power reserve
Functions: hours, minutes, subsidiary seconds; chronograph; date
Diameter: 29.94 mm
Height: 7.15 mm
Jewels: 59
Balance: with adjustable inertia
Frequency: 21,600 vph
Shock protection: Kif Elastor
Remarks: beveled and polished steel parts, perlage on plate, bridges with côtes de Genève

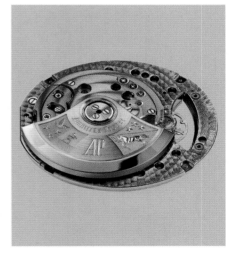

Caliber 4101

Automatic; inverted construction (escapement on dial side); bidirectional winding gold rotor with ceramic ball bearings; single spring barrel, 60-hour power reserve
Functions: hours, minutes, subsidiary seconds
Measurements: 37.25 x 32.9 mm
Height: 7.46 mm
Jewels: 34
Balance: with variable inertia
Frequency: 28,800 vph
Shock protection: Kif Elastor
Remarks: all components decorated by hand; dial side of plate with horizontal côtes de Genève, perlage on back; rhodium-plated bridges, beveled and with decorative graining

Azimuth Watch Co. Sàrl
Rue des Draizes n° 5
CH-2000 Neuchâtel
Switzerland

Tel.:
+41-79-765-1466

E-Mail:
gpi@azimuthwatch.com
sales@azimuthwatch.com

Website:
www.azimuthwatch.com

Founded:
2004

Number of employees:
10

U.S. distributor:
Coast Time
800 S. Pacific Coast Highway, Suite 8446
Redondo Beach, CA 90277
888-609-1010

Most important collections/price range:
SP-1 / $3,800 to $102,000

Azimuth

Creativity can take on all forms and accept all forms as well. That appears to be the philosophy behind Azimuth, a brand that has sprouted an eclectic and surprising bouquet of watch designs. The company is named for the mathematical term defining the arc of a horizon from a reference point. *Azimuth* is a word of Arabic origin meaning "the route taken by a traveler" or even "the way." It is a term, and indeed a concept, that suggests unbeaten paths, and Azimuth delivers, with avant-garde designs for luxury timepieces. The Mr. Roboto and Chrono Gauge Mecha-1 are tongue-in-cheek statements about the meaning of a mechanical watch. The SP-1 Mecanique Spaceship and its adventurous mix of displays, powered by a highly modified ETA Unitas 6497, feature a variety of imaginative dials. The single three-dimensional titanium hand vaguely recalls a spaceship. The SP-1 Landship made it over the top (yes, it refers to a WWI tank) in time for the 2014 centennial commemorations. Given all these complicated devices, the single-hand Back-In-Time pieces appear as mysterious as a koan.

The journey continues: Giuseppe Picchi, an experienced watchmaker, invested in the company and was named CTO in 2015. His brief is to create new movements to support Azimuth's particular approach to design and to develop new timepieces. "The brand founders and I share the same vision of taking contemporary watchmaking as far as we possibly can," says Picchi. The prospect is exciting for Azimuth fans.

Retrograde Minutes MOP Metal Element Dragon

Reference number: RN.RM.SS.L002
Movement: automatic, in-house modified (base ETA); 21,600/28,800 vph; ø 33.1 mm, height 6.4 mm
Functions: retrograde minutes, hours, seconds
Case: stainless steel, ø 42 mm, height 14.8 mm; domed sapphire crystal; water-resistant to 3 atm
Band: calf leather, folding clasp
Remarks: dragon motif engraved on single piece of MOP
Price: $7,000; limited to 25 pieces
Variations: fire red dragon MOP dial, limited to 25 pieces

Back In Time (BIT) Silver Rose

Reference number: RN.BT.SS.D003
Movement: automatic, in-house modified (base ETA/Sellita); 21,600/28,800 vph; ø 34.4 mm; height 4.5 mm
Functions: single hand in counterclockwise motion; date
Case: stainless steel, ø 42 mm, height 14.4 mm; domed sapphire crystal; water-resistant to 3 atm
Band: calf leather, buckle
Price: $2,050
Variations: beige, black, blue, anthracite, etc., dials

SP-1 Spaceship Predator

Reference number: SP.SS.SS.N004
Movement: manual winding, AZM 768 modified and skeletonized; 18,000 vph; ø 36.6 mm; height 4.5 mm
Functions: jumping hours, minutes, seconds
Case: stainless steel, ø 47.8 mm; domed sapphire crystal; water-resistant to 3 atm
Band: reptile skin or calf leather, folding clasp
Remarks: 3D titanium minute hand
Price: $6,700
Variations: PVD case

SP-1 King Casino

Reference number: SP.KC.SS.001
Movement: automatic, in-house modified (base ETA); 21,600 vph; ø 25.6 mm, height 6.0 mm
Functions: hours, minutes, seconds; casino game function by depressing crown
Case: stainless steel, 45 x 45 mm; domed sapphire crystal; water-resistant to 3 atm
Band: calf leather, folding clasp
Remarks: roulette and baccarat game functions
Price: $3,800
Variations: chocolate color or yellow gold plated

SP-1 King Casino

Reference number: SP.KC.PV.002
Movement: automatic, in-house modified (base ETA); 21,600 vph; ø 25.6 mm, height 6.0 mm
Functions: hours, minutes, seconds; casino game function by depressing crown
Case: stainless steel plated, 45 x 45 mm; domed sapphire crystal; water-resistant to 3 atm
Band: calf leather, folding clasp
Remarks: roulette and baccarat game functions
Price: $3,800
Variations: stainless steel or yellow gold plated

SP-1 Crazy Rider

Reference number: SP.MC.SS.001
Movement: automatic, in-house modified (base ETA); 28,800 vph; length 47.7 mm, height 4.35 mm
Functions: 24-hour chain drive hour system, minutes
Case: stainless steel, 55 x 36 mm; sapphire crystal; water-resistant to 3 atm
Band: calf leather, folding clasp
Price: $5,500
Variations: brown dial

SP-1 Twin Barrel Tourbillon

Reference number: SP.TB.TI.L001
Movement: manual winding tourbillon; in-house modified; 5-day power reserve; twin barrels; 28,800 vph; 36.3 x 32.0 mm; height 6.4 mm
Functions: jumping hours, minutes; specially modified twin-disc jumping hour system on 3D minute hand
Case: titanium with carbon fiber side inserts, 45 x 50 mm, height 18.3 mm; domed sapphire crystal; water-resistant to 5 atm
Band: calf leather, folding clasp
Price: $102,000; limited to 25 pieces

SP-1 Mr. Roboto

Reference number: ME.RB.SS.N001
Movement: automatic, in-house modified (base ETA); 21,600/28,800 vph; ø 32.5 mm, height 6.7 mm
Functions: regulator hours, retrograde minutes, seconds; GMT
Case: stainless steel; 43 x 50 mm; sapphire crystal; water-resistant to 5 atm
Band: calf leather, buckle
Price: $5,150
Variations: stainless steel bracelet

SP-1 Landship

Reference number: SP.LS.TI.L001
Movement: automatic, in-house modified (base ETA); 21,600/28,800 vph; ø 32.5 mm, height 6.4 mm
Functions: wandering hour, retrograde minutes
Case: titanium, 55 x 40 mm; water-resistant to 3 atm
Band: rubber, folding clasp
Price: $7,300
Variations: handpainted military camouflage case

Ball Watch Company SA
Rue du Châtelot 21
CH-2300 La Chaux-de-Fonds
Switzerland

Tel.:
+41-32-724-53-00

Fax:
+41-32-724-53-01

E-Mail:
info@ballwatch.ch

Website:
www.ballwatch.com

Founded:
1891

U.S. distributor:
Ball Watch USA
1920 Dr. Martin Luther King Jr. St. N
Suite D
St. Petersburg, FL 33704
727-896-4278

Most important collections/price range:
Engineer, Fireman, Trainmaster, Conductor /
$1,300 to $6,500

Ball Watch Co.

Engineer, Fireman, Trainmaster, Conductor . . . these names for the Ball Watch Co. collections trace back to the company's origins and evoke the glorious age when trains puffing smoke and steam crisscrossed America. Back then, the pocket watch was a necessity to maintain precise rail schedules. By 1893, many companies had adopted the General Railroads Timepiece Standards, which included such norms as regulation in at least five positions, precision to within thirty seconds per week, Breguet balance springs, and so on. One of the chief players in developing the standards was Webster Clay Ball. This farmboy-turned-watchmaker from Fredericktown, Ohio, decided to leave the homestead for a more lucrative occupation. He apprenticed as a watchmaker, became a salesperson for Dueber watch cases, and finally opened the Webb C. Ball Company in Cleveland. In 1891, he added the position of chief inspector of the Lake Shore Lines to his CV. When a hogshead's watch stopped resulting in an accident, Ball decided to establish quality benchmarks for watches that included antimagnetic technology, and he set up an inspection system for the timepieces.

Today, Ball Watch Co. has maintained its lineage, although now producing in Switzerland. These rugged, durable watches aim to be "accurate in adverse conditions," so the company tagline says—and at a very good price. Functionality remains a top priority, so Ball will go to special lengths to work special technologies into its timepieces. Ball has also developed special oils for cold temperatures, for instance. And it is one of few brands to use tritium gas tubes to light up dials, hands, and markers. For those who need to read the time accurately in dark places—divers, pilots, commandos, hunters, etc.—this is essential.

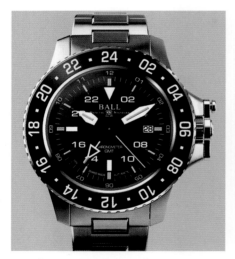

Engineer Hydrocarbon AeroGMT

Reference number: DG2016A-SCJ-BK
Movement: automatic, BALL Caliber RR1201-C; ø 25.6 mm, height 4.1 mm; 21 jewels; 28,800 vph; 42-hour power reserve; COSC-certified chronometer
Functions: hours, minutes, sweep seconds; date; 2nd time zone indication
Case: stainless steel, ø 42 mm, height 13.85 mm; sapphire bidirectional bezel with micro gas tube illumination; sapphire crystal; crown protection system; water-resistant to 30 atm
Band: stainless steel, folding clasp and extension
Remarks: micro gas tube illumination; shock-resistant; antimagnetic
Price: $3,999

Engineer Hydrocarbon Airborne

Reference number: DM2076C-S1CAJ-BK
Movement: automatic, BALL Caliber RR1102-CSL; ø 25.6 mm, height 5.05 mm; 25 or 26 jewels; 28,800 vph; 38-hour power reserve; COSC-certified chronometer
Functions: hours, minutes, sweep seconds; day, date
Case: stainless steel, ø 42 mm, height 13.85 mm; SpringLOCK® antishock system; ceramic unidirectional bezel; sapphire crystal; crown protection system; water-resistant to 12 atm
Band: stainless steel, folding clasp and extension
Remarks: micro gas tube illumination; shock-resistant; antimagnetic
Price: $4,399

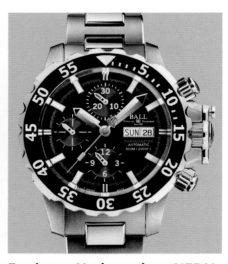

Engineer Hydrocarbon NEDU

Reference number: DC3026A-SC-BK
Movement: automatic, BALL Caliber RR1402-C; ø 30 mm, height 7.9 mm; 25 jewels; 28,800 vph; 48-hour power reserve; COSC-certified chronometer
Functions: hours, minutes, subsidiary seconds; day, date; 12-hour chronograph operable underwater
Case: stainless steel, ø 42 mm, height 17.30 mm; patented helium system; ceramic unidirectional bezel; sapphire crystal; crown protection system; water-resistant to 60 atm
Band: titanium/stainless steel, folding clasp, extension
Remarks: micro gas tube illumination; shock-resistant; antimagnetic
Price: $4,799

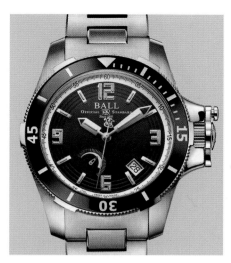

Engineer Hydrocarbon Hunley

Reference number: PM2096B-S1J-BK
Movement: automatic, BALL Caliber RR1702; ø 25.6 mm, height 4.85 mm; 21 jewels; 28,800 vph; 42-hour power reserve; Amortiser® antishock system
Functions: hours, minutes, sweep seconds; date; power reserve indication
Case: stainless steel, ø 42 mm, height 17.3 mm; ceramic unidirectional bezel; sapphire crystal; patented crown protection; water-resistant to 20 atm
Band: stainless steel, folding clasp and extension
Remarks: micro gas tube illumination; antimagnetic
Price: $3,899; limited to 500 pieces

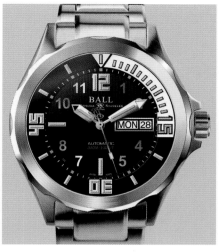

Engineer Master II Diver

Reference number: DM3020A-SAJ-BK
Movement: automatic, BALL Caliber RR1102; ø 25.6 mm, height 5.05 mm; 25 or 26 jewels; 28,800 vph; 38-hour power reserve
Functions: hours, minutes, sweep seconds; day, date
Case: stainless steel, ø 42 mm, height 14.55 mm; inner bezel with micro gas tube illumination; sapphire crystal; screw-in crown; water-resistant to 30 atm
Band: stainless steel, folding clasp
Remarks: micro gas tube illumination; shock-resistant; antimagnetic
Price: $2,399

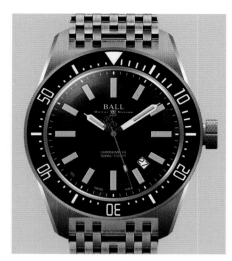

Engineer Master II Skindiver II

Reference number: DM3108A-SCJ-BK
Movement: automatic, BALL Caliber RR1103-C; ø 25.6 mm, height 4.6 mm; 25 or 26 jewels; 28,800 vph; 38-hour power reserve; COSC-certified chronometer
Functions: hours, minutes, sweep seconds; date
Case: stainless steel, ø 43 mm, height 14 mm; ceramic unidirectional bezel; helium valve, sapphire crystal; screw-in crown; water-resistant to 50 atm
Band: stainless steel, folding clasp
Remarks: micro gas tube illumination; shock-resistant; antimagnetic
Price: $2,799

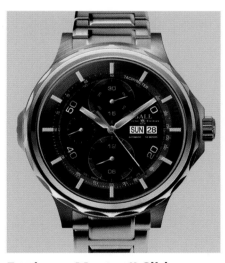

Engineer Master II Slide Chronograph

Reference number: CM3888D-S1J-BK
Movement: automatic, BALL Caliber RR1402; ø 30 mm, height 7.9 mm; 25 jewels; 28,800 vph; 48-hour power reserve
Functions: hours, minutes, subsidiary seconds; day, date; 12-hour patented slide chronograph
Case: stainless steel, ø 47.6 mm, height 15.5 mm; sapphire crystal; screw-in crown; water-resistant to 5 atm
Band: stainless steel, folding clasp
Remarks: micro gas tube illumination; shock-resistant
Price: $3,399

Engineer Master II Pilot GMT

Reference number: GM3090C-LLAJ-BK
Movement: automatic, BALL Caliber RR1201; ø 25.6 mm, height 4.1 mm; 21 jewels; 28,800 vph; 42-hour power reserve
Functions: hours, minutes, sweep seconds; magnified date; 2nd time zone
Case: stainless steel, ø 43.5 mm, height 11.9 mm; aluminum unidirectional bezel; sapphire crystal; screw-in crown; transparent back; water-resistant to 10 atm
Band: reptile skin, buckle
Remarks: micro gas tube illumination; shock-resistant; antimagnetic
Price: $2,499

Engineer II Green Berets

Reference number: NM2028C-L4CJ-BK
Movement: automatic, BALL Caliber RR1103-C; ø 25.6 mm, height 4.6 mm; 25 or 26 jewels; 28,800 vph; 38-hour power reserve; COSC-certified chronometer
Functions: hours, minutes, sweep seconds; magnified date
Case: titanium carbide, ø 43 mm, height 12.35 mm; sapphire crystal; screw-in crown; water-resistant to 10 atm
Band: nubuck leather, buckle
Remarks: micro gas tube illumination; shock-resistant; antimagnetic
Price: $2,199

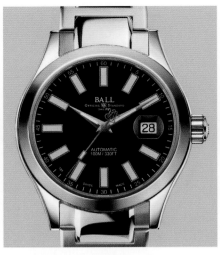

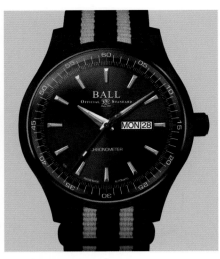

Engineer II Magneto S

Reference number: NM3022C-N1CJ-BK
Movement: automatic, BALL Caliber RR1103-CSL; ø 25.6 mm, height 4.6 mm; 25 or 26 jewels; 28,800 vph; 38-hour power reserve; COSC-certified chronometer
Functions: hours, minutes, sweep seconds; date
Case: stainless steel, ø 42 mm, height 12.9 mm; A-PROOF® antimagnetic system; SpringLOCK® antishock system; sapphire crystal; screw-in crown; transparent case back; water-resistant to 10 atm
Band: fabric, buckle
Remarks: micro gas tube illumination; shock-resistant
Price: $3,399

Engineer II Marvelight

Reference number: NM2026C-S6-BK
Movement: automatic, BALL Caliber RR1103; ø 25.6 mm, height 4.6 mm; 25 or 26 jewels; 28,800 vph; 38-hour power reserve
Functions: hours, minutes, sweep seconds; date
Case: stainless steel, ø 40 mm, height 13.15 mm; sapphire crystal; screw-in crown; water-resistant to 10 atm
Band: stainless steel, folding clasp
Remarks: micro gas tube illumination; shock-resistant; antimagnetic
Price: $1,799
Variations: blue, gray, or silver dial

Engineer II Volcano

Reference number: NM3060C-PCJ-GY
Movement: automatic, BALL Caliber RR1102-C; ø 25.6 mm, height 5.05 mm; 25 or 26 jewels; 28,800 vph; 38-hour power reserve; COSC-certified chronometer
Functions: hours, minutes, sweep seconds; day, date
Case: patented Mumetal & Carbide composite, ø 45 mm, height 12.4 mm; sapphire crystal; screw-in crown; water-resistant to 10 atm
Band: textile, buckle
Remarks: micro gas tube illumination; shock-resistant; antimagnetic
Price: $3,599

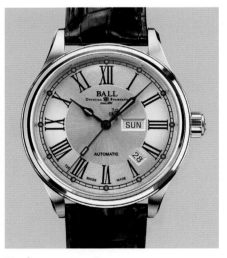

Trainmaster Cannonball

Reference number: CM1052D-S3J-WH
Movement: automatic, BALL Caliber RR1401-SL; ø 30 mm, height 7.5 mm; 49 jewels; 28,800 vph; 38-hour power reserve
Functions: hours, minutes, subsidiary seconds; date; 45-minute chronograph
Case: stainless steel, ø 43 mm, height 14.8 mm; SpringLOCK® antishock system; sapphire crystal; transparent case back; screw-in crown; water-resistant to 5 atm
Band: stainless steel, folding clasp
Remarks: micro gas tube illumination; shock-resistant
Price: $3,899
Variations: black or gray dial

Trainmaster Cleveland Express

Reference number: NM1058D-LCJ-SL
Movement: automatic, BALL Caliber RR1102-C; ø 25.6 mm, height 5.05 mm; 25 or 26 jewels; 28,800 vph; 38-hour power reserve; COSC-certified chronometer
Functions: hours, minutes, sweep seconds; day, date
Case: stainless steel, ø 41 mm, height 12.5 mm; antireflective convex sapphire crystal; sapphire crystal case back; screw-in crown; water-resistant to 5 atm
Band: reptile skin, buckle or clasp
Remarks: satin dial; micro gas tube illumination; shock-resistant
Price: $2,799

Trainmaster Roman

Reference number: NM1058D-L4J-WH
Movement: automatic, BALL Caliber RR1102; ø 25.6 mm, height 5.05 mm; 25 or 26 jewels; 28,800 vph; 38-hour power reserve
Functions: hours, minutes, sweep seconds; day, date
Case: stainless steel, ø 41 mm, height 12.55 mm; antireflective sapphire crystal; screw-in crown; sapphire crystal case back; water-resistant to 5 atm
Band: reptile skin, buckle or clasp
Remarks: micro gas tube illumination; shock-resistant
Price: $1,899
Variations: gray dial

Fireman Storm Chaser Pro

Reference number: CM3090C-L1J-BK
Movement: automatic, BALL Caliber RR1402;
ø 30 mm, height 7.9 mm; 25 jewels; 28,800 vph;
48-hour power reserve
Functions: hours, minutes, subsidiary seconds; day,
date; 12-hour chronograph; telemeter
Case: stainless steel, ø 42 mm, height 15.65 mm;
aluminum bezel, sapphire crystal; screw-in crown;
transparent case back; water-resistant to 10 atm
Band: calf leather, buckle
Remarks: micro gas tube illumination; shock-
resistant
Price: $3,199
Variations: gray or white dial

Fireman NECC

Reference number: DM3090A-SJ-BK
Movement: automatic, BALL Caliber RR1103;
ø 25.6 mm, height 4.6 mm; 25 or 26 jewels;
28,800 vph; 38-hour power reserve
Functions: hours, minutes, sweep seconds; date
Case: stainless steel, ø 42 mm, height 13.2 mm;
stainless steel carbide rotating bezel, sapphire
crystal; transparent case back; screw-in crown;
water-resistant to 30 atm
Band: stainless steel, folding clasp
Remarks: micro gas tube illumination; shock-
resistant
Price: $1,599
Variations: blue or silver dial

Ball for BMW TimeTrekker

Reference number: DM3010B-SCJ-BK
Movement: automatic, BALL Caliber RR1102-C;
ø 25.6 mm, height 5.05 mm; 25 or 26 jewels;
28,800 vph; 38-hour power reserve; COSC-certified
chronometer
Functions: hours, minutes, sweep seconds; day,
date
Case: stainless steel, ø 44 mm, height 13.45 mm;
Amortiser® antishock system; ceramic unidirectional
bezel; antireflective sapphire crystal; screw-in crown;
transparent case back; water-resistant to 20 atm
Band: stainless steel, folding clasp
Remarks: micro gas tube illumination; antimagnetic
Price: $3,099
Variations: blue dial

Ball for BMW GMT

Reference number: GM3010C-SCJ-SL
Movement: automatic, BALL Caliber RR1201-C;
ø 25.6 mm, height 4.1 mm; 21 jewels; 28,800 vph;
42-hour power reserve; COSC-certified chronometer
Functions: hours, minutes, sweep seconds; date;
2nd time zone indication
Case: stainless steel, ø 42 mm, height 12.64 mm;
Amortiser® antishock system; antireflective
sapphire crystal; screw-in crown; sapphire crystal
case back; water-resistant to 10 atm
Band: stainless steel, folding clasp
Remarks: micro gas tube illumination; antimagnetic
Price: $4,399
Variations: black DLC case; black dial

Ball for BMW Chronograph

Reference number: CM3010C-P1CJ-BK
Movement: automatic, BALL Caliber RR1402-C;
ø 30 mm, height 7.9 mm; 25 jewels; 28,800 vph;
48-hour power reserve; COSC-certified chronometer
Functions: hours, minutes, subsidiary seconds; day,
date; 12-hour chronograph
Case: stainless steel with black DLC, ø 44 mm,
height 16 mm; Amortiser® antishock system;
sapphire crystal; screw-in crown; transparent case
back; water-resistant to 10 atm
Band: rubberized leather, folding clasp
Remarks: micro gas tube illumination; antimagnetic
Price: $4,999
Variations: stainless steel case

Ball for BMW TMT

Reference number: NT3010C-P1CJ-BKF
Movement: automatic, BALL Caliber RR1601-C;
ø 25.6 mm, height 5.1 mm; 21 jewels; 28,800 vph;
42-hour power reserve; COSC-certified chronometer
Functions: hours, minutes, sweep seconds;
mechanical thermometric indication
Case: stainless steel with black DLC, ø 44 mm,
height 13.25 mm; Amortiser® antishock system;
sapphire crystal; screw-in crown; transparent case
back; water-resistant to 10 atm
Band: rubberized leather, folding clasp
Remarks: micro gas tube illumination; antimagnetic
Price: $5,299; limited to 1,000 pieces
Variations: TMT Celsius scale

Baume & Mercier
chemin de la Chênaie 50
CH-1293 Bellevue
Switzerland

Tel.:
+41-022-999-5151

Fax:
+41-44-972-2086

Website:
www.baume-et-mercier.com
register on the website to contact via e-mail

Founded:
1830

U.S. distributor:
Baume & Mercier
Richemont North America
New York, NY 10022
800-MERCIER

Most important collections/price range:
Clifton (men) / $2,700 to $13,950; Capeland (men) / $4,350 to $19,990; Hampton (men and women) / $3,450 to $15,000; Linea (women) / $1,950 to $15,750; Classima / $1,750 to $5,950

Baume & Mercier

Baume & Mercier and its elite watchmaking peers Cartier and Piaget make up the quality timepiece nucleus in the Richemont Group's impressive portfolio. The tradition-rich brand counts among the most accessible and most affordable watches of the Genevan luxury brands. In the past decade, it has created a number of remarkable—and often copied—classics. The twelve-sided Riviera and the Catwalk have had to step off the stage, but the classic rectangular Hampton continues to evolve. In recent years, the company has worked hard to gain acceptance in the men's market for its Classima Executives line and to build on watchmaking glory of days gone by, when Baume & Mercier was celebrated as a chronograph specialist.

Though the brand has taken up residence in Geneva, most of the watches are produced in a reassembly center built a few years ago in Les Brenets near Le Locle. Individual parts are made by specialized suppliers according to the strictest of quality guidelines. Some of these manufacturers are sister companies within the Richemont Group.

Keeping the brand abreast of trends is key to its design strategy. The newly interpreted, iconic Classima, with its streamlined look, is very much in tune with the modern zeitgeist. The company's 185th anniversary was feted with a new Clifton featuring a *manufacture* movement made in Schaffhausen and offered as a limited edition. Elsewhere, too, the brand has been busy. A Clifton with a large date and a series of new Hamptons have been added to its portfolio.

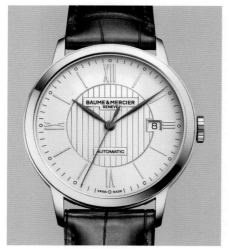

Classima
Reference number: 10214
Movement: automatic, Sellita Caliber SW 200-1; ø 25.6 mm, height 4.6 mm; 26 jewels; 28,000 vph; côtes de Genève on rotor; 38-hour power reserve
Functions: hours, minutes, sweep seconds; date
Case: stainless steel, ø 40 mm, height 8.95 mm; sapphire crystal; transparent case back; water-resistant to 5 atm
Band: reptile skin, double folding clasp
Price: $2,350
Variations: stainless steel bracelet ($2,700)

Classima
Reference number: 10220
Movement: automatic, ETA Caliber 2892; ø 25.6 mm, height 3.6 mm; 25 jewels; 28,800 vph; côtes de Genève; 42-hour power reserve
Functions: hours, minutes, sweep seconds; date
Case: stainless steel, ø 36.5 mm, height 7.95 mm; sapphire crystal; transparent case back; water-resistant to 5 atm
Band: stainless steel, double folding clasp
Price: $2,600
Variations: mother-of-pearl dial set with diamonds ($2,950)

Hampton
Reference number: 10155
Movement: automatic, ETA Caliber 2892-A2; ø 25.6 mm, height 3.6 mm; 21 jewels; 28,800 vph; côtes de Genève on rotor; 42-hour power reserve
Functions: hours, minutes, sweep seconds; date
Case: stainless steel, 31 x 47 mm, height 10 mm; sapphire crystal; transparent case back; water-resistant to 5 atm
Band: reptile skin, double folding clasp
Price: $2,650
Variations: brown leather band

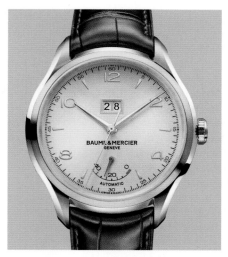

Clifton Large Date RDM

Reference number: 10205
Movement: automatic, Soprod Caliber 9090 (base ETA 2892-A2); ø 25.6 mm, height 5.1 mm; 30 jewels; 28,800 vph; finely finished; côtes de Genève on rotor; 42-hour power reserve
Functions: hours, minutes, sweep seconds; power reserve indicator; large date
Case: stainless steel, ø 43 mm, height 12.05 mm; sapphire crystal; transparent case back; water-resistant to 5 atm
Band: reptile skin, double folding clasp
Price: $4,100

Clifton 8 Days Power Reserve

Reference number: 10195
Movement: manually wound, IWC Caliber 59210; ø 37.8 mm, height 5.8 mm; 30 jewels; 28,800 vph; finely decorated; 192-hour power reserve
Functions: hours, minutes, subsidiary seconds; power reserve indicator; date
Case: red gold, ø 45 mm, height 13 mm; sapphire crystal; transparent case back; water-resistant to 5 atm
Band: reptile skin, buckle
Remarks: limited to 185 pieces
Price: $17,900

Clifton Moon Phase

Reference number: 10213
Movement: automatic, Dubois Dépraz Caliber 9000 (base ETA 2892-A2); ø 25.6 mm, height 5.35 mm; 25 jewels: 28,800 vph; finely finished; 42-hour power reserve
Functions: hours, minutes, sweep seconds; full calendar with date, weekday, month, moon phase
Case: stainless steel, ø 43 mm, height 12.3 mm; sapphire crystal; transparent case back; water-resistant to 5 atm
Band: reptile skin, double folding clasp
Price: $4,950

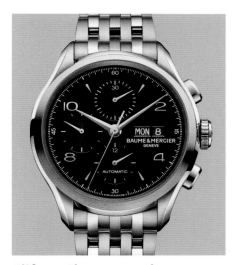

Clifton Chronograph

Reference number: 10212
Movement: automatic, ETA Caliber 7750; ø 30 mm, height 7.9 mm; 25 jewels; 28,800 vph; finely finished; 42-hour power reserve
Functions: hours, minutes, subsidiary seconds; chronograph; date, weekday
Case: stainless steel, ø 43 mm, height 14.95 mm; sapphire crystal; transparent case back; water-resistant to 5 atm
Band: stainless steel, double folding clasp
Price: $3,950

Promesse

Reference number: 10183
Movement: automatic, ETA Caliber 2671; ø 17.5 mm, height 4.8 mm; 25 jewels; 28,800 vph; 38-hour power reserve
Functions: hours, minutes, sweep seconds
Case: stainless steel, ø 30 mm, height 9.8 mm; pink gold bezel; sapphire crystal; transparent case back; water-resistant to 5 atm
Band: stainless steel with red gold elements, folding clasp
Price: $4,450

Promesse

Reference number: 10182
Movement: automatic, ETA Caliber 2671; ø 17.5 mm, height 4.8 mm; 25 jewels; 28,800 vph; 38-hour power reserve
Functions: hours, minutes, sweep seconds
Case: stainless steel, ø 30 mm, height 9.8 mm; sapphire crystal; transparent case back; water-resistant to 5 atm
Band: stainless steel, double folding clasp
Price: $2,990

Bell & Ross Ltd.
8 rue Copernic
F-75116 Paris
France

Tel.:
+33-1-73-73-93-00

Fax:
+33-1-73-73-93-01

E-Mail:
sav@bellross.com

Website:
www.bellross.com

Founded:
1992

U.S. distributor:
Bell & Ross, Inc.
605 Lincoln Road, Suite 300
Miami Beach, FL 33139
888-307-7887; 305-672-3840 (fax)
www.bellross.com

Most important collections/price range:
Instrument BR 01 and BR 03 / approx.
$3,100 to $200,000

Bell & Ross

Known for robust, "large-print" watches with a military look, Paris-headquartered Bell & Ross develops, manufactures, assembles, and regulates its famed timepieces in a modern factory in La Chaux-de-Fonds in the Jura mountains of Switzerland. In recent years, working with outside specialists, the company has dared to design even more complicated watches such as tourbillons and wristwatches with uncommon shapes. This kind of ambitious innovation has only been possible since perfume and fashion specialist Chanel—which also maintains a successful watch line in its own right—became a significant Bell & Ross shareholder and brought the watchmaker access to the production facilities where designers Bruno Belamich and team can to create more complicated, more interesting designs for their aesthetically unusual "instrument" watches.

Belamich continues to prove his skills where technical features and artful proportions are concerned, and what sets Bell & Ross timepieces apart from those of other, more traditional professional luxury makers is their special, roguish look—a delicate balance between striking, martial, and poetic. And it is this beauty for the eye to behold that makes the company's wares popular with style-conscious "civilians" as well as with the pilots, divers, astronauts, sappers, and other hard-riding professionals drawn to Bell & Ross timepieces for their superior functionality.

PW1 Minute Répetition 5 Minutes Skeleton

Reference number: BRPW1-REPET-ARG-MI
Movement: manually wound, Dubois Dépraz Caliber; ø 36.6 mm, height 8.25 mm; partially skeletonized; 56-hour power reserve
Functions: hours, minutes, subsidiary seconds; 5-minute repeater
Case: silver, ø 52 mm, sapphire crystal; transparent case back; water-resistant to 3 atm
Remarks: limited to 25 pieces
Price: $43,000

Vintage WW1 Edición Limitada

Reference number: BRWW1-GRM-PG
Movement: manually wound, Caliber BR-CAL.202; ø 30 mm, height 5.65 mm; 34 jewels; 28,800 vph; partly skeletonized mainplate with opening over escapement; twin spring barrels; beveled bridges, fine finishing with blued screws, côtes de Genéve 120-hour power reserve
Functions: hours, minutes, sweep seconds; power reserve indicator
Case: pink gold, ø 42 mm, height 10 mm; sapphire crystal; transparent case back; water-resistant to 5 atm
Band: reptile skin, buckle
Price: $24,000; limited to 99 pieces

Vintage WW1 Argentium

Reference number: BRWW1-ME-AG
Movement: manually wound, ETA Caliber 7001; ø 23.3 mm, height 2.5 mm; 17 jewels; 21,600 vph; 42-hour power reserve
Functions: hours, minutes, subsidiary seconds
Case: silver, ø 41 mm, height 10.2 mm; sapphire crystal; water-resistant to 3 atm
Band: reptile skin, folding clasp
Price: $5,900

Vintage BR 126 Sport Heritage GMT & Flyback

Movement: automatic, modified ETA Caliber 2894; ø 28.6 mm, height 6.1 mm; 37 jewels; 28,800 vph; 40-hour power reserve
Functions: hours, minutes, subsidiary seconds; additional 24-hour display (2nd time zone); flyback chronograph; date
Case: stainless steel, ø 43 mm; bezel with aluminum inlay, sapphire crystal; transparent case back; water-resistant to 10 atm
Band: calf leather, folding clasp
Remarks: limited to 500 pieces
Price: $7,900

BR 01 10th Anniversary

Reference number: BR0192-10TH-CE
Movement: automatic, BR Caliber 302 (based on ETA 2892-A2); ø 25.6 mm, height 3.6 mm; 21 jewels; 28,800 vph; 42-hour power reserve
Functions: hours, minutes, sweep seconds
Case: ceramic, 46 x 46 mm, height 10.5 mm; bezel attached to monocoque case with 4 screws; sapphire crystal; screw-in crown; water-resistant to 10 atm
Band: rubber, buckle
Remarks: limited to 500 pieces
Price: $5,300

BR 03-94 Rafale

Reference number: BR0394-RAFALE-CE
Movement: automatic, Caliber BR-CAL.301 (based on ETA 2894-2); ø 28.6 mm, height 6.1 mm; 37 jewels: 28,800 vph; 42-hour power reserve
Functions: hours, minutes, subsidiary seconds; chronograph; date
Case: ceramic, 42 x 42 mm, height 12.3 mm; bezel attached to monocoque case with 4 screws; sapphire crystal; water-resistant to 10 atm
Band: rubber, buckle
Remarks: limited to 500 pieces
Price: $6,200

BR S Golden Heritage

Reference number: BRS92-G-HE-ST
Movement: automatic, Caliber BR-CAl.302 (based on ETA 2892-A2); ø 25.6 mm, height 3.6 mm; 21 jewels, 28,800 vph; 38-hour power reserve
Functions: hours, minutes, sweep seconds; date
Case: stainless steel, 39 x 39 mm, height 10.5 mm; bezel attached to monocoque case with 4 screws; sapphire crystal; water-resistant to 5 atm
Band: calf leather, buckle
Price: $3,300

BR-X1 Tourbillon Titanium

Reference number: BRX1-CE-CF-BLACK
Movement: automatic, Caliber BR-CAL.313; ø 30 mm, height 7.9 mm; 56 jewels; 28,800 vph; partly skeletonized
Functions: hours, minutes, subsidiary seconds; chronograph; date
Case: titanium and carbon fiber, 45 x 45 mm, height 12 mm; bezel attached to monocoque case with 4 screws; sapphire crystal; transparent back; water-resistant to 10 atm
Band: rubber, buckle
Price: $19,500; limited to 250 pieces
Variations: carbon forgé ($23,000)

BR-X1 Chronograph Tourbillon

Reference number: BRX1-CHTB-TI
Movement: automatic, Caliber BR-CAL.MHC; ø 34 mm, height 7.4 mm; 1-minute tourbillon; 100-hour power reserve
Functions: hours, minutes; power reserve indicator; chronograph
Case: titanium, 45 x 45 mm; sapphire crystal; transparent case back
Band: rubber, buckle
Price: $163,000; limited to 20 pieces
Variations: rose gold ($180,000; limited to 20 pieces)

Blancpain SA
Le Rocher 12
CH-1348 Le Brassus
Switzerland

Tel.:
+41-21-796-3636

Website:
www.blancpain.com

Founded:
1735

U.S. distributor:
Blancpain
The Swatch Group (U.S.), Inc.
1200 Harbor Boulevard
Weehawken, NJ 07086
201-271-1400

Most important collections/price range:
L'Evolution, Villeret, Fifty Fathoms
Bathyscaphe, Le Brassus, Women / $9,800
to $400,000

Blancpain

In its advertising, the Blancpain watch brand has always proudly declared that, since 1735, the company has never made quartz watches and never will. Indeed, Blancpain is Switzerland's oldest watchmaker, and by sticking to its ideals, the company was put out of business by the "quartz boom" of the 1970s.

The Blancpain brand we know today came into being in the mid-eighties, when Jean-Claude Biver and Jacques Piguet purchased the venerable name. The company was subsequently moved to the Frédéric Piguet watch factory in Le Brassus, where it quickly became largely responsible for the renaissance of the mechanical wristwatch. This success caught the attention of the Swatch Group—known at that time as SMH. In 1992, it swooped in and purchased both companies to add to its portfolio. Movement fabrication and watch production were melded to form the Blancpain Manufacture in mid-2010.

Over the past several years, Blancpain president Marc A. Hayek has put a great deal of energy into the company's technical originality. He is frank about the fact that the development of the new *manufacture* caliber harnessed most of Blancpain's creative potential, leaving little to apply to its existing collection of watches. Still, in terms of complications, Blancpain watches have always been in a class of their own. And now even more models are being introduced, watches that feature the company's own basic movement and a choice of manual or automatic winding, like the new collection, the Fifty Fathoms Bathyscaphe, a modern interpretation of the classic diver's watch of 1953. As part of the planned consolidation of the entire collection, the other major families—the Villeret, Le Brassus, L'Evolution, and Sport—will be reworked over time.

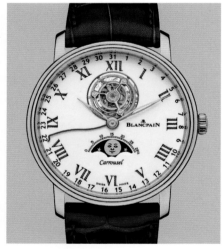

Le Brassus Carrousel Répétition Minutes Chronograph Flyback

Reference number: 2358-3631-55B
Movement: automatic, Blancpain Caliber 2358; ø 32.8 mm; height 11.7 mm; 59 jewels; 21,600 vph; escapement system with 1-minute flying tourbillon, 1-minute carrousel
Functions: hours, minutes; minute repeater; flyback chronograph with 30-minute sweep counter
Case: pink gold, ø 45 mm, height 17.8 mm; sapphire crystal; transparent back; water-resistant to 3 atm
Band: reptile skin, folding clasp
Remarks: enamel dial
Price: $449,600

Villeret Tourbillon Volant Une Minute 12 Jours

Reference number: 66240-3431-55B
Movement: automatic, Blancpain Caliber 242; ø 30.6 mm; height 6.1 mm; 43 jewels; 28,800 vph; flying 1-minute tourbillon; 288-hour power reserve
Functions: hours, minutes; power reserve display (on case back)
Case: platinum, ø 42 mm, height 11.65 mm; sapphire crystal; transparent back; water-resistant to 3 atm
Band: reptile skin, folding clasp
Remarks: enamel dial
Price: $148,800; limited to 188 pieces
Variations: pink gold ($127,400)

Villeret Carrousel Phases de Lune

Reference number: 6622L-3631-55B
Movement: automatic, Blancpain Caliber 225L; ø 31.9 mm, height 6.86 mm; 40 jewels; 28,800 vph; flying 1-minute carrousel; 120-hour power reserve
Functions: hours, minutes; date; moon phase
Case: pink gold, ø 42 mm, height 12.74 mm; sapphire crystal; transparent case back; water-resistant to 3 atm
Band: reptile skin, folding clasp
Remarks: enamel dial
Price: $129,600
Variations: platinum ($151,000; limited to 88 pieces)

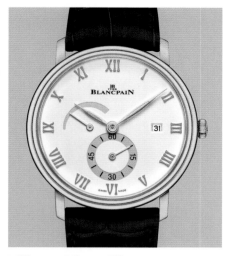

L'Evolution Tourbillon Carrousel

Reference number: 92322-34B39-55B
Movement: manually wound, Blancpain Caliber 2322V2; ø 35.3 mm, height 5.05 mm; 70 jewels; 21,600 vph; escapement system with flying 1-minute tourbillon with differential compensation; 3 spring barrels; 168-hour power reserve
Functions: hours, minutes; power reserve display (on movement side)
Case: platinum, ø 47.4 mm, height 11.66 mm; sapphire crystal; transparent case back; water-resistant to 3 atm
Band: reptile skin, folding clasp
Price: $373,130; limited to 50 pieces

Villeret Perpetual Calendar 8 Days Power Reserve

Reference number: 6659-3631-55B
Movement: automatic, Blancpain Caliber 5939A; ø 32 mm, height 7.25 mm; 42 jewels; 28,800 vph; 192-hour power reserve
Functions: hours, minutes, subsidiary seconds; perpetual calendar with date, weekday, month, moon phase, leap year
Case: pink gold, ø 42 mm, height 13.5 mm; sapphire crystal; transparent back; water-resistant to 3 atm
Band: reptile skin, folding clasp
Price: $58,900
Variations: pink gold Milanese mesh bracelet ($78,200); platinum ($80,300; limited to 188 pieces)

Villeret Ultra-Slim

Reference number: 6606A-1127-55B
Movement: manually wound, Blancpain Caliber 11C5; ø 26.2 mm, height 3.3 mm; 23 jewels; 21,600 vph; 72-hour power reserve
Functions: hours, minutes, subsidiary seconds; power reserve indicator; date
Case: stainless steel, ø 40 mm, height 8.55 mm; sapphire crystal; transparent case back; water-resistant to 3 atm
Band: reptile skin, folding clasp
Price: $9,600
Variations: stainless steel bracelet ($12,000); pink gold on strap ($19,200); pink gold on pink gold bracelet ($38,500)

Villeret Retrograde Seconds

Reference number: 6653Q-1127-55B
Movement: automatic, Blancpain Caliber 7663Q; ø 27 mm, height 4.75 mm; 34 jewels; 28,800 vph; 65-hour power reserve
Functions: hours, minutes, subsidiary seconds (retrograde); date
Case: stainless steel, ø 40 mm, height 10.88 mm; sapphire crystal; transparent case back; water-resistant to 3 atm
Band: reptile skin, folding clasp
Price: $12,860
Variations: stainless steel bracelet ($15,240)

Villeret Large Date

Reference number: 6669-3642-55B
Movement: automatic, Blancpain Caliber 6950; ø 32 mm, height 4.75 mm; 35 jewels; 28,800 vph; 2 spring barrels; 72-hour power reserve
Functions: hours, minutes, sweep seconds; large date
Case: pink gold, ø 40 mm, height 10.88 mm; sapphire crystal; transparent case back; water-resistant to 3 atm
Band: reptile skin, folding clasp
Price: $21,300
Variations: stainless steel ($11,660); stainless steel on stainless steel bracelet ($14,050); pink gold on pink gold bracelet ($40,640)

X Fathoms

Reference number: 5018-1230-64A
Movement: automatic, Blancpain Caliber 9918B (base Blancpain 1315); ø 36 mm, height 13 mm; 48 jewels; 28,800 vph; 3 spring barrels; 120-hour power reserve
Functions: hours, minutes, sweep seconds; mechanical depth gauge (split scale) with display of max. diving depth; 5-minute countdown
Case: titanium, ø 55.65 mm, height 24 mm; unidirectional bezel with 60-minute divisions; sapphire crystal; helium valve; water-resistant to 30 atm
Band: rubber, buckle
Price: $40,700

Fifty Fathoms Bathyscaphe Chronograph Ocean Commitment

Reference number: 5200-0240-52A
Movement: automatic, Blancpain Caliber F385;
ø 31.8 mm, height 6.65 mm; 37 jewels; 36,000 vph;
silicon spring; 50-hour power reserve
Functions: hours, minutes, subsidiary seconds;
flyback chronograph; date
Case: titanium, ø 43.6 mm, height 14.85 mm;
unidirectional ceramic bezel, 60-minute divisions;
sapphire crystal; transparent case back; water-
resistant to 30 atm
Band: textile, buckle
Price: $20,200

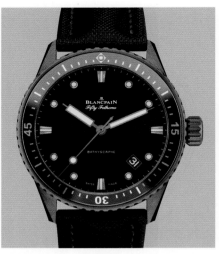

Fifty Fathoms Bathyscaphe

Reference number: 5000-0130-B52A
Movement: automatic, Blancpain Caliber
1315; ø 30.6 mm, height 5.65 mm; 35 jewels;
28,800 vph; silicon spring; 120-hour power reserve
Functions: hours, minutes, sweep seconds; date
Case: ceramic, ø 43 mm, height 13.4 mm;
unidirectional bezel with 60-minute divisions;
sapphire crystal; transparent case back; screw-in
crown; water-resistant to 30 atm
Band: textile, buckle
Price: $12,860
Variations: various textile bands; stainless steel
($10,500)

L'Evolution Rattrapante Chronograph

Reference number: 8886F-1503-52B
Movement: automatic, Blancpain Caliber 69F9;
ø 32 mm, height 8.4 mm; 44 jewels; 21,600 vph;
40-hour power reserve
Functions: hours, minutes, subsidiary seconds;
rattrapante chronograph; large date
Case: white gold, ø 43 mm, height 16.04 mm;
carbon-fiber bezel; sapphire crystal, transparent
case back; water-resistant to 30 atm
Band: textile, folding clasp
Remarks: carbon-fiber dial
Price: $55,700
Variations: pink gold ($55,700)

Women Day Night

Reference number: 3740-3744-58B
Movement: automatic, Blancpain Caliber 1163JN;
ø 34 mm, height 5.96 mm; 47 jewels; 28,800 vph;
40-hour power reserve
Functions: hours (retrograde), minutes, subsidiary
seconds (retrograde); day/night indicator
Case: pink gold, ø 40 mm, height 11.35 mm;
diamonds on bezel; sapphire crystal; transparent
case back; transparent case back; water-resistant
to 3 atm
Band: ostrich leather, buckle
Remarks: mother-of-pearl dial with sapphires and
diamonds
Price: $51,500
Variations: white gold ($51,500)

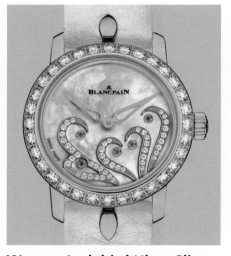

Women Ladybird Ultra-Slim

Reference number: 0063B-2954-63A
Movement: automatic, Blancpain Caliber 6150;
ø 15.7 mm, height 3.9 mm; 29 jewels; 28,800 vph;
40-hour power reserve
Functions: hours, minutes
Case: pink gold, ø 21.5 mm, height 18.7 mm;
diamonds on bezel; sapphire crystal; transparent
case back; water-resistant to 3 atm
Band: leather, buckle
Remarks: mother-of-pearl dial with rubies and
diamonds
Price: $22,500
Variations: white gold ($22,500)

Women

Reference number: 3650-1944L-58B
Movement: automatic, Blancpain Caliber 2653;
ø 26 mm, height 4.47 mm; 28 jewels; 28,800 vph;
72-hour power reserve
Functions: hours and minutes (off-center)
Case: white gold, ø 36.8 mm, height 10.3 mm;
diamonds on bezel; sapphire crystal; diamond
cabochon on crown; water-resistant to 3 atm
Band: ostrich leather, folding clasp
Remarks: mother-of-pearl dial
Price: $35,300

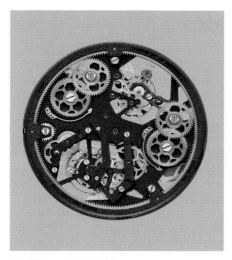

Caliber 2322V2

Manually wound; 2 independent escapement systems (1-minute carrousel and 1-minute tourbillon) with differential gearbox between the 2; 3 spring barrels; 168-hour power reserve
Functions: hours, minutes, date
Diameter: 35.3 mm
Height: 5.85 mm
Jewels: 70
Balance: glucydur with regulating screws (2x)
Frequency: 21,600 vph
Remarks: skeletonized movement; bridges with black coating; 350 components

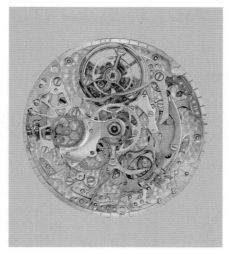

Caliber 2358

Automatic; escapement with 1-minute carrousel; single spring barrel; 65-hour power reserve
Functions: hours, minutes, minute repeater with cathedral gong; flyback chronograph 30-minute sweep counter
Diameter: 32.8 mm
Height: 11.7 mm
Jewels: 59
Balance: glucydur with gold regulating screws
Frequency: 28,800 vph
Balance spring: flat hairspring
Shock protection: Kif
Remarks: hand-engraved bridges and rotor; 546 components

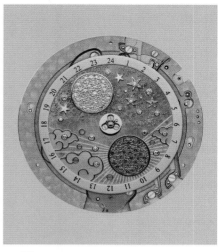

Caliber 1163JN

Automatic; single barrel spring, 40-hour power reserve
Functions: hours (retrograde), minutes, subsidiary seconds (retrograde); day/night indicator (jumping disc display)
Diameter: 34 mm
Height: 5.96 mm
Jewels: 47
Balance: glucydur
Frequency: 28,800 vph
Remarks: disc display for day/night indication with starry sky and set with precious stones; 372 components

Caliber 152B

Manually wound; inverted structure with time display on case back, bridges with black ceramic inserts; single spring barrel; 40-hour power reserve
Functions: hours, minutes
Diameter: 35.64 mm
Height: 2.95 mm
Jewels: 21
Balance: screw balance
Frequency: 21,600 vph
Balance spring: flat hairspring
Shock protection: Kif

Caliber 225l

Automatic; flying 1-minute tourbillon, 2 separate gearworks; single spring barrel; 120-hour power reserve
Functions: hours, minutes; date, moon phase
Diameter: 31.9 mm
Height: 6.86 mm
Jewels: 40
Balance: glucydur with weighted screw
Frequency: 28,800 vph
Balance spring: silicon
Shock protection: Kif
Remarks: 281 components

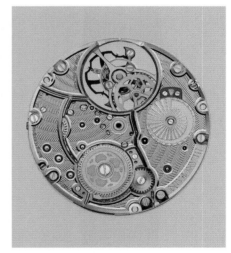

Caliber 242

Automatic; flying 1-minute tourbillon with silicon balance and anchor horns; hubless peripheral rotor at edge; 4 spring barrels; 288-hour power reserve
Functions: hours, minutes; power reserve indicator (on case back)
Diameter: 30.6 mm
Height: 6.1 mm
Jewels: 43
Balance: silicon
Frequency: 21,600 vph
Remarks: very fine finishing, hand-guillochéed bridges; 243 components

Botta Design
Klosterstraße 15a
D-61462 Königstein im Taunus
Germany

Tel.:
+49-6174-961-188

Fax:
+49-6174-961-189

Website:
www.botta-design.de

E-Mail:
info@botta-design.de

Founded:
1986

Number of employees:
5

Annual production:
approx. 5,000 watches

U.S. distributor:
Direct distribution through selected retailers.
Contact the company.

Most important collections:
UNO and UNO 24 one-hand series, NOVA

Botta Design

Botta Design develops and creates wristwatches with a very well-defined designer look. And the company has been very strict about living up to its motto "Designed in Germany—Made in Germany." Klaus Botta chalks up his success to the long years of collaboration with German firms mostly in Pforzheim and in the Black Forest, traditional sources of components for wristwatches.

What Botta and his small team come up with falls somewhere on or around the juncture between engineering and design. Botta first studied engineering physics and then industrial design before starting his own business in 1986. The company focuses on the end-to-end development of products for the audiovisual, medical technology, furniture, and engineering markets, but wristwatches were a part of the portfolio right from the start. The first entry-level watch models, Botta's "Watch People," express his concept of sleek, technological design and became the hallmark of the following generations of watches—featuring one, two, or three hands. At the company headquarters in Königstein near Frankfurt, a flexible team takes care of conceptual work, design, development, quality control, sales, and service for the watches.

To ensure the longevity of the watches, only top-drawer materials are used—sapphire crystal, stainless steel, and titanium. The movements are Swiss ETAs or Rondas. Botta's strategy works: The company has already won forty-five awards for design. The latest was a Red Dot for the Duo 24, a unique, one-hand watch with, remarkably, a second time zone. The Nova collection takes minimalism a step further, by almost blanking out the dial.

UNO+ Alpin Automatic
Movement: automatic, ETA Caliber 2824-2; ø 25.6 mm, height 4.6 mm; 25 jewels; 28,800 vph; 38-hour power reserve
Functions: hours (each line stands for 5 minutes); date
Case: stainless steel, ø 44 mm, height 8.8 mm; sapphire crystal; transparent case back; water-resistant to 3 atm
Band: calf leather, buckle
Price: $960
Variations: black PVD coating ($960); rubber strap ($960)

NOVA Carbon Automatic
Movement: automatic, ETA Caliber 2824-2; ø 25.6 mm, height 4.6 mm; 25 jewels; 28,800 vph; 38-hour power reserve
Functions: hours (each line stands for 1 hour); date
Case: stainless steel, with black PVD coating, ø 44 mm, height 8.8 mm; sapphire crystal; transparent case back; water-resistant to 3 atm
Band: calf leather, buckle
Price: $960
Variations: white dial w/o PVD coating ($960); rubber strap ($960)

UNO 24 NEO
Movement: quartz, Ronda Caliber 515.24H
Functions: 24 hours (each line stands for 10 minutes), date
Case: stainless steel, ø 40 mm, height 7.2 mm; sapphire crystal; water-resistant to 3 atm
Band: calf leather, buckle
Price: $430
Variations: stainless steel bracelet ($540), with rubber strap ($510); with black PVD coating ($490)

Bovet

If any brand can claim real connections to China, it is Bovet, founded by Swiss businessman Edouard Bovet. He emigrated to Canton, China in 1818 and sold four watches of his own design there. On his return to Switzerland in 1822, he set up a company for shipping his Fleurier-made watches to China. The company name, pronounced "Bo Wei" in Mandarin, became a synonym for "watch" in Asia. At one point, Bovet even had offices in Canton. For more than eighty years, Bovet and his successors supplied the Chinese ruling class with valuable timepieces.

In 2001, the brand was bought by entrepreneur Pascal Raffy. He ensured the company's industrial independence by acquiring several other companies as well, notably the high-end watchmaker Swiss Time Technology (STT) in Tramelan, which he renamed Dimier 1738. In addition to creating its own line of watches, this *manufacture* produces complex technical components such as tourbillons for Bovet watches. Assembly of Bovet creations takes place at the headquarters in the thirteenth-century Castle of Môtiers in Val-de-Travers not far from Fleurier.

Bovet watches have several distinctive features—undoubtedly a reason for their growing fame. The first is intricate dial work, featuring not only complex architecture, but also very fine enameling. The second is the lugs and crown at 12 o'clock, recalling Bovet's tasteful pocket watches of the nineteenth century. On some models, the wristbands are made to be easily removed so the watch can be worn on a chain or cord. Other watches convert to table clocks.

Bovet Fleurier S.A.
109 Pont-du-Centenaire
CP183 CH-1228 Plan-les-Ouates
Switzerland

Tel.:
+41-22-731-4638

Fax:
+41-22-884-1450

E-Mail:
info@bovet.com

Website:
www.bovet.com

Founded:
1822

Annual production:
2,500 timepieces

U.S. distributor:
Bovet LLC USA
3363 NE 163rd Street, Suite 703
North Miami Beach, FL 33160
888-909-1822

Most important collections/price range:
Amadeo Fleurier, Dimier, Pininfarina, Sportster / $18,500 to $1,000,000

Dimier Récital 12 "Monsieur Dimier"

Reference number: R120007
Movement: manually wound, Bovet Caliber Virtuoso II "Spécialités Horlogères" 13DM01 ; ø 30 mm, height 3.9 mm; 21,600 vph; 7-day power reserve; inverted design with balance/escapement on dial side
Functions: hours/minutes (off-center), subsidiary seconds; power reserve display
Case: pink gold, ø 42 mm, height 9.4 mm; sapphire crystal; transparent back; water-resistant to 3 atm
Band: reptile skin, pink gold buckle
Price: $43,700; limited to 100 pieces
Variations: diamonds ($101,200); white gold ($43,700; limited to 100); white gold/diamonds ($101,200)

Amadeo Fleurier "Monsieur Bovet"

Reference number: AI43002
Movement: manually wound, Bovet Caliber 13BM09AI; ø 31.02 mm, 41 jewels; 21,600 vph; 7-day power reserve
Functions: hours, minutes; power reserve display, subsidiary coaxial seconds, reversed watch: hours, minutes, seconds
Case: pink gold, ø 43 mm, height 12.35 mm; sapphire crystal; water-resistant to 3 atm
Band: reptile skin, pink or white gold buckle
Remarks: convertible case turns timepiece into reversible wristwatch, table clock, or pocket watch
Price: $57,500
Variations: white gold (from $61,000)

Dimier Récital 17

Reference number: R170002
Movement: manually wound, Bovet Caliber 13DM033FPL; ø 31.02 mm, height 12.7 mm; 37 jewels; 21,600 vph; 7-day power reserve
Functions: hours, minutes, subsidiary seconds (on movement side); 2nd/3rd time zone with reference city adjustment and day/night display; power reserve indicator (on movement side); double moon phase
Case: white gold, ø 45.3 mm, height 15.6 mm; sapphire crystal; sapphire cabochon on crown; water-resistant to 3 atm
Band: reptile skin, white gold buckle
Price: $69,000; limited to 100 pieces
Variations: pink gold (from $69,000; limited to 100)

Montres Breguet SA
CH-1344 L'Abbaye
Switzerland

Tel.:
+41-21-841-9090

Fax:
+41-21-841-9084

Website:
www.breguet.com

Founded:
1775 (Swatch Group since 1999)

U.S. distributor:
Breguet
The Swatch Group (U.S.), Inc.
1200 Harbor Boulevard, 7th Floor
Weehawken, NJ 07087
201-271-1400

Most important collections:
Classique, Tradition, Héritage, Marine, Reine
de Naples, Type XX

Breguet

We never quite lose that attachment to the era in which we were born and grew up, nor do some brands. Abraham-Louis Breguet (1747–1823), who hailed from Switzerland, brought his craft to Paris in the *Sturm und Drang* atmosphere of the late eighteenth century. It was fertile ground for one of the most inventive watchmakers in the history of horology, and his products soon found favor with the highest levels of society.

Little has changed two centuries later. After a few years of drifting, in 1999 the brand carrying this illustrious name became the prize possession of the Swatch Group and came under the personal management of Nicolas G. Hayek, CEO. Hayek worked assiduously to restore the brand's roots, going as far as rebuilding the legendary Marie Antoinette pocket watch and contributing to the restoration of the Petit Trianon at Versailles.

Breguet is a full-fledged *manufacture*, and this has allowed it to forge ahead uncompromisingly with upscale watches and even jewelry. In modern facilities on the shores of Lake Joux, traditional craftsmanship still plays a significant role in the production of its fine watches, but at the same time, Breguet is one of the few brands to work with modern materials for its movements. This is not just a PR trick, but rather a sincere attempt to improve quality and rate precision. Many innovations have debuted at Breguet, for instance pallet levers and balance wheels made of silicon, the first Breguet hairspring with the arched terminal curve made of this glassy material, or even a mechanical high-frequency balance beating at 72,000 vph. Other innovations include the electromagnetic regulation of a minute repeater or the use of two micro-magnets to achieve contactless anchoring of a balance wheel staff.

Breguet, now under the auspices of Nicolas G. Hayek's grandson, Marc A. Hayek, continues to explore the edges of the technologically possible in watchmaking.

Tradition
Independent Chronograph

Reference number: 7077BB G19XV
Movement: manually wound, Breguet Caliber 580 DR; 62 jewels; 21,600 vph; Breguet spring, silicon pallet lever and escapement wheel; independent gearwheels and escapement (36,000 vph) with blade spring energy store to drive chronograph, chrono functions controlled by anchor-shaped switch; 50-hour power reserve
Functions: hours and minutes (off-center); power reserve indicator; chronograph, with retrograde minute counter and function display
Case: white gold, ø 44 mm, height 13.95 mm; sapphire crystal; transparent case back; water-resistant to 3 atm
Band: reptile skin, folding clasp
Price: $79,700

Tradition
Seconde Rétrograde

Reference number: 7097BB G1 9WU
Movement: automatic, Breguet Caliber 505 SR; 38 jewels; 21,600 vph; Breguet spring, silicon pallet levers; 50-hour power reserve
Functions: hours and minutes (off-center), subsidiary seconds (retrograde)
Case: white gold, ø 40 mm, height 11.65 mm; sapphire crystal; transparent case back; water-resistant to 3 atm
Band: reptile skin, folding clasp
Price: $33,500
Variations: rose gold ($32,700)

Tradition
Minute Repeater Tourbillon

Reference number: 7087BR G1 9XV
Movement: automatic, Breguet Caliber 565DR; 60 jewels; 28,800 vph; 1-minute tourbillon; Breguet spring, silicon pallet lever and escape wheel, titanium mainplate, bridges, upper tourbillon bridge; repeater mechanism with magnet regulator; assymetrical loop-shaped gongs, axial hammer-strike (not radial) hubless peripheral rotor; 80-hour power reserve
Functions: hours, minutes; power reserve display; minute repeater
Case: rose gold, ø 44 mm, height 13.6 mm; sapphire crystal; transparent case back; water-resistant to 3 atm
Band: reptile skin, folding clasp
Price: $460,700

Classique Grande Complication Minute Repeater

Reference number: 7637BB 12 9ZU
Movement: manually wound, Breguet Caliber 567/2; ø 28 mm, height 5.8 mm; 31 jewels; 18,000 vph; hand-decorated; 40-hour power reserve
Functions: hours, minutes, subsidiary seconds; added 24-hour display (2nd time zone); hour, quarter-hour, and minute repeater
Case: white gold, ø 42 mm, height 12.35 mm; sapphire crystal; transparent case back; water-resistant to 3 atm
Band: reptile skin, folding clasp
Price: $237,000
Variations: rose gold ($236,400)

Classique Grande Complication Tourbillon Perpetual Calendar

Reference number: 3797BR 1E 9WU
Movement: manually wound, Breguet Caliber 558QP2; 37.09 mm; 21 jewels; 18,000 vph; 1-minute tourbillon, Breguet spring, balance with gold weight screws; 50-hour power reserve
Functions: hours and minutes (off-center), subsidiary seconds (on tourbillon cage); perpetual calendar with date (retrograde), weekday, month, leap year
Case: rose gold, ø 41 mm, height 11.6 mm; sapphire crystal; transparent case back; water-resistant to 3 atm
Band: reptile skin, double folding clasp
Price: $164,900
Variations: platinum ($179,200)

Classique Tourbillon Ultra-Thin

Reference number: 5377BR 12 9WU
Movement: automatic, Breguet Caliber 581 DR; ø 36 mm, height 3 mm; 42 jewels; 28,800 vph; 1-minute tourbillon in titanium cage, silicon hairspring; hubless peripheral rotor; 90-hour power reserve
Functions: hours, minutes, subsidiary seconds (on tourbillon cage); power reserve display
Case: platinum, ø 42 mm, height 7 mm; sapphire crystal; transparent case back; water-resistant to 3 atm
Band: reptile skin, double folding clasp
Remarks: currently thinnest automatic tourbillon movement
Price: $149,500
Variations: platinum ($163,800)

Classique Chronométrie

Reference number: 7727BR 12 9WU
Movement: manually wound, Breguet Caliber 574 DR; ø 31.6 mm, height 3.5 mm; 45 jewels; 72,000 vph; 2 spring barrels, double hairspring, silicon pallet lever and escape wheel; balance pivot held by magnet; 60-hour power reserve
Functions: hours, minutes, subsidiary seconds (display of 10th of seconds); power reserve indicator
Case: rose gold, ø 41 mm, height 9.65 mm; sapphire crystal; transparent case back; water-resistant to 3 atm
Band: reptile skin, folding clasp
Price: $40,000
Variations: white gold ($40,500)

Classique Moon Phase

Reference number: 7337BA 1E 9V6
Movement: automatic, Breguet Caliber 502.3 QSE1; ø 31 mm, height 3.8 mm; 35 jewels; 21,600 vph; silicon hairspring, rose gold hand-guillochéed rotor mass; numbered and signed
Functions: hours and minutes (off-center), subsidiary seconds; full calendar with date, weekday, moon phase, age
Case: rose gold, ø 39 mm, height 9.9 mm; sapphire crystal; transparent case back; water-resistant to 3 atm
Band: reptile skin, folding clasp
Remarks: silvered, hand-guillochéed gold dial
Price: $38,800
Variations: white gold ($39,900)

Classique Moon Phase

Reference number: 7787BR 29 9V6
Movement: automatic, Breguet Caliber 591 DRL; 28,800 vph; balance spring; silicon pallet lever and escape wheel; 38-hour power reserve
Functions: hours, minutes, sweep seconds; power reserve indicator; moon phase
Case: rose gold, ø 39 mm; sapphire crystal; transparent case back; water-resistant to 3 atm
Band: reptile skin, folding clasp
Remarks: enamel dial
Price: $29,700

Classique "La Musicale"

Reference number: 7800BR AA 9Y V02
Movement: automatic, Breguet Caliber 901;
ø 38.9 mm, height 8.7 mm; 59 jewels; 28,800 vph;
silicon anchor/anchor escape wheel, Breguet
balance with regulating screws; music box with
peg disc/gong strips, hand-guillochéed sonorous
liquid metal membrane, magnetic striking regulator;
45-hour power reserve
Functions: hours, minutes, sweep seconds; power
reserve display; alarm clock with music mechanism
and function display
Case: yellow gold, ø 48 mm, height 16.6 mm;
sapphire crystal, water-resistant to 3 atm
Band: reptile skin, folding clasp
Price: $89,600

Classique Hora Mundi

Reference number: 5717PT EU 9ZU
Movement: automatic, Breguet Caliber 77F0;
ø 36 mm, height 6.15 mm; 39 jewels; 28,800 vph;
silicon pallet lever, escape wheel, hairspring
Functions: hours, minutes, sweep seconds; world-
time display (2nd time zone); day/night indicator;
date
Case: platinum, ø 44 mm, height 13.55 mm;
sapphire crystal; transparent case back; water-
resistant to 3 atm
Band: reptile skin, folding clasp
Price: $94,200
Variations: rose gold ($78,900), 3 different dials
(Asia, America, Europe/Africa)

Classique

Reference number: 5177BR 15 9V6
Movement: automatic, Breguet Caliber 777Q26;
26 jewels; 28,800 vph; silicon anchor and lever
escapement; 55-hour power reserve
Functions: hours, minutes, sweep seconds; date
Case: rose gold, ø 38 mm, height 8.8 mm; sapphire
crystal; transparent case back; water-resistant to
3 atm
Band: reptile skin, folding clasp
Price: $23,200
Variations: white gold ($23,700); yellow gold
($22,700)

Tradition GMT

Reference number: 7067BR G1 9W6
Movement: manually wound, Breguet Caliber
507 DRF; ø 32.8 mm, height 6.92 mm; 40 jewels;
21,600 vph; Breguet balance spring, silicon pallet
lever and escape wheel, spring; 50-hour power
reserve
Functions: hours, minutes; additional 12-hour display
(2nd time zone); double power reserve display (on
dial and back)
Case: rose gold, ø 40 mm, height 12.65 mm;
sapphire crystal; transparent case back; water-
resistant to 3 atm
Band: reptile skin, folding clasp
Price: $39,200
Variations: white gold ($40,000)

Héritage Chronograph

Reference number: 5400BB 12 9V6
Movement: automatic, Breguet Caliber 550/1;
ø 23.9 mm, height 6 mm; 47 jewels; 21,600 vph;
Breguet spring, silicon pallet lever and escape
wheel; 52-hour power reserve
Functions: hours, minutes, subsidiary seconds;
chronograph; date
Case: white gold, 35 x 42 mm, height 14.45 mm;
sapphire crystal
Band: reptile skin, folding clasp
Price: $44,100
Variations: rose gold ($43,000)

Type XXII

Reference number: 3880BR Z2 9XV
Movement: automatic, Breguet Caliber 589F;
ø 30 mm, height 8.3 mm; 27 jewels; 72,000 vph;
high-frequency silicon escapement, sweep minute
counter; 40-hour power reserve
Functions: hours, minutes, subsidiary seconds;
added 12-hour display (2nd zone); flyback
chronograph; date
Case: rose gold, ø 44 mm, height 18.05 mm;
bidirectional bezel with 60-minute divisions;
sapphire crystal; transparent case back; screw-in
crown; water-resistant to 10 atm
Band: reptile skin, folding clasp
Price: $35,500
Variations: rose gold bracelet ($55,500)

Marine GMT

Reference number: 5857BR Z2 5ZU
Movement: automatic, Breguet Caliber 517F; ø 26.2 mm; 28 jewels; 28,800 vph; Breguet silicon lever escapement and hairspring; 65-hour power reserve
Functions: hours, minutes, sweep seconds; additional 12-hour display (2nd time zone); date
Case: pink gold, ø 42 mm, height 12.25 mm; sapphire crystal, transparent case back; water-resistant to 10 atm
Band: rubber, folding clasp
Price: $35,900
Variations: stainless steel, silver dial ($26,200); stainless steel, silver dial, rubber strap ($23,600); rose gold, black dial ($55,900)

Marine Royale

Reference number: 5847BR Z2 5ZV
Movement: automatic, Breguet Caliber 519 R; ø 27.6 mm, height 6.2 mm; 36 jewels; 28,800 vph
Functions: hours, minutes, sweep seconds; power reserve display; alarm clock; function indicator; date
Case: rose gold, ø 45 mm, height 17.45 mm; unidirectional bezel with 60-minute divisions, sapphire crystal; transparent case back; screw-in crown; water-resistant to 30 atm
Band: rubber, folding clasp
Price: $46,300
Variations: rose gold dial ($46,300); rose gold bracelet ($61,800); white gold with rubber strap ($42,900); white gold, black dial ($65,400)

Classique Dame

Reference number: 9068BB 12 976 DD00
Movement: automatic, Breguet Caliber 591A; ø 26 mm, height 3.15 mm; 25 jewels; 28,800 vph; silicon lever escapement and hairspring; 38-hour power reserve
Functions: hours, minutes, sweep seconds; date
Case: white gold, ø 33.5 mm, height 6.95 mm; 88 diamonds on bezel and lugs; sapphire crystal; water-resistant to 3 atm
Band: reptile skin, buckle
Price: $26,600
Variations: rose gold ($26,100)

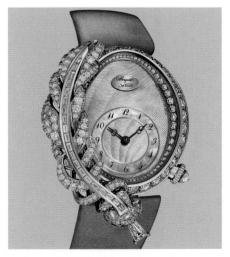

Reine de Naples Rêve de Plume

Reference number: GJ15 BB 8924 0DD8
Movement: automatic, Breguet Caliber 586/1; 29 jewels; 21,600 vph; silicon hairspring; 40-hour power reserve
Functions: hours, minutes
Case: white gold, 24.95 x 33 mm; bezel set with 76 brilliant-cut diamonds; sapphire crystal; diamond on crown
Band: satin, buckle
Remarks: mother-of-pearl dial
Price: $140,300
Variations: rose gold ($139,300)

Reine de Naples

Reference number: 8967ST 51 J50
Movement: automatic, Breguet Caliber 591C; ø 25.6 mm, height 2.95 mm; 25 jewels; 28,800 vph; silicon anchor and lever escapement; 38-hour power reserve
Functions: hours, minutes
Case: stainless steel, 34.95 x 43 mm, height 9.58 mm; sapphire crystal; transparent case back; sapphire cabochon on crown
Band: stainless steel, double folding clasp
Remarks: mother-of-pearl dial
Price: $18,500
Variations: various dials

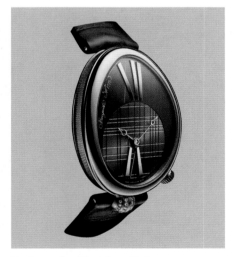

Reine de Naples Princess

Reference number: 8968BRX1 986 0D00
Movement: automatic, Breguet Caliber 591C; ø 26 mm, height 2.95 mm; 25 jewels; 28,800 vph; silicon anchor and lever escapement; 38-hour power reserve
Functions: hours, minutes
Case: rose gold, 34.95 x 43 mm, height 9.58 mm; sapphire crystal; transparent case back; diamond cabochon on crown, bezel set with 16 diamonds; water-resistant to 3 atm
Band: reptile skin, buckle set with 29 diamonds
Price: $27,200
Variations: silver-plated dial ($27,200)

Breitling
Schlachthausstrasse 2
CH-2540 Grenchen
Switzerland

Tel.:
+41-32-654-5454

Fax:
+41-32-654-5400

E-Mail:
info@breitling.com

Website:
www.breitling.com

Founded:
1884

Annual production:
700,000 (estimated)

U.S. distributor:
Breitling U.S.A. Inc.
206 Danbury Road
Stamford, CT 06897
800-641-7343
www.breitling.com

Most important collections:
Navitimer Avenger, Trancsocean, Superocean,
Cockpit, Breitling for Bentley

Breitling

In 1884, Léon Breitling opened his workshop in St. Imier in the Jura mountains and immediately began specializing in integrated chronographs. His business strategy was to focus consistently on instrument watches with a distinctive design. High quality standards and the rise of aviation completed the picture.

Today, Breitling's relationship with air sports and commercial and military aviation is clear from its brand identity. The watch company hosts a series of aviation days, owns an aerobatics team, and sponsors several aviation associations.

The unveiling of its own, modern chronograph movement at Basel in 2009 was a major milestone in the company's history and also a return to its roots. The new design was to be "100 percent Breitling" and industrially produced in large numbers at a reasonable cost. Although Breitling's operations in Grenchen and in La Chaux-de-Fonds both boast state-of-the-art equipment, the contract for the new chronograph was awarded to a small team in Geneva. By 2006, the brand-new Caliber B01 had made the COSC grade with flying colors, and it has enjoyed great popularity ever since. For the team of designers, the innovative centering system on the reset mechanism that requires no manual adjustment was one of the great achievements. Since then, the in-house caliber has evolved. It now comes as the B04 with a second time zone, the B05 with world time, and the B06 with a 30-second chrono display for the Breitling for Bentley series.

The year 1915 was another important one for the brand and watchmaking in general: Breitling unveiled a wrist chronograph with a separate pusher at 2 o'clock instead of in the crown. The Transocean Chronograph 1915 was finished just in time for the centennial. It comes in a limited edition equipped with the B14, manually wound chronograph caliber.

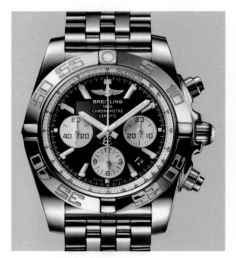

Chronomat 44

Reference number: AB011012/B967
Movement: automatic, Breitling Caliber 01;
ø 30 mm, height 7.2 mm; 47 jewels; 28,800 vph;
column wheel control of chronograph functions;
70-hour power reserve; COSC-certified chronometer
Functions: hours, minutes, subsidiary seconds;
chronograph; date
Case: stainless steel, ø 44 mm, height 16.95 mm;
unidirectional bezel with 60-minute divisions;
sapphire crystal; screw-in crown and pusher; water-resistant to 50 atm
Band: stainless steel, folding clasp
Price: $9,060
Variations: calf leather band and buckle ($7,775)

Chronoliner

Reference number: Y2431012/BE10
Movement: automatic, Breitling Caliber 24 (base ETA 7751); ø 30 mm, height 7.9 mm; 25 jewels; 28,800 vph; 42-hour power reserve
Functions: hours, minutes, subsidiary seconds; additional 24 hours display (2nd time zone); chronograph; date
Case: stainless steel, ø 46 mm, height 15.95 mm; bezel with ceramic inlay, bidirectional bezel with 24-hour divisions; sapphire crystal; water-resistant to 10 atm
Band: stainless steel Milanese mesh, folding clasp
Price: $7,575
Variations: stainless steel bracelet ($8,420)

Navitimer 01 (46 mm)

Reference number: AB012721/BD09
Movement: automatic, Breitling Caliber 01;
ø 30 mm, height 7.2 mm; 47 jewels; 28,800 vph;
column wheel control of chronograph functions;
70-hour power reserve; COSC-certified chronometer
Functions: hours, minutes, subsidiary seconds;
chronograph; date
Case: stainless steel, ø 46 mm, height 15.5 mm; bidirectional bezel with integrated slide rule/tachymeter scale; sapphire crystal, water-resistant to 3 atm
Band: calf leather, buckle
Price: $8,215
Variations: stainless steel bracelet ($9,620)

Navitimer GMT

Reference number: AB044121/BD24
Movement: automatic, Breitling Caliber 04 (base Breitling 01); ø 30 mm, height 7.4 mm; 47 jewels; 28,800 vph; column wheel control of chronograph functions; 70-hour power reserve; COSC-certified
Functions: hours, minutes, subsidiary seconds; additional 24 hours display; chronograph; date
Case: stainless steel, ø 48 mm, height 18.35 mm; bidirectional bezel, integrated slide rule/tachymeter scale; sapphire crystal; transparent back; screw-in crown/pushers; water-resistant to 3 atm
Band: calf leather, buckle
Price: $9,055
Variations: stainless steel bracelet ($10,460)

Avenger Blackbird 44

Reference number: V1731110/BD74
Movement: automatic, Breitling Caliber 17 (base ETA 2824-2); ø 25.6 mm, height 4.6 mm; 25 jewels; 28,800 vph; 40-hour power reserve; COSC-certified chronometer
Functions: hours, minutes, sweep seconds; date
Case: titanium with black PVD coating, ø 44 mm, height 14.2 mm; unidirectional bezel with 60-minute divisions; sapphire crystal; screw-in crown, helium valve; water-resistant to 200 atm
Band: textile, buckle
Price: $5,105

Super Avenger II

Reference number: A1337111/BC29
Movement: automatic, Breitling Caliber 13 (base ETA 7750); ø 30 mm, height 7.9 mm; 25 jewels; 28,800 vph; 42-hour power reserve; COSC-certified chronometer
Functions: hours, minutes, subsidiary seconds; chronograph; date
Case: stainless steel, ø 48 mm, height 17.75 mm; unidirectional bezel with 60-minute divisions, sapphire crystal; screw-in crown; water-resistant to 30 atm
Band: rubber, folding clasp
Price: $5,635
Variations: Steel Professional III bracelet ($5,835)

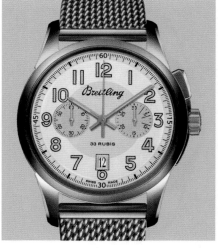

Transocean Chronograph Unitime

Reference number: AB0510U4/BB62
Movement: automatic, Breitling Caliber 05 (base Breitling 01); ø 30 mm, height 8.1 mm; 56 jewels; 28,800 vph; 70-hour power reserve; COSC-certified
Functions: hours, minutes, subsidiary seconds; 24 time zones shown on dial (world-time display); chronograph; date
Case: stainless steel, ø 46 mm, height 14.8 mm; crown rotates inner ring with reference city names; sapphire crystal; water-resistant to 10 atm
Band: calf leather, folding clasp
Price: $11,265
Variations: stainless steel bracelet ($11,575)

Transocean Chronograph 1915

Reference number: AB14112/G799
Movement: manually wound, Breitling Caliber 14; ø 30 mm, height 6.1 mm; 33 jewels; 28,800 vph; pusher control of chronograph functions; 70-hour power reserve
Functions: hours, minutes, subsidiary seconds; chronograph; date
Case: stainless steel, ø 43 mm, height 14.6 mm; sapphire crystal; transparent case back
Band: stainless steel Milanese mesh, folding clasp
Price: $9,275
Variations: calf leather band ($8,715)

Transocean Chronograph

Reference number: AB015212/BA99
Movement: automatic, Breitling Caliber 01; ø 30 mm, height 7.2 mm; 47 jewels; 28,800 vph; column wheel control of chronograph functions; 70-hour power reserve; COSC-certified chronometer
Functions: hours, minutes, subsidiary seconds; chronograph; date
Case: stainless steel, ø 43 mm, height 14.35 mm; sapphire crystal; transparent case back; water-resistant to 10 atm
Band: Ocean Classic bracelet, folding clasp
Price: $8,395
Variations: calf leather band and buckle ($7,835)

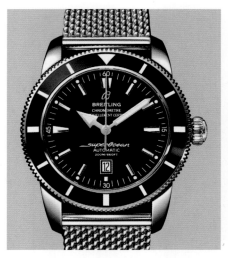

Superocean Heritage 46

Reference number: A1732024/B868
Movement: automatic, Breitling Caliber 17 (base ETA 2824-2); ø 25.6 mm, height 4.6 mm; 25 jewels; 28,800 vph; COSC-certified chronometer
Functions: hours, minutes, sweep seconds; date
Case: stainless steel, ø 46 mm, height 16.4 mm; unidirectional bezel with reference markers; sapphire crystal; screw-in crown; water-resistant to 20 atm
Band: Ocean Classic bracelet
Price: $4,405
Variations: rubber band and folding clasp ($4,080)

Superocean II 36

Reference number: A17321D2/A775
Movement: automatic, Breitling Caliber 17 (base ETA 2824-2); ø 25.6 mm, height 3.6 mm; 21 jewels; 28,800 vph; 40-hour power reserve; COSC-certified chronometer
Functions: hours, minutes, sweep seconds; date
Case: stainless steel, ø 36 mm, height 11.25 mm; unidirectional bezel with 60-minute divisions; sapphire crystal; screw-in crown, helium valve; water-resistant to 20 atm
Band: rubber, buckle
Price: $3,400
Variations: stainless steel bracelet ($3,900)

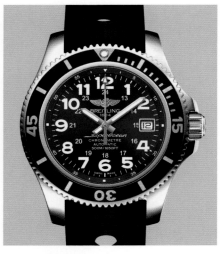

Superocean II 42

Reference number: A17365D1/C915
Movement: automatic, Breitling Caliber 17 (base ETA 2824-2); ø 25.6 mm, height 3.6 mm; 21 jewels; 28,800 vph; 40-hour power reserve; COSC-certified chronometer
Functions: hours, minutes, sweep seconds; date
Case: stainless steel, ø 42 mm, height 13.3 mm; unidirectional bezel with 60-minute divisions; sapphire crystal; screw-in crown, helium valve; water-resistant to 50 atm
Band: rubber, buckle
Price: $3,400
Variations: stainless steel bracelet ($3,900)

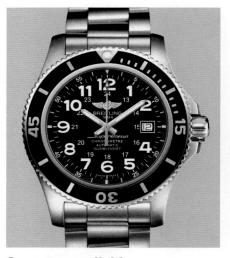

Superocean II 44

Reference number: A17392D7/BD68
Movement: automatic, Breitling Caliber 17 (base ETA 2824-2); ø 25.6 mm, height 4.6 mm; 25 jewels; 28,800 vph; 40-hour power reserve; COSC-certified chronometer
Functions: hours, minutes, sweep seconds; date
Case: stainless steel, ø 44 mm, height 14.2 mm; unidirectional bezel with 60-minute divisions; sapphire crystal; screw-in crown, helium valve; water-resistant to 100 atm
Band: stainless steel, folding clasp
Price: $4,150
Variations: rubber band and folding clasp ($3,950)

Galactic Unitime Sleek T

Reference number: WB3510U4/BD94
Movement: automatic, Breitling Caliber 35; ø 30 mm, height 8.1 mm; 41 jewels; 28,800 vph; 70-hour power reserve
Functions: hours, minutes, sweep seconds; world-time display (2nd time zone); date
Case: stainless steel, ø 44 mm, height 15.3 mm; tungsten carbide bezel, rotating inner ring with reference cities, rotates via crown; sapphire crystal; screw-in crown; water-resistant to 10 atm
Band: stainless steel, folding clasp
Price: $9,000
Variations: calf leather band and buckle ($7,715)

Galactic 36 Automatic

Reference number: A3733053/A717
Movement: automatic, Breitling Caliber 37 (base ETA 2892-A2); ø 25.6 mm, height 3.6 mm; 27 jewels; 28,800 vph; 42-hour power reserve
Functions: hours, minutes, subsidiary seconds; date
Case: stainless steel, ø 36 mm, height 12.3 mm; unidirectional bezel with diamonds; sapphire crystal
Band: calf leather, buckle
Price: $9,450
Variations: stainless steel bracelet ($10,735)

Colt Chronograph Automatic

Reference number: A1338811/G804
Movement: automatic, Breitling Caliber 13 (base ETA 7750); ø 30 mm, height 7.9 mm; 25 jewels; 28,800 vph; 42-hour power reserve; COSC-certified
Functions: hours, minutes, subsidiary seconds; chronograph; date
Case: stainless steel, ø 44 mm, height 14.7 mm; unidirectional bezel with 60-minute divisions; sapphire crystal; screw-in crown; water-resistant to 20 atm
Band: stainless steel, folding clasp
Price: $5,300
Variations: calf leather band and buckle ($4,865)

Bentley GMT Light Body B04 AS

Reference number: EB043335/BD78
Movement: automatic, Breitling Caliber B04 (base Breitling 01); ø 30 mm, height 7.4 mm; 47 jewels; 28,800 vph; column wheel control of chronograph functions; 70-hour power reserve; COSC-certified
Functions: hours, minutes, subsidiary seconds; additional 24-hour display; chronograph; date
Case: titanium, ø 49 mm, height 17.35 mm; rotating inner ring with reference cities, rotates via crown; sapphire crystal; transparent case back; screw-in crown; water-resistant to 10 atm
Band: rubber, folding clasp
Price: $11,615

Bentley GMT Light Body B04 Midnight Carbon

Reference number: VB043222/BD69
Movement: automatic, Breitling Caliber B04 (base Breitling 01); ø 30 mm, height 7.4 mm; 47 jewels; 28,800 vph; column wheel control of chronograph functions; 70-hour power reserve; COSC-certified
Functions: hours, minutes, subsidiary seconds; additional 24 hours display; chronograph; date
Case: titanium with black PVD coating, ø 49 mm, height 17.35; rotating inner ring with reference cities, rotates via crown; sapphire crystal; transparent case back; screw-in crown, water-resistant to 10 atm
Band: rubber, folding clasp
Price: $14,800

Caliber 01

Automatic; column wheel control of chronograph functions, horizontal clutch; single spring barrel, 70-hour power reserve; COSC-certified chronometer
Functions: hours, minutes, subsidiary seconds; chronograph; date
Diameter: 30 mm
Height: 7.2 mm
Jewels: 47
Balance: glucydur
Frequency: 28,800 vph

Caliber B04

Automatic, column wheel control of chronograph functions, horizontal clutch; single spring barrel; 70-hour power reserve; COSC-certified chronometer
Functions: hours, minutes, subsidiary seconds; additional 24-hour display (2nd time zone); chronograph; date
Diameter: 30 mm
Height: 7.4 mm
Jewels: 47
Balance: glucydur
Frequency: 28,800 vph

Caliber B05

Automatic; column wheel control of chronograph functions, horizontal clutch; time zone disc coupled with hands mechanism using planetary transmission; single spring barrel; 70-hour power reserve; COSC-certified chronometer
Functions: hours, minutes, subsidiary seconds; 2nd time zone; world-time display (adjusted by crown); chronograph; date
Diameter: 30 mm
Height: 8.1 mm
Jewels: 56
Balance: glucydur
Frequency: 28,800 vph

Bremont Watch Company

PO Box 4741
Henley-on-Thames
RG9 9BZ
Great Britain

Tel.:
+44-845-094-0690

Fax:
+44-870-762-0475

E-Mail:
info@bremont.com

Website:
www.bremont.com

Founded:
2002

Number of employees:
60+

Annual production:
several thousand watches

U.S. distributor:
Mike Pearson
1-855-BREMONT
michael@bremont.com

Most important collections/price range:
ALT1, Bremont Boeing, Bremont Jaguar, MB, SOLO, Supermarine, U-2, and limited editions / $3,900 to $30,000

Bremont

At the 2012 Olympic Games in London, stuntman Gary Connery parachuted into the stadium wearing an outfit that made him look suspiciously like the Queen. He was also the first to jet suit out of a helicopter. On both occasions he was wearing a Bremont watch. And so do many other adventurous types, like polar explorer Ben Saunders or Levison Wood, who was the first person to walk the length of the Nile.

Bremonts are tough stuff, created by brothers Nick and Giles English, themselves dyed-in-the-wool pilots and restorers of vintage airplanes. They understand that flying safety relies on outstanding mechanics, so they took their time engineering their watches. Naming their brand required some thought, however. The solution came when they remembered an adventure they had had in southern France when they were forced to land their vintage biplane in a field to avoid a storm. The farmer, a former WWII pilot and just as passionate about aircraft as Nick and Giles, was more than happy to put them up. His name: Antoine Bremont.

Ever since the watches hit the market in 2007, the brand has grown by leaps and bounds. These British-made timepieces reflect sobriety, functionality, history, and ruggedness. They would fit as well in an old Spitfire as on a vintage yacht. They use a sturdy, COSC-certified automatic movement, especially hardened steel, a patented shock-absorbing system, and a rotor whose design recalls a flight of planes. The brand continues to explore various cultural icons in British history, including the Spitfire, Bletchley Park (where the German codes were broken during World War II), or Jaguar sports cars. Recently, though, it tied the knot, so to speak, with Boeing and produced an elegant range of watches on an organic polymer strap and a seconds hand with a Boeing-blue tip shaped like part of the Seattle firm's famous logo.

Kingsman RG

Movement: automatic, modified Caliber BE-54AE; ø 28.04 mm, height 10.5 mm; 25 jewels; 28,800 vph; Bremont molded and decorated rotor; COSC-certified chronometer; 42-hour power reserve
Functions: hours, minutes, subsidiary seconds; 2nd time zone; world-time display; chronograph; date and world-time zone
Case: rose gold, DLC-treated case barrel, ø 43 mm, height 16 mm; transparent case back; sapphire crystal; water-resistant to 10 atm
Band: reptile skin, rose gold buckle
Price: $20,285
Variations: DLC and stainless steel case

Jaguar MKI

Movement: automatic, Bremont BWC/01-10; ø 33.4 mm; 25 jewels; 28,800 vph; 50-hour power reserve
Functions: hours, minutes, subsidiary seconds; date
Case: stainless steel; ø 43 mm, height 16 mm; transparent case back; sapphire crystal; water-resistant to 10 atm
Remarks: miniaturized Jaguar E-Type steering wheel rotor with Growler emblem
Price: $10,950

Boeing Ti Model 247

Movement: automatic, modified Caliber BE-54AE; ø 28.04 mm, height 10.5 mm; 25 jewels; 28,800 vph; Bremont molded and decorated rotor; COSC-certified chronometer; 42-hour power reserve
Functions: hours, minutes, subsidiary seconds; 2nd time zone; world-time display; chronograph; date
Case: stainless steel, DLC-treated case barrel, ø 43 mm, height 16 mm; transparent case back; sapphire crystal; water-resistant to 10 atm
Band: leather-polymer composite (Seattle Hybrid), buckle
Price: $7,495

U-22

Movement: automatic, modified Caliber BE-36AE; ø 28 mm, height 7.5 mm; 25 jewels; 28,800 vph; 38-hour power reserve; Bremont molded and decorated rotor; COSC-certified chronometer
Functions: hours, minutes, seconds; weekday, date
Case: stainless steel; ø 43 mm, height 16 mm; antimagnetic soft iron core; crown-adjustable bidirectional bezel; sapphire crystal; transparent case back; water-resistant to 10 atm
Band: leather strap, buckle
Remarks: optional Temple Island rubber strap
Price: $5,695

MBIII

Movement: automatic, modified Caliber BE-93-2AE; ø 29.89 mm; 21 jewels; 28,800 vph; Bremont skeletonized rotor; COSC-certified; 42-hours power reserve
Functions: hours, minutes, sweep seconds; sweep 24-hour hand (2nd time zone); date
Case: stainless steel; ø 43 mm, height 14.35 mm; crown-operated bidirectional inner bezel; antimagnetic cage; screwed-down case back; sapphire crystal; water-resistant to 10 atm
Band: leather, buckle
Remarks: with NATO military strap
Price: $6,395
Variations: bronze, orange, or anthracite barrel

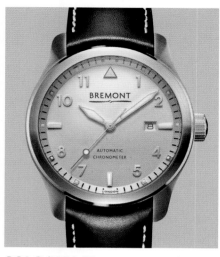

SOLO/WH-SI

Movement: automatic, modified Caliber BE-36AE; ø 28 mm, height 7.5 mm; 25 jewels; 28,800 vph; 38-hour power reserve; Bremont molded and decorated rotor; COSC-certified chronometer
Functions: hours, minutes, subsidiary seconds; date
Case: stainless steel; ø 43 mm, height 16 mm; crown-adjustable bezel; transparent case back; sapphire crystal; water-resistant to 10 atm
Band: leather, stainless steel buckle
Price: $4,295
Variations: white dial with silver markers; black dial with white or cream hands and markers

ALT1-ZT/BK

Movement: automatic, modified Caliber BE-54AE; ø 28.04 mm, height 10.5 mm; 25 jewels; 28,800 vph; Bremont molded and decorated rotor; COSC-certified chronometer; 42-hour power reserve
Functions: hours, minutes, subsidiary seconds; 2nd time zone; world-time display; chronograph; date
Case: stainless steel, DLC-treated case barrel. ø 43 mm, height 16 mm; transparent case back; sapphire crystal; water-resistant to 10 atm
Band: leather with stainless steel deployment buckle and security clasp
Price: $6,595

Supermarine S2000

Movement: automatic, modified Caliber BE-36AE; ø 28 mm, height 7.5 mm; 25 jewels; 28,800 vph; 38-hour power reserve; Bremont molded and decorated rotor; COSC-certified chronometer
Functions: hours, minutes, seconds; weekday, date
Case: stainless steel; ø 45 mm, height 16 mm; antimagnetic soft iron cage; unidirectional bezel; screw-down case back; sapphire crystal; water-resistant to 200 atm
Band: rubber, buckle
Price: $5,900

ALT1-C/PW

Movement: automatic, Caliber BE-50AE; ø 28.04 mm, height 10.5 mm; 28 jewels; 28,800 vph; 42-hour power reserve; Bremont decorated rotor; COSC-certified chronometer
Functions: hours, minutes, subsidiary seconds; chronograph; date
Case: stainless steel; ø 43 mm, height 16 mm; transparent case back; sapphire crystal; water-resistant to 10 atm
Band: reptile skin, stainless steel buckle
Price: $6,695
Variations: cream, anthracite, black, green, or silver dial

BRM
(Bernard Richards Manufacture)
2 Impasse de L'Aubette
ZA des Aulnaies
F-95420 Magny en Vexin
France

Tel.:
+33-1-61-02-00-25

Fax:
+33-1-61-02-00-14

Website:
www.brm-manufacture.com

Founded:
2003

Number of employees:
20

Annual production:
approx. 2,000 pieces

U.S. distributor:
BRM Manufacture North America
25 Highland Park Village, Suite 100-777
Dallas, TX 75205
214-231-0144
usa@brm-manufacture.com

Most important collections/price range:
$3,000 to $150,000

BRM

Is luxury on the outside or the inside? The answer to this question can tear the veil from the hype and reveal the true craftsman. For Bernard Richards, the true sign of luxury lies in "technical skills and perfection in all stages of manufacture." The exterior of the product is of course crucial, but all of BRM's major operations for making a wristwatch—encasing, assembling, setting, and polishing—are performed by hand in his little garage-like factory outside Paris in Magny-sur-Vexin.

The look: 1940s, internal combustion, axle grease, pinups, real pilots, and a can-do attitude. The design: three dimensions visible to the naked eye, big horological landscapes. The inside: custom-designed components, fitting perfectly into Richards's automotive ideal. And since 2009, BRM aficionados have been able to engage in this process to an even greater degree: On the BRM website, the client can now construct his or her own V12-44-BRM model. A luxury watch that is a collaboration between the client and Richards is simply a click away.

BRM's unusual timepieces have mainly been based on the trusted Valjoux 7750. But Richards has lofty goals: he intends to set up a true *manufacture* in his French factory. His Birotor model is thus outfitted with the Precitime, an autonomous caliber conceived and manufactured on French soil. The movement features BRM's own shock absorbers mounted on the conical springs of its so-called Isolastic system. Plates and bridges are crafted in Arcap; rotors are made of Fortale and tantalum. The twin rotors at 12 and 6 o'clock are mounted on double rows of ceramic bearings that require no lubrication.

RG 46
Reference number: RG46 MK AR
Movement: automatic, modified ETA Caliber 2824; ø 25.6 mm, height 4.6 mm; 25 jewels; 28,800 vph; 6 shock absorbers; BRM designed and manufactured rotor; 38-hour power reserve
Functions: hours, minutes, sweep seconds; stop mechanism function
Case: makrolon, ø 46 mm, height 14 mm; Fortale HR lugs and crown with black PVD; crystal sapphire; transparent case back; water-resistant to 10 atm
Band: seat belt material, buckle
Price: $13,550
Variations: rose gold

BiRotor
Reference number: BRT-01
Movement: automatic, Precitime Caliber Birotor; 24 x 32 mm; 35 jewels; 28,800 vph; 45-hour power reserve; Fortale HR and tantalum double rotors on ceramic ball bearings; patented Isolastic system with 4 shock absorbers, Arcap plates, bridges
Functions: hours, minutes, subsidiary seconds
Case: titanium with rose gold crown and strap lugs, 40 x 48 mm, height 9.9 mm; domed sapphire crystal, antireflective on both sides; domed sapphire crystal transparent case back; water-resistant to 30 m
Band: nomex, buckle
Price: $68,500

TriRotor
Movement: automatic, Precitime Caliber TriRotor; ø 48 mm; 29 jewels; 28,800 vph; 45-hour power reserve; Fortale HR main rotors with 3 macro rotors in Fortale HR with tantalum on ceramic ball bearings; patented Isolastic system with 3 shock absorbers, Arcap plates, bridges
Functions: hours, minutes, subsidiary seconds
Case: titanium with rose gold crown and strap lugs, ø 48 mm, height 9.9 mm; domed sapphire crystal, antireflective on both sides; domed sapphire crystal transparent case back; water-resistant to 10 atm
Band: nomex, buckle
Price: $47,950
Variations: rose gold; yellow, red, or orange hands

R50 MK

Movement: automatic, heavily modified ETA Caliber 2161; ø 38 mm; 35 jewels; 28,800 vph; 48-hour power reserve; patented Isolastic system with 3 shock absorbers; Fortale HR, tantalum, and aluminum rotor; hand-painted Gulf colors
Functions: hours, minutes, sweep seconds; power reserve indication
Case: makrolon with rose gold crown and strap lugs, ø 50 mm, height 13.2 mm; sapphire crystal, antireflective on both sides; exhibition case back; water-resistant to 3 atm
Band: leather, buckle
Price: $28,550; limited to 30 pieces
Variations: rose gold ($65,000)

TR1 Tourbillon

Movement: automatic, Precitime Caliber; ø 30 mm, height 7.9 mm; 26 jewels; 28,800 vph; 46-hour power reserve; 105-second tourbillon in Arcap with reversed cage for visible escapement and suspended by 2 micro springs; patented Isolastic system with 4 shock absorbers; automatic assembly with ceramic ball bearings
Functions: hours, minutes, sweep seconds
Case: titanium, ø 52 mm; sapphire crystal, antireflective on both sides; transparent case back; water-resistant to 10 atm
Band: leather, buckle
Price: $145,350
Variations: 48 mm ($136,150)

R46

Movement: automatic, heavily modified ETA Caliber 2161; ø 38 mm; 35 jewels; 28,800 vph; 48-hour power reserve; patented Isolastic system with 3 shock absorbers; Fortale HR, tantalum, and aluminum rotor; hand-painted Gulf colors
Functions: hours, minutes, sweep seconds; power reserve indicator
Case: makrolon with rose gold crown and strap lugs, ø 46 mm, height 10 mm; sapphire crystal, antireflective on both sides; exhibition case back; water-resistant to 3 atm
Band: leather, buckle
Price: $24,750; limited to 30 pieces

V6-SA SQ Gulf

Movement: automatic, ETA Valjoux Caliber 2824 modified; ø 30 mm, height 7.90 mm; 27 jewels; 28,800 vph; shock absorbers connected to block; 42-hour power reserve
Functions: hours, minutes, sweep seconds
Case: polished stainless steel case with black PVD; lugs/crown from single titanium block; sapphire crystal; transparent case back; water-resistant to 10 atm
Band: leather, buckle
Remarks: skeletonized dial with red hands
Price: $7,250

Ringmaster

Movement: automatic, ETA Valjoux Caliber 7753; ø 30 mm, height 7.90 mm; 27 jewels; 28,800 vph; 42-hour power reserve; Gulf logo and color strip
Functions: hours, minutes, subsidiary seconds; date; chronograph
Case: grade 5 titanium, black PVD, 46 mm; sapphire crystal; transparent case back; water-resistant to 10 atm
Band: seat belt material, buckle
Price: $8,950; limited to 100 pieces

MK-44-ABL

Movement: automatic, ETA Valjoux Caliber 7753; ø 30 mm, height 7.90 mm; 27 jewels; 28,800 vph; 42-hour power reserve
Functions: hours, minutes, subsidiary seconds; date; chronograph
Case: makrolon (polycarbonate), ø 45 mm; pushers, lugs, crown from single titanium block; sapphire crystal; exhibition case back; water-resistant to 10 atm
Band: technical fabrics for extra lightness
Remarks: lightest automatic chronograph ever made; skeleton dial with blue hands
Price: $13,450
Variations: many options with configurator

Bulgari Horlogerie SA
rue de Monruz 34
CH-2000 Neuchâtel
Switzerland

Tel.:
+41-32-722-7878

Fax:
+41-32-722-7933

E-Mail:
info@bulgari.com

Website:
www.bulgari.com

Founded:
1884 (Bulgari Horlogerie was founded in the early 1980s as Bulgari Time.)

U.S. distributor:
Bulgari Corporation of America
625 Madison Avenue
New York, NY 10022
212-315-9700

Most important collections/price range:
Bulgari-Bulgari / from approx. $4,700 to $30,300; Diagono / from approx. $3,200; Octo / from approx. $9,500 to $690,000 and above; Daniel Roth and Gérald Genta collections

Bulgari

Although Bulgari is one of the largest jewelry manufacturers in the world, watches have always played an important role for the brand. The purchase of Daniel Roth and Gérald Genta opened new perspectives for its timepieces, thanks to specialized production facilities and the watchmaking talent in the Vallée de Joux—especially where complicated timepieces are concerned.

The Bulgari family is originally from Greece, and the watches, though designed in Rome, echo classic Hellenistic architecture in many ways. They are timeless and elegant, with style elements that border on the abstract. Manufacturing is done in Switzerland. From its modern building in the industrial zone of La Chaux-de-Fonds, the company has produced, among others, the Caliber 168 automatic based on a Leschot design that managing director Guido Terrini calls "the tractor," because it provided the "pull" to guarantee the company's independence. The year 2014 saw the simple Octo built on the double-barreled Caliber 193.

In March 2011, luxury goods giant Louis Vuitton Moët Hennessy (LVMH) secured all the Bulgari family shares in exchange for 16.5 million LVMH shares and a say in the group's future. The financial backing of the mega-group boosted the company's strategy to become fully independent. In mid-2013, Jean-Christophe Babin, the man who turned TAG Heuer into a leading player in sports watches, was chosen to head the venerable brand. He had also managed to build up a manufacturing structure from scratch at TAG Heuer, which is exactly the direction Bulgari's watch division is headed in. Barring a few components and the "Velocissimo" caliber, Bulgari is now able to do everything on its own. Its latest venture has been into electronics, with an NFC chip for the Magnesium to store private data, like passwords and credit card numbers—and even open garage doors or start your car.

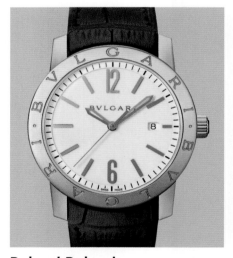

Bulgari Bulgari

Reference number: BBP39WGLD
Movement: automatic, Bulgari Caliber BVL 191; ø 26.2 mm, height 3.8 mm; 26 jewels; 28,800 vph; finely finished with côtes de Genève; 42-hour power reserve
Functions: hours, minutes, sweep seconds; date
Case: rose gold, ø 39 mm; sapphire crystal; water-resistant to 3 atm
Band: reptile skin, folding clasp
Price: $19,900
Variations: stainless steel ($6,600)

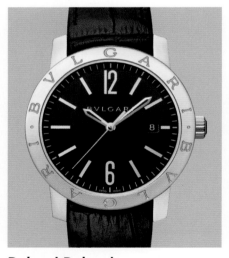

Bulgari Bulgari

Reference number: BB41WSLD
Movement: automatic, Bulgari Caliber BVL 191; ø 26.2 mm, height 3.8 mm; 26 jewels; 28,800 vph; finely finished with côtes de Genève; 42-hour power reserve
Functions: hours, minutes, sweep seconds; date
Case: stainless steel, ø 41 mm; sapphire crystal; water-resistant to 5 atm
Band: reptile skin, folding clasp
Price: $6,600
Variations: rose gold ($19,900)

Bulgari Bulgari Chronograph

Reference number: BB41BSSDCH
Movement: automatic, Bulgari Caliber BVL 328 (base Zenith "El Primero"); ø 30.5 mm, height 6.62 mm; 31 jewels; 36,000 vph; côtes de Genève; 50-hour power reserve
Functions: hours, minutes, subsidiary seconds; chronograph; date
Case: stainless steel, ø 41 mm; sapphire crystal; screw-in crown; water-resistant to 10 atm
Band: stainless steel, folding clasp
Price: $10,200

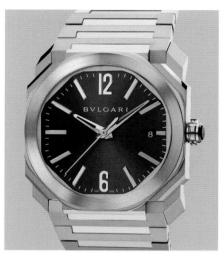

Octo Solotempo

Reference number: BGO38C3SSD
Movement: automatic, Bulgari Caliber BVL 193;
ø 25.6 mm, height 3.7 mm; 28 jewels; 28,800 vph;
double spring barrel; 50-hour power reserve
Functions: hours, minutes, sweep seconds; date
Case: stainless steel, ø 41.5 mm, height 10.55 mm;
sapphire crystal; transparent case back
Band: stainless steel, folding clasp
Price: $7,700
Variations: rose gold with rose gold bracelet
($46,500); rose gold with reptile skin band
($7,050)

Octo Solotempo

Reference number: BGOP41BGLD
Movement: automatic, Bulgari Caliber BVL 193;
ø 25.6 mm, height 3.7 mm; 28 jewels; 28,800 vph;
double spring barrel; 50-hour power reserve
Functions: hours, minutes, sweep seconds; date
Case: rose gold, ø 41.5 mm, height 10.55 mm;
sapphire crystal; transparent case back
Band: reptile skin, double folding clasp
Price: $23,900

Octo Velocissimo

Reference number: BGO41BSLDCH
Movement: automatic, Bulgari Caliber Velocissimo
(base Zenith "El Primero"); ø 30 mm, height
6.62 mm; 31 jewels, 36,000 vph; column
wheel control of chronograph functions, silicon
escapement; 50-hour power reserve
Functions: hours, minutes, subsidiary seconds;
chronograph; date
Case: stainless steel, ø 41.5 mm; screw-in crown
Band: reptile skin, buckle
Price: $9,900
Variations: stainless steel bracelet ($11,000); rose
gold ($29,000)

Octo Finissimo

Reference number: BGO40BPLXT
Movement: manually wound, Bulgari Caliber
Finissimo; ø 36.6 mm, height 2.23 mm; 26 jewels;
28,800 vph; fine finishing; 70-hour power reserve
Functions: hours, minutes, subsidiary seconds
Case: platinum, ø 40 mm, height 5 mm; sapphire
crystal; transparent case back; water-resistant to
3 atm
Band: reptile skin, buckle
Price: $26,200
Variations: platinum

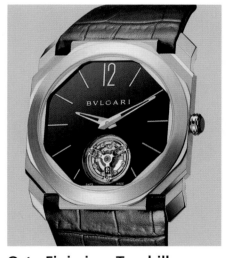

Octo Finissimo Tourbillon

Reference number: BGO40BPLTBXT
Movement: manually wound, Bulgari Caliber
Finissimo Tourbillon; ø 32 mm, height 1.95 mm; 26
jewels; 21,600 vph; flying 1-minute tourbillon; fine
finishing; 55-hour power reserve
Functions: hours, minutes
Case: platinum, ø 40 mm, height 5 mm; sapphire
crystal; transparent case back; water-resistant to
3 atm
Band: reptile skin, buckle
Price: $138,000
Variations: platinum with diamonds ($159,000);
rose gold ($127,000)

Octo Grande Sonnerie Tourbillon

Reference number: BGOW44BGLTBGS
Movement: automatic, Gérald Genta GG31002;
ø 31.5 mm, height 10.65 mm; 95 jewels;
21,600 vph; 1-minute tourbillon
Functions: hours (retrograde), hours/minutes
(digital, jumping); 2 power reserve indicators; large
repeater with Westminster chimes on 3 gongs
Case: white gold, ø 44 mm, height 15.76 mm;
sapphire crystal; transparent case back; falcon-eye
cabochon on crown; water-resistant to 3 atm
Band: reptile skin, double folding clasp
Price: on request

Commedia dell'Arte

Reference number: BGGW54GLCA/PU
Movement: manually wound, Bulgari Caliber BVL 618; ø 36 mm, height 11 mm; 91 jewels; 18,000 vph; 48-hour power reserve
Functions: hours (jumping), minutes (retrograde); automaton with 5 figures
Case: white gold, ø 54 mm, height 16.36 mm; sapphire crystal, transparent case back; water-resistant to 3 atm
Band: reptile skin, buckle
Price: price on request; limited to 8 pieces

Papillon Voyageur

Reference number: BRRP46C14GLGMTP
Movement: automatic, Daniel Roth Caliber DR 1307; ø 25.6 mm, height 6.78 mm; 26 jewels; 28,800 vph; 45-hour power reserve
Functions: hours (digital, jumping), minutes (retrograde), subsidiary seconds (segment display with double hand); additional 24-hour indicator (2nd time zone)
Case: rose gold, 43 x 46 mm, height 15.2 mm; sapphire crystal; transparent case back; pusher to advance 24-hour display; water-resistant to 3 atm
Band: reptile skin, double folding clasp
Price: $51,000

Daniel Roth Carillon Tourbillon

Reference number: BRRP48GLTBMR
Movement: manually wound, Caliber DR 3300; ø 34.6 mm, height 8.35 mm; 35 jewels; 21,600 vph; 1-minute tourbillon; double spring barrel; partially skeletonized, black finishing; 75-hour power reserve
Functions: hours, minutes; 3-hammer minute repeater
Case: rose gold, 45 x 48 mm, height 14.9 mm; sapphire crystal, transparent case back; water-resistant to 3 atm
Band: reptile skin, double folding clasp
Remarks: skeletonized dial; limited edition
Price: $257,000

Ammiraglio del Tempo

Reference number: BRRP50BGLDEMR
Movement: manually wound, Bulgari Caliber; ø 38 mm, height 9.38 mm; 56 jewels; 14,400 vph; minute repeater, Westminster chimes/chronometer escapement, 4 hammers/gongs; constant force mechanism; cylindrical balance spring; triple shock absorbing system; fine finishing; 48-hour power reserve
Functions: hours, minutes; minute repeater
Case: rose gold, 45.75 x 50 mm, height 14.9 mm; sapphire crystal; transparent case back
Remarks: mobile lug at 7 to activate chimes
Price: $359,000
Variations: white gold ($359,000)

Tourbillon Saphir Ultranero

Reference number: BGG53BTLTBSK/UN
Movement: manually wound, Gérald Genta Caliber GG 8000; ø 32.6 mm, height 6.2 mm; 19 jewels; 21,600 vph; 1-minute tourbillon; skeletonized; 72-hour power reserve
Functions: hours, minutes
Case: white gold, sapphire crystal sides, ø 53 mm, height 14.89 mm; black PVD coating on bezel; sapphire crystal; transparent case back; water-resistant to 3 atm
Band: reptile skin, double folding clasp
Remarks: limited to 25 pieces
Price: $198,000

Roma Finissimo 40th Anniversary

Reference number: BB41BGLXT
Movement: manually wound, Bulgari Caliber BVL 128; ø 36.6 mm; height 2.23 mm; 26 jewels; 28,800 vph; finely finished; 65-hour power reserve
Functions: hours, minutes, subsidiary seconds
Case: yellow gold, ø 41 mm, height 6.5 mm; sapphire crystal; transparent case back
Band: reptile skin, buckle
Remarks: limited to 100 pieces
Price: $27,200
Variations: rose gold ($13,400)

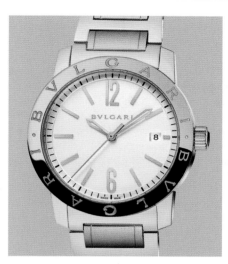

Bulgari Bulgari Solotempo

Reference number: BB39WGGD
Movement: automatic, Bulgari Caliber BVL 191;
ø 26.2 mm, height 3.8 mm; 26 jewels; 28,800 vph;
finely finished, with côtes de Genève; 42-hour power
reserve
Functions: hours, minutes, sweep seconds; date
Case: rose gold, ø 39 mm, height 6.5 mm; sapphire
crystal; transparent case back
Band: rose gold, folding clasp
Price: $39,000

Bulgari Roma Finissimo Tourbillon

Reference number: BBP41BGLTBXT
Movement: manually wound, Bulgari Caliber
Finissimo Tourbillon; ø 32.6 mm, height 1.95 mm;
26 jewels; 21,600 vph; flying 1-minute tourbillon;
fine finishing; 52-hour power reserve
Functions: hours, minutes
Case: rose gold, ø 41 mm, height 5.15 mm;
sapphire crystal; transparent case back; water-
resistant to 3 atm
Band: reptile skin, buckle
Price: $119,000

Diagono Magnesium

Reference number: DG41C3SMCVD
Movement: automatic, Bulgari Caliber 191;
ø 25.6 mm, height 4.6 mm; 25 jewels; 28,800 vph;
42-hour power reserve
Functions: hours, minutes, sweep seconds; date
Case: magnesium and poly ether ketone (PEEK),
ø 41 mm, ceramic bezel; sapphire crystal
Band: rubber, buckle
Price: $3,900

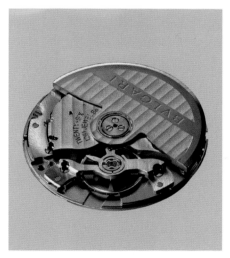

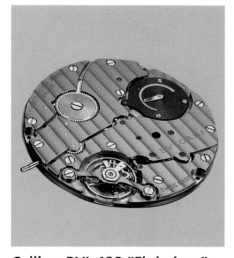

Caliber BVL 191

Automatic; single barrel spring, 42-hour power
reserve
Functions: hours, minutes, sweep seconds; date
Diameter: 26.2 mm
Height: 3.8 mm
Jewels: 26
Balance: glucydur
Frequency: 28,800 vph
Balance spring: flat hairspring with fine adjustment
Shock protection: Incabloc
Remarks: plate and bridges with perlage, polished
steel parts and screw heads

Caliber BVL 128 "Finissimo"

Manually wound; single spring barrel, 70-hour
power reserve
Functions: hours, minutes, subsidiary seconds;
power reserve indicator (on movement side)
Diameter: 36.6 mm
Height: 2.23 mm
Jewels: 26
Balance: glucydur
Frequency: 28,800 vph
Balance spring: flat hairspring with fine adjustment
Shock protection: Incabloc
Remarks: polished and beveled mainplate and
bridges, with sunburst polish, bridges with côtes de
Genève

Caliber BVL 193

Automatic; double spring barrel, 50-hour power
reserve
Functions: hours, minutes, sweep seconds; date
Diameter: 25.6 mm
Height: 3.7 mm
Jewels: 28
Balance: glucydur
Frequency: 28,800 vph
Balance spring: flat hairspring with fine adjustment
Shock protection: Incabloc
Remarks: perlage on plate, beveled and polished
bridges, with côtes de Genève

Bucherer Montres SA
Langensandstrasse 27
CH-6002 Lucerne
Switzerland

Tel.:
+41-41-369-7070

Fax:
+41-41-369-7072

E-Mail:
info@carl-f-bucherer.com

Website:
www.carl-f-bucherer.com

Founded:
1919, repositioned under the name Carl F.
Bucherer in 2001

Number of employees:
approx. 160

Annual production:
approx. 25,000 watches

U.S. distributor:
Carl F. Bucherer North America
1805 South Metro Parkway
Dayton, OH 45459
937-291-4366
info@cfbna.com; www.carl-f-bucherer.com

Most important collections/price range:
Patravi, Manero, and Alacria / core price
segment $5,000 to $30,000

Carl F. Bucherer

While luxury watch brand Carl F. Bucherer is still rather young, the Lucerne-based Bucherer jewelry dynasty behind it draws its vast know-how from more than ninety years of experience in the conception and design of fine wristwatches.

The summer of 2005 ushered in a new age for the watch brand: Company decision makers chose to develop and manufacture an in-house mechanical movement. Together with Bucherer's longtime, Sainte-Croix-headquartered cooperative partner, Techniques Horlogères Appliquées SA (THA), an ambitious plan was hatched. When it became clear that such sophisticated construction could not be realized using outside suppliers, the next logical step was to purchase its partner's renowned atelier in the Jura mountains.

THA was integrated into the Bucherer Group and the watch company renamed Carl F. Bucherer Technologies SA (CFBT). The Sainte-Croix operation is led by technical director Dr. Albrecht Haake, who oversees a staff of about twenty. Dr. Haake is currently focusing much of his energy on furthering the capacities at the workshop. "Industrialization is not a question of cost, but rather a question of quality," says Haake.

This family-run business celebrated its 125th anniversary in 2013. Its birthday present to itself included a classic tourbillon and a two-tone Alacria with an in-house quartz engine. The tenth anniversary of the Patravi TravelTec has also been celebrated in style with the Patravi TravelTec II featuring three time zones. The brand has also been quietly pursuing a strategy of boutique openings to give its customers the right surroundings. A new store launched in Macau in March 2013, while the group opened the world's largest watch store in Paris, a favorite shopping city for travelers from Asia.

Patravi TravelTec II

Reference number: 00.10633.08.33.01
Movement: automatic, Caliber CFB 1901.1;
ø 28.6 mm, height 7.3 mm; 39 jewels; 28,800 vph;
42-hour power reserve, COSC-certified chronometer
Functions: hours, minutes, subsidiary seconds; 3
time zones; chronograph; date
Case: stainless steel, ø 47.4 mm, height 15.9 mm;
pusher-activated inner bezel with 24-hour division
(3rd time zone); sapphire crystal; screw-in crown;
water-resistant to 10 atm
Band: rubber, folding clasp
Price: $12,900
Variations: stainless steel bracelet ($13,400)

Patravi TravelTec FourX Limited Edition

Reference number: 00.10620.22.93.01
Movement: automatic, Caliber CFB 1901.1;
ø 28.6 mm, height 7.3 mm; 39 jewels; 28,800 vph;
42-hour power reserve; COSC-certified chronometer
Functions: hours, minutes, subsidiary seconds; 3
time zones; chronograph; date
Case: rose gold, ø 46.6 mm, height 15.5 mm;
ceramic bezel, pusher-activated inner bezel with
24-hour divisions (3rd time zone); sapphire crystal;
screw-in crown; water-resistant to 5 atm
Band: rubber, buckle
Price: $52,900
Variations: palladium ($52,900)

Patravi ScubaTec

Reference number: 00.10632.22.33.01
Movement: automatic, Caliber CFB 1950.1;
ø 26.2 mm, height 4.8 mm; 25 jewels; 28,800 vph;
38-hour power reserve, COSC-certified chronometer
Functions: hours, minutes, sweep seconds; date
Case: rose gold, ø 44.6 mm, height 13.45 mm; rose
gold bezel with ceramic inserts, unidirectional bezel
with 60-minute division; sapphire crystal; screw-in
crown, helium valve; water-resistant to 50 atm
Band: rubber, rose gold/blackened titanium diving
clasp with extension link
Price: $25,900
Variations: stainless steel bracelet ($11,800);
stainless steel with stainless steel ($6,800) or
rubber band ($6,400); rose gold/stainless steel
with rubber ($9,800)

Patravi ScubaTec

Reference number: 00.10632.24.53.21
Movement: automatic, Caliber CFB 1950.1;
ø 26.2 mm, height 4.8 mm; 25 jewels; 28,800 vph;
38-hour power reserve; COSC-certified chronometer
Functions: hours, minutes, sweep seconds; date
Case: stainless steel, ø 44.6 mm, height 13.45 mm;
unidirectional bezel with ceramic inserts, with
60-minute divisions, sapphire crystal; screw-in
crown, helium valve; water-resistant to 50 atm
Band: rubber, folding clasp with extension link
Price: $6,400
Variations: stainless steel bracelet ($6,800);
rose gold with rubber strap ($25,900); rose gold/
stainless steel ($11,800)

Patravi ChronoGrade

Reference number: 00.10623.08.63.01
Movement: automatic, Caliber CFB 1902; ø 30 mm,
height 7.3 mm; 51 jewels; 28,800 vph; 42-hour
power reserve
Functions: hours, minutes, subsidiary seconds;
power reserve indicator; flyback chronograph with
retrograde hour totalizer; full calendar with large
date, month
Case: stainless steel, ø 44.6 mm, height 14.1 mm;
sapphire crystal; transparent case back; screw-in
crown; water-resistant to 5 atm
Band: leather, folding clasp
Price: $10,900
Variations: rose gold ($33,900)

Manero Tourbillon Limited Edition

Reference number: 00.10918.03.93.01
Movement: manually wound, Caliber CFB T1001;
ø 33 mm, height 6.2 mm; 35 jewels; 28,800 vph;
1-minute tourbillon; 70-hour power reserve
Functions: hours, minutes, subsidiary seconds (on
tourbillon cage); additional 24-hour display; power
reserve indicator; date
Case: rose gold, ø 41.8 mm, height 12.58 mm;
sapphire crystal; transparent case back; water-
resistant to 3 atm
Band: reptile skin, rose gold folding clasp
Price: $98,800
Variations: black or silver dial

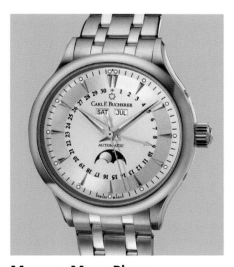

Manero MoonPhase

Reference number: 00.10909.03.13.21
Movement: automatic, Caliber CFB 1966;
ø 26.2 mm, height 5.2 mm; 21 jewels; 28,800 vph;
42-hour power reserve
Functions: hours, minutes, sweep seconds; full
calendar with date, weekday, month, moon phase
Case: rose gold, ø 38 mm, height 10.85 mm;
sapphire crystal; transparent case back; water-
resistant to 3 atm
Band: rose gold with folding clasp
Price: $27,200
Variations: reptile skin band ($12,900)

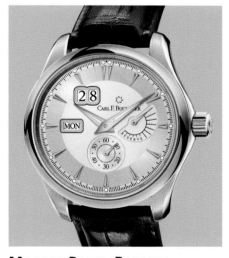

Manero PowerReserve

Reference number: 00.10912.03.13.01
Movement: automatic, Caliber CFB A1011;
ø 32 mm, height 6.3 mm; 33 jewels; 28,800 vph;
55-hour power reserve
Functions: hours, minutes, subsidiary seconds;
power reserve indicator; large date, weekday
Case: rose gold, ø 42.5 mm, height 12.54 mm;
sapphire crystal; transparent case back; water-
resistant to 3 atm
Band: reptile skin, rose gold pin folding clasp
Price: $26,100

Manero PowerReserve

Reference number: 00.10912.08.33.01
Movement: automatic, Caliber CFB A1011;
ø 32 mm, height 6.3 mm; 33 jewels; 28,800 vph;
55-hour power reserve
Functions: hours, minutes, subsidiary seconds;
power reserve indicator; large date, weekday
Case: stainless steel, ø 42.5 mm, height 12.54 mm;
sapphire crystal; transparent case back; water-
resistant to 3 atm
Band: leather, stainless steel folding clasp
Price: $11,000

Manero AutoDate

Reference number: 00.10908.08.13.01
Movement: automatic, Caliber CFB 1965;
ø 26.2 mm, height 3.6 mm; 21 jewels; 28,800 vph;
42-hour power reserve
Functions: hours, minutes, sweep seconds; date
Case: stainless steel, ø 38 mm, height 8.75 mm;
sapphire crystal; transparent case back; water-
resistant to 3 atm
Band: reptile skin, stainless steel buckle
Price: $2,800
Variations: rose gold ($9,000)

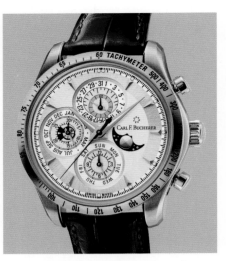

Manero ChronoPerpetual

Reference number: 00.10907.03.13.01
Movement: automatic, Caliber CFB 1904; ø 30 mm,
height 7.6 mm; 49 jewels; 28,800 vph; 50-hour
power reserve
Functions: hours, minutes, subsidiary seconds;
flyback chronograph; perpetual calendar with date,
weekday, month, moon phase, leap year; tachymeter
Case: rose gold, ø 42.5 mm, height 14.3 mm;
sapphire crystal; transparent case back; water-
resistant to 3 atm
Band: reptile skin, rose gold buckle
Price: $52,600

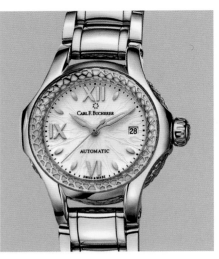

Pathos Queen

Reference number: 00.10550.07.25.21
Movement: automatic, Caliber CFB 1969;
ø 17.5 mm, height 4.8 mm; 25 jewels; 28,800 vph;
38-hour power reserve
Functions: hours, minutes, sweep seconds; date
Case: rose gold and stainless steel, ø 26.5 mm,
height 9.08 mm; rose gold bezel; sapphire crystal;
water-resistant to 3 atm
Band: rose gold and stainless steel, folding clasp
Price: $8,400
Variations: set with 38 diamonds ($13,100);
stainless steel ($4,400); stainless steel set with 38
diamonds ($9,400)

Alacria RoyalRose

Reference number: 00.10702.02.90.18
Movement: quartz
Functions: hours, minutes
Case: white gold, 26.5 x 38 mm, height 7.4 mm;
sapphire crystal
Band: goatskin, buckle set with diamonds and
sapphires
Remarks: white gold and mother-of-pearl dial set
with diamonds and sapphires; limited to 125 pieces
Price: $69,000

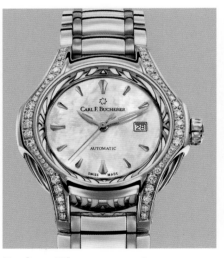

Pathos Diva

Reference number: 00.10580.03.73.31.02
Movement: automatic, Caliber CFB 1963; ø 20 mm,
height 4.8 mm; 25 jewels; 28,800 vph; 38-hour
power reserve
Functions: hours, minutes, sweep seconds; date
Case: rose gold, ø 34 mm, height 9.65 mm; sapphire
crystal; transparent case back; water-resistant to 3 atm
Band: rose gold, folding clasp
Remarks: case set with 54 diamonds
Price: $29,300
Variations: w/o diamonds ($24,800)

Caliber CFB A1000

Automatic, bidirectional rotor, peripheral rotor
on edge of movement with spring-held support
bearings; precision fine adjustment; single spring
barrel, 55-hour power reserve
Functions: hours, minutes, subsidiary seconds
Diameter: 30 mm; **Height:** 4.3 mm
Jewels: 33
Balance: glucydur
Balance spring: flat hairspring
Shock protection: Incabloc
Related calibers: CFB A1002 (with large date,
weekday, power reserve indicator); CFB A1003
(with large date and weekday)

Cartier

Since the Richemont Group's founding, Cartier has played an important role in the luxury concern as its premier brand and instigator of turnover. Although it took a while for Cartier to find its footing and convince the male market of its masculinity, any concerns about Cartier's seriousness and potential are being dispelled by facts. "We aimed to become a key player in *haute horlogerie*, and we succeeded," said CEO Bernard Fornas at a July 2012 press conference at the company's main manufacturing site in La Chaux-de-Fonds. The company is growing by leaps and bounds—a components manufacturing site employing 400 people is being built at the growing Richemont campus in Meyrin (Geneva).

It was Richemont Group's purchase of the Roger Dubuis *manufacture* in Geneva a few years ago that paved the way to the brand's independence and vertical integration. Under its brilliant head of fine watchmaking, Carole Forestier-Kasapi, Cartier has become a serious producer of movements, among them the 1904, which made its debut in the Calibre model. With a diameter of 42 mm, this strikingly designed men's watch is also well positioned in the segment. The designation 1904 MC is a reference to the year in which Louis Cartier developed the first wristwatch made for men—a pilot's watch custom designed for his friend and early pioneer of aviation, Alberto Santos-Dumont.

The automatic movement is a largely unadorned, yet efficient machine, powered by twin barrels. The central rotor sits on ceramic ball bearings, and the adjustment of the conventional escapement is by excenter screw. It is available for chronographs or diver's watches. The latest movement presented is the automatic 1847, which finds a home in the new Clé collection. And to prove that it can still innovate in jewelry, the brand has presented a stunning watch with a pavé of vibrating diamonds, each set separately on a spring.

Cartier SA
boulevard James-Fazy 8
CH-1201 Geneva
Switzerland

Tel.:
+41-022-818-4321

Fax:
+41-022-310-5461

E-Mail:
info@cartier.ch

Website:
www.cartier.de

Founded:
1847

Number of employees:
approx. 1,300 (watch manufacturing)

U.S. distributor:
Cartier North America
767 Fifth Avenue
New York, NY 10153
800-223-4000

Most important collections:
Ballon Bleu, Calibre, Clé, Pasha, Rotonde de Cartier, Santos, Tank

Rotonde de Cartier Reversed Tourbillon

Reference number: W1556246
Movement: manually wound, Cartier Caliber 9458 MC; ø 39 mm, height 5.58 mm; 19 jewels; 21,600 vph; flying 1-minute tourbillon; mirrored configuration; 50-hour power reserve; Geneva Seal
Functions: hours, minutes, subsidiary seconds (on tourbillon cage)
Case: white gold, ø 46 mm, height 12.73 mm; sapphire crystal; transparent case back; sapphire cabochon on crown; water-resistant to 3 atm
Band: reptile skin, folding clasp
Price: $150,000; limited to 100 pieces

Rotonde de Cartier Astrotourbillon Skeleton

Reference number: W1556250
Movement: manually wound, Cartier Caliber 9461 MC; ø 38 mm, height 8.89 mm; 21,600 vph; skeletonized with integrated roman numerals; 1-minute tourbillon; 49-hour power reserve
Functions: hours, minutes, subsidiary seconds (on tourbillon cage)
Case: white gold, ø 47 mm, height 15.5 mm; sapphire crystal; transparent case back; sapphire cabochon on crown
Band: reptile skin, double folding clasp
Price: $186,000

Rotonde de Cartier Mysterious Double Tourbillon

Reference number: W1556210
Movement: manually wound, Cartier Caliber 9454 MC; ø 35 mm, height 5 mm; 25 jewels; 21,600 vph; double flying tourbillon between 2 sapphire discs; 52-hour power reserve; Geneva Seal
Functions: hours, minutes (off-center)
Case: platinum, ø 45 mm, height 12.45 mm; sapphire crystal, transparent case back; sapphire cabochon on crown
Band: reptile skin, double folding clasp
Price: $183,000

Rotonde de Cartier Astrocalendaire

Reference number: W1556242
Movement: automatic, Cartier Caliber 9459 MC; ø 31.38 mm, height 8.1 mm; 53 jewels; 21,600 vph; 1-minute tourbillon; 50-hour power reserve; Geneva Seal
Functions: hours, minutes; perpetual calendar with date, weekday, month, leap year (on caliber side, switched backward and forward)
Case: platinum, ø 45 mm, height 15.1 mm; sapphire crystal; transparent case back; sapphire cabochon on crown; water-resistant to 3 atm
Band: reptile skin, folding clasp
Price: $170,000

Rotonde de Cartier 2nd Time Zone

Reference number: W1556368
Movement: automatic, Cartier Caliber 1904-FU MC; ø 25.6 mm, 28,800 vph; 48-hour power reserve
Functions: hours, minutes, subsidiary seconds; added retrograde 12-hour display (2nd time zone), day/night indicator; large date
Case: stainless steel, ø 42 mm, height 11.96 mm; sapphire crystal; transparent case back; sapphire cabochon on crown; water-resistant to 3 atm
Band: reptile skin, folding clasp
Price: $9,300
Variations: white gold ($27,000); pink gold ($25,200)

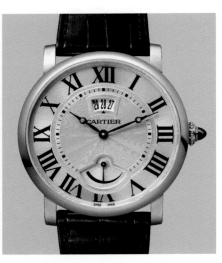

Rotonde de Cartier Power Reserve

Reference number: W1556369
Movement: manually wound, Cartier Caliber 9753 MC; ø 20.79 mm, 20 jewels; 21,600 vph; 40-hour power reserve
Functions: hours, minutes; power reserve indicator; date
Case: stainless steel, ø 40 mm, height 8.94 mm; sapphire crystal; sapphire cabochon on crown
Band: reptile skin, folding clasp
Price: $8,350
Variations: pink gold ($21,600)

Rotonde de Cartier Chronograph

Reference number: WSRO0002
Movement: automatic, Cartier Caliber 1904-CH MC; ø 25.6 mm, height 5.72 mm; 35 jewels; 28,800 vph; 2 spring barrels; 48-hour power reserve
Functions: hours, minutes; chronograph; date
Case: stainless steel, ø 40 mm, height 12.15 mm; sapphire crystal; transparent case back; water-resistant to 3 atm
Band: reptile skin, folding clasp
Price: $9,050
Variations: white and pink gold

Rotonde de Cartier Grande Complication Skeleton

Reference number: W1556251
Movement: automatic, Cartier Caliber 9406 MC; ø 35 mm, height 5.49 mm; 47 jewels; 21,600 vph; flying 1-minute tourbillon, microrotor; extra-flat construction; 50-hour power reserve; Geneva Seal
Functions: hours, minutes; minute repeater; perpetual calendar with date, weekday, month
Case: platinum, ø 45 mm, height 12.6 mm; sapphire crystal; transparent case back; sapphire cabochon on crown; water-resistant to 3 atm
Band: reptile skin, double folding clasp
Remarks: skeletonized white dial
Price: $600,000

Rotonde de Cartier Annual Calendar

Reference number: WSRO0002
Movement: automatic, Cartier Caliber 9908 MC; ø 30 mm, height 5.9 mm; 32 jewels; 28,800 vph; 48-hour power reserve
Functions: hours, minutes; full calendar with large date, weekday, month
Case: pink gold, ø 40 mm, height 13.26 mm; sapphire crystal; sapphire cabochon on crown; water-resistant to 3 atm
Band: reptile skin, double folding clasp
Price: $35,700
Variations: white gold ($42,800)

Clé de Cartier

Reference number: WGCL0005
Movement: automatic, Cartier Caliber1847 MC;
ø 25.6 mm, height 3.6 mm; 23 jewels; 28,800vph;
42-hour power reserve
Functions: hours, minutes, sweep seconds; date
Case: white gold, ø 40 mm, height 11.76 mm;
sapphire crystal; transparent case back; water-
resistant to 3 atm
Band: reptile skin, folding clasp
Price: $20,200
Variations: pink gold with pink gold bracelet
($34,900) or leather strap ($18,800); white gold
with white gold bracelet ($37,300)

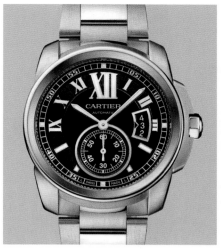

Calibre de Cartier

Reference number: W7100016
Movement: automatic, Cartier Caliber 1904-PS;
ø 25.6 mm, height 4 mm; 27 jewels; 28,800 vph; 2
spring barrels; 48-hour power reserve
Functions: hours, minutes, subsidiary seconds;
date
Case: stainless steel, ø 42 mm, height 9.64 mm;
sapphire crystal; transparent case back; water-
resistant to 3 atm
Band: stainless steel, folding clasp
Price: $7,800
Variations: white dial

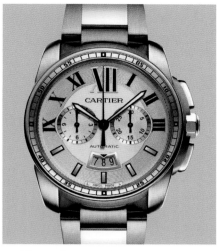

Calibre de Cartier Chronograph

Reference number: W7100045
Movement: automatic, Cartier Caliber 1904-
CH MC; ø 25.6 mm, height 5.71 mm; 35 jewels;
28,800 vph; côtes de Genève; 48-hour power
reserve
Functions: hours, minutes; chronograph; date
Case: stainless steel, ø 42 mm, height 12.66 mm;
sapphire crystal; transparent case back; water-
resistant to 10 atm
Band: stainless steel, folding clasp
Price: $10,900
Variations: reptile skin strap ($10,200); pink gold
with reptile skin strap ($13,500)

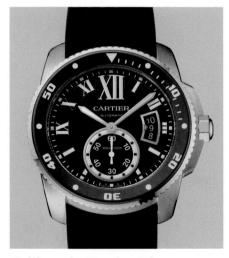

Calibre de Cartier Diver

Reference number: W7100052
Movement: automatic, Cartier Caliber 1904_
PS MC; ø 25.6 mm, height 4 mm; 27 jewels;
28,800 vph; 2 spring barrels; 48-hour power reserve
Functions: hours, minutes, subsidiary seconds;
date
Case: pink gold, ø 42 mm, height 11 mm;
unidirectional bezel with black ADLC coating, with
60-second divisions; sapphire crystal; screw-in
crown; water-resistant to 30 atm
Band: rubber, buckle
Price: $27,300
Variations: stainless steel ($10,200); stainless
steel with black ADLC coating ($7,900)

Calibre de Cartier Diver

Reference number: W2CA0004
Movement: automatic, Cartier Caliber 1904_
PS MC; ø 25.6 mm, height 4 mm; 27 jewels;
28,800 vph; 2 spring barrels; 48-hour power reserve
Functions: hours, minutes, subsidiary seconds;
date
Case: stainless steel with black DLC-coating, ø 42 mm,
height 11 mm; unidirectional pink gold bezel with black
numerals ring with 60-second divisions; sapphire
crystal; screw-in crown; water-resistant to 30 atm
Band: rubber, buckle
Price: $7,900
Variations: stainless steel w/o coating ($9,450);
pink gold ($10,200)

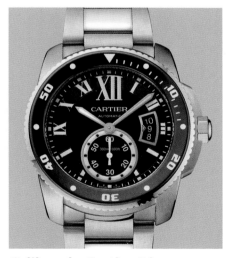

Calibre de Cartier Diver

Reference number: W7100057
Movement: automatic, Cartier Caliber 1904 MC;
ø 25.6 mm, height 4 mm; 27 jewels; 28,800 vph; 2
spring barrels; 48-hour power reserve
Functions: hours, minutes, sweep seconds; date
Case: stainless steel, ø 42 mm, height 11 mm;
black ADLC-coated unidirectional bezel with
60-minute division; sapphire crystal; screw-in
crown; water-resistant to 30 atm
Band: stainless steel, folding clasp
Price: $8,550
Variations: pink gold ($12,500); black ADLC
coating ($27,300)

Crash Skeleton

Reference number: W7200001
Movement: manually wound, Cartier Caliber 9618 MC; 18 jewels; 28,800 vph; skeletonized with integrated roman numerals; 2 spring barrels; 72-hour power reserve
Functions: hours, minutes
Case: platinum, 28.5 x 45.32 mm, height 9.62 mm; mineral glass; sapphire cabochon on crown
Band: reptile skin, folding clasp
Price: $78,500; limited to 67 pieces
Variations: with diamonds ($150,000; limited to 67 pieces)

Tank MC Skeleton

Reference number: W5310026
Movement: manually wound, Cartier Caliber 9619 MC; 28.6 x 28.6 mm, height 3.97 mm; 20 jewels; 28,800 vph; skeletonized with integrated roman numerals; 2 spring barrels; 72-hour power reserve
Functions: hours, minutes
Case: white gold, 34.5 x 43.8 mm, height 9.3 mm; sapphire crystal; transparent case back; sapphire cabochon on crown; water-resistant to 3 atm
Band: reptile skin, folding clasp
Price: $53,000
Variations: pink gold ($21,100)

Tank MC

Reference number: W5330003
Movement: automatic, Cartier Caliber 1904-PS MC; ø 25.6 mm, height 4 mm; 27 jewels; 28,800 vph; 2 spring barrels; 48-hour power reserve
Functions: hours, minutes, subsidiary seconds; date
Case: stainless steel, 34.3 x 44 mm, height 9.5 mm; sapphire crystal; transparent case back; sapphire cabochon on crown; water-resistant to 3 atm
Band: reptile skin, folding clasp
Price: $6,750
Variations: pink gold ($14,700)

Tank Louis Cartier Skeleton

Reference number: W5310012
Movement: manually wound, Cartier Caliber 9616 MC; 26 x 26.3 mm, height 3.6 mm; 21 jewels; 28,800 vph; skeletonized; 72-hour power reserve
Functions: hours, minutes
Case: white gold, 30 x 39.2 mm, height 7.45 mm; sapphire crystal; transparent case back; sapphire cabochon on crown; water-resistant to 3 atm
Band: reptile skin, folding clasp
Price: $51,500
Variations: pink gold ($50,500)

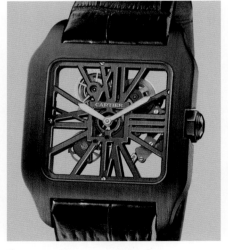

Santos Dumont Carbon Skeleton

Reference number: W2020052
Movement: manually wound, Cartier Caliber 9611 MC; 28 x 28 mm, height 3.97 mm; 20 jewels; 28,800 vph; skeletonized with integrated roman numerals; 2 spring barrels; 72-hour power reserve
Functions: hours, minutes
Case: titanium, with black ADLC coating, 38.7 x 47.4 mm, height 9.4 mm; sapphire crystal; transparent case back; water-resistant to 3 atm
Band: reptile skin, folding clasp
Price: $47,900
Variations: white gold ($53,500); pink gold ($25,300)

Santos Dumont Skeleton

Reference number: W2020033
Movement: manually wound, Cartier Caliber 9431 MC; 28.6 x 28.6 mm, height 3.97 mm; 20 jewels; 28,800 vph; skeletonized with integrated roman numerals; 2 spring barrels; 72-hour power reserve
Functions: hours, minutes
Case: white gold, 38.7 x 47.4 mm, height 9.4 mm; sapphire crystal; transparent case back; water-resistant to 3 atm
Band: reptile skin, double folding clasp
Price: $53,500
Variations: titanium with black coating ($47,900); pink gold ($25,300)

Caliber 1904-PS MC

Automatic; bidirectional rotor system; twin spring barrels; 48-hour power reserve
Functions: hours, minutes, subsidiary seconds; date
Diameter: 25.6 mm
Height: 4 mm
Jewels: 27
Balance: screw balance
Frequency: 28,800 vph
Balance spring: flat hairspring
Remarks: finely finished with côtes de Genève

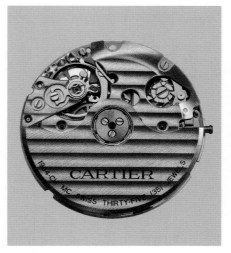

Caliber 1904-CH MC

Automatic; column wheel control of chronograph functions; double spring barrel; 48-hour power reserve
Functions: hours, minutes; chronograph; date
Diameter: 25.6 mm
Height: 5.71 mm
Jewels: 35
Balance: glucydur
Frequency: 28,800 vph
Balance spring: flat hairspring
Remarks: finely finished with côtes de Genève

Caliber 9908 MC

Automatic; double spring barrel; 48-hour power reserve
Functions: hours, minutes; full calendar with large date, weekday, month
Diameter: 30 mm
Height: 5.9 mm
Jewels: 32
Balance: glucydur
Frequency: 28,800 vph
Balance spring: flat hairspring
Remarks: finely finished with côtes de Genève

Caliber 9406 MC

Automatic; flying 1-minute tourbillon; microrotor; extra-flat construction; single spring barrel; 50-hour power reserve; Geneva Seal
Functions: hours, minutes; minute repeater; perpetual calendar with date, weekday, month
Diameter: 39.3 mm
Height: 5.49 mm
Jewels: 47
Balance: glucydur
Frequency: 21,600 vph
Balance spring: flat hairspring
Remarks: first "grande complication" designed and made in-house by Cartier Manufacture
Remarks: 578 components

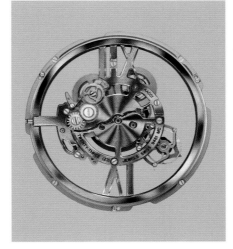

Caliber 9461 MC

Manually wound; skeletonized movement with integrated roman numeral hours; eccentrically rotating 1-minute tourbillon with a large hand indicating seconds; single spring barrel; 48-hour power reserve; Geneva Seal
Functions: hours, minutes, subsidiary seconds (on tourbillon cage)
Diameter: 38 mm
Height: 8.89 mm
Jewels: 23
Balance: glucydur
Frequency: 21,600 vph
Balance spring: flat hairspring

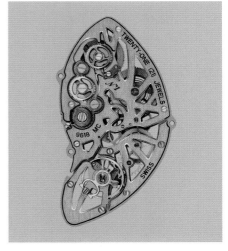

Caliber 9618 MC

Manually wound; skeletonized with integrated roman numeral hours; double spring barrel; 72-hour power reserve
Functions: hours, minutes
Measurements: 20.2 x 37.9 mm
Height: 3.97 mm
Jewels: 20
Balance: glucydur
Frequency: 28,800 vph
Balance spring: flat hairspring
Remarks: irregular movement contour

Chanel

135, avenue Charles de Gaulle
F-92521 Neuilly-sur-Seine Cedex
France

Tel.:
+33-1-41-92-08-33

Website:
www.chanel.com

Founded:
1914

Distribution:
retail and 200 Chanel boutiques worldwide

U.S. distributor:
Chanel Fine Jewelry and Watches
733 Madison Avenue
New York, NY 10021
800-550-0005
www.chanel.com

Most important collections:
J12, Première

Chanel

After putting the occasional jewelry watch onto the market earlier, the family-owned Chanel opened its own horology division in 1987, a move that gave the brand instant access to the world of watchmaking art. Chanel boasts its own studio and logistics center, both in La Chaux-de-Fonds. While the brand's first collections were directed exclusively at its female clientele, it was actually with the rather simple and masculine J12 that Chanel finally achieved a breakthrough. Designer Jacques Helleu says he mainly designed the unpretentious ceramic watch for himself. "I wanted a timeless watch in glossy black," shares the likable eccentric. Indeed, it's not hard to imagine that the J12 will still look modern a number of years down the road—especially given the fact that the watch now comes in white and shiny, polished titanium/ceramic as well.

The J12 collection showpiece, the Rétrograde Mystérieuse, was a stroke of genius—courtesy of the innovative think tank Renaud et Papi. It instantly propelled Chanel into the world of *haute horlogerie*. And the brand has not been resting on any laurels. Lately, it entirely redid the ladies' watch Première, even though the change is not obvious at first glance. The octagonal shape of Place Vendôme in Paris (home of the brand) and the famous Chanel No. 5 bottle stopper are still there, and the simple 1980s style, but with a narrower bezel and adapted hands.

J12 G.10 Blue Chromatic

Reference number: H4338
Movement: automatic, ETA Caliber 2824-2; ø 25.6 mm, height 4.6 mm; 25 jewels; 28,800 vph; 42-hour power reserve
Functions: hours, minutes, sweep seconds; date
Case: stainless steel, ø 38 mm, height 13 mm; bidirectional ceramic bezel with 60-minute division; sapphire crystal; screw-in crown; water-resistant to 20 atm
Band: textile, buckle
Price: $4,850
Variations: as Grey Chromatic

J12 Soft Mint

Reference number: H4465
Movement: automatic, ETA Caliber 2824-2; ø 25.6 mm, height 4.6 mm; 25 jewels; 28,800 vph; 42-hour power reserve
Functions: hours, minutes, sweep seconds
Case: ceramic, ø 38 mm, height 13 mm; white gold bezel with ceramic inlays; sapphire crystal; screw-in crown; water-resistant to 20 atm
Band: ceramic, double folding clasp
Remarks: limited to 1,200 pieces
Price: $5,500
Variations: various colors; with 29 mm case and diamond indices ($6,200); with 33 mm case ($5,200)

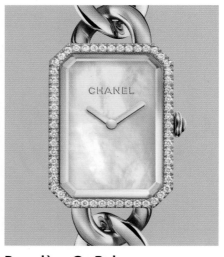

Première Or Beige

Reference number: H4412
Movement: quartz
Functions: hours, minutes
Case: beige gold, 20 x 28 mm, height 6.6 mm; bezel set with 56 brilliant-cut diamonds; sapphire crystal; water-resistant to 3 atm
Band: beige gold, push-slot clasp
Remarks: mother-of-pearl dial
Price: $30,500
Variations: with 16 x 22 mm case ($23,000)

Chopard

The Chopard *manufacture* was founded by Louis-Ulysse Chopard in 1860 in the tiny village of Sonvillier in the Jura mountains of Switzerland. In 1963, it was purchased by Karl Scheufele, a goldsmith from Pforzheim, Germany, and revived as a producer of fine watches and jewelry.

The past seventeen years have seen a breathtaking development, when Karl Scheufele's son, Karl-Friedrich, and his sister, Caroline, decided to create watches with in-house movements, thus restoring the old business launched by Louis-Ulysse back in the nineteenth century.

In the 1990s, literally out of nowhere, Chopard opened up its watchmaking *manufacture* in the sleepy town of Fleurier. Since 1996, the company has created no fewer than nine *manufacture* calibers, reassembled to configure more than fifty watch variations ranging from the three-hand automatic to the tourbillon. The aim of Chopard's Fleurier Ebauches SA is to revive the long-standing tradition of *ébauche* production in that town.

The factory's debut caliber, the 01.03-C, is featured in its Impériale ladies watch. In 2011, Chopard produced more than 3,000 "Fleurier" watches. In 2012 came the men's version, the 01.04-C. The number of movements was slated to reach 15,000 by the year 2015. And the engineers are not resting on their laurels: A chronograph caliber is already in the making. The company also continues to support the Geneva Watchmaking School with special *ébauches* for the students, a demonstration of its commitment to the industry. So, with its wide range of *manufacture* watch models and over 130 boutiques worldwide, the brand enjoys firm footing in the rarified air of *haute horlogerie*. Mission accomplished.

Chopard & Cie. SA
8, rue de Veyrot
CH-1217 Meyrin (Geneva)
Switzerland

Tel.:
+41-22-719-3131

E-Mail:
info@chopard.ch

Website:
www.chopard.ch

Founded:
1860

Distribution:
161 boutiques

U.S. distributor:
Chopard USA
21 East 63rd Street
New York, NY 10065
1-800-CHOPARD
www.us.chopard.com

Most important collections/price range:
Superfast / $9,230 to $33,190; L.U.C / $8,670 to $451,930; Imperiale / $4,390 to $803,270; Classic Racing / $5,070 to $40,860; Happy Sport / $5,120 to $438,750

Mille Miglia GTS Automatic

Reference number: 168565-3001
Movement: automatic; Chopard Manufacture Caliber 01.01-C; ø 28.8 mm, height 4.95 mm; 27 jewels; 28,800 vph; 60-hour power reserve; COSC-certified chronometer
Functions: hours, minutes, sweep seconds; date
Case: stainless steel, ø 43 mm, height 11.43 mm; sapphire crystal; transparent case back; screw-in crown, water-resistant to 10 atm
Band: rubber, folding clasp
Price: $6,080
Variations: stainless steel band ($7,690); rose gold ($21,830)

Mille Miglia GTS Chrono

Reference number: 161293-5001
Movement: automatic, ETA Caliber 7750; ø 30.4 mm, height 7.9 mm; 25 jewels; 28,800 vph; 48-hour power reserve; COSC-certified chronometer
Functions: hours, minutes, subsidiary seconds; chronograph; date
Case: rose gold, ø 44 mm, height 13.79 mm; sapphire crystal; screw-in crown; water-resistant to 10 atm
Band: rubber, folding clasp
Price: $23,630
Variations: stainless steel ($7,430)

Mille Miglia GTS Chrono

Reference number: 168571-3001
Movement: automatic, ETA Caliber 7750; ø 30.4 mm, height 7.9 mm; 25 jewels; 28,800 vph; 48-hour power reserve; COSC-certified chronometer
Functions: hours, minutes, subsidiary seconds; chronograph; date
Case: stainless steel, ø 44 mm, height 13.79 mm; sapphire crystal; screw-in crown; water-resistant to 10 atm
Band: rubber, folding clasp
Price: $7,430
Variations: stainless steel band ($8,980); rose gold ($23,630)

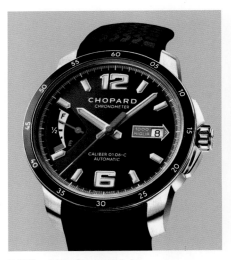

Mille Miglia GTS Power Control

Reference number: 168566-3001
Movement: automatic, Chopard Manufacture Caliber 01.08-C; ø 28.8 mm, height 4.95 mm; 40 jewels; 28,800 vph; 60-hour power reserve; COSC-certified
Functions: hours, minutes, sweep seconds; power reserve indicator; date
Case: stainless steel, ø 43 mm, height 11.43 mm; sapphire crystal; transparent case back; screw-in crown, water-resistant to 10 atm
Band: rubber folding clasp
Price: $6,640
Variations: stainless steel band ($8,250); rose gold ($22,390)

Mille Miglia 2015

Reference number: 161296-5002
Movement: automatic, Chopard Manufacture Caliber 01.08-C; ø 28.8 mm, height 4.95 mm; 40 jewels; 28,800 vph; 60-hour power reserve; COSC-certified chronometer
Functions: hours, minutes, sweep seconds, power reserve indicator, date
Case: rose gold, ø 43 mm, height 11.43 mm; sapphire crystal; transparent case back; screw-in crown, water-resistant to 10 atm
Band: calf leather, folding clasp
Price: $22,730; limited to 100 pieces
Variations: stainless steel ($6,980)

Classic Racing Porsche 919 Limited Edition

Reference number: 168535-3002
Movement: automatic, Chopard Manufacture Caliber 03.05-M; ø 28.8 mm, height 7.6 mm; 45 jewels; 28,800 vph; 60-hour power reserve; COSC-certified chronometer
Functions: hours, minutes, subsidiary seconds; flyback chronograph; date
Case: stainless steel, ø 45 mm, height 15.18 mm; sapphire crystal; transparent case back; screw-in crown, water-resistant to 10 atm
Band: rubber, folding clasp
Price: $12,890; limited to 919 pieces

Classic Racing Superfast Chrono

Reference number: 168535-3001
Movement: automatic, Chopard Manufacture Caliber 03.05-M; ø 28.8 mm, height 7.6 mm; 45 jewels; 28,800 vph; 60-hour power reserve; COSC-certified chronometer
Functions: hours, minutes, subsidiary seconds; flyback chronograph; date
Case: stainless steel, ø 45 mm, height 15.2 mm; sapphire crystal; transparent back; screw-in crown with rubber coating; water-resistant to 10 atm
Band: rubber, folding clasp
Price: $12,740
Variations: rose gold ($33,190)

L.U.C Quattro

Reference number: 161926-9001
Movement: manually wound, L.U.C Caliber 98.01-L; ø 28.6 mm, height 3.7 mm; 39 jewels; 28,800 vph; 4 spring barrels, gold rotor; 216-hour power reserve; Geneva Seal; COSC-certified chronometer
Functions: hours, minutes, subsidiary seconds; power reserve indicator; date
Case: platinum, ø 43 mm, height 8.84 mm; sapphire crystal; transparent case back; water-resistant to 5 atm
Band: reptile skin, buckle
Price: $32,630
Variations: rose gold ($26,510); white gold ($26,510)

L.U.C 8 HF Power Control

Reference number: 168575-9001
Movement: automatic, L.U.C Caliber 01.09-L; ø 28.8 mm, height 4.95 mm; 24 jewels, 57,600 vph; high-frequency escapement with silicone lever and escape wheel; 60-hour power reserve; COSC-certified chronometer
Functions: hours, minutes, subsidiary seconds; power reserve indicator; date
Case: ceramic, ø 42 mm, height 11.2 mm; sapphire crystal, transparent back; water-resistant to 10 atm
Band: textile, buckle
Price: $20,820

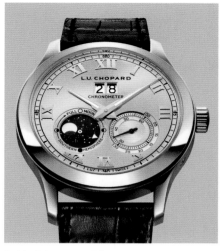

L.U.C Lunar One

Reference number: 161927-5001
Movement: automatic, L.U.C Caliber 96.13-L;
ø 33 mm, height 6 mm; 32 jewels; 28,800 vph;
65-hour power reserve; Geneva Seal; COSC-certified
Functions: hours, minutes, subsidiary seconds;
perpetual calendar with large date, weekday, month,
orbital moon phase display, leap year
Case: rose gold, ø 43 mm, height 11.47 mm;
sapphire crystal; transparent case back; water-
resistant to 5 atm
Band: reptile skin, folding clasp
Price: $63,600
Variations: diamonds on bezel ($98,550); white
gold ($63,600)

L.U.C Lunar Big Date

Reference number: 161969-1001
Movement: automatic, L.U.C Caliber 96.20-L;
ø 33 mm, height 5.25 mm; 33 jewels; 28,800 vph;
65-hour power reserve; COSC-certified chronometer
Functions: hours, minutes, subsidiary seconds;
large date; moon phase
Case: white gold, ø 42 mm, height 11.04 mm;
sapphire crystal; transparent case back; water-
resistant to 5 atm
Band: reptile skin, buckle
Price: $31,730
Variations: rose gold ($31,730)

L.U.C Perpetual T

Reference number: 161940-9001
Movement: manually wound, L.U.C Caliber 02.15-L;
ø 33 mm, height 9.35 mm; 31 jewels; 28,800 vph;
1-minute tourbillon, 4 spring barrels; 216-hour power
reserve; Geneva Seal; COSC-certified chronometer
Functions: hours, minutes, subsidiary seconds;
additional 24-hour display (2nd time zone); power
reserve display (on case back); perpetual calendar
with large date, weekday, month, leap year
Case: platinum, ø 43 mm, height 14.9 mm;
sapphire crystal; transparent case back; water-
resistant to 3 atm
Band: reptile skin, folding clasp
Price: $199,800; limited to 25 pieces
Variations: rose gold ($166,500)

L.U.C Tourbillon Qualité Fleurier Fairmined Gold

Reference number: 161929-5006
Movement: manually wound, L.U.C Caliber 02.13-L;
ø 29.7 mm, height 6.1 mm; 33 jewels; 28,800 vph;
1-minute tourbillon, bridges with côtes de Genève;
216-hour power reserve; COSC-certified, Qualité
Fleurier
Functions: hours, minutes, subsidiary seconds;
power reserve indicator
Case: rose gold, ø 43 mm, height 11.15 mm;
sapphire crystal; transparent case back; water-
resistant to 5 atm
Band: reptile skin, buckle
Remarks: case of Fairmined-certified gold
Price: $144,570; limited to 25 pieces

L.U.C 1963 Tourbillon

Reference number: 161970-5001
Movement: manually wound, L.U.C Caliber
02.19-L1; ø 29.7 mm, height 5.5 mm; 33 jewels;
28,800 vph; 1-minute tourbillon; 216-hour power
reserve; Geneva Seal; COSC-certified chronometer
Functions: hours, minutes, subsidiary seconds;
power reserve indicator
Case: pink gold, ø 40 mm, height 10.6 mm;
sapphire crystal; transparent case back; water-
resistant to 5 atm
Band: reptile skin, buckle
Price: $129,380; limited to 100 pieces

L.U.C Qualité Fleurier

Reference number: 161896-5003
Movement: automatic, L.U.C Caliber 96.09-L;
ø 27.4 mm, height 3.3 mm; 29 jewels; 28,800 vph;
65-hour power reserve; COSC-certified
chronometer, Qualité Fleurier
Functions: hours, minutes, subsidiary seconds
Case: rose gold, ø 39 mm, height 8.92 mm;
sapphire crystal, transparent case back; water-
resistant to 3 atm
Band: reptile skin, buckle
Price: $19,280

L.U.C 1963

Reference number: 161963-5001
Movement: manually wound, L.U.C Caliber 63.01-L;
ø 38 mm, height 5.5 mm; 20 jewels; 28,800 vph;
60-hour power reserve; Geneva Seal; COSC-certified
chronometer
Functions: hours, minutes, subsidiary seconds
Case: rose gold, ø 44 mm, height 11.5 mm;
sapphire crystal; transparent case back; water-
resistant to 5 atm
Band: reptile skin, buckle
Price: $37,580; limited to 50 pieces
Variations: platinum ($43,650; limited to 50
pieces)

L.U.C Regulator

Reference number: 161971-5001
Movement: manually wound, L.U.C Caliber 98.02-L;
ø 30.4 mm, height 4.9 mm; 39 jewels; 28,800 vph;
4 spring barrels, bridges with côtes de Genève; 216-
hour power reserve; Geneva Seal; COSC-certified
chronometer
Functions: hours (off-center), minutes, subsidiary
seconds; additional 24-hour display (2nd time
zone); power reserve indicator; date
Case: rose gold, ø 43 mm, height 9.78 mm;
sapphire crystal; transparent case back; water-
resistant to 3 atm
Band: reptile skin, buckle
Price: $33,530

L.U.C XPS

Reference number: 161920-5001
Movement: automatic, L.U.C Caliber 96.12-L;
ø 27.4 mm; height 3.3 mm; 29 jewels; 28,800 vph;
bridges with côtes de Genève; 65-hour power
reserve; COSC-certified chronometer
Functions: hours, minutes, subsidiary seconds
Case: rose gold, ø 39.5 mm, height 7.13 mm;
sapphire crystal; transparent case back; water-
resistant to 3 atm
Band: reptile skin, buckle
Price: $16,780
Variations: white gold ($16,780)

L.U.C XPS Fairmined Gold

Reference number: 161920-5006
Movement: automatic, L.U.C Caliber 96.12-L;
ø 27.4 mm, height 3.3 mm; 29 jewels; 28,800 vph;
gold rotor; bridges with côtes de Genève; 65-hour
power reserve; COSC-certified chronometer
Functions: hours, minutes, subsidiary seconds
Case: rose gold, ø 39.5 mm, height 7.13 mm;
sapphire crystal; transparent case back; water-
resistant to 3 atm
Band: reptile skin, buckle
Remarks: case made of Fairmined gold
Price: $18,900; limited to 250 pieces

L.U.C XPS 35 mm

Reference number: 131968-5001
Movement: automatic, L.U.C 96.12-L; ø 27.4 mm,
height 3.3 mm; 29 jewels; 28,800 vph; bridges with
côtes de Genève; 65-hour power reserve; COSC-
certified chronometer
Functions: hours, minutes, subsidiary seconds
Case: rose gold, ø 35 mm, height 7.1 mm; diamonds
on bezel; sapphire crystal; transparent case back;
water-resistant to 3 atm
Band: reptile skin, buckle
Remarks: dial set with diamonds
Price: $27,080
Variations: white gold ($27,080); w/o diamonds
($16,710)

L.U.C XPS Esprit de Fleurier

Reference number: 131968-1002
Movement: automatic, L.U.C Caliber 96.23-L;
ø 27.4 mm, height 3.3 mm; 29 jewels; 28,800 vph;
bridges with Fleurier finishing, gold rotor; 65-hour
power reserve; COSC-certified chronometer
Functions: hours, minutes, subsidiary seconds
Case: white gold, ø 35 mm, height 7.1 mm; 62
diamonds on bezel; sapphire crystal; transparent
case back; water-resistant to 3 atm
Band: reptile skin, buckle
Remarks: mother-of-pearl dial with 22 diamonds
Price: $50,630; limited to 25 pieces

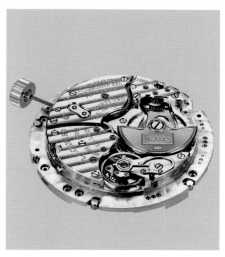

Caliber L.U.C 96.13-L

Automatic; microrotor; 2 double spring barrels; 65-hour power reserve; Geneva Seal; COSC-certified chronometer
Functions: hours, minutes, subsidiary seconds, perpetual calendar with large date, weekday, month, moon phase, leap year
Diameter: 33 mm
Height: 6 mm
Jewels: 32
Balance: glucydur
Frequency: 28,800 vph
Balance spring: flat hairspring, Nivarox 1

Caliber L.U.C 96.12-L

Automatic; microrotor; 2 double spring barrels; 65-hour power reserve; COSC-certified chronometer
Functions: hours, minutes, subsidiary seconds
Diameter: 27.4 mm
Height: 3.3 mm
Jewels: 29
Balance: glucydur
Frequency: 28,800 vph
Balance spring: flat hairspring, Nivarox 1

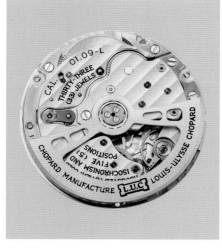

Caliber L.U.C 01.09-L

Automatic; high-frequency escapement with silicon pallet lever and balance wheel; single spring barrel; 60-hour power reserve; COSC-certified chronometer
Functions: hours, minutes, subsidiary seconds; power reserve indicator; date
Diameter: 28.8 mm
Height: 4.95 mm
Jewels: 33
Balance: glucydur
Frequency: 57,600 vph
Balance spring: flat hairspring, Nivarox 1

Caliber 03.05-M

Automatic; column wheel control of chronograph functions, vertical chronograph clutch; single spring barrel; 65-hour power reserve; COSC-certified chronometer
Functions: hours, minutes, subsidiary seconds; flyback chronograph; date
Diameter: 28.8 mm
Height: 7.6 mm
Jewels: 45
Balance: glucydur
Frequency: 28,800 vph
Balance spring: flat hairspring
Remarks: slitted movement bridges; gray finishing; skeletonized winding rotor

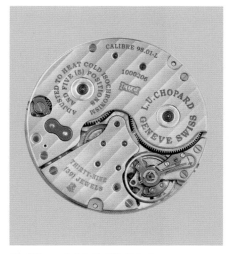

Caliber L.U.C 98.01-L

Manually wound; swan-neck fine adjustment; quadruple spring barrel operating in twin series, 200-hour power reserve; Geneva Seal; COSC-certified chronometer
Functions: hours, minutes, subsidiary seconds; power reserve indicator; date
Diameter: 28.6 mm
Height: 3.7 mm
Jewels: 39
Frequency: 28,800 vph
Balance spring: Breguet spring

Caliber L.U.C 02.15-L

Manually wound; 1-minute tourbillon; quadruple spring barrel, operating in twin series, 216-hour power reserve; Geneva Seal; COSC-certified chronometer
Functions: hours, minutes, subsidiary seconds; additional 24-hour display (2nd time zone), power reserve indicator (on movement side); perpetual calendar with large date, weekday, month, leap year
Diameter: 33 mm; **Height:** 9.35 mm; **Jewels:** 31
Balance: Variner; **Frequency:** 28,800 vph
Balance spring: balance spring with Philips terminal curve
Remarks: 353 components

**Christiaan van der Klaauw
Astronomical Watches**
P.O. Box 87
NL-8440 AB Heerenveen
The Netherlands

Tel.:
+31-513-624-906

E-Mail:
info@klaauw.com

Website:
www.klaauw.com

Founded:
1974

Annual production:
up to 300

U.S. distributor:
Tourneau
510 Madison Avenue
New York, NY 10022
212-758-5830

Most important collections:
astronomical watches

Christiaan van der Klaauw

Christiaan van der Klaauw was one of the earliest members of the famous AHCI, the Académie Horlogère des Créateurs Indépendents (Horological Academy of Independent Creators), in Switzerland. His main focus since 1976 has been on astronomical watches. He did not have to search long for a role model: The most obvious choice was Christiaan Huygens. The famous physicist and mathematician built the first pendulum clock. Like van der Klaauw, he too came from the Netherlands. And so did the astronomer Eise Eisinga, who set up a model of the solar system in his living room in 1774 to prove to people that the moon, Mars, Jupiter, Mercury, and Venus would not collide with our own planet.

During his studies of microengineering, van der Klaauw worked in the world's oldest observatory (founded by J. H. Oort in 1633) and had already begun building astrolabes, planetaria, and complicated calendar watches.

The astronomical watch he completed in 1990 turned out to be his passport to the AHCI. From then on, van der Klaauw drove the watch world forward with his many elaborate creations. A new era began in 2009 for Christiaan van der Klaauw: A partnership with the Dutch designer Daniel Reintjes evolved into a full-fledged investment model with two other partners. The very modest master watchmaker could then concentrate on what he likes to do best: designing, inventing, tinkering. The brand's portfolio of astronomical watches has grown steadily. Van de Klaauw has also put time and talent into developing modern interpretations of astronomical displays for other brands, like the complex planetarium module for Van Cleef & Arpels.

Ceres
Reference number: CKCR3326
Movement: automatic, Caliber CK1068 (base Soprod A10); ø 25.6 mm, 25 jewels; 28,800 vph; hand-engraved gold rotor; 42-hour power reserve
Functions: hours, minutes; moon phase
Case: stainless steel, ø 40 mm, height 13 mm; sapphire crystal; transparent case back
Band: reptile skin, folding clasp
Price: $7,900
Variations: rose gold ($24,900)

Orion
Reference number: CKOR3326
Movement: automatic, Caliber CK1072 (base Soprod A10); ø 25.6 mm, height 3.6 mm; 25 jewels; 28,800 vph; planisphere turns counterclockwise once per sidereal day (23 hours, 56 minutes, 4 seconds); 42-hour power reserve
Functions: hours, minutes, sweep seconds; planisphere (map of skies) with zodiac
Case: stainless steel, ø 40 mm, height 13.5 mm; sapphire crystal; transparent case back
Band: reptile skin, buckle folding clasp
Price: $16,500
Variations: rose gold ($33,500)

Retro Moon
Reference number: CKRT1144
Movement: automatic, Caliber CK1086 (base Soprod A10); ø 25.6 mm, 25 jewels; 28,800 vph; hand-engraved gold rotor; 42-hour power reserve
Functions: hours, minutes, sweep seconds; moon phase (retrograde)
Case: rose gold, ø 40 mm, height 13.5 mm; sapphire crystal; transparent case back
Band: reptile skin, buckle
Price: $35,900
Variations: stainless steel ($18,900)

Real Moon Joure MOP

Reference number: CKRJ3394
Movement: automatic, Caliber CK7382 (base TT 738); ø 30 mm, height 4.35 mm; 35 jewels; 28,800 vph; double spring barrel, hand-engraved gold rotor; 96-hour power reserve
Functions: hours, minutes, moon phase
Case: stainless steel, ø 40 mm, height 14.8 mm; sapphire crystal; transparent case back
Band: reptile skin, folding clasp
Remarks: mother-of-pearl dial, 3D moon
Price: $26,900
Variations: various colors

Real Moon Joure

Reference number: CKRJ1124
Movement: automatic, Caliber CK7382 (base TT 738); ø 30 mm, height 4.35 mm; 35 jewels; 28,800 vph; twin spring barrels; hand-engraved gold rotor; 96-hour power reserve
Functions: hours, minutes, sweep seconds; moon phase
Case: rose gold, ø 40 mm, height 14.8 mm; sapphire crystal; transparent back; water-resistant to 5 atm
Band: reptile skin, buckle
Remarks: 3D moon
Price: $42,900
Variations: white gold ($48,900); stainless steel ($25,900)

Real Moon Tides

Reference number: CKRS1124
Movement: automatic, Caliber CK7383 (base TT 738); ø 30 mm, height 4.35 mm; 35 jewels; 28,800 vph; twin spring barrels; hand-engraved gold rotor; 96-hour power reserve
Functions: hours, minutes; indication of tides; moon phase
Case: rose gold, ø 40 mm, height 14.8 mm; sapphire crystal; transparent case back; water-resistant to 5 atm
Band: reptile skin, buckle
Remarks: 3D moon
Price: $53,900
Variations: stainless steel ($36,900)

Real Moon 1980

Reference number: CKRL1124
Movement: automatic, Caliber CK7384 (base TT 738); ø 30 mm, height 4.35 mm; 35 jewels; 28,800 vph; double spring barrel, hand-engraved gold rotor; 96-hour power reserve
Functions: hours, minutes; perpetual calendar with date, month, moon phase, sun at zenith (depending on version), solar and lunar eclipse indicators
Case: rose gold, ø 40 mm, height 13 mm; sapphire crystal; transparent case back
Band: reptile skin, buckle
Remarks: 3D; homage to 1980 astronomical watch by Christiaan van der Klaauw
Price: $64,900

Planetarium

Reference number: CKPT3304
Movement: automatic, Caliber CK7386 (base TT 738); ø 30 mm, height 4.35 mm; 35 jewels; 28,800 vph; double spring barrel, hand-engraved gold rotor; 96-hour power reserve
Functions: hours, minutes; planetarium with orbits of Mercury, Venus, Earth, Mars, Jupiter, Saturn; perpetual calendar with date, month
Case: stainless steel, ø 40 mm, height 14.8 mm; sapphire crystal; transparent back; water-resistant to 5 atm
Band: reptile skin, folding clasp
Remarks: world's smallest heliocentric planetarium
Price: $46,500

Planetarium

Reference number: CKPT1124
Movement: automatic, Caliber CK7386 (base TT 738); ø 30 mm, height 4.35 mm; 35 jewels; 28,800 vph; double spring barrel, hand-engraved gold rotor; 96-hour power reserve
Functions: hours, minutes; planetarium with orbits of Mercury, Venus, Earth, Mars, Jupiter, Saturn; perpetual calendar with date, month
Case: rose gold, ø 40 mm, height 14.8 mm; sapphire crystal; transparent back; water-resistant to 5 atm
Band: reptile skin, buckle
Remarks: world's smallest heliocentric planetarium
Price: $56,500
Variations: white gold ($62,500); platinum ($76,500)

Christophe Claret SA
Route du Soleil d'Or 2
CH-2400 Le Locle
Switzerland

Tel.:
+41-32-933-0000

Fax:
+41-32-933-8081

E-Mail:
info@christopheclaret.com

Website:
www.christopheclaret.com

Founded:
manufacture 1989, brand 2010

Number of employees:
100

Distribution:
Contact the *manufacture* directly.

Most important collections:
Allegro, Aventicum, Maestoso, Kantharos,
Soprano; X-TREM-1/DualTow; Poker, Baccara,
Blackjack; Margot

Christophe Claret

Individuals like Christophe Claret are authentic horological engineers who eat, drink, and breathe watchmaking and have developed careers based on pushing the envelope to the very edge of what's possible.

By the age of twenty-three, the Lyon-born Claret was in Basel alongside Journe, Calabrese, and other independents, where he was spotted by the late Rolf Schnyder of Ulysse Nardin and commissioned to make a minute repeater with jacquemarts. In 1989, he opened his *manufacture*, a nineteenth-century mansion tastefully extended with a state-of-the-art machining area. Indeed, Claret embraces wholeheartedly the potential in modern tools to create the precise pieces needed to give physical expression to exceedingly complex ideas.

Over the years, Claret created complications and movements for many companies. In 2004, he came out with the Harry Winston Opus IV, a reversible moon phase with tourbillon and minute repeater.

Twenty years after establishing his business, Claret finally launched his own complex watches: models like the DualTow, with its hours and minutes on two tracks, minute repeater, and complete view of the great ballet of arms and levers inside. Then came the Adagio, again a minute repeater, with a clear dial that manages a second time zone and large date. In 2011, Claret wowed the watch world with a humorous, on-the-wrist gambling machine telling time and playing blackjack, craps, or roulette. It was followed by the stunning X-TREM-1, a turbocharged DualTow with two spheres controlled by magnets hovering along the numeral tracks to tell the time plus a tourbillon. Whatever he produces—the Margot, for women, the art-laden Aventicum, or the latest minute repeater, the Allegro—the Claret signature is always present: a total dedication to power mechanics and an infallible sense of style.

Allegro

Reference number: MTR.ALG89.000-020
Movement: manually wound, Christophe Claret
Caliber ALG 89; ø 34 mm, height 8.2 mm; 39 jewels;
21,600 vph; minute repeater centrifugal regulator;
skeletonized bridge; 60-hour power reserve
Functions: hours, minutes, subsidiary seconds;
additional 12-hour display (2nd time zone), day/
night indicator, minute repeater; large date
Case: rose gold, titanium, PVD-coated, ø 45 mm,
height 14.1 mm; sapphire crystal; transparent case
back
Band: reptile skin, folding clasp
Price: $250,000; limited to 20 pieces
Variations: white gold and titanium (limited to
20 pieces); rose gold

Aventicum

Reference number: MTR.AVE15.070-107
Movement: automatic, Christophe Claret Caliber
AVE 15; ø 26.2 mm, height 3.37 mm; 28 jewels;
28,800 vph; double spring barrel; invisible sapphire
crystal rotor with 5 weights; 72-hour power reserve
Functions: hours, minutes
Case: white gold, titanium, PVD-coated, ø 44 mm,
height 18.5 mm; sapphire crystal; transparent back
Band: reptile skin, folding clasp
Remarks: sculptural, hologram projection of
miniature bust of Marcus Aurelius in middle of dial
Price: $50,000; limited to 38 pieces
Variations: rose gold and titanium ($46,000;
limited to 68 pieces)

X-Trem-1 Blue

Reference number: MTR.FLY11.120-128
Movement: manually wound, Christophe Claret
Caliber FLY 11; 26.6 x 46.4 mm, height 11.94 mm;
64 jewels; 21,600 vph; flying tourbillon tilted at
30°; 50-hour power reserve
Functions: hours, minutes (linear display using steel
beads hovering in lateral sapphire crystal tube)
Case: white gold, titanium, blue PVD-coated,
40.8 x 56.8 mm, height 15 mm; sapphire crystal;
transparent case back
Band: reptile skin, folding clasp
Price: $250,000; limited to 8 pieces
Variations: platinum/titanium (8 pieces); rose gold;
gray gold; rose/gray gold/titanium (8 pieces)

The Lure of Gold
An Artistic and Cultural History
By Hans-Gert Bachmann
Cloth · $75.00
ISBN 978-0-7892-0900-9

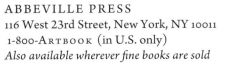

Chronoswiss AG
Löwenstrasse 16a
CH-6004 Lucerne
Switzerland

Tel.:
+41-41-552-2100

Fax:
+41-41-552-2109

E-Mail:
mail@chronoswiss.com

Website:
www.chronoswiss.com

Founded:
1983

Number of employees:
approx. 40

Annual production:
4,000–6,000 wristwatches

U.S. distributor:
Please contact brand headquarters in
Switzerland.

Most important collections/price range:
approx. 30 models including Sirius
Régulateur, Sirius Triple Date, Sirius
Artist, Timemaster Big Date, Timemaster
Chronograph GMT / approx. $3,550 to
$39,900

Chronoswiss

Chronoswiss has been assembling its signature watches—which boast such features as coin edge bezels and onion crowns—since 1983. Chronoswiss founder Gerd-Rüdiger Lang loved to joke about having "the only Swiss watch factory in Germany" as the brand has always adhered closely to the qualities of the Swiss watch industry while still contributing a great deal to reviving mechanical watches from its facilities in Karlsfeld near Munich, with concepts and designs "made in Germany." The fact is, however, that the watches are equipped with Swiss movements and cases, as well as many other important parts. The company's financial brawn is also Swiss, ever since Eva and Oliver Ebstein bought up all Chronoswiss shares in order to ensure the brand's survival. Oliver, as a passionate watch man, is continuing the brand tradition and producing top-drawer mechanical timepieces. The spacious sun-drenched facilities in Karlsfeld are now focused on distribution and servicing.

With such developments as the *manufacture* caliber C.122—based on an old Enicar automatic movement with a patented rattrapante mechanism—and its Chronoscope chronograph, Chronoswiss has earned a solid reputation for technical prowess. The Pacific and Sirius models, additions to the classic collection, point the company in a new stylistic direction designed to help win new buyers and the attention of the international market. As for the successful Timemaster chrono, it has appeared in a new skeletonized version, giving a deep insight into the brand's own modification of an ETA Valjoux.

Sirius Régulateur Jumping Hour

Reference number: CH-8321R
Movement: automatic, Chronoswiss Caliber C.283; ø 29.4 mm, height 5.35 mm; 27 jewels; 28,800 vph; skeletonized rotor; finely finished; 42-hour power reserve
Functions: hours (digital, jumping), minutes (off-center), subsidiary seconds
Case: pink gold, ø 40 mm, height 10.35 mm; sapphire crystal; transparent case back; water-resistant to 3 atm
Band: reptile skin, buckle
Remarks: sterling silver dial
Price: $20,500
Variations: stainless steel ($9,500)

Sirius Chronograph Moon Phase

Reference number: CH-7541LR
Movement: automatic, Chronoswiss Caliber C.755 (base ETA 7750); ø 30 mm, height 7.9 mm; 25 jewels; 28,800 vph; côtes de Genève, perlage; skeletonized rotor
Functions: hours, minutes, subsidiary seconds; chronograph; date; moon phase
Case: pink gold, ø 42 mm, height 14.75 mm; sapphire crystal; transparent case back; water-resistant to 3 atm
Band: reptile skin, buckle
Price: $23,775
Variations: stainless steel ($8,700)

Sirius Chronograph Skeleton

Reference number: CH-7543S
Movement: automatic, Chronoswiss Caliber C.741 S (base ETA 7750); ø 30 mm, height 7.9 mm; 25 jewels; 28,800 vph; entirely skeletonized and decorated with stripes
Functions: hours, minutes, subsidiary seconds; chronograph; date
Case: stainless steel, ø 42 mm, height 14.75 mm; sapphire crystal; transparent case back; water-resistant to 3 atm
Band: reptile skin, buckle
Remarks: skeletonized dial
Price: $12,925

Sirius Artist Régulateur Jumping Hour

Reference number: CH-8323E-BL
Movement: automatic, Chronoswiss Caliber C.283; ø 29.4 mm, height 5.35 mm; 27 jewels; 28,800 vph; skeletonized rotor; finely finished and partially hand-guilloché; 42-hour power reserve
Functions: hours (digital, jumping), minutes (off-center), subsidiary seconds
Case: stainless steel, ø 40 mm, height 10.35 mm; sapphire crystal; transparent back; water-resistant to 3 atm
Band: reptile skin, buckle
Remarks: guilloché and fired enamel dial
Price: $16,100
Variations: red gold ($29,000)

Sirius Big Date Small Seconds

Reference number: CH-8423
Movement: automatic, Chronoswiss Caliber C.284; ø 29.4 mm, height 5.35 mm; 26 jewels; 28,800 vph; perlage on bridges and plates; skeletonized rotor with côtes de Genève; 42-hour power reserve
Functions: hours, minutes, subsidiary seconds; large date
Case: stainless steel, ø 40 mm, height 10.35 mm; sapphire crystal; transparent case back; water-resistant to 3 atm
Band: reptile skin
Remarks: sterling silver dial
Price: $7,250
Variations: pink gold ($18,650)

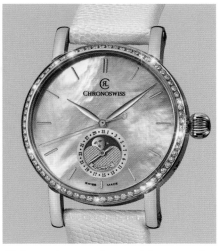

Sirius Moon Phase Diamonds

Reference number: CH-8521RD-MP
Movement: automatic, Chronoswiss Caliber C.932 S (base Sellita SW300); ø 25.6 mm, height 5.35 mm; 25 jewels: 28,800 vph; perlage on bridges and plates; skeletonized rotor with côtes de Genève; 42-hour power reserve
Functions: hours, minutes, sweep seconds; date; moon phase
Case: pink gold, ø 40 mm, height 10.35 mm; 72 brilliant-cut diamonds on bezel; sapphire crystal; transparent case back; water-resistant to 3 atm
Price: $26,650
Variations: diamonds on case ($39,900); stainless steel ($15,750)

Sirius Triple Date

Reference number: CH 9343
Movement: automatic, Chronoswiss Caliber C.931 (base ETA 2892-A2); ø 25.6 mm, height 5.75 mm; 21 jewels; 28,800 vph; skeletonized rotor, côtes de Genève; 42-hour power reserve
Functions: hours, minutes, sweep seconds; full calendar with date, weekday, month, moon phase
Case: stainless steel, ø 40 mm, height 9.9 mm; sapphire crystal, transparent case back; water-resistant to 3 atm
Band: reptile skin, buckle
Price: $9,025
Variations: pink gold ($18,675)

Sirius Small Seconds

Reference number: CH-8021R
Movement: automatic, Chronoswiss Caliber C.285; ø 30 mm; height 5.2 mm; 25 jewels; 28,800 vph; perlage on bridges and plates; skeletonized rotor with côtes de Genève; 42-hour power reserve
Functions: hours, minutes, subsidiary seconds
Case: pink gold, ø 40 mm, height 9.75 mm; sapphire crystal; transparent case back; water-resistant to 3 atm
Band: reptile skin, buckle
Price: $14,900
Variations: stainless steel ($5,400)

Sirius Retrograde Day

Reference number: CH-8121R-DS
Movement: automatic, Chronoswiss Caliber C.286; ø 30 mm, height 5.2 mm; 22 jewels; 28,800 vph; perlage on plate and bridges; skeletonized rotor with côtes de Genève; 42-hour power reserve
Functions: hours, minutes, sweep seconds; large date and weekday (retrograde)
Case: pink gold, ø 40 mm, height 10.30 mm; sapphire crystal; transparent case back
Band: reptile skin, buckle
Price: $17,800
Variations: stainless steel ($7,100)

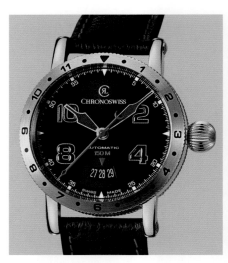

Timemaster 150

Reference number: CH-2733-AZ
Movement: automatic, Chronoswiss Caliber C.287 (base Sellita SW200); ø 25.6 mm, height 4.6 mm; 26 jewels: 28,800 vph; 38-hour power reserve
Functions: hours, minutes, sweep seconds; date
Case: stainless steel, ø 41 mm, height 13 mm; sapphire crystal; screw-in crown; water-resistant to 15 atm
Band: calf leather, buckle
Price: $3,550
Variations: black PVD coating ($3,800)

Timemaster Chronograph Skeleton

Reference number: CH-9043SB-BK
Movement: automatic, Chronoswiss Caliber C.741 S (base ETA 7750); ø 30 mm, height 7.9 mm; 25 jewels; 28,800 vph; perlage on bridges and plates; skeletonized rotor with côtes de Genève; 46-hour power reserve
Functions: hours, minutes, subsidiary seconds; chronograph; date
Case: stainless steel, ø 44 mm, height 15.3 mm; black DLC coating on bezel; sapphire crystal; screw-in crown; water-resistant to 10 atm
Price: $13,750
Variations: silver-plated dial; stainless steel ($13,900)

Timemaster Chronograph Day Date

Reference number: CH-9043B-DB
Movement: automatic, Chronoswiss Caliber C.771 (base ETA 7750); ø 30 mm, height 7.9 mm; 25 jewels; 28,800 vph; perlage on bridges and plates; skeletonized rotor with côtes de Genève; 46-hour power reserve
Functions: hours, minutes, subsidiary seconds; chronograph; weekday, date
Case: stainless steel, ø 44 mm, height 15.3 mm; black DLC coating on bezel; sapphire crystal; screw-in crown; water-resistant to 10 atm
Band: rubber, folding clasp
Price: $7,700
Variations: uncoated bezel ($7,300)

Timemaster GMT

Reference number: CH-2563/S0-2
Movement: automatic, Chronoswiss Caliber C.289 (base ETA 2893-2); ø 25.6 mm, height 4.1 mm; 21 jewels; 28,800 vph; perlage on bridges and plates; skeletonized rotor with côtes de Genève; 42-hour power reserve
Functions: hours, minutes, sweep seconds; additional 24-hour display (2nd time zone)
Case: stainless steel, ø 44 mm, height 13.9 mm; sapphire crystal; screw-in crown; water-resistant to 10 atm
Band: stainless steel, folding clasp
Price: $6,900

Timemaster GMT

Reference number: CH-2535
Movement: automatic, Chronoswiss Caliber C.289 (base ETA 2893-1); ø 25.6 mm, height 4.1 mm; 21 jewels; 28,800 vph; perlage on bridges and plates; skeletonized rotor with côtes de Genève; 42-hour power reserve
Functions: hours, minutes, sweep seconds; additional 24-hour display (2nd time zone)
Case: stainless steel with black DLC coating, ø 44 mm, height 13.9 mm; sapphire crystal; screw-in crown, water-resistant to 10 atm
Band: textile, folding clasp
Remarks: carbon fiber dial
Price: $7,400

Timemaster Big Date

Reference number: CH 3535.1
Movement: automatic, Chronoswiss Caliber C.351 S (base LJP 3513); ø 25.6 mm, height 4.95 mm; 21 jewels; 28,800 vph; rhodium-plated, skeletonized rotor with black DLC coating; côtes de Genève
Functions: hours, minutes, sweep seconds; power reserve indicator; large date
Case: stainless steel, black DLC coating; ø 44 mm, height 15.1 mm; bezel with 60-minute divisions, sapphire crystal, transparent case back; water-resistant to 10 atm
Band: rubber, buckle
Price: $6,475
Variations: w/o DLC coating ($5,750)

Caliber C.111

Base caliber: Marvin 700
Manually wound; power reserve 46 hours
Functions: hours, minutes, subsidiary seconds
Diameter: 29.4 mm
Height: 3.3 mm
Jewels: 17
Balance: glucydur, 3-legged
Frequency: 21,600 vph
Balance spring: Nivarox 1
Shock protection: Incabloc
Remarks: polished pallet lever, escapement wheel and screws, bridges with côtes de Genève

Caliber C.122

Automatic; skeletonized and gold-plated rotor on ball bearings, with côtes de Genève; power reserve approx. 40 hours
Functions: hours, minutes, subsidiary seconds
Diameter: 26.8 mm
Height: 5.3 mm
Jewels: 30
Balance: glucydur, 3-legged
Frequency: 21,600 vph
Balance spring: Nivarox 1
Shock protection: Incabloc
Remarks: pallet lever, escape wheel and screws, perlage on plate, bridges with côtes de Genève; individually numbered

Caliber C.126

Automatic; E94 striking module (Dubois Dépraz), all-or-nothing strike train and 2 gongs; power reserve 35 hours
Functions: hours, minutes, subsidiary seconds; quarter hour repeater
Diameter: 28 mm
Height: 8.35 mm
Jewels: 38
Balance: glucydur, 3-legged
Frequency: 21,600 vph
Balance spring: Nivarox 1
Shock protection: Incabloc
Remarks: base plate with perlage; beveled bridges with perlage; côtes de Genève decoration; individually numbered

Caliber C.127

Automatic; calendar module with a left-side moon phase; skeletonized and gold-plated rotor on ball bearings, with côtes de Genève; power reserve 40 hours
Functions: hours, minutes, sweep seconds; perpetual calendar with months, moon phase, weekday, date, leap year
Diameter: 26.8 mm; **Height:** 8.79 mm
Jewels: 30; **Balance:** glucydur, 3-legged
Frequency: 21,600 vph
Balance spring: Nivarox 1
Shock protection: Incabloc
Remarks: polished pallet lever, escapement wheel and screws, perlage on plate, bridges with côtes de Genève; individually numbered

Caliber C.673

Base caliber: ETA 6498
Manually wound; power reserve 46 hours
Functions: hours (off-center), minutes, subsidiary seconds
Diameter: 37.2 mm
Height: 4.5 mm
Jewels: 17
Balance: glucydur screw balance with stop second
Frequency: 18,000 vph
Balance spring: Nivarox 1
Shock protection: Incabloc
Remarks: polished pallet lever, escape wheel and screws; côtes de Genève and hand perlage on bridges, balance cocks, sunburst pattern on crown and ratchet wheel; individually numbered

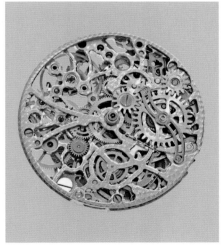

Caliber C.741 S

Base caliber: ETA 7750
Automatic; completely skeletonized; skeletonized and gold-plated rotor on ball bearings, with côtes de Genève; power reserve approx. 46 hours
Functions: hours, minutes, subsidiary seconds; chronograph; date
Diameter: 30 mm; **Height:** 7.9 mm; **Jewels:** 25
Balance: glucydur, 3-legged
Frequency: 28,800 vph
Balance spring: Nivarox 1
Shock protection: Incabloc
Remarks: polished pallet lever, escape wheel and screws; perlage on plate, skeletonized and beveled levers and wheels

C. H. Wolf GmbH
Feldstrasse 2
D-01768 Glashütte
Germany

Tel.:
+49-35053-31-553

Fax:
+49-35053-32-232

E-Mail:
info@c-h-wolf.de

Website:
www.c-h-wolf.de

Founded:
2004/2014

Number of employees:
15

U.S. distributor:
Horology Works
860-986-9676
mmargolis@horologyworks.com
www.horologyworks.com

Most important collections:
Urban, Nautic, Racing, Pilot, Flymatic

C. H. Wolf

Before the age of the affordable wristwatch, it was the church clock that kept people informed of the march of time. In the industrial age, they continued their function, but other venues also required clocks as tools to regulate day-to-day life. Of course, someone had to build these devices and service and maintain them. One such firm was the Turmuhren-Fabrik und Mechanische Werkstatt (Tower Clock Manufactory and Mechanical Workshop) founded in 1868 by Carl Heinrich Wolf in Glashütte, Germany.

The company passed on to Wolf's children and was later bought out. At one point it was known as Hemess. Finally, in October 2014, it was renamed after its original founder and given a new lease on life—with the clocks shrunk down to fit on a human wrist. New owners Christoph Pfeiffer and Jürgen Werner managed even to acquire the original premises of the old firm and carefully renovated the old structure, which now boasts top-of-the-line modern equipment. To relaunch the firm, they had several thousand square feet of light-filled, air-conditioned space with proper watchmaking workstations to maintain production of a small, well-rounded collection of wristwatches.

The first products, already released, are driven by mechanical calibers, all finely finished according to the rules of Glashütte watchmaking and given the typical decorative touches. The Swiss origins of these calibers are no longer identifiable, as is obvious when peering inside the watches through the standard transparent case backs. One specialty of this old-new Glashütte brand is the very elaborate dials that appear on the limited special editions. One was made out of the skiwear of a world-champion skier, another covered over with a very fine bit of cloth from a historic costume.

Pilot Red

Reference number: AP-450-06-302-30-02
Movement: manually wound, Caliber CHW 302 (base ETA 6498-1); ø 36.6 mm, height 4.5 mm; 17 jewels; 18,000 vph; three-quarter plate; swan-neck fine adjustment; 46-hour power reserve
Functions: hours, minutes, subsidiary seconds
Case: black PVD-coated stainless steel, ø 45 mm, height 10.8 mm; sapphire crystal; transparent case back; water-resistant to 5 atm
Band: calf leather with red artificial silk inserts, buckle
Remarks: dial layered with red artificial silk
Price: $3,250

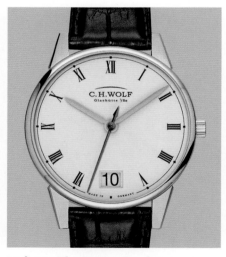

Urban Big Date Business

Reference number: HBB-410-01-208-02-01
Movement: automatic, Caliber Hematic CHW 3910 (base Eterna 39); ø 30.4 mm, height 5.6 mm; 30 jewels; 28,800 vph; finely finished rotor with special C. H. Wolf pattern; 65-hour power reserve
Functions: hours, minutes, sweep seconds; large date
Case: stainless steel, ø 41 mm, height 10.5 mm; sapphire crystal; transparent case back; water-resistant to 5 atm
Band: reptile skin, buckle
Price: $6,900

Flymatic Chrono

Reference number: FP-450-01-502-01-07
Movement: automatic, Caliber Hematic CHW 500 (base Sellita SW500); ø 30 mm, height 7.9 mm; 25 jewels; 28,800 vph; finely finished rotor with special C. H. Wolf pattern; 48-hour power reserve
Functions: hours, minutes, subsidiary seconds; chronograph; date
Case: stainless steel, ø 45 mm, height 15.3 mm; rotating inner ring with reference cities, turns via crown; sapphire crystal; transparent case back; water-resistant to 5 atm
Band: textile, buckle
Price: $7,350

Corum

Founded in 1955, Switzerland's youngest luxury watch brand, Corum, celebrated sixty years of unusual—and sometimes outlandish—case and dial designs in 2015. The brand has had quite a busy history, but still by and large remains true to the collections launched by founders Gaston Ries and his nephew René Bannwart: the Admiral's Cup, Bridges, and Heritage. Among Corum's most iconic pieces is the legendary Golden Bridge baguette movement, which has received a complete makeover in recent years with the use of modern materials and complicated mechanisms. The development of these extraordinary movements required great watchmaking craftsmanship and expansion and modernization of the product development department.

The Bridges collection has always been an eye-catcher with its unusual movement, originally the brainchild of the great watchmaker Vincent Calabrese. Its introduction was a milestone in watchmaking history. And the Golden Bridge recently acquired a new highlight: in the Golden Bridge Tourbillon Panoramique with all components appearing to float in thin air.

To secure its financial future, Corum was sold to China Haidian Group (now Citychamp Watch & Jewellery Group) for over $90 million in April 2013. Calce welcomed the move not only for the financial independence it was to bring, but also for the access it allows to the crucial Chinese market.

Today, the sporty Admiral's Cup collection is divided into two families: Legend in classical and elegant style and AC-One 45, which is for active use. The colorful nautical number flags have returned to the Admiral's Cup dials. For the brand's sixtieth birthday, it produced a Legend with a flying tourbillon and revived the remarkable Bubble in a limited series.

Montres Corum Sàrl
Rue du Petit-Château 1
Case postale 374
CH-2301 La Chaux-de-Fonds
Switzerland

Tel.:
+41-32-967-0670

Fax:
+41-32-967-0800

E-Mail:
info@corum.ch

Website:
www.corum.ch

Founded:
1955

Number of employees:
160 worldwide

Annual production:
16,000 watches

U.S. distributor:
Montres Corum USA
14050 NW 14th Street, Suite 110
Sunrise, Florida 33323
954-279-1220; 954-279-1780 (fax)
www.corum.ch

Most important collections/price range:
Admiral's Cup, Corum Bridges and Heritage, Romvlvs and Artisan, 150 models in total / approx. $4,100 to over $1,000,000

Golden Bridge

Reference number: 113.261.15/0001 0000R
Movement: manually wound, Caliber CO 113; 4.9 x 34 mm, height 3 mm; 19 jewels; 28,800 vph; baguette with gold bridges and plate; hand-engraved
Functions: hours, minutes
Case: ceramic, 34 x 51 mm, height 11.35 mm; sapphire crystal; transparent case back; water-resistant to 3 atm
Band: reptile skin, buckle
Remarks: lateral window on case for full view of movement
Price: $19,000

Golden Bridge Automatic

Reference number: 313.165.95 0001 GL10R
Movement: automatic, Caliber CO 313; 11.25 x 33.18 mm; 26 jewels; 28,800 vph; variable inertia balance; baguette with gold bridges and mainplate; linear winding with sliding platinum weight
Functions: hours, minutes
Case: pink gold, 51.8 x 37.2 mm, height 13.7 mm; sapphire crystal, transparent case back; water-resistant to 3 atm
Band: reptile skin, buckle
Remarks: lateral window on case
Price: $44,800
Variations: titanium with black PVD ($34,000); white gold ($46,600)

Golden Bridge Tourbillon Panoramique

Reference number: 100.160.55 OF01 0000
Movement: manually wound, Caliber CO 100; ø 29 mm; 22 jewels; 21,600 vph; flying 1-minute tourbillon; baguette; sapphire crystal bridges and plate; 90-hour power reserve
Functions: hours, minutes
Case: pink gold, 37.6 x 56 mm, height 12.35 mm; sapphire crystal, transparent case back; water-resistant to 3 atm
Band: reptile skin, folding clasp
Remarks: lateral window on case
Price: $185,300
Variations: white gold ($193,700)

Ti-Bridge
Automatic Dual Winder

Reference number: 207.201.04 OF61 0000
Movement: automatic, Caliber CO 207;
37.9 x 12.27 mm; 30 jewels, 28,800 vph; baguette;
titanium bridges and plate; 2 winding rotors with
tungsten oscillating weights coupled by pushrod;
72-hour power reserve
Functions: hours, minutes
Case: titanium, 52 x 42 mm, height 15 mm; sapphire
crystal; transparent case back; water-resistant to 3 atm
Band: leather/rubber, folding clasp
Price: $22,300
Variations: titanium bracelet ($23,000); pink gold/
leather strap ($51,000)

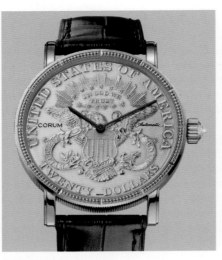

$20 Coin Watch

Reference number: 293.645.56/0001 MU51
Movement: automatic, Caliber CO 293 (base
Frédéric Piguet 1150); ø 25.6 mm, height 3.25 mm;
30 jewels; 28,800 vph; 70-hour power reserve
Functions: hours, minutes
Case: yellow gold, ø 36 mm, height 6.4 mm;
sapphire crystal; water-resistant to 3 atm
Band: reptile skin, buckle
Remarks: dial and case back made of original
Double Eagle dollar coin
Price: $20,800

Admiral's Cup AC-One
45 Skeleton

Reference number: 082.401.04/0F01 FH10
Movement: automatic, Caliber CO 082; ø 25.6 mm;
27 jewels, 28,800 vph; platinum, skeletonized
bridges and rotors; 42-hour power reserve
Functions: hours, minutes, sweep seconds; date
Case: titanium, ø 45 mm, height 13.3 mm; sapphire
crystal; transparent back; water-resistant to 30 atm
Band: reptile skin, double folding clasp
Remarks: skeletonized dial
Price: $11,500

Admiral's Cup AC-One
45 Tides

Reference number: 277.101.04/F376 AR12
Movement: automatic, Caliber CO 277 (base
ETA 2892-A2 with Dubois Dépraz tides module);
ø 25.9 mm, height 5.2 mm; 21 jewels; 28,800 vph
Functions: hours, minutes, sweep seconds; tides
display with current strength; date, moon phase
Case: titanium, ø 45 mm, height 14.3 mm; sapphire
crystal; transparent case back; screw-in crown;
water-resistant to 30 atm
Band: rubber, double folding clasp
Price: $9,350
Variations: blue dial/blue rubber strap ($9,350)

Admiral's Cup Legend
42 Chronograph

Reference number: 984.101.20/0F01 AB20
Movement: automatic, Caliber CO 984 (base ETA
2892-2); ø 28.6 mm, height 6.1 mm; 37 jewels;
28,800 vph; 42-hour power reserve; COSC-certified
chronometer
Functions: hours, minutes, subsidiary seconds;
chronograph; date
Case: stainless steel, ø 42 mm, height 11.6 mm;
sapphire crystal; transparent back; water-resistant
to 3 atm
Band: crocodile leather, double folding clasp
Price: $4,850
Variations: stainless steel bracelet ($5,125)

Bubble

Reference number: 082.301.98/0062 FG30
Movement: automatic, Caliber CO 082; ø 25.6 mm,
27 jewels; 28,800 vph; 42-hour power reserve
Functions: hours, minutes, sweep seconds; date
Case: stainless steel with brown PVD coating,
ø 47 mm, height 18.8 mm; sapphire crystal;
transparent case back
Band: calf leather, folding clasp
Remarks: domed sapphire crystal; limited to 350
pieces
Price: $3,425
Variations: black PVD-coating ($3,425; limited to
350 pieces)

Cuervo y Sobrinos

Cuervo y Sobrinos SA
Via Carlo Maderno 54
CH-6825 Capolago
Switzerland

Tel.:
+41-91-921-2773

Fax:
+41-91-921-2775

E-Mail:
info@cuervoysobrinos.ch

Website:
www.cuervoysobrinos.ch

Founded:
1882

Annual production:
3,500 watches

U.S. distribution:
Cuervo y Sobrinos Swiss Watches
P.O. Box 347890
Coral Gables, FL 33234
214-704-3000

Most important collections/price range:
Esplendidos, Historiador, Prominente,
Torpedo, Robusto / $3,200 to $16,000;
higher for perpetual calendars and tourbillon
models

Cuba means a lot of things to different people. Today it seems to be the last bastion of genuine retro in an age of frenzied technology. However, turn the clock back to the early twentieth century and you find that Ramón Rio y Cuervo and his sister's sons (the "sobrinos" or nephews of the brand name) kept a watchmaking workshop and an elegant store on Quinta Avenida where they sold fine Swiss pocket watches—and more modest American models as well. With the advent of tourism from the coast of Florida, their business developed with wristwatches, whose dials Don Ramón soon had printed with Cuervo y Sobrinos.

An Italian watch enthusiast, Marzio Villa, resuscitated Cuervo y Sobrinos in 2002 and started manufacturing in the Italian-speaking region of Switzerland in cooperation with various Swiss watchmakers. The tagline "Latin heritage, Swiss manufacture" says it all. These timepieces epitomize—or even romanticize—the island's heyday. The colors hint at cigar leaves and sepia photos in frames of old gold. The lines are at times elegant and sober, for the Esplendidos, or radiate the ease of those who still have time on their hands, in the Prominente. Playfulness is also a Cuervo y Sobrinos quality: The Piratas have buttons shaped like the muzzle of a blunderbuss, a cannonball crown, and a porthole flange. Lately, CyS has been modernizing (the Manjuari dive watch or the Robusto Day-Date have a younger feel), and they have introduced a line of writing implements as accessories for the genuine lover of fine things and the mechanical world.

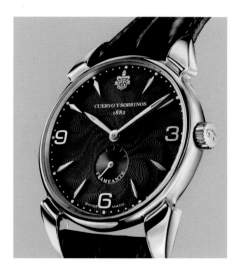

Historiador Flameante Blue Edition

Reference number: 3130.1FB-US
Movement: manually wound, ETA Caliber 7001; ø 23.3 mm, height 2.5 mm; 17 jewels; 28,800 vph; 42-hour power reserve
Functions: hours, minutes, small seconds; date
Case: stainless steel, ø 40 mm, height 6.2 mm; sapphire crystal; transparent case back; water-resistant to 3 atm
Band: reptile skin, folding clasp
Remarks: 10th Anniversary USA Commemorative
Price: $3,300

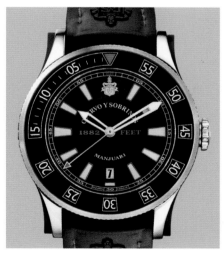

Robusto Manjuari

Reference number: 2808.1NR3
Movement: automatic, Sellita Caliber SW 200-1; ø 25.6 mm, height 4.6 mm; 26 jewels; 28,800 vph; 38-hour power reserve
Functions: hours, minutes, central seconds; date
Case: stainless steel and titanium, ø 43 mm, height 14.95 mm; titanium with sapphire bezel, black ring rubber with Cuervo y Sobrinos in relief; sapphire crystal; screwed-in case back with manjuari fish engraving; water-resistant to 60 atm
Band: rubber, folding clasp
Price: $5,100

Historiador Retrogrado

Reference number: 3194.1A
Movement: automatic, 9094/2892-A2 ETA; ø 25.6 mm, height 5.1 mm; 30 jewels; 28,800 vph; 42-hour power reserve
Functions: hours, minutes, central seconds; retrograde date; weekday; power reserve
Case: stainless steel, ø 40 mm, height 11.25 mm; double curved sapphire crystal; transparent case back; water-resistant to 3 atm
Band: reptile skin, folding buckle
Price: $5,500

Hasler & Co. SA
CH-2720 Tramelan
Switzerland

E-Mail:
info@davosa.com

Website:
www.davosa.com

Founded:
1861

U.S. distributor:
D. Freemont Inc.
P.O. Box 417
232 Karda Drive
Hollidaysburg, PA 16648
877-236-9248
david@freemontwatches.com
www.davosawatches.com

Most important collections/price range:
Argonautic, Classic, Gentleman, Pilot,
Simplex, Ternos, Titanium, Vanguard, X-Agon /
$650 to $2,600

Davosa

Davosa has come a long way from its beginnings in 1861. Back then, farmer Abel Frédéric Hasler spent the long winter months in Tramelan, in Switzerland's Jura mountains, making silver pocket watch cases. Later, two of his brothers ventured out to the city of Geneva and opened a watch factory. The third brother also opted to engage with the watch industry and moved to Biel. The entire next generation of Haslers went into watchmaking as well.

The name Hasler & Co. appeared on the occasional package mailed in Switzerland or overseas. Playing the role of unassuming private-label watchmakers, the Haslers remained in the background and let their customers in Europe and the United States run away with the show. It wasn't until after World War II that brothers Paul and David Hasler dared produce their own timepieces.

In 1987, the brothers developed their own line of watches under the brand name Davosa and took on the sales and marketing roles. The sustained development of the brand began in 1993, when the Haslers signed a partnership with the German distributor Bohle. In Germany, mechanical watches were experiencing a boom, so the brand was able to evolve quickly. In 2000, Corinna Bohle took over as manager of strategic development. Meanwhile, Davosa has reached well beyond Switzerland's borders and is now an integral part of the world of mechanical watches.

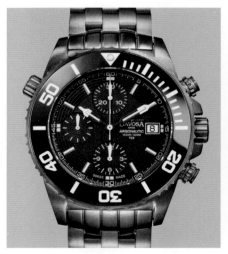

Argonautic Lumis Chronograph

Reference number: 161.508.80
Movement: automatic, ETA Caliber 7750; ø 30 mm, height 7.9 mm; 25 jewels; 28,800 vph; 42-hour power reserve
Functions: hours, minutes, subsidiary seconds; chronograph; date
Case: stainless steel with gray PVD coating; ø 42.5 mm, height 17.5 mm; unidirectional bezel with 60-minute division, sapphire crystal; screw-in crown, helium valve; water-resistant to 30 atm
Band: stainless steel, safety folding clasp
Price: $1,868
Variations: w/o PVD coating ($1,758); 3-hand automatic ($812)

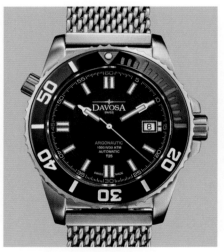

Argonautic Lumis Color

Reference number: 151.520.60
Movement: automatic, ETA Caliber 2824-2; ø 25.6 mm, height 4.6 mm; 25 jewels; 28,800 vph; 38-hour power reserve
Functions: hours, minutes, sweep seconds; date
Case: stainless steel, ø 43 mm, height 14 mm; unidirectional bezel with 60-minute division; sapphire crystal; screw-in crown, helium valve; water-resistant to 30 atm
Band: stainless steel Milanese mesh, folding clasp
Price: $823
Variations: indices in different luminescent colors

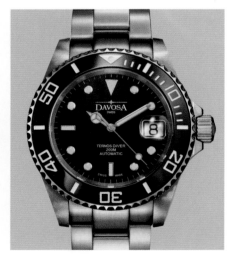

Ternos Ceramic

Reference number: 161.555.80
Movement: automatic, ETA Caliber 2824-2; ø 25.6 mm, height 4.6 mm; 25 jewels; 28,800 vph; 38-hour power reserve
Functions: hours, minutes, sweep seconds; date
Case: stainless steel, ø 40 mm, height 12.5 mm; unidirectional ceramic bezel with 60-minute division, sapphire crystal; screw-in crown; water-resistant to 20 atm
Band: stainless steel, safety folding clasp with extension link
Price: $768
Variations: various dial, bezel colors

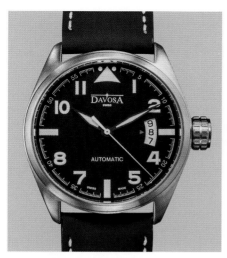

Military Automatic

Reference number: 161.511.54
Movement: automatic, ETA Caliber 2824-2;
ø 25.6 mm, height 4.6 mm; 25 jewels; 28,800 vph;
38-hour power reserve
Functions: hours, minutes, sweep seconds; date
Case: stainless steel, ø 42 mm, height 12.5 mm;
sapphire crystal; screw-in crown; water-resistant to
20 atm
Band: calf leather, buckle
Remarks: includes additional bracelet
Price: $713
Variations: green or black PVD-coated case

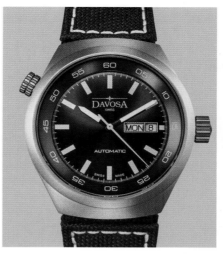

Trailmaster

Reference number: 161.518.45
Movement: automatic, ETA Caliber 2836-
2; ø 25.6 mm, height 5.05 mm; 25 jewels;
28,800 vph; 38-hour power reserve
Functions: hours, minutes, sweep seconds; date,
weekday
Case: stainless steel, ø 42 mm, height 12.8 mm;
crown-adjustable flange with 60-hour division;
sapphire crystal; transparent case back; water-
resistant to 10 atm
Band: textile, buckle
Price: $768
Variations: various dial, band colors

Grande Diva

Reference number: 165.500.60
Movement: automatic, Caliber DAV 6498 (base
ETA Caliber 6498); ø 36.6 mm; height 5.6 mm; 17
jewels; 21,600 vph; skeletonized and decorated;
38-hour power reserve
Functions: hours, minutes, subsidiary seconds
Case: stainless steel, ø 42 mm, height 10 mm;
sapphire crystal; transparent back; water-resistant
to 3 atm
Band: calf leather, buckle
Remarks: skeletonized dial set with 100 zirconia
Price: $988
Variations: white or black jewels ($988); stainless
steel, gold PVD coating, brown jewels ($1,098)

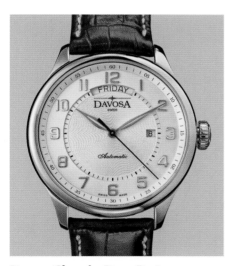

Pares Classic Day-Date

Reference number: 161.483.36
Movement: automatic, ETA Caliber 2834-2;
ø 29 mm, height 5.05 mm; 25 jewels; 28,800 vph;
rotor with côtes de Genève; 38-hour power reserve
Functions: hours, minutes, sweep seconds; date,
weekday
Case: stainless steel, ø 44 mm, height 11.1 mm;
sapphire crystal; transparent case back; water-
resistant to 5 atm
Band: calf leather, buckle
Price: $702
Variations: white dial and blackened hour markers;
black dial and luminescent hour markers

World Traveler Chronograph

Reference number: 161.502.45
Movement: automatic, ETA Caliber 7754; ø 30 mm,
height 7.9 mm; 25 jewels; 28,800 vph; finely
finished with côtes de Genève, blued screws,
perlage on bridges; 42-hour power reserve
Functions: hours, minutes, subsidiary seconds;
added 24-hour display; chronograph; date
Case: stainless steel, ø 44 mm, height 15.7 mm;
unidirectional bezel with 24-hour time zone,
sapphire crystal; transparent back; water-resistant
to 5 atm
Band: calf leather, buckle
Price: $2,198
Variations: silver or black dial; 3-hand ($1,208)

Vintage Rallye Pilot Chronograph

Reference number: 161.008.46
Movement: automatic, ETA Caliber 7750; ø 30 mm,
height 7.9 mm; 25 jewels; 28,800 vph; finely
finished with côtes de Genève, blued screws,
perlage on bridges, 42-hour power reserve
Functions: hours, minutes, subsidiary seconds;
chronograph; date
Case: stainless steel, ø 42 mm, height 15.6 mm;
sapphire crystal, transparent case back; water-
resistant to 10 atm
Band: calf leather, buckle
Price: $1,868
Variations: black dial

De Bethune SA

Granges Jaccard 6
CH-1454 La Chaux L'Auberson
Switzerland

Tel.:
+41-24-454-2281

Fax:
+41-24-454-2317

E-Mail:
info@debethune.ch

Website:
www.debethune.ch

Founded:
2002

Number of employees:
60

Annual production:
400

Distribution:
For all inquiries from the U.S., contact the *manufacture* directly.

De Bethune

De Bethune's technical director, Denis Flageollet, has more than twenty years of experience under his belt with regard to the research, conception, and successful implementation of more than 120 different, extremely prestigious timepieces—all for other firms. He and David Zanetta, a well-known consultant for a number of high-end watch brands, founded their own company in 2002, and De Bethune was born. Together, they bought what used to be the village pub and turned it into a stunning factory. The modern CNC machinery, combined with the expertise of an experienced watchmaking team, allows Flageollet to produce prototypes in the blink of an eye and make small movement series with great dispatch. In order to become even more independent of suppliers, the little factory now also produces its own cases, dials, and hands, which guarantees a high level of excellence with regard to quality control.

Since its founding, De Bethune has developed a manually wound caliber with a power reserve of up to eight days, a self-regulating double barrel, a balance wheel in titanium and platinum that allows for an ideal inertia/mass ratio, a balance spring with a patented De Bethune end curve, and a triple "parachute" shock-absorbing system, the lightest and one of the fastest silicon/titanium tourbillons on the market. Another project was research into acoustic vibrations as a power regulator. The control of the "Resonique" escapement utilizes a flying magnet that regulates the escape wheel without touching it. The logical extension of the titanium-platinum balance wheel is the eighteen-month development of an in-house silicon hairspring.

As for the recent Dreamwatch No. 5, it is a genuine sculpture for the wrist by Zanetta and Flageollet. Some elements from its predecessors were kept and form a harmonious ensemble in the new model. The dial is nothing but a cutout revealing jumping hours and minutes and a three-dimensional moon. Keeping things simple is a design guideline.

DB28 Skybridge

Reference number: DB28CE
Movement: manually wound, De Bethune Caliber DB 2105; ø 30 mm; 27 jewels; 28,800 vph; double spring barrel, silicon balance; 144-hour power reserve
Functions: hours, minutes; spherical moon phase
Case: titanium, ø 42.6 mm, height 11.4 mm; sapphire crystal; transparent case back
Band: reptile skin, buckle
Remarks: concave dial with golden spheres as heavenly bodies; completely sculptural moon
Price: $106,000

DB 28 T

Reference number: DB28TTIS8
Movement: manually wound, Caliber DB 2019; ø 30 mm, height 6.95 mm; 31 jewels; 36,000 vph; 30-second tourbillon with silicon balance and platinum frame; double spring barrel; 120-hour power reserve
Functions: hours, minutes, subsidiary seconds (on tourbillon cage); power reserve display (on case back)
Case: titanium, ø 42.60 mm, height 11.3 mm; sapphire crystal
Band: reptile skin, buckle
Price: $199,000

DB 27 Titan Hawk Silver

Reference number: DB27S1
Movement: automatic, De Bethune Caliber S233; ø 32.95 mm, height 3.55 mm; 31 jewels; 144-hour power reserve
Functions: hours, minutes; date
Case: titanium, ø 43 mm, height 11 mm; sapphire crystal; window at 6 o'clock reveals balance wheel
Band: reptile skin, buckle
Price: $39,900

de Grisogono

Watch connoisseurs frequently look down on jewelers who suddenly develop an interest for their trade. The brand de Grisogono had to deal with this somewhat odd prejudice when it made its debut in horology, but the critics quickly fell silent once it became obvious that brand head Fawaz Gruosi was not just producing quartz watches with lots of glitz, but was intending to grow his portfolio with a line of very high-end mechanical watches.

His jewelry pieces are renowned for showcasing precious stones of the highest quality. Gruosi applied the same standard to the manufacturing of his watches. Not only are they unusually sophisticated technically, but the actual manufacturing quality has stood the test of even the toughest experts.

Right from the start, Gruosi opted for unusual case shapes and novel ways of displaying time. He took the high road, as it were, producing, for instance, the Instrumento Doppio Tre, with a single spring barrel that drives three separate sets of hands to display three time zones, or watches with dials that open and close like camera shutters or can be turned to change the display.

For the most part, de Grisogono watches have no historical models—which is quite rare nowadays. The Meccanico dG, a large rectangular watch with a hint of 1970s chic, has an imitation digital display produced mechanically with extreme engineering. The Tondos seem to borrow from the brand's jewelry segment, with bright and trendy colors. The latest Instrumento No. Uno Tourbillon does, however, hark back to the genial work of the likes of Richard Daner or Walter Prendel. The flying tourbillon is set at a 30° angle in a rectangular case under a domed crystal. It's another sign of the company's will to find a unique technical and aesthetic niche for itself.

de Grisogono SA
Route de St-Julien 176 bis
CH-1228 Plan-les-Ouates (Geneva)
Switzerland

Tel.:
+41-22-817-8100

Fax:
+41-22-817-8188

E-Mail:
marco@degrisogono.com

Website:
www.degrisogono.com

Founded:
1993

Number of employees:
approx. 150

U.S. distributor:
De Grisogono, Inc.
824 Madison Avenue, 3rd Floor
New York, NY 10021
866-DEGRISO

Most important collections/price range:
Instrumento N°Uno / starting at $39,900;
Tondo / starting at $36,200

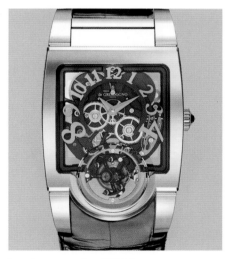

Instrumento N° Uno Tourbillon

Movement: automatic, Caliber TB 31-00; 26.8 x 35 mm, 21,600 vph; skeletonized; flying 1-minute tourbillon with axis inclined at 30°; 72-hour power reserve
Functions: hours, minutes
Case: white gold, 33 x 59.2 mm, height 12.5 mm; sapphire crystal; transparent case back; black diamonds on crown; water-resistant to 3 atm
Band: reptile skin, triple folding clasp
Remarks: sapphire crystal dome set over tourbillon covers entire case without visible mounts
Price: $162,700
Variations: rose gold

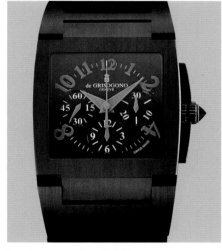

Instrumento N° Uno Carbon Chrono

Movement: automatic, Caliber CR 10-82; ø 26.2 mm, height 5.6 mm; 33 jewels; 28,800 vph; 42-hour power reserve
Functions: hours, minutes, subsidiary seconds; chronograph
Case: carbon fiber, 33 x 56.4 mm, height 11.2 mm; black diamond on crown; sapphire crystal; transparent case back; water-resistant to 3 atm
Band: rubber, stainless steel double folding clasp, PVD-coated
Remarks: limited to 100 pieces
Price: $20,400

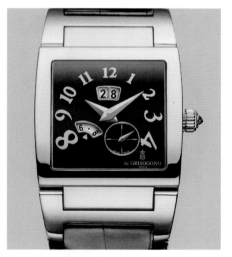

Instrumento N° Uno Annual Calendar

Movement: automatic, Caliber QA 20-89; ø 26.2 mm, height 5.6 mm; 28,800 vph; 42-hour power reserve
Functions: hours, minutes, subsidiary seconds; annual calendar with large date, month
Case: rose gold, 33 x 56.4 mm, height 16 mm; sapphire crystal; transparent case back; black diamonds on crown; water-resistant to 3 atm
Band: reptile skin, double folding clasp
Price: $43,000
Variations: off-white lacquered dial

Dodane 1857
2, Chemin des Barbizets
F-25870 Châtillon le Duc
France

Tel.:
+33-3-81-58-88-02

Fax:
+33-3-81-58-92-27

E-Mail:
info@dodane1857.com

Website:
www.Dodane1857.com

Founded:
1857

U.S. distributor:
Totally Worth It, LLC
76 Division Avenue
Summit, NJ 07901-2309
201-894-4710
info@totallyworthit.com
www.TotallyWorthIt.com

Most important collections:
Type 21 and Type 23 chronographs used
by the French military

Dodane 1857

For pilots of all aircraft, time is not money; it is life and death. So not surprisingly, the specifications for on-board instruments put out by the world's air forces are particularly stringent. In the 1950s, the French Air Force approached several companies to produce watches that could withstand the extreme accelerations and pressure changes imposed by the new generation of jet-propelled aircraft. Pilots also needed a flyback chronograph to measure speed and distances in case of instrument failure.

One of those companies was Dodane, a small family enterprise situated in Besançon just a few miles from the Swiss border and the horologically prolific "Jurassic Arc." The company had been founded in 1857 by Alphonse Dodane on the banks of the Doubs River and produced watch components and watches. It was Alphonse's son, Alphonse Gabriel, who set the course on aviation, though. During World War I, he developed a chronograph that allowed flyers to target their payload more accurately. From then on, inventing instruments for airplanes became the main business. Among the later Dodane developments was an altimetric chronograph used by night parachutists to tell them when to pull the cord.

The Dodane range of watches is limited to the Type 21 and the Type 23, also available in quartz with many functions for sporty types. These products are authentic military—rugged, resistant, and perhaps a touch rabble-rousing. After all, they have to appeal to pilots as well as meeting the high standards of the French defense ministry.

TYPE 21

Reference number: 21NLN
Movement: automatic, Caliber Dubois Dépraz 42022; ø 30 mm, height 6.8 mm; 57 jewels; 28,800 vph; 42-hour power reserve; chronometer; côtes de Genève, blued screws, cocks with perlage
Functions: hours, minutes, subsidiary seconds; date; 1/5th-second 3-hand flyback chronograph with 30-minute counter
Case: stainless steel, ø 41.5 mm, height 13.7 mm; unidirectional black anodized bezel with ratchet wheel; sapphire crystal; transparent case back; water-resistant to 10 atm
Band: reptile skin, with double folding buckle
Price: $5,750; limited to 400

TYPE 23

Reference number: 23-CF10R
Movement: automatic, Caliber Dubois Dépraz 42030; ø 30 mm, height 6.5 mm; 45 jewels; 28,800 vph
Functions: hours, minutes, sweep seconds; chronograph
Case: stainless steel, ø 42.5 mm, height 12.3 mm; sapphire crystal; transparent case back; bidirectional brushed steel bezel with ratchet wheel; sapphire crystal; transparent case back; hinged back cover for pilot ID tag; water-resistant to 10 atm
Band: reptile skin, double folding clasp
Price: $4,750
Variations: black anodized and polished steel bezel; various straps, NATO clasp

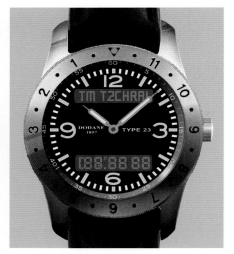

Dodane Type 23 Quartz

Reference number: 23-C7N
Movement: quartz, ETA 988.333; digital and analog display
Functions: hours, minutes, seconds; day, date, perpetual calendar; various chronograph functions (1/100th seconds); alarm; second time zone
Case: stainless steel, ø 42.5 mm, height 12.3 mm; sapphire crystal; transparent case back; bidirectional brushed steel bezel with ratchet wheel; sapphire crystal; transparent case back; water-resistant to 10 atm
Band: calf, rubber, double folding clasp
Price: $2,250

D. Dornblüth & Sohn

D. Dornblüth & Sohn is a two-generation team of master watchmakers. Their workshop in Kalbe, near Magdeburg in eastern Germany, turns out remarkable wristwatches with large manual winding mechanisms, three-quarter plates, screw balances, swan-neck fine adjustments, and a clever power reserve indicator.

The history of the "Dornblüth Caliber" goes back to the 1960s in the Erz mountains in East Germany. Dieter Dornblüth, the father in this father-and-son team, had sketched the first outlines for his own movement. But he only managed to complete the work in 1999 with the assistance of his son Dirk, and by that time Germany had already been reunified.

The strength of the tiny *manufacture* lies in the high level of skill that goes into producing these classical, manually wound watches in the old-fashioned way, i.e., without any CNC machines.

The 99 series is based on the reliable ETA Unitas 6497 pocket watch movement. Dirk redesigns about one-half of it by putting in a three-quarter plate and other elements. The dials are created in-house, using the 250-year-old "filled engraving" technique. They are then given a lustrous frosted layer of matte silver plating to complement the traditional *grainage* look.

The brand's fiftieth anniversary in 2012 saw the birth of the Q-2010, which features a special Maltese cross drive that reduces linear torque between two serially positioned spring barrels. The movement drives the latest models, like the Auf & Ab and Klassik. A specially designed lowered escape wheel minimizes position errors caused by the anchor escapement. The 99.0 collection has a new model, too: the 99.5, with a hand date and power reserve indicator on the traditionally classical Dornblüth dial.

D. Dornblüth & Sohn
Westpromenade 7
D-39624 Kalbe/Milde
Germany

Tel.:
+49-39080-3206

Fax:
+49-39080-72796

E-Mail:
info@dornblueth.com

Website:
www.dornblueth.com

Founded:
1962

Number of employees:
5

Annual production:
approx. 120 watches

U.S. distributor:
Dornblüth & Sohn
WatchBuys
888-333-4895
www.watchbuys.com

Most important collections/price range:
men's wristwatches / between $3,000 and $24,000

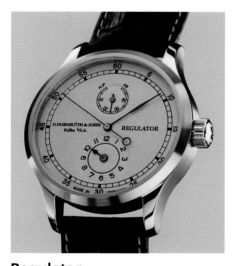

Regulator

Reference number: Regulator (GR) RG
Movement: manually wound, Dornblüth Caliber Regulator (based on ETA 6498); ø 37 mm, height 5.4 mm; 20 jewels; 18,000 vph; indirect sweep seconds driven by seconds wheel; screw balance; swan-neck fine adjustment; finely finished
Functions: hours (off-center), minutes, sweep seconds; power reserve indicator
Case: rose gold, ø 42 mm, height 12.5 mm; sapphire crystal; transparent case back
Band: reptile skin, buckle
Remarks: engraved and silver-plated dial
Price: $17,600
Variations: various dials; stainless steel ($9,950)

Classic

Reference number: Q-2010.2(GR)ST
Movement: manually wound, Dornblüth Caliber Q-2010 Classic; ø 34.3 mm, height 4.7 mm; 29 jewels; 18,000 vph; double spring barrel; driven by indirectly controlled Maltese cross spring producing almost linear torque; short anchor escapement with lowered escape wheel; Breguet spring
Functions: hours, minutes, subsidiary seconds
Case: stainless steel, ø 38.5 mm, height 10 mm; sapphire crystal; transparent case back
Band: reptile skin, buckle
Price: $11,750
Variations: various dials; rose gold (upon request)

Up & Down

Reference number: Q-2010.2(GR)ST
Movement: manually wound, Dornblüth Caliber Q-2010 Auf-Ab; ø 34.3 mm, height 4.7 mm; 29 jewels; 18,000 vph; double spring barrel; driven by indirectly controlled Maltese cross spring producing almost linear torque; short anchor escapement with lowered escape wheel; Breguet spring
Functions: hours, minutes, subsidiary seconds; power reserve indicator
Case: stainless steel, ø 38.5 mm, height 10 mm; sapphire crystal; transparent case back
Band: reptile skin, buckle
Price: $14,200
Variations: various dials; rose gold (upon request)

Doxa Watches USA

5847 San Felipe, 17th Floor
Houston, TX 77057

Tel.:
877-255-5017

Fax:
866-230-2922

E-Mail:
customersupport@doxawatches.com

Website:
www.doxawatches.com

Founded:
1889

Number of employees:
48

Distribution:
direct sales only

Most important collections/price range:
Doxa SUB dive watch collection / $1,500 to $3,500

Doxa

Watch aficionados who have visited the world-famous museum in Le Locle will know that the little castle in which it is housed once belonged to Georges Ducommun, the founder of Doxa. The *manufacture* was launched as a backyard operation in 1889 and originally produced pocket watches. Quality products and good salesmanship quickly put Doxa on the map, but the company's real game-changer came in 1967 with the uncompromising SUB 300, a heavy, bold diver's watch. It featured a unidirectionally rotating bezel with the official U.S. dive table engraved on it. The bright orange dial was notable for offering the best legibility under water. It also marked the beginning of a trend for colorful dials.

Doxa continued to develop successful diver's watches in the 1970s in collaboration with U.S. Divers, Spirotechnique, and Aqualung. Their popularity increased with the commercialization of diving. Thriller writer Clive Cussler, chairman and founder of the National Underwater and Marine Agency, NUMA, even chose a Doxa as gear for his action hero Dirk Pitt.

Doxa makes watches for other occasions as well. The Ultraspeed and Régulateur are just two examples combining a classic look, fine workmanship, and an affordable price. Today, the brand has also resurrected some of the older designs from the late sixties, but with improved technology, enabling divers to go down to 1,500 meters and still read the time.

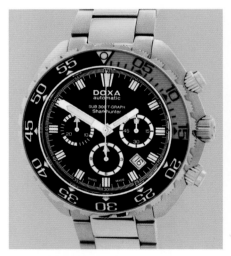

SUB 300T-Graph "Sharkhunter"

Reference number: 877.10.101.10
Movement: automatic, ETA Caliber 2894-2; ø 28.6 mm, height 6.1 mm; 37 jewels; 28,800 vph; 42-hour power reserve
Functions: hours, minutes, subsidiary seconds; chronograph; date
Case: stainless steel, ø 47 mm, height 19 mm; unidirectional bezel with 60-minute divisions; sapphire crystal; screwed-in crown; water-resistant to 30 atm
Band: stainless steel, folding clasp with safety lock and extension link
Price: $2,990; limited to 250 pieces
Variations: orange dial ($2,990); rubber strap ($2,790)

SUB 1500T Professional

Reference number: 1500.10.P.03
Movement: automatic, ETA Caliber 2894-2; ø 26.2 mm, height 3.6 mm; 21 jewels, 28,800 vph; 42-hour power reserve
Functions: hours, minutes, sweep seconds; date
Case: stainless steel, ø 45 mm, height 13 mm; unidirectional bezel, engraved decompression table; sapphire crystal; screw-in crown; water-resistant to 150 atm
Band: stainless steel, folding clasp with extension link
Remarks: reissue of 1969 original; with rubber strap
Price: $2,490
Variations: Searambler/silver dial ($2,490); Sharkhunter/black dial ($2,490)

SUB 4000T "Professional"

Reference number: 875.10.351.10
Movement: automatic, ETA Caliber 2897-2; ø 25.6 mm, height 4.85 mm; 21 jewels; 28,800 vph; 42-hour power reserve
Functions: hours, minutes, sweep seconds; date; power reserve indicator
Case: stainless steel, ø 47 mm, height 16 mm; unidirectional bezel with 60-minute divisions; sapphire crystal; screwed-in crown; helium valve; water-resistant to 120 atm
Band: stainless steel, folding clasp with extension link
Price: $2,590
Variations: orange dial ($2,590); Sharkhunter/black dial ($2,590)

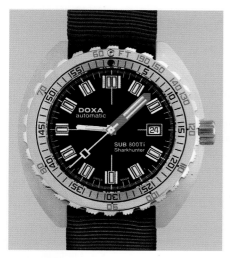

SUB 800Ti

Reference number: 880.10.101N-WH
Movement: automatic, ETA Caliber 2824-2;
ø 25.6 mm, height 4.6 mm; 25 jewels; 28,800 vph
Functions: hours, minutes, sweep seconds; date
Case: titanium, ø 44.7 mm, height 15 mm;
unidirectional bezel with engraved decompression
table; sapphire crystal; screwed-in crown; water-
resistant to 80 atm
Band: titanium, folding clasp with extension link
Remarks: reissue of 1969 original, limited to 1,000
pieces; with orange NATO fabric strap
Price: $2,790
Variations: Sharkhunter/black dial ($2,790);
Professional/orange hands ($2,790)

SUB MISSION 31

Reference number: 801.50.351-WH
Movement: automatic, ETA Caliber 2824-2;
ø 25.6 mm, height 4.6 mm; 25 jewels; 28,800 vph
Functions: hours, minutes, sweep seconds; date
Case: titanium, ø 44 mm, height 15 mm;
unidirectional bezel with engraved decompression
table; sapphire crystal; screwed-in crown; water-
resistant to 100 atm
Band: BOR titanium, folding clasp with extension
link
Remarks: reissue of 1969 original, limited to 331
pieces; with orange NATO fabric strap
Price: $2,890

SUB 5000T Military Sharkhunter Black Ed.

Reference number: 880.30.101N.11
Movement: automatic, ETA Caliber 2892-2;
ø 25.6 mm, height 4.85 mm; 21 jewels; 28,800 vph
Functions: hours, minutes, sweep seconds; date
Case: stainless steel, ø 45 mm; helium valve;
unidirectional bezel with engraved decompression
table; sapphire crystal; screwed-in crown; water-
resistant to 150 atm
Band: stainless steel, folding clasp with extension
link
Price: $2,490
Variations: Sharkhunter/orange dial ($2,490);
Caribbean/blue dial ($2,490)

SUB 750T GMT

Reference number: 850.10.351N.10
Movement: automatic, ETA Caliber 2893-2;
ø 25.6 mm, height 4.1 mm; 21 jewels; 28,800 vph
Functions: hours, minutes, sweep seconds; 24-hour
display (3 time zones); date
Case: stainless steel, ø 45 mm, height 16 mm;
unidirectional bezel with engraved decompression
table (patented); sapphire crystal; screwed-in
crown; water-resistant to 750 m
Band: stainless steel, folding clasp
Price: $2,790
Variations: Professional/orange dial ($2,790);
Sharkhunter/black dial ($2,790); Divingstar/yellow
dial ($2,790); Caribbean/blue dial ($2,790)

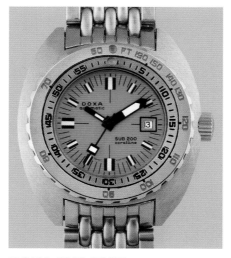

DOXA SUB 200T

Reference number: 802.10.021.10
Movement: automatic, ETA Caliber 2671;
ø 17.2 mm, height 4.8 mm; 25 jewels; 28,800 vph
Functions: hours, minutes, sweep seconds
Case: stainless steel, ø 35 mm, height 9 mm;
unidirectional bezel with engraved decompression
table (patented); sapphire crystal; screwed-in
crown; water-resistant to 20 atm
Band: stainless steel, folding clasp
Price: $1,649
Variations: Seamaid/black dial ($1,649)

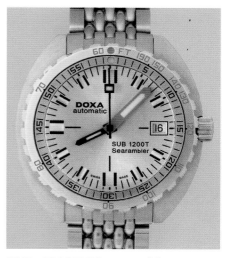

SUB 1200T "Searambler"

Reference number: 872.10.021.10
Movement: automatic, ETA Caliber 2824-2;
ø 25.6 mm, height 4.6 mm; 25 jewels; 28,800 vph;
42-hour power reserve
Functions: hours, minutes, sweep seconds; date
Case: stainless steel, ø 42 mm, height 14 mm;
unidirectional bezel with engraved decompression
scale; sapphire crystal; screwed-in crown; helium
valve; water-resistant to 120 atm
Band: stainless steel, folding clasp with extension
Remarks: reissue of 1969 original; with rubber strap
Price: $1,990
Variations: Sharkhunter/black dial; Professional/
orange dial

Eberhard & Co.
5, rue du Manège
CH-2502 Biel/Bienne
Switzerland

Tel.:
+41-32-342-5141

Fax:
+41-32-341-0294

E-Mail:
info@eberhard-co-watches.ch

Website:
www.eberhard-co-watches.ch

Founded:
1887

U.S. distributor:
ABS Distributors
22600 Savi Ranch Parkway
Suite 274
Yorba Linda, CA 92887
www.absdist.com
714-453-1622
714-998-0181 (fax)

Most important collections/price range:
Chrono 4, Champion V, Tazio Nuvolari, 8 Jours,
Extra Forte, Gilda, Contograph
(Prices are in Swiss francs. Use daily exchange
rate for calculations.)

Eberhard & Co.

Chronographs weren't always the main focus of the Eberhard & Co. brand. In 1887, Georges-Emile Eberhard rented a workshop in La Chaux-de-Fonds to produce a small series of pocket watches, but it was the unstoppable advancement of the automotive industry that gave the young company its inevitable direction. By the 1920s, Eberhard was producing timekeepers for the first auto races. In Italy, Eberhard & Co. functioned well into the 1930s as the official timekeeper for all important events relating to motor sports. And the Italian air force later commissioned some split-second chronographs from the company, one of which went for 56,000 euros at auction.

Eberhard & Co. is still doing well, thanks to the late Massimo Monti. In the 1990s, he associated the brand with legendary racer Tazio Nuvolari. The company dedicated a chronograph collection to Nuvolari and sponsored the annual Gran Premio Nuvolari oldtimer rally in his hometown of Mantua.

With the launch of its four-counter chronograph, this most Italian of Swiss watchmakers underscored its expertise and ambitions where short time/sports time measurement is concerned. Indeed, Eberhard & Co.'s Chrono 4 chronograph, featuring four little counters all in a row, has brought new life to the chronograph in general. CEO Mario Peserico has continued to develop it, putting out versions with new colors and slightly altered looks.

The brand is pure vintage, so it was no surprise when, in 2014, it reissued the two-totalizer Contograph chrono from the 1960s, which originally allowed the user to calculate phone units exactly (conto = bill).

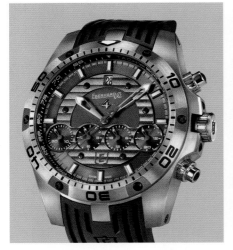

Chrono 4 Géant Titane

Reference number: 37060 CU
Movement: automatic, Eberhard Caliber EB 250-12 1/2 (base ETA 2894-2); ø 33 mm, height 7.5 mm; 53 jewels; 28,800 vph; 4 totalizers in row (patented)
Functions: hours, minutes, subsidiary seconds; additional 24-hour display; chronograph; date
Case: titanium, ø 46 mm, height 14.1 mm; unidirectional bezel with 60-minute divisions; sapphire crystal; screw-in crown and pusher; water-resistant to 20 atm
Band: rubber, buckle
Remarks: limited to 1,887 pieces
Price: CHF 9,130

Chrono 4 Grande Taille

Reference number: 31052 CU
Movement: automatic, Eberhard Caliber EB 251-12 1/2 (base ETA 2894-2); ø 33 mm, height 7.5 mm; 53 jewels; 28,800 vph; 4 totalizers in row (patented)
Functions: hours, minutes, subsidiary seconds; additional 24-hour display; chronograph; date
Case: stainless steel, ø 43 mm, height 13.32 mm; sapphire crystal; screw-in crown; water-resistant to 5 atm
Band: rubber, buckle
Price: CHF 7,120
Variations: various dial designs

8 Jours Grande Taille

Reference number: 21027 CP
Movement: manually wound, Eberhard Caliber EB 896 (base ETA 7001); ø 34 mm, height 5 mm; 25 jewels; 21,600 vph; 2 winding springs; 192-hour power reserve
Functions: hours, minutes, subsidiary seconds; 8-day power reserve indicator
Case: stainless steel, ø 41 mm, height 10.85 mm; sapphire crystal; transparent case back; water-resistant to 3 atm
Band: reptile skin, buckle
Price: CHF 4,860
Variations: black dial

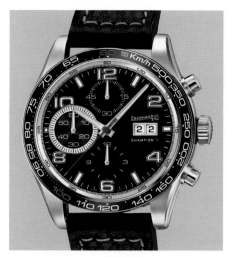

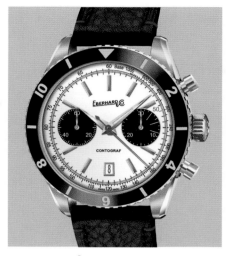

Champion V Grande Date

Reference number: 31064.2 CP
Movement: automatic, ETA Caliber 7750; ø 30 mm, height 7.9 mm; 25 jewels; 28,800 vph
Functions: hours, minutes, subsidiary seconds; chronograph; large date
Case: stainless steel, ø 42.8 mm, height 14.45 mm; sapphire crystal; screw-in crown; water-resistant to 5 atm
Band: calf leather, buckle
Price: CHF 4,150

Contograf

Reference number: 31069 CP
Movement: automatic, Eberhard Caliber 8147 (base ETA 7750); ø 30 mm, height 7.9 mm; 25 jewels; 28,800 vph; 42-hour power reserve
Functions: hours, minutes, subsidiary seconds; chronograph; date
Case: stainless steel, ø 42 mm, height 14.7 mm; unidirectional ceramic bezel with 12-hour divisions; sapphire crystal; screw-in crown; water-resistant to 5 atm
Band: calf leather, buckle
Price: CHF 5,460
Variations: various dials

Tazio Nuvolari Vanderbilt Cup "Naked"

Reference number: 31068 CPD
Movement: automatic, Eberhard Caliber 13 1/4 (base ETA 7750); ø 30 mm, height 7.9 mm; 25 jewels; 28,800 vph; crown pusher for zero reset; bridges with perlage, côtes de Genève on rotor; 42-hour power reserve
Functions: hours, minutes, subsidiary seconds; chronograph
Case: stainless steel, ø 42 mm, height 13.45 mm; sapphire crystal; transparent case back; water-resistant to 3 atm
Band: calf leather, folding clasp
Price: CHF 6,110

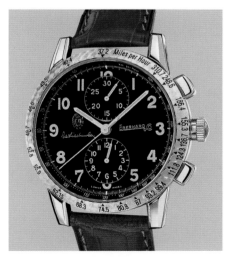

Tazio Nuvolari Gold Car

Reference number: 31038.5 CP
Movement: automatic, ETA Caliber 7750; ø 30 mm, height 7.9 mm; 25 jewels; 28,800 vph; 42-hour power reserve
Functions: hours, minutes; chronograph
Case: stainless steel, ø 43 mm, height 13 mm; sapphire crystal; transparent case back; screw-in crown; water-resistant to 3 atm
Band: reptile skin, buckle
Remarks: gold, stylized Alfa Romeo on rotor
Price: CHF 5,030

Tazio Nuvolari 336

Reference number: 41033 CP
Movement: automatic, ETA Caliber 2824-2 with Soprod module 9035; ø 25.6 mm; 25 jewels; 28,800 vph; 42-hour power reserve
Functions: hours, minutes, sweep seconds; additional 24-hour display (2nd time zone); power reserve indicator; date
Case: stainless steel, ø 45 mm, height 12 mm; ceramic bezel; sapphire crystal; screw-in crown, water-resistant to 10 atm
Band: reptile skin, buckle
Remarks: limited to 336 pieces (for 336 km/h record by Nuvolari in 1935 on autostrada Firenze-Mare)
Price: CHF 4,500

Tazio Nuvolari Automatic

Reference number: 41032 CP
Movement: automatic, ETA Caliber 2824-2; ø 25.6 mm, height 4.6 mm; 25 jewels; 28,800 vph; 42-hour power reserve
Functions: hours, minutes, sweep seconds; date
Case: stainless steel, ø 42.5 mm, height 11.35 mm; sapphire crystal; screw-in crown; water-resistant to 10 atm
Band: reptile skin, buckle
Price: CHF 2,500

Ernst Benz
7 Route de Crassier
CH-1262 Eysins
Switzerland

E-Mail:
info@ernstbenz.com

Website:
www.ernstbenz.com

Founded:
early 1960s

U.S. distributor:
Ernst Benz North America
177 S. Old Woodward
Birmingham, MI 48009
248-203-2323; 248-203-6633 (fax)

Most important collections:
Great Circle, ChronoScope, ChronoLunar,
ChronoRacer

Ernst Benz

Necessity is really the mother of creativity and then invention. Ernst Benz was an engineer by trade, an inventor by design, and a multitalented person who dabbled in many technologies including record player styluses. And as a passionate flier, he needed solid, reliable, and readable watches that could be used in the cockpits of small aircraft and gliders, so he gradually slipped into making timepieces. Size and clarity were determining factors, hence his clean dials and 47 mm diameters. Reliability is guaranteed by a no-nonsense Valjoux 7750. These elements save pilots' lives. At first, Benz made what he called the Great Circle Chronograph and later the ChronoScope just for fellow aviators. He also engineered other aviation instruments now standard in many small aircraft.

In 2005, the brand was bought by the Khankins, a watchmaking family with generations of experience in complicated horology. Leonid Khankin has spent a lifetime in the hands-on side of the business—starting right at the bottom, cleaning out cases in a small workshop. That's why he makes sure that the sapphire crystals are flush with the bezel, for instance, and will not get chipped accidentally. The family vigorously expanded the brand both geographically and by creating exciting new models. The ChronoScope received black PVC coating and was retooled as the ChronoDiver for those attracted to water rather than air. They were also quick to adopt ultra-hard DLC coating.

Khankin, who knows every nook and cranny of the horological world, is taking the brand places. He uses the broad dial of these distinct timepieces as a platform for adding thrilling design elements. On the style side, Ernst Benz has collaborated with fashion designer John Varvatos and Food Network chef Mario Batali on a series with distinct hands and color schemes.

ChronoScope ChronoRacer CR3

Reference number: GC10100/CR3
Movement: automatic, Valjoux Caliber 7750; ø 30 mm, height 7.9 mm; 25 jewels; 28,800 vph
Functions: hours, minutes, subsidiary seconds; date, day; chronograph with hours, minutes, sweep seconds
Case: brushed stainless steel, ø 47 mm, height 16 mm; sapphire crystal; screwed-down transparent case back; double O-ring sealed crown; water-resistant to 5 atm
Band: reptile skin, buckle
Price: $5,700; limited edition of 50 pieces, individually numbered dials

ChronoScope Instrument Titanium

Reference number: GC10179T
Movement: automatic, Valjoux Caliber 7750; ø 30 mm, height 7.9 mm; 25 jewels; 28,800 vph
Functions: hours, minutes, subsidiary seconds; date, day; chronograph with hours, minutes, sweep seconds
Case: brushed titanium, ø 47 mm, height 16 mm; sapphire crystal; screwed-down transparent case back; double O-ring sealed crown; water-resistant to 5 atm
Band: reptile skin, buckle
Price: $5,800; limited edition of 50 pieces, individually numbered dials

ChronoScope ChronoRacer

Reference number: GC10100/CR2
Movement: automatic, Valjoux Caliber 7750; ø 30 mm, height 7.9 mm; 25 jewels; 28,800 vph
Functions: hours, minutes, subsidiary seconds; date, day; chronograph with hours, minutes, sweep seconds
Case: brushed stainless steel, ø 47 mm, height 16 mm; sapphire crystal; screwed-down transparent case back; double O-ring sealed crown; water-resistant to 5 atm
Band: reptile skin, buckle
Price: $5,700; limited edition of 50 pieces, individually numbered dials

ChronoSport DLC

Reference number: GC10216-DLC
Movement: automatic, ETA Caliber 2836-2;
ø 30 mm, height 5.05 mm; 25 jewels; 28,800 vph;
38-hour power reserve
Functions: hours, minutes, sweep seconds;
weekday, date
Case: black DLC brushed stainless steel, ø 47 mm,
height 16 mm; sapphire crystal; screwed-down
transparent case back; double O-ring sealed crown;
water-resistant to 5 atm
Band: reptile skin, buckle
Price: $4,325
Variations: 44 mm black brushed DLC case
($3,725)

ChronoSport Officer

Reference number: GC10281
Movement: automatic, ETA Caliber 2836-2;
ø 30 mm, height 5.05 mm; 25 jewels; 28,800 vph;
38-hour power reserve
Functions: hours, minutes, sweep seconds;
weekday, date
Case: polished stainless steel, ø 47 mm, height
16 mm; sapphire crystal; screwed-down transparent
case back; double O-ring sealed crown; water-
resistant to 5 atm
Band: reptile skin, buckle
Price: $3,675
Variations: 44 mm case ($3,075)

ChronoLunar Traditional DLC

Reference number: GC10318-DLC
Movement: automatic, Valjoux 7751; ø 30 mm,
height 7.9 mm; 25 jewels; 28,800 vph
Functions: hours, minutes, subsidiary seconds;
day, date, month, moon phase; 24-hour display;
chronograph with hours, minutes, sweep seconds
Case: polished stainless steel; ø 47 mm, height
16 mm; water-resistant to 5 atm
Band: reptile skin, buckle
Price: $8,175
Variations: 44 mm case ($7,575)

ChronoLunar Officer

Reference number: GC10386
Movement: automatic, Valjoux 7751; ø 30 mm,
height 7.9 mm; 25 jewels; 28,800 vph
Functions: hours, minutes, subsidiary seconds;
day, date, month, moon phase; 24-hour display;
chronograph with hours, minutes, sweep seconds
Case: polished stainless steel, ø 47 mm, height
16 mm; sapphire crystal; screwed-down transparent
case back; double O-ring sealed crown; water-
resistant to 5 atm
Band: reptile skin, buckle
Price: $7,625

Ernst Benz by John Varvatos ChronoScope

Reference number: GC10410/JV2
Movement: automatic, Valjoux Caliber 7750;
ø 30 mm, height 7.9 mm; 25 jewels; 28,800 vph
Functions: hours, minutes, subsidiary seconds;
day, date; chronograph with hours, minutes, sweep
seconds
Case: polished/brushed stainless steel, ø 47 mm,
height 16 mm; angled/polished bezel, sapphire
crystal; screwed-down transparent case back;
double O-ring sealed crown; water-resistant to 5 atm
Band: reptile skin, buckle
Price: $6,800; limited edition of 250 pieces,
individually numbered dials

Ernst Benz by John Varvatos ChronoScope DLC

Reference number: GC10410/JV6-DLC
Movement: automatic, Valjoux Caliber 7750;
ø 30 mm, height 7.9 mm; 25 jewels; 28,800 vph
Functions: hours, minutes, subsidiary seconds;
day, date; chronograph with hours, minutes, sweep
seconds
Case: black DLC-coated brushed stainless steel,
ø 47 mm, height 16 mm; angled/polished bezel,
sapphire crystal; screwed-down transparent back;
double O-ring sealed crown; water-resistant to 5 atm
Band: reptile skin, buckle
Price: $7,800; limited edition of 25 pieces,
individually numbered dials

Erwin Sattler OHG

Grossuhrenmanufaktur
Lohenstr. 6
D-82166 Gräfelfing
Germany

Tel.:
+49-89-895-5806-0

Fax:
+49-89-895-5806-28

E-Mail:
info@erwinsattler.de

Website:
www.erwinsattler.de

Founded:
1958

Number of employees:
31

Annual production:
approx. 1,200 clocks and watches

Distribution:
direct through company in Germany

Most important collections/price range:
wristwatches, precision clocks, winders,
table clocks, marine chronometers / approx.
$1,000 to $200,000

Erwin Sattler

Anyone even slightly familiar with the history of watches knows that they are in fact miniaturized church clocks. On the way down from the spire, timekeepers became "grandfather" clocks, wall clocks, and table clocks, all of which still find an active clientele. Erwin Sattler, a company based near Munich, has specialized in high-precision clocks and winders. In 2008, for the fiftieth anniversary of their *manufacture*, managing directors Stephanie Sattler-Rick and Richard Müller presented something unexpected: an impressive, limited edition of the "Trilogy" set, comprising a table clock, watch winder, and wristwatch. The wristwatch was in high demand—leading Sattler to add an unlimited stainless steel version of the wristwatch regulator to its line in 2009.

The Sattler wristwatches were the result of a collaboration with the Austrian watchmaking couple Maria and Richard Habring. They turned to the ETA Valjoux Caliber 7750 as their base, modifying it to accommodate the regulator display and adding a special technical detail: The second hand jumps in one-second increments just like its role model, one of Sattler's full-size pendulum clocks.

The dial, a miniature version of the popular Sattler wall clock regulator, features four screws and is made of solid sterling silver. The steel hands are vaulted, hardened, and polished. Like those of their large clock cousins, the watches' hour and minute hands have steel sockets with polished grooves.

This small collection has been extended by an unusual automatic chronograph featuring a regulator dial and a classic crown control system between the two lower lugs.

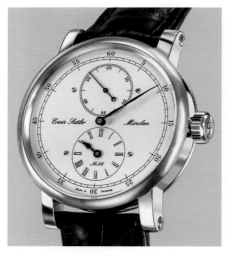

Régulateur "Classica Secunda"

Movement: automatic, Sattler Caliber ES 01 (base ETA 7750); ø 30 mm, height 7.9 mm; 28 jewels; 28,800 vph; modified for regulator display with jumping seconds; rotor skeletonized, engraved, and guillochéed by hand; 42-hour power reserve
Functions: hours (off-center), minutes, subsidiary seconds (retrograde)
Case: stainless steel, ø 44 mm, height 15 mm; sapphire crystal; water-resistant to 5 atm
Band: reptile skin, double folding clasp
Price: $9,800
Variations: rose gold bezel ($19,900)

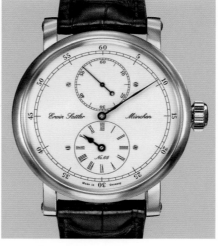

Régulateur "Classica Secunda" Medium

Movement: manually wound, Sattler Caliber ES 02 (base Habring A09MS); ø 30 mm, height 6.25 mm; 28 jewels; 28,800 vph; modified for regulator display with jumping seconds; rotor skeletonized, engraved, and guillochéed by hand
Functions: hours (off-center), minutes, subsidiary seconds (retrograde)
Case: stainless steel, ø 38 mm, height 12 mm; sapphire crystal; water-resistant to 5 atm
Band: reptile skin, double folding clasp
Price: $9,130

Chronograph "Classica Secunda"

Movement: automatic, Sattler Caliber ES 03 (base ETA 7750); ø 30 mm, height 7.9 mm; 25 jewels; 28,800 vph; modified for central time display and crown-activated chronograph control; hand-engraved and guillochéed rotor; 42-hour power reserve
Functions: hours, minutes (off-center), subsidiary seconds; chronograph
Case: stainless steel, ø 44 mm, height 15.5 mm; sapphire crystal; transparent back
Band: reptile skin, folding clasp
Price: $13,850

Eterna

The brand Eterna has truly left its mark on the watchmaking industry. Founded in 1856 as Dr. Girard & Schild, the company became a *manufacture*, producing pocket watches under Urs Schild in 1870. Among its earliest claims to fame was the first wristwatch with an alarm, released in 1908, by which time the company had taken on the name Eterna. Forty years later, came the legendary Eterna-matic, featuring micro ball bearings for an automatic winding rotor. At the slightest movement of the watch, the rotor began to turn and set in motion what was another newly developed system of two ratchet wheels, which, independent of the rotational direction, lifted the mainspring over the automatic gears. Today, the five micro ball bearings used to cushion that rotor are the inspiration for Eterna's stylized pentagon-shaped logo. The invention itself is now standard in millions of watch movements.

In 2007, the company launched its Caliber 39 project with two distinct goals: the first, to develop an automatic chronograph with three totalizers, and the second, to optimize manufacturing costs. Gradually, this led to the establishment of an entire family of movements whose particular design allowed them to be flexibly built up on a single base movement, the 88. Modules for additional indicators or functions could be affixed with just a few screws or connected by way of a bridge. The Royal KonTiki Two Time Zones is the first model making use of this base caliber. Thanks to the famous ball bearing mounted Spherodrive winding mechanism, the movement has a power reserve of sixty-eight hours.

So ironically perhaps, Eterna, whose original movement division became a separate company called ETA (now with the Swatch Group), has returned to building its own movements. In 1995, Eterna was acquired by F.A. Porsche Beteiligungen GmbH and started manufacturing for Porsche Design. But in 2011, International Volant Ltd., a wholly owned subsidiary of Citychamp, bought up the Porsche-owned shares in Eterna, opening many opportunities in Asia through its chain of retailers. In March 2014, Eterna and Porsche finally separated, freeing up Eterna's technical and financial resources to focus on its own growth.

Eterna SA
Schützenstrasse 40
CH-2540 Grenchen
Switzerland

Tel.:
+41-32-654-7211

Website:
www.eterna.com

Founded:
1856

Number of employees:
approx. 50

Distribution:
Contact headquarters for all enquiries.

Most important collections:
1948, Vaughan, Madison, KonTiki, Contessa

1948 Legacy Small Second

Reference number: 7682.47.11.1320
Movement: automatic, Eterna Caliber 3903A; ø 30 mm, height 5.6 mm; 27 jewels; 28,800 vph; ball-bearing mounted spring barrel (Spherodrive); 68-hour power reserve
Functions: hours, minutes, subsidiary seconds; date
Case: stainless steel, ø 41.5 mm, height 11.45 mm; rose gold bezel and crown; sapphire crystal; transparent case back; water-resistant to 5 atm
Band: reptile skin, folding clasp
Price: $6,900
Variations: stainless steel bezel; black or silver-plated dial

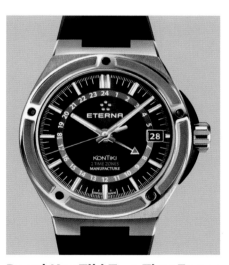

Royal KonTiki Two TimeZones

Reference number: 7740.40.41.1289
Movement: automatic, Eterna Caliber 3945A; ø 30 mm, height 5.9 mm; 28 jewels; 28,800 vph; 2 ball-bearing mounted spring barrels (Spherodrive); 68-hour power reserve
Functions: hours, minutes, sweep seconds; additional 24-hour display (2nd time zone); date
Case: stainless steel, ø 42 mm, height 12.3 mm; sapphire crystal, transparent case back; water-resistant to 10 atm
Band: rubber, buckle
Price: $5,400

Royal KonTiki Chronograph GMT Limited Edition 1856

Reference number: 7760.42.80.0280
Movement: automatic, Eterna Caliber 3927A; ø 30 mm, height 7.95 mm; 33 jewels; 28,800 vph; 68-hour power reserve
Functions: hours, minutes, subsidiary seconds; additional 24-hour display (2nd time zone); flyback chronograph
Case: stainless steel, ø 45 mm, height 14.75 mm; sapphire crystal; transparent case back; water-resistant to 10 atm
Band: stainless steel, folding clasp
Price: $6,500

Super KonTiki

Reference number: 1273.41.49.1363
Movement: automatic, Sellita Caliber SW200-1;
ø 25.6 mm, height 4.6 mm; 26 jewels; 28,800 vph;
38-hour power reserve
Functions: hours, minutes, sweep seconds; date
Case: stainless steel, ø 45 mm, height 12.6 mm;
unidirectional bezel with 60-minute division;
sapphire crystal; water-resistant to 20 atm
Band: calf leather, buckle
Price: $2,020

Adventic GMT

Reference number: 7661.41.56.1352
Movement: automatic, Eterna Caliber 3914A;
ø 30 mm, height 5.6 mm; 27 jewels; 28,800 vph;
ball-bearing mounted spring barrel (Spherodrive),
68-hour power reserve
Functions: hours, minutes, subsidiary seconds;
additional 24-hour display (2nd time zone); date
Case: stainless steel, ø 42 mm, height 12.6 mm;
sapphire crystal; transparent case back; water-
resistant to 5 atm
Band: calf leather, buckle
Price: $4,540

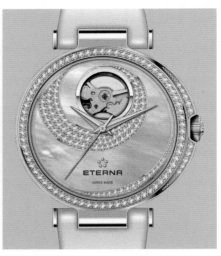

Grace Open Art

Reference number: 2943.61.69.1367
Movement: automatic, ETA Caliber 2824-2;
ø 25.6 mm, height 4.6 mm; 25 jewels; 28,800 vph;
38-hour power reserve
Functions: hours, minutes, sweep seconds
Case: stainless steel with rose gold-colored PVD
coating, ø 34 mm, height 10 mm; 69 diamonds
on bezel; sapphire crystal; transparent case back;
water-resistant to 5 atm
Band: calf leather, buckle
Remarks: dial with opening, diamonds
Price: $7,800

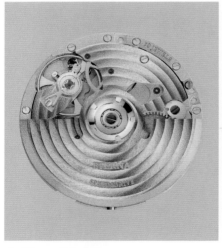

Caliber 3945A

Automatic; ball bearing-mounted spring barrel and
rotor; single spring barrel, 68-hour power reserve
Functions: hours, minutes, sweep seconds;
additional 24-hour indicator (2nd time zone); date
Diameter: 30 mm
Height: 5.9 mm
Jewels: 28
Balance: glucydur
Frequency: 28,800 vph
Balance spring: flat hairspring
Shock protection: Incabloc

Caliber 3927a

Automatic; ball bearing-mounted rotor; single spring
barrel; 68-hour power reserve
Functions: hours, minutes, subsidiary seconds;
additional 24-hour indicator (2nd time zone);
flyback chronograph
Diameter: 30 mm
Height: 7.95 mm
Jewels: 33
Balance: glucydur
Frequency: 28,800 vph
Balance spring: flat hairspring
Shock protection: Incabloc

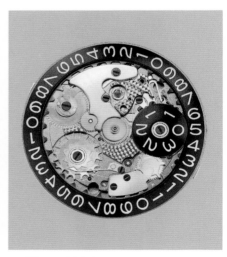

Caliber 3030

Automatic; ball bearing-mounted rotor; single spring
barrel; 48-hour power reserve
Functions: hours, minutes, sweep seconds; large
date
Diameter: 30 mm
Height: 4.4 mm
Jewels: 24
Balance: glucydur
Frequency: 28,800 vph
Balance spring: flat hairspring
Shock protection: Incabloc

Fabergé

Some names have achieved legendary status in that nebulous frontier zone where jewelry, art, and luxury meet. Peter Carl Fabergé (1846–1920), son of a St. Petersburg jeweler of French Protestant stock and supplier to the Romanovs, is one of those. In 1885, he was commissioned by Tsar Alexander III to produce a special Easter egg for the tsarina. He did so, employing the best craftspeople of the time, and in the process catapulted himself into the good graces of the Romanovs. This also meant exile when the Bolsheviks took over in 1918. His sons set up a jewelry and restoration business in Paris.

Fast-forward nearly ninety years. The name Fabergé has been repeatedly sold for at times dizzying sums. It has expanded into all sorts of luxury segments—perfume, jewelry, even watches. In 2007, Unilever sold it to Pallinghurst, a holding company with investments in mining that include the famous Gemfields, a specialist in colored stones.

In 2013, brand president and COO Robert Benvenuto decided to launch a new portfolio of watches. Utilizing colored stones and platinum was a foregone conclusion. Victor Mayer, a former licensee, took on the enamel guilloche dials of the Lady Fabergé core collection, which received a Vaucher movement. The eye-catching Summer in the Provence went to Art&D, an exclusive company located in Carouge next to Geneva. The model was clearly inspired by the iconic eggs, with the dial fully integrated into the bracelet to create a flowing landscape of diamonds, tourmalines, emeralds, mother-of-pearl flowers, and a turquoise enamel "stream." For the men's watch, Renaud & Papi produced a subtly modern tourbillon with a geometrically openworked dial. But the pièce de résistance, the Lady Compliquée, was assigned to Jean-Marc Wiederrecht of Agenhor, who created a movement driving a retrograde peacock's tail (Peacock) or a wave of frost (Winter) to display the minutes, while the hours circle the dial in the opposite direction.

Fabergé
54 Jermyn Street
London SW1Y 6LX
Great Britain

Tel.:
+44-20-7518-7297

E-Mail:
information@faberge.com

Website:
www.faberge.com

Founded:
1842, current watch department relaunched 2013

Annual production:
approx. 350 watches

U.S. distributor:
694 Madison Avenue
New York, NY 10065
646-559-8848
sales@faberge.com

Most important collections:
Lady Core Collection, Summer in the Provence, Lady Compliquée, Visionnaire I

Summer in the Provence

Movement: automatic, Vaucher Caliber 3000; ø 23.3 mm, height 3.9 mm; 28 jewels; 28,800 vph; white gold rotor set with diamonds; 50-hour power reserve
Functions: hours, minutes
Case: white gold, ø 37 mm; set in 374 diamonds, 17 Paraiba tourmalines, 10 emeralds; transparent case back; sapphire crystal
Band: white gold, set with diamonds and emeralds, mother-of-pearl flowers, folding clasp
Price: $290,000

Lady Compliquée Peacock

Movement: manually wound, Caliber 6901, custom by Agenhor ; ø 32.7 mm, height 3.58 mm; 38 jewels; 21,600 vph; white gold rotor with diamonds; 50-hour power reserve
Functions: hours (on disc at crown), minutes (retrograde)
Case: platinum, 38 mm, height 12.90 mm; 54 diamonds on bezel; transparent back; sapphire crystal; water-resistant to 3 atm
Band: reptile skin, platinum buckle
Remarks: after 1908 Fabergé Peacock Egg; gemstones, hand-engraved peacock on dial
Price: $98,000
Variations: 1913 Winter Egg/retrograde blades covering dial in frost ($67,500)

Visionnaire 1

Movement: manually wound, Caliber TOF14 (by APRP); ø 38 mm, height 8.05 mm; 29 jewels; 21,600 vph; 1-minute flying tourbillon; German silver bridges/mainplate; 72-hour power reserve
Functions: hours, minutes, power reserve indicator (movement side)
Case: blue PVD-treated titanium and platinum, 44 mm; transparent case back; sapphire crystal; water-resistant to 3 atm
Band: reptile skin, platinum and titanium folding clasp, blue PVD
Remarks: dial of NAC-treated German silver, bead-shot, blue PVD
Price: $245,000; limited to 15 pieces
Variations: rose gold and black PVD ($220,000)

Fortis Uhren AG

Lindenstrasse 45
CH-2540 Grenchen
Switzerland

Tel.:
+41-32-653-3361

Fax:
+41-32-652-5942

E-Mail:
info@fortis-watches.com

Website:
www.fortis-watches.com

Founded:
1912

U.S. distributor:
Gevril Group
9 Pinecrest Road
Valley Cottage, NY 10989
845-425-9882; 845-425-9897 (fax)
www.gevrilgroup.com

Most important collections/price range:
Flieger, Official Cosmonauts, Marinemaster, Stratoliner, Art Edition / $1,400 to $9,500

Fortis

From March to September 2012, anyone visiting the Museum of Cultural History in Grenchen, Switzerland, could have enjoyed an in-depth look at one century's worth of Fortis. The exhibition was appropriately called "From Grenchen into Space." And knowing Grenchen, that is quite a step.

The 102-year history of the Fortis brand has been marked by many memorable events. The biggest milestone dates to the 1920s, when the company began the first serial production of wristwatches with automatic winding.

The word *Fortis* comes from the Latin term for "strong." With its striking and sturdy watches, the brand itself has always enjoyed a reputation for reliability and consistency. But perhaps its greatest claim to fame comes from the clients it serves: These days, if you say "Fortis," the first thing that springs to mind is aeronautics and space travel. For the past seventeen years, Fortis has been collaborating with specialists from the European space agency to test how the company's first generation of space chronographs would hold up in truly extreme conditions. This resulted in approval for use aboard the Russian space station *Mir*. Since then, Fortis chronographs have become part of the official equipment of the Russian space program and, from there, on the *International Space Station*.

The competencies acquired from work in space continue to flow back into the company's traditional pilot's watches, which have long served as the role models for modern cockpit wristwatches. It's hardly astonishing that many international squadrons wear Fortis watches. Aside from such high-performance, space-traveling timepieces, Fortis also regularly enjoys creating limited edition art and design timepieces in collaboration with artists.

B-42 Monolith Day/Date

Reference number: 647.18.31 LP 01
Movement: automatic, ETA Caliber 2836-2; ø 30 mm, height 5.05 mm; 25 jewels; 28,800 vph; 38-hour power reserve
Functions: hours, minutes, sweep seconds; date, weekday
Case: stainless steel with black PVD coating, ø 42 mm, height 13 mm; unidirectional bezel with 60-minute divisions, sapphire crystal; water-resistant to 20 atm
Band: calf leather ("Performance"), buckle
Price: $2,495
Variations: various bands; chronograph

B-42 Monolith Chronograph

Reference number: 638.18.31 M
Movement: automatic, ETA Caliber 7750; ø 30 mm, height 7.9 mm; 25 jewels; 28,800 vph; 42-hour power reserve
Functions: hours, minutes, subsidiary seconds; chronograph; date, weekday
Case: stainless steel with black PVD coating, ø 42 mm, height 13 mm; unidirectional bezel with 60-minute divisions, sapphire crystal; water-resistant to 20 atm
Band: stainless steel with black PVD coating, safety folding clasp
Price: $4,495
Variations: various bands; day/date

B-42 Official Cosmonauts Chronograph

Reference number: 638.10.11 M
Movement: automatic, ETA Caliber 7750; ø 30 mm, height 7.9 mm; 25 jewels; 28,800 vph; 42-hour power reserve
Functions: hours, minutes, subsidiary seconds; chronograph; weekday, date
Case: stainless steel, ø 42 mm, height 16 mm; unidirectional bezel with 60-minute divisions, sapphire crystal, water-resistant to 20 atm
Band: stainless steel, folding clasp
Price: $3,995
Variations: various bands; day/date; alarm chronograph

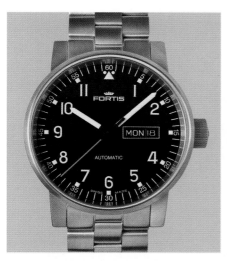

Spacematic Pilot Professional

Reference number: 623.10.71 M
Movement: automatic, ETA Caliber 2836-2; ø 25.6 mm, height 4.1 mm; 25 jewels; 28,800 vph; 42-hour power reserve
Functions: hours, minutes, sweep seconds; date, weekday
Case: stainless steel, ø 40 mm, height 13 mm; sapphire crystal; transparent case back; water-resistant to 10 atm
Band: stainless steel, folding clasp
Price: $1,995
Variations: various bands; with PVD coating

B-42 Marinemaster Chronograph

Reference number: 670.17.14 K
Movement: automatic, ETA Caliber 7750; ø 30 mm, height 7.9 mm; 25 jewels; 28,800 vph; 42-hour power reserve
Functions: hours, minutes, subsidiary seconds; chronograph; date, weekday
Case: stainless steel, ø 42 mm, height 13 mm; unidirectional bezel with 60-minute divisions; sapphire crystal; water-resistant to 20 atm
Band: silicon, folding clasp
Price: $2,195

B-47 Big Steel

Reference number: 675.10.81 L
Movement: automatic, Fortis Caliber F-2016 (base ETA 2836-2); ø 25.6 mm, height 5.05 mm; 26 jewels; 28,800 vph; 42-hour power reserve
Functions: hours, minutes, sweep seconds; weekday, date
Case: stainless steel, ø 47 mm, height 13.3 mm; unidirectional bezel with 60-minute divisions, sapphire crystal; water-resistant to 20 atm
Band: calf leather, buckle
Remarks: sapphire crystal dial
Price: $3,450; limited to 2,012 pieces
Variations: calf leather band ($3,450); stainless steel bracelet ($3,775)

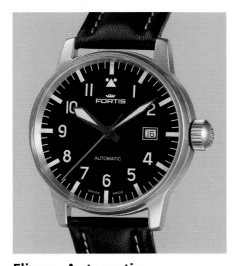

Flieger Automatic

Reference number: 595.11.41 L01
Movement: automatic, ETA Caliber 2824-2; ø 25.6 mm, height 4.6 mm; 25 jewels; 28,800 vph; 38-hour power reserve
Functions: hours, minutes, sweep seconds; date
Case: stainless steel, ø 40 mm, height 13 mm; sapphire crystal; water-resistant to 20 atm
Band: calf leather, buckle
Price: $1,295
Variations: various bands

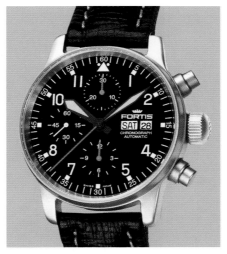

Flieger Automatic Chronograph

Reference number: 597.11.11 L01
Movement: automatic, ETA Caliber 7750; ø 30 mm, height 7.9 mm; 25 jewels, 28,800 vph; 42-hour power reserve
Functions: hours, minutes, subsidiary seconds; chronograph; weekday, date
Case: stainless steel, ø 40 mm, height 14.6 mm; sapphire crystal; water-resistant to 10 atm
Band: calf leather, buckle
Price: $2,995
Variations: various bands

F-43 Flieger Chrono Alarm GMT Certified Chronometer

Reference number: 703.10.11 LC01
Movement: automatic, Fortis Caliber F-2012 (base ETA 7750); ø 30 mm, height 7.9 mm; 39 jewels; 28,800 vph; 36-hour power reserve; COSC-certified chronometer
Functions: hours, minutes, subsidiary seconds; additional 24-hour display (2nd time zone); double power reserve indicator; alarm clock; chronograph; date, day/night indicator
Case: stainless steel, ø 43 mm, height 16.3 mm; sapphire crystal; water-resistant to 5 atm
Band: reptile skin, folding clasp
Price: $19,995; limited to 100 pieces
Variations: day/date ($2,495); chronograph ($3,525)

**Groupe Franck Muller
Watchland SA**

22, route de Malagny
CH-1294 Genthod
Switzerland

Tel.:
+41-22-959-8888

Fax:
+41-22-959-8882

E-Mail:
info@franckmuller.ch

Website:
www.franckmuller.com

Founded:
1997

Number of employees:
approx. 500 (estimated)

U.S. distributor:
Franck Muller USA, Inc.
207 W. 25th Street, 8th Floor
New York, NY 10001
212-463-8898
www.franckmuller.com

Most important collections:
Giga, Aeternitas, Revolution, Evolution 3-1

Franck Muller

Francesco "Franck" Muller has been considered one of the great creative minds in the industry ever since he designed and built his first tourbillon watch back in 1986. In fact, he never ceased amazing his colleagues and competition ever since, with his astounding timepieces combining complications in a new and fascinating manner.

Recently, the "master of complications" has been stepping away from the daily business of the brand, leaving space for the person who had paved young Muller's way to fame, Vartan Sirmakes. It was Sirmakes, previously a specialist in watch cases, who had contributed to the development of the double-domed, tonneau-shaped Cintrée Curvex case, with its elegant, 1920s retro look. The complications never stop either. The latest Gigatourbillons are 20 millimeters across; the Revolution series has a tourbillon that rises toward the crystal.

It was in 1997 that Muller and Sirmakes founded the Franck Muller Group Watchland, which now holds the majority interest in thirteen other companies, eight of which are watch brands. During the 2009 economic crisis, the company downsized somewhat and put all its ambitious plans for expansion on hold. Franck Muller remains the leading brand in the Watchland portfolio, but via far-reaching synergies within the group, two brands specializing in complicated movements, Pierre Kunz and Pierre-Michel Golay, play a part in the founding brand's success.

Giga Tourbillon

Reference number: 8889 T G SQT BR BR
Movement: manually wound, FM Caliber 2100 TS; 34.4 x 41.4 mm, height 8.5 mm; 29 jewels; 18,000 vph; flying 1-minute, 20 mm tourbillon; 4 spring barrels; fully skeletonized; 216-hour power reserve
Functions: hours, minutes; power reserve indicator
Case: rose gold, 43.7 x 59.2 mm, height 14 mm; sapphire crystal; transparent case back; water-resistant to 3 atm
Band: reptile skin, buckle
Price: $238,000
Variations: white gold ($238,000)

Giga Tourbillon

Reference number: 7048 T G SQT BR
Movement: manually wound, FM Caliber 2100 T RS; ø 40.5 mm, height 8.5 mm; 29 jewels; 18,000 vph; flying 1-minute, 20 mm tourbillon; 4 spring barrels; fully skeletonized; 216-hour power reserve
Functions: hours, minutes; power reserve indicator
Case: white gold, ø 49 mm, height 13 mm; sapphire crystal; transparent case back; water-resistant to 3 atm
Band: reptile skin, buckle
Price: $238,000
Variations: rose gold ($238,000)

Giga Gong Tourbillon

Reference number: 8889 T G GONG SQT
Movement: manually wound, FM Caliber 2100 TS; 34.4 x 41.4 mm, height 8.5 mm; 54 jewels; 18,000 vph; flying 1-minute, 20 mm tourbillon; 4 spring barrels; fully skeletonized; 144-hour power reserve
Functions: hours, minutes; power reserve display; alarm clock (hourly and half-hourly chime)
Case: rose gold, 43.7 x 59.2 mm, height 14 mm; sapphire crystal; transparent case back; water-resistant to 3 atm
Band: reptile skin, buckle
Price: $338,000

Cintrée Curvex
7 Days Power Reserve

Reference number: 7885 BS6 PR VIN
Movement: manually wound, FM Caliber 1700;
ø 31 mm, height 5 mm; 27 jewels; 18,000 vph;
double spring barrel, Breguet spring, finely finished
with côtes de Genève and perlage; 168-hour power
reserve
Functions: hours, minutes, subsidiary seconds;
power reserve indicator
Case: rose gold, 36 x 50.4 mm, height 10.3 mm;
sapphire crystal; transparent case back; water-
resistant to 3 atm
Band: reptile skin, buckle
Price: $19,800

Cintrée Curvex
7 Days Power Reserve
Skeleton

Reference number: 8880 B S6 SQT
Movement: manually wound, FM Caliber 1740
CS; 34.9 x 41.35 mm, height 5.3 mm; 21 jewels;
18,000 vph; Breguet spring, double spring barrel,
skeletonized mainplate and bridges, finely finished
with côtes de Genève and perlage; 168-hour power
reserve
Functions: hours, minutes, subsidiary seconds
Case: rose gold, 39.6 x 55.4 mm, height 13.7 mm;
sapphire crystal; transparent case back
Band: reptile skin, buckle
Price: $9,800

Aeternitas Mega 4

Reference number: 8888 Aternitas Mega 4 (8888
GSW T CC R QPS)
Movement: Automatic, FM Caliber 3420;
33.8 x 40.8 mm, height 13 mm; 21,600 vph; flying
1-minute tourbillon, microrotor; 96-hour power
reserve
Functions: hours, minutes; 2 24-hour displays;
equation of time indicator; minute repeater; grande
and petite sonnerie; split-second chronograph;
perpetual secular calendar with date (retrograde),
weekday, month, moon phase, year, leap year
Case: platinum, 42 x 61 mm, height 23.05 mm;
sapphire crystal; transparent case back
Band: reptile skin, buckle
Price: $2,600,000

Vanguard Chronograph

Reference number: V45 CC DT TT BR.TT
Movement: automatic, FM Caliber 7000;
ø 30.4 mm, height 7.9 mm; 27 jewels; 28,800 vph;
finely finished with côtes de Genève; 48-hour power
reserve
Functions: hours, minutes, subsidiary seconds;
chronograph; date
Case: titanium, 44 x 53.7 mm, height 15.8 mm;
sapphire crystal
Band: reptile skin, folding clasp
Price: $14,200
Variations: stainless steel ($14,200)

Cintrée Curvex Blue Dream

Reference number: 8880 SC BLEU
Movement: automatic, FM Caliber 2800;
ø 25.6 mm, height 3.6 mm; 21 jewels; 28,800 vph;
finely finished with côtes de Genève; 42-hour power
reserve
Functions: hours, minutes, sweep seconds
Case: stainless steel with blue PVD coating,
39.6 x 55.4 mm, height 11.9 mm; sapphire crystal;
water-resistant to 3 atm
Band: reptile skin, buckle
Price: on request

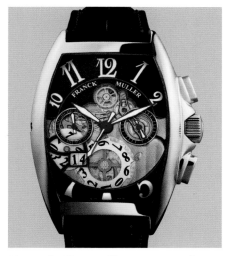

Grande Date Chronograph

Reference number: 8083 CC GD FO
Movement: automatic, FM Caliber; 28,800 vph;
46-hour power reserve
Functions: hours, minutes, subsidiary seconds;
chronograph; large date
Case: stainless steel, 39.5 x 55.5 mm; sapphire
crystal; transparent case back; water-resistant to
3 atm
Band: reptile skin, buckle
Price: $28,000
Variations: blue or red dial ($28,000)

Montres Journe SA
17 rue de l'Arquebuse
CH-1204 Geneva
Switzerland

Tel.:
+41-22-322-0909

Fax:
+41-22-322-0919

E-Mail:
info@fpjourne.com

Website:
www.fpjourne.com

Founded:
1999

Number of employees:
120

Annual production:
850–900 watches

U.S. distributor:
Montres Journe America
4330 NE 2nd Avenue
Miami, FL 33137
305-572-9802
phalimi@fpjourne.com

Most important collections/price range:
Souveraine, Octa, Vagabondage, Elégante
(Prices are in Swiss francs. Use daily exchange
rate for calculations.)

François-Paul Journe

Born in Marseilles in 1957, François-Paul Journe might have become something else had he concentrated in school. He was kicked out and apprenticed with a watchmaking uncle in Paris instead. And he has never looked back. By the age of twenty he had made his first tourbillon and soon was producing watches for connoisseurs.

He then moved to Switzerland, where he started out with handmade creations for a limited clientele and developing the most creative and complicated timekeepers for other brands before taking the plunge and founding his own in the heart of Geneva. The timepieces he basically single-handedly and certainly single-mindedly—hence his tagline *invenit et fecit*—conceives and produces are of such extreme complexity that it is no wonder that they leave his workshop in relatively small quantities. Journe has won numerous top awards, some several times over. He particularly values the Prix de la Fondation de la Vocation Bleustein-Blanchet since it came from his peers.

His collection is divided into two pillars: the automatic Octa line with its more readily understandable complications and the manually wound Souveraine line, containing horological treasures that can't be found anywhere else. The latter includes a *grande sonnerie*, a minute repeater, a constant force tourbillon with deadbeat seconds, and even a timepiece with two escapements beating in resonance—and providing chronometer-precise timekeeping. Journe never stops surprising the watch world.

He even surprises while remaining true to classical codes. His women's Elégante features a microprocessor that electronically notes when the watch is immobile, stops the mechanical movement to preserve energy, and restarts it when the watch is once again in motion.

Chronomètre à Résonance

Movement: manually wound, F.P.Journe Caliber 1499.3; ø 32.6 mm, height 4.2 mm; 36 jewels; 21,600 vph; unique concept of 2 escapements mutually influencing and stabilizing each other through resonance; pink gold plate and bridges
Functions: hours, minutes, subsidiary seconds; 2nd time zone; power reserve indicator
Case: platinum, ø 40 mm, height 9 mm; sapphire crystal; transparent case back
Band: reptile skin, platinum buckle
Price: CHF 84,200
Variations: pink gold (CHF 75,600)

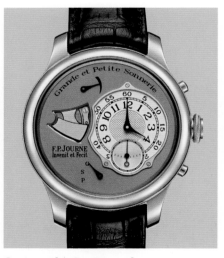

Sonnerie Souveraine

Movement: manually wound, F.P.Journe Caliber 1505; ø 35.8 mm, height 7.8 mm; 42 jewels; 21,600 vph; 18 kt rose gold plate and bridges; repeater chimes hours/quarter hours automatically, minute repeater on demand; on/off function; 422 components; 10 patents
Functions: hours, minutes (off-center), subsidiary seconds; grande sonnerie; power reserve indicator; chime indicator
Case: stainless steel, ø 42 mm, height 12.25 mm; sapphire crystal; screw-in crown and pusher; transparent case back
Band: 2 reptile skin straps, double folding clasp and 1 stainless steel bracelet
Price: CHF 734,400

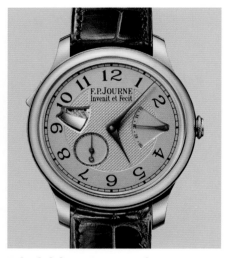

Répétition Souveraine

Movement: manually wound, F.P. Journe Caliber 1408; ø 32.2 mm, height 4 mm; 33 jewels; 21,600 vph; pink gold plate and bridges
Functions: hours, minutes, subsidiary seconds; hour, quarter-hour, minute repeater; power reserve indicator
Case: stainless steel, ø 40 mm, height 8.8 mm; sapphire crystal; transparent case back
Band: reptile skin, double folding clasp
Price: CHF 195,000

Tourbillon Souverain

Movement: manually wound, F.P.Journe Caliber 1403.2; ø 32.4 mm, height 7.15 mm; 26 jewels; 21,600 vph; pink gold plate and bridges; tourbillon with remontoire (constant force device) and deadbeat second
Functions: off-center hours and minutes, subsidiary seconds: power reserve
Case: platinum, ø 40 mm, height 10.7 mm; sapphire crystal; transparent case back
Band: reptile skin, buckle
Price: CHF 159,800
Variations: pink gold (CHF 148,500)

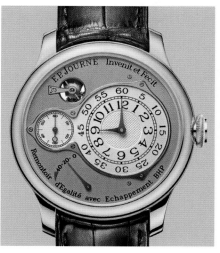

Chronomètre Optimum

Movement: manually wound, F.P.Journe Caliber 1510; ø 34.4 mm, height 3.75 mm; 44 jewels; 21,600 vph; pink gold plate and bridges; double barrel, constant force remontoire, EPHB high-performance biaxial escapement, balance spiral with Phillips curve, deadbeat seconds on back
Functions: hours, minutes, subsidiary seconds; power reserve indicator
Case: platinum, ø 40 mm, height 10.1 mm; sapphire crystal; transparent case back
Band: reptile skin, buckle
Price: CHF 90,200
Variations: pink gold (CHF 85,800)

Chronomètre Bleu

Movement: manually wound, F.P.Journe Caliber 1304; ø 30.4 mm, height 3.75 mm; 22 jewels; 21,600 vph; pink gold plate and bridges; chronometer balance with "invisible" connection to gear train; 2 spring barrels
Functions: hours, minutes, subsidiary seconds
Case: tantalum, ø 39 mm, height 8.6 mm; sapphire crystal; transparent case back
Band: reptile skin, tantalum buckle
Price: CHF 21,500

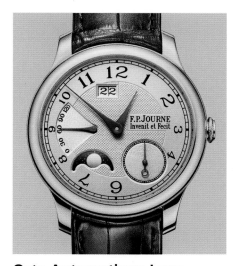

Octa Automatique Lune

Movement: automatic, F.P.Journe Caliber 1300.3; ø 30.8 mm, height 5.7 mm; 39 jewels; 21,600 vph; 120-hour power reserve; pink gold plate and bridge
Functions: hours, minutes, subsidiary seconds; large date; moon phase; power reserve indicator
Case: platinum, ø 40 mm, height 10.6 mm; sapphire crystal; transparent case back
Band: reptile skin, platinum buckle
Remarks: silver guilloché dial with clous de Paris
Price: CHF 50,600
Variations: pink gold (CHF 43,200)

Octa Sport

Movement: automatic, F.P.Journe Caliber 1303.3; ø 30.8 mm, height 5.70 mm; 40 jewels; 21,600 vph; entirely aluminum alloy; 120-hour power reserve
Functions: hours, minutes, subsidiary seconds; large date; power reserve; day/night indicator
Case: titanium, ø 42 mm, height 11.6 mm; sapphire crystal; transparent case back
Band: rubber, titanium clasp
Price: CHF 26,500
Variations: titanium bracelet (CHF 31,900)

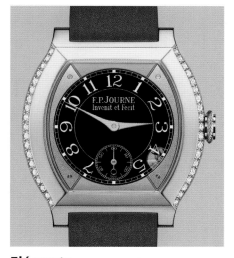

Elégante

Movement: electromechanical, F.P.Journe Caliber 1210; 28.5 x 28.3 mm, height 3.13 mm; 18 jewels; quartz frequency 32,000 Hz; autonomy 100 years/18-year standby mode; pink gold
Functions: hours, minutes, subsidiary seconds; motion detector with inertia weight at 4:30
Case: pink gold, 34 x 35 mm, height 7.35 mm; sapphire crystal; transparent case back
Band: chocolate rubber strap, pink gold buckle
Remarks: standby mode after 30 minutes motionless, microprocessor keeps time, restarts automatically, sets time when watch put back on; Luminova dial
Price: CHF 25,800
Variations: titanium (CHF 15,200); platinum (CHF 29,100)

Frédérique Constant SA
Chemin du Champ des Filles 32
CH-1228 Plan-les-Ouates (Geneva)
Switzerland

Tel.:
+41-22-860-0440

Fax:
+41-22-860-0464

E-Mail:
info@frederique-constant.com

Website:
www.frederique-constant.com

Founded:
1988

Number of employees:
100

Annual production:
110,000 watches

U.S. distributor:
Frederic Constant USA
877-61-WATCH; info@usa.frederique-constant.com

Most important collections/price range:
Slimline Manufacture Automatic / from approx.
$2,800; Heart Beat Manufacture / from approx.
$6,000; Lady Automatic / from approx. $2,800;
Runabout / from approx. $2,500; Vintage Rally /
from approx. $1,700; Art Deco / approx. $1,100;
Classics / from approx. $800; Smart Watch / from
approx. $995 to $1,295

Frédérique Constant

Time flies when you're having fun, even in the watch business. It's been just over ten years since the brand Frédérique Constant went public with its first movement entirely produced in-house and equipped with innovative silicon components. The move was in line with the strategy of staying independent, and it was crowned with success. In 2013, Frédérique Constant sold about 130,000 timepieces at 2,800 doors in roughly 100 countries. The production of Heart Beat calibers more than doubled, allowing the brand to get a lot closer to achieving its goal of offering affordable luxury to everyone.

Since 1991, the Dutch couple Peter und Aletta Stas have genuinely lived up to the tagline they use for their Swiss brand: "live your passion." The watch brand, named for Aletta's great-grandmother, Frédérique Schreiner, and Peter's great-grandfather, Constant Stas, was conceived in the late 1980s. The new company had its work cut out for it: Frédérique Constant had to compete in a watch market truly saturated with brands.

After their Heart Beat *manufacture* model met with award-winning enthusiasm in 2003, the Stases decided to invest in their own watch factory, an impressive, four-floor facility with ample room for a spacious atelier, administrative offices, conference rooms, fitness area, and cafeteria, in Geneva's industrial Plan-les-Ouates. Frédérique Constant moved into its new home in 2006, joined shortly after by sister brand Alpina. The Heart Beat collection continues to make waves, but the brand is growing in other directions as well, seeking to bridge the gap between fans of fine watchmaking and users of electronic nannies. The Horological Smartwatch, equipped with a quartz movement, connects with mobile phones and other electronic devices and can display data on its analog dial.

Manufacture Worldtimer

Reference number: FC-718NWM4H6
Movement: automatic, Caliber FC-718; ø 25.6 mm, height 4.1 mm; 26 jewels; 28,800 vph; 42-hour power reserve
Functions: hours, minutes, sweep seconds; world-time display (2nd time zone); date
Case: stainless steel, ø 42 mm, height 12.1 mm; rotating inner-ring with 24-hour division and reference city names, rotates via crown; sapphire crystal; transparent case back; water-resistant to 5 atm
Band: reptile skin, buckle
Price: $4,195

Vintage Rally Healey Chronograph

Reference number: FC-397HDG5B4
Movement: automatic, Caliber FC-397 (base Sellita SW500); ø 30 mm, height 7.9 mm; 25 jewels; 28,800 vph; 46-hour power reserve
Functions: hours, minutes, subsidiary seconds; chronograph
Case: stainless steel with rose gold-colored PVD coating, ø 42 mm, height 14.5 mm; sapphire crystal; water-resistant to 5 atm
Band: reptile skin, buckle
Remarks: limited to 2,888 pieces
Price: $3,295
Variations: w/o PVD coating ($2,995)

Horological Smartwatch

Reference number: FC-285S5B6
Movement: quartz
Functions: hours, minutes; electronic motion detector and sleep monitoring; date
Case: stainless steel, ø 42 mm, height 13.7 mm; sapphire crystal; water-resistant to 10 atm
Band: calf leather, folding clasp
Price: $995

Runabout Moonphase

Reference number: FC-365RM5B4
Movement: automatic, Caliber FC-365 (base ETA 2892-A2); ø 25.6 mm, 25 jewels; 28,800 vph; 42-hour power reserve
Functions: hours, minutes, sweep seconds; full calendar with date, weekday, month, moon phase
Case: stainless steel with rose gold-colored PVD coating, ø 40 mm, height 11.2 mm; sapphire crystal; transparent case back; water-resistant to 5 atm
Band: calf leather, folding clasp
Remarks: limited to 2,888 pieces
Price: $3,195

Heart Beat Manufacture

Reference number: FC-945MC4H9
Movement: automatic, Caliber FC-945; ø 30.5 mm, height 6.38 mm; 26 jewels; 28,800 vph; silicon escapement; finely finished with côtes de Genève; 42-hour power reserve
Functions: hours, minutes; additional 24-hour display (2nd time zone); date, moon phase
Case: rose gold, ø 42 mm, height 11.6 mm; sapphire crystal; transparent back; water-resistant to 5 atm
Band: reptile skin, buckle
Remarks: dial with opening
Price: $15,500
Variations: stainless steel

Healey GMT 24H

Reference number: FC-350HS5B6
Movement: automatic, Sellita Caliber SW 200; ø 25.6 mm, height 6.1 mm; 26 jewels; 28,800 vph; 38-hour power reserve
Functions: hours, minutes, sweep seconds; additional 24-hour display (2nd time zone); date
Case: stainless steel, ø 40 mm, height 12.5 mm; sapphire crystal; water-resistant to 5 atm
Band: calf leather, buckle
Price: $2,295

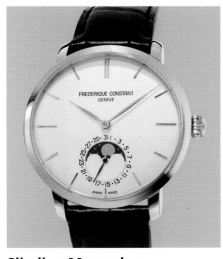

Slimline Moonphase Manufacture

Reference number: FC-705S4S6
Movement: automatic, Caliber FC705; ø 30 mm, height 6.3 mm; 26 jewels; 28,800 vph; côtes de Genève; 42-hour power reserve
Functions: hours, minutes; date; moon phase
Case: stainless steel, ø 42 mm, height 11.3 mm; sapphire crystal; transparent case back; water-resistant to 3 atm
Band: reptile skin, buckle
Price: $3,695
Variations: 38 mm case

Slimline Moonphase Manufacture

Reference number: FC-703VD3SD4
Movement: automatic, Caliber FC703; ø 27.5 mm, height 6.3 mm; 26 jewels; 28,800 vph; côtes de Genève; 42-hour power reserve
Functions: hours, minutes; date; moon phase
Case: rose gold, ø 38.8 mm, height 11.2 mm; 60 diamonds on bezel; sapphire crystal; transparent case back; water-resistant to 3 atm
Band: reptile skin, buckle
Price: $5,350

Slimline Ladies Moonphase

Reference number: FC-206MPWD1SD6B
Movement: quartz
Functions: hours, minutes; moon phase
Case: stainless steel, ø 30 mm, height 7.7 mm; diamonds on bezel; sapphire crystal; water-resistant to 3 atm
Band: stainless steel, buckle
Remarks: dial set with 8 diamonds
Price: $1,295

Genesis
Jaffestr. 6
D-21109 Hamburg
Germany

Tel.:
+49-40-414-9880-0

E-Mail:
info@genesis-uhren.de

Website:
www.genesis-uhren.de

Founded:
2005

Number of employees:
2

U.S. distributor:
direct sales only

Most important collections/price range:
$2,500 to $3,800
Prices may vary due to exchange rate
fluctuations.

Genesis

These days, the graduating classes of watchmaking schools comprise more and more women who are passionate about precision handcrafting. Many of them have already become masters of their trade. Hamburg-based watchmaker Christine Genesis is one of these women—and her last name, the biblical term for the story of creation, can be seen as the theme of her horological activities. In addition to teaming up with designer Jorn Lund to create her own series of timelessly elegant, reliable, and affordable wristwatches in an old factory building in Hamburg's south end, Genesis, who studied at the watchmaking school of Pforzheim, also makes use of her longtime experience repairing clocks, maintaining mechanical wristwatches, and working on such larger complications as perpetual calendars.

Genesis has bucked the trend toward ever larger watches and complicated dials, opting instead for uncluttered elegance, with complications subtly integrated in timepieces that are hardly ostentatious. She manufactures all the components in Germany with the exception of the movements. Everything goes through her hands: planning, design, production of the case, modifications to the movement, and fine-tuning all the parts. Each model is manufactured in limited editions and individually numbered.

Christine Genesis is always personally available to answer questions about the manufacturing process and the collection.

Genesis Carpe Diem

Reference number: 39.14.1
Movement: automatic, ETA Caliber 7750; ø 30 mm, height 7.9 mm; 25 jewels; 28,800 vph; finely finished with perlage and côtes de Genève; 42-hour power reserve
Functions: hours, minutes, subsidiary seconds; chronograph; weekday, date
Case: stainless steel, ø 39.6 mm, height 14 mm; sapphire crystal; transparent case back
Band: calf leather, buckle
Remarks: limited to 50 pieces
Price: $3,000
Variations: various colored hands; various dial colors

Genesis 4

Reference number: 38.04.2
Movement: automatic, Soprod Caliber 9090 (base ETA 2892-A2), ø 25.6 mm, height 5.1 mm; 28 jewels; 28,800 vph; finely finished with perlage and côtes de Genève, engraved rotor
Functions: hours, minutes, sweep seconds; power reserve indicator; large date
Case: stainless steel, ø 38.5 mm, height 10.5 mm; sapphire crystal; transparent case back
Band: calf leather, buckle
Remarks: limited to 44 pieces
Price: $2,600
Variations: light-colored dial; black DLC-coating

Genesis Classic

Reference number: 38.11.4
Movement: automatic, ETA Caliber 2892-A2; ø 25.6 mm, height 3.6 mm; 25 jewels; 28,800 vph; finely finished with perlage and côtes de Genève; 42-hour power reserve
Functions: hours, minutes, sweep seconds; date
Case: stainless steel, ø 38.5 mm, height 9.5 mm; sapphire crystal; transparent case back
Band: calf leather, buckle
Price: $2,100
Variations: various dial colors

Tempting Timekeepers From Around The World

If you love the art and engineering of a fine timepiece, WristWatch Magazine is a must-read.

$49.00 (6-issues)
for a one year subscription

From the rarest masterpieces, to popular trends, **WristWatch Magazine** will fan the flames of your watch passion. Famous brands will be joined by deserving up-and-comers on the pages of **WristWatch Magazine**. Education, collecting, watch news and events from around the world will come together on our pages to sharpen your watch knowledge and immerse you in the world of micro machines that are mechanical wristwatches.

ISOCHRON Media Llc

Publishers of: WristWatch Magazine and AboutTime Magazine
Office **(203) 485-6276** • E-mail **info@isochronmedia.com**

Girard-Perregaux

1, Place Girardet
CH-2300 La Chaux-de-Fonds
Switzerland

Tel.:
+41-32-911-3333

Fax:
+41-32-913-0480

Website:
www.girard-perregaux.com

Founded:
1791

Number of employees:
280

Annual production:
approx. 12,000 watches

U.S. distributor:
Girard-Perregaux
Tradema of America, Inc.
7900 Glades Road, Suite 200
Boca Raton, FL 33434
877-846-3447
www.girard-perregaux.com

Most important collections/price range:
Vintage 1945 / approx. $7,010 to $650,000;
ww.tc / $12,400 to $210,000; GP 1966 /
$13,600 to $290,850

Girard-Perregaux

When Girard-Perregaux CEO Luigi ("Gino") Macaluso died in 2010, the former minority partner of Sowind Group, PPR (Pinault, Printemps, Redoute), increased its equity stake to 51 percent. Under the leadership of Michele Sofisti since 2011, the brand has been charting a rather bold course that includes some technically sharp developments with the support of a strong development team and an excellently equipped production department. Under his guidance, the company has reduced its multitude of references but continues treading the fine line between fashionable watches and technical miracles. In January 2012, the manufacturing team was reinforced with one of the most scintillating figures in horology, master watchmaker Dominique Loiseau, who is working on a new, modular movement for the brand.

The various combinations of tourbillons and the gold bridges remain the company specialty. The elegant GP 1966 line and the very feminine Cat's Eye are still available, of course. The Vintage 45 is another standout, featuring striking rectangular and arched cases. But the most dazzling talking piece lately has undoubtedly been the Constant Escapement, a new concept that stores energy by buckling an ultrathin silicium blade and then releasing it to the balance wheel. Like many sophisticated systems, it was born of the banal: Inventor Nicolas Déhon was absentmindedly bending a train ticket one day when he was suddenly struck by the simple thought. As the ticket bent, it collected energy that was released in even bursts when it straightened out.

Another technical development is the triple-axis tourbillon. On the other side of the scale, one finds the manually wound chronograph caliber 03800, with column wheel and jumping minute counter, which maintains the brand's line of classic virtues.

Tourbillon Minute Repeater with Three Gold Bridges

Reference number: 99820-52-000-BA6A
Movement: manually wound, GP Caliber 09500-0002; ø 32 mm, height 9.35 mm; 37 jewels; 21,600 vph; 1-minute tourbillon; 58-hour power reserve
Functions: hours, minutes; minute repeater
Case: rose gold, ø 45 mm, height 15.63 mm; sapphire crystal; transparent case back; water-resistant to 3 atm
Band: reptile skin, double folding clasp
Price: $395,000; limited to 10 pieces

Neo-Tourbillon in Titanium

Reference number: 99270-21-000-BA6A
Movement: automatic, GP Caliber 9400-0001; ø 36.6 mm, height 8.21 mm; 27 jewels; 21,600 vph; 1-minute tourbillon under 3 PVD-coated titanium bridges, white gold microrotor; 70-hour power reserve
Functions: hours, minutes, subsidiary seconds (on tourbillon cage)
Case: titanium with black PVD coating, ø 45 mm, height 14.45 mm; sapphire crystal; transparent case back; water-resistant to 3 atm
Band: reptile skin, folding clasp
Price: $121,900
Variations: rose gold ($153,150)

Constant Escapement L.M.

Reference number: 93500-52-731-BA6D
Movement: manually wound, GP Caliber 09100-0002; ø 39.2 mm, height 7.9 mm; 28 jewels; 21,600 vph; escapement with constant force, 2 escape wheels and flat silicon blade spring to provide impulses; 2 spring barrels; 168-hour power reserve
Functions: hours and minutes (off-center), sweep seconds; linear power reserve indicator
Case: rose gold, ø 48 mm, height 14.63 mm; sapphire crystal; transparent case back; water-resistant to 3 atm
Band: reptile skin, folding clasp
Remarks: dedicated to Luigi ("Gino") Macaluso
Price: $123,500

GP 1966 "The Pearl of Wonders"

Reference number: 49534-52-R04-BB60
Movement: automatic, GP Caliber 03300-0060;
ø 25.6 mm, height 4.2 mm; 26 jewels; 28,800 vph;
46-hour power reserve
Functions: hours, minutes
Case: rose gold, ø 40 mm, height 9.94 mm;
sapphire crystal; transparent case back; water-
resistant to 3 atm
Band: reptile skin, buckle
Remarks: sodalite and papyrus, elaborately
handpainted dial
Price: $47,850; limited to 18 pieces

GP 1966 "Terrestrial Map"

Reference number: 49534-52-R05-BB60
Movement: automatic, GP Caliber 03300-0060;
ø 25.6 mm, height 4.2 mm; 26 jewels; 28,800 vph;
46-hour power reserve
Functions: hours, minutes
Case: rose gold, ø 40 mm, height 9.94 mm;
sapphire crystal; transparent case back; water-
resistant to 3 atm
Band: reptile skin, buckle
Remarks: elaborately handpainted jade dial
Price: $47,850; limited to 18 pieces

GP 1966 "The New World"

Reference number: 49534-52-R06-BB60
Movement: automatic, GP Caliber 03300-0060;
ø 25.6 mm, height 4.2 mm; 26 jewels; 28,800 vph;
46-hour power reserve
Functions: hours, minutes
Case: rose gold, ø 40 mm, height 9.94 mm;
sapphire crystal; transparent case back; water-
resistant to 3 atm
Band: reptile skin, buckle
Remarks: elaborately handpainted aventurine dial
Price: $47,850; limited to 18 pieces

GP 1966 Large Date and Moon Phase

Reference number: 49546-52-131-BB60
Movement: automatic, GP Caliber 03300-0110;
ø 25.6 mm, height 4.9 mm; 32 jewels; 28,800 vph;
46-hour power reserve
Functions: hours, minutes, subsidiary seconds;
large date, moon phase
Case: rose gold, ø 41 mm, height 11.22 mm;
sapphire crystal; transparent case back; water-
resistant to 3 atm
Band: reptile skin, buckle
Price: $24,360

GP 1966

Reference number: 49527-52-431-BB4A
Movement: automatic, GP Caliber 03300-0030;
ø 25.6 mm; 27 jewels; 28,800 vph; 46-hour power
reserve
Functions: hours, minutes, sweep seconds; date
Case: rose gold, ø 41 mm, height 11.22 mm;
sapphire crystal; transparent case back; water-
resistant to 3 atm
Band: reptile skin, buckle
Price: $16,500

GP 1966

Reference number: 49525-52-133-BB60
Movement: automatic, GP Caliber 03300-0030;
ø 25.6 mm; 27 jewels; 28,800 vph; 46-hour power
reserve
Functions: hours, minutes, sweep seconds; date
Case: rose gold, ø 38 mm, height 8.62 mm;
sapphire crystal; transparent case back; water-
resistant to 3 atm
Band: reptile skin, buckle
Price: $16,750
Variations: blue dial

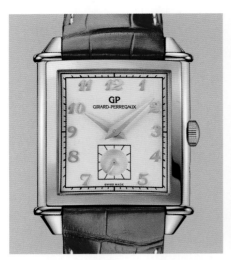

Vintage 1945 Small Seconds 70th Anniversary Edition

Reference number: 25880-56-111-BBBA
Movement: automatic, GP Caliber 03300-0051;
ø 25.6 mm, height 4.2 mm; 32 jewels; 28,800 vph;
46-hour power reserve
Functions: hours, minutes, subsidiary seconds
Case: stainless steel, 35.25 x 36.2 mm, height
10.83 mm; rose gold bezel; sapphire crystal;
transparent case back; water-resistant to 3 atm
Band: reptile skin, folding clasp
Price: $13,050
Variations: silver or anthracite dial; rose gold
($27,600)

Vintage 1945 XXL Large Date and Moon Phase

Reference number: 25882-11-121-BB6B
Movement: automatic, GP Caliber 03300-00062;
ø 25.6 mm, height 4.9 mm; 32 jewels; 28,800 vph;
46-hour power reserve
Functions: hours, minutes, subsidiary seconds;
large date; moon phase
Case: stainless steel, 35.25 x 36.1 mm, height
11.74 mm; sapphire crystal; transparent case back;
water-resistant to 3 atm
Band: reptile skin, folding clasp
Price: $12,200
Variations: rose gold ($29,950); anthracite-colored
dial

Vintage 1945 XXL Large Date and Moon Phase

Reference number: 25882-11-223-BB6B
Movement: automatic, GP Caliber 03300-00062;
ø 25.6 mm, height 4.9 mm; 32 jewels; 28,800 vph;
46-hour power reserve
Functions: hours, minutes, subsidiary seconds;
large date; moon phase
Case: stainless steel, 35.25 x 36.1 mm, height
11.74 mm; sapphire crystal; transparent case back;
water-resistant to 3 atm
Band: reptile skin, folding clasp
Remarks: sapphire crystal dial
Price: $16,000

Vintage 1945 Lady

Reference number: 25860D11A121-CK7A
Movement: automatic, GP Caliber 02700-003;
ø 19.4 mm; 26 jewels; 28,800 vph; 36-hour power
reserve
Functions: hours, minutes; date
Case: stainless steel, 27.85 x 28.2 mm, height
10.2 mm; 30 diamonds on bezel; sapphire crystal;
water-resistant to 3 atm
Band: reptile skin
Remarks: dial with 2 diamonds
Price: $10,700

Cat's Eye Power Reserve

Reference number: 80486D11A161-CK6A
Movement: automatic, GP Caliber 03300-0070;
ø 25.6 mm; 27 jewels; 28,800 vph; 46-hour power
reserve
Functions: hours, minutes, subsidiary seconds;
power reserve indicator; date
Case: stainless steel, 37.84 x 32.84 mm, height
9.1 mm; 64 diamonds on bezel; sapphire crystal;
transparent case back; water-resistant to 3 atm
Band: reptile skin, folding clasp
Remarks: dial with 8 diamonds
Price: $14,550

GP 1966 Lady

Reference number: 49528-D52A-131-CB6A
Movement: automatic, GP Caliber 03200-0005;
ø 25.3 mm, height 3.2 mm; 26 jewels; 28,800 vph;
42-hour power reserve
Functions: hours, minutes
Case: rose gold, ø 30 mm, height 8.9 mm; 60
diamonds on bezel; sapphire crystal; transparent
case back; water-resistant to 3 atm
Band: reptile skin, buckle
Price: $19,100

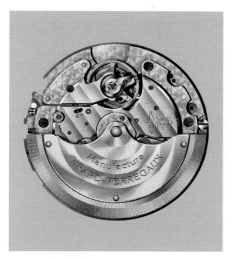

Caliber GP 3200

Automatic; rotor with ceramic ball bearing, stop-second system; single spring barrel, 42-hour power reserve
Functions: hours, minutes, sweep seconds or subsidiary seconds at 9 o'clock; date
Diameter: 23.3 mm
Height: 3.2 mm
Jewels: 27
Balance: glucydur
Frequency: 28,800 vph
Balance spring: flat hairspring, fine adjustment
Shock protection: Kif
Remarks: 185 components

Caliber GP 3300

Automatic; rotor with ceramic ball bearing, stop-second system; single spring barrel, 46-hour power reserve
Functions: hours, minutes, sweep seconds or subsidiary seconds at 9 o'clock; date
Diameter: 25.6 mm
Height: 3.2 mm
Jewels: 27
Balance: glucydur
Frequency: 28,800 vph
Balance spring: flat hairspring, fine adjustment
Shock protection: Kif
Remarks: 191 components

Caliber GP 3800

Manually wound; column wheel control of chronograph functions; single spring barrel, 58-hour power reserve
Functions: hours, minutes, subsidiary seconds; chronograph
Diameter: 25.6 mm
Height: 5.4 mm
Jewels: 31
Balance: Microvar with adjustable inertia
Frequency: 28,800 vph
Balance spring: flat hairspring
Shock protection: Kif
Remarks: 312 components

Caliber GP 09400

Automatic; 1-minute tourbillon, bidirectional winding rotor; tourbillon bridges in PVD-coated titanium; single spring barrel; 70-hour power reserve
Functions: hours, minutes, subsidiary seconds (on tourbillon cage)
Diameter: 36.6 mm
Height: 8.21 mm
Jewels: 27
Balance: screw balance
Frequency: 21,600 vph
Remarks: modern version of the classic Tourbillon under 3 Gold Bridges

Caliber GP 09300

Manually wound; 1-minute tourbillon held in 2 cages positioned at 90° with 30-second and 2-minute rotation speed; single spring barrel; 52-hour reserve
Functions: hours, minutes; power reserve indicator
Diameter: 36.1 mm
Height: 16.83 mm
Jewels: 34
Balance: screw balance
Frequency: 21,600 vph

Caliber GP 3330-6LM00

Automatic; unidirectional rotor, stop-second system; single spring barrel, 46-hour power reserve
Functions: hours, minutes, subsidiary seconds; large date; moon phase
Measurements: 25.6 x 28.8 mm
Height: 4.9 mm
Jewels: 32
Balance: glucydur
Frequency: 28,800 vph
Balance spring: flat hairspring, fine adjustment
Shock protection: Kif

Glashütter Uhrenbetrieb GmbH

Altenberger Strasse 1
D-01768 Glashütte
Germany

Tel.:
+49-350-53-460

Fax:
+49-350-53-46-205

E-Mail:
info@glashuette-original.com

Website:
www.glashuette-original.com

Founded:
1994

Annual production:
approx. 5,000 watches (estimated)

U.S. distributor:
Glashütte Original
The Swatch Group (U.S.), Inc.
1200 Harbor Boulevard
Weehawken, NJ 07087
201-271-1400

Most important collections/price range:
Senator, PanoMatic, Ladies / approx. $5,000
to $170,000

Glashütte Original

Is there a little nostalgia creeping into the designers at Glashütte Original? Or is it just understated ecstasy for older looks? The retro touches that started appearing again a few years ago with the Sixties Square Tourbillon are still in vogue as the company delves into its own past for inspiration, such as the use of a special silver treatment on dials.

The Glashütte Original *manufacture* was once subsumed in the VEB Glashütter Uhrenbetriebe, a group of Glashütte watchmakers and suppliers who were collectivized as part of the former East German system. After reunification, the company took up its old moniker of Glashütte Original, and in 1995, the *manufacture* released an entirely new collection. Later, it purchased Union Glashütte. In 2000, the *manufacture* was sold to the Swiss Swatch Group, which invested a sizable amount in production space expansion at Glashütte Original headquarters.

All movements are designed by a team of experienced in-house engineers, while the components comprising them such as plates, screws, pinions, wheels, levers, spring barrels, balance wheels, and tourbillon cages are manufactured in the upgraded production areas. These parts are lavishly finished by hand before assembly by a group of talented watchmakers. The large and elegant Senator Chronometer is a highlight of recent years with its classic design. It also boasts second and minute hands that automatically jump to zero when the crown is pulled, allowing for extremely accurate time setting. And to prove that the company is not just about tradition, it has even created a Senator-based app.

Grande Cosmopolite Tourbillon

Reference number: 1-89-01-03-03-04
Movement: manually wound, GO Caliber 89-01; ø 39.2 mm, height 7.5 mm; 70 jewels, 2 diamond endstones; 21,600 vph; flying 1-minute tourbillon; Breguet spring, 18 weighted screws on screw balance, gold chatons; 72-hour power reserve
Functions: hours, minutes, subsidiary seconds (on tourbillon cage); 37-zone world-time display, day/night indicator, power reserve indicator on back; perpetual calendar
Case: platinum, ø 48 mm, height 16 mm; sapphire crystal; transparent back; water-resistant to 5 atm
Band: reptile skin, folding clasp
Price: on request; limited to 25 pieces

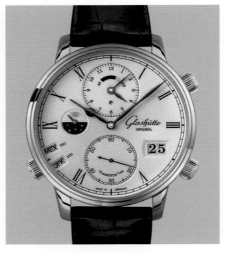

Senator Cosmopolite

Reference number: 1-89-02-01-05-30
Movement: automatic, GO Caliber 89-02; ø 39.2 mm, height 8 mm; 63 jewels; 28,800 vph; Glashütte three-quarter plate; screw balance with regulating screws, swan-neck fine adjustment; hand-engraved balance bridge, fine finishing; 72-hour power reserve
Functions: hours, minutes, subsidiary seconds; 2nd 12-hour time zone; 37-zone world-time display, day/night indicator, power reserve; panorama date
Case: pink gold, ø 44 mm, height 14 mm; sapphire crystal; transparent case back; water-resistant to 5 atm
Band: reptile skin, folding clasp
Price: $43,500
Variations: white gold ($45,300)

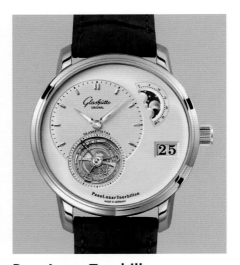

PanoLunarTourbillon

Reference number: 1-93-02-05-05-05
Movement: automatic, GO Caliber 93-02; ø 32.2 mm, height 7.65 mm; 48 jewels, 2 diamond endstones; 21,600 vph; flying 1-minute tourbillon; screw balance with 10 weighted screws, 8 regulation screws
Functions: hours and minutes (off-center), subsidiary seconds (on tourbillon cage); panorama date; moon phase
Case: pink gold, ø 40 mm, height 13.1 mm; sapphire crystal, transparent case back; water-resistant to 5 atm
Band: reptile skin, folding clasp
Price: $117,400
Variations: black reptile skin strap ($117,400)

PanoGraph

Reference number: 1-61-03-25-15-04
Movement: manually wound, GO Caliber 61-03;
ø 32.2 mm, height 7.2 mm; 41 jewels; 28,800 vph;
screw balance with 18 weighted screws, swan-neck
fine adjustment; hand-engraved balance bridge;
42-hour power reserve
Functions: hours, minutes, subsidiary seconds
(all off-center); flyback chronograph; 30-minute
counter; stop seconds; panorama date
Case: red gold, ø 40 mm, height 13.7 mm; sapphire
crystal; transparent back; water-resistant to 5 atm
Band: reptile skin, folding clasp
Price: $34,600
Variations: brown reptile skin strap ($34,600)

PanoReserve

Reference number: 1-65-01-26-12-30
Movement: manually wound, GO Caliber 65-01;
ø 32.2 mm, height 6.1 mm; 48 jewels; 28,800 vph;
Glashütte three-quarter plate, screw balance
with 18 weighted screws, duplex swan-neck fine
adjustment; hand-engraved balance bridge/second
cock, fine finishing; 42-hour power reserve
Functions: hours and minutes (off-center),
subsidiary seconds; power reserve indicator;
panorama date
Case: stainless steel, ø 40 mm, height 11.7 mm;
sapphire crystal; transparent back; water-resistant
to 5 atm
Band: reptile skin, folding clasp
Price: $11,500

PanoMaticInverse

Reference number: 1-91-02-01-05-30
Movement: automatic, GO Caliber 91-02;
ø 38.2 mm, height 7.1 mm; 49 jewels; 28,800 vph;
18 weighted screws on screw balance, duplex swan-
neck fine adjustment; inverted structure; three-
quarter plate with Glashütte ribbing, hand-engraved
balance bridge, skeletonized rotor with gold
oscillating weight; 42-hour power reserve
Functions: hours and minutes (off-center),
subsidiary seconds; panorama date
Case: pink gold, ø 42 mm, height 12.3 mm;
sapphire crystal; transparent back; water-resistant
to 5 atm
Band: reptile skin, folding clasp
Price: $29,700

Senator Chronograph Panorama Date

Reference number: 1-37-01-02-03-30
Movement: automatic, GO Caliber 37-01;
ø 31.6 mm, height 8 mm; 65 jewels; 28,800 vph;
screw balance with 4 gold regulating screws, swan-
neck fine adjustment; mainplate with côtes de
Genève, blued screws, skeletonized rotor with gold
oscillating weight; 70-hour power reserve
Functions: hours, minutes, subsidiary seconds;
power reserve indicator; flyback chronograph;
panorama date
Case: platinum, ø 42 mm, height 14 mm; sapphire
crystal; transparent back; stone cabochon on crown;
water-resistant to 5 atm
Band: reptile skin, folding clasp
Price: $55,600

Senator Chronometer

Reference number: 1-58-01-01-01-04
Movement: manually wound, GO Caliber 58-01;
ø 35 mm, height 6.5 mm; 58 jewels; 28,800 vph;
Glashütte three-quarter plate, second reset via
crown for precise minutes; screw balance with 18
weighted screws, swan-neck fine adjustment; hand-
engraved balance cock; 45-hour power reserve;
DIN-certified
Functions: hours, minutes, subsidiary seconds;
day/night indicator; power reserve; panorama date
Case: rose gold, ø 42 mm, height 12.3 mm;
sapphire crystal; transparent case back; water-
resistant to 5 atm
Band: reptile skin, folding clasp
Price: $30,300
Variations: white gold ($32,200)

Senator Chronometer Regulator

Reference number: 1-58-04-04-04-04
Movement: manually wound, GO Caliber 58-04;
ø 35 mm, height 6.5 mm; 58 jewels; 28,800 vph;
Glashütte three-quarter plate, swan-neck fine
adjustment; hand-engraved balance bridge; 18
weighted screws on screw balance; 45-hour power
reserve; DIN-certified
Functions: hours (off-center), minutes, subsidiary
seconds; day/night and power reserve indicators;
panorama date
Case: white gold, ø 42 mm, height 12.47 mm;
sapphire crystal; transparent case back; water-
resistant to 5 atm
Band: reptile skin, folding clasp
Price: $33,400
Variations: pink gold ($31,600)

Senator Observer

Reference number: 100-14-05-02-05
Movement: automatic, GO Caliber 100-14;
ø 31.15 mm, height 6.5 mm; 60 jewels; 28,800 vph;
screw balance, swan-neck fine adjustment; three-
quarter plate with Glashütte ribbing, skeletonized rotor
with gold oscillating weight; 55-hour power reserve
Functions: hours, minutes, subsidiary seconds; power
reserve indicator; hacking seconds; panorama date
Case: stainless steel, ø 44 mm, height 12 mm;
sapphire crystal; transparent case back; water-
resistant to 5 atm
Band: calf leather, folding clasp
Price: $11,800
Variations: reptile skin band; stainless steel bracelet
($13,300)

Senator Panorama Date

Reference number: 100-03-32-42-04
Movement: automatic, GO Caliber 100-03;
ø 31.15 mm, height 5.8 mm; 51 jewels; 28,800 vph;
screw balance with 18 weighted screws, swan-neck
fine adjustment; three-quarter plate with Glashütte
stripe, skeletonized rotor with gold oscillating
weight; 55-hour power reserve
Functions: hours, minutes, sweep seconds;
panorama date
Case: stainless steel, ø 40 mm, height 11.52 mm;
sapphire crystal; transparent back; water-resistant
to 5 atm
Band: reptile skin, folding clasp
Price: $10,300

Senator Panorama Date Moon Phase

Reference number: 100-04-32-15-04
Movement: automatic, GO Caliber 100-04;
ø 31.15 mm, height 5.8 mm; 55 jewels; 28,800 vph;
screw balance with 18 weighted screws, swan-neck
fine adjustment; three-quarter plate with Glashütte
stripe, skeletonized rotor with gold oscillating
weight; 55-hour power reserve
Functions: hours, minutes, sweep seconds;
panorama date; moon phase
Case: pink gold, ø 40 mm, height 11.52 mm;
transparent back; water-resistant to 5 atm
Band: reptile skin, folding clasp
Price: $23,900

Senator Perpetual Calendar

Reference number: 100-02-25-05-04
Movement: automatic, GO Caliber 100-02;
ø 31.15 mm, height 7.1 mm; 59 jewels; 28,800 vph;
screw balance with 18 weighted screws; swan-neck
fine adjustment; zero reset mechanism; skeletonized
rotor with gold oscillating weight; 55-hour power
reserve
Functions: hours, minutes, sweep seconds;
perpetual calendar with panorama date, weekday,
month, moon phase, leap year
Case: pink gold, ø 42 mm, height 13.6 mm;
sapphire crystal; transparent back; water-resistant
to 5 atm
Band: reptile skin band, folding clasp
Price: $37,100

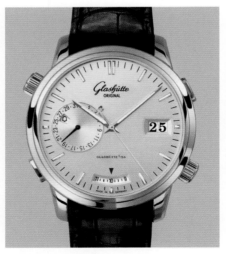

Senator Diary

Reference number: 100-13-01-01-04
Movement: automatic, GO Caliber 100-13;
ø 34 mm, height 8.4 mm; 86 jewels; 28,800 vph;
screw balance, swan-neck fine adjustment, zero
reset mechanism; three-quarter plate with Glashütte
stripe, skeletonized rotor with gold oscillating
weight; 55-hour power reserve
Functions: hours, minutes, sweep seconds;
panorama date; memory function (appointment
day/hour) with 80-second sonorous signal, on/off
switch
Case: rose gold, ø 42 mm, height 14.4 mm;
sapphire crystal, transparent back; water-resistant
to 5 atm
Band: reptile skin, folding clasp
Price: $39,000

PanoMaticCounter XL

Reference number: 1-96-01-02-02-04
Movement: automatic, GO Caliber 96-01;
ø 32.2 mm, height 8.9 mm; 72 jewels; 28,800 vph;
screw balance with 18 weighted screws, swan-
neck fine adjustment, skeletonized rotor with gold
oscillating weight; 42-hour power reserve
Functions: hours and minutes (off-center),
subsidiary seconds; 2-digit counter (pusher-
controlled, forward/backward); flyback
chronograph; hacking seconds on 2nd dial level;
panorama date
Case: stainless steel, ø 44 mm, height 16 mm;
sapphire crystal, transparent case back; water-
resistant to 5 atm
Band: reptile skin, folding clasp
Price: $25,100

Seventies Chronograph Panorama Date

Reference number: 1-37-02-03-02-30
Movement: automatic, GO Caliber 37-02;
ø 31.6 mm, height 8 mm; 65 jewels, 28,800 vph;
screw balance with 4 gold regulating screws, swan-neck fine adjustment; mainplate with côtes de Genéve, blued screws, skeletonized rotor with gold oscillating weight; 70-hour power reserve
Functions: hours, minutes, subsidiary seconds; power reserve indicator; flyback chronograph; panorama date
Case: stainless steel, 40 x 40 mm, height 13.5 mm; transparent case back; screw-in crown , water-resistant to 10 atm
Band: reptile skin, folding clasp
Price: $14,900

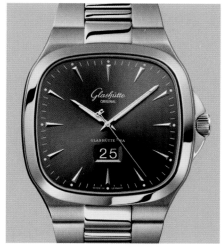

Seventies Panorama Date

Reference number: 2-39-47-12-12-14
Movement: automatic, GO Caliber 39-47;
ø 30.95 mm, height 5.9 mm; 39 jewels;
28,800 vph; swan-neck fine adjustment, three-quarter plate with Glashütte stripes, skeletonized rotor with gold oscillating weight; 40-hour power reserve
Functions: hours, minutes, sweep seconds; panorama date
Case: stainless steel, 40 x 40 mm, height 11.5 mm; sapphire crystal; transparent case back; screw-in crown; water-resistant to 10 atm
Band: reptile skin, folding clasp
Price: $10,100

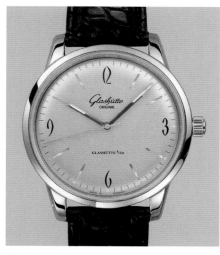

Sixties

Reference number: 1-39-52-01-02-04
Movement: automatic, GO Caliber 39-52; ø 26 mm, height 4.3 mm; 25 jewels; 28,800 vph; 40-hour power reserve
Functions: hours, minutes, sweep seconds
Case: stainless steel, ø 39 mm, height 9.4 mm; sapphire crystal; transparent case back
Band: reptile skin, buckle
Price: $7,500
Variations: black or blue dial ($7,500); rose gold ($15,000)

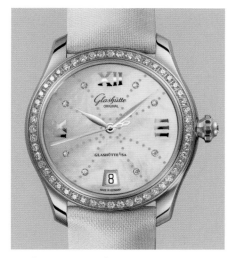

Lady Serenade

Reference number: 1-39-22-14-11-44
Movement: automatic, GO Caliber 39-22;
ø 26 mm, height 4.3 mm; 25 jewels; 28,800 vph; three-quarter plate, swan-neck fine adjustment, skeletonized rotor; 40-hour power reserve
Functions: hours, minutes, sweep seconds; date
Case: stainless steel, ø 36 mm, height 10.2 mm; 52 brilliant-cut diamonds on bezel; sapphire crystal; transparent case back; water-resistant to 5 atm
Band: reptile skin, buckle
Remarks: mother-of-pearl dial with diamonds
Price: $13,000
Variations: w/o diamond bezel ($7,300); rose gold with diamond bezel ($27,100); rose gold w/o diamonds ($20,600)

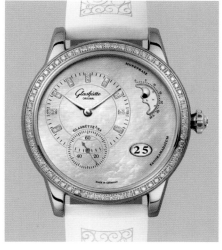

PanoMatic Luna

Reference number: 1-90-12-01-12-04
Movement: automatic, GO Caliber 90-12;
ø 32.6 mm, height 7 mm; 47 jewels; 28,800 vph; 42-hour power reserve
Functions: hours, minutes, subsidiary seconds; panorama date; moon phase
Case: stainless steel, ø 39.4 mm, height 12 mm; 64 brilliant-cut diamonds on bezel; sapphire crystal; transparent case back; water-resistant to 3 atm
Band: rubber, buckle
Price: $20,400
Variations: reptile skin band ($20,400); dark mother-of-pearl dial ($20,400)

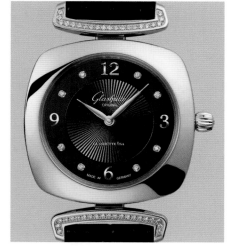

Pavonina

Reference number: 1-03-01-05-34-30
Movement: quartz
Functions: hours, minutes; date
Case: white gold, 31 x 31 mm, height 7.5 mm; sapphire crystal; water-resistant to 5 atm
Band: satin, buckle
Remarks: set with 513 brilliant-cut diamonds, only available in Glashütte Original boutiques
Price: $41,400
Variations: various bands, dials, and cases (from $5,200)

Caliber 37

Automatic; single barrel spring, 70-hour power reserve
Functions: hours, minutes, subsidiary seconds; power reserve indicator; flyback chronograph; panorama date
Diameter: 31.6 mm; **Height:** 8 mm; **Jewels:** 65
Balance: screw balance with 4 gold regulating screws
Frequency: 28,800 vph
Balance spring: flat hairspring, swan-neck fine adjustment
Remarks: finely finished movement, beveled edges, polished steel parts, blued screws, mainplate with Glashütte ribbing, skeletonized rotor with 21 kt gold oscillating mass

Caliber 39

Automatic; 40-hour power reserve
Functions: hours, minutes, sweep seconds (base caliber)
Diameter: 26.2 mm; **Height:** 4.3 mm
Jewels: 25
Frequency: 28,800 vph
Balance spring: flat hairspring, swan-neck fine adjustment
Shock protection: Incabloc
Related calibers: 39-55 (GMT, 40 jewels); 39-52 (automatic, 25 jewels); 39-50 (perpetual calendar, 48 jewels); 39-41/39-42 (panorama date, 44 jewels); 39-31 (chronograph, 51 jewels); 39-21/39-22 (date, 25 jewels)

Caliber 58-01

Manually wound; approx. 44-hour power reserve, second reset when crown is pulled allows precise setting of minutes and seconds
Functions: hours (off-center), minutes (off-center), subsidiary seconds; date (retrograde); power reserve indication with planetary gear; large date
Diameter: 35 mm; **Height:** 6.5 mm; **Jewels:** 58
Balance: screw balance with 18 weighted screws
Frequency: 28,800 vph
Remarks: components finely finished, beveled edges, polished steel parts, screw-mounted gold chatons, blued screws, swan-neck fine adjustment, three-quarter plate with Glashütte ribbing, hand-engraved balance cock

Caliber 61

Manually wound; 42-hour power reserve
Functions: hours, minutes, subsidiary seconds; chronograph with flyback function; panorama date
Diameter: 32.2 mm; **Height:** 7.2 mm
Jewels: 41
Balance: screw balance with 18 gold screws
Frequency: 28,800 vph
Balance spring: flat hairspring, swan-neck fine adjustment
Remarks: components finely finished, beveled edges, polished steel parts, screw-mounted gold chatons, blued screws, winding wheels with double sunburst pattern, bridges and cocks decorated with Glashütte ribbing, hand-engraved balance cock

Caliber 65

Manually wound; single spring barrel, 42-hour power reserve
Functions: hours (off-center), minutes (off-center), subsidiary seconds; power reserve indication
Diameter: 32.2 mm
Height: 6.1 mm
Jewels: 48
Balance: screw balance with 18 weighted screws
Frequency: 28,800 vph
Balance spring: flat hairspring, duplex swan-neck fine adjustment (for rate and beat)
Remarks: components finely finished, beveled edges, polished steel parts, screw-mounted gold chatons, blued screws

Caliber 89-02

Automatic; single barrel spring, 72-hour power reserve
Functions: hours, minutes, subsidiary seconds; world time display with 37 time zones, day/night indicator power reserve indicator; panorama date
Diameter: 39.2 mm
Height: 8 mm
Jewels: 63
Balance: screw balance with 4 gold regulating screws
Frequency: 28,800 vph
Balance spring: flat hairspring, duplex swan-neck fine regulator for rate and beat
Shock protection: Incabloc
Remarks: finely finished movement, three-quarter plate with Glashütte ribbing, hand-engraved escapement bridge

Caliber 90

Automatic; single spring barrel, 42-hour power reserve
Functions: hours, minutes (off-center), sweep seconds; panorama date; moon phase
Diameter: 32.6 mm; **Height:** 7 mm
Jewels: 41, 47, or 61; **Frequency:** 28,800 vph
Balance: screw balance with 18 gold screws
Balance spring: flat hairspring, duplex swan-neck fine adjustment (for rate and beat)
Shock protection: Incabloc
Remarks: components finely finished; hand-engraved balance cock; beveled edges, polished steel parts; three-quarter plate with Glashütte ribbing; off-center skeletonized rotor with gold oscillating weight

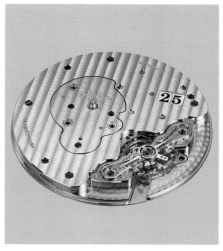

Caliber 91-02

Automatic; inverted movement with rate regulator on dial side; single spring barrel; 42-hour power reserve
Functions: hours and minutes (off-center), subsidiary seconds; panorama date
Diameter: 38.2 mm; **Height:** 7.1 mm
Jewels: 49
Balance: screw balance with 18 weighted screws
Frequency: 28,800 vph
Balance spring: flat hairspring, duplex swan-neck fine adjustment (for rate and beat)
Shock protection: Incabloc
Remarks: finely finished movement, beveled edges, polished steel parts, three-quarter plate with blued screws, with côtes de Genève, skeletonized rotor with gold oscillating mass, hand-engraved balance bridge

Caliber 93-02

Automatic; flying tourbillon, single spring barrel, 48-hour power reserve
Functions: hours, minutes (off-center), subsidiary seconds (on tourbillon cage); panorama date; moon phase
Diameter: 32.2 mm; **Height:** 7.65 mm
Jewels: 48
Balance: screw balance with 18 weighted screws in rotating frame
Frequency: 21,600 vph
Balance spring: flat hairspring
Remarks: finely finished movement, hand-engraved balance cock, beveled edges, polished steel parts, mainplate with Glashütte ribbing; oscillating, eccentric, skeletonized, gold weight

Caliber 94-03

Automatic; flying tourbillon; single spring barrel, 48-hour power reserve
Functions: hours, minutes, subsidiary seconds (on tourbillon cage); panorama date
Diameter: 32.2 mm
Height: 7.65 mm
Jewels: 50
Balance: screw balance with 18 weighted screws in rotating frame
Frequency: 21,600 vph
Balance spring: flat hairspring
Remarks: finely finished movement, beveled edges, polished steel parts, mainplate with Glashütte ribbing; oscillating, eccentric, skeletonized, gold weight

Caliber 96-01

Automatic; twin spring barrel, 2-speed bidirectional winding via stepped reduction gear, 42-hour power reserve
Functions: hours and minutes (off-center), subsidiary seconds; 2-digit counter (pusher-controlled, forward and backward); split-seconds chronograph with flyback function; large date
Diameter: 32.2 mm; **Height:** 8.9 mm; **Jewels:** 72
Balance: screw balance with 18 gold weight screws
Frequency: 28,800 vph
Balance spring: flat hairspring, swan-neck fine adjustment; **Shock protection:** Incabloc
Remarks: separate wheel bridges for winding and chronograph, finely finished, beveled edges, polished steel parts, screwed-in gold chatons, blued screws, hand-engraved balance cock

Caliber 100

Automatic; skeletonized rotor; reset mechanism for second hand via button on case; 55-hour power reserve
Functions: hours, minutes, sweep seconds; panorama date
Diameter: 31.15 mm
Height: 7.1 mm
Jewels: 59
Balance: screw balance with 18 gold screws
Frequency: 28,800 vph
Balance spring: flat hairspring
Related calibers: 100-01 (power reserve display); 100-02 (perpetual calendar); 100-03 (large date); 100-04 (moon phase); 100-05 (53 weeks); 100-06 (full calendar, moon phase)

Glycine Watch SA
Eckweg 8
CH-2500 Biel/Bienne
Switzerland

Tel.:
+41-32-341-2213

Fax:
+41-32-341-2216

E-Mail:
glycine@glycine-watch.ch

Website:
www.glycine-watch.ch

Founded:
1914

Number of employees:
8

U.S. Distributor:
DKSH Luxury & Lifestyle North America, Inc.
103 Carnegie Center, Suite 300
Princeton, NJ 08540
609-750-8800; 609-751-9370 (fax)
usc@glycine.us

Most important collections/price range:
Airman, Incursore, Combat / mechanical
watches between $1,250 and $4,950

Glycine

Founded in 1914 by Eugène Meylan, Glycine evolved into one of the industry's most innovative companies. It was already known early on for very large wristwatches, for instance. The venerable company also managed to weather the main crises of the twentieth century well, notably the Great Depression and World War II. In 1953, it came up with one of its iconic lines: 24-hour watches conceived for commercial pilots and swept up by early jet-setters. The collection is still the brand's flagship and available in both modern and newly produced retro versions.

In 1984, Hans Brechbühler took over a Glycine floundering during the quartz crisis and managed to save it from bankruptcy. Together with his youngest daughter, Katherina, he rebuilt the brand and positioned it as a specialist in robust pilot's and sports watches, which continued to be larger than those of the competition. In 2005, Katherina Brechbühler became CEO and added striking watches with an almost military look to the repertoire.

Over a century after the first Glycine watches hit the market, this dynamic company is forging ahead on a very independent path, with timekeepers that are always a little unconventional. Stephan Lack, who took over as CEO in 2011, presided over the 100th anniversary celebrations of this very traditional Swiss company.

Airman "Airfighter" Camouflage

Reference number: 3921
Movement: automatic, Caliber GL 754 (base ETA 7754); ø 30 mm, height 7.9 mm; 25 jewels; 28,800 vph; fine finishing; 46-hour power reserve
Functions: hours (24), minutes, sweep seconds; 24-hour display (2nd time zone); 3rd time zone with adjustable bezel; chronograph; date
Case: stainless steel with black PVD, ø 46 mm, height 14.95 mm; bidirectional bezel with 24-hour division, safety screws; sapphire crystal; transparent back; water-resistant to 20 atm
Band: textile, buckle
Remarks: chronograph control with sliding mechanism
Price: $4,950

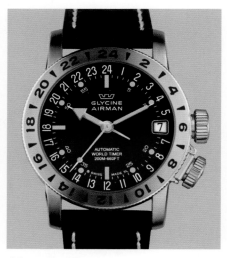

Airman 17

Reference number: 3917
Movement: automatic, Caliber GL 293 (base ETA 2893); ø 36.6 mm, height 7.9 mm; 24 jewels; 28,800 vph; finely finished with côtes de Genève and engraving; 42-hour power reserve
Functions: hours (24), minutes, sweep seconds; added 24-hour display (2nd time zone); 3rd time zone with adjustable bezel; chronograph; date
Case: stainless steel, ø 46 mm, height 15 mm; bidirectional bezel with 24-hour division; safety screws; sapphire crystal; water-resistant to 20 atm
Band: calf leather, buckle
Price: $2,825

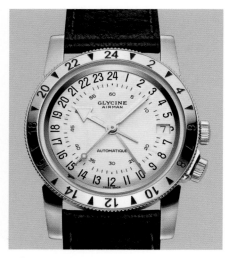

Airman No. 1

Reference number: 3944.11.LB77U
Movement: automatic, Caliber GL 293 (base ETA 2893); ø 25.6 mm, height 4.1 mm; 21 jewels; 28,800 vph; côtes de Genève; 42-hour power reserve
Functions: hours (24), minutes, sweep seconds; 24-hour display (2nd time zone); 3rd time zone with adjustable bezel; chronograph; date
Case: stainless steel, ø 36 mm, height 10.75 mm; bidirectional bezel with 24-hour division and safety screws; Plexiglas; transparent case back; screw-in crown; water-resistant to 10 atm
Band: calf leather, buckle
Remarks: dial coated entirely with luminescent mass
Price: $2,600

Graham

In the mid-1990s, unusual creations gave an old English name in watchmaking a brand-new life. In the eighteenth century, George Graham perfected the cylinder escapement and the dead-beat escapement as well as inventing the chronograph. For these contributions and more, Graham certainly earned the right to be considered one of the big wheels in watchmaking history.

Despite his merits in the development of precision timekeeping, it was the mechanism he invented to measure short times—the chronograph—that became the trademark of his wristwatch company. To this day, the fundamental principle of the chronograph hasn't changed at all: A second set of hands can be engaged to or disengaged from the constant flow of energy of the movement. Given The British Masters' aim to honor this English inventor, it is certainly no surprise that the Graham collection includes quite a number of fascinating chronograph variations.

In 2000, the company released its Chronofighter, whose striking thumb-controlled lever mechanism—a modern twist on a function designed for WWII British fighter pilots, who couldn't activate the crown button of their flight chronographs with their thick gloves on—is a perfect example of why luxury watches are one of the male world's most beloved toys. Recently, Graham has also added comparatively conventionally designed watches to its collection. For lovers of special pieces, there are the models of the Geo.Graham series. It was the name used by the brilliant watchmaker-inventor, and The Moon, developed in collaboration with Christophe Claret, is a perfect exemplar of the line featuring a beautifully finished flying tourbillon with a stunning retrograde moon phase.

Graham
Boulevard des Eplatures 38
CH-2300 La Chaux-de-Fonds
Switzerland

Tel.:
+41-32-910-9888

Fax:
+41-32-910-9889

E-Mail:
info@graham1695.com

Website:
www.graham1695.com

Founded:
1995

Number of employees:
approx. 30

Annual production:
5,000–7,000 watches

U.S. distributor:
Graham USA
510 W. 6th Street, Suite 309
Los Angeles, CA 90014
213-622-1716

Most important collections:
Tourbillograph, Chronofighter, Silverstone, Swordfish

Geo.Graham Tourbillon Orrery

Reference number: 2GGBP.B01A
Movement: manually wound, Graham Caliber G1800 (Christophe Claret base); ø 39 mm, height 10.5 mm; 35 jewels; 21,600 vph; 1-minute tourbillon, mechanical model of solar system with sculptural planets, 2 spring barrels; côtes de Genève; 72-hour power reserve
Functions: hours, minutes, (off-center); 100-year calendar with date/month indicator, zodiac/year display (case back); sculptural planets
Case: red gold, ø 48 mm, height 17.6 mm; sapphire crystal; transparent case back; water-resistant to 5 atm
Band: reptile skin, buckle
Price: on request; limited to 20 pieces

Geo.Graham Tourbillon

Reference number: 2GGCP.W01A
Movement: automatic, Graham Caliber G 1769; ø 30 mm, height 5.4 mm; 29 jewels; 21,600 vph; 1-minute tourbillon, 2 spring barrels, microrotor; côtes de Genève; 72-hour power reserve
Functions: hours, minutes
Case: pink gold, ø 40 mm, height 9.5 mm; sapphire crystal; transparent case back; water-resistant to 5 atm
Band: reptile skin, folding clasp
Price: $80,420; limited to 100 pieces

Chronofighter Oversize

Reference number: 2CCAU.B02A.T13N
Movement: automatic, Graham Caliber G 1747; ø 30 mm, height 8 mm; 25 jewels; 28,800 vph; 48-hour power reserve
Functions: hours, minutes, subsidiary seconds; chronograph; date
Case: stainless steel with black PVD coating, ø 47 mm, height 15 mm; ceramic bezel, sapphire crystal; transparent case back; crown, pusher, carbon finger lever on left; water-resistant to 10 atm
Band: textile, ceramic buckle
Price: $6,900

Chronofighter Oversize Black Arrow

Reference number: 2CCAU.G02A.K94N
Movement: automatic, Graham Caliber G 1747; ø 30 mm, height 8 mm; 25 jewels; 28,800 vph; 48-hour power reserve
Functions: hours, minutes, subsidiary seconds; chronograph; date
Case: stainless steel with black PVD coating; ø 47 mm, height 15 mm; ceramic bezel, sapphire crystal; transparent case back; crown, pusher, carbon finger lever on left; water-resistant to 10 atm
Band: rubber, ceramic buckle
Price: $8,050

Chronofighter Oversize Superlight Carbon

Reference number: 2CCBK.B11A.K95K
Movement: automatic, Graham Caliber G 1747; ø 30 mm, height 8 mm; 25 jewels; 28,800 vph; 48-hour power reserve
Functions: hours, minutes, subsidiary seconds; chronograph; date
Case: carbon nanofiber composite; ø 47 mm, height 15 mm; sapphire crystal; transparent case back; crown, pusher, carbon finger lever on left; water-resistant to 10 atm
Band: rubber, buckle
Price: $11,550

Silverstone RS Endurance 24H

Reference number: 2STCB.B03A.K89H
Movement: automatic, Graham Caliber G1751; ø 30 mm; 25 jewels; 28,800 vph; single pusher for chronograph functions; separate, controllable 24-hour counter with flyback function; 48-hour power reserve
Functions: hours, minutes, subsidiary seconds; chronograph; date
Case: stainless steel with black DLC coating, ø 46 mm, height 15 mm; ceramic bezel with aluminum ring, sapphire crystal; transparent case back; crown with bayonet locking; water-resistant to 10 atm
Band: rubber, folding clasp
Price: $14,580; limited to 250 pieces

Silverstone RS GMT

Reference number: 2STDC.B08A.L119F
Movement: automatic, Graham Caliber G 1721; ø 30 mm, height 8.85 mm; 28 jewels; 28,800 vph; 48-hour power reserve
Functions: hours, minutes, subsidiary seconds; added 24-hour display (2nd time zone); flyback chronograph; large date
Case: stainless steel, ø 46 mm, height 16.95 mm; sapphire crystal; transparent case back; screw-in crown; water-resistant to 10 atm
Band: calf leather, buckle
Price: $12,780; limited to 250 pieces

Silverstone RS Racing

Reference number: 2STEA.U02A.K107F
Movement: automatic, Graham Caliber G1749 (base ETA 7750); ø 30 mm, height 7.9 mm; 25 jewels; 28,800 vph; 48-hour power reserve
Functions: hours, minutes, subsidiary seconds; chronograph; weekday, date
Case: stainless steel, ø 46 mm, height 16.1 mm; sapphire crystal; transparent case back; water-resistant to 10 atm
Band: rubber, buckle
Price: $5,780

Chronofighter Oversize GMT

Reference number: 2OVGS.B39A.C118F
Movement: automatic, Graham Caliber G1733 (base ETA 7750); ø 30 mm, height 8.4 mm; 28 jewels; 28,800 vph; 48-hour power reserve
Functions: hours, minutes, subsidiary seconds; added 24-hour display (2nd time zone); chronograph; large date
Case: stainless steel, ø 47 mm, height 16.5 mm; bezel with 24-hour divisions; sapphire crystal; transparent case back; crown with chrono pusher and finger level on left side; water-resistant to 10 atm
Band: reptile skin, buckle
Price: $10,300

Greubel Forsey

Each year, at the SIHH, the journalists visit brands. But they congregate at the Greubel Forsey booth to take part in something close to a religious experience, an initiation into the esoteric art of *ultra-haute horlogerie*.

In 2004, when Alsatian Robert Greubel and Englishman Stephen Forsey presented a new movement at Baselworld, eyes snapped open: Their watch featured not one, but *two* tourbillon carriages working at a 30° incline. In their design, Forsey and Greubel not only took up the basic Abraham-Louis Breguet idea of cancelling out the deviations of the balance by the continuous rotation of the tourbillon cage, but they went further, creating a quadruple tourbillon.

In 2010, Greubel Forsey moved into new facilities at a renovated farmhouse between Le Locle and La Chaux-de-Fonds and a brand-new modern building. After capturing an Aiguille D'Or for the magical Double Tourbillon 30° and the Grand Prix d'Horlogerie in Geneva, these two specialists snatched up the top prize at the International Chronometry Competition in Le Locle for the Double Tourbillon 30°.

Greubel and Forsey continue to stun the highest-end fans with some spectacular pieces, like the Quadruple Tourbillon Secret, which shows the complex play of the tourbillons through the case back, and the Greubel Forsey GMT with the names of world cities and a huge floating globe. Their first Art Piece came out in 2013, a most natural collaboration with British miniaturist Willard Wigan, who can sculpt the head of a pin. The latest Art Piece celebrates Robert Filliou, an artist from the freewheeling, multilayered, anti-movement Fluxus—evidence that these two serious watchmaking masters have a deep sense of irony as well.

Greubel Forsey SA

Eplatures-Grise 16
CH-2301 La Chaux-de-Fonds
Switzerland

Tel.:
+41-32-925-4545

Fax:
+41-32-925-4500

E-Mail:
info@greubelforsey.com

Website:
www.greubelforsey.com

Founded:
2004

Number of employees:
approx. 75

Annual production:
approx. 100 watches

U.S. distributor:
Time Art Distribution
550 Fifth Avenue
New York, NY 10036
212-221-5842
info@timeartdistribution.com

Remarks:
Prices given only in Swiss francs. Use daily exchange rate for conversion.

GMT Black

Reference number: GF05 9100 6139
Movement: manually wound, Caliber GF 05; ø 36.4 mm, height 9.8 mm; 50 jewels; 21,600 vph; 24-second tourbillon cage inclined at 25° angle; 2 coaxial series-coupled fast rotating barrels; 72-hour power reserve
Functions: titanium rotating globe with universal time display, 24-time zone world-time display, DST indicator, day/night indicator; power reserve indicator; hour and minute display, small second indicator
Case: titanium with black ADLC coating, ø 43.5 mm, height 16.14 mm; sapphire crystal; transparent case back; water-resistant to 3 atm
Band: rubber, black ADLC titanium folding clasp
Price: CHF 510,000; limited to 22 pieces

Art Piece 1 Robert Filliou

Movement: manually wound, Caliber GF 02w; ø 36.4 mm, height 10.95 mm; 21,000 vph; 35 jewels; 24-second tourbillon cage inclined at 25° angle; 2 coaxial series-coupled fast rotating barrels; 72-hour power reserve
Functions: hours, minutes, subsidiary seconds; power reserve indicator
Case: white gold, ø 44 mm, height 16.78 mm; sapphire crystal; transparent case back
Band: calf leather, folding clasp
Remarks: integrated Willard Wigan bowler hat nanosculpture with works by Fluxus artists at Filliou's exhibition Chapeaux!; 23x magnification
Price: on request

Tourbillon 24 Secondes Vision

Reference number: 9100 5850
Movement: manually wound, Caliber GF 01r; ø 36.4 mm, height 7.09 mm; 41 jewels; 21,600 vph; 24-second tourbillon cage inclined at 25° angle; 72-hour power reserve
Functions: hours, minutes, subsidiary seconds
Case: white gold, ø 43.5 mm, height 13.65 mm; sapphire crystal; transparent case back with sapphire dome; water-resistant to 3 atm
Band: reptile skin, white gold buckle
Price: CHF 290,000; limited to 22 pieces

Habring Uhrentechnik OG

Hauptplatz 16
A-9100 Völkermarkt
Austria

Tel.:
+43-4232-51-300

Fax:
+43-4232-51-300-4

E-Mail:
info@habring.com

Website:
www.habring2.com; www.habring.com

Founded:
1997

Number of employees:
4

Annual production:
150 watches

U.S. distributors:
Martin Pulli (USA-East)
215-508-4610
www.martinpulli.com
Passion Fine Jewelry (USA-West)
858-794-8000
www.passionfinejewelry.com

Most important collections/price range:
Felix / from $5,450; Jumping Second / from
$6,450; Doppel 3 / from $8,250; Chrono
COS / from $7,150

Habring²

Fine mechanical works of art are created with smaller and larger complications in a small workshop in Austria's Völkermarkt, where the name Habring² stands for an unusual joint project. "We only come in a set," Maria Kristina Habring jokes. Her husband, Richard, adds with a grin, "You get double for your money here." The couple's first watch labeled with their own name came out in 2004: a simple, congenial three-handed watch based on a refined and unostentatiously decorated ETA pocket watch movement, the Unitas 6498-1. In connoisseur circles the news spread like wildfire that exceptional quality down to the smallest detail was hidden behind its inconspicuous specifications.

Since then, they have put their efforts into such projects as completely revamping the Time Only, powered by brand-new base movement Caliber A09. All the little details that differentiate this caliber are either especially commissioned or are made in-house. Caliber A09 is available both as a manually wound movement (A09M) and a bidirectionally wound automatic with an exclusive gear system. Its sporty version drives a pilot's watch. Also more or less in-house are the components of the Seconde Foudroyante. Because the drive needs a lot of energy, the foudroyante mechanism has been given its own spring barrel. In the Caliber A07F, the eighth of a second is driven by a gear train directly coupled with the movement without surrendering any reliability, power reserve, or amplitude.

For the twentieth anniversary of the IWC double chronograph, Habring² has built a limited, improved edition. The movement, based on the ETA 7750 "Valjoux," was conceived in 1991/1992 with an additional module between the chronograph and automatic winder. With new processes like deep reacting ion etching allowing many brands to create their own escapements, Habring² still remains true to traditional materials like steel. "Being able to make a pallet lever is not only having command of a key technology," says Maria, "it's the best way to remain competitive in an unevenly distributed field."

Felix

Reference number: Felix
Movement: manually wound, Habring Caliber A11B; ø 30 mm, height 4.2 mm; 18 jewels; 28,800 vph; Triovis fine adjustment; finely finished; 48-hour power reserve
Functions: hours, minutes, subsidiary seconds
Case: stainless steel, ø 38.5 mm, height 7 mm; sapphire crystal; transparent case back; water-resistant to 3 atm
Band: calf leather, buckle
Price: $5,450

Jumping Second Pilot

Reference number: Jumping Second Pilot
Movement: manually wound, Caliber A11MS; ø 36.6 mm, height 7 mm; 20 jewels; 28,800 vph; Triovis fine adjustment
Functions: hours, minutes, dead beat seconds
Case: stainless steel, ø 42 mm, height 13 mm; sapphire crystal; transparent case back; water-resistant to 5 atm
Band: calf leather, buckle
Price: $6,450
Variations: automatic; various dials

Jumping Second Date

Reference number: Jumping Second Date
Movement: automatic, Caliber A11SD; ø 36.6 mm, height 7.9 mm; 24 jewels; 28,800 vph
Functions: hours, minutes, sweep seconds (jumping); date
Case: stainless steel, ø 42 mm, sapphire crystal; transparent case back
Band: calf leather, buckle
Price: $7,250
Variations: w/o date display; various dials

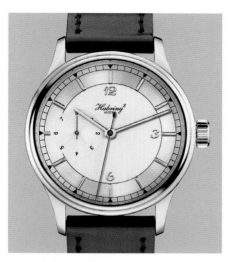

Foudroyante

Reference number: Foudroyante
Movement: manually wound, Caliber A11MF;
ø 30 mm, height 7 mm; 20 jewels; 28,800 vph;
Triovis fine adjustment
Functions: hours, minutes, dead beat seconds,
eighth of a second display (flashing second or
"foudroyante")
Case: stainless steel, ø 42 mm, height 13 mm;
sapphire crystal; transparent case back; water-
resistant to 5 atm
Band: calf leather, buckle
Price: $7,650
Variations: automatic; various dials

Chrono Mono

Reference number: Chrono Mono
Movement: automatic, Habring Caliber A08;
25 jewels; 28,800 vph; 1 pusher control of
chronograph functions; 42-hour power reserve
Functions: hours, minutes, subsidiary seconds;
chronograph
Case: stainless steel, ø 42 mm, height 13 mm;
sapphire crystal; water-resistant to 5 atm
Band: calf leather, buckle
Price: $5,450

Chrono COS

Reference number: Chrono COS
Movement: automatic, Caliber A08COS; ø 30 mm,
height 7.9 mm; 25 jewels; 28,800 vph; Triovis fine
adjustment; crown control of chronograph functions
Functions: hours, minutes, subsidiary seconds;
chronograph
Case: stainless steel, ø 42 mm, height 13 mm;
sapphire crystal; transparent case back; water-
resistant to 5 atm
Band: calf leather, buckle
Price: $7,150
Variations: titanium; manual winding; various dials

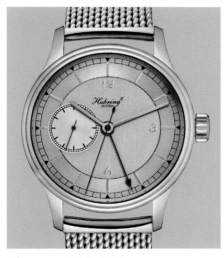

Chrono COS ZM

Reference number: Chrono COS ZM
Movement: manually wound, Caliber A08MCOSZM;
ø 30 mm, height 7 mm; 17 jewels; 28,800 vph;
Triovis fine adjustment; central minute totalizer;
crown control of chronograph functions
Functions: hours, minutes, sweep seconds;
chronograph
Case: stainless steel, ø 42 mm, height 13 mm;
sapphire crystal; transparent case back; water-
resistant to 5 atm
Band: stainless steel Milanese mesh, folding clasp
Price: $7,550
Variations: titanium; various dial variations

Doppel 3

Reference number: Doppel 3
Movement: manually wound, Caliber A08MR-
MONO; ø 30 mm, height 8.4 mm; 23 jewels;
28,800 vph; Triovis fine adjustment; 48-hour power
reserve
Functions: hours, minutes, subsidiary seconds;
split-seconds chronograph
Case: titanium, ø 42 mm, height 13 mm; sapphire
crystal; transparent case back; water-resistant to
5 atm
Band: leather, buckle
Remarks: limited to 20 pieces per year
Price: $8,250
Variations: various dials

Doppel 3.1

Reference number: Doppel 3.1
Movement: manually wound, Caliber A08MR;
ø 30 mm, height 8.4 mm; 23 jewels; 28,800 vph;
Triovis fine adjustment; chronograph with sweep
minute totalizer; 48-hour power reserve
Functions: hours, minutes, subsidiary seconds;
split-second chronograph
Case: stainless steel, ø 42 mm, height 13 mm;
sapphire crystal; transparent case back; water-
resistant to 5 atm
Band: calf leather, buckle
Remarks: limited to 20 pieces per year
Price: $8,650
Variations: various dial designs

Hamilton International Ltd.

Mattenstrasse 149
CH-2503 Biel/Bienne
Switzerland

Tel.:
+41-32-343-4004

Fax:
+41-32-343-4006

Email:
info@hamiltonwatch.com

Website:
www.hamiltonwatch.com

Founded:
1892

U.S. distributor:
Hamilton
The Swatch Group, Inc.
1200 Harbor Boulevard
Weehawken, NJ 07087
201-271-1400
www.hamilton-watch.com

Price range:
between approx. $500 and $2,500

Hamilton

The Hamilton Watch Co. was founded in 1892 in Lancaster, Pennsylvania, and, within a very brief period, grew into one of the world's largest *manufactures*. Around the turn of the twentieth century, every second railway employee in the United States was carrying a Hamilton watch in his pocket, not only to make sure the trains were running punctually, but also to assist in coordinating them and organizing schedules. And during World War II, the American army officers' kits included a service Hamilton.

Hamilton is the sole survivor of the large U.S. watchmakers—if only as a brand within the Swiss Swatch Group. At one time, Hamilton had itself owned a piece of the Swiss watchmaking industry in the form of the Büren brand in the 1960s and 1970s. As part of a joint venture with Heuer-Leonidas, Breitling, and Dubois Dépraz, Hamilton-Büren also made a significant contribution to the development of the automatic chronograph. Just prior in its history, the tuning fork watch pioneer was all the rage when it took the new movement technology and housed it in a modern case created by renowned industrial designer Richard Arbib. The triangular Ventura hit the watch-world ground running in 1957, in what was truly a frenzy of innovation. The American spirit of freedom and belief in progress this model embodies, something evoked in Hamilton's current marketing, are taken quite seriously by its designers—even those working in Biel, Switzerland. The collection today is dominated by models that recall the glory days of the 1950s and 1960s. As such, they are absolutely trendy.

Khaki Chrono Worldtimer

Reference number: H76714335
Movement: quartz, Hamilton Caliber H-41e
Functions: hours, minutes, subsidiary seconds; world-time display (2nd time zone); chronograph; date
Case: stainless steel, ø 45 mm; sapphire crystal; water-resistant to 10 atm
Band: rubber, buckle
Price: $1,295

Ventura "Elvis 80" Auto

Reference number: H24585331
Movement: automatic, Hamilton Caliber H-10 (base ETA 2824-2); ø 25.6 mm, height 4.6 mm; 25 jewels; 28,800 vph; 80-hour power reserve
Functions: hours, minutes, sweep seconds; date
Case: stainless steel with black PVD coating, 42.5 x 44.6 mm; sapphire crystal; transparent case back; water-resistant to 5 atm
Band: rubber, buckle
Price: $1,495

Khaki Navy Pioneer Auto Chrono

Reference number: H77706553
Movement: automatic, Hamilton Caliber H-21; ø 30 mm, height 7.9 mm; 25 jewels; 28,800 vph; 60-hour power reserve
Functions: hours, minutes, subsidiary seconds; chronograph; date
Case: stainless steel, ø 44 mm; sapphire crystal; transparent case back; water-resistant to 10 atm
Band: calf leather, buckle
Price: $1,895

Pan Europ

Reference number: H35405741
Movement: automatic, Hamilton Caliber H30 (base ETA 2834-2); ø 25.6 mm, height 5.05 mm; 29 jewels; 28,800 vph; 80-hour power reserve
Functions: hours, minutes, sweep seconds; date, weekday
Case: stainless steel, ø 42 mm; unidirectional bezel with 60-minute divisions, sapphire crystal; transparent case back; water-resistant to 5 atm
Band: calf leather, folding clasp
Remarks: comes with leather strap, canvas strap and changing tool
Price: $1,195

Railroad Skeleton

Reference number: H40655751
Movement: automatic, Hamilton Caliber H-10 (base ETA 2824-2); ø 25.6 mm, height 4.6 mm; 25 jewels; 28,800 vph; partially skeletonized; 80-hour power reserve
Functions: hours, minutes, sweep seconds
Case: stainless steel, ø 42 mm, height 11.2 mm; sapphire crystal; transparent case back; water-resistant to 5 atm
Band: calf leather, buckle
Remarks: skeletonized dial
Price: $1,345

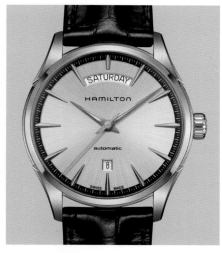

Jazzmaster Day-Date

Reference number: H42565751
Movement: automatic, Hamilton Caliber H-40 (base ETA 2834-2); ø 29 mm, height 5.05 mm; 25 jewels; 28,800 vph; 80-hour power reserve
Functions: hours, minutes, sweep seconds; date, weekday
Case: stainless steel, ø 42 mm; sapphire crystal; transparent case back; water-resistant to 5 atm
Band: calf leather, folding clasp
Price: $1,045

Khaki Takeoff Air Zermatt

Reference number: H76695733
Movement: automatic, Hamilton Caliber H-10 (base ETA 2824-2); ø 25.6 mm, height 4.6 mm; 25 jewels; 28,800 vph; 80-hour power reserve
Functions: hours, minutes, sweep seconds; date
Case: stainless steel, special alloy, with black PVD coating, ø 42 mm; bidirectional bezel with 60-minute divisions; sapphire crystal; water-resistant to 5 atm
Band: calf leather with rubber inlay, buckle
Price: $1,195

Jazzmaster Auto Chrono

Reference number: H32596181
Movement: automatic, Hamilton Caliber H-21 (base ETA 7750); ø 30 mm, height 7.9 mm; 25 jewels; 28,800 vph; 60-hour power reserve
Functions: hours, minutes, subsidiary seconds; chronograph; date
Case: stainless steel, ø 42 mm, height 15.23 mm; sapphire crystal; transparent case back; water-resistant to 10 atm
Band: stainless steel, folding clasp
Price: $1,495

Jazzmaster Skeleton Lady

Reference number: H42405991
Movement: automatic, Hamilton Caliber H-20-S (base ETA_2824); ø 25.6 mm, height 4.6 mm; 25 jewels; 28,800 vph; partially skeletonized; 40-hour power reserve
Functions: hours, minutes, sweep seconds
Case: stainless steel, ø 36 mm; 68 diamonds on bezel; sapphire crystal; transparent case back; water-resistant to 5 atm
Band: satin, buckle
Remarks: skeletonized dial
Price: $2,695

Hanhart 1882 GmbH

Hauptstrasse 33
D-78148 Gütenbach
Germany

Tel.:
+49-7723-93-44-20

Fax:
+49-7723-93-44-40

E-Mail:
info@hanhart.com

Website:
www.hanhart.com

Founded:
1882 in Diessenhofen, Switzerland;
in Germany since 1902

Number of employees:
35

Annual production:
approx. 1,000 chronographs and 150,000
stopwatches

U.S. distributor:
Thomas Plocher, Hanhart 1882 LLC
3801 East Florida Avenue, Suite 400
Denver, CO 80210
970-215-5317; 303-800-5889 (fax)

Most important collections/price range:
Mechanical stopwatches / from approx.
$600; Pioneer / from approx. $1,090;
Primus / from approx. $2,600

Hanhart

In 2012, Hanhart celebrated its 130th anniversary. But its reputation really goes back to the twenties and thirties. At the time, the brand manufactured affordable and robust stopwatches, pocket watches, and chronograph wristwatches. These core timepieces were what the fans of instrument watches wanted, and so they were thrilled as the company slowly abandoned its quartz dabbling of the eighties and reset its sights on the brand's rich and honorable tradition. A new collection was in the wings, raising expectations of great things to come. Support by the shareholding Gaydoul Group provided the financial backbone to get things moving.

The first step was to move company headquarters to the Swiss town of Diessenhofen, leaving the factory and technical offices in the Black Forest town of Gütenbach, Germany. The company's motto thus became "German engineering, Swiss made"; its goal, expanding exports into new key markets using three solid collections: two chronographs, the Pioneer and Primus, and the ClassicTimer stopwatches.

In spite of effort and money, however, Hanhart was not able to get back off the ground. Following bankruptcy, the company reorganized under the name Hanhart 1822 GmbH and moved everything to its German hometown. It has also returned to its stylistic roots: The characteristic red start/stop pusher grace the new collections, even on the bi-compax chronos of the Racemasters, which come with a smooth bezel.

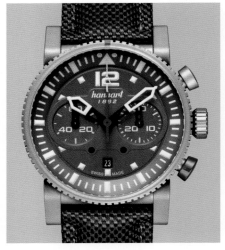

PRIMUS Survivor Pilot

Reference number: 740.290-3820
Movement: automatic, Caliber HAN3809 (based on ETA 7750); ø 30 mm, height 7.9 mm; 28 jewels; 28,800 vph; 42-hour power reserve
Functions: hours, minutes, subsidiary seconds; chronograph; date
Case: sand-blasted stainless steel, ø 44 mm, height 15 mm; sapphire crystal; transparent case back; screw-in crown; water-resistant to 10 atm
Band: textile, folding clasp
Remarks: flexible lugs
Price: $2,970

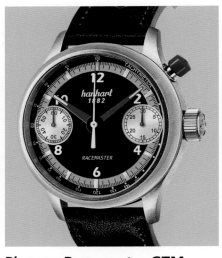

Pioneer Racemaster GTM

Reference number: 737.670-0010
Movement: automatic, Caliber HAN4212 (based on ETA 7750); ø 30 mm, height 8.7 mm; 31 jewels; 28,800 vph; single pusher control for chronograph functions; 42-hour power reserve
Functions: hours, minutes, subsidiary seconds; chronograph
Case: stainless steel, ø 45 mm, height 16 mm; sapphire crystal; water-resistant to 10 atm
Band: calf leather, buckle
Price: $3,080

Pioneer TachyTele

Reference number: 712.200-0110
Movement: automatic, Caliber HAN3703 (based on ETA 7753); ø 30 mm, height 7.9 mm; 27 jewels; 28,800 vph; 42-hour power reserve
Functions: hours, minutes, subsidiary seconds; chronograph
Case: stainless steel, ø 40 mm, height 15 mm; bidirectional bezel with reference marker; sapphire crystal; water-resistant to 10 atm
Band: calf leather, buckle
Price: $2,050
Variations: black dial

Harry Winston

Swatch Group's purchase of the luxury brand Harry Winston in early 2013 for $1 billion came as something of a surprise. But considering the upward flow of money worldwide, banking on a proven high-end luxury brand would seem obvious. On his many travels, founder Harry Winston (1896–1978) bought, recut, and set some of the twentieth century's greatest precious gems. He was succeeded by his son Ronald, a gifted craftsman himself with several patents in precious metals processing.

It was Ronald who added watches to the company's portfolio, inaugurating two lines: one showcasing the finest precious gems to dovetail with the company's overall focus and one containing clever, complicated timepieces. The result was the stunning Opus line launched by Harry Winston Rare Timepieces. Each of the thirteen models has been developed in conjunction with one exceptional independent watchmaker in very small series and contains an exclusive *manufacture* movement. The roster of artist-engineers who have participated reads like a *Who's Who* of independent watchmaking, including François-Paul Journe, Vianney Halter, Felix Baumgartner, and Greubel Forsey all the way to Denis Giguet and Emmanuel Bouchet. For the Opus XIII, the brand drew on the skills of Ludovic Ballouard. An extremely complex movement flicks fifty-nine metal pins to show the minutes and eleven triangles to show the hours. At twelve and noon, the dial cover opens to reveal the Harry Winston logo.

In May 2013, Nayla Hayek, daughter of Swatch founder Nicolas Hayek, became CEO of the brand. A year after, Harry Winston started presenting models that are benefiting from the new sister brands in the huge group, notably Blancpain.

Harry Winston, Inc.
718 Fifth Avenue
New York, NY 10019

Tel.:
800-848-3948

Website:
www.harrywinston.com

Founded:
1989

Most important collections:
Avenue, Midnight, Premier, Ocean, Opus

Histoire de Tourbillon 6

Reference number: HCOMTT55WW001
Movement: manually wound, Harry Winston Caliber HW4303; 40.9 x 45.08 mm, height 17.3 mm; 90 jewels; 21,600 vph; triaxial tourbillon (45, 75, 300 seconds), variable inertia balance with gold adjustment screws; Phillips end curve, 2 serially coupled spring barrels, 80 hours and 70 hours resp.
Functions: hours/minutes (off-center disc display), subsidiary seconds (on tourbillon cage at 8); power reserve indicator
Case: titanium with PVD coating; 55 x 49 mm, height 21.8 mm; white gold/rubber crown; sapphire crystals on hours/tourbillon; transparent back; water-resistant to 3 atm
Band: reptile skin, white gold buckle
Price: $722,900; limited to 20 pieces

Harry Winston Midnight Stalactites Automatic 36 mm

Reference number: MIDAHM36RR001
Movement: automatic, Harry Winston Caliber HW2008; ø 26.2 mm, height 3.37 mm; 28 jewels; 28,800 vph; balance spring, skeletonized rotor in white gold, circular côtes de Genève
Functions: hours, minutes (off-center); date (retrograde); moon phase
Case: white gold, ø 36 mm, height 9 mm; sapphire crystal; transparent case back; water-resistant to 3 atm
Band: reptile skin, buckle
Remarks: 84 diamonds on case, mother-of-pearl dial with 161 brilliant-cut diamonds in "stalactite" décor
Price: $34,400
Variations: pink gold

Project Z8

Reference number: OCEATZ44ZZ009
Movement: automatic, Harry Winston Caliber HW3502; ø 32 mm, height 5.2 mm; 32 jewels; 28,800 vph; balance spring, skeletonized rotor in white gold, circular côtes de Genève
Functions: hours, minutes (off-center); additional 12-hour indicator (2nd time zone, retrograde); day/night indicator; date, shuriken-shaped power reserve indicator
Case: Zalium, ø 44.2 mm, height 21.7 mm; sapphire crystal; transparent case back; water-resistant to 10 atm
Band: rubber, buckle
Price: $20,300; limited to 300 pieces

Premier Chronograph 40 mm

Reference number: PRNQCH40RR002
Movement: quartz
Functions: hours, minutes, subsidiary seconds; chronograph; date
Case: rose gold, ø 40 mm, height 9.5 mm; 57 brilliant-cut diamonds on bezel, sapphire crystal; diamond on crown; water-resistant to 3 atm
Band: reptile skin, buckle, with 42 brilliant-cut diamonds
Remarks: mother-of-pearl dial with 135 brilliant-cut diamonds
Price: $48,100
Variations: various bands and dials

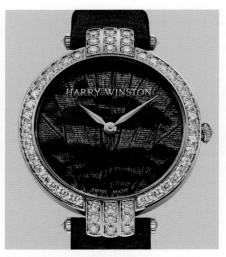

Premier Precious Butterfly Automatic 36 mm

Reference number: PRNAHM36WW004
Movement: automatic, Harry Winston Caliber HW2008; ø 26.2 mm, height 3.37 mm; 28 jewels; 28,800 vph; balance spring, skeletonized rotor in white gold, circular côtes de Genève, rhodium plating
Functions: hours, minutes
Case: white gold, ø 36 mm, height 8.4 mm; 57 brilliant-cut diamonds on bezel, sapphire crystal; diamond on crown; water-resistant to 3 atm
Band: black "tech" satin, white gold buckle, 17 diamonds
Remarks: *Chrysiridia madagascariensis* butterfly marquetry on dial
Price: $42,500

Harry Winston Avenue C Precious Marquetry

Reference number: AVCQHM19WW139
Movement: quartz
Functions: hours, minutes
Case: white gold, 19 x 39.5 mm, height 6.7 mm; 43 brilliant-cut diamonds on bezel, sapphire crystal; water-resistant to 3 atm
Band: reptile skin, buckle
Remarks: dial with marquetry of various mother-of-pearl color inlays and 44 brilliant-cut diamonds
Price: $41,500

Harry Winston Avenue Dual Time Automatic

Reference number: AVEATZ37RR001
Movement: automatic, Caliber HW3502; ø 32 mm, height 5.2 mm; 32 jewels; 28,800 vph; flat silicon spring, white gold rotor; côtes de Genève; circular grain, beveled bridges
Functions: hours, minutes; 2nd time zone (retrograde); day/night indicator; date
Case: Sedna gold, 53.8 x 35.8 mm, height 10.7 mm; sapphire crystal; transparent back; water-resistant to 3 atm
Band: reptile skin, Sedna gold buckle
Remarks: sapphire crystal dial, emerald appliques
Price: $38,300
Variations: Zalium, band with Zalium buckle ($22,200)

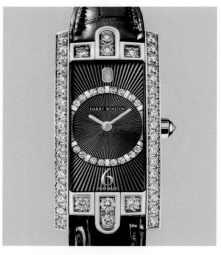

Harry Winston Avenue C Art Deco

Reference number: AVCQHM19WW130
Movement: quartz
Functions: hours, minutes
Case: white gold, 19 x 39.5 mm, height 7.8 mm; 43 brilliant-cut diamonds on bezel, sapphire crystal; diamond on crown; water-resistant to 3 atm
Band: reptile skin, folding clasp
Price: $34,800
Variations: rose gold; various bands and dials

Harry Winston Avenue C Mini Lily Cluster

Reference number: AVCQHM16RR042
Movement: quartz
Functions: hours, minutes
Case: rose gold, 15.6 x 32.3 mm, height 9.5 mm; 47 brilliant-cut diamonds on bezel, sapphire crystal; diamond on crown; water-resistant to 3 atm
Band: reptile skin, folding clasp
Remarks: mother-of-pearl dial with 34 brilliant-cut diamonds
Price: $31,100
Variations: white gold; various bands

Hautlence

Time can be read in so many ways. Back in 2004, after spending years in the Swiss watch industry, Guillaume Tetu and Renaud de Retz decided that their idea for tracking it was new and unique. They were not watchmakers, but they knew whom to bring on board for the genesis of Hautlence, an anagram of Neuchâtel, the town where their small company is located. And soon, the first HL model was produced: a fairly large, rectangular timepiece with the ratios of a television set and a lively and visible mechanical life. All good things in watchmaking being small, the big innovation was a "connecting rod," as Tetu calls it, to propel the hour disk. When the retrograde minute hand reaches the end of its arc, it triggers the rod, which advances the hour.

Having survived the Great Recession, Hautlence persisted thinned down and without de Retz. The watches evolved, developing shape and character. For the HLq, the movement was reengineered for a round case. Instead of a tourbillon, Hautlence has found a way to have the whole escapement rotate four times a day.

In 2012, Hautlence became the first member of the brand-new MELB Holding, headed by Georges-Henri Meylan (formerly of Audemars Piguet) and former Breguet CFO Bill Muirhead. The experience and contacts of these two horological powerhouses have energized the brand. Besides opening outlets in Dubai and Los Angeles, Hautlence has refreshed its collection with Atelier and Signature series. The stark industrial look is now tempered with daubs of color, but prices have been lowered by the use of trusty Soprod engines in some models. And in 2014, the brand acquired an ambassador, former French soccer star Eric Cantona, now an art collector as well and an edgy personality, which goes along well with the chic-steampunkish look and the brand's will to be different, come what may.

Hautlence
Rue Numa-Droz 150
CH-2300 La Chaux-de-Fonds
Switzerland

Tel.:
+41-32-924-00-60

Fax:
+41-32-924-00-64

E-Mail:
info@hautlence.com

Website:
www.hautlence.com

Founded:
2004

Number of employees:
10

Annual production:
400 watches

U.S. distributor:
Westime
132 South Rodeo Drive, Fourth Floor
Beverly Hills, CA 90212
310-205-5555
info@westime.com
www.westime.com

Most important collections:
Concepts d'Exception, Atelier, Signature

HL2.5

Movement: automatic, in-house caliber with gear train/automatic winding system; ID HL2.3 on No. plate; 37.8 x 33.2 mm, height 12.35 mm; 18,000 vph; 92 jewels; rotating mobile bridge, white gold oscillator; 2 spring barrels; 45-hour power reserve
Functions: half-trailing hours on 12-link chain, 3-4 seconds for change, retrograde minutes; power reserve indicator
Case: titanium in satin, polished, microbille finishing; 50 x 42 mm, height 17.8 mm; satin-brushing, ruthenium-anthracite/polished steel elements; 3D sapphire crystal; rose gold horns/case back screws; water-resistant to 3 atm
Band: reptile skin, folding buckle
Price: $189,900; limited to 28 pieces

Invictus Morphos

Movement: automatic, Soprod A10 with skeletonized Dubois Dépraz module; 45 jewels; 28,800 vph; circular/sandblasted skeletonized module; 42-hour power reserve
Functions: hours, minutes, small seconds; chronograph; date
Case: stainless steel; 42 x 49 mm, height 14 mm; titanium case middle; sapphire crystal with extra-hard antireflective treatment; rose gold horns/case back screws; water-resistant to 5 atm
Band: reptile skin, folding buckle
Remarks: sandblasted titanium back with inscription, star footballer Eric Cantona's fingerprint/signature
Price: $23,600; limited to 250 pieces

HL Black Edition

Movement: manually wound, in-house caliber; 24 jewels; 21,600 vph; hand-beveled bridges and connecting rods; côtes de Genève; 40-hour power reserve
Functions: jumping hour, retrograde minutes, trailing seconds; jumping date with quick corrector
Case: black ceramic, 37 x 43.5 mm, height 10.5 mm; polished DLC steel bezel, crown, lugs; antireflective, beveled sapphire crystal; screwed-down sapphire case back; water-resistant to 3 atm
Band: reptile skin, folding buckle
Remarks: mineral glass hour disc with rhodium-treated hour markers/orange Superluminova
Price: $44,100; limited to 88 pieces

La Montre Hermès
Erlenstrasse 31A
CH-2555 Brügg
Switzerland

Tel.:
+41-32-366-7100

Fax:
+41-32-366-7101

E-Mail:
info@montre-hermes.ch

Website:
www.hermes.ch

Founded:
1978

Number of employees:
150

U.S. distributor:
Hermès of Paris, Inc.
55 East 59th Street
New York, NY 10022
800-441-4488
www.hermes.com

Most important collections/price range:
Arceau, Cape Cod, Clipper, Dressage, Heure H, Kelly, Medor, Slim / $2,400 to $500,000

Hermès

Thierry Hermès's timing was just right. When he founded his saddlery in Paris in 1837, France's middle class was booming and spending money on beautiful things and activities like horseback riding. Hermès became a household name and a symbol of good taste—not too flashy, not trendy, useful. The advent of the automobile brought luggage, bags, headgear, and soon Hermès, still in family hands today, diversified its range of products into foulards, fashion, porcelain, glass, perfume, and gold jewelry. Watches were a natural, especially with the rise of the wristwatch in the years prior to WWI. Hermès even had a timepiece that could be worn on a belt. But some time passed before it engaged in "real" watchmaking. In 1978, La Montre Hermès opened its watch manufactory in Biel.

Rather than just produce fluffy lifestyle timepieces, Hermès has gone to the trouble to get an in-depth grip on the business. "Our philosophy is all about the quality of time," says Laurent Dordet, who took over as CEO from Luc Perramond in March 2015. "It's about imagination; we want people to dream." So rather than pull out all the complication stops, Hermès has come up with highly identifiable features, like the lively leaning numerals of the Arceau series or the bridoon recalling the company's equine roots at 12 o'clock for holding the strap. As for in-house complications, they are produced in collaboration with external designers, notably the great Jean-Marc Wiederrecht, and include unusual hand movements with varying speeds, an option to "suspend" time for a moment, or one to hide time. A chrono and tourbillon are de rigueur.

To ensure its independence, Hermès invested close to 25 million Swiss francs for 25 percent of the Vaucher Manufacture's stock. Movements not being everything, the company also wisely picked up shares in dial maker Natéber and case maker Joseph Erard. The bracelets, understated, elegant pieces that require two hours' work to complete by hand, are made in Biel.

La Montre Hermès is well positioned in an affordable luxury segment holding promise in the post-recession era. It never had to "go vintage," but the brand is creative as well and always prepared to go into new complications or extraordinary dials, like the Millefiori sapphire crystal one, or a discreet little gem like the Faubourg.

Slim d'Hermès Quantième Perpétuel

Reference number: CA3.870.220/MHA
Movement: automatic, Hermès Caliber H1950 with Agenhor module; ø 30 mm, height 4 mm; 32 jewels; 21,600 vph; microrotor; 42-hour power reserve
Functions: hours, minutes, subsidiary seconds; additional 12-hour display (2nd time zone); perpetual calendar with date, month, moon phase, leap year
Case: rose gold, ø 39.5 mm, height 9.06 mm; sapphire crystal; transparent case back; water-resistant to 3 atm
Band: reptile skin, buckle
Price: $38,900

Slim d'Hermès

Reference number: CA2.870.220/MHA
Movement: automatic, Hermès Caliber H1950; ø 30 mm, height 2.6 mm; 29 jewels; 21,600 vph; microrotor; 42-hour power reserve
Functions: hours, minutes, subsidiary seconds
Case: rose gold, ø 39.5 mm, height 8.11 mm; sapphire crystal; transparent case back; water-resistant to 3 atm
Band: reptile skin, buckle
Price: $18,500
Variations: stainless steel ($7,650)

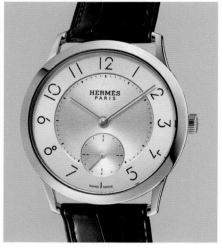

Slim d'Hermès

Reference number: CA2.810.220/MNO
Movement: automatic, Hermès Caliber H1950; ø 30 mm, height 2.6 mm; 29 jewels; 21,600 vph; microrotor; 42-hour power reserve
Functions: hours, minutes, subsidiary seconds
Case: stainless steel, ø 39.5 mm, height 8.11 mm; sapphire crystal; transparent case back; water-resistant to 3 atm
Band: reptile skin, buckle
Price: $7,650
Variations: rose gold ($18,500)

Arceau Automatic

Reference number: AR8.67AQ.222/MHA
Movement: automatic, Hermès Caliber H1837;
ø 25.6 mm, height 3.7 mm; 28 jewels; 28,800 vph;
finely finished; 50-hour power reserve
Functions: hours, minutes; date
Case: rose gold, ø 40 mm; sapphire crystal;
transparent case back; water-resistant to 3 atm
Band: reptile skin, buckle
Price: $18,300
Variations: stainless steel ($5,950)

Cape Cod Automatic

Reference number: CD7.810.220/MHA
Movement: automatic, Hermès Caliber H1912;
ø 23.3 mm, height 3.9 mm; 28 jewels; 28,800 vph;
50-hour power reserve
Functions: hours, minutes, sweep seconds;
large date
Case: stainless steel, 33 x 33 mm; sapphire crystal;
transparent case back; water-resistant to 3 atm
Band: reptile skin, buckle
Price: $6,200

Dressage "L'Heure Masquée"

Reference number: DR5.870.221/MHA
Movement: automatic, Hermès Caliber H1925;
ø 32 mm, height 6.5 mm; 35 jewels; 28,800 vph;
pressing crown reveals hour hand from hiding place
behind minute hand; 45-hour power reserve
Functions: hours (on demand), minutes; additional
24-hour display (2nd time zone; only on pressing
crown)
Case: rose gold, ø 40.5 mm; sapphire crystal;
water-resistant to 5 atm
Band: reptile skin, buckle
Price: $45,900
Variations: stainless steel ($21,750; limited to
1,000 pieces)

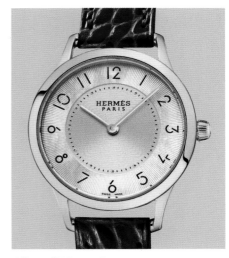

Slim d'Hermès

Reference number: CA2.230.220/ZZ8C
Movement: quartz
Functions: hours, minutes
Case: stainless steel, ø 32 mm; 70 diamonds on
bezel; sapphire crystal; transparent case back;
water-resistant to 3 atm
Band: reptile skin, buckle
Price: $8,700
Variations: various dials and colors

Slim d'Hermès

Reference number: CA2.210.220/5000
Movement: quartz
Functions: hours, minutes
Case: stainless steel, ø 32 mm; sapphire crystal;
transparent case back; water-resistant to 3 atm
Band: stainless steel, folding clasp
Price: $9,425
Variations: various dials and colors

Slim d'Hermès

Reference number: CA2.170.212/ZET
Movement: quartz
Functions: hours, minutes
Case: rose gold, ø 25 mm; sapphire crystal;
transparent case back; water-resistant to 3 atm
Band: reptile skin, buckle
Price: $9,100
Variations: various dials and colors

Hublot SA
Chemin de la Vuarpillière 33
CH-1260 Nyon
Switzerland

Tel.:
+41-22-990-9900

E-Mail:
info@hublot.ch

Website:
www.hublot.com

Founded:
1980

Number of employees:
approx. 450

Annual production:
approx. 40,000 watches

U.S. distributor:
Hublot of America, Inc.
The International Building, ST-402
2455 East Sunrise Blvd.
Fort Lauderdale, FL 33304
800-536-0636

Most important collections/price range:
Big Bang / $15,000 to $1,000,000; King
Power / $20,000 to $200,000; Classic
Fusion / $7,000 to $130,000; MasterPieces /
$100,000 to $450,000

Hublot

Ever since Hublot moved into a new, modern, spacious factory building in Nyon, near Geneva—in the midst of a recession, no less—the brand has evolved with stunning speed. The growth has been such that Hublot has even built a second factory, which is even bigger than the first. The ground-breaking ceremony took place on March 3, 2014, and the man holding the spade was Hublot chairman Jean-Claude Biver, who is also head of LVMH's Watch Division.

Hublot grew and continues to grow thanks to its innovative approach to watchmaking. In 2011, the brand introduced the first scratchproof precious metal, an alloy of gold and ceramic named "Magic Gold," which is produced in a dedicated facility in Nyon. And the experimentation continues. At Baselworld 2014, Hublot came out with a watch whose dial is made of osmium, one of the world's rarest metals. Using a new patented process, Hublot has also implemented a unique concept of cutting wafer-thin bits of glass that are set in the open spaces of a skeletonized movement plate. In 2015, the Big Bang concept, which pushed the brand to the top market rankings, turned ten. It was together with current CEO Ricardo Guadalupe that Biver developed the idea of fusing different and at times incompatible materials in a watch: carbon composite and gold, ceramic and steel, denim and diamonds . . . In order to present these surprising combinations in a flashy way, a case had to be created that was made up of more than the standard three parts. The container of the Big Bang I comprised about 70 parts and several layers, making it one of the most flexible cases in *haute horlogerie* in that its construction allows for all kinds of material mixes.

Big Bang Ferrari
Special Ceramic

Reference number: 401.CX.1123.VR
Movement: automatic, Caliber HUB 1241 "Unico"; ø 30 mm, height 8.05 mm; 38 jewels; 28,800 vph; black-coated plate and bridges; 72-hour power reserve
Functions: hours, minutes, subsidiary seconds; flyback chronograph; date
Case: ceramic, ø 45.5 mm, height 16.7 mm; bezel attached with 6 titanium screws, sapphire crystal; transparent case back; water-resistant to 10 atm
Band: calf leather, folding clasp
Price: $29,800; limited to 250 pieces

Big Bang Ferrari
Titanium Carbon

Reference number: 401.NJ.0123.VR
Movement: automatic, Caliber HUB 1241 "Unico"; ø 30 mm, height 8.05 mm; 38 jewels; 28,800 vph; black-coated plate and bridges; 72-hour power reserve
Functions: hours, minutes, subsidiary seconds; flyback chronograph; date
Case: titanium, ø 45.5 mm, height 16.7 mm; carbon titanium composite bezel attached with 6 titanium screws, sapphire crystal; transparent case back; water-resistant to 10 atm
Band: calf leather, folding clasp
Price: $28,600; limited to 1,000 pieces

Big Bang Ferrari
White Ceramic Carbon

Reference number: 401.HQ.0121.VR
Movement: automatic, Caliber HUB 1241 "Unico"; ø 30 mm, height 8.05 mm; 38 jewels; 28,800 vph; black-coated plate and bridges; 72-hour power reserve
Functions: hours, minutes, subsidiary seconds; flyback chronograph; date
Case: ceramic, ø 45.5 mm, height 16.7 mm; carbon fiber bezel attached with 6 titanium screws, sapphire crystal; transparent back; water-resistant to 10 atm
Band: calf leather, folding clasp
Price: $29,800; limited to 500 pieces

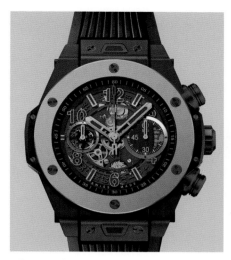

Big Bang Unico Ceramic Magic Gold

Reference number: 411.CM.1138.RX
Movement: automatic, Caliber HUB 1242 "Unico"; ø 30 mm, height 9.8 mm; 38 jewels; 28,800 vph; black-coated plate and bridges; 72-hour power reserve
Functions: hours, minutes, subsidiary seconds; flyback chronograph; date
Case: ceramic, ø 45 mm, height 15.45 mm; "Magic Gold" bezel attached with 6 titanium screws; sapphire crystal; transparent case back; water-resistant to 10 atm
Band: rubber, folding clasp
Price: $26,300

Big Bang Unico Titanium Ceramic Bracelet

Reference number: 411.NM.1170.NM
Movement: automatic, Caliber HUB 1242 "Unico"; ø 30 mm, height 9.8 mm; 38 jewels; 28,800 vph; black-coated plate and bridges; 72-hour power reserve
Functions: hours, minutes, subsidiary seconds; flyback chronograph; date
Case: titanium, ø 45 mm, height 15.45 mm; ceramic bezel attached with 6 titanium screws; sapphire crystal; transparent back; water-resistant to 10 atm
Band: titanium with rubber elements, folding clasp
Price: $24,600
Variations: various cases and dials

Big Bang Unico Carbon

Reference number: 411.QX.1170.RX
Movement: automatic, Caliber HUB 1242 "Unico"; ø 30 mm, height 9.8 mm; 38 jewels; 28,800 vph; black-coated plate and bridges; 72-hour power reserve
Functions: hours, minutes, subsidiary seconds; flyback chronograph; date
Case: carbon fiber, ø 45.5 mm, height 15.55 mm; bezel attached with 6 titanium screws, sapphire crystal; transparent case back; water-resistant to 10 atm
Band: rubber, folding clasp
Price: $24,000
Variations: various cases and dials

Big Bang Unico King Gold Ceramic

Reference number: 411.QX.1170.RX
Movement: automatic, Caliber HUB 1242 "Unico"; ø 30 mm, height 9.8 mm; 38 jewels; 28,800 vph; black-coated plate and bridges; 72-hour power reserve
Functions: hours, minutes, subsidiary seconds; flyback chronograph; date
Case: rose gold, ø 45.5 mm, height 15.45 mm; ceramic bezel attached with 6 titanium screws, sapphire crystal; transparent case back; water-resistant to 10 atm
Band: rubber, folding clasp
Price: $40,100
Variations: various cases and dials

Spirit of Big Bang White Ceramic

Reference number: 601.HX.0173.LR
Movement: automatic, Caliber HUB 4700 (based on Zenith El Primero); ø 30 mm, height 6.6 mm; 31 jewels; 36,000 vph; 50-hour power reserve
Functions: hours, minutes, subsidiary seconds; chronograph; date
Case: ceramic, 45 x 51 mm, height 14.25 mm; bezel attached with 6 titanium screws; sapphire crystal; transparent case back; water-resistant to 10 atm
Band: reptile skin, folding clasp
Price: $28,600
Variations: titanium ($24,000)

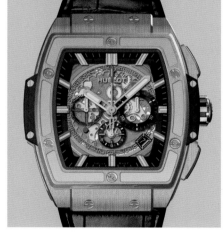

Spirit of Big Bang Titanium

Reference number: 601.NX.0173.LR
Movement: automatic, Caliber HUB 4700 (based on Zenith El Primero); ø 30 mm, height 6.6 mm; 31 jewels; 36,000 vph; 50-hour power reserve
Functions: hours, minutes, subsidiary seconds; chronograph; date
Case: titanium, 45 x 51 mm, height 14.25 mm; bezel attached with 6 titanium screws; sapphire crystal; transparent case back; water-resistant to 10 atm
Band: reptile skin, folding clasp
Price: $24,000
Variations: ceramic ($28,600)

Big Bang Jeans
Reference number: 301.SL.2770.NR.JEANS
Movement: automatic, Caliber HUB 4100 (base ETA 7750); ø 30 mm, height 8.4 mm; 27 jewels; 28,000 vph; 42-hour power reserve
Functions: hours, minutes, subsidiary seconds; chronograph; date
Case: stainless steel, ø 44 mm, height 14.6 mm; bezel attached with 6 titanium screws; sapphire crystal; transparent case back; water-resistant to 10 atm
Band: textile, folding clasp
Price: $16,000

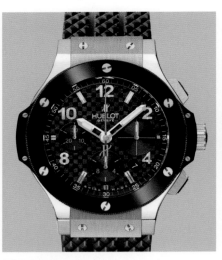

Big Bang Steel Ceramic
Reference number: 342.SB.131.RX
Movement: automatic, Caliber HUB 1145; ø 30 mm, 37 jewels; 28,800 vph; 42-hour power reserve
Functions: hours, minutes, subsidiary seconds; chronograph; date
Case: stainless steel, ø 41 mm, height 14 mm; ceramic bezel attached with 6 titanium screws; sapphire crystal; transparent case back; water-resistant to 3 atm
Band: rubber, folding clasp
Price: $13,700

King Power Unico All Carbon
Reference number: 701.QX.0140.RX
Movement: automatic, Caliber HUB 1242 "Unico"; ø 30 mm, height 9.8 mm; 38 jewels; 28,800 vph; black-coated plate and bridges; 72-hour power reserve
Functions: hours, minutes, subsidiary seconds; flyback chronograph; date
Case: carbon fiber, ø 48 mm, height 17.4 mm; bezel attached with 6 titanium screws; sapphire crystal; transparent case back; water-resistant to 10 atm
Band: rubber, folding clasp
Price: $26,300

Classic Fusion Tourbillon Cathedral Minute Repeater Carbon
Reference number: 504.QX.0110.LR
Movement: manual winding, Caliber HUB 8001; height 6.35 mm; 30 jewels; 21,600 vph; flying 1-minute tourbillon; 120-hour power reserve
Functions: hours, minutes; minute repeater
Case: carbon fiber, ø 45 mm, height 14.3 mm; bezel attached with 6 titanium screws, sapphire crystal; transparent case back; water-resistant to 3 atm
Band: reptile skin, folding clasp
Price: $276,000; limited to 99 pieces
Variations: rose gold ($299,000; limited to 50); titanium ($264,000; limited to 99)

Classic Fusion Blue Titanium
Reference number: 521.NX.7170.LR
Movement: automatic, Caliber HUB 1143; height 6.9 mm; 59 jewels; 28,800 vph; 42-hour power reserve
Functions: hours, minutes, subsidiary seconds; chronograph; date
Case: titanium, ø 45 mm, bezel attached with 6 titanium screws; sapphire crystal; transparent case back; water-resistant to 5 atm
Band: reptile skin, folding clasp
Price: $12,000

Classic Fusion AeroFusion Moonphase King Gold
Reference number: 517.OX.0180.LR
Movement: automatic, Caliber 1131; 25 jewels; 28,800 vph; 42-hour power reserve
Functions: hours, minutes, sweep seconds; full calendar with date, weekday, month, moon phase
Case: rose gold, ø 45 mm, height 12 mm; bezel attached with 6 titanium screws; sapphire crystal; transparent case back
Band: reptile skin, folding clasp
Price: $34,800
Variations: titanium ($17,600)

Classic Fusion Power Reserve 8 Days All Black

Reference number: 516.CM.1140.LR
Movement: automatic, Caliber HUB 1601;
ø 34.4 mm, height 4 mm; 33 jewels; 21,600 vph;
192-hour power reserve
Functions: hours, minutes, subsidiary seconds;
power reserve indicator; date
Case: ceramic, ø 45 mm, height 11.15 mm; bezel
attached with 6 titanium screws; sapphire crystal;
transparent case back
Band: reptile skin, folding clasp
Price: $18,300
Variations: rose gold ($32,500)

Classic Fusion Power Reserve 8 Days King Gold

Reference number: 516.OX.1480.LR
Movement: automatic, Caliber HUB 1601;
ø 34.4 mm, height 4 mm; 33 jewels; 21,600 vph;
192-hour power reserve
Functions: hours, minutes, subsidiary seconds;
power reserve indicator; date
Case: rose gold, ø 45 mm, height 11.15 mm; bezel
attached with 6 titanium screws, sapphire crystal;
transparent case back
Band: reptile skin, folding clasp
Price: $32,500

Classic Fusion Chronograph Forbidden X

Reference number: 521.OC.0589.VR.OPX14
Movement: automatic, Caliber HUB 1143; height
6.9 mm; 59 jewels; 28,800 vph; 42-hour power
reserve
Functions: hours, minutes, subsidiary seconds;
chronograph; date
Case: rose gold, ø 45 mm, height 13.05 mm;
ceramic bezel attached with 6 titanium screws,
sapphire crystal; transparent back; water-resistant
to 5 atm
Band: calf leather, folding clasp
Price: $36,700; limited to 250 pieces
Variations: titanium (limited to 250); black ceramic
(limited to 250)

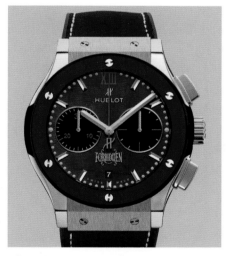

Classic Fusion Chronograph Forbidden X

Reference number: 521.NC.0589.VR.OPX14
Movement: automatic, Caliber HUB 1143; height
6.9 mm; 59 jewels; 28,800 vph; 42-hour power
reserve
Functions: hours, minutes, subsidiary seconds;
chronograph; date
Case: titanium, ø 45 mm, height 13.05 mm;
ceramic bezel attached with 6 titanium screws,
sapphire crystal; transparent back; water-resistant
to 5 atm
Band: calf leather, folding clasp
Price: $14,800; limited to 250 pieces
Variations: rose gold (limited to 150); black
ceramic (limited to 250)

Caliber HUB1240

Automatic; column wheel control of chronograph
functions; silicon anchor and anchor escape wheel;
removable escapement; double-pawl automatic
winding (Pellaton system), winding rotor with
ceramic ball bearing, simple spring barrel, 70-hour
power reserve
Functions: hours, minutes, subsidiary seconds;
flyback chronograph; date
Diameter: 30.4 mm; **Height:** 8.05 mm
Jewels: 38; **Balance:** glucydur
Frequency: 28,800 vph
Balance spring: flat hairspring with fine regulation
Shock protection: Incabloc
Remarks: 330 individual components

Caliber HUB1300

Manually wound, skeletonized movement; structural
sections with black PVD coating; double spring
barrel; 90-hour power reserve
Functions: hours, minutes, subsidiary seconds
Diameter: 28 mm
Height: 2.9 mm
Jewels: 23
Balance: glucydur
Frequency: 21,600 vph
Balance spring: flat hairspring with fine regulation
Shock protection: Incabloc
Remarks: 123 individual components

Itay Noy

P.O. Box 16661
Tel Aviv 61166
Israel

Tel.:
+972-352-47-380

Fax:
+972-352-47-381

E-Mail:
studio@itay-noy.com

Website:
www.itay-noy.com

Founded:
2000

Number of employees:
4

Annual production:
up to 300

U.S. distributor:
Bareti, California
949-715-7084
info@bareti.com
www.bareti.com

Most important collections/price range:
Hyper Scape, X-ray, Identity, Point of View /
$2,500 to $7,500

Itay Noy

Israeli watchmaker Itay Noy started his career as a jeweler, so it comes as no surprise that his earlier watches tended to emphasize form, while the functional aspects are left to solid Swiss movements. As a shaper, though, he reveals himself to be a pensive, philosophical storyteller making each timepiece a unique, encapsulated tale of sorts. The City Squares model, for example, gives the time on the backdrop of a map of the owner's favorite or native city, thus creating an intimate connection with, perhaps, a past moment. At Baselworld 2013, Noy showcased a square watch run on a Technotime automatic movement with a face-like dial that changes with the movement of the hands, a reminder of how our life has become dominated by the rectangular frame of mobile gadgets. The Cityscape, square as well, represents a modern urban landscape. The skeletonization of the Point of View dial, his 2014 model, creates a harmonious collage of the world's religious symbols superimposed on the inexorable passage of time. For 2015, Noy ratcheted up his craft designing a special module to create a fascinating, two-part square dial for his Part Time, dividing day and night and providing the time plus the position of the sun and the moon through little apertures.

Noy's timepieces inevitably express a personal concept, idea, or opinion, which creates an intimate relationship with future owners. The personal touch is all the more intense due to the fact that all pieces come in limited, numbered editions, yet always in a very accessible price range. Engineering with Noy is an art form, and so it's no wonder his collections find their way into museums and special exhibitions, notably the C. Bronfman Collection in New York, the Droog Design Collection in Amsterdam, and the collection of the Israel Museum in Jerusalem. The Museum of Art and Design in New York will be showing his works in April 2016.

Part Time

Reference number: PT-DN.BL
Movement: manually wound IN.DD&6498-1; ø 36.6 mm, height 5.2 mm; 17 jewels; 21,600 vph; 38-hour power reserve
Functions: analog hours, minutes, subsidiary seconds; moon disk, sun disk
Case: stainless steel, 41.6 x 44.6 mm, height 10.6 mm; sapphire crystal; transparent case back; water-resistant to 5 atm
Band: leather, double folding clasp
Remarks: limited to 24 numbered pieces
Price: $4,800
Variations: blue or black

Point Of View

Reference number: POV-R.G
Movement: automatic, Caliber 90S5; ø 25.6 mm, height 3.9 mm; 24 jewels; 28,800 vph; 42-hour power reserve
Functions: hours, minutes, sweep seconds
Case: stainless steel, ø 42.4 mm, height 10 mm; sapphire crystal; screw-down case back; water-resistant to 4 atm
Band: leather, folding clasp
Remarks: limited to 99 numbered pieces
Price: $2,400
Variations: black leather band

Heper Scape

Reference number: LANDSCAPE.B
Movement: automatic, Caliber TT651-24H; ø 26.2 mm, height 5.25 mm; 21 jewels; frequency 28,800 vph; 42-hour power reserve
Functions: hours, minutes, sweep seconds; quick-set big date; 2nd 24-hour time zone with day/night indication
Case: stainless steel, 42.4 x 42.4 mm, height 11.6 mm; sapphire crystal; transparent case back; water resistant to 5 atm
Band: rubber or handmade leather, double folding clasp
Remarks: limited to 24 numbered pieces
Price: $5,800
Variations: black or cream dial

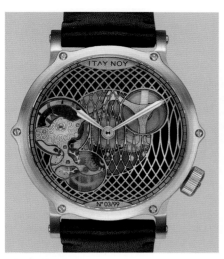

Skeleton

Reference number: SKEL6498G
Movement: manually wound, ETA Caliber 6498-1;
ø 36.6 mm, height 4.5 mm; 17 jewels; 21,600 vph;
38-hour power reserve
Functions: hours, minutes, subsidiary seconds
Case: stainless steel, 41.6 x 44.6 mm, height
10 mm; sapphire crystal; screw-down case back;
water-resistant to 50 m
Band: leather, double folding clasp
Remarks: limited to 99 numbered pieces
Price: $3,900
Variations: brown leather band

X-ray

Reference number: XRAY6498
Movement: manually wound, ETA Caliber 6498-1;
ø 36.6 mm, height 4.5 mm; 17 jewels; 21,600 vph;
38-hour power reserve
Functions: hours, minutes, subsidiary seconds
Case: stainless steel, 41.6 x 44.6 mm, height
10 mm; sapphire crystal; screw-down case back;
water-resistant to 5 atm
Band: leather, double folding clasp
Remarks: limited to 99 numbered pieces
Price: $3,640
Variations: gold plated dial ($3,900); brown
leather band

DiaLOG

Reference number: DiaLOG.Num
Movement: manually wound, ETA Caliber 6498-1;
ø 36.6 mm, height 4.5 mm; 17 jewels; 21,600 vph;
38-hour power reserve
Functions: hours, minutes, subsidiary seconds
Case: stainless steel, 41.6 x 44.6 mm, height
10 mm; sapphire crystal; screw-down case back;
water-resistant to 50 m
Band: dark blue leather, double folding clasp
Remarks: limited to 99 numbered pieces
Price: $3,900

Maximalism

Reference number: MAX-DECO
Movement: automatic, ETA Caliber 2824-2;
ø 25.6 mm, height 4.6 mm; 25 jewels; 28,800 vph;
38-hour power reserve
Functions: hours, minutes, sweep seconds; quick-
set date window
Case: stainless steel, ø 42.4 mm, height 10 mm;
sapphire crystal, screw-down case back, water-
resistant to 5 atm
Band: leather, double folding clasp
Remarks: limited to 99 numbered pieces
Price: $2,400
Variations: black leather band

Identity- Hebrew

Reference number: ID-HEB.G
Movement: automatic, ETA Caliber 2824-2;
ø 25.6 mm, height 4.6 mm; 25 jewels; 28,800 vph;
38-hour power reserve
Functions: hours, minutes, sweep seconds; quick-
set date window
Case: stainless steel, ø 42.4 mm, height 10 mm;
sapphire crystal; screw-down case back; water-
resistant to 5 atm
Band: leather, double folding clasp
Remarks: gold-plated dial, limited to 99 numbered
pieces
Price: $2,800
Variations: black leather band

City Squares
Columbus Square, New York

Reference number: CS-Rome
Movement: automatic, ETA Caliber 2824-2;
ø 25.6 mm, height 4.6 mm; 25 jewels; 28,800 vph;
38-hour power reserve
Functions: hours, minutes, sweep seconds; quick-
set date window
Case: stainless steel, ø 42.4 mm, height 10 mm;
sapphire crystal; screw-down case back; water-
resistant to 5 atm
Band: leather, double folding clasp
Remarks: limited to 99 numbered pieces
Price: $3,640
Variations: London, Paris, Rome, Tel Aviv, Copenhagen

International Watch Co.
Baumgartenstrasse 15
CH-8201 Schaffhausen
Switzerland

Tel.:
+41-52-635-6565

Fax:
+41-52-635-6501

E-Mail:
info@iwc.com

Website:
www.iwc.com

Founded:
1868

Number of employees:
approx. 750

U.S. distributor:
IWC North America
645 Fifth Avenue, 5th Floor
New York, NY 10022
800-432-9330

Most important collections/price range:
Da Vinci, Pilot's, Portuguese, Ingenieur,
Aquatimer / approx. $4,000 to $260,000

IWC

It was an American who laid the cornerstone for an industrial watch factory in Schaffhausen—now environmentally state-of-the-art facilities. In 1868, Florentine Ariosto Jones, watchmaker and engineer from Boston, crossed the Atlantic to the then low-wage venue of Switzerland to open the International Watch Company Schaffhausen.

Jones was not only a savvy businessperson, but also a talented designer, who had a significant influence on the development of watch movements. Soon, he gave IWC its own seal of approval, the *Ingenieursmarke* (Engineer's Brand), a standard it still maintains today. IWC is synonymous with excellently crafted watches that meet high technical benchmarks. Not even a large variety of owners over the past 100 years has been able to change the company's course, though it did ultimately end up in the hands of the Richemont Group in 2000.

Technical milestones from Schaffhausen include the Jones caliber, named for the IWC founder, and the pocket watch caliber 89, introduced in 1946 as the creation of then technical director Albert Pellaton. Four years later, Pellaton created the first IWC automatic movement and, with it, a company monument. Over the years, IWC has made a name for itself with its pilot's watches. The technical highlight of the present day is no doubt the Perpetual Calendar, which is programmed to run until the year 2499.

Georges Kern, the current CEO at IWC, has pursued the development of in-house movements, such as those found in the company's Da Vinci and Ingenieur models, and of course the Portuguese, which celebrated its seventy-fifth anniversary in style in 2015 with a spate of special editions. The watches are naturally retro-styled. Lately, IWC has revisited its Aquatimer and brought out the Deep Three, with two depth gauges, one of which records how deep the diver has gone. The health of the company was signaled by the groundbreaking ceremony in the fall of 2014 for a new technology center near Schaffhausen.

Portuguese Hand-Wound Eight Days Edition "75th Anniversary"

Reference number: IW510206
Movement: manually wound, IWC Caliber 59215; ø 37.8 mm, 30 jewels; 28,800 vph; screw balance; 192-hour power reserve
Functions: hours, minutes, subsidiary seconds; date
Case: pink gold, ø 43 mm, height 12 mm; sapphire crystal; transparent case back; water-resistant to 3 atm
Band: reptile skin, buckle
Remarks: limited to 175 pieces
Price: $24,100
Variations: stainless steel ($11,400; limited to 750)

Portuguese Grande Complication

Reference number: IW377601
Movement: automatic, IWC Caliber 79091; 75 jewels; 28,800 vph; 44-hour power reserve
Functions: hours, minutes, sweep seconds; minute repeater; chronograph; perpetual calendar with date, weekday, month, moon phase; year display (4 digits)
Case: platinum, ø 45 mm, height 16.5 mm; sapphire crystal; water-resistant to 3 atm
Band: reptile skin, folding clasp
Price: $255,000; limited to 250 pieces
Variations: pink gold ($225,000)

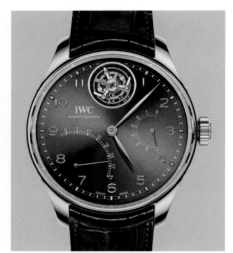

Portuguese Tourbillon Mystère Rétrograde

Reference number: IW504602
Movement: automatic, IWC Caliber 51900; ø 37.8 mm, height 9 mm; 44 jewels; 19.800 vph; 1-minute flying tourbillon; Breguet spring, Pellaton winding, pink gold oscillating mass; 168-hour power reserve
Functions: hours, minutes; power reserve indicator; date (retrograde)
Case: pink gold, ø 44.2 mm, height 15.3 mm; sapphire crystal; transparent case back; water-resistant to 3 atm
Band: reptile skin, folding clasp
Price: $99,800
Variations: platinum ($125,000)

Portuguese Perpetual Calendar

Reference number: IW503401
Movement: automatic, IWC Caliber 52615; ø 37.8 mm, 54 jewels; 28,800 vph; Breguet spring, screw balance, Pellaton winding, gold oscillating mass; 168-hour power reserve
Functions: hours, minutes, subsidiary seconds; power reserve indicator; perpetual calendar with month, weekday, date, double moon phase (for northern and southern hemispheres), year display (4 digits)
Case: white gold, ø 44.2 mm, height 15.3 mm; sapphire crystal; transparent case back; water-resistant to 3 atm
Band: reptile skin, folding clasp
Price: $41,900

Portugeser Perpetual Calendar Digital Date-Month Edition "75th Anniversary"

Reference number: IW397202
Movement: automatic, IWC Caliber 89801; ø 37 mm, height 9.9 mm; 51 jewels; 28,800 vph; Pellaton winding, pink gold oscillating mass; 68-hour power reserve
Functions: hours, minutes, subsidiary seconds; flyback chronograph; perpetual calendar with large date, month (digital), leap year
Case: pink gold, ø 45 mm, height 16.5 mm; sapphire crystal; transparent case back; water-resistant to 3 atm
Band: reptile skin, folding clasp
Price: $49,800; limited to 75 pieces
Variations: white dial; platinum ($66,800; limited to 25)

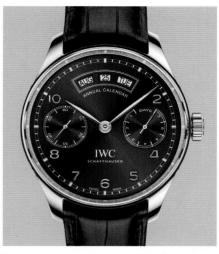

Portuguese Annual Calendar

Reference number: IW503502
Movement: automatic, IWC Caliber 52850; ø 37.8 mm, 36 jewels; 28,800 vph; 2 spring barrels, Breguet spring, screw balance, Pellaton winding, gold oscillating mass; 168-hour power reserve
Functions: hours, minutes, subsidiary seconds; power reserve indicator; annual calendar with date, weekday, month
Case: stainless steel, ø 44.2 mm, height 15.3 mm; sapphire crystal; transparent back; water-resistant to 3 atm
Band: reptile skin, folding clasp
Price: $21,300
Variations: light dial ($21,300); pink gold ($31,600)

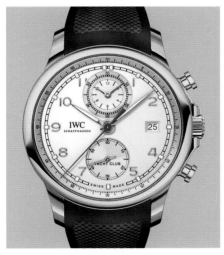

Portuguese Yacht Club Chronograph

Reference number: IW390501
Movement: automatic, IWC Caliber 89361; ø 30 mm, height 7.5 mm; 38 jewels; 28,800 vph; Pellaton winding; 68-hour power reserve
Functions: hours, minutes, subsidiary seconds; flyback chronograph; date
Case: pink gold, ø 43.5 mm, height 14.5 mm; sapphire crystal; screw-in crown; water-resistant to 6 atm
Band: rubber, buckle
Price: $24,500
Variations: stainless steel ($12,700)

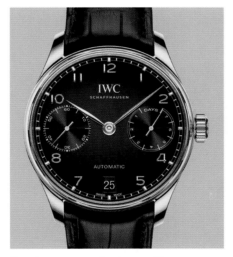

Portuguese Automatic

Reference number: IW500703
Movement: automatic, IWC Caliber 52010; 31 jewels; 28,800 vph; 2 spring barrels; Pellaton winding, Breguet spring, screw balance, gold oscillating mass; 168-hour power reserve
Functions: hours, minutes, subsidiary seconds; power reserve indicator; date
Case: stainless steel, ø 42.3 mm, height 14.5 mm; sapphire crystal; transparent case back; water-resistant to 3 atm
Band: reptile skin, folding clasp
Price: $13,000
Variations: light dial ($13,000); pink gold ($24,400)

Aquatimer Chronograph Edition "Galapagos Islands"

Reference number: IW379502
Movement: automatic, IWC Caliber 89365; ø 30 mm, height 7.5 mm; 35 jewels; 28,800 vph; 68-hour power reserve
Functions: hours, minutes, subsidiary seconds; chronograph; date
Case: stainless steel with black rubber coating, ø 44 mm, height 17 mm; bidirectional bezel for activating inside bezel; sapphire crystal; screw-in crown; water-resistant to 30 atm
Band: rubber, buckle
Price: $10,900

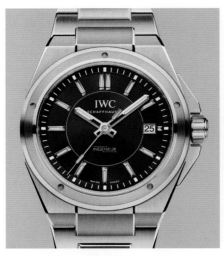

Ingenieur Automatic "Laureus Sport for Good" Edition

Reference number: IW323909
Movement: automatic, IWC Caliber 30110 (base ETA 2892-A2); ø 25.6 mm, height 3.6 mm; 21 jewels; 28,800 vph; 42-hour power reserve
Functions: hours, minutes, sweep seconds; date
Case: stainless steel, ø 40 mm, height 10 mm; sapphire crystal; water-resistant to 12 atm
Band: stainless steel, folding clasp
Price: $6,900; limited to 1,500 pieces

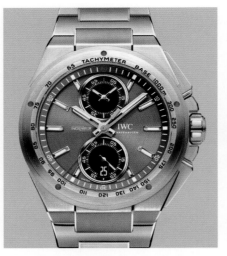

Ingenieur Chronograph Racer

Reference number: IW378508
Movement: automatic, IWC Caliber 89361; ø 30 mm, height 7.5 mm; 38 jewels; 28,800 vph; double-pawl automatic winding system; 68-hour power reserve
Functions: hours, minutes, subsidiary seconds; flyback chronograph; date
Case: stainless steel, ø 45 mm, height 14.5 mm; sapphire crystal; screw-in crown; water-resistant to 12 atm
Band: stainless steel, folding clasp
Price: $13,600
Variations: black dial; rubber strap ($12,300)

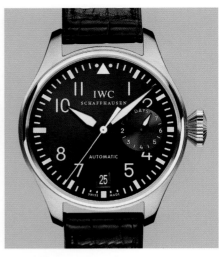

Big Pilot's Watch

Reference number: IW500901
Movement: automatic, IWC Caliber 51111; ø 37.8 mm, height 7.6 mm; 42 jewels; 21,600 vph; Pellaton winding; soft iron cap for antimagnetic protection; 168-hour power reserve
Functions: hours, minutes, sweep seconds; power reserve indicator; date
Case: stainless steel, ø 46 mm, height 16 mm; sapphire crystal; screw-in crown; water-resistant to 6 atm
Band: reptile skin, folding clasp
Price: $14,500

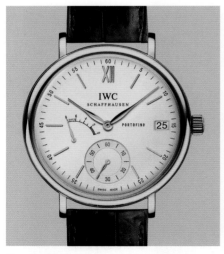

Portofino Hand-Wound Eight Days

Reference number: IW510107
Movement: manually wound, IWC Caliber 59210; ø 37.8 mm, height 5.8 mm; 30 jewels; 28,800 vph; 192-hour power reserve
Functions: hours, minutes, subsidiary seconds; power reserve indicator; date
Case: pink gold, ø 45 mm, height 12 mm; sapphire crystal; transparent case back; water-resistant to 3 atm
Band: reptile skin, buckle
Price: $19,800
Variations: stainless steel ($10,300)

Portofino Midsize Automatic Moonphase

Reference number: IW459002
Movement: automatic, IWC Caliber 35800; 25 jewels; 28,800 vph; 42-hour power reserve
Functions: hours, minutes, sweep seconds; moon phase
Case: pink gold, ø 37 mm, height 11 mm; 66 diamonds on bezel; sapphire crystal; water-resistant to 3 atm
Band: reptile skin, buckle
Remarks: mother-of-pearl dial with 12 diamonds
Price: $22,400
Variations: white gold case/diamond markers, numerals ($29,300); pink gold case/pink gold Milanese mesh bracelet ($38,700)

Portofino Midsize Automatic

Reference number: IW458107
Movement: automatic, IWC Caliber 35111; 25 jewels; 28,800 vph; 42-hour power reserve
Functions: hours, minutes, sweep seconds; date
Case: pink gold, ø 37 mm, height 9 mm; 66 diamonds on bezel; sapphire crystal; water-resistant to 3 atm
Band: reptile skin, buckle
Price: $6,600
Variations: various cases and dials

Caliber 51111

Base caliber: 5000
Automatic; double-pawl automatic winding (Pellaton system); single spring barrel, 7-day power reserve
Functions: hours, minutes, sweep seconds; date; power reserve indicator
Diameter: 37.8 mm
Height: 7.53 mm
Jewels: 44
Balance: balance with variable inertia
Frequency: 21,600 vph
Balance spring: Breguet
Shock protection: Incabloc

Caliber 52010

Automatic; double-pawl automatic winding (Pellaton system) with ceramic wheels; double spring barrel, 168-hour power reserve
Functions: hours, minutes, subsidiary seconds; power reserve indicator; date
Diameter: 37.8 mm
Height: 7.5 mm
Jewels: 31
Balance: balance with variable inertia
Frequency: 28,800 vph
Balance spring: Breguet
Shock protection: Incabloc
Remarks: new generation of calibers

Caliber 52615

Automatic; double-pawl automatic winding (Pellaton system) with ceramic wheels; double spring barrel, 168-hour power reserve
Functions: hours, minutes, subsidiary seconds; power reserve indicator; perpetual calendar with month, weekday, date, double moon phase (for northern and southern hemisphere), year display (4 digits)
Diameter: 37.8 mm; **Height:** 9 mm
Jewels: 54
Balance: balance with variable inertia
Frequency: 28,800 vph
Balance spring: Breguet
Shock protection: Incabloc
Remarks: new generation of calibers

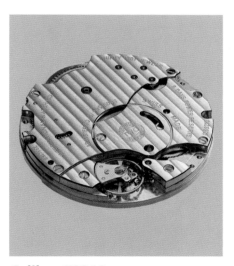

Caliber 59210

Manually wound; single spring barrel, 192-hour power reserve
Functions: hours, minutes, subsidiary seconds; date; power reserve indicator
Diameter: 37.8 mm
Height: 5.8 mm
Jewels: 30
Balance: balance with variable inertia
Frequency: 28,800 vph
Balance spring: Breguet
Shock protection: Incabloc

Caliber 89361

Automatic; double-pawl automatic winding (Pellaton system); column wheel control of chronograph functions; single spring barrel, 68-hour power reserve
Functions: hours, minutes, subsidiary seconds; flyback chronograph; date
Diameter: 30 mm; **Height:** 7.46 mm
Jewels: 38
Balance: balance with variable inertia
Frequency: 28,800 vph
Balance spring: flat hairspring
Shock protection: Incabloc
Remarks: concentric chronograph counter for minutes and hours

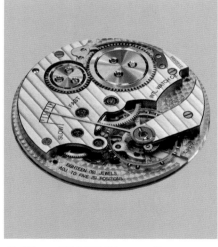

Caliber 98295 "Jones"

Manually wound; single spring barrel, 46-hour power reserve
Functions: hours, minutes, subsidiary seconds
Diameter: 38.2 mm
Height: 5.3 mm
Jewels: 18
Balance: screw balance with precision adjustment cams on balance arms
Frequency: 18,000 vph
Balance spring: Breguet
Shock protection: Incabloc
Remarks: characteristic long regulator index; three-quarter plate of German silver, hand-engraved balance cocks

Manufacture Jaeger-LeCoultre
Rue de la Golisse, 8
CH-1347 Le Sentier
Switzerland

Tel.:
+41-21-852-0202

Fax:
+41-21-852-0505

E-Mail:
info@jaeger-lecoultre.com
Website:
www.jaeger-lecoultre.com

Founded:
1833

Number of employees:
over 1,000

Annual production:
approx. 50,000 watches

U.S. distributor:
Jaeger-LeCoultre
645 Fifth Avenue
New York, NY 10022
800-JLC-TIME
www.jaeger-lecoultre.com

Most important collections/price range:
Reverso, Rendez-Vous, Duomètre, Master,
AMVOX / approx. $6,000 to $130,000
and higher for limited editions and Grandes
Complications models

Jaeger-LeCoultre

The Jaeger-LeCoultre *manufacture* has a long and tumultuous history. In 1833, Antoine LeCoultre opened his own workshop for the production of gear wheels. Having made his fortune, he then did what many other artisans did: In 1866, he had a large house built and brought together all the craftspeople needed to produce timepieces, from the watchmakers to the turners and polishers. He outfitted the workshop with the most modern machinery of the day, all powered by a steam engine. "La Grande Maison" was the first watch *manufacture* in the Vallée de Joux.

At the start of the twentieth century, the grandson of the company founder, Jacques-David LeCoultre, built slender, complicated watches for the Paris manufacturer Edmond Jaeger. The Frenchman was so impressed with these that, after a few years of fruitful cooperation, he engineered a merger of the two companies.

In the 1970s, the *manufacture* was taken over by the German VDO Group (later Mannesmann). Under the leadership of Günter Blümlein, Jaeger-LeCoultre weathered the quartz crisis, and during the mechanical watch renaissance in the 1980s, the company finally recouped its status as an innovative, high-performance *manufacture*.

Then, in 2000, Mannesmann's watch division (JLC, IWC, A. Lange & Söhne) sold Jaeger-LeCoultre to the Richemont Group. Given the group's strength, Jaeger-LeCoultre continued to grow. Fifty new calibers, including minute repeaters, tourbillons, and other *grandes complications*, a lubricant-free movement, and more than 400 patents tell their own story. Today, it is the largest employer in the Vallée de Joux—just as it was back in the 1860s.

Duomètre Sphérotourbillon Moon

Reference number: 608 65 20
Movement: manually wound, JLC Caliber 389; ø 33.7 mm, height 10.45 mm; 56 jewels; 21,600 vph; flying 3-axis tourbillon; 2 separate spring barrels, 2 separate gear works for regulating organ/time display; 45-hour power reserve
Functions: hours and minutes (off-center), subsidiary seconds; additional 24-hour display (2nd time zone); power reserve indicator; moon phase
Case: platinum, ø 42 mm, height 14.3 mm; sapphire crystal; transparent back; water-resistant to 3 atm
Band: reptile skin, buckle
Price: on request; limited to 75 pieces

Duomètre à Quantième Lunaire

Reference number: 604 25 22
Movement: manually wound, JLC Caliber 381; ø 33.7 mm, height 7.25 mm; 40 jewels; 21,600 vph; 2 separate spring barrels, 2 gear trains for watch/ foudroyante mechanism; 50-hour power reserve
Functions: hours and minutes (off-center), sweep seconds; "flashing" sixth of a second ("foudroyante"); double power reserve display, date, moon phase/age
Case: rose gold, ø 42 mm, height 13.5 mm; sapphire crystal; transparent back; water-resistant to 5 atm
Band: reptile skin, buckle
Price: $39,200

Duomètre Unique Travel Time

Reference number: 606 25 20
Movement: manually wound, JLC Caliber 383; ø 34.3 mm, height 7.25 mm; 54 jewels; 28,800 vph; 2 separate spring barrels, 2 gear works for 2 time displays; 50-hour power reserve
Functions: hours and minutes (off-center), sweep seconds; 2nd time zone (digital, jumping hours, minutes), world-time display; power reserve indicator for each spring barrel
Case: pink gold, ø 42 mm, height 13.6 mm; sapphire crystal
Band: reptile skin, buckle
Price: $42,700
Variations: white gold ($51,000)

Master Calendar

Reference number: 155 84 21
Movement: automatic, JLC Caliber 866; ø 26 mm,
height 5.65 mm; 32 jewels; 28,800 vph; 40-hour
power reserve
Functions: hours, minutes, subsidiary seconds; full
calendar with date, weekday, month, moon phase
Case: stainless steel, ø 39 mm, height 10.62 mm;
sapphire crystal; transparent case back; water-
resistant to 5 atm
Band: reptile skin, folding clasp
Remarks: dial of meteorite
Price: $12,600
Variations: pink gold ($24,500)

Master Calendar

Reference number: 155 25 40
Movement: automatic, JLC Caliber 866; ø 26 mm,
height 5.65 mm; 32 jewels; 28,800 vph; 40-hour
power reserve
Functions: hours, minutes, subsidiary seconds; full
calendar with date, weekday, month, moon phase
Case: pink gold, ø 39 mm, height 10.62 mm;
sapphire crystal; transparent case back; water-
resistant to 5 atm
Band: reptile skin, buckle
Remarks: dial of meteorite
Price: $24,500
Variations: stainless steel ($12,600)

Master Ultra Thin Calendar

Reference number: 126 35 20
Movement: automatic, JLC Caliber 891/2-448;
ø 26 mm, height 5.5 mm; 36 jewels; 28,800 vph;
38-hour power reserve
Functions: hours, minutes, subsidiary seconds; full
calendar with date, weekday, month, moon phase
Case: white gold, ø 39 mm, height 9.88 mm;
sapphire crystal; transparent case back; water-
resistant to 5 atm
Band: reptile skin, buckle
Price: $24,300

Master Ultra Thin Date

Reference number: 128 84 20
Movement: automatic, JLC Caliber 899; ø 26 mm,
height 3.3 mm; 32 jewels; 28,800 vph; 38-hour
power reserve
Functions: hours, minutes, sweep seconds; date
Case: stainless steel, ø 40 mm, height 7.45 mm;
sapphire crystal; transparent case back; water-
resistant to 5 atm
Band: reptile skin, folding clasp
Price: $8,100

Master Ultra Thin Moon 39

Reference number: 136 84 70
Movement: automatic, JLC Caliber 925; ø 26 mm,
height 4.9 mm; 30 jewels; 28,800 vph; 38-day
power reserve;
Functions: hours, minutes, sweep seconds; date,
moon phase
Case: stainless steel, ø 39 mm, height 9.9 mm;
sapphire crystal; transparent case back; water-
resistant to 5 atm
Band: reptile skin, folding clasp
Price: $9,250

Master Ultra Thin Perpetual

Reference number: 130 25 01
Movement: automatic, JLC Caliber 868; ø 27.8 mm,
height 4.72 mm; 46 jewels; 38-hour power reserve
Functions: hours, minutes, sweep seconds;
perpetual calendar with date, weekday, month,
moon phase, year display (4 digits)
Case: pink gold, ø 39 mm, height 9.2 mm;
diamonds on bezel; sapphire crystal; transparent
case back; water-resistant to 5 atm
Band: reptile skin, buckle
Price: $36,400
Variations: w/o diamonds ($30,000)

Hybris Mechanica 11

Reference number: 131 35 20
Movement: automatic, JLC Caliber 362; ø 33.3 mm, height 4.8 mm; 21,600 vph; flying tourbillon with flying balance; hubless peripheral rotor; 45-hour power reserve
Functions: hours, minutes; minute repeater
Case: white gold, ø 41 mm, height 7.9 mm; sapphire crystal; transparent case back; activation pusher for minute repeater sunken into case; water-resistant to 3 atm
Band: reptile skin, buckle
Price: on request; limited to 75 pieces

Master Control

Reference number: 154 84 70
Movement: automatic, JLC Caliber 899; ø 26 mm, height 3.3 mm; 32 jewels; 28,800 vph; 38-hour power reserve
Functions: hours, minutes, sweep seconds; date
Case: stainless steel, ø 39 mm, height 8.8 mm; sapphire crystal; transparent case back; water-resistant to 5 atm
Band: reptile skin, folding clasp
Price: $6,850

Master Compressor Extreme LAB 2

Reference number: 203 T5 41
Movement: automatic, JLC Caliber 780; height 9.08 mm; 70 jewels; 28,800 vph; 60-hour power reserve
Functions: hours, minutes, sweep seconds; additional 12-hour display (2nd time zone), power reserve indicator; chronograph with digital minute counter; date
Case: titanium, ø 46.8 mm, height 16.6 mm; black PVD coating on bezel; sapphire crystal; transparent case back; screw-in crown; water-resistant to 10 atm
Band: reptile skin, buckle
Price: $54,000; limited to 300 pieces
Variations: with rubber band

Master Grande Tradition à Répétition Minutes

Reference number: 509 25 20
Movement: automatic, JLC Caliber 942; height 7.17 mm; 58 jewels; 28,800 vph; 40-hour power reserve
Functions: hours, minutes, subsidiary seconds; minute repeater
Case: pink gold, ø 39 mm, height 12.1 mm; sapphire crystal; transparent case back; water-resistant to 5 atm
Band: reptile skin, buckle
Price: $180,000

Master Grande Tradition Tourbillon Cylindrique à Quantième Perpétuel

Reference number: 504 35 80
Movement: automatic, JLC Caliber 985; ø 30.7 mm, height 8.25 mm; 49 jewels; 28,800 vph; flying 1-minute tourbillon; cylindrical balance spring, 45-hour power reserve
Functions: hours, minutes, subsidiary seconds (on tourbillon); perpetual calendar with date, weekday, month, moon phase, year display (digital, 4 digits)
Case: white gold, ø 42 mm, height 13.1 mm; sapphire crystal; transparent back; water-resistant to 5 atm
Band: reptile skin, buckle
Price: $137,000

Master Grande Tradition Grande Complication

Reference number: 502 25 80
Movement: manually wound, JLC Caliber 945; height 12.62 mm; 49 jewels; 28,800 vph; flying orbital 1-minute tourbillon; repeating mechanism with trebuchet hammers/cathedral gongs; 40-hour power reserve
Functions: hours, minutes; additional 24-hour indicator (2nd time zone); minute repeater, tourbillon turns counterclockwise/shows sidereal time of stars; firmament/zodiac calendar
Case: pink gold, ø 45 mm, height 15.8 mm; sapphire crystal; transparent back; water-resistant to 5 atm
Band: reptile skin, buckle
Price: on request

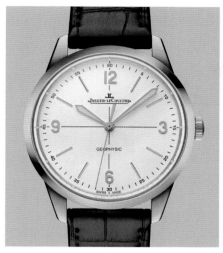

Geophysic 1958

Reference number: 800 85 20
Movement: automatic, JLC Caliber 898/1;
ø 26 mm, height 3.3 mm; 30 jewels; 28,800 vph;
43-hour power reserve
Functions: hours, minutes, sweep seconds
Case: stainless steel, ø 38.5 mm, height 11.32 mm;
sapphire crystal; transparent case back; water-
resistant to 10 atm
Band: reptile skin, buckle
Price: $9,800; limited to 800 pieces
Variations: pink gold ($20,800)

Geophysic 1958

Reference number: 800 25 20
Movement: automatic, JLC Caliber 898/1;
ø 26 mm, height 3.3 mm; 30 jewels; 28,800 vph;
43-hour power reserve
Functions: hours, minutes, sweep seconds
Case: pink gold, ø 38.5 mm, height 11.32 mm;
sapphire crystal; transparent case back; water-
resistant to 10 atm
Band: reptile skin, buckle
Price: $20,800; limited to 300 pieces
Variations: stainless steel ($9,800)

Grande Reverso Ultra Thin 1931

Reference number: 278 25 60
Movement: manually wound, JLC Caliber 822-
2; height 2.95 mm; 19 jewels; 21,600 vph; fine
finishing by hand; 45-hour power reserve
Functions: hours, minutes, subsidiary seconds
Case: pink gold, 27.4 x 46.8 mm, height 7.3 mm;
sapphire crystal; water-resistant to 3 atm
Band: reptile skin, buckle
Remarks: case turns and swivels 180°; comes with
2nd strap
Price: $17,200

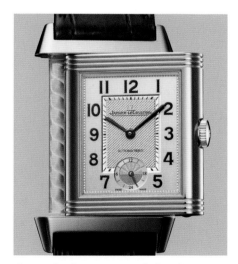

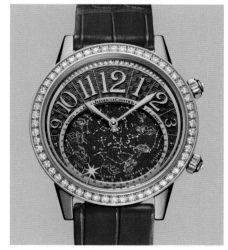

Grande Reverso Night & Day

Reference number: 380 25 20
Movement: automatic, JLC Caliber 967B; height
4.05 mm; 28 jewels; 28,800 vph; fine finishing by
hand; 42-hour power reserve
Functions: hours, minutes; additional 24-hour
display, day/night indicator
Case: pink gold, 27.4 x 46.8 mm, height 9.14 mm;
sapphire crystal; transparent case back; water-
resistant to 3 atm
Band: reptile skin, buckle
Remarks: case can turn and pivot by 180°
Price: $17,700
Variations: stainless steel ($8,850)

Rendez-Vous Moon

Reference number: 352 34 90
Movement: automatic, JLC Caliber 935; ø 30 mm,
height 4.63 mm; 41 jewels; 28,800 vph; pink gold
rotor; 42-hour power reserve
Functions: hours, minutes; moon phase
Case: white gold, ø 36 mm, height 10.5 mm; 166
diamonds on bezel and lugs; sapphire crystal;
transparent case back; water-resistant to 3 atm
Band: satin, folding clasp
Price: $44,100
Variations: 39 mm case ($54,000)

Rendez-Vous Celestial

Reference number: 348 25 60
Movement: automatic, JLC Caliber 809/I; ø 26 mm,
height 5.23 mm; 31 jewels; 28,800 vph; 40-hour
power reserve
Functions: hours, minutes, heavenly chart with
zodiac
Case: pink gold, ø 37.5 mm, height 10.54 mm; 60
diamonds on bezel; sapphire crystal; transparent
case back; water-resistant to 5 atm
Band: reptile skin, buckle
Price: $53,500

Caliber 362

Automatic; ultra-thin construction; flying 1-minute tourbillon with flying (one-sided) balance; hubless peripheral winding rotor; repeater mechanism with reduced waiting times; single spring barrel; 45-hour power reserve
Functions: hours, minutes; hour, quarter-hour, and minute repeater
Diameter: 33.3 mm; **Height:** 4.8 mm
Jewels: 68
Balance: glucydur
Frequency: 21,600 vph
Balance spring: glucydur
Remarks: 471 components

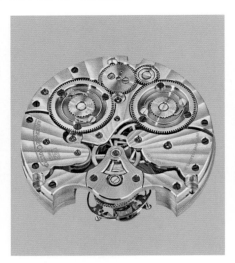

Caliber 382

Manually wound; 2 spring barrels and 2 separate mechanisms for watch and double-axis tourbillon, double-axis tourbillon with 20° tilt, 15- or 30-second revolution; second hand resert via crown; twin spring barrels, 50-hour power reserve
Functions: hours, minutes, subsidiary seconds; 2nd time zone (additional 24-hour display); annual calendar with date; double power reserve display
Diameter: 33.7 mm; **Height:** 10.45 mm
Jewels: 33; **Balance:** glucydur
Frequency: 21,600 vph
Balance spring: cylindrical

Caliber 383

Manually wound; 2 separate spring barrels and 2 separate gear works for 2 time displays, second hand resert via crown; 50-hour power reserve
Functions: hours and minutes (off-center), sweep seconds; 2nd time zone (digital, jumping hours, minutes) world-time display, separate power reserve indicator for each spring barrel
Diameter: 34.3 mm
Height: 7.25 mm
Jewels: 54
Balance: glucydur
Frequency: 28,800 vph

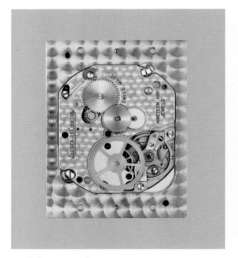

Caliber 986

Manually wound; 48-hour power reserve
Functions: hours, minutes, subsidiary seconds; 24-hour display (2nd time zone); date
Measurements: 22.6 x 25.6 mm
Height: 4.15 mm
Jewels: 19
Frequency: 28,800 vph
Balance spring: flat hairspring
Shock protection: Kif
Remarks: perlage on plate

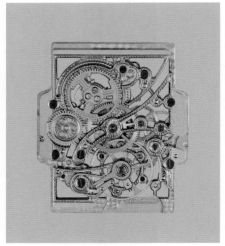

Caliber 849 RSQ

Manually wound; fully skeletonized and engraved by hand; simple spring barrel, 35-hour power reserve
Functions: hours, minutes
Measurements: 20 x 23.5 mm
Height: 2.09 mm
Jewels: 19
Balance: glucydur
Frequency: 21,600 vph
Balance spring: flat spring with swan-neck fine adjustment
Shock protection: Kif
Remarks: 128 components

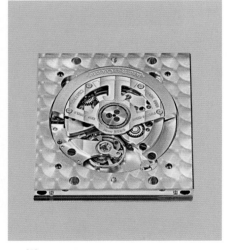

Caliber 967B

Automatic; single spring barrel, 42-hour power reserve
Functions: hours, minutes; additional 12-hour indicator (2nd time zone), day/night indicator
Diameter: 23 mm
Height: 4.05 mm
Jewels: 28
Balance: glucydur, with a smooth rim
Frequency: 28,800 vph
Balance spring: flat hairspring
Shock protection: Kif
Remarks: perlage on plate

Caliber 757

Automatic; column wheel control of chronograph functions; 2 spring barrels, 65-hour power reserve
Functions: hours, minutes, subsidiary seconds; additional 12-hour display (2nd time zone), day/night indicator; chronograph; date
Diameter: 28 mm
Height: 6.26 mm
Jewels: 45
Balance: glucydur with 4 weighted screws
Frequency: 28,800 vph
Balance spring: flat hairspring
Shock protection: Kif

Caliber 849

Manually wound; single spring barrel, 35-hour power reserve
Functions: hours, minutes
Diameter: 26 mm
Height: 1.85 mm
Jewels: 19
Balance: glucydur
Frequency: 21,600 vph
Balance spring: flat hairspring
Shock protection: Kif
Remarks: finely finished movement, bridges with côtes de Genève; 123 components

Caliber 898A

Automatic; single spring barrel, 43-hour power reserve
Functions: hours, minutes, sweep seconds; day/night indicator
Diameter: 26 mm
Height: 3.3 mm
Jewels: 30
Balance: glucydur with 4 weighted screws
Frequency: 28,800 vph
Balance spring: flat hairspring
Shock protection: Kif

Caliber 866

Automatic; single spring barrel, 43-hour power reserve
Functions: hours, minutes, subsidiary seconds; full calendar with date, weekday, month, moon phase
Diameter: 26 mm
Height: 5.65 mm
Jewels: 32
Balance: glucydur
Frequency: 28,800 vph
Balance spring: flat hairspring
Shock protection: Kif
Remarks: fine finishing on movement, bridges with côtes de Genève

Caliber 982

Automatic; 1-minute tourbillon; full gold rotor; single spring barrel, 48-hour power reserve
Functions: hours, minutes, subsidiary seconds (on tourbillon cage)
Diameter: 30 mm
Height: 6.4 mm
Jewels: 33
Balance: glucydur with weighted screws
Frequency: 28,800 vph
Balance spring: Breguet spring
Shock protection: Kif
Remarks: perlage on plate, bridges with côtes de Genève

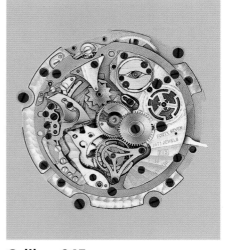

Caliber 945

Manually wound; silicon pallet lever with integrated pallets; flying tourbillon rotates with dial in 56 minutes (sidereal/astronomical time); single spring barrel; 48-hour power reserve
Functions: hours, minutes; hour, quarter-hour, and minute repeater; perpetual calendar with date, month, map of sky with signs of zodiac
Diameter: 31 mm; **Height:** 12.62 mm
Jewels: 49
Balance: screw balance
Frequency: 28,800 vph
Balance spring: flat hairspring
Remarks: 527 components; repetition with trebuchet hammer to reinforce impulse

Montres Jaquet Droz SA
CH-2300 La Chaux-de-Fonds
Switzerland

Tel.:
+41-32-924-2888

Fax:
+41-32-924-2882

E-Mail:
info@jaquet-droz.com

Website:
www.jaquet-droz.com

Founded:
1738

U.S. distributor:
The Swatch Group (U.S.), Inc.
1200 Harbor Boulevard
Weehawken, NJ 07086
201-271-1400
www.swatchgroup.com

Most important collections:
Les Ateliers d'Art, Grande Seconde, Grande
Seconde SW, Astrale Collection, Petite Heure
Minute, Lady 8

Jaquet Droz

Though this watch brand first gained real notice when it was bought by the Swatch Group in 2001, Jaquet Droz looks back on a long tradition. Pierre Jaquet-Droz (1721–1790) was actually supposed to be a pastor, but instead followed the call to become a mechanic and a watchmaker. In the mid-eighteenth century, he began to push the limits of micromechanics, and his enthusiasm for it quickly led him to work on watch mechanisms and more complicated movements, which he attempted to operate through purely mechanical means.

Jaquet-Droz became famous in Europe for his automatons. More than once, he had to answer to religious institutions, whose guardians of public morals suspected there might be some devil's work and witchcraft behind his mechanical children, scribes, and organists. He even designed prostheses. A small enterprise in La Chaux-de-Fonds still produces items of this applied art, proof that the name Jaquet-Droz is still alive and well in the Jura mountains. The true wealth of the Jaquet-Droz family's output, however, was shown in the stunning exhibition "Automats and Marvels" organized in Neuchâtel, La Chaux-de-Fonds, and Le Locle in 2012.

The Swatch Group has developed an aesthetically and technically sophisticated collection based on an outstanding Frédéric Piguet movement. In recent years, the classically beautiful watch dials have taken on a slightly modern look without losing any of their identity. The spirit of the maverick founder of the brand still hovers about. In fact, Jaquet Droz is a top representative in the Swatch Group's portfolio. Its CEO is Marc A. Hayek, who is also CEO of Breguet and Blancpain.

The Bird Repeater "Geneva"

Reference number: J031033204
Movement: manual winding, Jaquet Droz Caliber RMA88; ø 35 mm, height 8.8 mm; 69 jewels; 18,000 vph; 48-hour power reserve
Functions: hours and minutes (off-center); minute repeater
Case: pink gold, ø 47 mm, height 18.7 mm; sapphire crystal
Band: reptile skin, folding clasp
Remarks: handpainted mother-of-pearl dial
Price: $472,500; limited to 8 pieces

Grande Seconde Tourbillon "Pietersit"

Reference number: J013014271
Movement: automatic, Jaquet Droz Caliber 25JD; ø 28 mm, height 5.85 mm; 31 jewels; 21,600 vph; 1-minute tourbillon, white gold oscillating mass, 192-hour power reserve
Functions: hours, minutes, subsidiary seconds
Case: white gold, ø 39 mm, height 13.2 mm; 260 diamonds on bezel and lugs; sapphire crystal; transparent case back; water-resistant to 3 atm
Band: reptile skin, folding clasp
Remarks: pietersite dial with 90 diamonds
Price: $117,300; limited to 8 pieces

Lady 8 Flower

Reference number: J032003200
Movement: automatic, Jaquet Droz Caliber 2653; ø 26.2 mm, height 15.7 mm; 29 jewels; escapement with silicon regulating screws and balance spring; platinum oscilating mass; added automaton mechanism with opening flower; 38-hour power reserve
Functions: hours, minutes
Case: pink gold, ø 35 mm; 114 diamonds on bezel; sapphire crystal; water-resistant to 3 atm
Band: reptile skin, folding clasp
Remarks: hand-engraved and enameled petals, pink gold butterfly; mother-of-pearl dial under the flower
Price: $157,500; limited to 28 pieces
Variations: white gold ($262,500)

Jörg Schauer

Jörg Schauer's watches are first and foremost cool. The cases have been carefully worked, the look is planned to draw the eye. After all, he is a perfectionist and leaves nothing to chance. He works on every single case himself, polishing and performing his own brand of magic for as long as it takes to display his personal touch. This time-consuming process is one that Schauer believes is absolutely necessary. "I do this because I place a great deal of value on the fact that my cases are absolutely perfect," he explains. "I can do it better than anyone, and I would never let anyone else do it for me."

Schauer, a goldsmith by training, has been making watches since 1990. He began by doing one-off pieces in precious metals for collectors and then opened his business and simultaneously moved to stainless steel. His style is to produce functional, angular cases with visibly screwed-down bezels and straightforward dials in plain black or white. Forget finding any watch close to current trends in his collection; Schauer only builds timepieces that he genuinely likes.

Purchasing a Schauer is not that easy. He has chosen a strategy of genuine quality over quantity and only produces to about 500 annually. This includes special watches like the One-Hand Durowe, with a movement from one of Germany's movement manufacturers, Durowe, which Schauer acquired in 2002. His production structure is a vital part of his success and includes prototyping, movement modification, finishing, case production, dial painting and printing—all done in Schauer's own workshop in Engelsbrand. Any support he needs from the outside he prefers to search out among regional specialists.

Jörg Schauer
c/o Stowa GmbH & Co. KG
Gewerbepark 16
D-75331 Engelsbrand
Germany

Tel.:
+49-7082-9306-0

Fax:
+49-7082-9306-2

E-Mail:
info@schauer-germany.com

Website:
www.schauer-germany.com

Founded:
1990

Number of employees:
20

Annual production:
approx. 500 watches

Distribution:
direct sales; please contact the address in Germany

Edition 12

Reference number: Ed12
Movement: automatic, ETA Caliber 7753; ø 30 mm, height 7.9 mm; 27 jewels; 28,800 vph; ornamental stripes, blued screws, exclusive engraved Schauer rotor; 48-hour power reserve
Functions: hours, minutes, subsidiary seconds; chronograph
Case: stainless steel, ø 41 mm, height 15 mm; bezel fixed with 12 screws; sapphire crystal; transparent case back; water-resistant to 5 atm
Band: calf leather, double folding clasp
Price: $3,423
Variations: reptile skin band ($3,495); stainless steel band ($3,702)

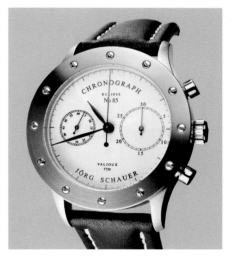

Edition 10

Reference number: Ed10
Movement: automatic, ETA Caliber 7753; ø 30 mm, height 7.9 mm; 27 jewels; 28,800 vph; ornamental stripes, blued screws, exclusive engraved Schauer rotor; 42-hour power reserve
Functions: hours, minutes, subsidiary seconds; chronograph
Case: stainless steel, ø 42 mm, height 15 mm; bezel fixed with 12 screws; sapphire crystal on front and back, antireflective inside; water-resistant to 5 atm
Band: calf leather, double folding clasp
Price: $3,350
Variations: reptile band ($3,405); stainless steel bracelet ($3,612); manually wound ($3,693)

Edition 15

Reference number: Ed15
Movement: automatic, ETA Caliber 7753; ø 30 mm, height 7.9 mm; 27 jewels; 28,800 vph; ornamental stripes, blued screws, exclusive engraved Schauer rotor; 40-hour power reserve
Functions: hours, minutes, subsidiary seconds; chronograph; date
Case: stainless steel, ø 44 mm, height 15 mm; bezel fixed with 12 screws; sapphire crystal on front and back, antireflective inside; water-resistant to 5 atm
Band: calf leather, double folding clasp
Price: $3,342
Variations: leather strap ($3,423); stainless steel bracelet ($3,441)

Kobold Watch Company, LLC

1801 Parkway View Drive
Pittsburgh, PA 15205

Tel.:
724-533-3000

E-Mail:
info@koboldwatch.com

Website:
www.koboldwatch.com

Founded:
1998

Number of employees:
12

Annual production:
maximum 2,500 watches

Distribution:
factory-direct, select retailers

Most important collections/price range:
Soarway / $1,950 to $35,000

Kobold

Like many others in the field, Michael Kobold had already developed an interest in the watch industry in childhood. As a young man, he found a mentor in Chronoswiss founder Gerd-Rüdiger Lang, who encouraged him to start his own brand. This he did in 1998—at the age of nineteen while he was still a student at Carnegie Mellon University.

Kobold Watch Company grew to twelve employees split between Amish Country in Pennsylvania and a subsidiary in Kathmandu, Nepal. In 2014, Kobold inaugurated a new headquarters on a 170-year-old farm. There, the company manufactures cases, movement components, dials, hands, and even straps. Kobold has contributed to the renaissance of American watchmaking and has set its sights even higher, namely, on an in-house U.S.-made movement. The Kathmandu operation was run by two former sherpas, Namgel and Thundu, who trained under Kobold watchmakers in Pittsburgh in 2011 and went on to oversee the first mechanical watch company in the Himalayas. Alas, the violent earthquake of April 2015 destroyed the budding industry. At the time of writing, the future of this enterprise is unknown, and Michael Kobold is very busy organizing relief for the people of Nepal.

The company's motto—Embrace Adventure—is reflected in the adventure-themed watches it turns out worn by explorers such as Sir Ranulph Fiennes, whom the *Guinness Book of Records* describes as "the world's greatest living explorer." The brand's centerpiece is the Soarway collection and the fabled Soarway case, which was originally created in 1999 by Sir Ranulph, master watchmaker and Chronoswiss founder Lang, as well as company founder Kobold. The Soarway collection includes several novelties, including the Soarway Transglobe, a watch with a second time zone that displays minutes as well as hours.

Soarway Transglobe

Reference number: KN 266853
Movement: automatic, Caliber K.793 (base ETA 2892-A2); ø 36 mm, height 4.95 mm; 26 jewels; 28,800 vph; 46-hour power reserve
Functions: hours, minutes, sweep seconds; date; 2nd time zone with hours and minutes
Case: stainless steel, ø 44 mm, height 14.3 mm; sapphire crystal; screwed-down case back; water-resistant to 30 atm
Band: canvas, signed buckle
Price: $3,950

Himalaya

Reference number: KN 880121
Movement: automatic, ETA Caliber 2824-A2; ø 30.4 mm, height 10.35 mm; 25 jewels; 28,800 vph; 42-hour power reserve
Functions: hours, minutes, sweep seconds
Case: stainless steel, ø 44 mm, height 11.3 mm; antireflective sapphire crystal; screwed-down case back; water-resistant to 10 atm
Band: calf leather, buckle
Price: $3,250
Variations: black or white dial

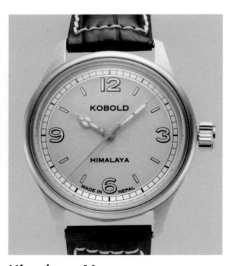

Himalaya 41

Reference number: KN 830854
Movement: automatic, ETA Caliber 2824-A2; ø 30.4 mm, height 10.35 mm; 25 jewels; 28,800 vph; 42-hour power reserve
Functions: hours, minutes, sweep seconds
Case: stainless steel, ø 41 mm, height 12.6 mm; antireflective sapphire crystal; screwed-down case back; water-resistant to 10 atm
Band: reptile, buckle
Price: $2,950

Phantom Tactical Chronograph

Reference number: KD 924451
Movement: automatic, ETA Valjoux Caliber 7750; ø 30 mm, height 8.1 mm; 25 jewels; 28,800 vph; 46-hour power reserve; côtes de Genève, perlage, engraved and skeletonized gold-plated rotor
Functions: hours, minutes, subsidiary seconds; date, day; chronograph
Case: PVD-coated stainless steel, made in USA, ø 41 mm, height 15.3 mm; unidirectional bezel with 60-minute divisions; screwed-in crown/buttons; sapphire crystal; screwed-down back; water-resistant to 300 m
Band: PVD-coated stainless steel, folding clasp
Price: $4,250

Phantom Chronograph

Reference number: KD 924453
Movement: automatic, ETA Valjoux Caliber 7750; ø 30 mm, height 8.1 mm; 25 jewels; 28,800 vph; 46-hour power reserve
Functions: hours, minutes, subsidiary seconds; perpetual calendar, date, weekday; chronograph
Case: stainless steel, made in USA, ø 41 mm, height 15.3 mm; unidirectional bezel with 60-minute divisions; screwed-in crown and buttons; sapphire crystal; screwed-down case back; water-resistant to 30 atm
Band: canvas, folding clasp
Price: $3,450

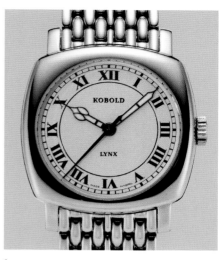

Lynx

Reference number: KD 415752
Movement: automatic, ETA Caliber 2892-A2; ø 28 mm, height 3.6 mm; 25 jewels; 28,800 vph; 46-hour power reserve
Functions: hours, minutes, sweep seconds
Case: stainless steel, made in USA, ø 36 mm, height 10.2 mm; antireflective sapphire crystal; screwed-down case back; water-resistant to 10 atm
Band: stainless steel bracelet, folding clasp
Price: $2,450
Variations: dial made from Mt. Everest summit rock, mother-of-pearl, diamond bezel

Polar Surveyor

Reference number: KD 915151
Movement: automatic, Caliber K.751 (base ETA 7750); ø 26.2 mm, height 5.3 mm; 28 jewels; 28,800 vph; 42-hour power reserve
Functions: hours, minutes, sweep seconds; perpetual calendar, date; chronograph; day/night indicator
Case: stainless steel, made in USA, ø 41 mm, height 15.3 mm; antireflective sapphire crystal; screwed-down case back; screwed-in crown; water-resistant to 30 atm
Band: canvas, signed buckle
Price: $4,150

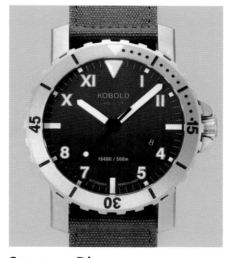

Soarway Diver

Reference number: KD 212441
Movement: automatic, ETA Caliber 2892-A2; ø 28 mm, height 3.6 mm; 25 jewels; 28,800 vph; 46-hour power reserve
Functions: hours, minutes, sweep seconds; date
Case: stainless steel, made in USA; ø 43.5 mm, height 15 mm; unidirectional bezel; soft iron core; antireflective sapphire crystal; screwed-down case back; screw-in crown; water-resistant to 50 atm
Band: canvas, buckle
Price: $2,150
Variations: standard, non-California dial; Arctic Blue dial

SMG-2

Reference number: KD 956853
Movement: automatic, Caliber ETA 2893-A2; ø 26.2 mm, height 6.1 mm; 21 jewels; 28,800 vph; 40-hour power reserve
Functions: hours, minutes, sweep seconds; 2nd time zone; date
Case: stainless steel, made in USA; ø 43 mm, height 12.75 mm; unidirectional bezel; soft iron core; antireflective sapphire crystal; screwed-down case back; screwed-in crown; water-resistant to 30 atm
Band: canvas, buckle
Price: $3,650

Konstantin Chaykin Manufacture

Rechnikov Street 2, Building 15
RU-115407 Moscow
Russia

Tel.:
+7-495-988-73-72

E-Mail:
info@chaykin.ru

Website:
www.konstantin-chaykin.com

Founded:
2003

Number of employees:
10

Annual production:
approx. 20 timepieces

U. S. distribution:
Contact company directly.

Most important collections:
small series of uniquely themed watches and clocks

Konstantin Chaykin

Twelve years ago, in St. Petersburg, the budding watchmaker Konstantin Chaykin created the first Russian table clock with a flying tourbillon. The world did not even notice this engineering artist at first, but collector circles in Russia were thrilled. Soon the young man began repairing and restoring watches, which gave him the opportunity to learn all about the tricks of the trade as applied by the old masters.

There is no watchmaking school in Russia; the craft is transmitted directly. Chaykin became a highly coveted teacher himself. He went to Moscow and founded the first modern Russian watch *manufacture* producing *haute horlogerie* pieces. He gathered a team of his most talented apprentices and focused on the development, design, and manufacturing of in-house watches. Every year, his workshop with a view of the Kolomenskoye Natural History Museum produces about twenty highly complicated timepieces, each imbued with a deep sense of poetry, both in their visual appearance as well as their functionality.

In fact, Chaykin already holds forty-five patents for his unusual designs, which quite often break the mold of traditional watchmaking. His creations range from complicated animations and all manner of little technical devices to simple but ingenious ways to display things on the dial, like the sculptural moon of the Lunokhod, which gets covered by a shadow, or the Carpe Diem, which artistically displays Father Time holding an hourglass. These complications are unique in the six hundred years of watchmaking history.

Chaykin's star rose internationally when he became a member of the Académie Horlogère des Créateurs Indépendants (AHCI). His watches began appearing at exhibitions and trade fairs, and soon his products were known to aficionados from all over. Chaykin's strategy is set: build up a small core collection, without neglecting unique pieces and complicated clocks.

Cinema

Movement: manually wound, Caliber K06-0; 32 x 42.5 mm; height 8.8 mm; 37 jewels; 21,600 vph; separate gears with locking system show 12 motifs of animation with galloping horse, 0.8 seconds shutter speed, 20 seconds clip fully wound; 45-hour power reserve
Functions: hours, minutes; animation (image sequence)
Case: white gold, 37.6 x 47.6 mm, height 13.8 mm; sapphire crystal
Band: reptile skin, buckle
Remarks: animation from Eadweard Muybridge's Zoopraxiscope; limited to 12 pieces
Price: $66,200

Genius Temporis

Movement: manually wound, Caliber K01-5; ø 36 mm, height 9.5 mm; 29 jewels; 21,600 vph; 1-hand mechanism hour hand displays minutes by pusher at 2 o'clock; 48-hour power reserve
Functions: hours (minutes on request)
Case: rose gold, ø 44 mm, height 12.2 mm; sapphire crystal; sapphire cabochon on crown
Band: reptile skin, buckle
Remarks: limited to 12 pieces
Price: $28,500

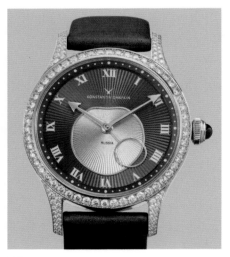

Diana

Movement: manually wound, Caliber K01-6; ø 31 mm, height 7.3 mm; 17 jewels; 21,600 vph; 48-hour power reserve
Functions: hours, minutes, moon phase
Case: white gold, ø 40 mm, height 11 mm; 138 diamonds on bezel and lugs; sapphire crystal; sapphire cabochon on crown
Band: satin, buckle
Remarks: moon phase using ring display that travels over dial in contrasting colors; limited to 12 pieces
Price: $28,500

Kudoke

Stefan Kudoke, a watchmaker from Frankfurt/Oder, has made a name for himself as an extremely skilled and imaginative creator of timepieces. He apprenticed with two experienced watchmakers and graduated as the number one trainee in the state of Brandenburg. This earned him a stipend from a federal program promoting gifted individuals. He then moved on to one of the large *manufactures* in Glashütte, where he refined his skills in its workshop for complications and prototyping. At the age of twenty-two, with a master's diploma in his pocket, he decided to get an MBA and then devote himself to building his own company.

His guiding principle is individuality, and that is not possible to find in a serial product. So Kudoke began building unique pieces. By realizing the special wishes of customers, he manages to reflect each person's uniqueness in each watch. And he has produced some out-of-the-ordinary pieces, like the ExCentro1 and 2, whose dials are off-center and hint at a feeling for the absurd, à la Dalí.

His specialties include engraving and goldsmithing. Within his creations bridges may in fact be graceful bodies, or the fine skeletonizing of a plate fragment, a world of figures and garlands. In 2012, he presented the ladies' White Flower, frankly romantic and surprisingly simple. A close look at the bridges and fragments of the mainplate reveals small works of art—the shape of a grasping octopus, the sensuous body of a woman, or a skull with a bone, giving the term "skeleton watch" a special meaning.

Kudoke Uhren
Tannenweg 5
D-15236 Frankfurt (Oder)
Germany

Tel.:
+49-335-280-0409

E-Mail:
info@kudoke.eu

Website:
www.kudoke.eu

Founded:
2007

Number of employees:
1

Annual production:
30–50 watches

U.S. distributor:
Kudoke
WatchBuys
888-333-4895
www.watchbuys.com

Most important collections/price range:
between approx. $4,500 and $11,500

ExCentro II

Movement: automatic, ETA Caliber 2824-2; ø 25.6 mm, height 4.6 mm; 25 jewels; 28,800 vph; partly hand-skeletonized and engraved, gold-plated rotor; 38-hour power reserve
Functions: hours, minutes, sweep seconds; date
Case: stainless steel, ø 42 mm, height 10.5 mm; sapphire crystal; transparent case back; water-resistant to 5 atm
Band: reptile skin, buckle
Remarks: ring to hold movement, customizable
Price: $4,430

HR1-Ring

Movement: manually wound, modified ETA Caliber 6498; ø 36.6 mm, height 4.5 mm; 17 jewels; 18,000 vph; hand-skeletonized and engraved; 38-hour power reserve
Functions: hours, minutes
Case: stainless steel, ø 42 mm, height 10.5 mm; sapphire crystal; transparent case back
Band: reptile skin, buckle
Remarks: hand-guilloché silver dial
Price: $6,370

Real Skeleton

Movement: manually wound, modified ETA Caliber 6498; ø 36.6 mm, height 4.5 mm; 17 jewels; 18,000 vph; screw balance, polished pallet lever and escape wheel, hand-skeletonized and engraved; 38-hour power reserve
Functions: hours, minutes
Case: stainless steel, ø 42 mm, height 10.5 mm; sapphire crystal; transparent case back
Band: reptile skin, buckle
Remarks: real bone hands, handmade, skull eyes with diamonds
Price: $9,740

Linde Werdelin
Studio 7, 27a Pembridge Villas
London W11 3EP
United Kingdom

Tel.:
+44-207-727-6577

Fax:
+44-207-900-1722

E-Mail:
info@lindewerdelin.com

Website:
www.lindewerdelin.com

Founded:
2002

Number of employees:
20+

Annual production:
600–1000

U.S. distributor:
Totally Worth It, LLC
76 Division Avenue
Summit, NJ 07901-2309
201-894-4710
info@totallyworthit.com

Most important collections/price range:
SpidoSpeed, SpidoLite, Oktopus / $11,000
to $44,200

Linde Werdelin

There are sports watches, and then there are watches for sports. Morton Linde and Jorn Werdelin, two Danes, were just teenagers when they started comparing their iconic acquisitions, like their Cartier Santos Octogonal, their Reversos, their Royal Oaks. Werdelin went on to study business; Linde became an industrial designer—the chairs in Copenhagen's park are from his drawing board.

The two men also shared a love of sports, particularly skiing. One day, when Werdelin was recovering from a severe skiing accident, the two friends dreamed up the idea of launching a sports watch. Thus Linde Werdelin was founded in 2002, and their idea gradually grew into a full-fledged concept, bold and quite literally out-of-the-box. Why confine oneself to mechanics, when electronics do some things better? A separate clip-on instrument box with a sophisticated mini-computer could be affixed to the base watch to display and log all the parameters of the activity being performed: The Reef, for divers, displays dive time, ascent rate, temperature, decompression stops, and more. For climbers, the Rock features a chronometer, altimeter, thermometer, three-point compass, incline indicator, and much more. As for the watch itself, without its IT unit, it spices up refinement with a dose of industrial ruggedness and hell-raiser edginess. So the collections were born: the Founders—the Elemental and 2-Timer—the Oktopus, and the SpidoSpeed, a three-way summit between tradition, high-tech, and style for the active and athletic with clip-ons for diving and skiing.

Divers looking for the thrill and romance of a moonlit plunge now have the Oktopus MoonLite, launched at Baselworld 2014 alongside the new-generation SpidoSpeed RoseGold Black and Green. In addition to its budding romance with color (blues, reds, even "champagne" gold), the brand is experimenting with unusual materials like Alloy Linde Werdelin (ALW), an ultralight aerospace zirconium, aluminum, and magnesium-based alloy, or the special ceramic material TiN. All timepieces are manufactured in Geneva and Zurich.

SpidoLite Titanium

Movement: automatic, LW07; ø 30 mm; 27 jewels; skeletonized and customized; 28,800 vph; 48-hour power reserve
Functions: hours, minutes, sweep seconds
Case: titanium satin, polished with microbille finishing; 44 x 46 mm, height 15 mm; antireflective sapphire crystal; screwed-in crown with logo; screwed-down case back; water-resistant to 10 atm
Band: rubber, titanium buckle
Price: $17,400; limited to 75 numbered pieces

Oktopus Double Date Carbon - Green

Movement: automatic, LW-modified Dubois Dépraz caliber 14580; 26.2 mm; 26 jewels; 28,800 vph; 42-hour power reserve
Functions: hours, minutes, sweep seconds; double date
Case: multilayer carbon, 44 x 46 mm, height 15 mm; black ceramic bezel; titanium screws with TIN treatment; antireflective sapphire crystal; titanium case back with TIN and microbillé finishing, octopus motif engraving; water-resistant to 30 atm
Band: rubber, buckle
Remarks: special double date complication; 5-layered dial with côtes de Genève
Price: $15,900; limited to 88 numbered pieces

Oktopus BluMoon

Movement: automatic, bespoke caliber with in-house moon phase complication; 23 jewels; 28,800 vph; 44-hour power reserve
Functions: hours, minutes, sweep seconds; moon phase
Case: titanium satin, polished with microbillé finishing; 44 x 46 mm, height 15 mm; antireflective sapphire crystal; titanium grade 5 crown engraved with octopus icon; titanium case back engraved with octopus motif; water resistant to 30 atm
Band: rubber strap; buckle
Price: $18,200; limited to 59 numbered pieces

Longines

The Longines winged hourglass logo is the world's oldest trademark, according to the World Intellectual Property Organization (WIPO). Since its founding in 1832, the brand has manufactured somewhere in the region of 35 million watches, making it one of the genuine heavyweights of the Swiss watch world. In 1983, Nicolas G. Hayek merged the two major Swiss watch manufacturing groups ASUAG and SIHH into what would later become the Swatch Group. Longines, the leading ASUAG brand, barely missed capturing the same position in the new concern; that honor went to Omega, the SIHH frontrunner. However, from a historical and technical point of view, this brand has what it takes to be at the helm of any group. Was it not Longines that equipped polar explorer Roald Amundsen and air pioneer Charles Lindbergh with their watches? It has also been the timekeeper at many Olympic Games and, since 2007, the official timekeeper for the French Open at Roland Garros. In fact, this brand is a major sponsor at many sports events, from riding to archery.

It is not surprising then to find that this venerable Jura company also has an impressive portfolio of in-house calibers in stock, from simple manual winders to complicated chronographs. This broad technological base has benefited the company. As a genuine "one-stop shop," the brand can supply the Swatch Group with anything from cheap, thin quartz watches to heavy gold chronographs and calendars with quadruple retrograde displays. Longines does have one particular specialty, besides elegant ladies' watches and modern sports watches, in that it often has the luxury of rebuilding the classics from its own long history.

Longines Watch Co.
CH-2610 St.-Imier
Switzerland

Tel.:
+41-32-942-5425

Fax:
+41-32-942-5429

E-Mail:
info@longines.com

Website:
www.longines.com

Founded:
1832

Number of employees:
worldwide approx. 900

U.S. distributor:
Longines
The Swatch Group (U.S.), Inc.
1200 Harbor Boulevard
Weehawken, NJ 07087
201-271-1400
www.longines.com

Most important collections/price range:
Saint-Imier, Master Collection, PrimaLuna, Conquest Classic Collection, Heritage Collection / from approx. $1,350 to $6,500

Hydro Conquest

Reference number: L3.642.4.56.6
Movement: automatic, Caliber L633 (base ETA 2824-2); ø 25.6 mm, height 4.6 mm; 25 jewels; 28,800 vph; 38-hour power reserve
Functions: hours, minutes, sweep seconds; date
Case: stainless steel, ø 41 mm, height 11.9 mm; unidirectional bezel with 60-minute division; sapphire crystal; screw-in crown; water-resistant to 30 atm
Band: stainless steel, safety double folding clasp with extension link
Price: $1,275

Hydro Conquest Chronograph

Reference number: L3.696.4.59.2
Movement: automatic, Caliber L688 (base ETA A08.L01); ø 30 mm, height 7.9 mm; 27 jewels; 28,800 vph; 54-hour power reserve
Functions: hours, minutes, subsidiary seconds; chronograph; date
Case: stainless steel, ø 41 mm, height 15.6 mm; unidirectional bezel with aluminum inlay, with 60-minute division; sapphire crystal; screw-in crown; water-resistant to 30 atm
Band: rubber, double folding clasp
Price: $2,325
Variations: stainless steel bracelet

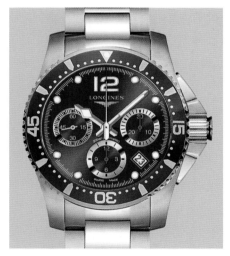

Hydro Conquest Chronograph

Reference number: L3.744.4.96.6
Movement: automatic, Caliber L688 (base ETA A08.L01); ø 30 mm, height 7.9 mm; 27 jewels; 28,800 vph; 54-hour power reserve
Functions: hours, minutes, subsidiary seconds; chronograph; date
Case: stainless steel, ø 41 mm, height 15.6 mm; unidirectional bezel with aluminum inlay, with 60-minute division; sapphire crystal; screw-in crown; water-resistant to 30 atm
Band: stainless steel, safety double folding clasp
Price: $2,050

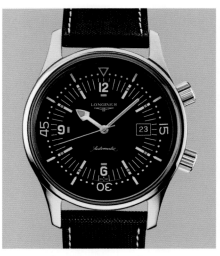

Legend Diver Watch

Reference number: L3.674.4.50.0
Movement: automatic, Caliber L633 (base ETA 2824-2); ø 25.6 mm, height 4.6 mm; 25 jewels; 28,800 vph; 38-hour power reserve
Functions: hours, minutes, sweep seconds; date
Case: stainless steel, ø 42 mm, height 13.6 mm; inner ring rotated with the crown, with 60-minute division; sapphire crystal; screw-in crown; water-resistant to 30 atm
Band: textile, folding clasp
Price: $2,300

Pulsometer Chronograph

Reference number: L2.801.4.23.2
Movement: automatic, Caliber L788.2 (base ETA A08.L11); ø 30 mm, height 7.9 mm; 27 jewels; 28,800 vph; 54-hour power reserve
Functions: hours, minutes, subsidiary seconds; chronograph; date
Case: stainless steel, ø 40 mm, height 13.73 mm; sapphire crystal; transparent case back; water-resistant to 3 atm
Band: reptile skin, buckle
Price: $4,200

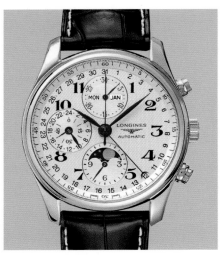

Master Collection Moonphase

Reference number: L2.673.4.78.3
Movement: automatic, Caliber L678 (base ETA 7751); ø 30 mm, height 7.9 mm; 25 jewels; 28,800 vph; 48-hour power reserve
Functions: hours, minutes, subsidiary seconds; additional 24-hour display (2nd time zone); chronograph; full calendar with date, weekday, month, moon phase
Case: stainless steel, ø 40 mm, height 14.24 mm; sapphire crystal; transparent case back; water-resistant to 3 atm
Band: reptile skin, folding clasp
Price: $3,325
Variations: stainless steel bracelet ($2,150)

Master Collection Retrograde

Reference number: L2.715.4.71.3
Movement: automatic, Caliber L707 (base ETA A07.L31); ø 36.6 mm, height 7.9 mm; 25 jewels; 28,800 vph; 48-hour power reserve
Functions: hours, minutes, subsidiary seconds, (retrograde), additional 24-hour display (2nd time zone) (retrograde); date/weekday (retrograde)
Case: stainless steel, ø 41 mm, height 15.4 mm; sapphire crystal; transparent case back; water-resistant to 3 atm
Band: reptile skin, folding clasp
Price: $3,325

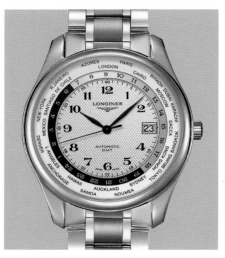

Master Collection GMT

Reference number: L2.802.4.70.6
Movement: automatic, Caliber L635 (base ETA 2824-2); ø 33 mm, height 6.55 mm; 25 jewels; 28,800 vph; 33-hour power reserve
Functions: hours, minutes, sweep seconds; world-time display (2nd time zone); date
Case: stainless steel, ø 42 mm, height 11.5 mm; sapphire crystal; transparent case back; water-resistant to 3 atm
Band: stainless steel, double folding clasp
Price: $2,425

Elegant Collection

Reference number: L4.910.4.11.2
Movement: automatic, Caliber L619 (base ETA 2802-A2); ø 25.6 mm, height 3.6 mm; 21 jewels; 28,800 vph; 42-hour power reserve
Functions: hours, minutes, sweep seconds; date
Case: stainless steel, ø 39 mm, height 8.6 mm; sapphire crystal; transparent case back; water-resistant to 3 atm
Band: reptile skin, buckle
Price: on request

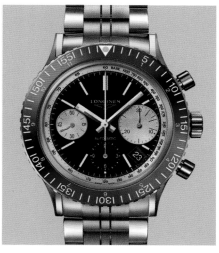

Heritage Diver

Reference number: L2.796.4.52.9
Movement: automatic, Caliber L651 (base ETA 2894-2); ø 28.6 mm, height 6.1 mm; 37 jewels; 28,800 vph; 42-hour power reserve
Functions: hours, minutes, subsidiary seconds; chronograph; date
Case: stainless steel, ø 43 mm, height 15.5 mm; inner ring rotated via crown, with 24-hour division; sapphire crystal; screw-in crown; water-resistant to 30 atm
Band: rubber, safety double folding clasp
Price: $3,750

Heritage Military COSD

Reference number: L2.832.4.53.5
Movement: automatic, Caliber L619 (base ETA 2892-A2); ø 25.6 mm, height 3.6 mm; 21 jewels; 28,800 vph; 42-hour power reserve
Functions: hours, minutes, sweep seconds; date
Case: stainless steel, ø 40 mm, height 10 mm; sapphire crystal; transparent case back; water-resistant to 3 atm
Band: textile, buckle
Price: $1,700

Heritage Diver 1967

Reference number: L2.808.4.52.6
Movement: automatic, Caliber L688 (base ETA A08.L01); ø 30 mm, height 7.9 mm; 27 jewels; 28,800 vph; 54-hour power reserve
Functions: hours, minutes, subsidiary seconds; chronograph; date
Case: stainless steel, ø 42 mm, height 16.2 mm; unidirectional aluminum bezel, with 60-minute division; sapphire crystal; screw-in crown; water-resistant to 30 atm
Band: stainless steel, safety double folding clasp with extension link
Price: $3,150

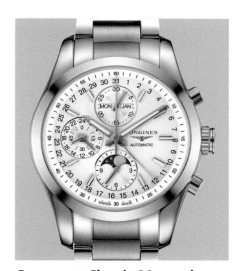

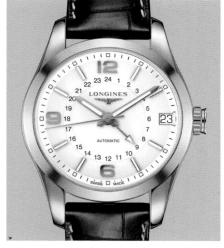

Conquest Classic Moonphase

Reference number: L2.798.4.72.6
Movement: automatic, Caliber L678 (base ETA 7751); ø 30 mm, height 7.9 mm; 25 jewels; 28,800 vph; 48-hour power reserve
Functions: hours, minutes, subsidiary seconds; chronograph; full calendar with date, weekday, month, moon phase
Case: stainless steel, ø 42 mm, height 14.4 mm; sapphire crystal; transparent case back; water-resistant to 5 atm
Band: stainless steel, double folding clasp
Price: $3,900

Conquest Classic Chronograph

Reference number: L2.786.4.56.6
Movement: automatic, Caliber L688 (base ETA A08.L01); ø 30 mm, height 7.9 mm; 27 jewels; 28,800 vph; 54-hour power reserve
Functions: hours, minutes, subsidiary seconds; chronograph; date
Case: stainless steel, ø 41 mm, height 14.2 mm; sapphire crystal; transparent case back; water-resistant to 5 atm
Band: stainless steel, folding clasp
Price: $3,175

Conquest Classic GMT

Reference number: L2.799.5.76.3
Movement: automatic, Caliber 704.2 (base ETA A07.171); ø 36.6 mm, height 7.9 mm; 24 jewels; 28,800 vph; 46-hour power reserve
Functions: hours, minutes, sweep seconds; additional 24-hour display (2nd time zone); date
Case: stainless steel, ø 42 mm, height 14.5 mm; rose gold-colored PVD coating on bezel; sapphire crystal; transparent case back; water-resistant to 5 atm
Band: reptile skin, folding clasp
Price: $3,375

Louis Vuitton Malletier
2, rue du Pont Neuf
F-75034 Paris, Cedex 01
France

Tel.:
+33-1-55-80-41-40

Fax:
+33-1-55-80-41-40

Website:
www.vuitton.com

Founded:
1854

U.S. distributor:
Louis Vuitton
1-866-VUITTON
www.louisvuitton.com

Most important collection/price range:
Tambour / starting at $3,250

Louis Vuitton

The philosophy of this over 150-year-old brand states that any product bearing the name Louis Vuitton must be manufactured in the company's own facilities. That is why Louis Vuitton has allowed itself the luxury of building its own workshop in Switzerland, specifically in La Chaux-de-Fonds, at the technology center of LVMH (Louis Vuitton, Moët & Hennessy).

Designing is carried out in Paris at the company headquarters, and it is obvious that it would not suit an upscale watch to simply cobble together various parts supplied by outside workshops. The cases and dials with all the details and the hands are all exclusive Louis Vuitton designs, as are other components, such as the pushers and the band clasps, in other words, all that is needed to ensure a unique look. In 2011, Louis Vuitton purchased the dial maker Léman Cadran and the movement specialist Fabrique du Temps (both in Geneva), giving the company a great deal of independence vis-à-vis other brands in the group.

You cannot buy a Louis Vuitton watch at your corner jewelry store, but solely through one of the 450 Louis Vuitton boutiques worldwide. What you will find there, for instance, is the 2014 novelty, the unconventional Escale world-time watch with handpainted scale fields in the style of the monograms that Louis Vuitton uses to mark its bags to avoid loss or confusion when loading the bags for an overseas voyage. Those little labels were also always painted by hand.

Escale Time Zone

Reference number: Q5D200
Movement: automatic, LV Caliber 87; ø 34.6 mm, height 5.45 mm; 21 jewels; 28,800 vph; 42-hour power reserve
Functions: hours, minutes; world-time display (2nd time zone) for 24 zones with handpainted rotating discs
Case: stainless steel, ø 39 mm, height 8.4 mm; sapphire crystal; transparent case back; water-resistant to 5 atm
Band: reptile skin, folding clasp
Price: $7,700

Tambour Evolution GMT in Black

Reference number: Q10580
Movement: automatic, LV Caliber 71; ø 26.2 mm, height 4.65 mm; 25 jewels; 28,800 vph; 42-hour power reserve
Functions: hours, minutes, sweep seconds; additional 24-hour display (2nd time zone), day/night indicator; date
Case: stainless steel with black DLC coating, ø 43 mm, height 13.53 mm; sapphire crystal; transparent case back; water-resistant to 10 atm
Band: calf leather, buckle
Price: $10,300

Tambour Monogram Sun Tourbillon

Reference number: Q1EBB0
Movement: automatic, LV Caliber 80; ø 28 mm, height 5.87 mm; 28 jewels; 28,800 vph; flying 1-minute tourbillon; microrotor; 35-hour power reserve
Functions: hours, minutes
Case: pink gold, ø 38 mm, height 12.21 mm; 106 diamonds on bezel and lugs; sapphire crystal; transparent case back; water-resistant to 10 atm
Band: reptile skin, buckle (with 103 diamonds)
Remarks: mother-of-pearl dial with 386 diamonds
Price: $82,000

Manufacture Royale

François-Marie Arouet (1694–1778), best known simply as Voltaire, was a brilliant playwright, historian, freewheeling philosopher, and all-round thinker. He was also one of the richest men in Europe, which allowed him to express his very progressive views— he opposed slavery and the death penalty—and fire off many satirical barbs directed at the powers-that-be, from iniquitous aristocrats and crowned heads to the budding, conservative middle class. Wherever he perceived injustice, he drew his pen. In Geneva, where he had often found refuge from the French king, he went further: The local established bourgeoisie steadfastly refused to give political and economic rights to a class of artisan known as the *natifs*, whose origins were not local but who made up nearly half the population. In 1770, at his estate in neighboring Ferney-Voltaire (France), Voltaire opened a series of workshops for them, including the "Manufacture Royale," which produced very respectable watches.

The enterprise did not survive Voltaire's death in 1778, but 132 years later, in 2010, four highly experienced and related watch executives, Gérard, David, and Alexis Gouten and Marc Guten, decided to revive the brand. Their basic idea: high-end complications, affordable prices, and *manufacture* movements assembled in-house.

They set up shop in Vallorbe and soon had three respected collections out. The 1770 is the most classic, with a simple dial as backdrop to a flying tourbillon. The Androgyne, an edgy timepiece with flexible lugs, a screwed-down bezel, and a generally steampunkish look, offers insight into the movement thanks to extensive skeletonizing. Finally, there is the Opera, a minute repeater with a clever case made of sixty parts that unfolds to form a kind of shell that amplifies the sound of the chimes. When fully deployed, the watch looks like the Sydney Opera House. It's clever, practical, and witty.

Manufacture Royale SA
ZI Le Day
CH-1337 Vallorbe
Switzerland

Tel.:
+41-21-843-01- 01

E-Mail:
info@manufacture-royale.com

Website:
www.manufacture-royale.com

Founded:
1770 by Voltaire, revived 2010

Number of employees:
5

Annual production:
150 watches

Most important collections/price range:
Androgyne / from $52,000; 1770 / from $58,000; Opera / $30,000

Opera

Reference number: OP50.0805P
Movement: manually wound, Caliber MR01; 1-minute tourbillon; 29 jewels; 108-hour power reserve; 21,600 vph
Functions: hours, minutes; slide-actuated minute repeater with 2 notes
Case: rose and white gold, ø 50 mm; 3 sapphire crystals, movable transparent sapphire case back; water-resistant to 3 atm
Band: reptile skin, rose gold buckle
Price: $423,500

Androgyne Steel

Reference number: AN43.01P01.A
Movement: manual winding, MR02 Caliber; 27 jewels; 21,600 vph; 108-hour power reserve
Functions: hours, minutes
Case: stainless steel, ø 43 mm; transparent case back; water resistant to 3 atm
Band: alligator leather strap, stainless steel pin-buckle
Price: $52,000

1770 Rose Gold with Openwork Skeleton Dial

Reference number: 177043.08P.S2
Movement: manual winding, MR02 Caliber; 19 jewels; 21,600 vph; 1-minute flying tourbillon; 108-hour power reserve
Functions: hours, minutes; power reserve indicator
Case: rose gold, ø 43 mm; sapphire crystal; transparent case back; water resistant to 3 atm
Band: reptile skin, rose gold buckle
Remarks: silver openwork skeleton dial
Price: $58,000

Maurice Lacroix SA
Rüschlistrasse 6
CH-2502 Biel/Bienne
Switzerland

Tel.:
+41-44-209-1111

E-Mail:
info@mauricelacroix.com

Website:
www.mauricelacroix.com

Founded:
1975

Number of employees:
about 250 worldwide

Annual production:
approx. 90,000 watches

U.S. distributor:
DKSH Luxury & Lifestyle North America Inc.
103 Carnegie Center, Ste. 300
Princeton, NJ 08540
609-750-8800

Most important collections/price range:
Miros / $1,000 to $2,000; Les Classiques /
$1,500 to $3,500; Fiaba (ladies) / $1,500
to 3,500; Pontos / $2,500 to $5,000;
Masterpiece *manufacture* models / $6,800
to $30,000

Maurice Lacroix

Maurice Lacroix watches are found in sixty countries. The heart of the company, however, remains the production facilities in the highlands of the Jura, in Saignelégier and Montfaucon, where the brand built La Manufacture des Franches-Montagnes SA (MFM) outfitted with state-of-the-art CNC technology for the production of very specific individual parts and movement components.

The watchmaker can thank the clever interpretations of "classic" pocket watch characteristics for its steep ascent in the 1990s. Since then, the *manufacture* has redesigned the complete collection, banning every lick of Breguet-like bliss from its watch designs. In the upper segment, *manufacture* models such as the chronograph and the retrograde variations on Unitas calibers set the tone. In the lower segment, modern "little" complications outfitted with module movements based on ETA and Sellita are the kings. The brand is mainly associated with the hypnotically turning square wheel, the "roue carrée." The idea was used for the latest ladies watch, the Power of Love, which has three turning hearts forming the word "love" at regular intervals.

Maurice Lacroix's drive to freshen up its look has earned the brand a number of awards in the past years, all good news for its fortieth anniversary, celebrated in 2015.

In 2011, DKSH (Diethelm Keller & SiberHegner) took over the brand. This Swiss holding company specializing in international market expansions with 600 establishments throughout the world has ensured Maurice Lacroix a strong position in all major markets, with flagship stores and its own boutiques. A special partnership with the Barcelona football club is bound to have an impact on sales as well, justifying the production of 90,000 watches per year.

Masterpiece Gravity

Reference number: MP6118-SS001-112
Movement: automatic, Caliber ML 230; ø 37.2 mm, height 9.05 mm; 35 jewels; 18,000 vph; inverted design with dial-side escapement, silicon pallet lever and escape wheel; 50-hour power reserve
Functions: hours and minutes (off-center), subsidiary seconds
Case: stainless steel, ø 43 mm, height 16.2 mm; sapphire crystal; transparent case back; water-resistant to 5 atm
Band: reptile skin, folding clasp
Price: $13,900
Variations: various cases and dials

Masterpiece Mystery

Reference number: MP6558-SS001-095
Movement: automatic, Caliber ML 215; ø 38.2 mm, height 9.33 mm; 48 jewels; 18,000 vph; rhodium-plated, côtes de Genève; 50-hour power reserve
Functions: hours and minutes (off-center), subsidiary seconds ("mysterious" time display with "floating" seconds hand)
Case: stainless steel, ø 43 mm, height 13.86 mm; sapphire crystal, transparent case back; water-resistant to 5 atm
Band: reptile skin, folding clasp
Price: $13,900
Variations: various cases and dials

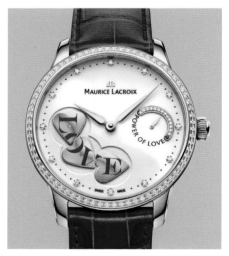

Masterpiece "Power of Love" Ladies

Reference number: MP7258-SD501-150
Movement: manually wound, Caliber ML 256; ø 36.6 mm, height 6.15 mm; 34 jewels; 18,000 vph; 50-hour power reserve
Functions: hours, minutes; heart-shaped disc display with special motif; power reserve indicator
Case: stainless steel, ø 43 mm, height 14.1 mm; 72 diamonds on bezel; sapphire crystal; transparent case back; water-resistant to 5 atm
Band: reptile skin, folding clasp
Remarks: 25 diamonds on dial
Price: $14,900

Masterpiece Square Wheel

Reference number: MP7158-SS001-301
Movement: manually wound, Caliber ML 156;
ø 36.6 mm, height 6.15 mm; 34 jewels; 18,000 vph;
45-hour power reserve
Functions: hours, minutes, subsidiary seconds
(with square wheel display); power reserve display
Case: stainless steel, ø 43 mm, height 14.1 mm;
sapphire crystal; transparent case back; water-
resistant to 5 atm
Band: reptile skin, folding clasp
Remarks: dial directly engraved on mainplate, with
"grand colimaçon" decoration
Price: $9,900
Variations: various dials

Pontos S Regatta

Reference number: PT6019-CAB01-330
Movement: automatic, Caliber ML 162; ø 36 mm;
44 jewels; 28,800 vph; 38-hour power reserve
Functions: hours, minutes, sweep seconds; regatta
countdown
Case: carbon fiber, ø 45 mm, height 12.5 mm;
crown-adjustable inner bezel with 60-second
divisions; sapphire crystal; water-resistant to 20 atm
Band: rubber, buckle
Price: $7,900

Pontos S Extreme

Reference number: PT6028-ALB11-331
Movement: automatic, Caliber ML 112 (base
ETA 7750); ø 30 mm, height 7.9 mm; 25 jewels;
28,800 vph; 46-hour power reserve
Functions: hours, minutes, subsidiary seconds;
chronograph; date
Case: composite material ("Powerlite"); ø 43 mm,
height 15.7 mm; crown-adjustable inner bezel with
60-minute divisions, sapphire crystal; screw-in
crown; water-resistant to 20 atm
Band: calf leather, buckle
Price: $5,900
Variations: various cases

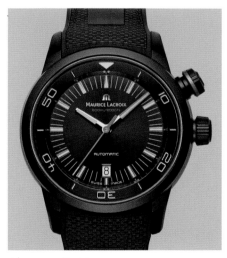

Pontos S Diver

Reference number: PT6248-PVB01-332
Movement: automatic, Caliber ML 115 (base Sellita
SW200); ø 25.6 mm, height 4.6 mm; 26 jewels;
28,800 vph; 38-hour power reserve
Functions: hours, minutes, sweep seconds; date
Case: stainless steel with black PVD coating,
ø 43 mm, height 15 mm; crown-adjustable inner
bezel with 60-second divisions; sapphire crystal;
screw-in crown; water-resistant to 60 atm
Band: rubber, buckle
Price: $3,400

Pontos Chronographe

Reference number: PT6288-SS001-130
Movement: automatic, Caliber ML 112 (base Sellita
SW500); ø 30 mm, height 7.9 mm; 25 jewels;
28,800 vph; 46-hour power reserve
Functions: hours, minutes, subsidiary seconds;
chronograph; date
Case: stainless steel, ø 43 mm, height 14.9 mm;
sapphire crystal; transparent case back; water-
resistant to 5 atm
Band: calf leather, folding clasp
Price: $3,900
Variations: black dial

Pontos Day Date

Reference number: PT6158-SS001-231
Movement: automatic, Caliber ML143 (based on
ETA 2836-2); ø 25.6 mm, height 5.05 mm; 25
jewels; 28,800 vph; 38-hour power reserve
Functions: hours, minutes, sweep seconds;
weekday, date
Case: stainless steel, ø 40 mm, height 12 mm;
sapphire crystal; transparent case back; water-
resistant to 5 atm
Band: reptile skin, folding clasp
Price: $2,900
Variations: various dials

Pontos Date Full Black

Reference number: PT6148-PVB01-330
Movement: automatic, Caliber ML115 (base Sellita SW300); ø 25.6 mm, height 3.6 mm; 25 jewels; 28,800 vph; 38-hour power reserve
Functions: hours, minutes, sweep seconds; date
Case: stainless steel with black PVD coating, ø 40 mm, height 11.8 mm; sapphire crystal; transparent case back; water-resistant to 5 atm
Band: calf leather, buckle
Remarks: hands/indices coated with black luminescent mass
Price: $2,900

Les Classiques Chronographe Phases de Lune

Reference number: LC6078-SS001-131
Movement: automatic, Caliber ML 154 (base ETA 7751); ø 30 mm, height 7.9 mm; 25 jewels; 28,800 vph
Functions: hours, minutes; additional 24-hour indicator (2nd time zone); chronograph; full calendar with date, weekday, month, moon phase
Case: stainless steel, ø 41 mm, height 14.8 mm; sapphire crystal; transparent case back; water-resistant to 3 atm
Band: stainless steel, folding clasp
Price: $3,880
Variations: various bands and dials

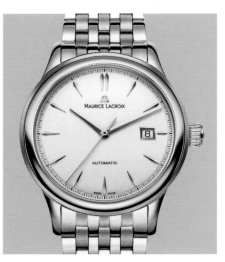

Les Classiques Date

Reference number: LC6098-SS002-130
Movement: automatic, Caliber ML 115 (base Sellita SW200); ø 25.6 mm, height 4.6 mm; 25 jewels; 28,800 vph; 38-hour power reserve
Functions: hours, minutes, sweep seconds; date
Case: stainless steel, ø 40 mm, height 10.6 mm; sapphire crystal; transparent case back; water-resistant to 3 atm
Band: stainless steel, folding clasp
Price: $1,680
Variations: leather strap ($1,480)

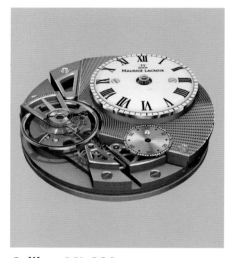

Caliber ML 230

Manually wound; inverted movement design with dial-side escapement, silicon pallet lever and escape wheel, single spring barrel; 50-hour power reserve
Functions: hours and minutes (off-center); subsidiary seconds
Jewels: 35
Balance: glucydur
Frequency: 18,000 vph
Remarks: rhodium finish, three-quarter plate (movement side) with côtes de Genève; dial assembled directly onto mainplate

Caliber ML 215

Manually wound; skeletonized movement; single spring barrel; 50 hours power reserve
Functions: hours and minutes (off-center), subsidiary seconds ("mysterious" display with floating double hands)
Diameter: 38.2 mm
Height: 9.33 mm
Jewels: 48
Balance: screw balance
Frequency: 18,000 vph
Balance spring: flat hairspring
Remarks: rhodium finish

Caliber ML 156

Manually wound; single spring barrel; 45-hour power reserve
Functions: hours, minutes, subsidiary seconds; power reserve indicator
Diameter: 36.6 mm
Height: 6.3 mm
Jewels: 34
Balance: screw balance
Frequency: 18,000 vph
Remarks: rhodium finish, three-quarter plate with "grand colimaçon" decoration, dial engraved directly on mainplate

MB&F

Maximilian Büsser & Friends goes beyond the standard idea of a brand. Perhaps calling it a tribe would be better: one aiming to create unique works of horology. MB&F is doing something unconventional in an industry that usually takes its innovation in small doses.

After seeing the Opus projects to fruition at Harry Winston, Büsser decided it was time to set the creators free. At MB&F he acts as initiator and coordinator. His Horological Machines are developed and realized in cooperation with highly specialized watchmakers, inventors, and designers in an "idea collective" creating unheard-of mechanical timepieces of great inventiveness, complication, and exclusivity. The composition of this collective varies as much as each machine. Number 5 ("On the Road Again") is an homage to the 1970s, when streamlining rather than brawn represented true strength. The display in the lateral window is reflected by a prism. The "top" of the watch opens to let in light to charge the Superluminova numerals on the discs. As for the Space Pirate, Number 6, it is a talking piece that makes a genial nod to sci-fi moviemakers, and all the talk was real: The model won a coveted Red Dot "Best of the Best" award in 2015. Contrasting sharply with the modern productions are the Legacy Machines, which reach into horological history and reinterpret past mechanical feats.

The spirit of Büsser is always present in each new watch, but it is now vented freely in the M.A.D. Gallery in Geneva, where "mechanical art objects" on display are beautiful, intriguing, technically impeccable, and sometimes perfectly useless. They have their own muse and serve as worthy companions to the sci-fi-inspired table clocks that MB&F produces with L'épée 1938.

MB&F
Boulevard Helvétique 22
Case postale 3466
CH-1211 Geneva 3
Switzerland

Tel.:
+41-22-786-3618

Fax:
+41-22-786-3624

E-Mail:
info@mbandf.com

Website:
www.mbandf.com

Founded:
2005

Number of employees:
20

Annual production:
approx. 280 watches

U.S. Distributors:
Westime Los Angeles
310-470-1388; 310-475-0628 (fax)
info@westime.com
Provident Jewelry, Florida
561-747-4449; nick@providentjewelry.com

Most important collections/price range:
Horological Machines / from $63,000; Legacy Machines / from $64,000

Legacy Machine N°1 Platinum

Reference number: 01.PL.W
Movement: manually wound, MB&F Caliber LM1; ø 34 mm, height 12.6 mm; 23 jewels; 18,000 vph; inverted with balance hovering over dial; finely decorated with côtes de Genève; 45-hour power reserve
Functions: hours and minutes (twice, 2 time zones); power reserve (2nd time zone)
Case: platinum, ø 44 mm, height 16 mm; sapphire crystal; transparent case back
Band: reptile skin, buckle
Remarks: limited to 33 pieces
Price: $114,000

HM3 MegaWind Final Edition

Reference number: 35.WBTL.B
Movement: automatic, MB&F Caliber HM3 (modified); 39.3 x 42.7 mm, height 11.6 mm; 36 jewels; 28,800 vph; 3-part winding rotor (titanium hub, 2 gold oscillating weights)
Functions: hours (left-hand display dome), minutes (right-hand display dome)
Case: white gold, 47 x 50 mm, height 17 mm; sapphire crystal; transparent case back; screw-in crown; water-resistant to 3 atm
Band: reptile skin, folding clasp
Price: $98,000

HM6 Space Pirate

Reference number: 60.TLB
Movement: automatic, MB&F Caliber HM6; 44.5 x 45.3 mm, height 17.3 mm; 68 jewels; 18,000 vph; flying 1-minute tourbillon under central glass dome protected by retractable shield; platinum rotor; 72-hour power reserve
Functions: hours (left lower display dome), minutes (right lower display dome)
Case: titanium, 49.5 x 52.3 mm, height 20.4 mm; sapphire crystal; transparent case back; screw-in crown
Band: calf leather, folding clasp
Price: $230,000

Meccaniche Veloci S.A.
Rue du Mont-Blanc, 3
CH-1201 Geneva

Tel.:
+41-22-900-0800

E-Mail:
info@meccanicheveloci.com

Website:
www.meccanicheveloci.com

Founded:
2006

Distribution:
Please contact headquarters directly.

Most important collections/price range:
Corsacorta Evo / from $1,450; Quattro
Valvole / from $2,300; Due Valvole / from
$1,900; Only One / on request

Meccaniche Veloci

The recipe almost seems too simplistic: watches and cars. With speed and exhaust fumes, the race clock ticking away . . . suddenly men become boys again. For a watch brand, choosing this aesthetic strategy is a risky game. It can look tacky, even predictable. Perhaps the trick is to be really frank about it, possibly even "in your face." Meccaniche Veloci, founded in 2006, is one brand that has succeeded in carving out a position for itself with some original ideas. Its name is a sort of tagline: fast engineering. Its timepieces are all saturated with the techno look—inside are Swiss movements; outside, Italian design.

The company made its automotive theme clear from the outset. It has blended the fascination with speed with the excitement of using materials from automotive sports. A series of unique models and a partnership with the Italian helmet maker Suomy have managed to captivate fans of both watches and high-power cars.

Meccaniche Veloci's first watch, the Quattro Valvole made use of piston ring grooves and four embedded valve seat pockets. It pushed all the right buttons with its target audience. Later designs, like the Duo Valvole "Only One," were exclusive pieces, because every dial is cut out of the body of a real Formula-1 racer, producing unique patterns of red and white. The latest collection is a mix of a dress watch with a touch of the bad boy. The Corsacorta Evo, named for an engine design featuring a short piston stroke, has the usual grooves on a thinner, more elegant case. The dial is decorated with a stylized gear wheel, harmonizing perfectly with the elegant textile band.

In a bid to grow sales, the brand moved its headquarters to Geneva in early 2015 and appointed a new president, Cesare Cerrito, and a new CEO, Riccardo Monfardino. Together, the two have a wide range of experience in finance, luxury goods, and, of course, watches.

Corsacorta Evo
Reference number: W129K477
Movement: automatic, ETA Caliber 2824-2;
ø 25.6 mm, height 4.6 mm; 25 jewels; 28,800 vph;
42-hour power reserve
Functions: hours, minutes, sweep seconds; date
Case: titanium with black IPB coating, ø 44 mm,
height 12 mm; sapphire crystal; transparent case
back; screw-in crown; water-resistant to 10 atm
Band: textile, buckle
Price: $1,450

Quattro Valvole Chronograph 44 RIM
Reference number: W123K488
Movement: automatic, ETA Caliber 7750; ø 30 mm,
height 7.9 mm; 25 jewels; 28,800 vph; 42-hour
power reserve
Functions: hours, minutes, subsidiary seconds
chronograph
Case: titanium with black IPB coating, ø 44 mm,
height 15.1 mm; sapphire crystal; transparent case
back; screw-in crown; water-resistant to 10 atm
Band: rubber, buckle
Remarks: limited to 250 pieces
Price: $3,750

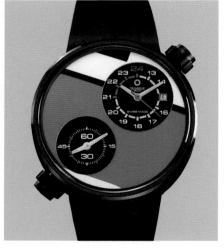

Due Valvole "Only One"
Reference number: W125KO19
Movement: automatic, 2 x ETA Caliber 2671;
ø 17.2 mm, height 4.8 mm; 25 jewels; 28,800 vph;
38-hour power reserve
Functions: hours and minutes (2x, 2 time zones),
sweep seconds; date
Case: titanium with black PVD coating, ø 44 mm,
height 16.3 mm; sapphire crystal; screw-in crown,
water-resistant to 10 atm
Band: rubber, buckle
Remarks: dial made of original Formula-1 body,
picture from side plate of rear wing of a Ferrari
F2003 GA from 2003 season
Price: on request

MeisterSinger

MeisterSinger GmbH & Co. KG
Hafenweg 46
D-48155 Münster
Germany

Tel.:
+49-251-133-4860

E-Mail:
info@meistersinger.de

Website:
www.meistersinger.de

Founded:
2001

Number of employees:
13

Annual production:
approx. 8,000 watches

U.S. distributor:
Duber Time
1920 Dr. MLK Jr. Street North
St. Petersburg, FL 33704
727-202-3262
damir@meistersingertime.com

Most important collections/price range:
from approx. $1,200 to $7,000

In 2014, MeisterSinger completed a long process of reorientation, setting the German brand in redux mode. At Baselworld 2014, it presented a portfolio of exclusively one-hand watches, the actual core of the brand. These watches express a relaxed and self-determined approach to the perception of time apparent in the special diurnal rituals that everyone knows, young, old, in private, or at work. These rituals actually divide up and define certain moments. And it is the reiteration of these moments which leads to order, or at least avoiding chaos.

Founder Martin Brassler launched his little collection of stylistically neat one-hand dials at the beginning of the new millennium. Looking at these ultimately simplified dials does tempt one to classify the one-hand watch as an archetype. The single hand simply cannot be reduced any further, and the 144 minutes for 12 hours around the dial do have a normative function of sorts. In a frenetic era when free time has become so rare, these watches slow things down a little. The most recent one-hander does provide the hour, jumping very precisely in a window under 12 o'clock—hence its Italian name "Salthora," or jumping hour.

Nevertheless, Brassler has put a few three-hand watches on the market, like the Paleograph, but the hour hand remains the dominant feature on the dials. Design, product planning, service, and management all happen in Münster, Germany. The watches, however, are Swiss made, with ETA and Sellita movements. The Circularis, however, is the brand's first model with an in-house movement, a manually wound caliber with two spring barrels developed in collaboration with the Swiss firm Synergies Horlogères.

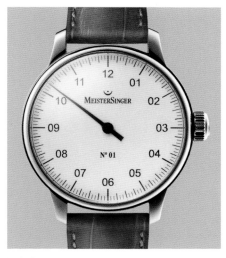

N° 01

Reference number: AM 3301
Movement: manually wound, ETA Caliber 2801-2; ø 35.6 mm, height 3.35 mm; 17 jewels; 28,800 vph; 42-hour power reserve
Functions: hours (each line stands for 5 minutes)
Case: stainless steel, ø 43 mm, height 11.5 mm; sapphire crystal, transparent case back; water-resistant to 5 atm
Band: calf leather, buckle
Price: $1,595
Variations: ivory-colored or anthracite dial; reptile skin or stainless steel Milanese mesh band

Salthora Meta

Reference number: SH 907
Movement: automatic, ETA Caliber 2824-2 or Sellita SW200-1 with module for jumping hour; ø 25.6 mm, height 6.9 mm; 26 jewels; 28,800 vph; 38-hour power reserve; côtes de Genève
Functions: hours (digital, jumping), minutes
Case: stainless steel, ø 43 mm, height 13 mm; sapphire crystal; transparent case back; water-resistant to 5 atm
Band: calf leather, double folding clasp
Price: $3,675
Variations: various dial colors, reptile skin or stainless steel Milanese mesh band

Adhaesio

Reference number: AD902
Movement: automatic, modified ETA Caliber 2893-2; ø 25.6 mm, height 4.6 mm; 25 or 26 jewels; 28,800 vph; côtes de Genève; 38-hour power reserve
Functions: hours (each line stands for 5 minutes); additional 24-hour display; date
Case: stainless steel, ø 43 mm, height 15.8 mm; sapphire crystal; transparent case back; water-resistant to 5 atm
Band: calf leather, double folding clasp
Price: $3,575
Variations: reptile skin strap; stainless steel Milanese bracelet

Milus International SA
Rue de Reuchenette 19
CH-2502 Biel/Bienne
Switzerland

Tel.:
+41-32-344-3939

Fax:
+41-32-344-3938

E-Mail:
info@milus.com

Website:
www.milus.com

Founded:
1919

U.S. distributor:
Totally Worth It, LLC
76 Division Avenue
Summit, NJ 07901-2309
201-894-4710
info@totallyworthit.com

Most important collections/price range:
Milus Tirion Répétition Minutes TriRetrograde /
from approx. $305,000; Tirion TriRetrograde /
from approx. $9,300; Merea TriRetrograde /
from approx. $7,000; Snow Star Heritage
$2,790

Milus

Milus was founded by Paul William Junod in Biel/Bienne and remained in family hands until the year 2002. A new era began then with the founding of Milus International SA under Jan Edöcs and with investments from the giant Peace Mark Group from Hong Kong.

Within a few years, the brand had made a new name for itself with a triple retrograde seconds indicator, which was developed together with the specialists at Agenhor in Geneva. And that made all the difference in the Milus image. In the 1970s, the brand had a considerable reputation for jewelry. Now, however, it has become a genuine and respected watchmaker, one producing top-drawer horological complications. The TriRetrograde function is a Milus trademark and can be found in a host of models all named after constellations (Tirion, Merea, Zetios). Fans of retrogrades will have a feast. There are watches with three separate second hands showing twenty seconds each before passing the baton to the next one.

After the Peace Mark Group collapsed in 2008, Milus quickly found another investor in the Chow Tai Fook Group owned by Dr. Cheng Yu-tung. In 2011, Cyril Dubois took over at the head of the company. Quietly, but surely, the brand has been expanding on several fronts with the triretrogrades in the lead, and the more sporty-elegant Zetios line coming in a close second. A new Zetios Automatic for women features a cascade of white diamonds. And the latest chronograph in the collection reflects Milus's sponsorship of the M2 Speed Tour Regatta in Switzerland. Models like the Merea look back to a time when Milus made top-of-the-line jewelry as well. The brand's Snow Star Instant Date from the 1940s was also rebuilt for vintage fans and will be available in a modern version later in 2015.

Zetios Chronographe Edition M2

Reference number: ZETC100
Movement: automatic, ETA Caliber 2892 with Dubois Depraz 4500 module; ø 30 mm, height 7.5 mm; 49 jewels; 28,800 vph; 40-hour power reserve
Functions: hours, minutes, subsidiary seconds at 3; chronograph; 30-minute counter at 9 and 12-hour at 6; date
Case: stainless steel, ø 45 mm, height 14.5 mm; sapphire crystal; screwed-down case back; water-resistant to 3 atm
Band: blue reptile skin cream stitching, buckle
Remarks: hour totalizer with M2 Speed Tour logo
Price: $5,350
Variations: white strap/blue stitching, white hour totalizer, subsidiary seconds frames ($5,350)

Zetios Regulator

Reference number: ZETR400
Movement: automatic, ETA Caliber 2892-A2 with Dubois Depraz 14070 module; ø 26.2 mm, height 5.2 mm; 25 jewels; 28,800 vph; 42-hour power reserve
Functions: hours, minutes, subsidiary seconds; date
Case: pink gold, ø 42 mm; sapphire crystal; screwed-down case back; water-resistant to 3 atm
Band: reptile skin, buckle
Remarks: galvanic dial with *grain de riz* decoration, blued hands
Price: $23,000

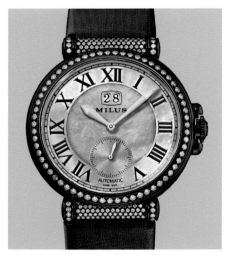

Zetios Automatic

Reference number: ZET011
Movement: automatic, Dubois Depraz 14000; ø 26.2 mm, height 5.2 mm; 25 jewels; 28,800 vph; 40-hour power reserve
Functions: hours, minutes, subsidiary seconds; large date
Case: stainless steel with polished DLC, ø 42 mm, 12.4 mm; screwed-down case back; sapphire crystal; water-resistant to 3 atm
Band: satin-finished, folding clasp
Remarks: 2-toned mother-of-pearl dial; 300 white diamonds on bezel, case, lugs
Price: $4,250

Tirion Répétition Minutes TriRetrograde

Reference number: TIRM600
Movement: manually wound, Milus Caliber M08-35RM module; ø 26.2 mm, height 5.2 mm; 25 jewels; 28,800 vph; 96-hour power reserve; COSC-certified
Functions: hours, minutes, subsidiary triretrograde seconds; date; minute repeater
Case: pink gold, ø 46 mm, height 13.92 mm; sapphire crystal; screwed-down case back; water-resistant to 3 atm
Band: reptile skin, buckle
Remarks: blued hands, retrograde seconds displayed on 3 20-second gold arcs
Price: $305,000

Tirion TriRetrograde

Reference number: TIRI022
Movement: automatic, ETA Caliber 2892-A2 with Milus special module 3838; ø 30 mm; 37 jewels; 28,800 vph; 40-hour power reserve
Functions: hours, minutes, triretrograde seconds (on black bridges); date
Case: DLC-treated stainless steel, ø 45 mm, height 13.91 mm; carbon bezel; screwed-in transparent case back; water-resistant to 3 atm
Band: reptile skin, folding clasp
Remarks: skeleton hour, minute, and second hands
Price: $11,800

Tirion TriRetrograde 200

Movement: automatic, ETA Caliber 2892-A2 with Milus special module 3838; ø 30 mm; 37 jewels; 28,800 vph, 38-hour power reserve
Functions: hours, minutes, triple retrograde subsidiary seconds; date
Case: stainless steel with DLC, ø 45 mm, height 13.91 mm; sapphire crystal; screwed-down case back; water-resistant to 3 atm
Band: reptile skin, buckle
Remarks: carbon dial, skeletonized hands
Price: $10,500

Merea TriRetrograde

Reference number: MER027
Movement: automatic, ETA Caliber 2892-A2 with Milus special module 3838; ø 30 mm; 37 jewels; 28,800 vph, 40-hour power reserve
Functions: hours, minutes, triple retrograde subsidiary seconds
Case: stainless steel, 35.8 x 36.8 mm, height 12.9 mm; case, crown, attachments partially set with 115 white diamonds; sapphire crystal; screwed-down case back; water-resistant to 3 atm
Band: reptile skin, buckle
Price: $12,800

Snow Star Heritage

Reference number: HKIT001
Movement: automatic, Sellita SW200; ø 25.6 mm, height 4.6 mm; 28,800 vph
Functions: hours, minutes, seconds; date
Case: stainless steel, ø 40 mm; sapphire crystal with magnifying glass at 3; water-resistant to 3 atm
Band: calf leather, buckle
Remarks: comes with interchangeable NATO strap, compass and propeller cufflinks, and military ID tag
Price: $2,740; limited to 1,940 pieces
Variations: pink gold ($32,900; limited to 99 pieces)

Milus Cufflinks

Reference number: CUF011D
Movement: with original Milus rotor rotating 360°, ø 19 mm; set with 104 diamonds
Case: stainless steel, rotor with côtes de Genève decoration
Remarks: Milus started manufacturing cufflinks in 2006 using original movement parts
Price: $1,550
Variations: white gold, pink gold, PVD-coated, rose gold and yellow gold plated (starting at $485)

Mk II Corporation
303 W. Lancaster Avenue, #283
Wayne, PA 19087

E-Mail:
info@mkiiwatches.com

Website:
www.mkiiwatches.com

Founded:
2002

Number of employees:
3

Annual production:
800 watches

Distribution:
direct sales

Most important collections/price range:
Professional series / $1,200 to $2,000;
Specialist series / $599 to $1,345

Mk II

If vintage and unserviceable watches had their say, they would probably be naturally attracted to Mk II for the name alone, which is a military designation for the second generation of equipment. The company, which was founded by watch enthusiast and maker Bill Yao in 2002, not only puts retired designs back into service, but also modernizes and customizes them. Before the screwed-down crown, diving watches were not nearly as reliably sealed, for example. And some beautiful old pieces were made with plated brass cases or featured Bakelite components, which are either easily damaged or have aged poorly. The company not only substitutes proven modern materials, but also modern manufacturing methods and techniques to ensure a better outcome.

These are material issues that the team at Mk II handles with great care. They will not, metaphorically speaking, airbrush a Model-T. As genuine watch lovers themselves, they make sure that the final design is in the spirit of the watch itself, which still leaves a great deal of leeway for many iterations given a sufficient number of parts. In the company's output, vintage style and modern functionality are key. The watches are assembled by hand at the company's workshop in Pennsylvania—and subjected to a rigorous regime of testing. The components are individually inspected, the cases tested at least three times for water resistance, and at the end the whole watch is regulated in six positions. Looking to the future, Mk II aspires to carry its clean vintage style into the development of what it hopes will be future classics of its own.

Tornek-Rayville Series 2

Reference number: CD02.1-2001N
Movement: automatic, Caliber Soprod A10;
ø 26.2 mm, height 3.6 mm; 25 jewels; 28,800 vph;
42-hour power reserve; rhodium-plated; rotor
decorated with côtes de Genève
Functions: hours, minutes, sweep seconds
Case: stainless steel, ø 42.0 mm, height 13.90 mm;
60-click unidirectional bezel; domed sapphire
crystal with antireflective coating; luminous sapphire
inlay, screwed-down case back; screwed-in crown;
antimagnetic shielding, water-resistant to 30 atm
Band: nylon NATO-style strap
Price: $1,295
Variations: stainless steel bracelet

Nassau

Reference number: CD05.1-1004B
Movement: automatic, Caliber ETA 2836-2;
ø 26 mm, height 5.05 mm; 25 jewels; 28,800 vph;
38-hour power reserve; rhodium-plated, rotor
decorated with côtes de Genève
Functions: hours, minutes, sweep seconds; date
Case: stainless steel; ø 39.2 mm, height 14.50 mm;
unidirectional steel/aluminium bezel; domed
sapphire crystal with antireflective coating; screwed-
down case back; screwed-in crown; water-resistant
to 20 atm
Band: steel bracelet
Price: $1,195
Variations: nylon strap

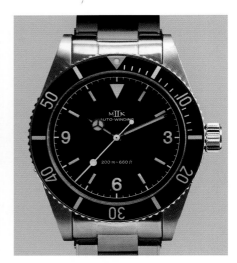

Nassau 369 Non-Date

Reference number: CD05.1-2003B
Movement: automatic, Caliber ETA 2836-2;
ø 26 mm, height 5.05 mm; 25 jewels; 28,800 vph;
38-hour power reserve; rhodium-plated, rotor
decorated with côtes de Genève
Functions: hours, minutes, sweep seconds
Case: stainless steel; ø 39.2 mm, height 14.50 mm;
2-tone lacquered dial, unidirectional bezel; domed
sapphire crystal with antireflective coating; screw-
down case back; screwed-in crown; water-resistant
to 20 atm
Band: steel bracelet
Price: $1,195
Variations: nylon strap

Montana Watch Company

Back in the nineteenth and early twentieth centuries, the American watch industry was a sizable affair, with manufacturers producing timepieces of superior craftsmanship, reliability, and simplicity, including their own movements in some instances. A century later, the Montana Watch Company in Livingston, Montana, decided to produce wristwatches that hark back to the days of old, boldly retro and therefore distinctive. Just looking at a Montana can make you hear horses galloping and banjos twanging.

The trick is in the design and the choice of materials. Think rich hand-engraved motifs, gems, and custom-designed cases. These often unique pieces are created by designer and horologist Jeffrey Nashan, who works individually with each client from concept to completion to achieve heirloom timepieces.

The traditional exterior, however, belies the state-of-the-art interior. Each case is machined in-house from a single piece of solid stock. Custom design with SolidWorks 3D modeling CAD software and state-of-the-art CNC machines allows production of small runs in all variety of metals, notably silver.

Nashan has assembled a team of master engravers well versed in every style of metal engraving, inlay, and gem setting, and one of the most highly skilled and innovative leathersmiths in the American West to produce the brand's bespoke straps. The watches featuring vignettes from John Banovich wildlife paintings using a special engraving technique are very popular. For the brand's fifteenth anniversary in 2013, Nashan rereleased newer versions of the watch that started the company—the 1915—with some especially florid engraving.

Montana Watch Company
124 N. Main Street
Livingston, MT 59047

Tel.:
406-222-8899

E-Mail:
info@montanawatch.com

Website:
www.montanawatch.com

Founded:
1998

Number of employees:
6

Annual production:
100 watches

Distribution:
direct distribution

Most important collection/price range:
Model 1915 / starting at $6,500; Bridger Field Watch / starting at $3,200; Model 1925 / starting at $5,150; Officer's Watch / starting at $6,100; Model 1920 / starting at $3,850; Model 1930 / starting at $5,650; Highline Aviator / starting at $3,550; Miles City Pocket Watch / starting at $3,350; Montana Travler / starting at $3,750

Highline Aviator "Spaghetti Western"

Movement: manually wound, ETA Caliber 6498; ø 36.6 mm, height 4.5 mm; 17 jewels; 18,000 vph
Functions: hours, minutes, subsidiary seconds
Case: sterling silver, ø 43 mm, height 10.5 mm; gold crown; wire lugs; sapphire crystal; transparent case back; water-resistant to 3 atm
Band: saddle leather, silver buckle
Remarks: custom hand-engraved dial with horse motif; engraved case
Price: $24,200
Variations: all custom variations available (from $3,650)

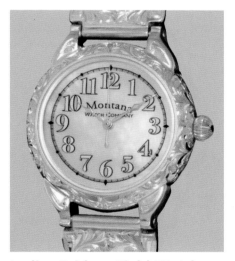

Ladies Bridger Field Watch

Movement: automatic, ETA Caliber 2824-2; ø 25.6 mm, height 4.6 mm; 25 jewels; 28,800 vph
Functions: hours, minutes, sweep seconds
Case: argentium silver, ø 37 mm, height 9.75 mm; gold crown; sapphire crystal; transparent case back; water-resistant to 3 atm
Band: silver bracelet, buckle
Remarks: case with western bright-cut engraving
Price: $9,900
Variations: custom variations available (from $3,300)

Western Design Premium Reissue

Movement: automatic, Soprod Caliber A10-2; ø 25.6 mm, height 3.6 mm; 25 jewels; 28,800 vph
Functions: hours, minutes, sweep second
Case: argentium silver, ø 37 mm, height 9.75 mm; gold crown; sapphire crystal; transparent case back
Band: saddle leather, buckle
Remarks: case with western single-point hand-engraving in deep relief, gold overlays, set with rubies; grand feu enamel dial; sterling silver buckle
Price: $15,000
Variations: unadorned variations (from $6,500)

Montblanc Montre SA

10, chemin des Tourelles
CH-2400 Le Locle
Switzerland

Tel.:
+41-32-933-8888

Fax:
+41-32-933-8880

E-Mail:
service@montblanc.com

Website:
www.montblanc.com

Founded:
1997 (1906 in Hamburg)

Number of employees:
worldwide approx. 3,000

U.S. distributor:
Montblanc International
26 Main Street
Chatham, NJ 07928
908-508-2301
www.montblanc.com

Most important collections:
Heritage Chronométrie, Meisterstück, Star,
Star Nicolas Rieussec, Star 4810, TimeWalker,
Collection Villeret

Montblanc

It was with great skill and cleverness that Nicolas Rieussec (1781–1866) used the invention of a special chronograph—the "Time Writer," a device that released droplets of ink onto a rotating sheet of paper—to make a name for himself. Montblanc, once famous only for its exclusive writing implements, borrowed that name on its way to becoming a distinguished watch brand. Within a few years, it had created an impressive range of chronographs driven by in-house calibers: from simple automatic stopwatches to flagship pieces with two independent spring barrels for time and "time-writing."

The Richemont Group, owner of Montblanc, has placed great trust in its "daughter" company, having put the little *manufacture* Minerva, which it purchased at the beginning of 2007, at the disposal of Montblanc. The Minerva Institute serves as a kind of think tank for the future, a place where young watchmakers can absorb the old traditions and skills, as well as the wealth of experience and mind-set of the masters.

In the summer of 2013, Jerôme Lambert from sister brand Jaeger-LeCoultre took over the presidency and focused the brand on the top and lower price segments. The Vasco da Gama theme opened in 2015 with numerous new developments in all segments, from a moon phase to a tourbillon with a cylindrical balance spring and simultaneous display of three time zones. Then, the new Heritage Chronométrie collection models take 500 hours of testing to guarantee top quality. And finally, Montblanc has created the e-Strap to connect the TimeWalker to the user's mobile phone.

Metamorphosis II

Reference number: 112442
Movement: manually wound, Montblanc Caliber MB M67.40; ø 38.4 mm; height 12.45 mm; 86 jewels; 18,000 vph; screw balance, crown pusher control; 50-hour power reserve
Functions: hours (off-center), minutes (retrograde), sweep seconds; chronograph; date
Case: pink gold, ø 52 mm, height 15.8 mm; sapphire crystal; transparent case back; pusher-activated mechanical dial elements switch from time display to chronograph function; water-resistant to 30 atm
Band: reptile skin, pink gold triple folding clasp
Price: on request; limited to 18 pieces

Tourbillon Cylindrique Geosphères "Vasco da Gama"

Reference number: 111675
Movement: manually wound, Montblanc Caliber MB M68.40; ø 38.4 mm; height 10.5 mm; 18 jewels; 18,000 vph; 1-minute tourbillon, screw balance; 48-hour power reserve
Functions: hours, minutes; separate (24-hour) world-time display for northern and southern hemispheres
Case: pink gold, ø 47 mm, height 15.38 mm; sapphire crystal; transparent case back; water-resistant to 3 atm
Band: reptile skin, pink gold buckle
Price: on request; limited to 18 pieces

Heritage Chronométrie ExoTourbillon Minute Chronograph

Reference number: 112542
Movement: automatic, Montblanc Caliber MB R230; ø 33.7 mm; height 8.65 mm; 44 jewels; 21,600 vph; 1-minute tourbillon with external balance spring, double spring barrel, screw balance, fine finishing; 50-hour power reserve
Functions: hours and minutes (off-center), subsidiary seconds (on tourbillon cage); chronograph; date
Case: pink gold, ø 44 mm, height 14.79 mm; sapphire crystal; transparent case back; water-resistant to 3 atm
Band: reptile skin, pink gold buckle
Price: $44,100

Heritage Chronométrie ExoTourbillon Minute Chronograph "Vasco Da Gama" Limited Edition

Reference number: 112649
Movement: automatic, Montblanc Caliber MB R230; ø 33.7 mm, height 8.65 mm; 44 jewels; 21,600 vph; 1-minute tourbillon/external balance spring, double spring barrel, screw balance, finishing; 50-hour power reserve
Functions: hours and minutes (off-center), subsidiary seconds (on tourbillon cage); chronograph; date
Case: white gold, ø 44 mm, height 14.79 mm; sapphire crystal; transparent case back; water-resistant to 3 atm
Band: reptile skin, white gold buckle
Remarks: aventurine dial
Price: $52,200; limited to 60 pieces

Heritage Spirit Orbis Terrarum

Reference number: 112308
Movement: automatic, Montblanc Caliber MB 29.20 (based on Sellita SW300 with module); ø 25.6 mm, height 3.6 mm; 25 jewels; 28,800 vph; 42-hour power reserve
Functions: hours, minutes; world-time display; day/night
Case: stainless steel, ø 41 mm, height 11.99 mm; sapphire crystal; transparent back; water-resistant to 3 atm
Band: reptile skin, triple folding clasp
Remarks: crystal dial with city names/world map
Price: $5,800
Variations: stainless steel bracelet, triple folding clasp ($6,100); pink gold/pink gold buckle ($16,100)

Heritage Chronométrie Quantième Annuel "Vasco da Gama"

Reference number: 112537
Movement: automatic, Montblanc Caliber MB 29.18 (base ETA 2892 with Dubois Dépraz module); ø 25.6 mm, height 5.2 mm; 25 jewels; 28,800 vph; 42-hour power reserve
Functions: hours, minutes; annual calendar with date, weekday, month, moon phase
Case: pink gold, ø 40 mm, height 9.55 mm; sapphire crystal; transparent case back; water-resistant to 3 atm
Band: reptile skin, buckle
Price: $12,900; limited to 238 pieces
Variations: stainless steel ($7,700)

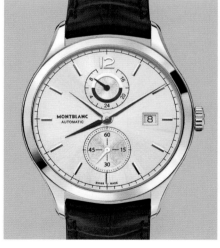

Heritage Chronométrie Quantième Complet "Vasco da Gama"

Reference number: 112539
Movement: automatic, Montblanc Caliber MB 29.16 (base ETA 2892 with Dubois Dépraz module); ø 25.6 mm, height 5.35 mm; 25 jewels; 28,800 vph; 42-hour power reserve
Functions: hours, minutes; full calendar with date, weekday, month, moon phase
Case: stainless steel, ø 40 mm, height 9.7 mm; sapphire crystal; transparent case back; water-resistant to 3 atm
Band: reptile skin, triple folding clasp
Price: $5,100

Heritage Chronométrie Dual Time

Reference number: 112540
Movement: automatic, Montblanc Caliber MB 29.19 (based on Sellita SW300 with module); ø 26.2 mm, height 5.2 mm; 34 jewels; 28,800 vph; 42-hour power reserve
Functions: hours, minutes, subsidiary seconds; added 12-hour (2nd time) display, day/night indicator; date
Case: stainless steel, ø 41 mm, height 9.97 mm; sapphire crystal; transparent case back; water-resistant to 3 atm
Band: reptile skin, triple folding clasp
Price: $4,600
Variations: pink gold bezel ($6,400)

Heritage Chronométrie Ultra Slim

Reference number: 112516
Movement: manually wound, Montblanc Caliber MB 23.01; ø 23.5 mm, height 2.5 mm; 17 jewels; 21,600 vph; 42-hour power reserve
Functions: hours, minutes
Case: rose gold, ø 38 mm, height 5.8 mm; sapphire crystal; transparent case back; water-resistant to 3 atm
Band: reptile skin, pink gold buckle
Price: $6,400
Variations: stainless steel/stainless steel buckle ($2,260)

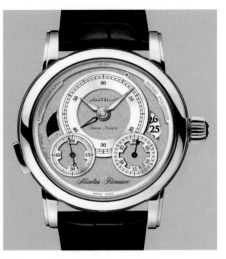

Heritage Spirit Perpetual Calendar

Reference number: 112310
Movement: automatic, Montblanc Caliber MB 29.15 (based on ETA 2892 with Dubois Dépraz module); ø 25.6 mm, height 5.2 mm; 25 jewels; 28,800 vph; 42-hour power reserve
Functions: hours, minutes; perpetual calendar with date, weekday, month, moon phase, leap year
Case: pink gold, ø 39 mm, height 10.27 mm; sapphire crystal; transparent case back; water-resistant to 3 atm
Band: reptile skin, pink gold buckle
Remarks: sapphire crystal dial
Price: $23,100

TimeWalker Urban Speed Chronograph e-Strap

Reference number: 113827
Movement: automatic, Montblanc Caliber MB 25.07 (base ETA 7750); ø 30 mm; height 7.9 mm; 25 jewels; 28,800 vph; 46-hour power reserve
Functions: hours, minutes, subsidiary seconds; chronograph; date
Case: stainless steel, ø 43 mm, height 14.4 mm; ceramic bezel; sapphire crystal; transparent case back; water-resistant to 3 atm
Band: Montblanc Extreme leather/stainless steel buckle
Remarks: special leather strap with "e-strap device" (electronic module with touchscreen for link to smartphone)
Price: $5,400

"Homage to Nicolas Rieussec II" Limited Edition

Reference number: 111873
Movement: automatic, Montblanc Caliber MB R200; ø 31 mm, height 8.46 mm; 40 jewels; 28,800 vph; 2 spring barrels; column wheel control of chronograph functions via single pusher, 72-hour power reserve
Functions: hours and minutes (off-center), subsidiary seconds; chronograph; date
Case: stainless steel, ø 43 mm, height 14.8 mm; sapphire crystal; transparent back; water-resistant to 3 atm
Band: reptile skin, buckle
Price: $11,300; limited to 565 pieces
Variations: pink gold ($32,100; limited to 190 pieces)

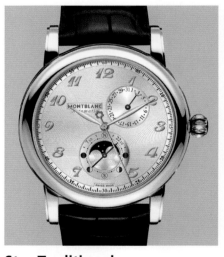

Star Traditional Twin Moonphase "Carpe Diem Edition"

Reference number: 113848
Movement: automatic, Montblanc Caliber MB 29.13; ø 26.2 mm, height 4.9 mm; 27 jewels; 28,800 vph; 42-hour power reserve
Functions: hours, minutes, sweep seconds; date, moon phase with northern and southern hemisphere display
Case: stainless steel, ø 42 mm, height 12.17 mm; sapphire crystal; transparent case back; water-resistant to 3 atm
Band: reptile skin, triple folding clasp
Price: $4,900

Star Traditional Chronograph Automatic "Carpe Diem Edition"

Reference number: 113847
Movement: automatic, Caliber MB 25.03 (base ETA 7750); ø 30 mm, height 7.9 mm; 25 jewels; 28,800 vph; 42-hour power reserve
Functions: hours, minutes, subsidiary seconds; chronograph; weekday, date
Case: stainless steel, ø 39 mm, height 13.95 mm; sapphire crystal; transparent back; water-resistant to 3 atm
Band: reptile skin, triple folding clasp
Price: $4,100

Star Roman Quantième Complet "10th Anniversary Celebration" Special Edition

Reference number: 113645
Movement: automatic, Montblanc Caliber MB 29.12 (based on ETA 2892 with Dubois Dépraz module); ø 25.6 mm, height 5.35 mm; 25 jewels; 28,800 vph; 42-hour power reserve
Functions: hours, minutes, sweep seconds; full calendar with date, weekday, month, moon phase
Case: stainless steel, ø 42 mm, height 12.17 mm; sapphire crystal; transparent back; water-resistant to 3 atm
Band: reptile skin, triple folding clasp
Price: $5,300

Caliber MB M68.40

Manually wound; 1-minute tourbillon; 2 additional time zone displays on hemispheres; single spring barrel, 50-hour power reserve

Functions: hours, minutes, sweep seconds; 2 additional 24-hour displays; day/night indicator
Diameter: 38.4 mm
Height: 10.5 mm
Jewels: 18
Balance: screw balance
Frequency: 18,000 vph
Balance spring: cylindrical with double Phillips terminal curve
Remarks: 281 components, including 91 for tourbillon cage

Caliber MB M67.40

Manually wound; bolt pusher for transformation between time display and chronograph; single spring barrel; 50-hour power reserve

Functions: hours (off-center), minutes (retrograde), sweep seconds; chronograph; date
Diameter: 38.4 mm
Height: 12.45 mm
Jewels: 85
Balance: screw balance
Frequency: 18,000 vph
Balance spring: with Phillips terminal curve
Remarks: 746 components, including 494 for transformation mechanisms

Caliber MB R230

Automatic; 1-minute tourbillon with balance outside turning cage (exo-tourbillon), stop-seconds device; column-wheel control using individual chronograph pushers, vertical chronograph clutch; double spring barrel, 50-hour power reserve

Functions: hours, minutes (off-center); chronograph; date
Diameter: 33.7 mm
Height: 8.65 mm
Jewels: 44
Balance: screw balance
Frequency: 21,600 vph
Balance spring: flat hairspring
Remarks: 296 components

Caliber MB R200

Automatic; column wheel control using separate chronograph pushers; vertical chronograph clutch; stop-seconds; double spring barrel, 72-hour power reserve

Functions: hours, minutes, sweep seconds; additional 12-hour display; chronograph; date; power reserve indicator
Diameter: 31 mm
Height: 8.46 mm
Jewels: 40
Balance: screw balance
Frequency: 28,800 vph
Balance spring: flat hairspring
Remarks: rhodium-plated plate with perlage, bridges with côtes de Genève

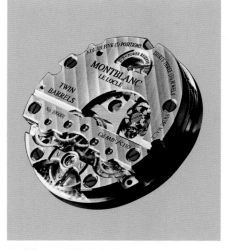

Caliber MB R110

Automatic; column wheel control using separate chronograph pushers; vertical disc clutch; double spring barrel, 72-hour power reserve

Functions: hours, minutes, subsidiary seconds; chronograph; date; power reserve indicator on case back
Diameter: 31 mm
Height: 7.6 mm
Jewels: 33
Balance: balance with variable inertia
Frequency: 28,800 vph
Balance spring: flat hairspring
Shock protection: Incabloc
Remarks: rhodium-plated plate with perlage, bridges with côtes de Genève

Caliber MB M66.25

Manually wound; 2 separate balance wheels and escapements for movement and chronograph with 1/100th second display; 100-hour power reserve, 45 minutes for chronograph; double spring barrel

Functions: hours, minutes, subsidiary seconds; ultra-high frequency chronograph (1/100)
Diameter: 38.4 mm
Height: 7.63 mm
Jewels: 37
Balance: screw balance with weights, ring balance (chronograph)
Frequency: 18,000 vph, 360,000 vph (chronograph)

Mühle Glashütte GmbH

Nautische Instrumente und Feinmechanik

Altenberger Strasse 35
D-01768 Glashütte
Germany

Tel.:
+49-35053-3203-0

Fax:
+49-35053-3203-136

E-Mail:
info@muehle-glashuette.de

Website:
www.muehle-glashuette.de

Founded:
first founding 1869; second founding 1993

Number of employees:
47

U.S. distributor:
Mühle Glashütte
Old Northeast Jewelers
1131 4th Street North
Saint Petersburg, FL 33701
800-922-4377
www.muehle-glashuette.com

Most important collections/price range:
mechanical wristwatches / approx. $1,399 to $5,400

Mühle Glashütte

Mühle Glashütte has survived all the ups and downs of Germany's history. The firm Rob. Mühle & Sohn was founded by its namesake in 1869. At that time, the company made precision measuring instruments for the local watch industry and the German School of Watchmaking. In the early 1920s, the firm established itself as a supplier for the automobile industry, making speedometers, automobile clocks, tachometers, and other measurement instruments.

Having manufactured instruments for the military during the war, the company was not only bombarded by the Soviet air force, but was also nationalized in 1945, as it was in the eastern part of the country. After the fall of the Iron Curtain, it was reestablished as a limited liability corporation. In 2007, Thilo Mühle took over the helm from his father, Hans-Jürgen Mühle.

The company's wristwatch business was launched in 1996 and now overshadows the nautical instruments that had made the name Mühle Glashütte famous. Its collection comprises mechanical wristwatches at entry and mid-level prices. For these, the company uses Swiss base movements that are equipped with such in-house developments as a patented woodpecker-neck regulation and the Mühle rotor. The modifications are so extensive, they have led to the calibers having their own names. A new traditional line named "R. Mühle & Sohn" was introduced in 2014 beginning with the Robert Mühle Auf/Ab and the Small Seconds equipped with the RMK 1 and RMK 2 calibers.

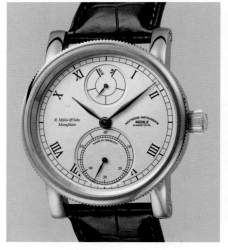

Robert Mühle Auf/Ab

Reference number: M1-11-15-LB
Movement: manually wound, Mühle Caliber RMK 01; ø 36.6 mm, height 8.35 mm; 29 jewels; 21,600 vph; woodpecker-neck fine adjustment, three-fifth plate, Glashütte stopwork; hand-engraved balance cock, 3 screwed-down gold chatons; 56-hour power reserve
Functions: hours, minutes, subsidiary seconds; power reserve indicator
Case: stainless steel, ø 44 mm, height 13 mm; sapphire crystal; transparent case back; water-resistant to 10 atm
Band: reptile skin, folding clasp
Price: $9,499

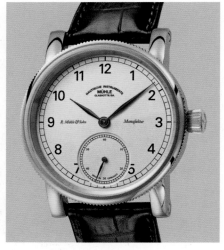

Robert Mühle Kleine Sekunde

Reference number: M1-11-05-LB
Movement: manually wound, Mühle Caliber RMK 02; ø 36.6 mm, height 6.65 mm; 18 jewels; 21,600 vph; woodpecker-neck fine adjustment, three-fifth plate, Glashütte stopwork; hand-engraved balance cock, 3 screwed-down gold chatons; 56-hour power reserve
Functions: hours, minutes, subsidiary seconds
Case: stainless steel, ø 44 mm, height 11.8 mm; sapphire crystal; transparent case back; water-resistant to 10 atm
Band: reptile skin, folding clasp
Price: $6,499

Teutonia II Grossdatum Chronometer

Reference number: M1-33-75-LB
Movement: automatic, ETA Caliber 2892 with Jaquet module 3532; ø 25.6 mm, 21 jewels; 28,800 vph; woodpecker-neck fine adjustment, Mühle rotor; special Mühle finish; 42-hour power reserve; DIN-certified chronometer
Functions: hours, minutes, subsidiary seconds; large date
Case: stainless steel, ø 41 mm, height 12.7 mm; sapphire crystal; transparent case back; screw-in crown; water-resistant to 10 atm
Band: reptile skin, double folding clasp
Price: $5,299; limited to 250 pieces

Teutonia II Chronograph

Reference number: M1-30-95-LB
Movement: automatic, Caliber MU 9413 (base ETA 7750); ø 30 mm, height 7.9 mm; 25 jewels; 28,800 vph; woodpecker-neck fine adjustment; three-quarter Glashütte plate; special Mühle finish; 48-hour power reserve
Functions: hours, minutes, subsidiary seconds; chronograph; weekday, date
Case: stainless steel, ø 42 mm, height 15.5 mm; sapphire crystal; transparent case back; screw-in crown; water-resistant to 10 atm
Band: reptile skin, double folding clasp
Price: $4,599
Variations: stainless steel bracelet ($4,799)

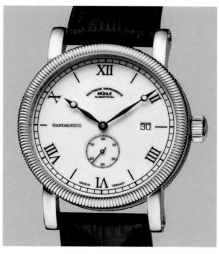

Teutonia III Handaufzug Kleine Sekunde

Reference number: M1-08-11-LB
Movement: manually wound, Caliber MU 9415; ø 25.6 mm, height 3.4 mm; 23 jewels; 28,800 vph; woodpecker neck regulator, three-quarter Glashütte plate; special Mühle finish; 42-hour power reserve
Functions: hours, minutes, subsidiary seconds; date
Case: stainless steel, ø 42 mm, height 12.2 mm; sapphire crystal; transparent case back; water-resistant to 10 atm
Band: calf leather, double folding clasp
Price: $3,099
Variations: stainless steel bracelet ($3,199)

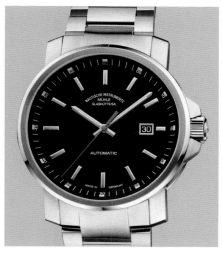

29er Big

Reference number: M1-25-33-MB
Movement: automatic, Sellita Caliber SW200-1; ø 25.6 mm, height 4.6 mm; 26 jewels; 28,800 vph; woodpecker-neck fine adjustment, Mühle rotor; special Mühle finish; 38-hour power reserve
Functions: hours, minutes, sweep seconds; date
Case: stainless steel, ø 42.4 mm, height 11.3 mm; sapphire crystal; transparent case back; screw-in crown; water-resistant to 10 atm
Band: stainless steel, double folding clasp
Price: $2,199
Variations: calf leather band ($2,099)

M 29 Classic Small Seconds

Reference number: M1-25-67-LB
Movement: automatic, Sellita Caliber SW290-1; ø 25.6 mm, 28,800 vph; woodpecker-neck fine adjustment; special Mühle finish; 38-hour power reserve
Functions: hours, minutes, subsidiary seconds; date
Case: stainless steel, ø 42.4 mm, height 12.2 mm; sapphire crystal; transparent case back; screw-in crown; water-resistant to 10 atm
Band: calf leather, double folding clasp
Price: $2,699
Variations: stainless steel bracelet ($2,799)

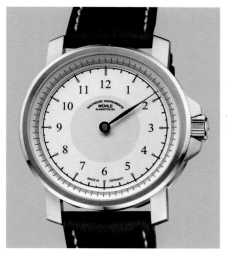

M 29 Classic Einzeiger

Reference number: M1-25-59-LB
Movement: automatic, Sellita Caliber SW200-1; ø 25.6 mm, height 4.6 mm; 26 jewels; 28,800 vph; woodpecker-neck fine adjustment, Mühle rotor; special Mühle finish; 38-hour power reserve
Functions: hours (each line stands for 2 minutes); date
Case: stainless steel, ø 42.4 mm, height 11.3 mm; sapphire crystal; transparent case back; screw-in crown, water-resistant to 10 atm
Band: calf leather, buckle
Price: $2,099
Variations: stainless steel bracelet ($2,299)

S.A.R. Rescue-Timer

Reference number: M1-41-03-MB
Movement: automatic, modified Sellita Caliber SW 200-1; ø 25.6 mm, height 4.6 mm; 26 jewels; 28,800 vph; woodpecker-neck fine adjustment; Mühle rotor; special Mühle finish; 38-hour power reserve
Functions: hours, minutes, sweep seconds; date
Case: stainless steel, ø 42 mm, height 13.5 mm; rubber bezel, sapphire crystal; screw-in crown; water-resistant to 100 atm
Band: stainless steel, folding clasp with extension link
Price: $2,799
Variations: rubber strap ($2,699)

S.A.R. Flieger-Chronograph

Reference number: M1-41-33-KB
Movement: automatic, Caliber MU9413 (based on Sellita SW500); ø 30 mm, height 7.9 mm; 25 jewels; 28,800 vph; woodpecker-neck fine adjustment; three-quarter plate, Mühle rotor; special Mühle finish; 48-hour power reserve
Functions: hours, minutes, subsidiary seconds; chronograph; date
Case: stainless steel, ø 44 mm, height 16.2 mm; bidirectional bezel with 60-minute divisions, sapphire crystal; transparent back; screw-in crown; water-resistant to 10 atm
Band: rubber, safety folding clasp with extension
Price: $4,699
Variations: stainless steel bracelet ($4,899)

Seebataillon GMT

Reference number: M1-28-62-KB
Movement: automatic, ETA Caliber 2893-2; ø 25.6 mm, height 4.1 mm; 21 jewels; 28,800 vph; woodpecker-neck fine adjustment; Mühle rotor; special Mühle finish; 42-hour power reserve
Functions: hours, minutes, sweep seconds; additional 24-hour display (2nd time zone); date
Case: titanium, ø 44 mm, height 12.7 mm; bidirectional bezel with 60-minute divisions, sapphire crystal; screw-in crown; water-resistant to 30 atm
Band: rubber, folding clasp
Price: $3,999

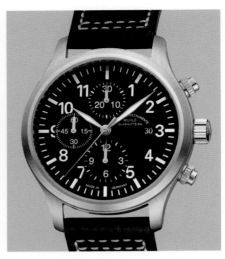

Terrasport I Chronograph

Reference number: M1-37-77-LB
Movement: automatic, Caliber 9413 (based on Sellita SW500); ø 30 mm, height 7.9 mm; 25 jewels; 28,800 vph; woodpecker-neck fine adjustment, three-quarter plate, Mühle rotor; special Mühle finish; 48-hour power reserve
Functions: hours, minutes, subsidiary seconds; chronograph; date
Case: stainless steel, ø 44 mm, height 13.6 mm; sapphire crystal; transparent case back; screw-in crown; water-resistant to 5 atm
Band: calf leather, buckle
Price: $4,099
Variations: stainless steel bracelet ($4,299)

Terrasport I Beobachter

Reference number: M1-37-34/4-LB
Movement: automatic, Sellita Caliber SW200-1; ø 25.6 mm, height 4.6 mm; 26 jewels; 28,800 vph; woodpecker-neck fine adjustment, three-quarter plate, Mühle rotor; special Mühle finish; 38-hour power reserve
Functions: hours, minutes, sweep seconds
Case: stainless steel, ø 44 mm, height 10.4 mm; sapphire crystal; transparent case back; screw-in crown; water-resistant to 5 atm
Band: calf leather, buckle
Price: $1,999
Variations: stainless steel bracelet ($2,199)

Terranaut III Trail

Reference number: M1-40-14/1-NB
Movement: automatic, Sellita Caliber SW200-1; ø 25.6 mm, height 4.6 mm; 26 jewels; 28,800 vph; woodpecker-neck fine adjustment, Mühle rotor; special Mühle finish; 38-hour power reserve
Functions: hours, minutes, sweep seconds; date
Case: stainless steel, ø 40 mm, height 10 mm; sapphire crystal; transparent case back; screw-in crown; water-resistant to 10 atm
Band: textile, buckle
Price: $1,799
Variations: stainless steel bracelet ($1,999)

Caliber RMK 02

Manually wound; woodpecker-neck fine adjustment; single spring barrel; 56-hour power reserve
Functions: hours, minutes, subsidiary seconds
Diameter: 36.6 mm
Height: 6.65 mm
Jewels: 18, including 3 screwed-mounted gold chatons
Balance: glucydur
Frequency: 21,600 vph
Balance spring: Nivarox
Remarks: three-fifth plate, Glashütte stopwork, hand-engraved balance cock

Nienaber Bünde

For over a quarter-century, Rainer Nienaber has manufactured, sold, and repaired watches in Bünde, Germany. Although his work has spanned large, small, simple, complicated, expensive, and inexpensive watches, they all share one trait: uniqueness. One of his particular specialties is retrograde displays, which he continually rearranges in various combinations to create new models. Nienaber uses Swiss movements; the rest is, however, "made in Germany" (cases, dials, bands). He doesn't like being called a "*manufacture*," opting instead for the term "atelier."

No one can doubt his inventiveness. He has produced watches with decimal time, a pair of watches called the Day and Night Watch (for more, visit the collections on his website). His Anterograde is designed to look like the tachometer of a classic car. Although this conceit is not that unusual in the watchmaking industry, in this case the result happens to be an unusual one-handed watch. The five-minute divisions along the dial still allow the user to read the time with considerable precision. But Nienaber has added another extraordinary feature: When the hour hand reaches the 12 o'clock mark, which is a little off-center to the left, it jumps ahead to a "0" mark to the right of center, to begin the next 12-hour period of the day. Hence the name "anterograde." This is no mean feat given the unavoidable tooth flank backlash in the display movement.

Nienaber Bünde
Bahnhofstrasse 33a
D-32257 Bünde
Germany

Tel.:
+49-5223-12292

E-Mail:
info@nienaber-uhren.de

Website:
www.nienaber-uhren.de

Founded:
1984

Number of employees:
1

Annual production:
approx. 50 watches

Distribution:
Please contact Nienaber Bünde directly.

Most important collections/price range:
watches with retrograde displays / approx. $4,000 to $27,000
Prices are determined from the daily euro exchange rate.

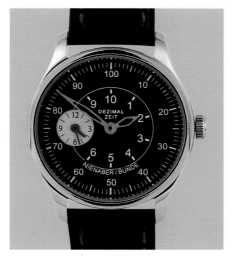

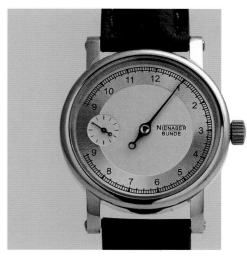

Monozeiger

Movement: manually wound, Caliber AS 1130; ø 29 mm, height 4.2 mm; 17 jewels; 18,000 vph; finely finished
Functions: hours, quarter-hour; dial turns counterclockwise allowing precise reading of time within a few minutes
Case: stainless steel, ø 42 mm, height 12 mm; sapphire crystal; transparent case back; water-resistant to 3 atm
Band: calf leather, buckle
Remarks: limited to 30 pieces
Price: $3,450

Decimal Watch

Movement: manually wound, Unitas Caliber 6325; ø 29.6 mm, height 4.2 mm; 17 jewels; 21,600 vph
Functions: hours, minutes (decimal); additional hours and minutes (sexagesimal)
Case: stainless steel, ø 43 mm, height 14 mm; sapphire crystal
Band: calf leather, buckle
Price: $3,150
Variations: various dial colors; black PVD coating

Antero

Movement: manually wound, based on ETA Caliber 6497; ø 36.5 mm, height 4.5 mm; 17 jewels; 18,000 vph; finely finished
Functions: hours (retrograde), subsidiary seconds
Case: stainless steel, ø 44 mm, height 12 mm; sapphire crystal; transparent case back; water-resistant to 3 atm
Band: calf leather, buckle
Remarks: anterograde means jumping forward: single hour hand jumps over segment of several degrees at 9

Nivrel Uhren

Gerd Hofer GmbH
Kossmannstrasse 3
D-66119 Saarbrücken
Germany

Tel.:
+49-681-584-6576

Fax:
+49-681-584-6584

E-Mail:
info@nivrel.com

Website:
www.nivrel.com

Founded:
1978

Number of employees:
10, plus external staff members

Distribution:
Please contact headquarters for enquiries.

Most important collections/price range:
mechanical watches, most with
complications / approx. $600 to $45,000

Nivrel

In 1891, master goldsmith Friedrich Jacob Kraemer founded a jewelry and watch shop in Saarbrücken that proved to be the place to go for fine craftsmanship. Gerd Hofer joined the family business in 1956, carrying it on into the fourth generation. However, his true passion was for watchmaking. In 1993, he and his wife, Gitta, bought the rights to use the Swiss name Nivrel, a brand that had been established in 1936, and integrated production of these watches into their German-based operations.

Today, Nivrel is led by the Hofers' daughter Anja, who is keeping both lineages alive. Mechanical complications with Swiss movements of the finest technical level and finishing as well as gold watches in the high-end design segment of the industry are manufactured with close attention to detail and an advanced level of craftsmanship. In addition to classic automatic watches, the brand has introduced everything from complicated chronographs and skeletonized watches to perpetual calendars and tourbillons. The movements and all the "habillage" of the watches—case, dial, crystal, crown, etc.—are made in Switzerland. Watch design, assembly, and finishing are done in Saarbrücken.

Nivrel watches are a perfect example of how quickly a watch brand incorporating a characteristic style and immaculate quality can make a respected place for itself in the industry. Affordable prices also play a significant role in this brand's success, but they do not keep the brand from innovating. Nivrel has teamed up with the Department of Metallic Materials of Saarland University to develop a special alloy for repeater springs that is softer and does not need as much energy to press.

Héritage Minier

Reference number: N 323.001 SAAB
Movement: manually wound, ETA Caliber 6497-1; ø 36.6 mm, height 4.5 mm; 17 jewels; 18,000 vph; 46-hour power reserve
Functions: hours, minutes, subsidiary seconds
Case: sterling silver; ø 45 mm, height 13 mm; mineral crystal
Band: stainless steel chain with 2 snap hooks
Remarks: limited to 200 pieces
Price: $1,100

Réplique Manuelle

Reference number: N 322.001 CASDS
Movement: manually wound, ETA Caliber 6497-1; ø 36.6 mm, height 4.5 mm; 17 jewels; 18,000 vph; blued screws, côtes de Genève; 46-hour power reserve
Functions: hours, minutes, subsidiary seconds
Case: stainless steel, ø 44 mm, height 13 mm; sapphire crystal; transparent case back; water-resistant to 5 atm
Band: calf leather, buckle
Price: $800
Variations: white dial

Réplique Lémania Limited

Reference number: N 151.001 CAAHS
Movement: manually wound, Lemania Caliber 8810; ø 25.6 mm, height 2.95 mm; 17 jewels; 28,800 vph; double spring barrel; 40-hour power reserve
Functions: hours, minutes, sweep seconds; date
Case: stainless steel, ø 40 mm, height 7.4 mm; sapphire crystal; transparent case back; water-resistant to 5 atm
Band: calf leather, buckle
Remarks: limited to 30 pieces
Price: $2,150

Héritage Grande Automatique

Reference number: N 112.001
Movement: automatic, Soprod Caliber A10; ø 25.6 mm, height 3.6 mm; 21 jewels; 28,800 vph; finely finished with côtes de Genève; 42-hour power reserve
Functions: hours, minutes, sweep seconds; date
Case: stainless steel, ø 40 mm, height 9 mm; sapphire crystal; transparent case back; screw-in crown; water-resistant to 5 atm
Band: reptile skin, buckle
Price: $1,450

Héritage Grand Chronographe

Reference number: N 512.001 AAAAS
Movement: automatic, ETA Caliber 7750; ø 30 mm, height 7.9 mm; 25 jewels; 28,800 vph; finely finished; 42-hour power reserve
Functions: hours, minutes, subsidiary seconds; chronograph; date, weekday
Case: stainless steel, ø 42 mm, height 13.5 mm; sapphire crystal; transparent case back; screw-in crown; water-resistant to 5 atm
Band: calf leather, buckle
Price: $2,200

Heritage Perpétuel

Reference number: N 401.001
Movement: automatic, ETA 2892-A2 with calendar module; ø 25.6 mm, 21 jewels; 28,800 vph; finely finished with côtes de Genève on rotor; 42-hour power reserve
Functions: hours, minutes, sweep seconds; perpetual calendar with date, weekday, month, moon phase, leap year
Case: stainless steel, ø 38 mm, height 10 mm; sapphire crystal; transparent case back; water-resistant to 5 atm
Band: reptile skin, buckle
Price: $10,500
Variations: black reptile skin band

Coeur de la Sarre: Sarrelouis

Reference number: N 130.001 CASDS
Movement: automatic, ETA Caliber 2824-2; ø 25.6 mm, height 4.6 mm; 25 jewels; 28,800 vph; rotor with côtes de Genève; 38-hour power reserve
Functions: hours, minutes, sweep seconds
Case: stainless steel, ø 42 mm, height 12.5 mm; mineral crystal; transparent case back; water-resistant to 5 atm
Band: calf leather, buckle
Price: $750

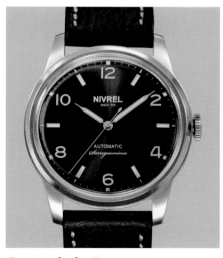

Coeur de la Sarre: Sarreguemines

Reference number: N 130.001 CABDS
Movement: automatic, ETA Caliber 2824-2; ø 25.6 mm, height 4.6 mm; 25 jewels; 28,800 vph; rotor with côtes de Genève; 38-hour power reserve
Functions: hours, minutes, sweep seconds
Case: stainless steel, ø 42 mm, height 12.5 mm; mineral crystal; transparent case back; water-resistant to 5 atm
Band: calf leather, buckle
Price: $750

Chronographe Réplique III

Reference number: N 512.001 AASDS
Movement: automatic, ETA Caliber 7750; ø 30 mm, height 7.9 mm; 25 jewels; 28,800 vph; finely finished, côtes de Genève on rotor; 42-hour power reserve
Functions: hours, minutes, subsidiary seconds; chronograph; date, weekday
Case: stainless steel, ø 42 mm, height 13.5 mm; sapphire crystal; transparent case back; screw-in crown; water-resistant to 5 atm
Band: calf leather, buckle
Price: $2,200

NOMOS Glashütte/SA

Roland Schwertner KG
Ferdinand-Adolph-Lange-Platz 2
D-01768 Glashütte
Germany

Tel.:
+49-35053-4040

Fax:
+49-35053-40480

E-Mail:
nomos@glashuette.com

Website:
www.nomos-glashuette.com

Founded:
1990

Number of employees:
close to 200

U.S. distributor:
For the U.S. market, please contact NOMOS
Glashütte directly.

Most important collections/price range:
Ahoi / $4,060 to $4,660; Club / $1,550 to
$3,550; Lambda / $18,500 to $20,000;
Ludwig / $1,700 to $3,780; Metro / $3,480
to $3,780; Orion / $1,920 to $3,060;
Sundial / $185 to $310; Tangente / $1,760
to $3,500; Tangomat / $3,280 to $4,920;
Tetra / $1,980 to $2,920; Zürich / $4,480
to $6,100

Nomos

Still waters run deep, and discreet business practices at times travel far. Nomos, founded in 1990, has suddenly become a full-fledged *manufacture* with brand-new facilities and a smart policy of only so much growth as the small team gathered around the founder Roland Schwertner and his associate Uwe Ahrendt can easily absorb.

The collection is based on five or six basic models, though the number of calibers available is growing at an impressive rate, including two luxury manually wound movements with fine finishings. The most striking advance, however, has been in Nomos's core business. Over the past years the brand has invested heavily in the design and construction of an in-house escapement with a spring "made in Germany." The escapement made its debut at Baselworld 2014 under the name DUW 4401 (Deutsche Uhrenwerke Nomos Glashütte) and will gradually be used in all the movements, including the new, automatic ultrathin DUW 3001.

In 2005, Nomos moved into new space in the former Glashütte train station, but already, the factory is bursting at the seams. Since 2010, the staff virtually doubled in size to close to 200 people, including about 30 design and communication staff in Berlin and Zurich. Nomos has also managed to double its revenues during the same period and intends to repeat that feat by 2017. Its phenomenal growth could be a lesson to many brands: Use outstanding watches at an affordable price, a simple look full of subtle details, and marketing that is bold and humorous. The 2009 Orion models with dials in various shades of gray celebrating the anniversary of the fall of the Berlin Wall were a real hit. The more recent Ahoi (as in "ship ahoy!"), a swimmer's watch with an optional synthetic strap like those that carry locker keys at Germany's public swimming pools, has won several prizes.

Minimatik

Reference number: 1201
Movement: automatic, Nomos Caliber DUW 3001; ø 28.8 mm, height 3.2 mm; 27 jewels; 21,600 vph; 42-hour power reserve
Functions: hours, minutes, subsidiary seconds
Case: stainless steel, ø 35.5 mm, height 8.86 mm; sapphire crystal; transparent case back; water-resistant to 3 atm
Band: horse leather, buckle
Price: $4,060

Tangente Automatik

Reference number: 171
Movement: automatic, Nomos Caliber DUW 3001; ø 28.8 mm, height 3.2 mm; 27 jewels; 21,600 vph; 42-hour power reserve
Functions: hours, minutes, subsidiary seconds
Case: stainless steel, ø 35 mm, height 6.9 mm; sapphire crystal; transparent case back; water-resistant to 3 atm
Band: horse leather, buckle
Price: $3,780

Metro 38 Datum Stadtschwarz

Reference number: 1103
Movement: manually wound, Nomos Caliber DUW 4101; ø 32.1 mm, height 2.8 mm; 23 jewels; 21,600 vph; 42-hour power reserve
Functions: hours, minutes, subsidiary seconds; date
Case: stainless steel, ø 38.5 mm, height 7.75 mm; sapphire crystal; transparent case back; water-resistant to 3 atm
Band: horse leather, buckle
Price: $3,480

Ahoi Datum

Reference number: 551
Movement: automatic, Nomos Caliber Zeta; ø 31 mm, height 4.3 mm; 26 jewels; 21,600 vph; 42-hour power reserve
Functions: hours, minutes, subsidiary seconds; date
Case: stainless steel, ø 40 mm, height 10.64 mm; sapphire crystal; transparent case back; screw-in crown; water-resistant to 20 atm
Band: textile, buckle
Price: $4,660

Tangomat

Reference number: 601
Movement: automatic, Nomos Caliber Epsilon; ø 31 mm, height 4.3 mm; 26 jewels; 21,600 vph; 43-hour power reserve
Functions: hours, minutes, subsidiary seconds
Case: stainless steel, ø 38.3 mm, height 8.3 mm; sapphire crystal; transparent case back; water-resistant to 3 atm
Band: horse leather, buckle
Price: $3,280

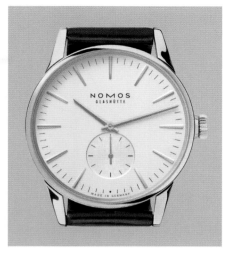

Zürich

Reference number: 801
Movement: automatic, Nomos Caliber Epsilon; ø 31 mm, height 4.3 mm; 26 jewels; 21,600 vph; 43-hour power reserve
Functions: hours, minutes, subsidiary seconds
Case: stainless steel, ø 39.7 mm, height 9.65 mm; sapphire crystal; transparent case back; water-resistant to 3 atm
Band: horse leather, buckle
Price: $4,480

Ahoi Atlantik

Reference number: 552
Movement: automatic, Nomos Caliber Epsilon; ø 31 mm, height 4.3 mm; 26 jewels; 21,600 vph; 43-hour power reserve
Functions: hours, minutes, subsidiary seconds
Case: stainless steel, ø 40 mm, height 10.64 mm; sapphire crystal; transparent case back; screw-in crown; water-resistant to 20 atm
Band: textile, buckle
Price: $4,060

Tangomat GMT

Reference number: 635
Movement: automatic, Nomos Caliber DUW 5201; ø 31 mm, height 5.7 mm; 26 jewels; 21,600 vph; 42-hour power reserve
Functions: hours, minutes, subsidiary seconds; world-time display (2nd time zone)
Case: stainless steel, ø 40 mm, height 10.85 mm; sapphire crystal; transparent case back; water-resistant to 3 atm
Band: horse leather, buckle
Price: $4,920

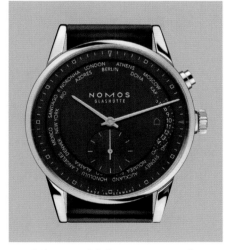

Zurich Worldtimer True Blue

Reference number: 807
Movement: automatic, Nomos Caliber DUW 5201; ø 31 mm, height 5.7 mm; 26 jewels; 21,600 vph; 42-hour power reserve; Glashütte stopwork
Functions: hours, minutes, subsidiary seconds; world-time display (2nd time zone)
Case: stainless steel, ø 39.9 mm, height 10.85 mm; sapphire crystal; transparent case back; water-resistant to 3 atm
Band: leather, buckle
Price: $6,100

Tangente 38 Datum

Reference number: 130
Movement: manually wound, Nomos Caliber Beta;
ø 32.1 mm, height 2.8 mm; 23 jewels; 21,600 vph;
42-hour power reserve
Functions: hours, minutes, subsidiary seconds;
date
Case: stainless steel, ø 37.5 mm, height 6.75 mm;
sapphire crystal; transparent case back; water-
resistant to 3 atm
Band: horse leather, buckle
Price: $2,780

Metro Datum Gangreserve

Reference number: 1101
Movement: manually wound, Nomos Caliber DUW
4401; ø 32.1 mm, height 2.8 mm; 23 jewels;
21,600 vph; 42-hour power reserve; Glashütte
stopwork
Functions: hours, minutes, subsidiary seconds;
power reserve indicator; date
Case: stainless steel, ø 37 mm, height 7.65 mm;
sapphire crystal; transparent case back; water-
resistant to 3 atm
Band: horse leather, buckle
Price: $3,780

Orion 38 Grau

Reference number: 383
Movement: manually wound, Nomos Caliber Alpha;
ø 23.3 mm, height 2.6 mm; 17 jewels; 21,600 vph;
43-hour power reserve
Functions: hours, minutes, subsidiary seconds
Case: stainless steel, ø 38 mm, height 8.86 mm;
sapphire crystal; transparent case back; water-
resistant to 3 atm
Band: horse leather, buckle
Price: $2,620

Club Datum

Reference number: 733
Movement: manually wound, Nomos Caliber Beta;
ø 33.1 mm, height 2.8 mm; 23 jewels; 21,600 vph;
42-hour power reserve
Functions: hours, minutes, subsidiary seconds;
date
Case: stainless steel, ø 38.5 mm, height 8.45 mm;
sapphire crystal; transparent case back; water-
resistant to 10 atm
Band: horse leather, buckle
Price: $2,560

Tetra Kleene

Reference number: 492
Movement: manually wound, Nomos Caliber DUW
4301; ø 23.3 mm, height 2.8 mm; 17 jewels;
21,600 vph; 43-hour power reserve
Functions: hours, minutes, subsidiary seconds;
power reserve display
Case: stainless steel, 29.5 x 29.5 mm, height
6.3 mm; sapphire crystal; transparent case back;
water-resistant to 3 atm
Band: suede, buckle
Price: $2,920

Orion 33 1989

Reference number: 326
Movement: manually wound, Nomos Caliber Alpha;
ø 23.3 mm, height 2.6 mm; 17 jewels; 21,600 vph;
43-hour power reserve
Functions: hours, minutes, subsidiary seconds
Case: stainless steel, ø 32.8 mm, height 8.54 mm;
sapphire crystal; transparent case back; water-
resistant to 3 atm
Band: suede, buckle
Price: $2,300

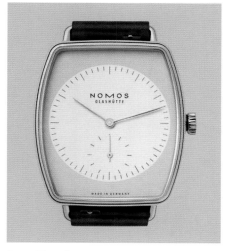

Lambda Roségold

Reference number: 932
Movement: manually wound, Nomos Caliber DUW 1001; ø 32 mm, height 3.6 mm; 29 jewels; 21,600 vph; screw balance; swan-neck fine adjustment; twin spring barrels, 84-hour power reserve; hand-engraved balance cock
Functions: hours, minutes, subsidiary seconds; power reserve indicator
Case: rose gold, ø 42 mm, height 8.9 mm; sapphire crystal; transparent case back; water-resistant to 3 atm
Band: horse leather, buckle
Price: $18,500
Variations: rose gold hands

Lambda Deep Blue

Reference number: 935
Movement: manually wound, Nomos Caliber DUW 1001; ø 32 mm, height 3.6 mm; 29 jewels; 21,600 vph; screw balance; swan-neck fine adjustment; twin mainspring barrels, 84-hour power reserve; hand-engraved balance cock
Functions: hours, minutes, subsidiary seconds; power reserve indicator
Case: white gold, ø 42 mm, height 8.9 mm; sapphire crystal; transparent case back; water-resistant to 3 atm
Band: horse leather, buckle
Price: $20,000

Lux Ermine

Reference number: 940
Movement: manually wound, Nomos Caliber DUW 2002; 32.6 x 22.6 mm, height 3.6 mm; 23 jewels; 21,600 vph; screw balance; swan-neck fine adjustment; twin spring barrels, 84-hour power reserve
Functions: hours, minutes, subsidiary seconds
Case: rose gold, 38.5 x 34 mm, height 9 mm; sapphire crystal; transparent case back; water-resistant to 3 atm
Band: horse leather, buckle
Price: $19,500

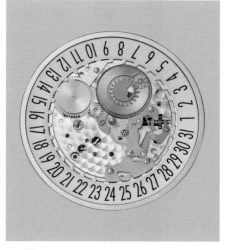

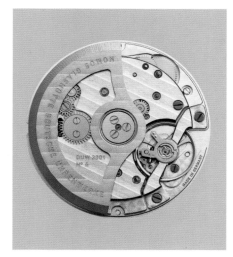

Caliber DUW 1001

Manually wound; swan-neck fine adjustment; double spring barrel, 84-hour power reserve
Functions: hours, minutes, subsidiary seconds; power reserve indicator
Diameter: 32 mm
Height: 3.6 mm
Jewels: 29, including 5 screwed-mounted gold chatons
Balance: glucydur with weighted screws
Frequency: 21,600 vph
Balance spring: Nivarox 1A
Shock protection: Incabloc
Remarks: hand-engraved balance cock, beveled and polished edges, rhodium-plated movement surfaces with Glashütte sun-brushing and perlage

Caliber DUW 4401

Manually wound; single spring barrel, 42-hour power reserve
Functions: hours, minutes, subsidiary seconds; power reserve indicator; date
Diameter: 32.1 mm
Height: 2.8 mm
Jewels: 23
Balance: glucydur
Frequency: 21,600 vph
Shock protection: Incabloc
Remarks: three-quarter plate, movement surfaces rhodium-plated, with Glashütte ribbing and perlage

Caliber DUW 3001

Automatic; single spring barrel, 42-hour power reserve
Functions: hours, minutes, subsidiary seconds
Diameter: 28.8 mm
Height: 3.2 mm
Jewels: 27
Balance: glucydur
Frequency: 21,600 vph
Shock protection: Incabloc
Remarks: three-quarter plate, movement surfaces rhodium-plated, with Glashütte ribbing and perlage

Omega SA
Jakob-Stämpfli-Strasse 96
CH-2502 Biel/Bienne
Switzerland

Tel.:
+41-32-343-9211

E-Mail:
info@omegawatches.com

Website:
www.omegawatches.com

Founded:
1848

Annual production:
750,000 (estimated)

U.S. distributor:
Omega
The Swatch Group (U.S.), Inc.
1200 Harbor Boulevard
Weehawken, NJ 07086
201-271-1400
www.omegawatches.com

Most important collections/price range:
Seamaster / approx. $2,750 to $95,000;
Constellation / approx. $2,700 to $130,000;
Speedmaster / approx. $4,650 to $36,000

Omega

When it comes to price—and perhaps prestige as well—there are some *manufactures* within the Swatch Group that have overtaken Omega. Nevertheless, the brand still manages to command respect as the flagship of the group and as the timekeeper for the more recent incarnations of James Bond as well as the Vancouver Winter Olympics in 2010.

It has also played a major role in the history of the watch business in Switzerland. The brand was originally founded in 1848. In 1930, it merged with Tissot to form SIHH, which in turn merged with watch conglomerate ASUAG to form the Swatch Group in 1983, of which Omega was the leading brand. In the 1990s, the brand managed to expand incrementally into the Chinese market and thus established a firm foothold in Asia. This also led to a steep growth in production numbers, putting it neck-and-neck with Rolex.

And today, Omega has once again put itself back in the competition with technology as the key. It introduced the innovative coaxial escapement to several collections, which has pushed the brand back into the technological frontrunners in its segment. Swatch Group subsidiary Nivarox-FAR has finally mastered the production of the difficult, oil-free parts of the system designed by Englishman George Daniels, although the escapement continues to include lubrication as the long-term results of "dry" coaxial movements are less than satisfactory. Thus the most important plus for this escapement design remains high rate stability after careful regulation. Omega has even revived the Ladymatic, adding a silicon spring and the trademark coaxial escapement.

In July 2013, Omega officially unveiled a brand-new 15,000 Gauss antimagnetic movement, which will be spread throughout the brand's models in years to come. Meanwhile, the Swatch Group's company grounds in Biel have been entirely restructured and will include a testing and certification unit as of 2016. After promulgating the benefits of decentralization for years, Omega appears to be returning to the good old *manufacture* system of all crafts under a single roof.

Speedmaster Moonwatch "Dark Side of the Moon"

Reference number: 311.92.44.51.01.003
Movement: automatic, Omega Caliber 9300; ø 32.5 mm, height 7.6 mm; 54 jewels; 28,800 vph; coaxial escapement, silicon balance/balance spring; 60-hour power reserve; COSC-tested chronometer
Functions: hours, minutes, subsidiary seconds; chronograph; date
Case: ceramic, ø 44.25 mm, height 15.79 mm; sapphire crystal; transparent case back; water-resistant to 5 atm
Band: nylon, folding clasp
Price: $12,000

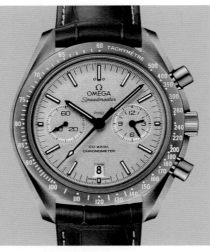

Speedmaster "Grey Side of the Moon"

Reference number: 311.93.44.51.99.001
Movement: automatic, Omega Caliber 9300; ø 32.5 mm, height 7.6 mm; 54 jewels; 28,800 vph; coaxial escapement, silicon balance/balance spring; 60-hour power reserve; COSC-certified chronometer
Functions: hours, minutes, subsidiary seconds; chronograph; date
Case: ceramic, ø 44.25 mm, height 16.14 mm; sapphire crystal; water-resistant to 5 atm
Band: reptile skin, folding clasp
Price: $12,000

Speedmaster "Dark Side of the Moon" Sedna Black

Movement: automatic, Omega Caliber 9300; ø 32.5 mm, height 7.6 mm; 54 jewels; 28,800 vph; coaxial escapement, silicon balance/balance spring; 60-hour power reserve; COSC-certified chronometer
Functions: hours, minutes, subsidiary seconds; chronograph; date
Case: ceramic, ø 41.5 mm, height 16.17 mm; red gold bezel; sapphire crystal; transparent case back, water-resistant to 5 atm
Band: reptile skin, folding clasp
Price: $15,000

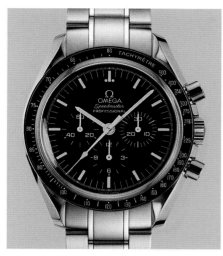

Speedmaster Moonwatch Professional

Reference number: 311.30.42.30.01.006
Movement: manually wound, Omega Caliber 1863 (base Lémania 1873); ø 27 mm, height 6.87 mm; 18 jewels; 21,600 vph; 48-hour power reserve; COSC-certified chronometer
Functions: hours, minutes, subsidiary seconds; chronograph
Case: stainless steel, ø 42 mm, height 14.15 mm; sapphire crystal; water-resistant to 5 atm
Band: stainless steel, folding clasp
Price: $6,250

Speedmaster 57

Reference number: 331.12.42.51.01.002
Movement: automatic, Omega Caliber 9300; ø 32.5 mm, height 7.6 mm; 54 jewels; 28,800 vph; coaxial escapement, silicon balance/balance spring; 60-hour power reserve; COSC-tested chronometer
Functions: hours, minutes, subsidiary seconds; chronograph; date
Case: stainless steel, ø 41.5 mm, height 16.17 mm; sapphire crystal; water-resistant to 10 atm
Band: calf leather, folding clasp
Price: $8,900

Speedmaster Moonwatch Professional "Silver Snoopy Award" 45th Anniversary Limited Edition

Reference number: 311.32.42.30.04.003
Movement: manually wound, Omega Caliber 1861 (base Lémania 1873); ø 27 mm, height 6.87 mm; 18 jewels; 21,600 vph; 48-hour power reserve
Functions: hours, minutes, subsidiary seconds; chronograph
Case: stainless steel, ø 42 mm, height 14.81 mm; ceramic bezel; sapphire crystal; transparent case back; water-resistant to 5 atm
Remarks: luminescent hour markers/image of Snoopy
Price: $7,350; limited to 1,970 pieces

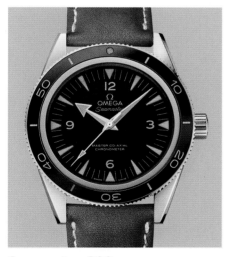

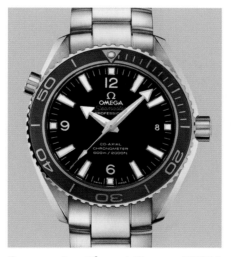

Seamaster 300

Reference number: 233.32.41.21.01.002
Movement: automatic, Omega Caliber 8400; ø 29 mm, height 5.5 mm; 38 jewels; 25,200 vph; coaxial escapement, silicon balance/balance spring; antimagnetic to 15,000 Gauss; 60-hour power reserve; COSC-certified chronometer
Functions: hours, minutes, sweep seconds
Case: stainless steel, ø 41 mm, height 14.65 mm; unidirectional bezel with 60-minute divisions; sapphire crystal; water-resistant to 30 atm
Band: calf leather, folding clasp
Price: $6,500
Variations: titanium ($9,000); Sedna gold/Sedna gold bracelet ($34,200)

Seamaster Planet Ocean 600M

Reference number: 232.30.42.21.01.001
Movement: automatic, Omega Caliber 8500; ø 29 mm, height 5.5 mm; 39 jewels; 25,200 vph; coaxial escapement, silicon balance/balance spring; antimagnetic to 15,000 Gauss; 60-hour power reserve; COSC-certified chronometer
Functions: hours, minutes, sweep seconds; date
Case: stainless steel, ø 42 mm, height 12.95 mm; unidirectional bezel with 60-minute divisions; sapphire crystal; transparent case back; screw-in crown, helium valve; water-resistant to 60 atm
Band: stainless steel, folding clasp
Price: $6,200
Variations: titanium/rubber strap ($10,000)

Seamaster Planet Ocean "Good Planet" GMT

Reference number: 232.30.44.22.03.001
Movement: automatic, Omega Caliber 8605; ø 29 mm, height 6 mm; 38 jewels; 25,200 vph; coaxial escapement, silicon balance/balance spring; 60-hour power reserve; COSC-certified chronometer
Functions: hours, minutes, sweep seconds; additional 24-hour display (2nd time zone); date
Case: stainless steel, ø 43.5 mm, height 17.25 mm; bidirectional bezel with 24-hour divisions, sapphire crystal; screw-in crown; water-resistant to 60 atm
Band: stainless steel, folding clasp
Price: $8,100
Variations: titanium/rubber strap ($10,100)

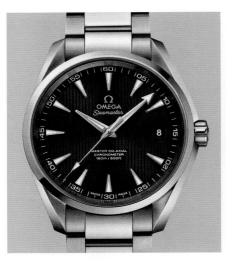

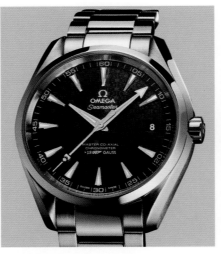

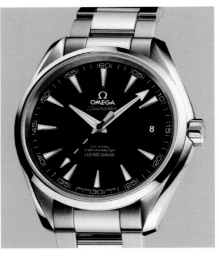

Seamaster Aqua Terra

Reference number: 231.10.42.21.03.003
Movement: automatic, Omega Caliber 8500;
ø 29 mm, height 5.5 mm; 39 jewels; 25,200 vph;
coaxial escapement, silicon balance/balance
spring; antimagnetic to 15,000 Gauss; 60-hour
power reserve; COSC-certified chronometer
Functions: hours, minutes, sweep seconds; date
Case: stainless steel, ø 41.5 mm, height 12.95 mm;
sapphire crystal; screw-in crown; automatic helium
valve; water-resistant to 15 atm
Band: stainless steel, folding clasp
Price: $6,000
Variations: various dials; steel/leather band
($6,100); steel-rose gold/steel-rose gold band
($12,000); yellow gold/yellow gold bracelet
($33,500)

Seamaster Aqua Terra "James Bond" Limited Edition

Reference number: 231.10.42.21.03.004
Movement: automatic, Omega Caliber 8507;
ø 29 mm, height 5.5 mm; 39 jewels; 25,200 vph;
coaxial escapement, silicon balance/balance spring,
antimagnetic to 15,007 Gauss, special rotor with
James Bond decoration; 60-hour power reserve;
COSC-certified chronometer
Functions: hours, minutes, sweep seconds; date
Case: stainless steel, ø 41.5 mm, height 13.46 mm;
sapphire crystal; transparent back; water-resistant
to 15 atm
Band: stainless steel, folding clasp
Price: $7,350; limited to 15,007 pieces

Seamaster Aqua Terra 15.000 Gauss

Reference number: 231.10.42.21.01.002
Movement: automatic, Omega Caliber 8500;
ø 29 mm, height 5.5 mm; 39 jewels; 25,200 vph;
coaxial escapement, silicon balance/balance
spring; antimagnetic to 15,000 Gauss; 60-hour
power reserve; COSC-certified chronometer
Functions: hours, minutes, sweep seconds; date
Case: stainless steel, ø 41.5 mm, height 14.3 mm;
sapphire crystal; screw-in crown; automatic helium
valve; water-resistant to 15 atm
Band: stainless steel, folding clasp
Price: $6,600
Variations: leather strap ($6,500)

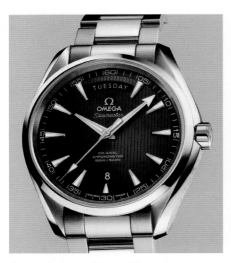

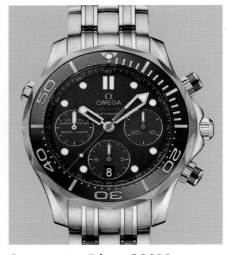

Seamaster Aqua Terra Day-Date

Reference number: 231.10.42.22.03.001
Movement: automatic, Omega Caliber 8602;
ø 29 mm, height 6.5 mm; 39 jewels; 25,200 vph;
coaxial escapement, silicon balance/balance spring;
55-hour power reserve; COSC-certified chronometer
Functions: hours, minutes, sweep seconds;
weekday, date
Case: stainless steel, ø 41.5 mm, height 14.3 mm;
sapphire crystal, transparent case back; screw-in
crown; water-resistant to 15 atm
Band: stainless steel, folding clasp
Price: $7,800
Variations: pink gold/pink gold bracelet ($36,000)

Seamaster Aqua Terra Master Co-Axial Chronometer

Reference number: 231.13.39. 21.57.001
Movement: automatic, Omega Caliber 8500;
ø 29 mm, height 5.5 mm; 39 jewels; 25,200 vph;
coaxial escapement, silicon balance/balance spring,
antimagnetic to 15,000 Gauss; 60-hour power
reserve; COSC-certified chronometer
Functions: hours, minutes, sweep seconds; date
Case: stainless steel, ø 38.5 mm, height 12.84 mm;
sapphire crystal; water-resistant to 15 atm
Band: reptile skin, buckle
Remarks: mother-of-pearl dial with 11 diamonds
Price: $7,600

Seamaster Diver 300M Co-Axial Chronograph

Reference number: 212.30.44.50.03.001
Movement: automatic, Omega Caliber 3330;
ø 30 mm, height 7.9 mm; 31 jewels; 28,800 vph;
coaxial escapement, silicon balance/balance spring;
60-hour power reserve; COSC-certified chronometer
Functions: hours, minutes, subsidiary seconds;
chronograph; date
Case: stainless steel, ø 44 mm, height 17.27 mm;
unidirectional bezel with 60-minute divisions,
sapphire crystal; screw-in crown; automatic helium
valve; water-resistant to 30 atm
Band: stainless steel, folding clasp
Price: $6,000
Variations: black dial ($6,000); 41.5 mm case
($6,000)

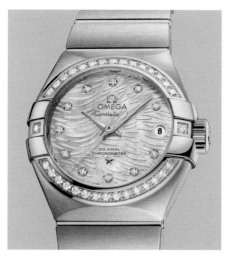

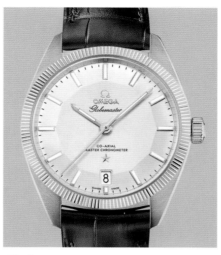

Constellation Pluma "Light Coral"

Reference number: 123.25.27.20.57.004
Movement: automatic, Omega Caliber 8520; ø 20 mm, height 5.3 mm; 28 jewels; 25,200 vph; coaxial escapement, silicon balance/balance spring, antimagnetic to 15,000 Gauss; 50-hour power reserve; COSC-certified chronometer
Functions: hours, minutes, sweep seconds; date
Case: stainless steel, ø 27 mm, height 12.25 mm; 32 diamonds on red gold bezel; sapphire crystal; water-resistant to 10 atm
Band: stainless steel/red gold elements, folding clasp
Remarks: mother-of-pearl dial with 11 diamonds
Price: $11,600
Variations: w/o diamonds ($10,000)

Globemaster

Reference number: 130.53.39.21.02.001
Movement: automatic, Omega Caliber 8901; ø 29 mm, height 5.5 mm; 39 jewels; 25,200 vph; coaxial escapement, silicon balance/balance spring, antimagnetic to 15,000 Gauss; 60-hour power reserve; COSC-certified chronometer
Functions: hours, minutes, sweep seconds; date
Case: yellow gold, ø 39 mm, height 12.53 mm; sapphire crystal; water-resistant to 10 atm
Band: reptile skin, buckle
Price: $21,600
Variations: stainless steel band/white dial ($7,700)

Globemaster

Reference number: 130.30.39.21.03.001
Movement: automatic, Omega Caliber 8900; ø 29 mm, height 5.5 mm; 39 jewels; 25,200 vph; coaxial escapement, silicon balance/balance spring, antimagnetic to 15,000 Gauss; 60-hour power reserve; COSC-certified chronometer
Functions: hours, minutes, sweep seconds; date
Case: stainless steel, ø 39 mm, height 12.53 mm; tungsten carbide bezel; sapphire crystal; water-resistant to 10 atm
Band: stainless steel, folding clasp
Price: $7,700
Variations: yellow gold/stainless steel bracelet ($12,000)

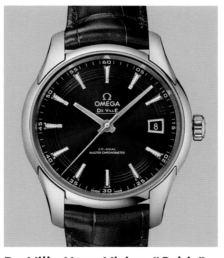

De Ville Trésor

Reference number: 432.53.40.21.02.001
Movement: automatic, Omega Caliber 8511; ø 29 mm; 25,200 vph; coaxial escapement, silicon balance/balance spring; antimagnetic to 15,000 Gauss; 60-hour power reserve; COSC-certified chronometer
Functions: hours, minutes, sweep seconds; date
Case: yellow gold, ø 40 mm, height 10.6 mm; sapphire crystal
Band: reptile skin, folding clasp
Price: $13,800
Variations: white gold ($15,000); pink gold ($13,900)

De Ville Hour Vision "Orbis"

Reference number: 433.33.41.21.03.001
Movement: automatic, Omega Caliber 8900; ø 29 mm, height 5.5 mm; 39 jewels; 25,200 vph; coaxial escapement, silicon balance/balance spring, antimagnetic to 15,000 Gauss; 60-hour power reserve; COSC-certified chronometer
Functions: hours, minutes, sweep seconds; date
Case: stainless steel, ø 41 mm, height 12.2 mm; tungsten carbide bezel; sapphire crystal; transparent case back; water-resistant to 10 atm
Band: reptile skin, buckle
Price: $7,700

De Ville Prestige Power Reserve

Reference number: 424.53.40.21.03.002
Movement: automatic, Omega Caliber 2627; 29 jewels; 25,200 vph; coaxial escapement; 48-hour power reserve; COSC-certified chronometer
Functions: hours, minutes, subsidiary seconds; power reserve indicator; date
Case: pink gold, ø 39.5 mm, height 10.6 mm; sapphire crystal; water-resistant to 3 atm
Band: reptile skin, buckle
Price: $11,200
Variations: steel with leather ($4,800)

Caliber 9300

Automatic; coaxial escapement; column wheel control of chronograph functions; twin spring barrels, 60-hour power reserve; COSC-certified chronometer
Functions: hours, minutes, subsidiary seconds; chronograph; date
Diameter: 32.5 mm
Height: 7.7 mm
Jewels: 54
Balance: silicon, without regulator
Frequency: 28,800 vph
Balance spring: silicon
Shock protection: Nivachoc
Remarks: base plate, bridges, and rotor with "arabesque" côtes de Genève, balance and screws blackened

Caliber 9301

Base caliber: 9300
Automatic; coaxial escapement; column wheel control of chronograph functions; twin spring barrels, 60-hour power reserve; COSC-certified chronometer
Functions: hours, minutes, subsidiary seconds; chronograph; date
Diameter: 32.5 mm; **Height:** 7.7 mm
Jewels: 54; **Balance:** silicon, without regulator
Frequency: 28,800 vph
Balance spring: silicon
Shock protection: Nivachoc
Remarks: base plate, bridges, and rotor with "arabesque" côtes de Genève, rotor and balance bridges in pink gold, balance and screws blackened

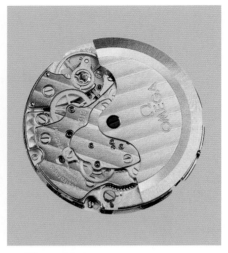

Caliber 3313

Automatic; coaxial escapement; column wheel control of chronograph functions; single spring barrel, 52-hour power reserve; COSC-certified chronometer
Functions: hours, minutes, subsidiary seconds; chronograph; date
Diameter: 27 mm
Height: 6.85 mm
Jewels: 37
Balance: without regulator
Frequency: 28,800 vph
Balance spring: freely oscillating
Remarks: perlage on plate, bridges and balance cock with côtes de Genève, gold-plated engravings; rotor hub screw of blued steel

Caliber 8605

Automatic; coaxial escapement; twin spring barrels, 60-hour power reserve; COSC certified chronometer
Functions: hours, minutes, sweep seconds; second time zone (additional 24-hour indicator); date
Diameter: 29 mm; **Height:** 5.9 mm
Jewels: 38
Balance: silicon, without regulator
Frequency: 25,200 vph
Balance spring: silicon
Shock protection: Nivachoc
Remarks: base plate, bridges, and rotor with "arabesque" côtes de Genève, rhodium-plated, balance and screws blackened (Caliber 8615 with rotor and balance bridge in pink gold)

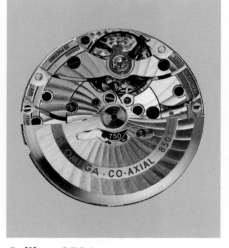

Caliber 8501

Base caliber: 8500
Automatic; coaxial escapement; twin spring barrels, 60-hour power reserve; COSC-certified chronometer
Functions: hours, minutes, sweep seconds; date
Diameter: 29 mm; **Height:** 5.6 mm
Jewels: 39
Balance: silicon, without regulator
Frequency: 25,200 vph
Balance spring: silicon
Shock protection: Nivachoc
Remarks: platinum, bridges and rotor with "arabesque" côtes de Genève, rotor and balance bridges in pink gold, balance and screws blackened (base Caliber 8500 without gold finishing)

Caliber 8520

Automatic; coaxial escapement; twin spring barrels, 60-hour power reserve; COSC-certified chronometer
Functions: hours, minutes sweep seconds; date
Diameter: 20 mm
Height: 5.3 mm
Jewels: 28
Balance: silicon, without regulator
Frequency: 25,200 vph
Balance spring: silicon
Shock protection: Nivachoc
Remarks: platinum, bridges and rotor with "arabesque" côtes de Genève, rhodium-plated, balance and screws blackened (Caliber 8251 with rotor and balance bridge in pink gold)

Oris SA
Ribigasse 1
CH-4434 Hölstein
Switzerland

Tel.:
+41-61-956-1111

E-Mail:
info@oris

Website:
www.oris.ch

Founded:
1904

Number of employees:
90

U.S. distributor:
Oris Watches USA
50 Washington Street, Suite 412
Norwalk, CT 06854
203-857-4769; 203-857-4782 (fax)

Most important collections/price range:
Diver, Big Crown, Artelier, BC3, BC4 / approx.
$1,100 to $5,500

Oris

Oris has been producing mechanical watches in the little town of Hölstein in northwestern Switzerland, near Basel, since 1904, so 2014 was a celebratory year. The brand's strategy has always been to keep prices low and quality high, so Oris has managed to expand in a segment relinquished by other big-name competitors as they sought their fortune in the higher-end markets. The result has been growing international success for Oris, whose portfolio is divided up into four "product worlds," each with its own distinct identity: aviation, motor sports, diving, and culture. In utilizing specific materials—a tungsten bezel for the divers, for example—and functions based on these types, Oris makes certain that each will fit perfectly into the world for which it was designed. Yet the heart of every watch houses a small, high-quality "high-mech" movement identifiable by the brand's standard red rotor.

The brand surprised everyone for its 110th birthday by signing off on in-house Caliber 110, an unembellished and technically efficient manually wound movement. In 2015 came the Caliber 111. These movements are special: In collaboration with the engineers from the Technical College of Le Locle, Oris developed a massive spring barrel containing a 6-foot (1.8 m) spring. With numerous trials and lots of tweaking, the unwinding of this very long spring was optimized, providing a full ten days of power of even torque. The power reserve indicator on the right of the dial does not move evenly, however, due to the transmission ratio. Toward the end, the markers are somewhat longer to give a more accurate idea of the remaining power in the spring.

Caliber 111

Reference number: 111 7700 6061
Movement: manually wound, Oris Caliber 111; ø 34 mm, 40 jewels; 21,600 vph; 240-hour power reserve
Functions: hours, minutes, subsidiary seconds; power reserve indicator; date
Case: rose gold, ø 43 mm, height 12.3 mm; sapphire crystal; transparent case back; water-resistant to 3 atm
Band: reptile skin, buckle
Price: $5,800
Variations: stainless steel ($15,500)

Caliber 111

Reference number: 111 7700 4063
Movement: manually wound, Oris Caliber 111; ø 34 mm, 40 jewels; 21,600 vph; 240-hour power reserve
Functions: hours, minutes, subsidiary seconds; power reserve indicator; date
Case: stainless steel, ø 43 mm, height 12.3 mm; sapphire crystal; transparent case back; water-resistant to 3 atm
Band: reptile skin, buckle
Price: $5,800
Variations: rose gold ($15,500)

Audi Sport Limited Edition II

Reference number: 778 7661 7784
Movement: automatic, Oris Caliber 778 (base Sellita SW500); ø 30 mm, height 7.9 mm; 25 jewels; 28,800 vph; 48-hour power reserve
Functions: hours, minutes, subsidiary seconds (linear display); chronograph; date, weekday
Case: titanium with black DLC coating, ø 44 mm; ceramic bezel with rubber ring; sapphire crystal; screw-in crown; water-resistant to 10 atm
Band: calf leather, folding clasp
Remarks: limited to 2,000 pieces
Price: $4,100

Williams Chronograph

Reference number: 774 7717 4154
Movement: automatic, Oris Caliber 774 (base Sellita SW500); ø 30 mm, height 7.9 mm; 25 jewels; 28,800 vph; 48-hour power reserve
Functions: hours, minutes, subsidiary seconds; chronograph; date
Case: stainless steel, ø 44 mm, height 15 mm; sapphire crystal; transparent case back; water-resistant to 10 atm
Band: stainless steel, folding clasp
Price: $4,200
Variations: rubber strap

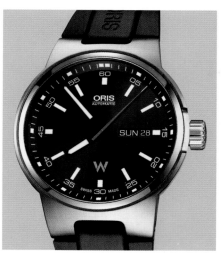

Williams Day Date

Reference number: 735 7716 4155
Movement: automatic, Oris Caliber 735 (base Sellita SW220-1); ø 25.6 mm, height 5.05 mm; 26 jewels; 28,800 vph; 38-hour power reserve
Functions: hours, minutes, sweep seconds; date, weekday
Case: stainless steel, ø 42 mm, height 11.6 mm; sapphire crystal; transparent case back; water-resistant to 10 atm
Band: rubber, folding clasp
Price: $1,350
Variations: stainless steel bracelet ($1,550)

Calobra Chronograph Limited Edition II

Reference number: 676 7661 4494
Movement: automatic, Oris Caliber 676 (base ETA 7753); ø 30 mm, height 7.9 mm; 27 jewels; 28,800 vph; 48-hour power reserve
Functions: hours, minutes, subsidiary seconds; chronograph; date
Case: stainless steel, ø 44 mm, height 14.9 mm; ceramic bezel; sapphire crystal; water-resistant to 10 atm
Band: calf leather, folding clasp
Remarks: limited to 250 pieces
Price: $4,500

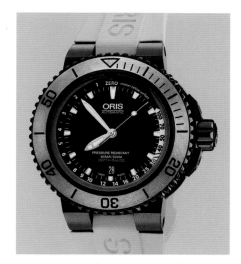

Aquis Depth Gauge Yellow

Reference number: 733 7675 4754
Movement: automatic, Oris Caliber 733 (base Sellita SW200-1); ø 25.6 mm, height 4.6 mm; 26 jewels; 28,800 vph; 38-hour power reserve
Functions: hours, minutes, sweep seconds; date
Case: stainless steel with black DLC coating, ø 46 mm, height 15 mm; unidirectional bezel with ceramic inlay and 60-minute division; sapphire crystal; screw-in crown, water-resistant to 50 atm
Band: rubber, safety folding clasp with extension link
Remarks: includes additional rubber bracelet
Price: $3,500

Carlos Coste L.E. IV

Reference number: 743 7709 7184
Movement: automatic, Oris Caliber 743 (base Sellita SW220-1); ø 25.6 mm, height 5.50 mm; 28 jewels; 28,800 vph; 38-hour power reserve
Functions: hours, minutes, subsidiary seconds; date
Case: titanium, ø 46 mm, height 15.9 mm; unidirectional bezel with ceramic inlay and 60-minute division; sapphire crystal; screw-in crown, helium valve; water-resistant to 50 atm
Band: titanium, folding clasp with extension link
Remarks: limited to 2,000 pieces
Price: $2,700
Variations: rubber strap ($2,900)

Divers Sixty-Five

Reference number: 733 7707 4064
Movement: automatic, Oris Caliber 733 (base Sellita SW200-1); ø 25.6 mm, height 4.6 mm; 26 jewels; 28,800 vph; 38-hour power reserve
Functions: hours, minutes, sweep seconds, date
Case: stainless steel, ø 40 mm, height 12.8 mm; unidirectional bezel with aluminum inlay, 60-minute divisions; sapphire crystal; screw-in crown; water-resistant to 10 atm
Band: rubber, buckle
Remarks: built after original 1960s model
Price: $1,850
Variations: textile band ($1,850)

Aquis Date

Reference number: 733 7653 4135
Movement: automatic, Oris Caliber 733 (base Sellita SW200-1); ø 25.6 mm, height 4.6 mm; 26 jewels; 28,800 vph; 38-hour power reserve
Functions: hours, minutes, sweep seconds; date
Case: stainless steel, ø 43 mm, height 12.6 mm; unidirectional bezel with ceramic inlay and 60-minute division; sapphire crystal; transparent case back; screw-in crown; water-resistant to 30 atm
Band: stainless steel, folding clasp
Price: $1,850
Variations: rubber strap ($1,650)

Force Recon GMT

Reference number: 747 7715 7754
Movement: automatic, Oris Caliber 747 (base Sellita SW220-1); ø 25.6 mm, height 5.05 mm; 28 jewels; 28,800 vph; 38-hour power reserve
Functions: hours, minutes, subsidiary seconds; additional 24-hour display (2nd time zone)
Case: titanium with black PVD coating, ø 49 mm, height 16 mm; unidirectional ceramic bezel, 60-minute divisions; sapphire crystal; screw-in crown, helium valve; water-resistant to 100 atm
Band: rubber, safety folding clasp with extension link
Remarks: additional textile bracelet
Price: $4,200

Big Crown ProPilot Altimeter

Reference number: 733 7705 4164
Movement: automatic, Oris Caliber 733 (base Sellita SW200-1); ø 25.6 mm, height 4.6 mm; 26 jewels; 28,800 vph; 38-hour power reserve
Functions: hours, minutes, sweep seconds; altimeter; date
Case: stainless steel, ø 47 mm, height 17.7 mm; ceramic bezel, inner ring rotated via crown to adjust altimeter; sapphire crystal; screw-in crown; water-resistant to 10 atm
Band: textile, folding clasp
Remarks: barometric altimeter with pressure capsule and mechanical gearworks
Price: $3,800

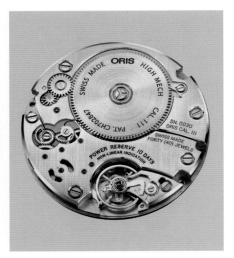

Big Crown ProPilot Date

Reference number: 751 7697 4164
Movement: automatic, Oris Caliber 751 (base Sellita SW220-1); ø 32.2 mm, height 4.6 mm; 26 jewels; 28,800 vph; 38-hour power reserve
Functions: hours, minutes, sweep seconds; date
Case: stainless steel, ø 41 mm, height 12.2 mm; sapphire crystal; transparent case back; screw-in crown; water-resistant to 10 atm
Band: textile, folding clasp
Price: $1,550
Variations: stainless steel bracelet ($1,750)

Thelonious Monk Limited Edition

Reference number: 732 7712 4085
Movement: automatic, Oris Caliber 733 (base Sellita SW200-1); ø 25.6 mm, height 4.6 mm; 26 jewels; 28,800 vph; 38-hour power reserve
Functions: hours, minutes
Case: stainless steel, ø 40 mm, height 10.9 mm; sapphire crystal; water-resistant to 3 atm
Band: calf leather, folding clasp
Remarks: back engraved with Monk quip "Monk Always Know"; 11 minute markers between 10 and 12 reference Monk's use of dissonance
Price: $1,900; limited to 1,000 pieces

Caliber 111

Manually wound; single spring barrel, 240 hours power reserve
Functions: hours, minutes, subsidiary seconds; power reserve indicator; date
Diameter: 34 mm
Height: 11.1 mm
Jewels: 40
Balance: glucydur with weighted screws
Frequency: 21,600 vph

Officine Panerai

Viale Monza, 259
I-20126 Milan
Italy

Tel.:
+39-02-363-138

Fax:
+39-02-363-13-297

Website:
www.panerai.com

Founded:
1860 in Florence, Italy

Number of employees:
approx. 250

U.S. distributor:
Panerai
645 Fifth Avenue
New York, NY 10022
877-PANERAI
concierge.usa@panerai.com; www.panerai.com

Most important collections/price range:
Luminor / $5,000 to $25,000; Luminor 1950 / $8,000 to $30,000; Radiomir / $7,000 to $25,000; Radiomir 1940 / $8,000 to $133,000; special editions / $10,000 to $125,000; clocks and instruments / $20,000 to $250,000

Panerai

Officine Panerai (in English: Panerai Workshops) joined the Richemont Group in 1997. Since then, it has made an unprecedented rise from an insider niche brand to a lifestyle phenomenon. The company, founded in 1860 by Giovanni Panerai, supplied the Italian navy with precision instruments. In the 1930s, the Florentine engineers developed a series of waterproof wristwatches that could be used by commandos under especially extreme and risky conditions. After 1997, under the leadership of Angelo Bonati, the company came out with a collection of oversize wristwatches, both stylistically and technically based on these historical models.

In 2002, Panerai opened a *manufacture* in Neuchâtel, and by 2005 it was already producing its own movements (caliber family P.2000). In 2009, the new "little" Panerai *manufacture* movements (caliber family P.9000) were released. From the start, the idea behind them was to provide a competitive alternative to the base movements available until a couple of years ago.

In 2014, a new *manufacture* was inaugurated in Neuchâtel to handle development, manufacturing, assembly, and quality control under one roof.

Panerai has recently been expanding its portfolio with a series of new calibers. The first was a chronograph with a flyback function, the P.9100. This was followed by a new caliber, the P.5000, in 2013, with an eight-day power reserve and manual winding, two features that have been with the brand ever since it received its first commissions from the Italian navy. In 2014, came caliber P.4000, with an off-center winding rotor. At 3.95 millimeters, it is very thin for Panerai, but then again, it was developed for a new set of models.

Mare Nostrum Titanio

Reference number: PAM00603
Movement: manually wound, Panerai Caliber OP XXV (based on Minerva 13-22); ø 28.76 mm, height 6.4 mm; 22 jewels; 18,000 vph; swan-neck fine adjustment, column wheel control; 55-hour power reserve
Functions: hours, minutes, subsidiary seconds; chronograph
Case: titanium, ø 52 mm, height 13.1 mm; sapphire crystal; screw-in crown; water-resistant to 3 atm
Band: calf leather, buckle
Remarks: limited to 150 pieces
Price: $43,300

Luminor Submersible 1950 Carbotech 3 Days Automatic

Reference number: PAM00616
Movement: automatic, Panerai Caliber P.9000; ø 31.02 mm, height 7.9 mm; 28 jewels; 28,800 vph; 2 spring barrels; 72-hour power reserve
Functions: hours, minutes, subsidiary seconds; date
Case: Carbotech (carbon fiber and polyether ether ketone, PEEK, composite), ø 47 mm, height 16.8 mm; unidirectional bezel with 60-minute divisions; sapphire crystal; crown protector with hinged lever; water-resistant to 30 atm
Band: rubber, buckle
Price: $18,400

Luminor Submersible 1950 3 Days Chrono Flyback Automatic Titanio

Reference number: PAM00615
Movement: automatic, Panerai Caliber P.9100; ø 31.02 mm, height 8.15 mm; 37 jewels; 28,800 vph; 2 spring barrels; zero reset of second hand via crown; 72-hour power reserve
Functions: hours, minutes, subsidiary seconds; flyback chronograph
Case: titanium, ø 47 mm, height 19 mm; ceramic bezel, unidirectional bezel with 60-minute divisions; sapphire crystal; crown protector with hinged lever; water-resistant to 30 atm
Band: rubber, buckle
Price: $18,400
Variations: titanium ($16,000)

Radiomir Firenze
3 Days Acciaio

Reference number: PAM00604
Movement: manually wound, Panerai Caliber
P.3000; ø 37.2 mm, height 5.3 mm; 21 jewels;
21,600 vph; 2 spring barrels; 72-hour power reserve
Functions: hours, minutes
Case: stainless steel with engravings, ø 47 mm,
height 15.9 mm; sapphire crystal; transparent case
back; screw-in crown; water-resistant to 10 atm
Band: reptile skin, buckle
Remarks: limited to 99 pieces; only available at
Officine Panerai Firenze San Giovanni
Price: on request

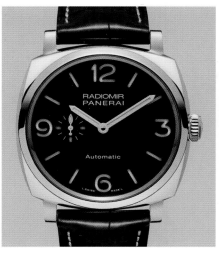

Radiomir 1940 3 Days
Automatic Acciaio

Reference number: PAM00572
Movement: automatic, Panerai Caliber P.4000;
ø 31.02 mm, height 3.95 mm; 31 jewels;
28,800 vph; 2 spring barrels; 72-hour power reserve
Functions: hours, minutes, subsidiary seconds
Case: stainless steel, ø 45 mm, height 12.2 mm;
sapphire crystal; transparent case back; screw-in
crown; water-resistant to 10 atm
Band: reptile skin, buckle
Price: $10,900
Variations: pink gold ($24,400)

Radiomir 1940 3 Days Acciaio

Reference number: PAM00514
Movement: manually wound, Panerai Caliber
P.3000; ø 37.2 mm, height 5.4 mm; 21 jewels;
21,600 vph; 2 spring barrels; 72-hour power reserve
Functions: hours, minutes, subsidiary seconds; date
Case: stainless steel, ø 47 mm, height 13.6 mm;
sapphire crystal; transparent case back; screw-in
crown; water-resistant to 10 atm
Band: leather, buckle
Price: $8,400
Variations: pink gold ($23,200)

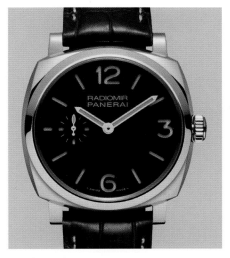

Radiomir 1940 Oro Rosso

Reference number: PAM00513
Movement: manually wound, Panerai Caliber P.999;
ø 27.07 mm, height 3.4 mm; 19 jewels; 21,600 vph;
swan-neck fine adjustment; 60-hour power reserve
Functions: hours, minutes, subsidiary seconds
Case: polished pink gold, ø 42 mm, height 11.1 mm;
sapphire crystal; transparent case back; screw-in
crown; water-resistant to 10 atm
Band: reptile skin, buckle
Price: $18,900
Variations: stainless steel ($7,800)

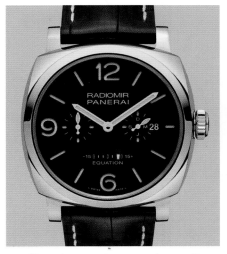

Radiomir 1940 Equation of
Time 8 Days Acciaio

Reference number: PAM00516
Movement: manually wound, Panerai Caliber
P.2002/E; ø 31.02 mm, height 8.3 mm; 31 jewels;
28,800 vph; 3 spring barrels; zero reset of second
hand via crown; 192-hour power reserve
Functions: hours, minutes, subsidiary seconds;
equation of time; power reserve indicator (on case
back); date, month
Case: stainless steel, ø 48 mm, height 16.8 mm;
sapphire crystal; transparent case back; screw-in
crown; water-resistant to 10 atm
Band: reptile skin, buckle
Price: $21,500; limited to 200 pieces

Luminor 1950 Equation of
Time 8 Days Acciaio

Reference number: PAM00601
Movement: manually wound, Panerai Caliber
P.2002/E; ø 31.02 mm, height 8.3 mm; 31 jewels;
28,800 vph; 3 spring barrels; zero reset of second
hand via crown; 192-hour power reserve
Functions: hours, minutes, subsidiary seconds;
equation of time; power reserve indicator (on case
back); date, month
Case: stainless steel, ø 47 mm, height 16.8 mm;
sapphire crystal; transparent case back; crown
protector with hinged lever; water-resistant to 10 atm
Band: reptile skin, buckle
Price: $22,000

Luminor 1950 3 Days Chrono Flyback Automatic Ceramica

Reference number: PAM00580
Movement: automatic, Panerai Caliber P.9100; ø 31.02 mm, height 8.15 mm; 37 jewels; 28,800 vph; 2 spring barrels; zero reset of second hand via crown; 72-hour power reserve
Functions: hours, minutes, subsidiary seconds; flyback chronograph; date
Case: matt black ceramic, ø 44 mm, height 18.4 mm; sapphire crystal; transparent case back; crown protector with hinged lever; water-resistant to 10 atm
Band: calf leather, buckle
Price: $15,800
Variations: stainless steel ($11,900); pink gold ($28,900)

Luminor 1950 3 Days Chrono Flyback Automatic Oro Rosso

Reference number: PAM00525
Movement: automatic, Panerai Caliber P.9100; ø 31.02 mm, height 8.15 mm; 37 jewels; 28,800 vph; 2 spring barrels; zero reset of second hand via crown; 72-hour power reserve
Functions: hours, minutes, subsidiary seconds; flyback chronograph; date
Case: pink gold, ø 44 mm, height 16.8 mm; sapphire crystal; transparent case back; crown protector with hinged lever; water-resistant to 5 atm
Band: reptile skin, buckle
Price: $28,900
Variations: ceramic ($15,800); stainless steel ($11,900)

Luminor 1950 10 Days GMT Automatic Acciaio

Reference number: PAM00533
Movement: automatic, Panerai Caliber P.2003; ø 31.02 mm, height 8 mm; 25 jewels; 28,800 vph; 2 spring barrels; zero reset of second hand via crown; 240-hour power reserve
Functions: hours, minutes, subsidiary seconds; additional 12-hour display (2nd time zone); day/night indicator; power reserve indicator; date
Case: stainless steel, ø 44 mm, height 17 mm; sapphire crystal; transparent case back; crown protector with hinged lever; water-resistant to 10 atm
Band: calf leather, buckle
Price: $14,600

Luminor 1950 3 Days GMT 24H Automatic Acciaio

Reference number: PAM00531
Movement: automatic, Panerai Caliber P.9003; ø 31.02 mm, height 7.9 mm; 28 jewels; 28,800 vph; 2 spring barrels; zero reset of second hand via crown; 72-hour power reserve
Functions: hours, minutes, subsidiary seconds; additional 24-hour display (2nd time zone); power reserve display (on case back); date
Case: stainless steel, ø 44 mm, height 17.9 mm; sapphire crystal; transparent case back; crown protector with hinged lever; water-resistant to 30 atm
Band: calf leather, buckle
Price: $9,800

Luminor Base 8 Days Acciaio

Reference number: PAM00560
Movement: manually wound, Panerai Caliber P.5000; ø 35.53 mm; height 4.5 mm; 21 jewels; 21,600 vph; 2 spring barrels, 192-hour power reserve
Functions: hours, minutes
Case: stainless steel, ø 44 mm, height 13.7 mm; sapphire crystal; transparent case back; hinged-lever crown protector; water-resistant to 30 atm
Band: calf leather, buckle
Remarks: additional bracelet
Price: $7,100
Variations: white dial ($7,500); titanium ($7,700)

Luminor Marina 8 Days Titanio

Reference number: PAM00564
Movement: manually wound, Panerai Caliber P.5000; ø 35.53 mm, height 4.5 mm; 21 jewels; 21,600 vph; 2 spring barrels; 192-hour power reserve
Functions: hours, minutes, subsidiary seconds
Case: titanium, ø 44 mm, height 13.7 mm; sapphire crystal; transparent case back; hinged-lever crown protector; water-resistant to 30 atm
Band: reptile skin, buckle
Remarks: additional bracelet
Price: $8,100
Variations: stainless steel; stainless steel/white dial ($7,600)

Caliber P.9100

Automatic; twin spring barrels, serially connected, 72-hour power reserve
Functions: hours, minutes, subsidiary seconds; flyback chronograph; date
Diameter: 31.1 mm
Height: 8.15 mm
Jewels: 37
Balance: glucydur
Frequency: 28,800 vph
Balance spring: flat hairspring
Shock protection: Kif
Remarks: reset second hand to zero by pulling crown ("zero reset"); 302 components

Caliber P.5000

Manually wound; 2 serially connected spring barrels; 192-hour power reserve
Functions: hours, minutes, subsidiary seconds
Diameter: 37.2 mm
Height: 4.5 mm
Jewels: 21
Balance: glucydur with weighted screws
Frequency: 21,600 vph
Balance spring: flat hairspring
Remarks: 127 components

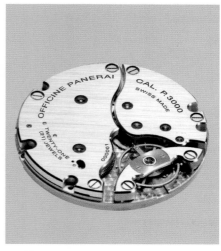

Caliber P.3000

Manually wound; 2 serially connected spring barrels, 72-hour power reserve
Functions: hours, minutes
Diameter: 37.2 mm
Height: 5.3 mm
Jewels: 21
Balance: glucydur
Frequency: 21,600 vph
Remarks: 160 components

Caliber P.9000

Automatic; 2 serially connected spring barrels, 72-hour power reserve
Functions: hours, minutes, subsidiary seconds; date
Diameter: 31 mm
Height: 7.9 mm
Jewels: 28
Balance: glucydur
Frequency: 28,800 vph
Remarks: 197 components

Caliber P.2002

Manually wound; 3 serially connected spring barrels; 192-hour power reserve
Functions: hours, minutes, subsidiary seconds; additional 24-hour display (2nd time zone); power reserve indicator (on movement side); date
Diameter: 31 mm
Height: 6.6 mm
Jewels: 21
Balance: glucydur
Frequency: 28,800 vph
Remarks: reset second hand to zero by pulling crown ("zero reset"); 247 components

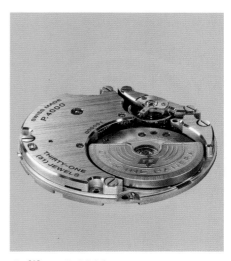

Caliber P.4000

Automatic; 2 serially connected spring barrels, 72-hour power reserve
Functions: hours, minutes, subsidiary seconds
Diameter: 30 mm
Height: 3.95 mm
Jewels: 31
Balance: glucydur
Frequency: 28,800 vph
Balance spring: flat hairspring
Shock protection: Kif
Remarks: 203 components

Parmigiani Fleurier SA
Rue du Temple 11
CH-2114 Fleurier
Switzerland

Tel.:
+41-32-862-6630

Fax:
+41-32-862-6631

E-Mail:
info@parmigiani.ch

Website:
www.parmigiani.ch

Founded:
1996

Number of employees:
600

Annual production:
approx. 6,000 watches

U.S. distributor:
Parmigiani Fleurier
Distribution Americas LLC
285 NW 26th Street
Miami, FL 33127
305-260-7770; 305-269-7770
americas@parmigiani.com

Most important collections/price range:
Kalpa, Tonda, Pershing, Toric, Bugatti /
approx. $7,800 to $700,000 for *haute
horlogerie* pieces, no limit for unique pieces

Parmigiani

What began as the undertaking of a single man—a gifted watchmaker and reputable restorer of complicated vintage timepieces—in the small town of Fleurier in Switzerland's Val de Travers has now grown into an empire of sorts comprising several factories and more than 400 employees.

Michel Parmigiani is in fact just doing what he has done since 1976 when he began restoring vintage works. An exceptional talent, his output soon attracted the attention of the Sandoz Family Foundation, an organization established by a member of one of Switzerland's most famous families in 1964. The foundation bought 51 percent of Parmigiani Mesure et Art du Temps SA in 1996, turning what was practically a one-man show into a full-fledged and fully financed watch *manufacture*.

After the merger, Swiss suppliers were acquired by the partners, furthering the quest for horological autonomy. Atokalpa SA in Alle (Canton of Jura) manufactures parts such as pinions, wheels, and micro components. Bruno Affolter SA in La Chaux-de-Fonds produces precious metal cases, dials, and other specialty parts. Les Artisans Boitiers (LAB) and Quadrance et Habillage (Q&H) in La Chaux-de-Fonds manufacture cases out of precious metals and dials as well. Elwin SA in Moutier specializes in turned parts. In 2003, the movement development and production department officially separated from the rest as Vaucher Manufacture, now an autonomous entity.

Parmigiani has enjoyed great independence and, hence, strong growth, notably in the United States. The brand also set its sights on Latin America, notably Brazil, where it signed a partnership with the Confederação Brasileira de Futebol. In addition to making watches and unique pieces, like the famed Islamic clock based on a lunar calendar, Parmigiani also devotes a part of its premises to restoring ancient timepieces.

Tonda 1950 Skeleton
Reference number: PFC280-1200100-HA1441
Movement: automatic, Parmigiani Caliber PF705; ø 30 mm, height 2.6 mm; 29 jewels; 21,600 vph; microrotor, entirely skeletonized by hand; 42-hour power reserve
Functions: hours, minutes
Case: white gold, ø 39 mm, height 7.8 mm; sapphire crystal; transparent case back; water-resistant to 3 atm
Band: reptile skin, pin buckle
Remarks: sapphire crystal dial
Price: $39,500

Tonda 1950 Skeleton
Reference number: PFC280-1060100-HA3921
Movement: automatic, Parmigiani Caliber PF705; ø 30 mm, height 2.6 mm; 29 jewels; 21,600 vph; microrotor, entirely skeletonized by hand; 42-hour power reserve
Functions: hours, minutes
Case: rose gold, ø 39 mm, height 8.4 mm; 84 diamonds on bezel; sapphire crystal; transparent case back; water-resistant to 3 atm
Band: reptile skin, pin buckle
Remarks: matted sapphire crystal dial
Price: $42,500

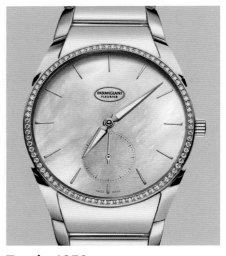

Tonda 1950
Reference number: PFC267-1063300-B10002
Movement: automatic, Parmigiani Caliber PF701; ø 30 mm, height 2.6 mm; 29 jewels; 21,600 vph; 42-hour power reserve
Functions: hours, minutes, subsidiary seconds
Case: rose gold, ø 39 mm, height 8.4 mm; 90 diamonds on bezel; sapphire crystal; transparent case back; water-resistant to 3 atm
Band: rose gold, folding clasp
Price: $45,500

Tonda 1950

Reference number: PFC267-1002400-HA1241
Movement: automatic, Parmigiani Caliber PF701; ø 30 mm, height 2.6 mm; 29 jewels; 21,600 vph; 42-hour power reserve
Functions: hours, minutes, subsidiary seconds
Case: rose gold, ø 39 mm, height 7.8 mm; sapphire crystal; transparent case back; water-resistant to 3 atm
Band: reptile skin, pin buckle
Price: $17,500
Variations: white gold ($17,500)

Tonda 1950 Meteorite

Reference number: PFC267-3000600-HA3141
Movement: automatic, Parmigiani Caliber PF701; ø 30 mm, height 2.6 mm; 29 jewels; 21,600 vph; 42-hour power reserve
Functions: hours, minutes, subsidiary seconds
Case: titanium, ø 39 mm, height 7.8 mm; sapphire crystal; transparent case back; water-resistant to 3 atm
Band: reptile skin, pin buckle
Remarks: meteorite dial
Price: $19,500

Tonda Centum

Reference number: PFH227-1201300-HA1241
Movement: automatic, Parmigiani Caliber PF333; ø 27 mm, height 5.5 mm; 32 jewels; 28,800 vph; double spring barrel; 50-hour power reserve
Functions: hours, minutes, sweep seconds; perpetual calendar with retrograde date, weekday, month, double moon phase, leap year
Case: white gold, ø 42 mm, height 11.15 mm; sapphire crystal; transparent case back; water-resistant to 3 atm
Band: reptile skin, folding clasp
Price: $66,500
Variations: rose gold ($66,500)

Tonda Hemispheres

Reference number: PFC231-0060700-HC2822
Movement: automatic, Parmigiani Caliber PF337; ø 35.6 mm, height 5.1 mm; 38 jewels; 28,800 vph; double spring barrel; côtes de Genève; 50-hour power reserve
Functions: hours, minutes, subsidiary seconds; added 12-hour display (2nd time zone), double day/night indicator; date
Case: stainless steel, ø 42 mm, height 11.15 mm; 90 diamonds on bezel; sapphire crystal; transparent case back; water-resistant to 3 atm
Band: calf leather, pin buckle
Price: $28,000

Tonda Metrographe

Reference number: PFC274-0005600-B33002
Movement: automatic, Parmigiani Caliber PF315; ø 28 mm, height 6 mm; 46 jewels; 28,800 vph; double spring barrel; côtes de Genève; 42-hour power reserve
Functions: hours, minutes, subsidiary seconds; chronograph; date
Case: stainless steel, ø 40 mm, height 12.2 mm; sapphire crystal; transparent case back; water-resistant to 3 atm
Band: stainless steel with titanium elements, folding clasp
Price: $12,500
Variations: various dials

Tonda Metrographe

Reference number: PFC274-0002400-HE6042
Movement: automatic, Parmigiani Caliber PF315; ø 28 mm, height 6 mm; 46 jewels; 28,800 vph; double spring barrel; côtes de Genève; 42-hour power reserve
Functions: hours, minutes, subsidiary seconds; chronograph; date
Case: stainless steel, ø 40 mm, height 12.2 mm; sapphire crystal; transparent case back; water-resistant to 3 atm
Band: calf leather, folding clasp
Price: $11,900
Variations: various dials

Tonda Resonance 8

Reference number: PFH233-1002400-HA1441
Movement: manually wound, Parmigiani Caliber PF350; ø 24.85 mm, height 5 mm; 21,600 vph; 45-hour power reserve
Functions: hours, minutes, subsidiary seconds; minute repeater
Case: rose gold, ø 40 mm, height 11.28 mm; sapphire crystal; transparent case back; water-resistant to 3 atm
Band: reptile skin, pin buckle
Price: on request

Tonda Métropolitaine

Reference number: PFC273-0065600-B00002
Movement: automatic, Parmigiani Caliber PF310; ø 23.9 mm, height 3.9 mm; 28 jewels; 28,800 vph; double spring barrel; côtes de Genève; 50-hour power reserve
Functions: hours, minutes, subsidiary seconds; date
Case: stainless steel, ø 33.1 mm, height 8.65 mm; 72 diamonds on bezel; sapphire crystal; transparent case back; water-resistant to 3 atm
Band: stainless steel, folding clasp
Price: $11,300
Variations: w/o diamonds ($8,900); various dials

Tonda Métropolitaine

Reference number: PFC273-0001400-HE1421
Movement: automatic, Parmigiani Caliber PF310; ø 23.9 mm, height 3.9 mm; 28 jewels; 28,800 vph; double spring barrel; côtes de Genève; 50-hour power reserve
Functions: hours, minutes, subsidiary seconds; date
Case: stainless steel, ø 33.1 mm, height 8.65 mm; sapphire crystal; transparent case back; water-resistant to 3 atm
Band: calf leather, folding clasp
Price: $8,500
Variations: stainless steel band ($8,900); diamonds ($10,900); various dials

Tonda 39 Qualité Fleurier

Reference number: PFC222-1602400-HA1431
Movement: automatic, Parmigiani Caliber PF331QF; ø 25.6 mm, height 3.5 mm; 28,800 vph; 55-hour power reserve; COSC-certified chronometer, Qualité Fleurier
Functions: hours, minutes, sweep seconds; date
Case: pink gold, ø 39 mm, height 8.85 mm; sapphire crystal; transparent case back; water-resistant to 3 atm
Band: reptile skin, pin buckle
Remarks: limited to 50 pieces
Price: $19,500

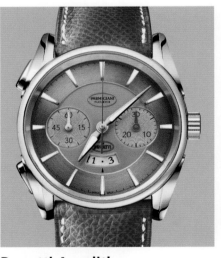

Bugatti Aerolithe

Reference number: PFC329-3405600-HC6032
Movement: automatic, Parmigiani Caliber PF335; ø 30.3 mm, height 6.81 mm; 68 jewels; 28,800 vph; double spring barrel; bridges with côtes de Genève; 50-hour power reserve
Functions: hours, minutes, subsidiary seconds; flyback chronograph; date
Case: titanium, ø 41 mm, height 12.55 mm; white gold bezel; sapphire crystal; transparent case back; water-resistant to 3 atm
Band: calf leather, folding clasp
Price: $26,000
Variations: blue dial ($26,000)

Ovale Pantographe

Reference number: PFH775-1005400-HA3131
Movement: manually wound, Parmigiani Caliber PF111; 23.6 x 29.3 mm, height 4.9 mm; 28 jewels; 21,600 vph; double spring barrel; 216-hour power reserve
Functions: telescopic length-adjustable hands; power reserve indicator; date
Case: rose gold, 37.6 x 45 mm, height 12 mm; sapphire crystal; transparent case back; water-resistant to 3 atm
Band: reptile skin, pin buckle
Price: $55,000

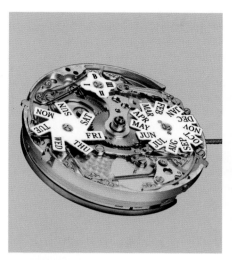

Caliber PF333

Base caliber: 331
Automatic; module for perpetual calendar with retrograde date and precision moon phase; double spring barrel; 50-hour power reserve
Functions: hours, minutes, sweep seconds; perpetual calendar with month, moon phase, leap year
Diameter: 27.1 mm
Height: 5.5 mm
Jewels: 32
Frequency: 28,800 vph
Balance spring: flat hairspring

Caliber PF511

Manually wound; 30-second tourbillon; skeletonized mainplate and bridges; double spring barrel; 7-day power reserve
Functions: hours, minutes, sweep seconds; power reserve indicator
Diameter: 33.9 mm
Height: 5.55 mm
Jewels: 30
Frequency: 21,600 vph
Balance spring: flat hairspring

Caliber PF705

Automatic; microrotor; single spring barrel; 42-hour power reserve
Functions: hours, minutes
Diameter: 30 mm
Height: 2.6 mm
Jewels: 29
Frequency: 21,600 vph
Remarks: skeletonized movement, 144 components

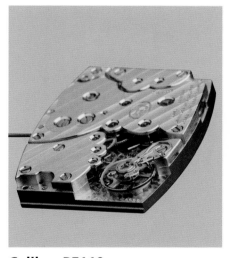

Caliber PF110

Manually wound; double spring barrel; 8-day power reserve
Functions: hours, minutes, subsidiary seconds; date; power reserve indicator
Measurements: 29.3 x 23.6 mm
Height: 4.9 mm
Jewels: 28

Caliber PF334

Base caliber: 331
Automatic; module for chronograph; double spring barrel; 50-hour power reserve
Functions: hours, minutes, subsidiary seconds; chronograph; date
Diameter: 30.3 mm
Height: 6.8 mm
Jewels: 68
Frequency: 28,800 vph

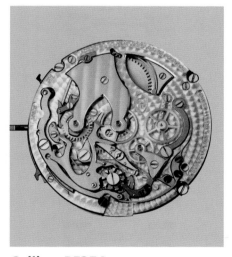

Caliber PF354

Manually wound; module for chronograph; double spring barrel; 72-hour power reserve
Functions: hours, minutes, subsidiary seconds; chronograph; power reserve indicator
Diameter: 29.9 mm
Height: 7.6 mm
Jewels: 29
Frequency: 21,600 vph

Patek Philippe SA
Chemin du pont-du-centenaire 141
CH-1228 Plan-les-Ouates
Switzerland

Tel.:
+41-22-884-20-20

Fax:
+41-22-884-20-40

Website:
www.patek.com

Founded:
1839

Number of employees:
approx. 2,000 (estimated)

Annual production:
approx. 45,000 watches worldwide per year

U.S. distributor:
Patek Philippe USA
45 Rockefeller Center, Suite 401
New York, NY 10111
212-218-1272; 212-218-1283 (fax)

Most important collections/price range:
Calatrava, Nautilus, Gondolo, Ellipse,
Aquanaut / ladies' timepieces begin at
$13,000 (Twenty~4) and men's at $20,800
(basic Calatrava)

Patek Philippe

Not many companies can boast a 175th anniversary. In the Swiss watchmaking landscape, Patek Philippe has a special status as the last independent family-owned business. The company was founded by Count Norbert Antoine de Patek in 1839, and in 1845, master watchmaker Jean Adrien Philippe came on board. Literally since then, Patek Philippe has been known for creating high-quality mechanical watches, some with extremely sophisticated complications. Even among its competition, the *manufacture* enjoys the greatest respect.

In 1932, Charles-Henri Stern took over the *manufacture*. His son Henri and grandson Philippe continued the tradition of solid leadership, steering the company through the notorious quartz crisis without ever compromising quality. The next in line, also Henri, heads the enterprise these days.

In 1997, Patek Philippe moved into new quarters, based on the most modern standards. The facility boasts the world's largest assembly of watchmakers under one roof, and yet production figures are comparatively modest. A small section of the building is reserved for restoring old watches using either parts from a large and valuable collection of components or rebuilding them from scratch.

The company recently opened a highly industrialized second branch between La Chaux-de-Fonds and Le Locle, where case components are manufactured, cases are polished, and gem setting is done. Patek Philippe's main headquarters remain in Geneva, but the *manufacture* no longer has a need for that city's famed seal: All of the company's mechanical watches now feature the "Patek Philippe Seal," the criteria for which far exceed the requirements of the *Poinçon de Genève* and include specifications for the entire watch, not just the movement.

Nautilus

Reference number: 5711/1R-001
Movement: automatic, Patek Philippe Caliber 324 S C; ø 27 mm, height 3.3 mm; 29 jewels; 28,800 vph; 35-hour power reserve
Functions: hours, minutes, sweep seconds; date
Case: rose gold, ø 40 mm, height 8.3 mm; sapphire crystal; transparent case back; screw-in crown; water-resistant to 12 atm
Band: rose gold, folding clasp
Price: $51,000
Variations: stainless steel ($24,800)

Nautilus Travel Time Chronograph

Reference number: 5990/1A
Movement: automatic, Patek Philippe Caliber 28-520 S C FUS; ø 31 mm, height 6.95 mm; 34 jewels; 28,800 vph; 45-hour power reserve
Functions: hours, minutes, subsidiary seconds; additional 12-hour display (2nd time zone), day/night indicator; flyback chronograph; date
Case: stainless steel, ø 40.5 mm, height 12.53 mm; sapphire crystal; transparent case back; screw-in crown , water-resistant to 12 atm
Band: stainless steel, folding clasp
Price: $53,300

Ladies' Nautilus

Reference number: 7118/1A-001
Movement: automatic, Patek Philippe Caliber 324 S C; ø 27 mm, height 3.3 mm; 29 jewels; 28,800 vph; 35-hour power reserve
Functions: hours, minutes, sweep seconds; date
Case: stainless steel, ø 35.2 mm, height 8.62 mm; sapphire crystal; transparent case back; screw-in crown; water-resistant to 6 atm
Band: stainless steel, folding clasp
Price: $24,800

Gondolo

Reference number: 5124G-011
Movement: manually wound, Patek Philippe Caliber 25-21 REC PS; 21.5 x 24.6 mm; height 2.57 mm; 18 jewels; 28,800 vph; 44-hour power reserve
Functions: hours, minutes, subsidiary seconds
Case: white gold, 33.4 x 43 mm, height 7.38 mm; sapphire crystal; transparent case back; water-resistant to 3 atm
Band: reptile skin, buckle
Price: $27,200

Calatrava

Reference number: 5153R-001
Movement: automatic, Patek Philippe Caliber 324 S C; ø 27 mm, height 3.3 mm; 29 jewels; 28,800 vph; Spiromax silicon spring; 35-hour power reserve
Functions: hours, minutes, sweep seconds; date
Case: rose gold, ø 38 mm, height 9.7 mm; sapphire crystal; transparent case back; water-resistant to 3 atm
Band: reptile skin, buckle
Remarks: hinged case back cover
Price: $34,400
Variations: white gold ($34,400); yellow gold ($32,200)

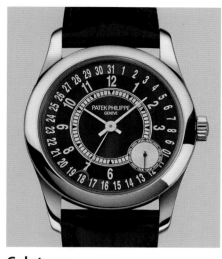

Calatrava

Reference number: 6000G-012
Movement: automatic, Patek Philippe Caliber 240 PS C; ø 30 mm, height 3.43 mm; 27 jewels; 21,600 vph; gold microrotor; 38-hour power reserve
Functions: hours, minutes, subsidiary seconds; date
Case: white gold, ø 37 mm, height 8.75 mm; sapphire crystal; transparent case back; water-resistant to 3 atm
Band: reptile skin, folding clasp
Price: $27,900

Calatrava

Reference number: 5227G-010
Movement: automatic, Patek Philippe Caliber 324 S C; ø 27 mm, height 3.3 mm; 29 jewels; 28,800 vph; Spiromax silicon spring
Functions: hours, minutes, sweep seconds; date
Case: white gold, ø 39 mm, height 9.24 mm; sapphire crystal; transparent case back; water-resistant to 3 atm
Band: reptile skin, buckle
Remarks: hinged case back cover
Price: $34,700
Variations: white dial; yellow gold ($32,900); rose gold ($34,700)

Calatrava Pilot Travel Time

Reference number: 5524G-001
Movement: automatic, Patek Philippe Caliber S C FUS; ø 31 mm, height 4.82 mm; 29 jewels; 28,800 vph; Spiromax silicon spring; 35-hour power reserve
Functions: hours, minutes, sweep seconds; additional 12-hour display (2nd time zone); day/night indicator; date
Case: white gold, ø 42 mm, height 10.78 mm; sapphire crystal; transparent case back; water-resistant to 3 atm
Band: calf leather, buckle
Price: $47,600

Aquanaut Ladies

Reference number: 5067A-023
Movement: quartz
Functions: hours, minutes, sweep seconds; date
Case: stainless steel, ø 35.6 mm, height 7.7 mm; 46 diamonds on bezel; sapphire crystal; water-resistant to 12 atm
Band: rubber, folding clasp
Price: $16,200

Annual Calendar

Reference number: 4947G-001
Movement: automatic, Patek Philippe Caliber 324 S QA LU; ø 30 mm, height 5.32 mm; 34 jewels; 28,800 vph; Spiromax silicon spring; 35-hour power reserve
Functions: hours, minutes, sweep seconds; annual calendar with date, weekday, month, moon phase
Case: white gold, ø 38 mm, height 11 mm; diamonds on bezel; sapphire crystal; transparent case back; water-resistant to 3 atm
Band: reptile skin, buckle
Price: $49,800

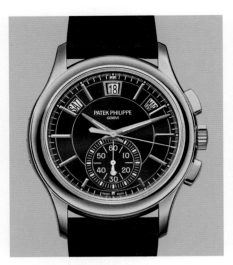

Annual Calendar Chronograph

Reference number: 5905P-001
Movement: automatic, Patek Philippe Caliber CH 28-520 QA 24H; ø 33 mm, height 7.68 mm; 37 jewels; 28,800 vph; Spiromax silicon spring; 45-hour power reserve
Functions: hours, minutes, sweep seconds; chronograph; annual calendar with date, weekday, month
Case: platinum, ø 42 mm, height 14.03 mm; sapphire crystal; transparent case back; water-resistant to 3 atm
Band: reptile skin, buckle
Price: $78,200

Annual Calendar Chronograph

Reference number: 5960/1A
Movement: automatic, Patek Philippe Caliber CH 28 520 IRM QA 24H; ø 33 mm, height 7.68 mm; 40 jewels: 28,800 vph; 45-hour power reserve
Functions: hours, minutes, sweep seconds; power reserve indicator; flyback chronograph; annual calendar with date, weekday, month
Case: stainless steel, ø 40.5 mm, height 13.5 mm; sapphire crystal; transparent case back; water-resistant to 3 atm
Band: stainless steel, folding clasp
Price: $51,000

Rattrapante Chronograph

Reference number: 5370P-001
Movement: manually wound, Patek Philippe Caliber 29-535 PS; ø 29.6 mm, height 7.1 mm; 34 jewels; 28,800 vph; 55-hour power reserve
Functions: hours, minutes, subsidiary seconds; rattrapante chronograph
Case: platinum, ø 41 mm, height 13.56 mm; sapphire crystal; transparent case back; water-resistant to 3 atm
Band: reptile skin, folding clasp
Price: $249,200

Chronograph Perpetual Calendar

Reference number: 5270R-001
Movement: manually wound, Patek Philippe Caliber CH 29 535 PS Q; ø 32 mm, height 7 mm; 33 jewels; 28,800 vph; 55-hour power reserve
Functions: hours, minutes, subsidiary seconds; day/night indicator; chronograph; perpetual calendar with date, weekday, month, moon phase, leap year
Case: rose gold, ø 41 mm, height 12.4 mm; sapphire crystal; transparent case back; water-resistant to 3 atm
Band: reptile skin, folding clasp
Price: $164,000
Variations: white gold ($164,000)

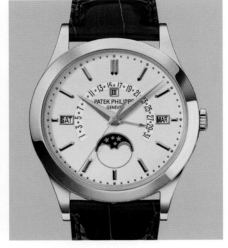

Perpetual Calendar

Reference number: 5496R
Movement: automatic, Patek Philippe Caliber 324 S QR; ø 28 mm, height 5.35 mm; 30 jewels; 28,800 vph; 35-hour power reserve
Functions: hours, minutes, sweep seconds; perpetual calendar with retrograde date, weekday, month, moon phase, leap year
Case: rose gold, ø 39.5 mm, height 11.19 mm; sapphire crystal; transparent case back; water-resistant to 3 atm
Band: reptile skin, folding clasp
Price: $107,600
Variations: platinum ($107,600)

Perpetual Calendar

Reference number: 5940G-010
Movement: automatic, Patek Philippe Caliber 240 Q; ø 27.5 mm, height 3.88 mm; 27 jewels; 21,600 vph; 38-hour power reserve
Functions: hours, minutes; additional 24-hour display; perpetual calendar with date, weekday, month, moon phase, leap year
Case: white gold, 37 x 44.6 mm, height 8.48 mm; sapphire crystal; transparent case back; water-resistant to 3 atm
Band: reptile skin, buckle
Remarks: additional case back
Price: $87,200

Perpetual Calendar

Reference number: 5140R
Movement: automatic, Patek Philippe Caliber 240 Q; ø 27.5 mm, height 3.88 mm; 27 jewels; 21,600 vph; 38-hour power reserve
Functions: hours, minutes; additional 24-hour display; perpetual calendar with date, weekday, month, moon phase, leap year
Case: rose gold, ø 37.2 mm, height 8.8 mm; sapphire crystal; transparent case back; water-resistant to 3 atm
Band: reptile skin, folding clasp
Price: $84,600

Rattrapante Chronograph

Reference number: 5950/1A
Movement: manually wound, Patek Philippe Caliber CH 27-525 PS; ø 27.3 mm, height 5.25 mm; 27 jewels; 21,600 vph; single pusher for chronograph functions; 48-hour power reserve
Functions: hours, minutes, subsidiary seconds; rattrapante chronograph
Case: stainless steel, 37 x 44.6 mm, height 10.13 mm; sapphire crystal; transparent case back; water-resistant to 3 atm
Band: stainless steel, folding clasp
Price: on request
Variations: opaline silver-gray or rose gold dial

Minute Repeater with Tourbillon and Perpetual Calendar

Reference number: 5207/700P-001
Movement: manually wound, Patek Philippe Caliber R TO 27 PS QI; ø 32 mm, height 9.33 mm; 35 jewels; 21,600 vph; 1-minute tourbillon; instant calendar display; 38-hour power reserve
Functions: hours, minutes, subsidiary seconds; day/night indicator; minute repeater; full calendar with date, weekday, month, moon phase
Case: platinum, ø 41 mm, height 13.81 mm; sapphire crystal
Band: reptile skin, buckle
Price: on request
Variations: rose gold (on request)

Perpetual Calendar with Minute Repeater

Reference number: 5073P-010
Movement: automatic, Patek Philippe Caliber R 27 PS QR LU; ø 28 mm, height 7.23 mm; 41 jewels; 21,600 vph; 38-hour power reserve
Functions: hours, minutes, subsidiary seconds; minute repeater; perpetual calendar with date, weekday, month, moon phase, leap year
Case: platinum, ø 42 mm, height 11.11 mm; 103 diamonds on bezel and lugs; sapphire crystal; transparent case back
Band: reptile skin, folding clasp with 42 diamonds
Remarks: full case back
Price: on request

Celestial

Reference number: 6102R-001
Movement: automatic, Patek Philippe Caliber 240 LU CL C; ø 38 mm, height 6.81 mm; 45 jewels; 21,600 vph; Spiromax silicon spring; 38-hour power reserve
Functions: hours, minutes; perpetual calendar with date, moon phase/orbit, moon/Sirius passages on map of stars
Case: rose gold, ø 44 mm, height 10.58 mm; sapphire crystal; transparent case back; water-resistant to 3 atm
Band: reptile skin, folding clasp
Price: $283,200
Variations: platinum ($306,500)

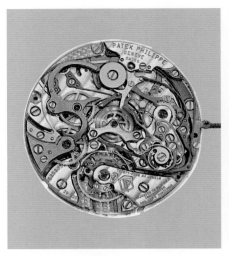

Caliber CH 29-535 PS

Manually wound; column wheel control of chronograph functions; precisely jumping 30-minute totalizer; single spring barrel, 65-hour power reserve
Functions: hours, minutes, subsidiary seconds; split-seconds chronograph
Diameter: 29.6 mm
Height: 7.1 mm
Jewels: 34
Balance: Gyromax, 4-armed, with 4 regulating weights
Frequency: 28,800 vph
Balance spring: Breguet
Shock protection: Incabloc
Remarks: 312 components

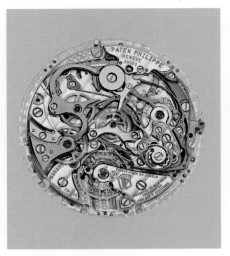

Caliber CHR 29-535 PS Q

Manually wound; 2 column wheels to control chronograph functions, split-second hand mechanism with isolator; single barrel spring; 65-hour power reserve
Functions: hours, minutes, subsidiary seconds; day/night indicator; split-second chronograph; perpetual calendar with date, weekday, month, moon phase, leap year
Diameter: 32 mm; **Height:** 8.7 mm; **Jewels:** 34
Balance: Gyromax, 4-armed, with 4 regulating weights; **Frequency:** 28,800 vph
Balance spring: Breguet
Remarks: 496 components, 182 alone for perpetual calendar and 42 for split-seconds mechanism with isolator

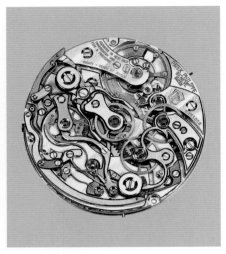

Caliber CHR 27-525 PS

Ultra-flat mechanical movement with manual winding; 48-hour power reserve; double column wheel control of chronograph functions with crown pusher (start-stop-reset) and separate split-seconds hand pusher
Functions: hours, minutes, subsidiary seconds; split-seconds chronograph
Diameter: 27.3 mm; **Height:** 5.25 mm; **Jewels:** 27
Balance: Gyromax, 2-armed, with 8 regulating weights
Frequency: 21,600 vph
Balance spring: Breguet
Shock protection: Kif
Remarks: 252 individual components; outstandingly high-quality finishing

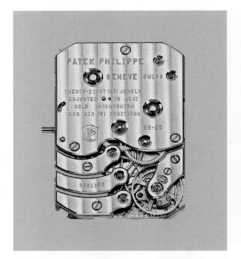

Caliber 28-20 REC 8J PS IRM C J

Manually wound; double spring barrel; 192-hour power reserve
Functions: hours, minutes, subsidiary seconds; power reserve indicator; weekday, date
Measurements: 20 x 28 mm
Height: 5.05 mm
Jewels: 28
Balance: Gyromax
Frequency: 28,800 vph
Balance spring: Spiromax silicon spring

Caliber 240 HU

Automatic; unidirectional winding off-center ball-bearing rotor in 22 kt gold; 48-hour power reserve
Functions: hours, minutes, world-time display (2nd time zone)
Diameter: 27.5 mm
Height: 3.88 mm
Jewels: 33
Balance: Gyromax
Frequency: 21,600 vph
Remarks: 239 individual parts

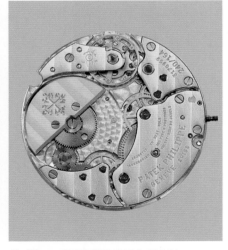

Caliber 240 PS IRM C LU

Automatic; unidirectional winding off-center ball-bearing rotor in 22 kt gold; 48-hour power reserve
Functions: hours, minutes, subsidiary seconds; power reserve display; date; moon phase
Diameter: 31 mm
Height: 3.98 mm
Jewels: 29
Balance: Gyromax
Frequency: 21,600 vph
Remarks: 265 individual parts

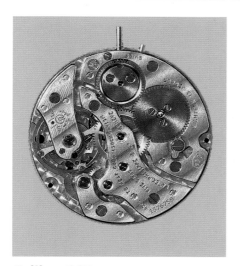

Caliber 215

Manually wound; single spring barrel; 44-hour power reserve
Functions: hours, minutes, subsidiary seconds
Diameter: 21.9 mm
Height: 2.55 mm
Jewels: 18
Balance: Gyromax with 8 masselotte regulating weights
Frequency: 28,800 vph
Balance spring: flat hairspring
Shock protection: Kif
Remarks: base plate with perlage, beveled bridges with côtes de Genève, 130 individual parts

Caliber 315 SC

Automatic; central rotor in 21 kt gold; single spring barrel; 48-hour power reserve
Functions: hours, minutes, sweep seconds; date
Diameter: 27 mm
Height: 3.22 mm
Jewels: 29
Balance: Gyromax
Frequency: 21,600 vph
Remarks: 213 individual parts

Caliber 315 S QA LU

Automatic; central rotor in 21 kt gold; single spring barrel; 48-hour power reserve
Functions: hours, minutes, sweep seconds; annual calendar with date, day, month, moon phase
Diameter: 30 mm
Height: 5.22 mm
Jewels: 34
Balance: Gyromax
Frequency: 21,600 vph
Remarks: 328 individual parts

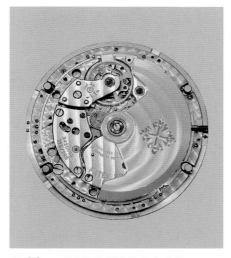

Caliber 315 S IRM QA LU

Manually wound; central rotor in 21 kt gold; single spring barrel; 48-hour power reserve
Functions: hours, minutes, sweep seconds, calendar with date, weekday, month, moon phase; power reserve display
Diameter: 30 mm
Height: 5.22 mm
Jewels: 36
Balance: Gyromax
Frequency: 21,600 vph
Remarks: 355 individual parts

Caliber 324 S IRM QA LU

Automatic; central rotor in 21 kt gold; single spring barrel; 45-hour power reserve
Functions: hours, minutes, sweep seconds; calendar with date, day, month, moon phase; power reserve display
Diameter: 32 mm
Height: 5.3 mm
Jewels: 36
Balance: Gyromax
Frequency: 28,800 vph
Balance spring: Spiromax (silicon)
Remarks: silicon escape wheel; 355 individual parts

Caliber 324 S QA LU 24H-303

Automatic; central rotor in 21 kt gold; single spring barrel; 45-hour power reserve
Functions: hours, minutes, sweep seconds; calendar with date, day, month (programmed for 1 year), moon phase; 24-hour display
Diameter: 32.6 mm
Height: 5.78 mm
Jewels: 34
Balance: Gyromax
Frequency: 28,800 vph
Balance spring: Spiromax (silicon)
Remarks: silicon escape wheel; 347 individual parts

Caliber 330 SC

Automatic; central rotor in 21 kt gold; single spring barrel; 48-hour power reserve
Functions: hours, minutes, sweep seconds; date
Diameter: 27 mm
Height: 3.5 mm
Jewels: 29
Balance: Gyromax
Frequency: 21,600 vph
Balance spring: Breguet
Remarks: 217 individual parts

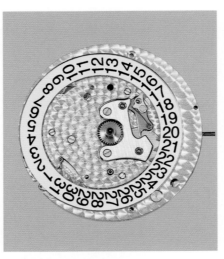

Caliber CH 28-520 C

Automatic; column-wheel control of chronograph functions; central rotor in 21 kt gold; single spring barrel; 55-hour power reserve
Functions: hours, minutes, sweep seconds; chronograph with combined hour and minute counter; date
Diameter: 30 mm
Height: 6.63 mm
Jewels: 35
Balance: Gyromax
Frequency: 28,800 vph
Balance spring: Breguet
Remarks: 327 individual parts

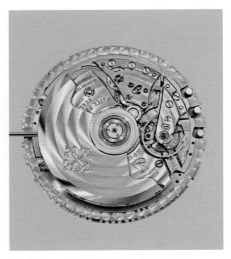

Caliber CH 28-520 IRM QA 24H

Manually wound; column-wheel control of chronograph functions; central rotor in 21 kt gold; single spring barrel; 55-hour power reserve
Functions: hours, minutes, sweep seconds; chronograph with combined hour and minute counter; calendar with date, day, month, moon phase; day/night indication; power reserve display
Diameter: 33 mm; **Height:** 7.68 mm
Jewels: 40
Balance: Gyromax
Frequency: 28,800 vph
Balance spring: Breguet
Remarks: 456 individual parts

Caliber CH 28-520 C FUS

Automatic; column wheel control of chronograph functions, 21 kt gold central rotor; single spring barrel; 45-hour power reserve
Functions: hours, minutes; additional 12-hour indicator (2nd time zone); double day/night indicator; flyback chronograph; date
Diameter: 31 mm
Height: 6.95 mm
Jewels: 34
Balance: Gyromax
Frequency: 28,800 vph
Balance spring: Spiromax
Remarks: 370 components

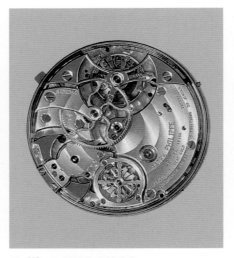

Caliber RTO 27 PS

Manually wound; 1-minute tourbillon; single spring barrel; 48-hour power reserve; COSC-certified chronometer
Functions: hours, minutes, subsidiary seconds; minute repeater
Diameter: 28 mm
Height: 6.58 mm
Jewels: 28
Balance: Gyromax
Frequency: 21,600 vph
Balance spring: Breguet
Remarks: 336 individual parts

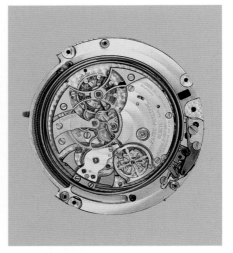

Caliber RTO 27 QR SID LU CL

Manually wound; 1-minute tourbillon; chime with 2 cathedral gongs, actuating mechanism integrated into movement; single spring barrel; 48-hour power reserve; COSC-certified chronometer
Functions: hours, minutes; minute repeater; perpetual calendar with date (retrograde), weekday, month, moon phase and leap year (dial side), sidereal time, sky map with moon phase and age (movement side)
Diameter: 38 mm; **Height:** 12.61 mm; **Jewels:** 55
Balance: Gyromax
Frequency: 21,600 vph
Remarks: 686 components

Paul Picot

The 1976 establishment of the Société des Montres Paul Picot required a large dose of pioneering spirit on the part of its initiators. The new brand was born of the will to save the rich history of the Swiss watch industry and let its true values once again come to light. The age-old tradition of watchmaking was threatening to collapse; qualified masters of the craft were disappearing from the workplace, and the once-fascinating atmosphere of watchmakers' workshops had given way to the industrial hustle and bustle of anonymous brand names. For company founder and president Mario Boiocchi, the only chance for the survival of European watch culture was to rediscover quality and precision. While Japanese and American competitors were forcing the Swiss watch industry to make compromises in order to meet the demands of mass consumption, Paul Picot chose to walk a different path.

The market—that vague, undefinable, yet despotic entity—was calling for futuristic design and electronic technology. However, Paul Picot went in the exact opposite direction and produced fine gold cases and mechanical watch movements. In the years to follow, the collections attracted the attention of watch buyers the world over with their good balance of elegance and sportiness. This company located in Le Noirmont in the heart of watchmaking country is writing its own history. For a relatively small concern, it has manages to produce a very wide range of models each with a unique look. The Firshire series comes in sober round cases or as the 1937 or 3000 Regulateur in a comfortable tonneau with a dial tightly packed with displays. It even has divers and chronographs to cap its portfolio. And while many brands have to drop their prices to attract a coveted target group, Paul Picot has already staked out this territory.

**Société des Montres
Paul Picot SA**
Rue du Doubs 6
CH-2340 Le Noirmont
Switzerland

Tel.:
+41-32-911-1818

Fax:
+41-32-911-1819

E-Mail:
info@paulpicot.ch

Website:
www.paulpicot.ch

Founded:
1976

U.S. distributor:
Time Innovations LLC
After Sales Services
444 Madison Avenue, Ste. 601
New York, NY 10022
718-725-7509
info@timeinnovationsllc.com

Most important collections:
Atelier, C-Type, Gentleman, Technicum, Firshire, unique pieces

Megarotor GMT Grand Feu

Reference number: P0482.RG.2000
Movement: automatic, ETA Caliber 2892 with Dubois-Dépraz module; ø 25.6 mm, height 6.2 mm; 21 jewels; 28,800 vph; crown-switchable hour hand; winding rotor with tungsten oscillating mass; 42-hour power reserve
Functions: hours, minutes, sweep seconds; world-time display (2nd time zone)
Case: rose gold, ø 42 mm, height 11.5 mm; sapphire crystal; transparent back; water-resistant to 5 atm
Band: reptile skin, folding clasp
Remarks: dial motif of champlevé enamel
Price: $28,119; limited to 88 pieces
Variations: stainless steel ($10,598; limited to 300)

Firshire Extraflat Date

Reference number: P3754.RG.5624
Movement: automatic, Caliber PP 1650 (base Lemania 8810); ø 25.6 mm, height 2.9 mm; 17 jewels; 28,800 vph; 2 spring barrels; winding rotor with côtes de Genève; 38-hour power reserve
Functions: hours, minutes; date
Case: rose gold, ø 40.5 mm, height 6.9 mm; sapphire crystal; transparent case back; water-resistant to 3 atm
Band: reptile skin, folding clasp
Price: $7,354
Variations: stainless steel ($4,434); various dial colors

Plongeur Full Black Orange

Reference number: P4118.SFB.3410
Movement: automatic, ETA Caliber 2824; ø 25.6 mm, height 4.6 mm; 25 jewels; 28,800 vph; 42-hour power reserve
Functions: hours, minutes, sweep seconds; date
Case: stainless steel, black DLC-coating, ø 42 mm, height 14 mm; bezel with colored HDT-coated antifriction ring, unidirectional bezel with 60-minute divisions; sapphire crystal; screw-in crown; water-resistant to 30 atm
Band: calf leather, folding clasp
Price: $3,136
Variations: blue bezel; as chronograph ($5,299)

Perrelet SA
Rue Bubenberg 7
CH-2502 Biel/Bienne
Switzerland

Tel.:
+41-32-346-2626

Fax:
+41-32-346-2627

E-Mail:
perrelet@perrelet.com

Website:
www.perrelet.com

Founded:
1995

Number of employees:
18

U.S. distributor:
H5 Group, Corp.
3230 West Commercial Blvd., Suite 160
Fort Lauderdale, FL 33309
954-575-7980; 954-575-7981 (fax)
info@perreletusa.com

Most important collections:
Turbine, Turbine XL, Turbine XS, Turbine
Chrono, Turbine Skeleton, Turbine Pilot,
Double Rotor, First Class, Diamond Flower

Perrelet

The Perrelet story will sound familiar to anyone who has read about Swiss watchmaking: Abraham-Louis Perrelet (1729–1826) was the son of a middle-class farmer from Le Locle who developed an interest in watchmaking early on in life. He was the first watchmaker in Le Locle to work on cylinder and duplex escapements, and there is a persistent rumor that he was responsible for a repeater that could be heard echoing in the mountains.

Many watchmakers later to become famous were at one time Perrelet's apprentices, and some historians even suggest that Abraham-Louis Breguet was in this illustrious group. Suffice to say, Perrelet invented a great deal, including the "perpetual" watch from around 1770, a pocket watch that wound itself utilizing the motion of the wearer.

When the brand hit the market in 1995, it came out with a double rotor and a movement, the P-181, which made waves in the industry. The Turbines soon followed featuring a kind of jet engine fan that decoratively turns over the dial, creating all sorts of effects and giving lots of potential for creative designing.

Today, the P-181 continues to power the Classic Double Rotor models and the Diamond Flowers, which balance sensual beauty with technical prowess—it was, after all, designed by a woman. And to celebrate the brand's twentieth birthday in 2015, a new caliber, the P-481, was made for the new First Class Double Rotor.

Turbillon

Reference number: A3037/1
Movement: automatic, P-371 in-house caliber; ø 32.8 mm, height 5.3 mm; 27 jewels; 28,800 vph; 65-hour power reserve; silicon escapement wheel and pallet lever; exclusive patented Perrelet oscillating weight; 2nd sapphire crystal Perrelet rotor acts as "turbine" on dial side
Functions: hours, minutes, seconds on tourbillon carriage
Case: stainless steel with DLC coating, ø 46 mm, height 13.4 mm; rose gold bezel and back; sapphire crystal; water-resistant to 5 atm
Band: rubber, buckle
Price: $98,350

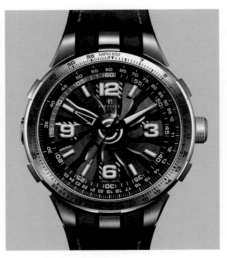

Turbine Yacht

Reference number: A1088/1
Movement: automatic, P-331 in-house caliber; ø 25.60 mm, height 3.85 mm; 25 jewels; 28,800 vph; 42-hour power reserve; exclusive patented Perrelet double rotor; 2nd black titanium rotor acts as "turbine" on dial side
Functions: hours, minutes, sweep seconds
Case: stainless steel with black PVD coating, ø 47 mm, height 15.45 mm; crown-activated rotating wind rose ring; sapphire crystal; transparent back; water-resistant to 30 atm
Band: blue rubber, black PVD buckle
Price: $7,350

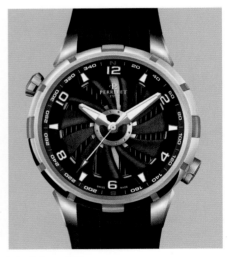

Turbine Pilote

Reference number: A1085/2A
Movement: automatic, P-331 in-house caliber; ø 25.60 mm, height 3.85 mm; 25 jewels; 28,800 vph; 42-hour power reserve; exclusive patented Perrelet double rotor; 2nd black titanium rotor acts as "turbine" on dial side
Functions: hours, minutes, sweep seconds; bidirectional dial ring; aviation slide rule
Case: stainless steel, ø 48 mm, height 13.65 mm; sapphire crystal; screwed-down sapphire crystal case back; water-resistant to 5 atm
Band: rubber, buckle
Price: $6,650

Turbine Chrono

Reference number: A1074/2
Movement: automatic, Perrelet Caliber P-361;
ø 30 mm, height 7.55 mm; 41 jewels; 28,800 vph;
mainplate with perlage, skeletonized and branded
rotor; 42-hour power reserve
Functions: hours, minutes; sweep chronograph
hand, 60-minute counter on central sapphire disk;
date
Case: stainless steel with DLC coating, ø 47 mm,
height 16 mm; bezel with tachymeter scale; sapphire
crystal; screwed-down sapphire crystal case back;
water-resistant to 5 atm
Band: rubber, buckle
Price: $7,950

Turbine Skeleton

Reference number: A1082/1
Movement: automatic, P-381 in-house caliber;
ø 26.2 mm, height 3.85 mm; 25 jewels; 28,800 vph;
42-hour power reserve
Functions: hours, minutes, sweep seconds
Case: stainless steel with PVD coating, steel
bezel and back with DLC coating, ø 44 mm, height
13.3 mm; sapphire crystal; antireflective sapphire
crystal; transparent case back; water-resistant to
5 atm
Band: reptile skin, DLC-treated folding clasp
Remarks: 10 black turbines rotate over skeletonized
movement
Price: $7,550
Variations: rose gold ($9,950)

First Class Lady Open Heart

Reference number: A2067/3
Movement: automatic, Perrelet Caliber P-391;
ø 25 jewels; 28,800 vph; 42-hour power reserve
Functions: hours, minutes, sweep seconds
Case: stainless steel, ø 35 mm, height 10 mm;
sapphire crystal; transparent case back; water-
resistant to 5 atm
Band: reptile skin, folding clasp
Remarks: dial with opening onto movement
Price: $3,150

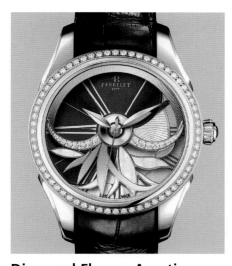

Diamond Flower Amytis

Reference number: A2066/4
Movement: automatic, Perrelet Caliber P-181-H
in-house caliber; ø 31.6 mm, height 4.75 mm; 21
jewels; 28,800 vph; Perrelet decorated hollowed out
oscillating mass; 42-hour power reserve
Functions: hours, minutes, sweep seconds
Case: ceramic, with stainless steel bezel and case
back; ø 36.5 mm, height 12.3 mm; sapphire crystal;
transparent case back; water-resistant to 5 atm
Band: reptile skin, folding clasp
Remarks: anthracite and white engraved mother-
of-pearl dial set with 80 diamonds or 24 diamonds
Price: $11,500

First Class Double Rotor
Skeleton

Reference number: A3050/1
Movement: automatic, Perrelet Caliber P-481;
25 jewels; 28,800 vph; 42-hour power reserve;
skeletonized Perrelet double rotor with côtes de
Genève; exclusive patented Perrelet double rotor;
2nd silver rotor in dial center
Functions: hours, minutes, sweep seconds
Case: rose gold, ø 42.5 mm, height 10.7 mm;
sapphire crystal; sapphire crystal back; water-
resistant to 5 atm
Band: reptile skin, buckle
Remarks: 20th anniversary double rotor edition
Price: $19,950; limited to 77 pieces
Variations: stainless steel ($8,950)

First Class Double Rotor

Reference number: A1090/1A
Movement: automatic, Caliber P-181-H; ø 31.6 mm,
height 4.9 mm; 25 jewels; 28,800 vph; Perrelet
exclusive double rotor, 2nd rotor on dial side;
rhodium-plated mainplate; 42-hour power reserve
Functions: hours, minutes, sweep seconds; date
Case: stainless steel, ø 42.5 mm, height 10.7 mm;
sapphire crystal; antireflective sapphire crystal;
transparent case back; water-resistant to 5 atm
Band: reptile skin, stainless steel folding clasp
Remarks: white grained/guilloché dial, hour-
markers; double rotor with côtes de Genève
Price: $4,250

Speake-Marin
Chemin en-Baffa 2
CH-1183 Bursins
Switzerland

Tel.:
+41-21-825-5069

E-Mail:
info@speake-marin.com

Website:
www.speake-marin.com

Founded:
2002

Number of employees:
5

Annual production:
500 watches

U.S. distributor:
Martin Pulli, Inc.
4337 Main Street
Philadelphia, PA 19127
215-508-4610
martinpulli@aol.com
www.martinpulli.com

Most important collections/price range:
HMS, Spirit Mark 2, Triad, Resilience, Serpent
Calendar, Renaissance, Marin-1, Marin-2
(Prices are in Swiss francs. Use daily exchange
rate for calculations.)

Peter Speake-Marin

Peter Speake-Marin brings realism, genius, and a sense of romance to his work. As a horological innovator—he could have been a poet or adventurer—he has managed within little more than a decade to establish an outstanding reputation for originality, virtuosity, and being an outstanding colleague. He has contributed to such iconic pieces as the HM1 of MB&F, the Chapter One for Maîtres du Temps, and the Harry Winston Excenter Tourbillon.

Born in Essex in 1968, Speake-Marin attended Hackney College, London, and WOSTEP in Switzerland, before earning his spurs restoring antique watches at a Somlo in Piccadilly. In 1996, he moved to Le Locle, Switzerland, to work with Renaud et Papi, when he also set about making his own pieces. A dual-train tourbillon (the Foundation Watch) opened the door to the prestigious AHCI.

The recession taught him something crucial: "I was a watchmaker, not an entrepreneur," he shares. "I had to become entrepreneurial to become a watchmaker again." And so he reorganized himself as a brand with three watch families. The Spirit has a military, adventurous feel; the J-Class recalls the discreet elegance of J-Class yachts. And for his flashes of creative madness, he has the grab-bag Cabinet des Mystères.

Speake-Marin has never stopped reflecting on, creating, recreating, and questioning his pieces. His first independent product, the Piccadilly, features a cylinder case with a narrow bezel and a frank dial. The Serpent Calendar saw a twisted sweep date hand in blued metal, a modern "surprise" in tune with the eighteenth-century marine look. The Spirit Mark 2 paid honors the hardiness of his fellows, bearing the inscription "Fight, Love & Persevere." Those who obey that exhortation will have luck, it seems. Speake-Marin was chosen to coach ex-007 Pierce Brosnan in his role as a watchmaker in the espionage yarn Survivor. The film may have its critics, but Brosnan became a Speake-Marin fan and an ambassador for the brand.

Magister
Reference number: PIC.10030
Movement: automatic, Caliber SM 3, ø 30.4 mm, height 5.4 mm; 25 jewels; 21,600 vph; 1-minute tourbillon; platinum microrotor; 72-hour power reserve
Functions: hours, minutes
Case: titanium, ø 42 mm, height 12 mm; sapphire crystal; transparent case back; water-resistant to 3 atm
Band: reptile skin, titanium buckle
Remarks: enamel dial
Price: CHF 67,000
Variations: pink gold 42 mm (CHF 89,000); pink gold 38 mm (CHF 86,500)

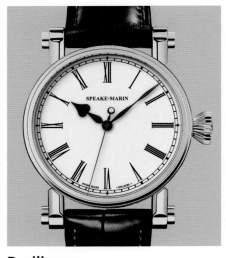

Resilience
Reference number: PIC.10010
Movement: automatic, Vaucher Caliber 3002, ø 26 mm, height 4.3 mm; 28 jewels; 28,800 vph; 50-hour power reserve
Functions: hours, minutes, sweep seconds
Case: pink gold, ø 38 mm, height 12 mm; sapphire crystal; transparent case back; water-resistant to 3 atm
Band: reptile skin, pink gold buckle
Price: CHF 19,600
Variations: stainless steel (CHF 10,200); pink gold 42 mm (CHF 21,900)

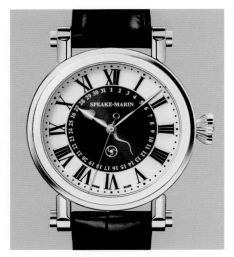

Serpent Calendar
Reference number: PIC.10006-04
Movement: automatic, Vaucher Caliber 3002, ø 26 mm, height 4.3 mm; 28 jewels; 28,800 vph; 50-hour power reserve
Functions: hours, minutes, sweep seconds; date
Case: titanium, ø 42 mm, height 12 mm; sapphire crystal; transparent case back; water-resistant to 3 atm
Band: reptile skin, titanium buckle
Price: CHF 9,700
Variations: black dial; stainless steel 38 mm (CHF 9,500); pink gold 38 mm (CHF 19,100)

Piaget SA

CH-1228 Plan-les-Ouates
Switzerland

Tel.:
+41-32-867-21-21

E-Mail:
info@piaget.com

Website:
www.piaget.com

Founded:
1874

Number of employees:
900

Annual production:
watches not specified; plus about 20,000
movements for Richemont Group

U.S. distributor:
Piaget North America
645 5th Avenue, 6th Floor
New York, NY 10022
212-909-4362; 212-909-4332 (fax)
www.piaget.com

Most important collections/price range:
Altiplano / approx. $13,500 to $22,000

Piaget

One of the oldest watch manufacturers in Switzerland, Piaget began making watch movements in the secluded Jura village of La Côte-aux-Fées in 1874. For decades, those movements were delivered to other watch brands. The *manufacture* itself, strangely enough, remained in the background. Until the middle of its fifth decade in business, Piaget provided movements to almost every renowned Swiss watchmaker. It wasn't until the 1940s that the Piaget family began to offer complete watches under their own name.

Even today, Piaget, which long ago moved the business side of things to Geneva, still makes its watch movements at its main facility high in the Jura mountains. Among its specialties in the 1960s were the ultrathin calibers 9P and 12P (automatic), which were 2 mm and 2.3 mm thin, respectively. The production of movements for other brands has been largely discontinued. Only associated brands within the Richemont Group are supplied with special movements.

Because the brand came a little late in the day to the manufacturing of its own timepieces, it has often gotten less attention than it deserved. The brand's strategy to focus stubbornly on outstandingly thin movements has been working out, however. It lends these watches the kind of understated elegance that is the hallmark of the new post-recession times. The 900P Altiplano became the world's thinnest mechanical movement at 3.65 mm. It is inverted to enable repairs, making the back the mainplate with the dial set on the upper side. In 2015, the Chrono Altiplano equipped with the 883P caliber became the thinnest chronograph ever, at 8.25 millimeters. As for the Limelight's case, with the playfully dynamic single lug on each side, it testifies to the creative acumen at Piaget.

Altiplano Chronograph

Reference number: G0A40030
Movement: manually wound, Piaget Caliber 883P; ø 27 mm, height 4.65 mm; 30 jewels; 28,800 vph; twin spring barrels; extra-flat construction; 50-hour power reserve; Geneva Seal
Functions: hours, minutes, subsidiary seconds; additional 24-hour display (2nd time zone); flyback chronograph
Case: pink gold, ø 41 mm, height 8.25 mm; sapphire crystal; transparent case back; water-resistant to 3 atm
Band: reptile skin, buckle
Price: $28,600
Variations: white gold with diamonds ($40,400)

Altiplano

Reference number: G0A35130
Movement: automatic, Piaget Caliber 1208P; ø 29.9 mm, height 2.35 mm; 27 jewels; 21,600 vph; rose gold microrotor; côtes de Genève; 42-hour power reserve
Functions: hours, minutes, subsidiary seconds
Case: white gold, ø 43 mm, height 5.25 mm; sapphire crystal; transparent case back
Band: reptile skin, folding clasp
Price: $22,800
Variations: pink gold ($21,900)

Altiplano Date

Reference number: G0A38131
Movement: automatic, Piaget Caliber 1205P; ø 29.9 mm, height 3 mm; 27 jewels; 21,600 vph; rose gold microrotor; côtes de Genève; 44-hour power reserve
Functions: hours, minutes, subsidiary seconds; date
Case: pink gold, ø 40 mm, height 6.36 mm; sapphire crystal; transparent case back
Band: reptile skin, buckle
Price: $23,800
Variations: white gold ($24,700)

Altiplano Skeleton

Reference number: G0A40033
Movement: automatic, Piaget Caliber 1200S;
ø 31.9 mm, height 2.4 mm; 26 jewels; 21,600 vph;
black platinum microrotor; fully skeletonized;
44-hour power reserve; Geneva Seal
Functions: hours, minutes
Case: white gold, ø 38 mm, height 5.34 mm;
sapphire crystal; transparent case back; water-
resistant to 3 atm
Band: reptile skin, buckle
Price: $52,500
Variations: pink gold ($57,000)

Altiplano 38 mm 900P

Reference number: G0A39111
Movement: manually wound, Piaget Caliber 900P;
ø 38 mm; 20 jewels; 21,600 vph; case back serves
as mainplate; fine finishing; 48-hour power reserve;
Geneva Seal
Functions: hours and minutes (off-center)
Case: white gold, ø 38 mm, height 3.65 mm;
sapphire crystal; reptile skin, buckle
Band: reptile skin, buckle
Remarks: currently world's thinnest mechanical
watch
Price: $26,500
Variations: with diamonds ($31,100); rose gold
($24,900)

Altiplano

Reference number: G0A34113
Movement: manually wound, Piaget Caliber 838P;
ø 26.8 mm, height 2.5 mm; 19 jewels; 21,600 vph;
60-hour power reserve; Geneva Seal
Functions: hours, minutes, subsidiary seconds
Case: pink gold, ø 40 mm, height 6.6 mm; sapphire
crystal; transparent case back; water-resistant to
3 atm
Band: reptile skin, buckle
Price: $18,100
Variations: white gold ($19,000); white ($27,600)
or pink ($26,600) gold with diamonds

Emperador Coussin XL Tourbillon

Reference number: G0A40041
Movement: automatic, Piaget Caliber 1270S;
ø 34.9 mm, height 5.05 mm; 35 jewels;
21,600 vph; flying 1-minute tourbillon, blackened
platinum microrotor; skeletonized; 42-hour power
reserve; Geneva Seal
Functions: hours and minutes (off-center),
subsidiary seconds (on tourbillon cage); power
reserve display (on movement side)
Case: white gold, ø 46.5 mm, height 8.85 mm;
sapphire crystal; transparent case back; water-
resistant to 3 atm
Band: reptile skin, folding clasp
Price: on request

Emperador Coussin Minutenrepetition XL

Reference number: G0A38019
Movement: automatic, Piaget Caliber 1290P;
34.9 x 34.9 mm, height 4.8 mm; 44 jewels;
21,600 vph; partially skeletonized, platinum
microrotor; 40-hour power reserve; Geneva Seal
Functions: hours, minutes; minute repeater
Case: rose gold, ø 48 mm, height 9.4 mm; sapphire
crystal; transparent back; water-resistant to 3 atm
Band: reptile skin, folding clasp
Remarks: currently world's thinnest automatic
movement
Price: on request

Emperador Coussin

Reference number: G0A32016
Movement: automatic, Piaget Caliber 850P;
ø 26.8 mm, height 4 mm; 30 jewels; 21,600 vph;
85-hour power reserve; Geneva Seal
Functions: hours, minutes, subsidiary seconds;
additional 12-hour display (2nd time zone), day/
night indicator; date
Case: white gold, ø 42 mm, height 8.9 mm;
sapphire crystal; transparent back; water-resistant
to 3 atm
Band: reptile skin, folding clasp
Price: $30,300
Variations: pink gold ($29,300); white gold with
diamonds ($63,000); pink gold with diamonds
($62,000)

Gouverneur Perpetual Calendar

Reference number: G0A40018
Movement: automatic, Piaget Caliber 855P;
ø 28.4 mm, height 5.6 mm; 38 jewels; 21,600 vph;
80-hour power reserve; Geneva Seal
Functions: hours, minutes, subsidiary seconds;
additional 12-hour display (2nd time zone), day/
night indicator; perpetual calendar with date/
weekday (retrograde), month, leap year
Case: pink gold, ø 43 mm, height 10.5 mm;
sapphire crystal; transparent back; water-resistant
to 3 atm
Band: reptile skin, folding clasp
Price: $55,500
Variations: white gold with diamonds ($70,000)

Gouverneur

Reference number: G0A38110
Movement: automatic, Piaget Caliber 800P;
ø 26.8 mm, height 4 mm; 25 jewels; 21,600 vph;
twin spring barrels; 85-hour power reserve; Geneva
Seal
Functions: hours, minutes, sweep seconds; date
Case: white gold, ø 43 mm, height 9 mm; sapphire
crystal; transparent case back; water-resistant to
3 atm
Band: reptile skin, buckle
Price: $26,000
Variations: pink gold ($25,700)

Gouverneur Chronograph

Reference number: G0A37112
Movement: automatic, Piaget Caliber 882P;
ø 27 mm, height 5.6 mm; 33 jewels; 28,800 vph;
50-hour power reserve; Geneva Seal
Functions: hours, minutes; flyback chronograph;
date
Case: pink gold, ø 43 mm, height 10.4 mm;
sapphire crystal; transparent case back; water-
resistant to 3 atm
Band: reptile skin, folding clasp
Price: $34,200
Variations: with diamonds ($48,500)

Altiplano

Reference number: G0A39105
Movement: manually wound, Piaget Caliber 450P
20.5 mm, height 2.1 mm; 18 jewels; 21,600 vph;
40-hour power reserve
Functions: hours, minutes, subsidiary seconds
Case: rose gold, ø 34 mm, height 6.3 mm; sapphire
crystal; transparent case back; water-resistant to
3 atm
Band: reptile skin, buckle
Price: $14,600
Variations: with diamonds ($25,700); white gold
with diamonds ($26,600)

Limelight Gala

Reference number: G0A38160
Movement: quartz, Piaget Caliber 690P
Functions: hours, minutes
Case: white gold, ø 32 mm, height 7.4 mm; 62
diamonds on bezel; sapphire crystal; water-resistant
to 3 atm
Band: satin, buckle (with diamonds)
Price: $33,300
Variations: pink gold ($32,300)

Limelight Gala

Reference number: G0A39197
Movement: manually wound, Piaget Caliber
438P; 20.3 x 23.7 mm, height 2.1 mm; 9 jewels;
21,600 vph; 43-hour power reserve
Functions: hours, minutes
Case: pink gold, 27 x 28.2 mm, height 8.1 mm; 86
brilliant-cut diamonds on bezel; sapphire crystal;
transparent case back
Band: satin, buckle
Price: $35,800
Variations: white gold ($35,400)

Caliber 883P

Manually wound; stop-seconds; double spring barrel, 50-hour power reserve; Geneva Seal
Functions: hours, minutes, subsidiary seconds; 2nd time zone; additional 24-hour display; flyback chronograph
Diameter: 27 mm
Height: 4.65 mm
Jewels: 30
Frequency: 28,800 vph
Shock protection: Incabloc
Remarks: world's thinnest manually wound chronograph movement currently produced

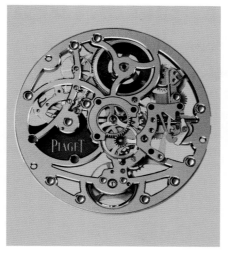

Caliber 1200S

Automatic; platinum microrotor; single spring barrel; 44-hour power reserve; Geneva Seal
Functions: hours, minutes
Diameter: 31.9 mm
Height: 2.4 mm
Jewels: 26
Balance: glucydur
Frequency: 21,600 vph
Balance spring: flat hairspring
Remarks: fully skeletonized movement

Caliber 1270S

Automatic; flying 1-minute tourbillon with titanium cage; platinum microrotor visible through dial; single spring barrel; 44-hour power reserve; Geneva Seal
Functions: hours, minutes, subsidiary seconds (on tourbillon cage at 1 o'clock)
Measurements: 34.9
Height: 5.05 mm
Jewels: 35
Balance: glucydur
Frequency: 21,600 vph
Remarks: fully skeletonized movement

Caliber 855P

Automatic; double spring barrel, 80-hour power reserve; Geneva Seal
Functions: hours, minutes, subsidiary seconds; 2nd time zone; additional 24-hour display; day/night indicator; perpetual calendar with retrograde date and weekday, month, leap year
Diameter: 28.4 mm
Height: 5.6 mm
Jewels: 38
Balance: glucydur
Frequency: 21,600 vph
Balance spring: flat hairspring
Remarks: variation as Caliber 856P with gold rotor set with diamonds

Caliber 1208P

Automatic; microrotor; 42-hour power reserve
Functions: hours, minutes, subsidiary seconds
Diameter: 29.9 mm
Height: 2.35 mm
Jewels: 27
Balance: glucydur
Frequency: 21,600 vph
Balance spring: flat hairspring
Shock protection: Incabloc
Remarks: world's thinnest automatic movement currently produced

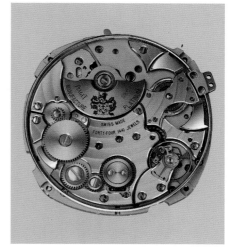

Caliber 1290P

Base caliber: 1208P
Automatic; platinum microrotor; single spring barrel, 40-hour power reserve; Geneva Seal
Functions: hours, minutes; minute repeater
Diameter: 34.9 mm
Height: 4.8 mm
Jewels: 44
Balance: glucydur
Frequency: 21,600 vph
Balance spring: flat hairspring

Pierre DeRoche SA

Le Revers 1
CH-1345 Le Lieu
Switzerland

Tel.:
+41-21-841-1169

Fax:
+41-21-841-2052

E-Mail:
ca.dubois@pierrederoche.com

Website:
www.pierrederoche.com

Founded:
2004

Number of employees:
3

Annual production:
250 watches

Distribution:
retail

Most important collections/price range:
TNT Royal Retro / approx. $20,500; SplitRock
Big Numbers / approx. $11,500; GrandCliff
QA / approx. $17,600

Pierre DeRoche

Apples apparently, are simply destined to fall not far from the tree, no matter what they intend. Pierre Dubois was born into a family with deep roots in watchmaking and a name that reinforced that fact. Dubois Dépraz, the outstanding manufacturer of movements and special modules, was founded by his great-grandfather, and two of his brothers now head that company. He went into finance, but the horological muse set him to work for fourteen years as CFO and COO for Audemars Piguet. "It's there that the genetic makeup from the four generations of watchmakers that he comes from rose to the surface, and with it the passion for watchmaking," says his wife Carole Dubois, who developed the same passion. The couple decided to leverage family ties and create a brand of watches—chic, complicated, yet fun—produced in the Vallée de Joux, the heart of watch country.

His name, which translates as "rock from wood," was a problem. When he was a child, an old peasant once remarked to him that wood and rock don't mix and a better name would be "rock pebble of stone": "*Pierre Caillou de Roche.*" The pebble got lost, Pierre DeRoche remained.

Working with the R&D department at Dubois Dépraz has been crucial for the ten-plus years of the brand's existence. Nevertheless, the two companies remain separate. They began with complicated chronographs featuring retrograde functions, multilayered, animated dials, and solid movements. The GrandCliff collection now exists in a host of different versions, from sober-elegant to sporty-intricate. For the TNT series, they decided on a genuine dance of six-second hands that deliver ten retrograde seconds each. For a slightly tamer experience, Pierre DeRoche has the SplitRock, whose large numbers and rectangular cases give it a retro art deco feel.

GrandCliff TNT Royal Retro

Reference number: TNT10005ACTIO-001CRO
Movement: automatic, exclusive Dubois Dépraz caliber; ø 36.6 mm, height 6.15 mm; 58 jewels; chamfered bridges, minute wheel with Pierre DeRoche logo; engraved oscillating weight
Functions: hours, minutes, retrograde seconds in 6 ten-second arcs; date
Case: titanium with black PVD, ø 47.5 mm, height 13.1 mm; steel bezel, crown and crown shield; sapphire crystal; transparent case back; water-resistant to 3 atm
Band: reptile skin, folding clasp
Price: $20,500; limited to 201 pieces

GrandCliff QA

Reference number: GRC10001ACIO-004CRO
Movement: exclusive Dubois Dépraz caliber; ø 30.0 mm, height 7.30 mm; 51 jewels; open-worked, decorated oscillating weight
Functions: hours, minutes, subsidiary seconds; flyback chronograph, 6 hour totalizer (retrograde), 60 minute totalizer; annual calendar, large date, month; power reserve indicator
Case: steel, ø 42.5 mm, height 13.3 mm; sapphire crystal; transparent case back; water-resistant to 10 atm
Band: reptile skin, folding clasp
Price: $17,600

SplitRock Big Numbers

Reference number: SPR30001ACIO-007CRO
Movement: exclusive Dubois Dépraz caliber; length 31.5 mm, height 6.95 mm; 39 jewels; open-worked, decorated oscillating weight
Functions: hours, minutes, subsidiary seconds; chronograph; power reserve indicator
Case: stainless steel, 45.5 x 31.5 mm, height 13.5 mm; sapphire crystal; transparent case back
Band: reptile skin, folding clasp
Price: $11,500

Rado

Rado is a relatively young brand, especially for a Swiss one. The company, which grew out of the Schlup clockwork factory, launched its first watches in 1957, but it achieved international fame only five years later, in 1962, when it surprised the world with a revolutionary invention. Rado's oval DiaStar was the first truly scratch-resistant watch ever, sporting a case made of the impervious alloy hardmetal. In 1985, its parent company, the Swatch Group, decided to put Rado's know-how and extensive experience in developing materials to good use, and from then on the brand intensified its research activities at its home in Lengnau, Switzerland, and continued to produce only watches with extremely hard cases. A record of sorts was even set in 2004, when they managed to create a 10,000-Vickers material, which is as hard as natural diamonds.

Within the Swatch Group, Rado was the most successful individual brand in the upper price segment for a long time. But at some point, the brand's image became a little blurred, and it began suffering from the almost unbridgeable gap that had suddenly opened up between its jeweled watches and high-tech line. However, the pioneering spirit of the brand's ceramic researchers and engineers has won out. The company already holds more than thirty patents arising from research and production of new case materials. Nowadays, the cases begin as powders, already premixed with binding agents and additives to later achieve the desired color. They are then pressed into molds and fired. The final touch is polishing with diamond powder to make the outside of Rado timepieces even more robust and scratchproof. And the techno inside is reflected in an unabashed techno look outside.

Rado Uhren AG

Bielstrasse 45
CH-2543 Lengnau
Switzerland

Tel.:
+41-32-655-6111

Fax:
+41-32-655-6112

E-Mail:
info@rado.com

Website:
www.rado.com

Founded:
1957

Number of employees:
approx. 470

U.S. distributor:
Rado
The Swatch Group (U.S.), Inc.
1200 Harbor Boulevard
Weehawken, NJ 07086
201-271-1400

Most important collections/price range:
Centrix / from approx. $900; Diamaster / from approx. $1,350; D-Star / from approx. $1,700; Integral / from approx. $2,000; Sintra / from approx. $3,000; True / from approx. $1,400; Hyperchrome / from approx $1,600

HyperChrome Court Collection

Reference number: R32525169
Movement: automatic, ETA Caliber 2894-2; ø 28.6 mm, height 6.2 mm; 37 jewels; 28,800 vph; fine decoration; 42-hour power reserve
Functions: hours, minutes, subsidiary seconds; chronograph; date
Case: ceramic, ø 45 mm, height 13 mm; sapphire crystal; transparent case back; water-resistant to 10 atm
Band: rubber, folding clasp
Price: $4,300

Coupole Classic

Reference number: R22861115
Movement: automatic, ETA Caliber C07.611; ø 25.6 mm, 25 jewels; 21,600 vph; 80-hour power reserve
Functions: hours, minutes, sweep seconds; date
Case: stainless steel with rose gold-colored PVD coating, ø 38 mm, height 10.2 mm; sapphire crystal; water-resistant to 5 atm
Band: calf leather, folding clasp
Price: $1,250

Diamaster Grande Seconde

Reference number: R14129106
Movement: automatic, ETA Caliber 2899 (base ETA 2892-A2); ø 25.6 mm, 21 jewels; 28,800 vph; 42-hour power reserve
Functions: hours and minutes (off-center), subsidiary seconds; date
Case: ceramic, titanium case back, ø 43 mm, height 11.8 mm; sapphire crystal; transparent case back; water-resistant to 10 atm
Band: calf leather, folding clasp
Price: $3,000

RGM Watch Company

801 W. Main Street
Mount Joy, PA 17552

Tel.:
717-653-9799

Fax:
717-653-9770

E-Mail:
sales@rgmwatches.com

Founded:
1992

Number of employees:
12

Annual production:
200–300 watches

Distribution:
RGM deals directly with customers.

Most important collections/price range:
Pennsylvania Series (completely made in the U.S.) / $2,500 to $125,000 range

RGM

If there is any part of the United States that can somehow be considered its "watch valley," it may be the state of Pennsylvania. And one of the big players there is no doubt Roland Murphy, founder of RGM. Murphy, born in Maryland, went through the watchmaker's drill, studying at the Bowman Technical School, then in Switzerland, and finally working with Swatch before launching his own business in 1992.

His first series, Signature, paid homage to local horological genius through vintage pocket watch movements developed by Hamilton. His second big project was the Caliber 801, the first "high-grade mechanical movement made in series in America since Hamilton stopped production of the 992 B in 1969," Murphy grins. The next goal was to manufacture an all-American-made watch, the Pennsylvania Tourbillon.

And so, model by model, Murphy continues to expand his "Made in U.S.A." portfolio. In 2012, the brand's twentieth anniversary, RGM went retro with the 801 Aircraft. The current pinnacle is the brand-new Caliber "20," which revives an old invention once in favor for railroad watches. The motor barrel is a complex but robust system in which the watch is wound by the barrel and the barrel arbor then drives the gear train. Less friction and wear and a slimmer chance of damage to the watch if the mainspring breaks are the two main advantages. Even the finishing on components is done following research into earlier American models. And in 2015, Murphy came out with a watch that pays homage to baseball—perhaps the pinnacle of Americana.

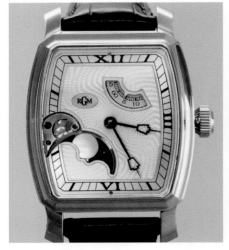

Caliber 20

Reference number: Caliber 20
Movement: manually wound, RGM motor barrel caliber; 34.4 x 30.4 mm; 19 jewels; 18,000 vph; perlage and côtes de Genève; 42-hour power reserve
Functions: hours, minutes, subsidiary seconds on disk; moon phase
Case: stainless steel, 42 x 38.5 mm, height 9.7 mm; sapphire crystal; transparent case back
Band: reptile skin, buckle
Remarks: blued steel hands
Price: $27,500
Variations: rose gold ($42,500)

Pennsylvania Tourbillon

Reference number: mm2
Movement: manual winding, American-made; ø 37.22 mm; 19 jewels; 18,000 vph; 1-minute tourbillon; German silver and rose gold finish with perlage and côtes de Genève; 42-hour power reserve
Functions: hours, minutes
Case: stainless steel, ø 43.5 mm, height 13.5 mm; sapphire crystal; transparent case back
Band: reptile skin, buckle
Remarks: blued steel minute/hour hands; guilloché dial
Price: $95,000
Variations: rose gold ($125,000); platinum (on request)

Enamel Corps of Engineers

Reference number: 801CoE
Movement: manually wound, RGM Caliber 801; ø 37 mm; 19 jewels; lever escapement; screw balance; U.S. bridges, mainplate, settings, 7-tooth winding click; circular côtes de Genève, silver guilloché; 42-hour power reserve
Functions: hours, minutes, subsidiary seconds
Case: stainless steel, ø 42 mm, height 10.5 mm; sapphire crystal; transparent back; water-resistant to 5 atm
Band: leather, buckle
Remarks: grand feu white glass enamel partially skeletonized dial with aged luminous numbers
Price: $9,700
Variations: stainless steel bracelet ($10,450)

Professional Diver

Reference number: 300-3 Series 3
Movement: automatic, modified ETA Caliber 2892; ø 25.6 mm, height 3.6 mm; 21 jewels; 28,800 vph; bridges and plates with perlage and côtes de Genève; 42-hour power reserve
Functions: hours, minutes, sweep seconds; date
Case: brushed stainless steel, ø 43.5 mm, height 17 mm; sapphire crystal; unidirectional bezel with 60-minute divisions (240 clicks); screwed-down back; screwed-in crown; water-resistant to more than 70 atm
Band: rubber strap, buckle
Remarks: comes with no date as well
Price: $3,700; limited to 75 pieces
Variations: stainless steel bracelet ($4,450)

Pennsylvania Series 801

Reference number: PS 801 ES
Movement: manually wound, RGM Caliber 801; ø 37 mm; 19 jewels; lever escapement; screw balance; U.S. bridges, mainplate, settings, 7-tooth winding click; circular côtes de Genève, silver guilloche; 42-hour power reserve
Functions: hours, minutes, subsidiary seconds
Case: stainless steel, ø 43.3 mm, height 12.3 mm; sapphire crystal; sapphire crystal transparent case back; water-resistant to 5 atm
Band: reptile or ostrich skin, folding clasp
Remarks: partially skeletonized dial
Price: $9,700
Variations: rose gold ($22,500); white gold ($24,500)

801 Aircraft

Reference number: 801 A
Movement: manually wound, RGM Caliber 801; ø 37 mm; 19 jewels; lever escapement; screw balance; U.S. bridges, mainplate, settings, 7-tooth winding click; circular côtes de Genève, silver guilloché; 42-hour power reserve
Functions: hours, minutes, subsidiary seconds
Case: stainless steel, ø 42 mm, height 10.5 mm; sapphire crystal; transparent back; water-resistant to 5 atm
Band: distressed leather, buckle
Remarks: partially skeletonized dial
Price: $7,450
Variations: green or red dials; stainless steel bracelet ($8,250)

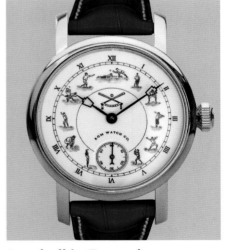

Vintage Chronograph

Reference number: 455
Movement: automatic, RGM/ETA Caliber 7750; 30 mm; 25 jewels; 28,800 vph; rhodium finish with perlage and côtes de Genève; 46-hour power reserve
Functions: hours, minutes, sweep seconds; chronograph, 30-minute/12-hour totalizers
Case: polished stainless steel, ø 38.5 mm, height 13.9 mm; sapphire crystal
Band: calfskin, buckle
Remarks: telemeter and tachymeter in blue or black
Price: $3,950; limited to 100 pieces

Pilot Professional

Reference number: 151 A
Movement: automatic, RGM/ETA Caliber 2892-A2; ø 25.6 mm; 21 jewels; 28,800 vph; rhodium finish with perlage and côtes de Genève; 42-hour power reserve
Functions: hours, minutes, sweep seconds; date
Case: brushed stainless steel, ø 38.5 mm, height 9.9 mm; domed sapphire crystal; transparent case back
Band: leather, buckle
Remarks: date at 4:30, 2-toned technical dial with Superluminova
Price: $3,350
Variations: titanium ($4,350)

Baseball in Enamel

Reference number: PS801BB
Movement: manually wound, RGM Caliber 801; ø 37 mm; 19 jewels; lever escapement; screw balance; U.S. bridges, mainplate, settings, 7-tooth winding click; circular côtes de Genève, silver guilloché; 42-hour power reserve
Functions: hours, minutes, subsidiary seconds
Case: stainless steel, ø 43.3 mm, height 12.3 mm; sapphire crystal; transparent back; water-resistant to 5 atm
Band: leather, buckle
Remarks: grand feu white glass enamel partially skeletonized dial; Keystone hands
Price: $13,900
Variations: rose gold ($23,900)

Richard Mille Watches
c/o Horométrie SA
11, rue du Jura
CH-2345 Les Breuleux
Switzerland

Tel.:
+41-32-959-4353

Fax:
+41-32-959-4354

E-Mail:
info@richardmille.ch

Website:
www.richardmille.com

Founded:
2000

Annual production:
over 2,600 watches

U.S. distributor:
Richard Mille Americas
132 South Rodeo Drive, 4th Floor
Beverly Hills, CA 90212
310-205-5555

Richard Mille

Mille never stops delivering the wow to the watch world with what he calls his "race cars for the wrist." His timepieces are usually built of exotic high-tech materials borrowed from automobile racing or even space travel. Mille is not an engineer by profession, but rather a marketing expert who earned his first paychecks in the watch division of the French defense, automobile, and aerospace concern Matra in the early 1980s. This was a time of fundamental changes in technology, and the European watch industry was being confronted with gigantic challenges. "I have no historical relationship with watchmaking whatsoever," says Mille, "and so I have no obligations either. The mechanics of my watches are geared towards technical feasibility."

In the 1990s, Mille had to go to the expert workshop of Audemars Piguet Renaud & Papi (APRP) in Le Locle to find a group of watchmakers and engineers who would take on the Mille challenge. Audemars Piguet even succumbed to the temptation of testing those scandalous innovations—materials, technologies, functions—in a Richard Mille watch before daring to use them in its own collections (Tradition d'Excellence).

Since 2007, Audemars Piguet has also become a shareholder in Richard Mille, and so the three firms are now closely bound. The assembly of the watches is done in the Franches-Montagnes region in the Jura, where Richard Mille opened the firm Horométrie. For years Mille has entertained at times personal friendships with various specialists in exotic materials. This has given rise to very ambitious projects, like the processing of carbon nanofibers or highly tough NTPT carbon fibers for ultralight and very sturdy watch cases. Richard Mille timepieces have also found their way onto the wrists of elite athletes, like tennis star Rafael Nadal and sprinter Yohan Blake.

In 2015, the brand presented the Tourbillon Fleur with a tourbillon that rises out of the opening petals of a magnolia. Here is proof high-tech can still be imbued with poetry.

RM 031 High Performance
Reference number: RM 031
Movement: manually wound, Richard Mille Caliber RM031; ø 36 mm, height 6.35 mm; 26 jewels; 36,000 vph; Arcap mainplate and bridges, AP direct-impulse escapement; crown-actuated function selection switch; 50-hour power reserve
Functions: hours, minutes, subsidiary seconds
Case: titanium, ø 50 mm, height 13.9 mm; sapphire crystal; transparent back; water-resistant to 5 atm
Band: rubber, folding clasp
Remarks: chronometric self-check (rate accuracy better than 30 seconds per month)
Price: $1,050,000

RM 033 Automatic Extra Flat
Reference number: RM 033
Movement: automatic, Richard Mille Caliber RMXP1; ø 33 mm, height 2.6 mm; 29 jewels; 21,600 vph; titanium mainplate, platinum microrotor; 42-hour power reserve
Functions: hours, minutes
Case: titanium, ø 45.7 mm, height 6.3 mm; sapphire crystal; transparent case back; ceramic bezel; water-resistant to 3 atm
Band: rubber, folding clasp
Price: $100,000
Variations: white gold; red gold

RM 63-01 Dizzy Hands
Reference number: RM 63-01
Movement: automatic, Caliber CRMA3; ø 31 mm, height 6.7 mm; 35 jewels, 28,800 vph; 50-hour power reserve
Functions: hours, minutes
Case: titanium, ø 42.7 mm, height 11.7 mm; rose gold bezel/case back; sapphire crystal, transparent back
Band: rubber, folding clasp
Remarks: "dizzy hands" function, pressing crown launches counterclockwise rotation of hour disc, hour hand turns clockwise; pressing crown again resets time
Price: $120,000

RM 030 Polo St. Tropez

Reference number: RM 030
Movement: automatic, Richard Mille Caliber RM 030; 28.45 x 30.25 mm, height 5.59 mm; 40 jewels; 28,800 vph; titanium bottom plate/bridges, 2 spring barrels; winding rotor with variable inertia automatically disengages when fully-wound
Functions: hours, minutes, sweep seconds; power reserve display, rotor clutch indicator; large date
Case: titanium, 42.7 x 50 mm, height 13.95 mm; ceramic bezel and case back (ATZ); sapphire crystal; transparent case back; water-resistant to 5 atm
Band: rubber, buckle
Remarks: RM St. Tropez polo club official timekeeper
Price: on request; limited to 50 pieces

RM 011 Carbon NTPT

Reference number: RM 011
Movement: automatic, Richard Mille Caliber RMAC1; ø 39.15 mm, height 9 mm; 62 jewels; 28,800 vph; titanium bridges and plate; 2 spring barrels; 55-hour power reserve
Functions: hours, minutes, subsidiary seconds; flyback chronograph; full calendar with large date, month
Case: carbon fiber (NTPT multilayer carbon), 42.7 x 50 mm, height 16.4 mm; sapphire crystal; water-resistant to 3 atm
Band: rubber, folding clasp
Remarks: Lotus F1 Team (driver Romain Grosjean)
Price: $160,000

RM 50-01 Tourbillon Chrono G-Sensor

Reference number: RM 50-01
Movement: manually wound, Richard Mille Caliber RM50-01; 32 x 36.7 mm, height 7.53 mm; 35 jewels, 21,600 vph; 1-minute tourbillon; winding, hand setting, rapid adjustment switch; 70-hour power reserve
Functions: hours, minutes, subsidiary seconds; accelerometer (G-sensor); chronograph
Case: rose gold, 42.7 x 50 mm, height 16.4 mm; NTPT carbon fiber bezel/case back; sapphire crystal; transparent back; water-resistant to 5 atm
Band: silicon, folding clasp
Remarks: mechanical accelerometer; Lotus F1 Team
Price: $920,000; limited to 10 pieces
Variations: NTPT carbon fiber ($940,000; limited to 20)

Flyback Chronograph with Regatta Countdown

Reference number: RM 60-01
Movement: automatic, Richard Mille Caliber RMAC2; ø 39.15 mm; height 9 mm; 62 jewels, 28,800 vph; titanium mainplate; adjustable rotor geometry; 50-hour power reserve
Functions: hours, minutes, subsidiary seconds; additional 24-hour display (2nd time zone); flyback chronograph with countdown function; full calendar with large date, month
Case: titanium, ø 50 mm, height 16.33 mm; bidirectional bezel with 360-degree division; sapphire crystal, transparent back; water-resistant to 3 atm
Band: rubber, folding clasp
Price: $150,000; limited to 35 pieces

RM 36-01 Competition G-Force

Reference number: RM 36-01
Movement: manually wound, Caliber RM36-01; ø 36.6 mm; height 3.96 mm; 37 jewels, 21,600 vph; 1-minute tourbillon; 50-component affixed module (ø 17 mm, height 10 mm) for G-sensor; 70-hour power reserve
Functions: hours, minutes; power reserve display; acceleration sensor
Case: titanium, ø 47.7 mm, height 17.4 mm; carbon nanofiber bezel, bidirectional to assess G-force direction; sapphire crystal, transparent back; water-resistant to 5 atm
Band: rubber, folding clasp
Remarks: Sébastien Loeb edition
Price: $625,000; limited to 30 pieces

RM 19-02 Tourbillon Fleur

Reference number: RM 19-02
Movement: manually wound, Richard Mille Caliber RM19-02; 29.6 x 31.5 mm, height 5.72 mm; 40 jewels; 21,600 vph; flying 1-minute tourbillon rises every hour or on request from opening magnolia flower with 5 petals; 42-hour power reserve
Functions: hours and minutes (off-center)
Case: white gold, 38.3 x 45.4 mm, height 12.55 mm; brilliant-cut diamonds on bezel and case sides; sapphire crystal; transparent case back; crown with dynamometer (slide clutch); water-resistant to 3 atm
Band: reptile skin, folding clasp
Remarks: brilliant-cut diamonds, hand-painted petals
Price: $1,080,000; limited to 30 pieces

Manufacture ROGER DUBUIS

2, rue André-De-Garrini - CP 149
CH-1217 Meyrin 2 (Geneva)
Switzerland

Tel.:
+41-22-783-2828

Fax:
+41-22-783-2882

E-Mail:
info@rogerdubuis.com

Website:
www.rogerdubuis.com

Founded:
1995

Annual production:
over 5,000 watches (estimated)

U.S. distributor:
Roger Dubuis N.A.
645 Fifth Avenue
New York, NY 10022
888-RDUBUIS
info@rogerdubuis.com

Most important collections:
Hommage, Excalibur, La Monégasque,
Pulsion, Velvet

Roger Dubuis

Roger Dubuis, a *manufacture* fully committed to luxury and *"très haute horlogerie,"* was taken over by the Richemont Group in 2007. The lure was without a doubt the company's state-of-the-art workshops, where the finest movement components are made—bearing the coveted Seal of Geneva. These credentials are interesting to other brands in the Richemont Group as well, especially to Cartier, which gets its skeletonized movements from the Roger Dubuis *manufacture.*

This Geneva-based company was founded in 1995 as SOGEM SA (Société Genevoise des Montres) by name-giver Roger Dubuis and financier Carlos Dias. These two exceptional men created a complete collection of unusual watches in no time flat—timepieces with unheard-of dimensions and incomparable complications. The meteoric development of this *manufacture* and the incredible frequency of its new introductions—even technical ones—continue to astound the traditional, rather conservative watch industry. Today, Roger Dubuis develops all of its own movements, currently numbering more than thirty different mechanical calibers. In addition, it produces just about all of its individual components in-house, from base plates to escapements and balance springs. With this heavy-duty technological know-how in its quiver, the brand has been able to build some remarkable movements, like the massive RD101, with four balance springs and all manner of differentials and gear works to drive the Excalibur Quatuor, the equivalent in horology to a monster truck. Even in more delicate versions, like the new Brocéliande, featuring colorful ivy leaves embracing the movement, Roger Dubuis watches always seem ready to jump off your wrist.

Excalibur Spider Skeleton Flying Double Tourbillon

Reference number: RDDBEX0481
Movement: manually wound, Caliber RD01SQ; ø 37.8 mm, height 7.67 mm; 28 jewels; 21,600 vph; flying double tourbillon with compensation differential; skeletonized, galvanic blackening, beveling, perlage; 50-hour power reserve; Geneva Seal
Functions: hours, minutes
Case: titanium, ø 47 mm, height 14.95 mm; bezel with 60-minute division; sapphire crystal; transparent case back; water-resistant to 5 atm
Band: rubber, folding clasp
Price: $298,500; limited to 188 pieces

Excalibur Spider Skeleton Flying Double Tourbillon

Reference number: RDDBEX0479
Movement: manually wound, Caliber RD505SQ; ø 36.1 mm, height 4.28 mm; 19 jewels; 21,600 vph; flying 1-minute tourbillon; skeletonized; 60-hour power reserve; Geneva Seal
Functions: hours, minutes
Case: titanium, ø 45 mm, height 13.75 mm; bezel with 60-minute division; sapphire crystal; transparent case back; water-resistant to 5 atm
Band: rubber, folding clasp
Price: $159,500

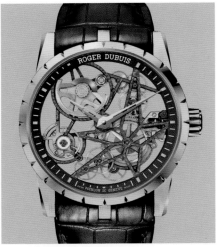

Excalibur Skeleton Automatic

Reference number: RDDBEX0422
Movement: automatic, Caliber RD820SQ; ø 36.1 mm, height 6.38 mm; 35 jewels; 28,800 vph; skeletonized; microrotor; 60-hour power reserve; Geneva Seal
Functions: hours, minutes
Case: rose gold, ø 42 mm, height 11.44 mm; sapphire crystal; transparent case back; water-resistant to 3 atm
Band: reptile skin, folding clasp
Price: $73,600
Variations: blackened titanium ($60,200)

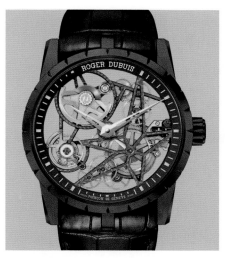

Excalibur Skeleton Automatic

Reference number: RDDBEX0473
Movement: automatic, Caliber RD820SQ;
ø 36.1 mm, height 6.38 mm; 35 jewels;
28,800 vph; skeletonized; microrotor; 60-hour
power reserve; Geneva Seal
Functions: hours, minutes
Case: titanium with black DLC coating, ø 42 mm,
height 11.44 mm; sapphire crystal; transparent
case back; water-resistant to 3 atm
Band: reptile skin, folding clasp
Price: $60,200
Variations: rose gold ($73,600)

Excalibur Skeleton Flying Double Tourbillon

Reference number: RDDBEX0395
Movement: manually wound, Caliber RD01SQ;
ø 37.8 mm, height 7.67 mm; 28 jewels; 21,600 vph;
flying double tourbillon with compensation differential;
skeletonized, galvanic blackening, beveling, perlage;
48-hour power reserve; Geneva Seal
Functions: hours, minutes
Case: rose gold, ø 45 mm, height 14.7 mm;
sapphire crystal; transparent case back; water-
resistant to 5 atm
Band: reptile skin, folding clasp
Price: $328,500
Variations: white gold ($338,000); titanium
($286,500)

Excalibur Quatuor

Reference number: RDDBEX0425
Movement: manually wound, Caliber RD101;
ø 37.9 mm, height 10.6 mm; 113 jewels;
28,800 vph; 4 coupled escapement systems with
4 Hz frequency; power transmission/synchronization
via 3 satellite differentials; 40-hour power reserve;
Geneva Seal
Functions: hours, minutes; power reserve indicator
Case: titanium with black PVD coating, ø 48 mm,
height 18.38 mm; sapphire crystal; transparent
case back; water-resistant to 3 atm
Band: reptile skin, folding clasp
Price: $447,500; limited to 188 pieces
Variations: rose gold ($489,500)

Hommage Automatic

Reference number: RDDBHO0565
Movement: automatic, Caliber RD 620; ø 31 mm,
height 4.5 mm; 35 jewels; 28,800 vph; microrotor;
52-hour power reserve; Geneva Seal
Functions: hours, minutes, subsidiary seconds
Case: rose gold, ø 42 mm, height 11.12 mm;
sapphire crystal; transparent case back; water-
resistant to 3 atm
Band: reptile skin, buckle
Remarks: Roger Dubuis signature on case back
Price: $30,800
Variations: white gold ($31,900)

Hommage Chronographe

Reference number: RDDBHO0569
Movement: automatic, Caliber RD 680; ø 31 mm,
height 6.3 mm; 44 jewels; 28,800 vph; microrotor,
column wheel control of chronograph; 52-hour
power reserve; Geneva Seal
Functions: hours, minutes, subsidiary seconds;
chronograph
Case: white gold, ø 42 mm, height 12.12 mm;
sapphire crystal; transparent case back; water-
resistant 3 atm
Band: reptile skin, buckle
Remarks: Roger Dubuis signature on case back
Price: $46,700
Variations: rose gold ($48,500)

Hommage Flying Double Tourbillon

Reference number: RDDBHO0563
Movement: manually wound, Caliber RD 100;
ø 36.1 mm, height 8.8 mm; 52 jewels; 21,600 vph;
2 flying 1-minute tourbillons with compensation
differential; 50-hour power reserve; Geneva Seal
Functions: hours, minutes
Case: rose gold, ø 45 mm, height 16.31 mm;
sapphire crystal; transparent case back; water-
resistant to 3 atm
Band: reptile skin, folding clasp
Remarks: Roger Dubuis signature on case back
Price: $328,500
Variations: white gold ($338,000)

Velvet Automatic

Reference number: RDDBVE0034
Movement: automatic, Caliber RD 821;
ø 25.93 mm, height 3.43 mm; 33 jewels;
28,800 vph; 48-hour power reserve; Geneva Seal
Functions: hours, minutes
Case: pink gold, ø 36 mm, height 8.77 mm;
sapphire crystal; water-resistant to 3 atm
Band: reptile skin, buckle
Remarks: flange set with diamonds
Price: $21,700

Velvet Automatic

Reference number: RDDBVE0020
Movement: automatic, Caliber RD 821;
ø 25.93 mm, height 3.43 mm; 33 jewels;
28,800 vph; 48-hour power reserve; Geneva Seal
Functions: hours, minutes
Case: pink gold, ø 36 mm, height 8.77 mm; bezel
set with diamonds; sapphire crystal; water-resistant
to 3 atm
Band: reptile skin, buckle
Price: $42,600
Variations: white gold ($43,800)

Excalibur Brocéliande

Reference number: RDDBEX0474
Movement: manually wound, Caliber RD505SQ;
ø 36.1 mm, height 4.28 mm; 19 jewels; 21,600 vph;
flying 1-minute tourbillon; skeletonized; 60-hour
power reserve; Geneva Seal
Functions: hours, minutes
Case: rose gold, ø 42 mm, height 11.66 mm;
sapphire crystal; transparent case back; water-
resistant to 3 atm
Band: reptile skin, folding clasp
Remarks: case/dial set with 349 diamonds
Price: $270,000; limited to 28 pieces

Excalibur 36 Automatic

Reference number: RDDBEX0355
Movement: automatic, Caliber RD 821; ø 25.93 mm,
height 3.43 mm; 33 jewels; 28,800 vph; 48-hour
power reserve; Geneva Seal
Functions: hours, minutes
Case: rose gold, ø 36 mm, height 9 mm; diamonds
on bezel; sapphire crystal; water-resistant to 3 atm
Band: reptile skin, folding clasp
Price: $31,900
Variations: rose gold bracelet ($50,300); stainless
steel ($23,700)

Excalibur 42 Automatic

Reference number: RDDBEX0443
Movement: automatic, Caliber RD620; ø 31.1 mm,
height 4.5 mm; 35 jewels; 28,800 vph; microrotor;
52-hour power reserve; Geneva Seal
Functions: hours, minutes, subsidiary seconds
Case: stainless steel, ø 42 mm; sapphire crystal;
transparent case back; water-resistant to 3 atm
Band: reptile skin, folding clasp
Price: $16,600
Variations: dark dial ($16,600)

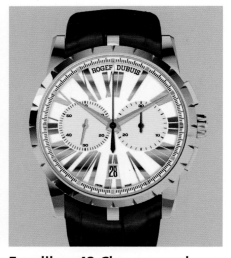

Excalibur 42 Chronograph

Reference number: RDDBEX0390
Movement: automatic, Caliber RD 681; ø 30.6 mm,
height 6.3 mm; 44 jewels; 28,800 vph; microrotor;
column wheel control of chronograph functions;
52-hour power reserve; Geneva Seal
Functions: hours, minutes, subsidiary seconds;
chronograph
Case: rose gold, ø 42 mm; sapphire crystal;
transparent case back; water-resistant to 3 atm
Band: reptile skin, folding clasp
Price: $45,900
Variations: stainless steel ($31,900)

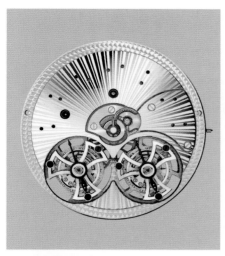

Caliber RD100

Manually wound; 2 flying tourbillons with differential; single spring barrel; 50-hour power reserve; Geneva Seal; COSC-certified chronometer
Functions: hours, minutes; power reserve indicator (on case back)
Diameter: 36.1 mm
Height: 8.8 mm
Jewels: 52
Balance: screw balance
Frequency: 21,600 vph

Caliber RD 101

Manually wound; 4 radially mounted and inclined lever escapements, synchronized with 3 balancing differentials; planetary gears for winding and power reserve; skeletonized movement; double spring barrel, 40-hour power reserve; Geneva Seal
Functions: hours, minutes; power reserve indicator
Diameter: 37.9 mm
Height: 10.6 mm
Jewels: 113
Balance: glucydur (4x)
Frequency: 28,800 vph (4x)
Balance spring: flat hairspring
Remarks: galvanic blackening and beveling of frame parts, perlage, 590 components

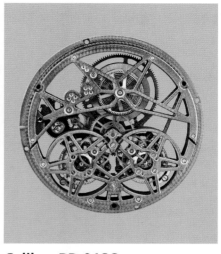

Caliber RD 01SQ

Manually wound; 2 flying tourbillons with differential; skeletonized
Functions: hours, minutes
Diameter: 37.8 mm
Height: 7.67 mm
Jewels: 28
Frequency: 21,600 vph
Remarks: galvanic blackening and beveling of frame parts, perlage, Geneva Seal, 319 components

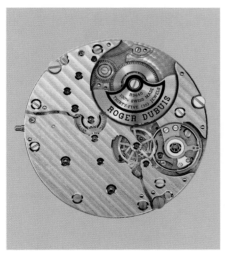

Caliber RD640

Automatic; microrotor; single spring barrel, 52-hour power reserve; Geneva Seal
Functions: hours, minutes, subsidiary seconds; date
Diameter: 31.1 mm
Height: 4.5 mm
Jewels: 35
Balance: glucydur, with smooth rim
Frequency: 28,800 vph
Balance spring: flat hairspring
Shock protection: Incabloc
Remarks: finely finished with côtes de Genève, 198 components

Caliber RD 681

Automatic; column wheel control of chronograph functions, microrotor; single spring barrel, 52-hour power reserve; Geneva Seal
Functions: hours, minutes, subsidiary seconds; chronograph
Diameter: 30.6 mm
Height: 6.3 mm
Jewels: 44
Balance: glucydur
Frequency: 28,800 vph
Balance spring: flat hairspring
Remarks: finely worked with côtes de Genève, 280 components

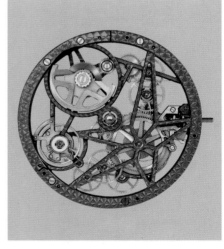

Caliber RD820SQ

Automatic; microrotor; single spring barrel, 60-hour power reserve; Geneva Seal
Functions: hours, minutes
Diameter: 35.7 mm
Height: 6.38 mm
Jewels: 35
Frequency: 28,800 vph
Remarks: skeletonized, rhodium-plated, finely finished with côtes de Genève, 167 components

Rolex SA
Rue François-Dussaud 3
CH-1211 Geneva 26
Switzerland

Website:
www.rolex.com

Founded:
1908

Number of employees:
over 2,000 (estimated)

Annual production:
approx. 1,000,000 watches (estimated)

U.S. distributor:
Rolex Watch U.S.A., Inc.
Rolex Building
665 Fifth Avenue
New York, NY 10022-5358
212-758-7700; 212-980-2166 (fax)
www.rolex.com

Rolex

Essentially, the Rolex formula for success has always been "what you see is what you get"—and plenty of it. For over a century now, the company has made wristwatch history without a need for *grandes complications*, perpetual calendars, tourbillons, or exotic materials. And its output in sheer quantity is phenomenal, at not quite a million watches per year. But make no mistake about it: The quality of these timepieces is legendary.

For as long as anyone can remember, this brand has held the top spot in the COSC's statistics, and year after year Rolex delivers just about half of all of the official institute's successfully tested mechanical chronometer movements. The brand has also pioneered several fundamental innovations: Rolex founder Hans Wilsdorf invented the hermetically sealed Oyster case in the 1920s, which he later outfitted with a screwed-in crown and an automatic movement wound by rotor. Shock protection, water resistance, the antimagnetic Parachrom hairspring, and automatic winding are some of the virtues that make wearing a Rolex timepiece much more comfortable and reliable. Because Wilsdorf patented his inventions for thirty years, Rolex had a head start on the competition.

Rolex watches and movements were at first produced in two different companies at two different sites. Only in 2004 did Geneva-based Rolex buy and integrate the Rolex movement factory in Biel. Then, in 2008, for its 100th birthday, the company built three gigantic new buildings with loads of steel and dark glass in the industrial suburb of Plan-les-Ouates. The latest automatic caliber 3255 suggests a brand still in innovation mode: It features new materials (nickel-phosphorus), special micromanufacturing technology (LIGA) to make the pallet fork and balance wheel of the Chronergy escapement, and a barrel spring that can store up more energy than ever.

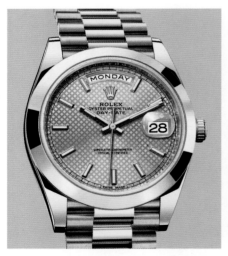

Oyster Perpetual Day-Date 40

Reference number: 228206
Movement: automatic, Rolex Caliber 3255, 31 jewels; 28,800 vph; Parachrom Breguet spring, Paraflex shock absorber, Chronergy escapement, glucydur balance with microstella regulating screws; 70-hour power reserve; COSC-certified chronometer
Functions: hours, minutes, sweep seconds; date, weekday
Case: platinum, ø 40 mm; sapphire crystal; screw-in crown; water-resistant to 10 atm
Band: President platinum, folding clasp
Price: $62,500
Variations: various dials; rose or white gold ($37,550); yellow gold ($34,850)

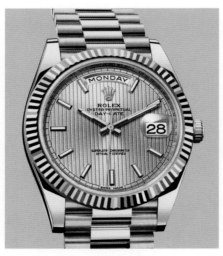

Oyster Perpetual Day-Date 40

Reference number: 228235
Movement: automatic, Rolex Caliber 3255, 31 jewels; 28,800 vph; Parachrom Breguet spring, Paraflex shock absorber, Chronergy escapement, glucydur balance with microstella regulating screws; 70-hour power reserve; COSC-certified chronometer
Functions: hours, minutes, sweep seconds; date, weekday
Case: rose gold, ø 40 mm; sapphire crystal; screw-in crown; water-resistant to 10 atm
Band: President rose gold, folding clasp
Price: $37,550
Variations: various dials; platinum ($62,500); white gold ($37,550); yellow gold ($34,850)

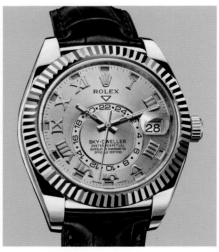

Oyster Perpetual Sky-Dweller

Reference number: 326138
Movement: automatic, Rolex Caliber 9001; ø 33 mm, height 8 mm; 40 jewels; 28,800 vph; Parachrom Breguet spring, Paraflex shock absorber, glucydur balance with microstella regulating screws; 72-hour power reserve; COSC-certified chronometer
Functions: hours, minutes, sweep seconds; 2nd time zone; annual calendar with date, month
Case: yellow gold, ø 42 mm, height 14.1 mm; bidirectional bezel controls functions; sapphire crystal; screw-in crown; water-resistant to 10 atm
Band: reptile skin, folding clasp
Price: $38,150

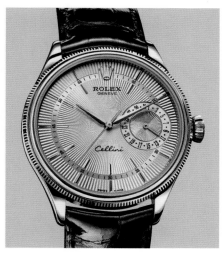

Cellini Time

Reference number: 50509
Movement: automatic, Rolex Caliber 3132 (base Caliber 3100); ø 28.5 mm; 31 jewels; 28,800 vph; Parachrom Breguet spring; 48-hour power reserve; COSC-certified chronometer
Functions: hours, minutes, sweep seconds
Case: white gold, ø 39 mm; sapphire crystal; screw-in crown; water-resistant to 5 atm
Band: reptile skin, buckle
Price: $15,200
Variations: various dials

Cellini Time

Reference number: 50505
Movement: automatic, Rolex Caliber 3132 (base Caliber 3100); ø 28.5 mm; 31 jewels; 28,800 vph; Parachrom Breguet spring; 48-hour power reserve; COSC-certified chronometer
Functions: hours, minutes, sweep seconds
Case: rose gold, ø 39 mm; sapphire crystal; screw-in crown; water-resistant to 5 atm
Band: reptile skin, buckle
Price: $15,200
Variations: various dials

Cellini Date

Reference number: 50519
Movement: automatic, Rolex Caliber 3165 (base Caliber 3187); 31 jewels; 28,800 vph; Parachrom Breguet spring; 48-hour power reserve; COSC-certified chronometer
Functions: hours, minutes, sweep seconds; date
Case: white gold, ø 39 mm; sapphire crystal; screw-in crown; water-resistant to 5 atm
Band: reptile skin, buckle
Price: $17,800
Variations: various dials

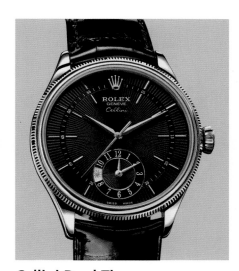

Cellini Date

Reference number: 50515
Movement: automatic, Rolex Caliber 3165 (base Caliber 3187); ø 31 jewels; 28,800 vph; Parachrom Breguet spring; 48-hour power reserve; COSC-certified chronometer
Functions: hours, minutes, sweep seconds; date
Case: rose gold, ø 39 mm; sapphire crystal; screw-in crown; water-resistant to 5 atm
Band: reptile skin, buckle
Price: $17,800
Variations: various dials

Cellini Dual Time

Reference number: 50529
Movement: automatic, Rolex Caliber 3180 (base Caliber 3187); 28,800 vph; Parachrom Breguet spring; 48-hour power reserve; COSC-certified chronometer
Functions: hours, minutes, sweep seconds; additional 12 hour display (2nd time zone), day/night indicator
Case: white gold, ø 39 mm; sapphire crystal; screw-in crown; water-resistant to 5 atm
Band: reptile skin, buckle
Price: $19,400
Variations: various dials

Cellini Dual Time

Reference number: 50525
Movement: automatic, Rolex Caliber 3180 (base Caliber 3187); 28,800 vph; Parachrom Breguet spring; 48-hour power reserve; COSC-certified chronometer
Functions: hours, minutes, sweep seconds; additional 12-hour display (2nd time zone); day/night indicator
Case: rose gold, ø 39 mm; sapphire crystal; screw-in crown; water-resistant to 5 atm
Band: reptile skin, buckle
Price: $19,400
Variations: various dials

Oyster Perpetual 39

Reference number: 114300
Movement: automatic, Rolex Caliber 3132 (base Caliber 3100); ø 28.5 mm, 31 jewels; 28,800 vph; Parachrom Breguet spring, Paraflex shock absorber, glucydur balance with microstella regulating screws; 48-hour power reserve, COSC-certified chronometer
Functions: hours, minutes, sweep seconds
Case: stainless steel, ø 39 mm; sapphire crystal; screw-in crown; water-resistant to 10 atm
Band: Oyster stainless steel, folding clasp
Price: $5,700

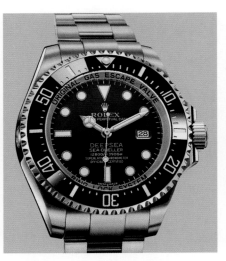

Oyster Perpetual DeepSea

Reference number: 116660
Movement: automatic, Rolex Caliber 3135; ø 28.5 mm, height 6 mm; 31 jewels; 28,800 vph; Parachrom Breguet spring, glucydur balance with microstella regulating screws; 48-hour power reserve; COSC-certified chronometer
Functions: hours, minutes, sweep seconds; date
Case: stainless steel, ø 44 mm; bezel with ceramic inlay, unidirectional bezel with 60-minute division; sapphire crystal; screw-in crown, helium valve; water-resistant to 390 atm
Band: Oyster stainless steel, safety folding clasp with extension link
Price: $12,050 (black dial); $12,350 (D-blue dial)

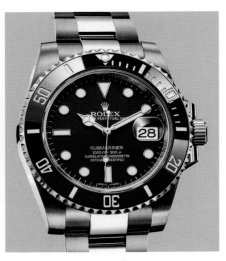

Oyster Perpetual Submariner Date

Reference number: 116619LB
Movement: automatic, Rolex Caliber 3135; ø 28.5 mm, height 6 mm; 31 jewels; 28,800 vph; Parachrom Breguet spring, glucydur balance with microstella regulating screws; 48-hour power reserve; COSC-certified chronometer
Functions: hours, minutes, sweep seconds; date
Case: white gold, ø 40 mm, height 12.5 mm; ceramic inlay on bezel, unidirectional bezel with 60-minute division; sapphire crystal; screw-in crown; water-resistant to 30 atm
Band: Oyster white gold, safety folding clasp
Price: $36,850

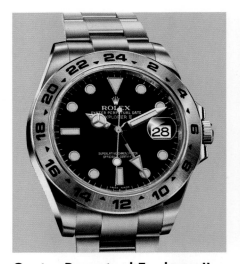

Oyster Perpetual Explorer II

Reference number: 216570
Movement: automatic, Rolex Caliber 3187 (base Caliber 3135); ø 28.5 mm, height 6.4 mm; 31 jewels; 28,800 vph; Parachrom Breguet spring; glucydur balance with microstella regulating bolts, Paraflex shock absorber; 48-hour power reserve; COSC-certified chronometer
Functions: hours, minutes, sweep seconds; additional 24-hour display (2nd time zone); date
Case: stainless steel, ø 42 mm, height 12.3 mm; bezel with 24-hour divisions; sapphire crystal; screw-in crown; water-resistant to 10 atm
Band: Oyster stainless steel, folding clasp with safety lock and extension link
Price: $8,100

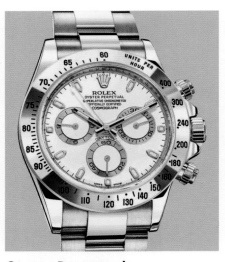

Oyster Perpetual Cosmograph Daytona

Reference number: 116523
Movement: automatic, Rolex Caliber 4130; ø 30.5 mm, height 6.5 mm; 44 jewels; 28,800 vph; Parachrom Breguet spring, glucydur balance with microstella regulating screws; 72-hour power reserve; COSC-certified chronometer
Functions: hours, minutes, subsidiary seconds; chronograph
Case: stainless steel, ø 40 mm, height 12.8 mm; yellow gold bezel, crown, pusher; sapphire crystal; screw-in crown, pusher; water-resistant to 10 atm
Band: Oyster stainless steel with yellow gold center links, safety folding clasp with extension link
Price: $16,900

Oyster Perpetual Yacht-Master 40

Reference number: 116655
Movement: automatic, Rolex Caliber 3135; ø 28.5 mm, height 6 mm; 31 jewels; 28,800 vph; Parachrom Breguet spring, glucydur balance with microstella regulating screws; 48-hour power reserve; COSC-certified chronometer
Functions: hours, minutes, sweep seconds; date
Case: rose gold, ø 40 mm, height 11.7 mm; bidirectional bezel with ceramic inlay and 60-minute division; sapphire crystal; screw-in crown; water-resistant to 10 atm
Band: Oysterflex strap with an Oysterlock clasp
Price: $24,950

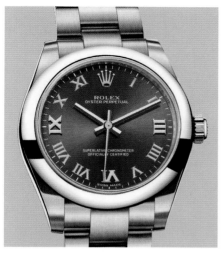

Oyster Perpetual 31

Reference number: 177200
Movement: automatic, Rolex Caliber 2231 (base Rolex Caliber 2230); ø 20 mm, height 5.95 mm; 31 jewels; 28,800 vph; glucydur balance with microstella regulating screws; 48-hour power reserve; COSC-certified chronometer
Functions: hours, minutes, sweep seconds
Case: stainless steel, ø 31 mm; sapphire crystal; screw-in crown; water-resistant to 10 atm
Band: Oyster stainless steel, folding clasp
Price: $4,950
Variations: various dials

Oyster Perpetual Datejust

Reference number: 116244
Movement: automatic, Rolex Caliber 3135; ø 28.5 mm, height 6 mm; 31 jewels; 28,800 vph; Parachrom Breguet spring, glucydur balance with microstella regulating screws; 42-hour power reserve; COSC-certified chronometer
Functions: hours, minutes, sweep seconds; date
Case: stainless steel, ø 36 mm, height 11.6 mm; white gold bezel with 52 diamonds; sapphire crystal; screw-in crown; water-resistant to 10 atm
Band: Oyster stainless steel, folding clasp with extension link
Remarks: mother-of-pearl dial with 10 diamonds
Price: $19,500

Oyster Perpetual 34

Reference number: 114200
Movement: automatic, Rolex Caliber 3132 (base Rolex Caliber 3135); ø 28.5 mm, 31 jewels; 28,800 vph; Parachrom Breguet spring, glucydur balance with microstella regulating screws; 48-hour power reserve; COSC-certified chronometer
Functions: hours, minutes, sweep seconds
Case: stainless steel, ø 34 mm; sapphire crystal; screw-in crown; water-resistant to 10 atm
Band: Oyster stainless steel, folding clasp
Price: $5,050
Variations: various dials

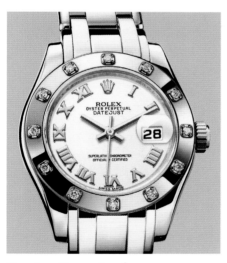

Oyster Perpetual Datejust Pearlmaster 34

Reference number: 81318
Movement: automatic, Rolex Caliber 2235 (base Caliber 2230); ø 20 mm, height 5.95 mm; 31 jewels; 28,800 vph; glucydur balance with microstella regulating screws; COSC-certified chronometer
Functions: hours, minutes, sweep seconds; date
Case: yellow gold, ø 34 mm, height 10.5 mm; 12 diamonds on bezel; sapphire crystal; screw-in crown, water-resistant to 10 atm
Band: Oyster yellow gold, folding clasp with extension link
Price: $34,550
Variations: various bands and dials

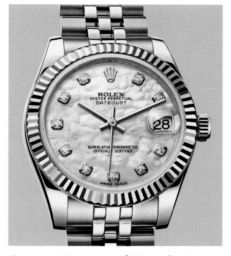

Oyster Perpetual Datejust Lady 31

Reference number: 178271
Movement: automatic, Rolex Caliber 2235 (base Caliber 2230); ø 20 mm, height 5.95 mm; 31 jewels; 28,800 vph; glucydur balance with microstella regulating screws; COSC-certified chronometer
Functions: hours, minutes, sweep seconds; date
Case: stainless steel, ø 31 mm, height 10.5 mm; rose gold bezel; sapphire crystal; screw-in crown; water-resistant to 10 atm
Band: Oyster stainless steel and rose gold, folding clasp with extension link
Remarks: dial set with 10 diamonds
Price: $11,400
Variations: various bands and dials

Oyster Perpetual Day-Date

Reference number: 118235
Movement: automatic, Rolex Caliber 3155 (base Caliber 3135); ø 28.5 mm, height 6.45 mm; 31 jewels; 28,800 vph; Parachrom Breguet spring, glucydur balance with microstella regulating screws; COSC-certified chronometer
Functions: hours, minutes, sweep seconds; date, weekday
Case: rose gold, ø 36 mm; sapphire crystal; screw-in crown; water-resistant to 10 atm
Band: Oyster rose gold, folding clasp
Price: $32,550
Variations: various bands and dials

Caliber 3255

Automatic; optimized Chronergy escapement, pallet lever and escape wheel made of nickel-phosphorus using LIGA process; single spring barrel, 70-hour power reserve; COSC-tested chronometer
Functions: hours, minutes, sweep seconds; weekday, date
Diameter: 29.1 mm
Height: 5.4 mm
Jewels: 31
Balance: glucydur balance with microstella regulating bolts
Frequency: 28,800 vph
Balance spring: Parachrom Breguet spring
Shock protection: Paraflex
Remarks: used in Day-Date 40

Caliber 4130

Automatic; single spring barrel, 42-hour power reserve; COSC-tested chronometer
Functions: hours, minutes, subsidiary seconds; chronograph
Diameter: 30.5 mm
Height: 6.5 mm
Jewels: 44
Balance: glucydur balance with microstella regulating screws
Frequency: 28,800 vph
Balance spring: Parachrom with Breguet overcoil
Shock protection: KIF
Remarks: used in Daytona

Caliber 4161

Base caliber: Caliber 4130
Automatic; single spring barrel, 72-hour power reserve; COSC-tested chronometer
Functions: hours, minutes, subsidiary seconds; programmable regatta countdown with memory
Diameter: 31.2 mm
Height: 8.05 mm
Jewels: 42
Balance: glucydur balance with microstella regulating bolts
Frequency: 28,800 vph
Balance spring: Parachrom Breguet spring
Shock protection: KIF
Remarks: used in Yacht-Master II

Caliber 3135

Automatic; single spring barrel, 42-hour power reserve; COSC-tested chronometer
Functions: hours, minutes, sweep seconds; date
Diameter: 28.5 mm
Height: 8.05 mm
Jewels: 42
Balance: glucydur balance with microstella regulating screws
Frequency: 28,800 vph
Balance spring: Parachrom with Breguet overcoil
Shock protection: KIF

Caliber 3156

Automatic; single spring barrel, 42-hour power reserve; COSC-tested chronometer
Functions: hours, minutes, sweep seconds; date, weekday
Diameter: 28.5 mm
Height: 6.45 mm
Jewels: 31
Balance: glucydur balance with microstella regulating screws
Frequency: 28,800 vph
Balance spring: Parachrom spring
Remarks: used in Day-Date II

Caliber 9001

Automatic; single spring barrel, 72-hour power reserve; COSC-tested chronometer
Functions: hours, minutes, sweep seconds; additional 24-hour display (2nd time zone); annual calendar with date, month
Diameter: 33 mm
Height: 8 mm
Jewels: 40
Balance: glucydur balance with microstella regulating bolts
Frequency: 28,800 vph
Balance spring: Parachrom Breguet spring
Shock protection: KIF
Remarks: used in Sky-Dweller

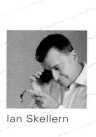

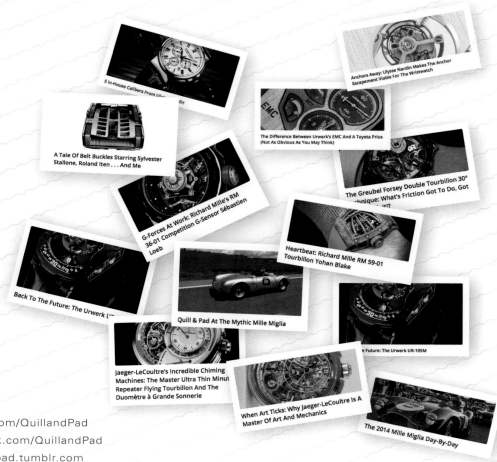

RJ Watches SA

11 Rue du Marché
CH-1204 Geneva
Switzerland

Tel.:
+41-22-319-29-39

Fax:
+41-22-319-29-30

E-Mail:
info@romainjerome.ch

Website:
www.romainjerome.ch

Founded:
2004

Number of employees:
approx. 20

Annual production:
3,000 watches and accessories

Distribution:
Please contact RJ-Romain Jerome
headquarters in Switzerland for any enquiries.

Most important collections/price range:
Titanic-DNA, Moon-DNA, Capsules,
Steampunk, Pac Man, DNA series / from
$8,000 to approx. $300,000 for highly
complicated watches

Romain Jerome

Tchaikovsky once said that he always put his best ideas into his work—and took them out again when editing. This singular approach to creativity makes its own kind of sense, but in a world where the hypest is the hippest, it may not be the most successful. When the fiery Yvan Arpa took hold of the barely known Romain Jerome in 2006, he quickly transformed its products, digging up unique and strange materials that caused the kind of chatter that means business—because there is no such thing as negative feedback. Quality and design, however, followed strict rules. The watches came in historical materials that connect the wearer to the bigger picture: bits of *Apollo 11*, moon dust, fibers from the space suits worn during the *International Space Station* mission.

Under the new CEO Manuel Emch, the brand weaned itself slowly from the antics that put it on the map. The oversize Moon Invader saw a shift toward a cooler techno design using the company's stock of lunar module shreds. The Steampunk Chrono won the "Couture Time Award for Watch Architecture" in Las Vegas in 2012. The transparent Skylab reflects the immaculateness of a scientific research space.

History remains a theme. To celebrate the twenty-fifth anniversary of the fall of the Berlin Wall, the designers at RJ have come up with a map of the city tracing where the divide once stood. For the Spacecraft, a seventies-style sci-fi time-telling trapezoidal object with a linear hour line on the side and a minute disc on top, Emch collaborated with Eric Giroud and Jean-Marc Wiederrecht. As for the Pac Man, it is an especially delightful way to remember the stylistically somewhat underendowed eighties. And with the streamlining of the look has come the added attraction of readjusted prices.

Subcraft Titanium

Reference number: RJ.T.AU.SC.001.01
Movement: automatic; Caliber RJ2000-A;
36.4 x 33.26 mm, height 5.9 mm; 54 jewels;
28,800 vph; 38-hour power reserve
Functions: linear, retrograde, and jumping hour indicated by white-lacquered cursor; dragging minutes on black disc with white numerals
Case: bead-blasted titanium; 52.3 x 40.1 mm, height 17 mm; sapphire crystal; water-resistant to 3 atm
Band: calf leather, buckle
Price: $26,950; limited to 99 pieces

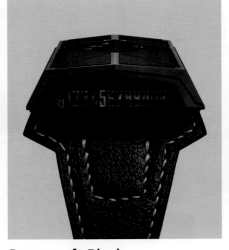

Spacecraft Black

Reference number: RJ.M.AU.SC.002.01
Movement: automatic; Caliber RJ2000-A;
36.4 x 33.26 mm, height 5.9 mm; 54 jewels;
28,800 vph; 38-hour power reserve
Functions: linear, retrograde, and jumping hour indicated by orange-lacquered cursor; dragging minutes on black disc with white numerals
Case: trapezoidal, titanium with black PVD, 50 x 44.5 x 32.85 mm; height 18.5 mm; metallized sapphire crystal; water-resistant to 3 atm
Band: buffalo, titanium buckle
Price: $29,500; limited to 25 pieces

Skylab 48 Speed Metal

Reference number: RJ.M.AU.030.01
Movement: manual, Caliber RJ004-M; ø 34.4 mm, height 5.6 mm; 21 jewels; 28,800 vph; skeletonized and black chrome finished; 48-hour power reserve
Functions: hours, minutes, subsidiary seconds
Case: steel, ø 48 mm, height 12 mm; sapphire case back; water-resistant to 3 atm
Band: reptile skin, buckle
Price: $20,950; limited to 99 pieces

Steampunk Auto Gunmetal

Reference number: RJ.T.AU.SP.006.01
Movement: automatic, Caliber RJ003-A;
ø 26.2 mm, height 5.05 mm; 30 jewels;
28,800 vph; 40-hour power reserve
Functions: hours, minutes, subsidiary seconds
Case: steel and black PVD-coated steel, ø 46 mm,
height 12.8 mm; gunmetal bezel; water-resistant
to 3 atm
Band: calf-leather, buckle
Price: $10,950; limited to 999 pieces

Moon Orbiter Speed Metal

Reference number: RJ.M.TO.MO.002.01
Movement: automatic, Caliber RJ3000;
42.2 x 29.8 mm, height 13.2 mm; 32 jewels;
28,800 vph; 1-minute flying tourbillon; 42-hour
power reserve
Functions: hours, minutes; power reserve indicator
Case: black PVD-coated steel, 44.5 x 48.5 mm,
height 20.3 mm; 5 shaped antireflective sapphire
crystals; sapphire crystal back; water-resistant to
3 atm
Band: reptile skin, buckle
Remarks: moon dust with laser engraved "stellar
pattern" on dial, elements from *Apollo 11* spacecraft
Price: $133,500; limited to 25 pieces

Steampunk Chrono Red

Reference number: RJ.T.CH.SP.003.01
Movement: automatic; Caliber RJ001-CS;
ø 30.4 mm, height 6.6 mm; 39 jewels; 28,800 vph;
42-hour power reserve
Functions: hours, minutes, subsidiary seconds;
chronograph, 30-minute totalizer at 3 o'clock
Case: steel; ø 50 mm, height 16.6 mm;
antireflective sapphire crystal; water-resistant to
3 atm
Band: black rubber, pink folding clasp
Remarks: bezel stabilized steel from *Titanic*;
integrated dial; bead-blasted, satin-brushed
ruthenium-colored bridge; mobile propeller at 6
Price: $32,950; limited to 2,012 pieces

Berlin-DNA

Reference number: RJ.T.AU.BE.001
Movement: automatic; Caliber RJ001-A;
ø 30.4 mm, height 7.9 mm; 23 jewels; 28,800 vph;
42-hour power reserve
Functions: hours, minutes
Case: black PVD-coated steel; ø 46 mm; height
17.1 mm; sapphire crystal; case back with *The
Brother Kiss* engraving by Dmitri Vrubel; water-
resistant to 3 atm
Band: reptile skin, black PVD-coated steel folding
clasp
Remarks: 3D map of Berlin on dial; cement from
Berlin Wall integrated into dial
Price: $15,950; limited edition of 25 pieces

Batman-DNA

Reference number: RJ.T.AU.WB.001.01
Movement: automatic; Caliber RJ001-A;
ø 30.4 mm, height 7.9 mm; 23 jewels; 28,800 vph;
42-hour power reserve
Functions: hours, minutes
Case: black PVD-coated steel, ø 46 mm, height
17.1 mm; water-resistant to 3 atm
Band: reptile skin, black PVD-coated steel folding
clasp
Remarks: faceted bezel in black-PVD-coated steel;
graphite engraving and Batman logo applique on
dial with black Superluminova C1 "blue emission"
Price: $18,500; limited edition of 75 pieces

Pac Man Level II

Reference number: RJ.M.AU.IN.009.05
Movement: automatic, automatic; Caliber RJ001-A;
ø 30.4 mm, height 7.9 mm; 23 jewels; 28,800 vph;
42-hour power reserve
Functions: hours, minutes
Case: black PVD-coated steel; ø 46 mm, height
16.6 mm; antireflective sapphire crystal; Pac Man
medallion on case back; water-resistant to 3 atm
Band: black rubber, black PVD-coated steel folding
clasp
Price: $18,950; limited to 20 pieces

Seiko Holdings
Ginza, Chuo, Tokyo
Japan

Website:
www.seikowatches.com

Founded:
1881

U.S. distributor:
Seiko Corporation of America
1111 Macarthur Boulevard
Mahwah, NJ 07430
201-529-5730
custserv@seikousa.com
www.seikousa.com

Most important collections/price range:
Grand Seiko / approx. $5,000 to $14,500;
Ananta / approx. $2,400 to $8,500;
Astron / approx. $1,850 to $3,400; Seiko
Elite (Sportura, Premier, Velatura, Arctura) /
approx. $430 to $1,500; Prospex / approx.
$395 to $6,000

Seiko

The Japanese watch giant is a part of the Seiko Holding Company, but the development and production of its watches are fully self-sufficient. Seiko makes every variety of portable timepiece and offers mechanical watches with both manual and automatic winding, quartz watches with battery and solar power or with the brand's own mechanical "Kinetic" power generation, as well as the groundbreaking "Spring Drive" hybrid technology. This intelligent mix of mechanical energy generation and electronic regulation is reserved for Seiko's top models.

Also in the top segment of the brand is the Grand Seiko line, a group of watches that enjoys cult status among international collectors. For the line's fiftieth anniversary, the Tokyo-based company put together an extensive collection of new models and, for the first time, officially offered them to the global market. Today, there are several watches with the interesting Spring Drive technology, but most new Grand Seikos are conventional, mechanical hand-wound and automatic watches.

Classic Seikos are designed for tradition-conscious buyers. The Astron, however, with its automatic GPS-controlled time setting, suggests the watch of the future. In its second incarnation, the Astron is 30 percent more compact, and the energy required by the GPS system inside is supplied by a high-tech solar cell on the dial. As for the new Prospex collection, released for the 50th anniversary of the first Seiko diver's watches, it has an unmistakably modern look. The old protective case of the Marinemaster is now of ceramic instead of plastic.

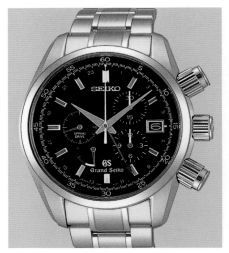

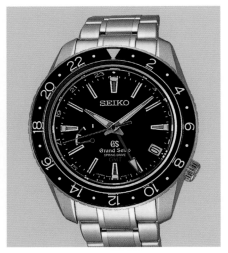

Grand Seiko Spring Drive Chronograph

Reference number: SBGC003
Movement: manually wound, Seiko Spring Drive Caliber 9R86; ø 30 mm, height 7.6 mm; 50 jewels; electromagnetic Tri-Synchro Regulator escapement system with sliding wheel; column wheel control of chronograph functions/vertical clutch
Functions: hours, minutes, subsidiary seconds; 12-hour display; chronograph; date; power reserve indicator
Case: stainless steel, ø 43.5 mm, height 16 mm; sapphire crystal; transparent case back, water-resistant to 10 atm
Band: stainless steel, folding clasp
Price: $7,700
Variations: light dial, titanium ($9,100)

Grand Seiko Automatic Hi-Beat 36,000 GMT

Reference number: SBGT001
Movement: automatic, Seiko Caliber 9S86; ø 28.4 mm, height 5.9 mm; 37 jewels; 36,000 vph; antimagnetic up to 4,800 A/m; 55-hour power reserve
Functions: hours, minutes, sweep seconds; additional 12-hour display (2nd time zone); date
Case: stainless steel, ø 40 mm, height 14 mm; sapphire crystal; transparent case back; screw-in crown; water-resistant to 10 atm
Band: titanium, safety folding clasp
Price: $6,000
Variations: black dial ($6,000)

Grand Seiko Spring Drive GMT

Reference number: SBGE011
Movement: manually wound, Seiko Caliber 9R66; ø 30 mm, height 5.1 mm; 30 jewels; electromagnetical Tri-Synchro Regulator escapement system with sliding wheel; 72-hour power reserve
Functions: hours, minutes, sweep seconds; additional 24-hour display (2nd time zone), power reserve indicator; date
Case: stainless steel, ø 43.5 mm, height 14.5 mm; unidirectional bezel with 24-hour divisions; sapphire crystal; transparent case back; screw-in crown; water-resistant to 20 atm
Band: stainless steel, folding clasp
Price: $5,100

Astron GPS Solar Chronograph

Reference number: SSE003J1
Movement: quartz, Seiko Caliber 8X82; solar energy-saving function
Functions: hours, minutes, sweep seconds; additional 24-hour display; world-time display (GPS in 39 time zones), flight mode, signal reception indicator; power reserve display, DST indicator; chronograph; date
Case: titanium with titanium carbide coating; ø 45 mm, height 14 mm; ceramic bezel, sapphire crystal; screw-in crown; water-resistant to 10 atm
Band: titanium, folding clasp
Price: $2,300
Variations: various cases and dials

Astron GPS Solar Dual Time

Reference number: SSE041J1
Movement: quartz, Seiko Caliber 8X53; independent energy generation using solar cells in dial
Functions: hours, minutes, sweep seconds; additional 12-hour display; world-time display (GPS alignment of 40 time zones), flight mode; signal reception indicator, DST indicator; power reserve display; perpetual calendar with date, weekday
Case: titanium with titanium carbide layer, ø 45 mm, height 13.3 mm; ceramic bezel; sapphire crystal; screw-in crown; water-resistant to 10 atm
Band: titanium with ceramic inserts, folding clasp
Price: on request
Variations: various cases and dials

Prospex Automatic Marinemaster Professional 1000m

Reference number: SBDX014G
Movement: automatic, Seiko Caliber 8L35; ø 28.4 mm, height 5.39 mm; 26 jewels; 50-hour power reserve
Functions: hours, minutes, sweep seconds; date
Case: ceramic, titanium inner case; ø 48.2 mm, height 17.4 mm; rose gold-colored PVD coating on bezel and crown, unidirectional bezel with 60-minute divisions; sapphire crystal; screw-in crown; water-resistant to 100 atm
Band: rubber, buckle
Price: $3,250

Seiko Prospex Kinetic GMT

Reference number: SUN019
Movement: quartz, Seiko Caliber 5M85; own energy source from rotor-driven micro-generator; up to 6-month power reserve
Functions: hours, minutes, sweep seconds; additional 24-hour display (2nd time zone), power reserve indicator; date
Case: stainless steel with titanium carbide coating, ø 45.6 mm, height 13.6 mm; unidirectional bezel with 360 divisions; plexiglass; transparent case back
Band: stainless steel, folding clasp
Price: $725
Variations: black coated case; leather strap

Premier Kinetic Direct Drive Mondphase

Reference number: SRX011P1
Movement: quartz, Seiko Caliber 5D88; own energy source from micro-generator with rotor-drive; hand winding; 1-month power reserve
Functions: hours, minutes, sweep seconds; additional 24-hour display (2nd time zone), power reserve indicator; full calendar with date, weekday, moon phase
Case: stainless steel, ø 41.5 mm, height 12.5 mm; sapphire crystal
Band: stainless steel, folding clasp
Price: $995

Sportura Solar Chronograph with Perpetual Calendar

Reference number: SSC357P1
Movement: quartz, independent energy generation using solar cells in dial
Functions: hours, minutes, subsidiary seconds; power reserve indicator; chronograph with alarm; perpetual calendar with date, weekday, leap year
Case: stainless steel, ø 45 mm, height 12.2 mm; sapphire crystal; screw-in crown; water-resistant to 10 atm
Band: stainless steel, folding clasp
Price: $575
Variations: light dial and leather strap

Sinn Spezialuhren GmbH
Im Füldchen 5-7
D-60489 Frankfurt / Main
Germany

Tel.:
+49-69-9784-14-200

Fax:
+49-69-9784-14-201

E-Mail:
info@sinn.de

Website:
www.sinn.de

Founded:
1961

Number of employees:
approx. 100

Annual production:
approx. 12,500 watches

U.S. distributor:
WatchBuys
888-333-4895
www.watchbuys.com

Most important collections/price range:
Financial District, U-Models, Diapal / from
approx. $700 to $27,500

Sinn

Pilot and flight instructor Helmut Sinn began manufacturing watches in Frankfurt am Main because he thought the pilot's watches on the market were too expensive. The resulting combination of top quality, functionality, and a good price-performance ratio turned out to be an excellent sales argument. Sinn Spezialuhren zu Frankfurt am Main is a brand with origins in technology. There is hardly another source that offers watch lovers such a sophisticated and reasonable collection of sporty watches, many conceived to survive in extreme conditions by conforming to German DIN industrial norms.

In 1994, Lothar Schmidt took over the brand, and his product developers began looking for inspiration in other industries and the sciences. They did so out of a practical technical impulse without any plan for launching a trend. Research and development are consistently aimed at improving the functionality of the watches. This includes application of special Sinn technology like moisture-proofing cases by pumping in an inert gas, like argon. Other Sinn innovations include the Diapal (a lubricant-free lever escapement), the Hydro (an oil-filled diver's watch), and tegiment processing (for hardened steel and titanium surfaces). Having noticed a lack of norms for aviator watches, Schmidt negotiated a partnership with the Aachen Technical University to create the Technischer Standard Fliegeruhren (TESTAF, or Technical Standards for Aviator Watches), which is housed at the Eurocopter headquarters.

Recently, Sinn Spezialuhren tied a tighter knot with its "native" city by opening a workshop and sales rooms in the historic Haus zum Goldenen Rad (House of the Golden Wheel) right in the center of the old town, next to the famous Town Hall.

240 St

Reference number: 240.010
Movement: automatic, Sellita Caliber SW220-1; ø 25.6 mm, height 5.05 mm; 26 jewels; 28,800 vph; shockproof and antimagnetic; 38-hour power reserve
Functions: hours, minutes, sweep seconds; date, weekday
Case: stainless steel, pearl-blasted, ø 43 mm, height 11 mm; inner ring rotated via crown, with 60-minute division, sapphire crystal; water-resistant to 10 atm
Band: calf leather, buckle
Price: $1,560

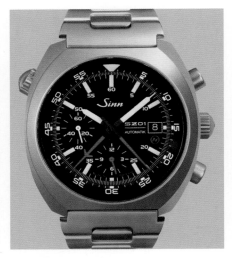

140 St

Reference number: 140.020
Movement: automatic, Sinn Caliber SZ 01 (base ETA 7750); ø 30 mm, height 8.5 mm; 28 jewels; 28,800 vph; sweep minute counter, shockproof, antimagnetic
Functions: hours, minutes, subsidiary seconds; chronograph; date
Case: tegimented stainless steel, ø 44 mm, height 15 mm; inner ring rotated with the crown, with 60-minute division, sapphire crystal; pusher with D3 seal; water-resistant to 10 atm
Band: stainless steel tegimented, folding clasp with safety lock and extension link
Remarks: Ar-dehumidifying technology
Price: $5,430

U212 S E

Reference number: 212.030
Movement: automatic, Sellita Caliber SW300-1; ø 25.6 mm, height 3.6 mm; 25 jewels; 28,800 vph; 42-hour power reserve
Functions: hours, minutes, seconds; date
Case: stainless steel tegimented, submarine steel with black PVD coating, ø 47 mm, height 14.5 mm; unidirectional bezel with 60-minute division; sapphire crystal; screw-in crown; water-resistant to 100 atm
Band: silicon, safety folding clasp with extension link
Remarks: EU diving certified; Ar-dehumidifying
Price: $2,870; limited to 300 pieces

EZM 10 TESTAF

Reference number: 950.011
Movement: automatic, Sinn Caliber SZ 01 (base ETA 7750); ø 30 mm, height 8.5 mm; 28 jewels; 28,800 vph; shockproof, antimagnetic; lubricant-free escapement (Diapal), sweep minute counter
Functions: hours, minutes, subsidiary seconds; additional 24-hour display; chronograph; date
Case: tegimented/pearl-blasted titanium, ø 46.5 mm, height 15.6 mm; bidirectional bezel with 60-minute division, sapphire crystal; screw-in crown; hard-coated pushers; water-resistant to 20 atm
Band: calf leather, buckle
Remarks: TESTAF-certified; Ar-dehumidifying
Price: $5,830
Variations: tegimented titanium bracelet ($6,850)

EZM 9 TESTAF

Reference number: 949.010
Movement: automatic, Sellita Caliber SW200-1; ø 25.6 mm, height 4.6 mm; 26 jewels; 28,800 vph; shockproof and antimagnetic; 38-hour power reserve
Functions: hours, minutes, sweep seconds; date
Case: tegimented titanium; ø 44 mm, height 12 mm; unidirectional bezel with 60-minute division, sapphire crystal; water-resistant to 20 atm
Band: tegimented titanium, folding clasp with safety lock and extension link
Remarks: TESTAF-certified; Ar-dehumidifying
Price: $4,600
Variations: leather strap ($3,940)

EZM 3 F

Reference number: 703.010
Movement: automatic, ETA Caliber 2824-2; ø 25.6 mm, height 4.6 mm; 25 jewels; 28,800 vph; shockproof and antimagnetic; 38-hour power reserve
Functions: hours, minutes, sweep seconds; date
Case: stainless steel, ø 41 mm, height 13 mm; unidirectional bezel with 60-minute division; sapphire crystal; screw-in crown; water-resistant to 20 atm
Band: calf leather, buckle
Remarks: EU diving-certified; Ar-dehumidifying; magnetic field protection to 80,000 A/m
Price: $1,830

EZM 13 Diver's Chronograph

Reference number: 613.010
Movement: automatic, Sinn Caliber SZ 02 (base ETA 7750); ø 30.4 mm, height 7.9 mm; 25 jewels; 28,800 vph; 60-minute counter; shockproof, antimagnetic; 42-hour power reserve
Functions: hours, minutes, subsidiary seconds; chronograph; date
Case: stainless steel, ø 41.5 mm, height 15 mm; unidirectional bezel with 60-minute division, sapphire crystal; water-resistant to 50 atm
Band: silicon, buckle
Remarks: EU diving-certified; Ar-dehumidifying; magnetic field protection to 80,000 A/m
Price: $2,960
Variations: stainless steel band ($3,150)

U1000 S

Reference number: 1011.020
Movement: automatic, Sinn Caliber SZ 02 (base ETA 7750); ø 30.4 mm, height 7.9 mm; 25 jewels; 28,800 vph; shockproof, antimagnetic; 60-minute totalizer; lubrication; 42-hour power reserve
Functions: hours, minutes, subsidiary seconds; chronograph; date
Case: submarine steel, tegimented with black PVD coating; ø 44 mm, height 18 mm; unidirectional bezel with 60-minute division, sapphire crystal; screw-in crown, D-3 seal pushers; water-resistant to 100 atm
Band: silicon, folding clasp
Remarks: EU diving-certified; Ar-dehumidifying
Price: $5,250
Variations: w/o coating ($4,970); black bezel ($5,540)

T1 (EZM 14)

Reference number: 1014.010
Movement: automatic, SOP A10-2A (base Soprod A10); ø 25.6 mm, height 3.6 mm; 25 jewels; 28,800 vph; shockproof, antimagnetic; 42-hour power reserve
Functions: hours, minutes, sweep seconds; date
Case: bead-blasted titanium, ø 45 mm, height 12.5 mm; unidirectional bezel with 60-minute division, sapphire crystal; screw-in crown; water-resistant to 100 atm
Band: silicon, folding clasp with safety lock/ extension link
Remarks: EU diving-certified; Ar-dehumidifying
Price: $3,560
Variations: titanium bracelet ($3,560); "T2" model ($3,370)

856 UTC

Reference number: 856.010
Movement: automatic, ETA Caliber 2893-2;
ø 25.6 mm, height 4.1 mm; 21 jewels; 28,800 vph;
shockproof, antimagnetic; 42-hour power reserve
Functions: hours, minutes, sweep seconds; added
24-hour display; date
Case: tegimented stainless steel, ø 40 mm, height
11 mm; sapphire crystal
Band: silicon, folding clasp
Remarks: Ar-dehumidifying technology
Price: $2,775
Variations: w/o 2nd time zone (model 856:
$1,770); rotating bezel (model 857; $2,190)

757 DIAPAL

Reference number: 757.030
Movement: automatic, ETA Caliber 7750;
ø 30.4 mm, height 7.9 mm; 25 jewels; 28,800 vph;
lubricant-free escapement (Diapal)
Functions: hours, minutes; added 12-hour display;
chronograph; date
Case: stainless steel, ø 43 mm, height 15 mm;
bidirectional bezel with 60-minute division, sapphire
crystal; screw-in crown; water-resistant to 20 atm
Band: tegimented stainless steel, double folding clasp
Remarks: Ar-dehumidifying; antimagnetic to
80,000 A/m
Price: $4,390
Variations: 757 w/o Diapal escapement ($2,940),
757 UTC with 2nd time zone ($3,650)

EZM 7 S

Reference number: 857.050
Movement: automatic, ETA Caliber 2893-2;
ø 26.2 mm, height 4.1 mm; 21 jewels; 28,800 vph;
shockproof, antimagnetic; 38-hour power reserve
Functions: hours, minutes, sweep seconds; added
24-hour display (2nd time zone); date
Case: tegimented stainless steel with black PVD
coating, ø 43 mm, height 12 mm; unidirectional
bezel with 60-minute division; sapphire crystal;
screw-in crown; water-resistant to 20 atm
Band: stainless steel tegimented, black PVD coating
Remarks: Ar-dehumidifying; antimagnetic to
80,000 A/m
Price: $2,860; limited to 300 pieces
Variations: stainless steel w/o coating ($2,790)

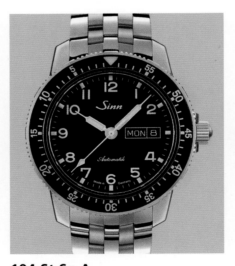

556 I

Reference number: 556.010
Movement: automatic, ETA Caliber 2824-2;
ø 25.6 mm, height 4.6 mm; 25 jewels; 28,800 vph;
shockproof, antimagnetic; 38-hour power reserve
Functions: hours, minutes, sweep seconds; date
Case: stainless steel, ø 38.5 mm, height 11 mm;
sapphire crystal, transparent case back; water-
resistant to 20 atm
Band: calf leather, buckle
Price: $1,020

104 St Sa A

Reference number: 104.011
Movement: automatic, Sellita Caliber SW220-
1; ø 25.6 mm, height 5.05 mm; 26 jewels;
28,800 vph; shockproof, antimagnetic; 38-hour
power reserve
Functions: hours, minutes, sweep seconds; date,
weekday
Case: stainless steel, ø 41 mm, height 11.5 mm;
bidirectional bezel with 60-minute division; sapphire
crystal; transparent case back; screw-in crown;
water-resistant to 20 atm
Band: stainless steel, folding clasp
Price: $1,560
Variations: index dial

103 St Sa

Reference number: 103.061
Movement: automatic, ETA Caliber 7750;
ø 30.4 mm, height 7.9 mm; 25 jewels; 28,800 vph;
42-hour power reserve
Functions: hours, minutes, subsidiary seconds;
chronograph; date, weekday
Case: stainless steel, ø 41 mm, height 17 mm;
bidirectional bezel with 60-minute division; sapphire
crystal; transparent case back; screw-in crown and
pusher; water-resistant to 20 atm
Band: calf leather, buckle
Price: $2,150
Variations: as 103 St with plexiglass ($1,640); as
103 Diapal in titanium ($3,920); as 103 TESTAF
pilot's watch ($2,980)

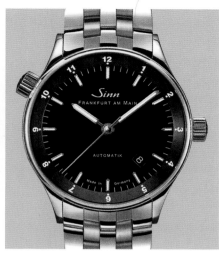

6000 Rose Gold

Reference number: 6000.040
Movement: automatic, modified SW 500;
ø 30.4 mm, height 7.9 mm; 26 jewels; 28,800 vph;
fine finishing; shockproof, antimagnetic; 42-hour
power reserve
Functions: hours, minutes, subsidiary seconds;
added 12-hour display (2nd time zone);
chronograph; date
Case: rose gold, ø 38.5 mm, height 16.5 mm;
crown-adjustable inner bezel with 12-hour divisions;
sapphire crystal; transparent case back; water-
resistant to 10 atm
Band: reptile skin, buckle
Price: $15,400
Variations: stainless steel ($4,320)

6052

Reference number: 6052.010
Movement: automatic, Sinn Caliber SZ 03 (base
ETA 7751); ø 30 mm, height 7.9 mm; 26 jewels;
28,800 vph; shockproof, antimagnetic; 42-hour
power reserve
Functions: hours, minutes, subsidiary seconds;
chronograph; annual calendar with date, weekday,
month
Case: stainless steel, ø 41.5 mm, height 14.5 mm;
sapphire crystal; transparent case back; water-
resistant to 10 atm
Band: calf leather, buckle
Remarks: extra stainless steel bracelet, changing
tool
Price: $4,980

6068

Reference number: 6068.010
Movement: automatic, Sellita Caliber SW300-1;
ø 25.6 mm, height 3.6 mm; 25 jewels; 28,800 vph;
shockproof, antimagnetic; 42-hour power reserve
Functions: hours, minutes, sweep seconds; date
Case: stainless steel, ø 38.5 mm, height 12 mm;
inner ring rotated with the crown, with 12-hour
division; sapphire crystal; transparent case back;
water-resistant to 10 atm
Band: stainless steel, folding clasp
Price: $1,980
Variations: as 6033 with ø 34 mm case ($2,370)

1746 Classic

Reference number: 1746.011
Movement: automatic, ETA Caliber 2892-A2;
ø 26.2 mm, height 3.6 mm; 21 jewels; 28,800 vph;
shockproof, antimagnetic
Functions: hours, minutes; date
Case: stainless steel, ø 42 mm, height 9.5 mm;
sapphire crystal; transparent case back; water-
resistant to 10 atm
Band: calf leather, buckle
Remarks: enamel dial
Price: $2,140
Variations: smaller 1736 Classic model ($2,375)

903 St B E

Reference number: 903.045
Movement: automatic, Sellita Caliber SW500;
ø 30 mm, height 7.9 mm; 26 jewels; 28,800 vph;
38-hour power reserve
Functions: hours, minutes, subsidiary seconds;
chronograph; date
Case: stainless steel, ø 41 mm, height 14.5 mm;
crown-adjustable inner bezel with slide rule function;
sapphire crystal; transparent case back; screw-in
crown; water-resistant to 10 atm
Band: calf leather, buckle
Price: $3,120
Variations: black or silver-plated dial

6110 Classic B

Reference number: 6110.010
Movement: manually wound, ETA Caliber 6498-1;
ø 36.6 mm, height 4.5 mm; 17 jewels; 18,000 vph;
shockproof, antimagnetic; 38-hour power reserve
Functions: hours, minutes, subsidiary seconds
Case: stainless steel, ø 44 mm, height 10.6 mm;
sapphire crystal; transparent case back; water-
resistant to 10 atm
Band: calf leather, buckle
Price: $2,620

Stowa GmbH & Co. KG

Gewerbepark 16
D-75331 Engelsbrand
Germany

Tel.:
+49-7082-9306-0

Fax:
+49-7082-9306-2

E-Mail:
info@stowa.com

Website:
www.stowa.com

Founded:
1927

Number of employees:
20

Annual production:
around 4,500 watches

Distribution:
direct sales; please contact company in Germany; orders taken by phone Monday-Friday 9 a.m. to 5 p.m. European time. Note: prices determined according to daily exchange rate.

Stowa

When a watch brand organizes a museum for itself, it is usually with good reason. The firm Stowa may not be the biggest fish in the horological pond, but it has been around for more than eighty years, and its products are well worth taking a look at as expressions of German watchmaking culture. Stowa began in Pforzheim, then moved to the little industrial town of Rheinfelden, and now operates in Engelsbrand, a "suburb" of Pforzheim. After a history as a family-owned company, today the brand is headed by Jörg Schauer, who has maintained the goal and vision of original founder Walter Storz: delivering quality watches at a reasonable price.

Stowa is one of the few German brands to have operated without interruption since the start of the twentieth century, albeit with a new owner as of 1990. Besides all the political upheavals, it survived the quartz crisis of the 1970s, during which Europe was flooded with cheap watches from Asia and many traditional German watchmakers were put out of business. Storz managed to keep Stowa going, but even a quality fanatic has to pay a price during times of trouble: With huge input from his son, Werner, Storz restructured the company so that it was able to begin encasing reasonably priced quartz movements rather than being strictly an assembler of mechanical ones.

Schauer bought the brand in 1996. Spurred on by the success of his own eponymous line, he also steered Stowa back toward mechanical watches, taking inspiration from older Stowa timepieces but using Swiss ETA movements. But the way out of the retro trap was about to become apparent: In 2015, Schauer joined forces with Hartmut Esslinger to create the Rana (frog) model, with an almost ethereal case and a modern dial, whose dot markers (DynaDots they are called) grow larger by the hour.

Flieger Without Logo

Reference number: FliegerohneLogo
Movement: automatic, ETA Caliber 2824-2; ø 25.6 mm, height 4.6 mm; 25 jewels; 28,800 vph; blued screws; handmade German silver rotor
Functions: hours, minutes, sweep seconds
Case: stainless steel, ø 40 mm, height 10.2 mm; sapphire crystal; water-resistant to 5 atm
Band: calf leather, buckle (optionally folding clasp)
Price: $837
Variations: reptile band or stainless steel bracelet ($945)

Antea Small Seconds

Reference number: AnteaKS
Movement: automatic, ETA Caliber 7001; ø 23.3 mm, height 2.5 mm; 17 jewels, 21,600 vph; finely finished with côtes de Genéve, blued screws; 42-hour power reserve
Functions: hours, minutes, subsidiary seconds
Case: stainless steel, ø 35.5 mm, height 6.9 mm; sapphire crystal; transparent case back; water-resistant to 3 atm
Band: deer skin, buckle
Price: $882
Variations: reptile skin band or stainless steel bracelet ($990)

Antea "Back to Bauhaus"

Reference number: Antea355b2b
Movement: manually wound, ETA Caliber 7001; ø 23.3 mm, height 2.5 mm; 17 jewels; 21,600 vph; finely finished with côtes de Genéve, blued screws; 42-hour power reserve
Functions: hours, minutes, subsidiary seconds
Case: stainless steel, ø 35.5 mm, height 6.9 mm; sapphire crystal; transparent case back; water-resistant to 3 atm
Band: calf leather, buckle or folding clasp
Price: $855
Variations: reptile skin band ($909)

Marine Original

Reference number: MarineOriginalpolweissarabisch
Movement: manually wound, ETA Caliber 6498-1;
ø 36.6 mm, height 4.5 mm; 17 jewels; 18,000 vph;
screw balance, swan-neck fine adjustment; côtes de
Genéve, blued screws; 46-hour power reserve
Functions: hours, minutes, subsidiary seconds
Case: stainless steel, ø 41 mm, height 12 mm;
sapphire crystal; transparent case back; water-
resistant to 5 atm
Band: calf leather, buckle
Price: $1,153
Variations: reptile skin band or stainless steel
bracelet ($1,225)

Rana

Reference number: RANA
Movement: automatic, ETA Caliber 2824-2;
ø 25.6 mm, height 4.6 mm; 25 jewels; 28,800 vph;
handmade rotor; blued screws, côtes de Genéve,
40-hour power reserve; COSC-certified
Functions: hours, minutes, sweep seconds
Case: stainless steel, 37.5 x 42.5 mm, height
10.2 mm; sapphire crystal; transparent case back;
water-resistant to 5 atm
Band: rubber, buckle
Remarks: with Hartmut Esslinger (Frog Design)
Price: $3,783
Variations: calf-leather band; white dial; Arabic
numerals ($3,423)

Seatime BlackForest

Reference number: SeatimeBlackForest
Movement: automatic, ETA Caliber 2836-2;
ø 25.6 mm, height 4.6 mm; 25 jewels; 28,800 vph;
finely finished with côtes de Genéve, blued screws;
40-hour power reserve
Functions: hours, minutes, sweep seconds; date
Case: titanium, ø 42 mm, height 13.5 mm;
unidirectional bezel with 60-minute division;
sapphire crystal; transparent case back; screw-in
crown; water-resistant to 20 atm
Band: rubber, safety double folding clasp with
extension link
Price: $1,252

Flieger TO2

Reference number: Flieger TO2
Movement: automatic, ETA Caliber 2824-2;
ø 25.6 mm, height 4.6 mm; 25 jewels; 28,800 vph;
finely finished with côtes de Genéve, blued screws;
40-hour power reserve
Functions: hours, minutes, sweep seconds
Case: stainless steel, ø 43 mm, height 13 mm;
sapphire crystal; transparent case back; water-
resistant to 20 atm
Band: rubber, safety folding clasp
Price: $1,162
Variations: buffalo leather band

Flieger GMT

Reference number: FliegerGMT
Movement: automatic, ETA Caliber A07.171;
ø 36.6 mm, height 7.9 mm; 24 jewels; 28,800 vph;
rhodium-plated, blued screws, côtes de Genéve;
46-hour power reserve
Functions: hours, minutes, sweep seconds; added
24-hour display (2nd time zone)
Case: titanium, ø 46 mm, height 12.9 mm;
bidirectional bezel with 24-hour division; sapphire
crystal; transparent case back; water-resistant to
20 atm
Band: rubber, safety folding clasp
Price: $1,576
Variations: buffalo leather band

Marine Chronograph

Reference number: MarineChronograph
Movement: automatic, ETA Caliber 7753; ø 30 mm,
height 7.9 mm; 27 jewels; 28,800 vph; 48-hour
power reserve
Functions: hours, minutes, subsidiary seconds;
chronograph
Case: stainless steel, ø 41 mm, height 14.7 mm;
sapphire crystal; transparent case back; water-
resistant to 5 atm
Band: reptile skin, buckle
Price: $1,720
Variations: manually wound ($1,990)

TAG Heuer

Branch of LVMH SA
6a, rue L.-J.-Chevrolet
CH-2300 La Chaux-de-Fonds
Switzerland

Tel.:
+41-32-919-8164

Fax:
+41-32-919-9000

E-Mail:
info@tagheuer.com

Website:
www.tagheuer.com

Founded:
1860

Number of employees:
approx. 1,000

U.S. distributor:
TAG Heuer/LVMH Watch & Jewelry USA
966 South Springfield Avenue
Springfield, NJ 07081
973-467-1890

Most important collections/price range:
TAG Heuer Formula 1, Aquaracer, Link, Carrera, Grand Carrera, Monaco / from approx. $1,000 to $20,000

TAG Heuer

Measuring speed accurately in ever greater detail was always the goal of TAG Heuer. The brand also established numerous technical milestones, including the first automatic chronograph caliber with a microrotor (created in 1969 with Hamilton-Büren, Breitling, and Dubois Dépraz). Of more recent vintage is the fascinating mechanical movement V4 with its belt-driven transmission, unveiled in a limited edition for the brand's 150th anniversary. At the same time TAG Heuer released its first chronograph with an in-house movement, Caliber 1887, the basis of which was an existing chronograph movement by Seiko. Some of the components are made by the company itself in Switzerland, while assembly is done entirely in-house.

Lately, TAG Heuer has increased its manufacturing capacities to meet the strong and growing demand and to maintain its independence. It also serves as an extended workbench for companion brands Zenith and Hublot, also part of the LVMH Group.

TAG Heuer has continued to break world speed records for mechanical escapements. In 2005, the Caliber 360 combined a standard movement with a 360,000 vph (50 Hz) chronograph mechanism able to measure 100ths of a second. In 2011, the Micrograph 1/100th brought time display and measurement on a single plate. Shortly after, the Mikrotimer Flying 1000 broke the 1,000th of a second barrier. A year later, the Mikrogirder 2000 doubled the frequency using a vibrating metal strip instead of a balance wheel. The MikrotourbillonS features a separate chronograph escapement driven at a record-breaking 360,000 vph.

But these flights of fancy slowed when, at the end of 2014, the new LVMH coordinator Jean-Claude Biver devised a new strategy for TAG Heuer to cut back on the top end of the pricing scale. He nominated development head Guy Sémon as new CEO and prescribed a return to former pricings, with a broader choice of models in the lower and medium segments. A project for a second chronograph caliber was dropped, but there are rumors that the brand is working on a low-cost tourbillon and other technical tidbits.

TAG Heuer Formula 1 Limited Edition McLaren

Reference number: CAZ1112.FC8188
Movement: quartz, Ronda Caliber 5040D
Functions: hours, minutes, subsidiary seconds; chronograph; date
Case: stainless steel, ø 42 mm, height 12 mm; unidirectional bezel, tachymeter scale; sapphire crystal; screw-in crown; water-resistant to 20 atm
Band: textile, buckle
Price: $1,550

TAG Heuer Formula 1 Limited Edition CR7

Reference number: CAZ1113.FC8189
Movement: quartz, Ronda Caliber 5040D
Functions: hours, minutes, subsidiary seconds; chronograph; date
Case: stainless steel with black titanium carbide coating; ø 42 mm, height 12 mm; bidirectional bezel, tachymeter scale; sapphire crystal; screw-in crown; water-resistant to 20 atm
Band: textile, buckle
Price: $1,550

TAG Heuer Formula 1 Calibre 7 GMT Special Edition David Guetta

Reference number: WAZ201A.FC8195
Movement: automatic, TAG Heuer Caliber 7 (base ETA 2893-2); ø 26.2 mm, height 4.1 mm; 21 jewels; 18,000 vph
Functions: hours, minutes, sweep seconds; additional 24-hour display (2nd time zone); date
Case: stainless steel with black titanium carbide coating; ø 43 mm, height 12 mm; unidirectional bezel with aluminum insert, 24-hour divisions; sapphire crystal; screw-in crown; water-resistant to 20 atm
Band: calf leather, buckle
Price: $2,450

TAG Heuer Formula 1 Calibre 5 Full Black

Reference number: WAZ2115.FT8023
Movement: automatic, TAG Heuer Caliber 5 (base ETA 2824-2); ø 26 mm, height 4.6 mm; 25 jewels; 28,800 vph
Functions: hours, minutes, sweep seconds; date
Case: stainless steel with black titanium carbide coating; ø 41 mm, height 12 mm; unidirectional bezel with 60-minute divisions; sapphire crystal; screw-in crown; water-resistant to 20 atm
Band: calf leather, buckle
Price: $2,000
Variations: stainless steel with stainless steel bracelet ($2,000) or rubber strap ($2,000)

Aquaracer 300M Calibre 5

Reference number: WAY211A.BA0928
Movement: automatic, TAG Heuer Caliber 5 (base ETA 2824-2); ø 26 mm, height 4.6 mm; 25 jewels; 28,800 vph
Functions: hours, minutes, sweep seconds; date
Case: stainless steel, ø 40.5 mm, height 12 mm; unidirectional bezel with 60-minute divisions, sapphire crystal; screw-in crown; water-resistant to 30 atm
Band: stainless steel, folding clasp with safety lock and extension link
Price: $2,550
Variations: blue dial ($2,550); nylon strap ($2,400)

Aquaracer 300M Calibre 5 Black Phantom

Reference number: WAY218B.FC6364
Movement: automatic, TAG Heuer Caliber 5 (base ETA 2824-2); ø 26 mm, height 4.6 mm; 25 jewels; 28,800 vph
Functions: hours, minutes, sweep seconds; date
Case: titanium with black titanium carbide coating, ø 41 mm, height 12 mm; unidirectional bezel with ceramic insert, 60-minute divisions; sapphire crystal; screw-in crown; water-resistant to 30 atm
Band: nylon, folding clasp
Price: $3,000

Aquaracer 300M Calibre 16

Reference number: CAY211A.BA0927
Movement: automatic, TAG Heuer Caliber 16 (base ETA 7750); ø 30.4 mm, height 7.9 mm; 25 jewels; 28,800 vph
Functions: hours, minutes, subsidiary seconds; chronograph; date
Case: stainless steel, ø 43 mm, height 16 mm; unidirectional bezel with ceramic insert, with 60-minute divisions; sapphire crystal; screw-in crown; water-resistant to 30 atm
Band: stainless steel, folding clasp with extension link
Price: $3,650
Variations: nylon strap ($3,500)

Carrera Lady Special Edition Cara Delevingne

Reference number: WAR101B.FC6367
Movement: quartz, ETA Caliber 955.112
Functions: hours, minutes, sweep seconds; date
Case: stainless steel, ø 41 mm; bezel with black titanium carbide coating, 72 diamonds; sapphire crystal; water-resistant to 10 atm
Band: reptile skin, folding clasp
Price: $4,000
Variations: blackened stainless steel bracelet ($4,150); stainless steel w/o diamonds ($2,250)

Carrera Calibre 5 Day-Date

Reference number: WAR201E.FC6292
Movement: automatic, TAG Heuer Caliber 5 (base ETA 2834-2); ø 29 mm, height 5.05 mm; 25 jewels; 28,800 vph
Functions: hours, minutes, sweep seconds; weekday, date
Case: stainless steel, ø 41 mm, height 13 mm; sapphire crystal; transparent case back; water-resistant to 10 atm
Band: reptile skin, folding clasp with safety lock
Price: $2,600
Variations: various dials; stainless steel bracelet ($2,600)

Carrera Calibre 6 C.O.S.C.

Reference number: WV5111.FC6350
Movement: automatic, TAG Heuer Caliber 6 (base ETA 2895-2); ø 26.2 mm, height 4.35 mm; 27 jewels; 28,800 vph; COSC-certified chronometer
Functions: hours, minutes, subsidiary seconds; date
Case: stainless steel, ø 39 mm, height 11.5 mm; sapphire crystal; water-resistant to 10 atm
Band: calf leather, folding clasp
Price: $3,400

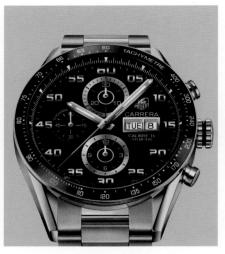

Carrera Calibre 16 Day-Date

Reference number: CV2A1R.BA0799
Movement: automatic, TAG Heuer Caliber 16 (base ETA 7750); ø 30.4 mm, height 7.9 mm; 25 jewels; 28,800 vph
Functions: hours, minutes, subsidiary seconds; chronograph; weekday, date
Case: stainless steel, ø 43 mm, height 16.5 mm; bezel with ceramic insert; sapphire crystal; transparent case back; water-resistant to 10 atm
Band: stainless steel, folding clasp
Price: $4,750
Variations: reptile skin band ($4,750)

Carrera Calibre 1887 Elegance

Reference number: CAR2012.FC6235
Movement: automatic, TAG Heuer Caliber 1887; ø 29.3 mm, height 7.13 mm; 39 jewels; 28,800 vph
Functions: hours, minutes, subsidiary seconds; chronograph; date
Case: stainless steel, ø 43 mm, height 16 mm; sapphire crystal; transparent case back; water-resistant to 10 atm
Band: reptile skin, folding clasp
Price: $4,800

Carrera Calibre Heuer 01

Reference number: CAR2A1Z.FT6044
Movement: automatic, TAG Heuer Caliber Heuer 01; ø 29.3 mm, 39 jewels; 28,800 vph
Functions: hours, minutes, subsidiary seconds; chronograph; date
Case: stainless steel, ø 45 mm, height 16 mm; bezel with black titanium carbide coating; sapphire crystal; transparent case back; water-resistant to 10 atm
Band: rubber, folding clasp
Price: $5,250

Monaco Calibre 11

Reference number: CAW211P.FC6356
Movement: automatic, TAG Heuer Caliber 11 (base Sellita SW300 with Dubois Dépraz module 2006); ø 30 mm, height 7.3 mm; 59 jewels; 28,800 vph
Functions: hours, minutes, subsidiary seconds; chronograph; date
Case: stainless steel, 39 x 39 mm, height 14.5 mm; sapphire crystal; transparent case back; water-resistant to 10 atm
Band: calf leather, folding clasp
Price: $5,550

Monaco V4 Carbon Phantom

Reference number: WAW2091.FC6369
Movement: automatic, TAG Heuer Caliber V4; 35 x 31.5 mm; 48 jewels; 18,000 vph; tungsten carbide linear winding mass, 4 spring barrels; 13 miniature belts transmit power; 39 micro ball bearings
Functions: hours, minutes
Case: carbon matrix composite material, 41 x 41 mm, height 16.5 mm; sapphire crystal; transparent case back; water-resistant to 10 atm
Band: reptile skin, folding clasp
Price: $48,000

Temption

Temption has been operating under the leadership of Klaus Ulbrich since 1997. Ulbrich is an engineer with special training in the construction of watches and movements, and right from the start, he intended to develop timekeepers that were modern in their aesthetics but not subject to the whims of zeitgeist. Retro watches would have no place in his collections. The design behind all Temption models is inspired more by the Bauhaus or the Japanese concept of wabi sabi. Reduction to what is absolutely necessary is the golden rule here. Beauty emerges from clarity, or in other words, less is more.

Ulbrich sketches all the watches himself. Some of the components are even made in-house, but all the pieces are assembled in the company facility in Herrenberg, a town just to the east of the Black Forest. The primary functions are always easy to read, even in low light. The company logo is discreetly included on the dial.

Ulbrich works according to a model he calls the "information pyramid." Hours and minutes are at the tip, with all other functions subordinated. To maintain this hierarchy, the dials are dark, the date windows are in the same hue, and all subdials are not framed in any way.

The Cameo rectangular model is a perfect example of Ulbrich's aesthetic ideas and his consistent technological approach: Because rectangular sapphire crystals can hardly be made water-resistant, the Cameo's crystal is chemically bonded to the case and water-resistant to 10 atm. The frame for the sapphire was metalized inside to hide the bonded edge. The overall look is one of stunning simplicity and elegance.

Temption GmbH
Raistinger Str. 46
D-71083 Herrenberg
Germany

Tel.:
+49-7032-977-954

Fax:
+49-7032-977-955

E-Mail:
ftemption@aol.com

Website:
www.temption.info

Founded:
1997

Number of employees:
4

Annual production:
700 watches

U.S. distributor:
TemptionUSA
Debby Gordon
2053 North Bridgeport Drive
Fayetteville, AR 72704
888-400-4293
temptionusa@sbcglobal.net

Most important collections/price range:
automatics (three-hand), GMT, chronographs, and chronographs with complications / approx. $1,900 to $4,200

CM05

Reference number: 16
Movement: automatic, Temption Caliber T15.1 (base Soprod A10); ø 25.6 mm, height 3.6 mm; 21 jewels; 28,800 vph; finely decorated; 42-hour power reserve
Functions: hours, minutes, sweep seconds; date
Case: stainless steel, ø 42 mm, height 11 mm; unidirectional bezel, 12-hour division, sapphire crystal; transparent case back; screw-in crown; water-resistant to 10 atm
Band: stainless steel, double folding clasp
Price: $2,400

CM01

Reference number: CM01
Movement: automatic, Temption Caliber T15.2; ø 25.6 mm, height 3.6 mm; 25 jewels, 28,800 vph; finely finished; 42-hour power reserve
Functions: hours, minutes, sweep seconds; date
Case: ø 43 mm, height 9.8 mm; sapphire crystal, transparent case back; screw-in crown; water-resistant to 10 atm
Band: calf leather, folding clasp
Price: $2,150

Chronograph CGK205 V2 Caribe

Reference number: 205
Movement: automatic, Temption Caliber T18.1 (base ETA 7751); ø 30 mm, height 7.8 mm; 25 jewels; 28,800 vph; finely decorated; 42-hour power reserve
Functions: hours, minutes, additional 24-hour display; chronograph; full calendar with date, weekday, month, moon phase
Case: stainless steel, ø 43 mm, height 14 mm; sapphire crystal; transparent case back; screw-in crown and pusher; with colored cabochons; water-resistant to 10 atm
Band: stainless steel, double folding clasp
Price: $3,950

Thomas Ninchritz
Niebüller Strasse 7
D-90425 Nuremberg
Germany

Tel.:
+49-911-552-363

Fax:
+49-911-581-7622

E-Mail:
th.ninchritz@t-online.de

Website:
www.ninchritz-uhren.de

Founded:
2005

Number of employees:
1

Distribution:
WatchBuys
888-333-4895
www.watchbuys.com

Most important collections/price range:
Black & Diamonds, Fliegeruhr, Grande
Seconde, Kathedral, Ornatis / $2,400 to
$23,250

Thomas Ninchritz

In 1520, the locksmith Peter Henlein of Nuremberg was the first craftsman in Europe who could create "portable clocks." About half a millennium later, a trip to Nuremberg is still well worth the effort for watch aficionados: In his atelier, watchmaker Thomas Ninchritz produces a small collection of fascinating wristwatches.

The core of Ninchritz's watches is the extremely robust ETA Unitas caliber—though when he adds his own well-proportioned three-quarter plate, it is hardly recognizable. The master's meticulous work lends the classic manually wound movement a finish that does not need to shy away from comparisons even to expensive *manufacture* movements. Screw-mounted gold chatons, hand-engraved balance cocks, and swan-neck fine adjustments are among the elements that make a watch enthusiast's heart beat faster.

The creative watchmaker came up with a very interesting idea for his Vice Versa model: Using a relatively simple method, he routes the dial train of ETA Caliber 6498 (the hunter version featuring subsidiary seconds at 6 o'clock) across two transmission wheels and a long stem through to the back of the movement. There is enough room to poke it through between the spring barrel and the balance, with the hand arbors now appearing in a small dial on the gear train bridge, which Ninchritz has extended to become a true three-quarter plate decorated with a stripe pattern, engraving, and chatons secured by little blued screws. Additionally, the index is accompanied by a beautiful swan-neck spring, to ensure that no one will mistake this work of art for the "back" of the movement.

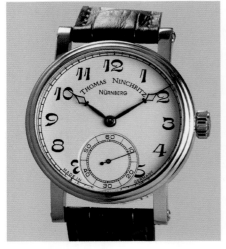

Kathedral

Reference number: NI 2000.4
Movement: manually wound, Caliber 200, ø 36.6 mm, height 4.03 mm; 17 jewels; 18,000 vph; three-quarter plate with screwed-in gold chatons; hand-engraved balance cock; swan-neck fine adjustment
Functions: hours, minutes, subsidiary seconds
Case: stainless steel, ø 42 mm, height 10.5 mm; sapphire crystal; transparent case back
Band: calf leather, buckle
Price: $4,350
Variations: stainless steel/gold or yellow or rose gold (on request)

Grande Seconde

Reference number: NI 2000.31
Movement: manually wound, TN Caliber 200 (base ETA 6498-1); ø 36.6 mm, height 4.03 mm; 17 jewels; 18,000 vph; three-quarter plate with gold chatons; hand-engraved balance cock; swan-neck fine adjustment
Functions: hours, minutes, subsidiary seconds
Case: stainless steel, ø 42 mm, height 10.5 mm; rose gold bezel; sapphire crystal; transparent case back
Band: calf leather, buckle
Price: $7,900
Variations: yellow gold bezel; stainless steel ($4,350); yellow or rose gold (on request)

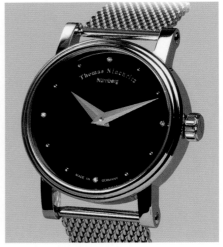

Black & Diamond

Reference number: NI 2000.7
Movement: manually wound, TN Caliber 200 (base ETA 6498-1); ø 36.6 mm, height 4.03 mm; 17 jewels; 18,000 vph; three-quarter plate with screwed-in gold chatons; hand-engraved balance cock, swan-neck fine adjustment, finely finished
Functions: hours, minutes
Case: stainless steel, ø 42 mm, height 10.5 mm; sapphire crystal; water-resistant to 3 atm
Band: stainless steel Milanese bracelet, folding clasp
Price: $7,700

Tissot

The Swiss watchmaker Tissot was founded in 1853 in the town of Le Locle in the Jura mountains. In the century that followed, it gained international recognition for its Savonnette pocket watch. And even when the wristwatch became popular in the early twentieth century, time and again Tissot managed to attract attention to its products. To this day, the Banana Watch of 1916 and its first watches in the art deco style (1919) remain design icons of that epoch. The watchmaker has always been at the top of its technical game as well: The first antimagnetic watch (1930), the first mechanical plastic watch (Astrolon, 1971), and its touch-screen T-Touch (1999) all bear witness to Tissot's remarkable capacity for finding unusual and modern solutions.

Today, Tissot belongs to the Swatch Group and, with its wide selection of quartz and inexpensive mechanical watches, serves as the group's entry-level brand. Within this price segment, Tissot offers something special for the buyer who values traditional watchmaking, but is not of limitless financial means. The brand, which celebrated its 160th anniversary in style in 2013 with a comprehensive retrospective in Geneva, has gravitated toward the sports crowd. Tissot is timing everything from basketball to superbike racing, from ice hockey to fencing—and water sports, of course. The Sailing Touch, a watch that provides sailors with a vast array of needed information, came out in 2010. The chronograph Couturier line is outfitted with the new ETA chronograph caliber C01.211. This caliber features a number of plastic parts: another step in simplifying, and lowering the cost of, mechanical movements.

Tissot SA
Chemin des Tourelles, 17
CH-2400 Le Locle
Switzerland

Tel.:
+41-32-933-3111

Fax:
+41-32-933-3311

E-Mail:
info@tissot.ch

Website:
www.tissot.ch

Founded:
1853

U.S. distributor:
Tissot
The Swatch Group (U.S.), Inc.
1200 Harbor Boulevard
Weehawken, NJ 07087
201-271-1400
www.us.tissotshop.com

Most important collection/price range:
T-Touch / from $575; T-Race / from $575;
T-Complication / from $1,950

T-Touch Expert Solar

Reference number: T091.420.46.051.00
Movement: quartz, ETA Caliber E84.301; multifunctional with LCD display and solar cell
Functions: hours, minutes; additional 12-hour indicator (2nd time zone); weather report, altimeter and altitude difference meter, compass, regatta function; 2 alarms; chronograph with countdown timer; perpetual calendar with date, weekday, week
Case: titanium, ø 45 mm, height 13 mm; sapphire crystal; water-resistant to 10 atm
Band: calf leather, folding clasp
Price: $1,150

PRS 516 Automatic Chronograph

Reference number: T100.427.36.201.00
Movement: automatic, ETA Caliber A05.H31; ø 30 mm, height 7.9 mm; 27 jewels; 28,800 vph; 60-hour power reserve
Functions: hours, minutes, subsidiary seconds; chronograph; date
Case: stainless steel with black PVD coating, ø 45 mm, height 15.84 mm; carbon fiber bezel; sapphire crystal; transparent case back; water-resistant to 10 atm
Band: calf leather, double folding clasp
Price: $2,150

T-Complication Skeleton

Reference number: T070.405.16.411.00
Movement: manually wound, ETA Caliber 6497-1; ø 36.6 mm, height 4.5 mm; 17 jewels; 18,000 vph; partly skeletonized; 46-hour power reserve
Functions: hours, minutes, subsidiary seconds
Case: stainless steel, ø 43 mm, height 11.99 mm; sapphire crystal; transparent case back; water-resistant to 5 atm
Band: calf leather, double folding clasp
Remarks: skeletonized dial
Price: $1,950

Chemin des Tourelles Powermatic 80 Gent Chronometer

Reference number: T099.408.36.038.00
Movement: automatic, Tissot Powermatic 80 (base ETA 2824-2); ø 25.6 mm; height 4.6 mm; 23 jewels; 21,600 vph; variable inertia balance; 80-hour power reserve; COSC-certified chronometer
Functions: hours, minutes, sweep seconds; date
Case: stainless steel with rose gold-colored PVD coating, ø 42 mm, height 10.89 mm; sapphire crystal; transparent case back; water-resistant to 5 atm
Band: calf leather, double folding clasp
Price: $1,100

Chemin des Tourelles Automatic Chronograph

Reference number: T099.427.11.038.00
Movement: automatic, ETA Caliber C01.211; ø 30 mm, height 8.44 mm; 15 jewels; 21,600 vph; 45-hour power reserve
Functions: hours, minutes, subsidiary seconds; chronograph; date
Case: stainless steel, ø 44 mm, height 15.18 mm; sapphire crystal; transparent case back; water-resistant to 5 atm
Band: stainless steel, double folding clasp
Price: $1,100

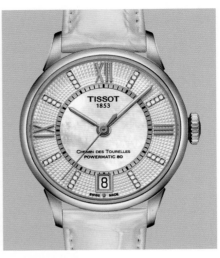

Chemin des Tourelles Powermatic 80 Lady

Reference number: T099.207.16.116.00
Movement: automatic, Tissot Powermatic 80 (base ETA 2824-2); ø 25.6 mm; height 4.6 mm; 23 jewels; 21,600 vph; variable inertia balance; 80-hour power reserve
Functions: hours, minutes, sweep seconds; date
Case: stainless steel, ø 32 mm, height 10.69 mm; sapphire crystal; transparent case back; water-resistant to 5 atm
Band: calf leather, double folding clasp
Remarks: dial set with 32 diamonds
Price: $950

Bridgeport Automatic Chronograph

Reference number: T097.427.26.033.00
Movement: automatic, ETA Caliber 7753; ø 30 mm, height 7.9 mm; 27 jewels; 28,800 vph; 48-hour power reserve
Functions: hours, minutes, subsidiary seconds; chronograph; date
Case: stainless steel, ø 42 mm, height 13.19 mm; bezel and crown with rose gold-colored PVD coating; sapphire crystal; transparent case back; water-resistant to 5 atm
Band: calf leather, double folding clasp
Price: $2,200

Le Locle Automatic Chronometer

Reference number: T006.408.36.057.00
Movement: automatic, ETA Caliber 2824-2; ø 25.6 mm, height 4.6 mm; 25 jewels; 28,800 vph; 42-hour power reserve; COSC-certified chronometer
Functions: hours, minutes, sweep seconds; date
Case: stainless steel with rose gold-colored PVD coating, ø 39.3 mm, height 9.75 mm; sapphire crystal; transparent case back; water-resistant to 3 atm
Band: calf leather, double folding clasp
Price: $1,295

T-Race MotoGP Automatic Chronograph Limited Edition 2015

Reference number: T092.427.27.061.00
Movement: automatic, ETA Caliber C01.211; ø 30 mm, height 8.44 mm; 15 jewels; 21,600 vph; 45-hour power reserve
Functions: hours, minutes, subsidiary seconds; chronograph; date
Case: stainless steel, ø 45.3 mm, height 16.09 mm; bezel with black PVD coating; sapphire crystal; transparent case back; water-resistant to 10 atm
Band: rubber, folding clasp
Price: $1,395

Towson Watch Company

Towson Watch Co.
502 Dogwood Lane
Towson, MD 21286

Tel.:
410-823-1823

Fax:
410-823-8581

E-Mail:
towsonwatchco@aol.com

Website:
www.twcwatches.com

Founded:
2000

Number of employees:
4

Annual production:
200 watches

Distribution:
retail

Most important collections/price range:
Skipjack GMT / approx. $2,950; Mission / approx. $2,500; Potomac / approx. $2,000; Choptank / approx. $4,500; Martin / approx. $3,950; custom design / $10,000 to $35,000

"The old charm, in truth, still survives in the town, despite the frantic efforts of boosters and boomers who, in late years, have replaced all its ancient cobblestones with asphalt," commented H. L. Mencken on his native Baltimore back in the 1920s. No doubt he would have sprayed his caustic ink at some of the more recent urban renewal projects, but he would still have welcomed the Towson Watch Company, founded in 2000 by two men with a deep-seated passion for mechanical timepieces. After over forty years repairing high-grade watches, repeaters, and chronographs and making his own tourbillons, George Thomas, a master watchmaker, met Hartwig Balke, a mechanical engineer and also a talented watchmaker, by chance.

Thomas built his first tourbillon pocket watches, now displayed at the National Watch and Clock Museum in Columbia, Pennsylvania, in 1985. In 1999, Balke made his first wrist chronograph, the STS-99 Mission, for a NASA astronaut and mission specialist, and it was worn during the first space mission in the new millennium.

With Towson these two men's passion has gone into timepieces named for local sites and sights, like the Choptank or Potomac rivers. The latest Potomac features a guilloché dial by watchmaker Jochen Benzinger. Their timepieces are very imaginative, a touch retro, a bit nostalgic perhaps, and very personal—not to mention affordable. Their latest project is a return to the past: a pilot chronograph inspired by gauges on the Lockheed Martin China Clipper flying boats, which served as an air connection between the United States and Asia starting in November 1935—Martin being a Baltimore-based company, of course.

Pride II

Reference number: PR250
Movement: automatic ETA Caliber 2892-A2; ø 25.6 mm, height 3.6 mm; 21 jewels; 28,800 vph; fine finishing with côtes de Genève
Functions: hours, minutes, sweep second; date
Case: stainless steel, 39 x 44 mm, height 9.2 mm, sapphire crystal, screwed-down case back with engraving, water resistant to 5 atm
Band: calf leather, folding clasp.
Price: $3,850
Variations: silver-colored dial; mesh stainless steel bracelet ($4,150)

Potomac Classic

Reference number: PO10
Movement: manually wound Unitas 6498, ø 36.6 mm, height 4.5 mm; 17 jewels; 18,000 vph; skeletonized, guilloché dial by Jochen Benzinger
Functions: hours, minutes, subsidiary seconds
Case: rose gold, ø 42 mm, height 11 mm, sapphire crystal, transparent back, water resistant to 3 atm
Band: reptile skin, folding clasp.
Price: on request
Variations: stainless steel ($10,850)

Martin M-130

Reference number: CC100
Movement: automatic, ETA Caliber 7750 Valjoux; ø 30 mm; height 7.9 mm; 25 jewels; 28,800 vph; fine finishing with côtes de Genève
Functions: hours, minutes, subsidiary second; chronograph; date
Case: stainless steel, ø 42 mm, height 13.5 mm, sapphire crystal, screwed-down case back with engraving, water resistant to 5 atm
Band: leather, folding clasp
Price: $3,950
Variations: mesh stainless steel bracelet ($4,250)

Montres Tudor SA
Rue François-Dussaud 3-7
Case postale 1755
CH-1211 Geneva
Switzerland

Tel.:
+41-22-302-2200

Fax:
+41-22-300-2255

E-Mail:
info@tudorwatch.com

Website:
www.tudorwatch.com

Founded:
1946

U.S. distributor:
Tudor Watch U.S.A., LLC
665 Fifth Avenue
New York, NY 10022
212-897-9900; 212-371-0371(fax)
www.tudorwatch.com

Most important collections/price range:
Fastrider / $3,675 to $4,925; Grantour /
$2,475 to $8,000; Heritage / $2,825 to
$6,075; North Flag / $3,550 to $3,675;
Pelagos / $4,125 to $4,400; Style / $2,100
to $3,400; Glamour / $2,150 to $5,100

Tudor

The Tudor brand came out of the shadow cast by its "big sister" Rolex in 2007 and worked hard to develop its own personality. The strategy focuses on distinctive models that draw inspiration from the brand's rich past but remain in the "affordable quality watch segment."

Rolex founder Hans Wilsdorf started Tudor in 1946 as a second brand in order to offer the legendary reliability of his watches to a broader public at a more affordable price. To this day, Tudor still benefits from the same industrial platform as Rolex, especially in the area of cases and bracelets, assembly and quality assurance, not to mention distribution and after-sales. However, the movements themselves are usually delivered by ETA and "tudorized" according to the company's own aesthetic and technical criteria.

In the era of vintage and retro, it's no wonder that the brand has started tapping into its own treasure trove of icons. Following the success of the Heritage Black Bay diver's watch, based on a 1954 model, came the turn of the blue-highlighted 1973 Chronograph Montecarlo. In 2014, Tudor completed the Heritage collection with the Ranger, a sports watch with an urban-adventurer feel, inspired by the same "tool watch" from the 1960s. In a bit of sibling rivalry, the brand has now come out with its own caliber, designed and built in-house, the MT-5621, which made its debut in the simple North Flag and will be built as a three-hander (MT-5612) for the Pelagos models in the future.

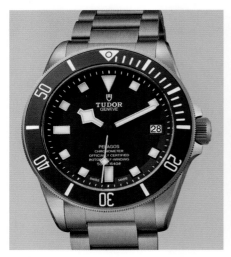

Pelagos

Reference number: 25600TB / 25600TN
Movement: automatic, Tudor Caliber MT5612; ø 31.8 mm, height 6.5 mm; 26 jewels; 28,800 vph; silicon balance hairspring; 70-hour power reserve; COSC-certified chronometer
Functions: hours, minutes, sweep seconds; date
Case: titanium and stainless steel, ø 42 mm; bezel with ceramic inlay, unidirectional bezel with 60-minute division; sapphire crystal; screw-in crown, helium valve; water-resistant to 50 atm
Band: titanium, folding clasp with safety catch and extension link
Remarks: added rubber strap with diving extension
Price: $4,400

North Flag

Reference number: 91210N
Movement: automatic, Tudor Caliber MT5621; ø 33.8 mm, height 6.5 mm; 28 jewels; 28,800 vph; silicon balance hairspring; 70-hour power reserve; COSC-certified chronometer
Functions: hours, minutes, sweep seconds; power reserve indicator; date
Case: stainless steel, ø 40 mm; bezel with ceramic ring; sapphire crystal; transparent case back; screw-in crown; waterproof to 10 atm
Band: stainless steel, folding clasp with safety catch
Price: $3,675
Variations: leather strap ($3,550)

Fastrider Chrono

Reference number: 42010N
Movement: automatic, Tudor Caliber 7753 (base ETA 7750); ø 30.4 mm, height 7.9 mm; 27 jewels; 28,800 vph; 46-hour power reserve
Functions: hours, minutes, subsidiary seconds; chronograph; date
Case: stainless steel, ø 42 mm; ceramic bezel; sapphire crystal; screw-in crown; water-resistant to 15 atm
Band: leather, folding clasp with safety catch
Price: $4,100
Variations: rubber strap, various dials

Fastrider Chrono

Reference number: 42010N
Movement: automatic, Tudor Caliber 7753 (base ETA 7750); ø 30.4 mm, height 7.9 mm; 27 jewels; 28,800 vph; 46-hour power reserve
Functions: hours, minutes, subsidiary seconds; chronograph; date
Case: stainless steel, ø 42 mm; ceramic bezel; sapphire crystal; screw-in crown; water-resistant to 15 atm
Band: leather, folding clasp with safety clasp
Price: $4,100
Variations: rubber strap, various dials

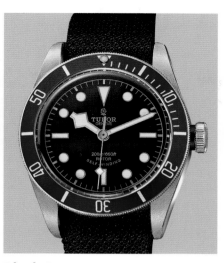

Black Bay

Reference number: 79220R
Movement: automatic, Tudor Caliber 2824 (base ETA 2824-2); ø 25.6 mm, height 4.6 mm; 25 jewels; 28,800 vph; 38-hour power reserve
Functions: hours, minutes, sweep seconds
Case: stainless steel, ø 41 mm; unidirectional bezel with 60-minute division; domed sapphire crystal; screw-in crown; water-resistant to 20 atm
Band: fabric, folding clasp with safety catch
Remarks: extra fabric strap and buckle
Price: $3,425
Variations: stainless steel bracelet

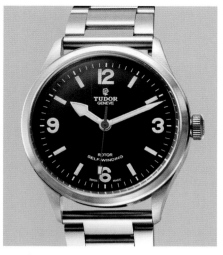

Heritage Ranger

Reference number: 79910
Movement: automatic, Tudor Caliber 2824 (base ETA 2824-2); ø 26 mm, height 4.6 mm; 25 jewels; 28,800 vph; 38-hour power reserve
Functions: hours, minutes, sweep seconds
Case: stainless steel, ø 41 mm, height 12.15 mm; domed sapphire crystal; screw-in crown; water-resistant to 15 atm
Band: stainless steel, folding clasp with safety catch
Remarks: extra fabric strap and buckle
Price: $2,950
Variations: different leather straps ($2,825)

Heritage Chrono Blue

Reference number: 70330B
Movement: automatic, Tudor Caliber 2892 (base ETA 2892-A2 with chronograph module); ø 30 mm, height 6.9 mm; 55 jewels; 28,800 vph; 42-hour power reserve
Functions: hours, minutes, subsidiary seconds; chronograph; date
Case: stainless steel, ø 42 mm, height 13.38 mm; bidirectional bezel with 12-hour divisions, sapphire crystal; screw-in crown and pushers; water-resistant to 15 atm
Band: fabric, buckle
Price: $4,425

Fastrider Black Shield

Reference number: 42000CR
Movement: automatic, Tudor Caliber 7753 (base ETA 7750); ø 30.4 mm, height 7.9 mm; 27 jewels; 28,800 vph; 46-hour power reserve
Functions: hours, minutes, subsidiary seconds; chronograph; date
Case: ceramic, ø 42 mm; sapphire crystal; water-resistant to 15 atm
Band: leather, folding clasp and safety catch
Price: $4,925
Variations: rubber strap and buckle

Caliber MT5621

Automatic; single spring barrel, 70-hour power reserve; COSC-certified chronometer
Functions: hours, minutes, sweep seconds; power reserve indicator; date
Diameter: 33.8 mm
Height: 6.5 mm
Jewels: 28
Balance: glucydur with regulating screws
Frequency: 28,800 vph
Balance spring: silicon related caliber: MT5612 (without power reserve indicator)

Tutima Uhrenfabrik GmbH
Ndl. Glashütte

Altenberger Straße 6
D-01768 Glashütte
Germany

Tel.:
+49-35053-320-20

Fax:
+49-35053-320-222

E-Mail:
info@tutima.com

Website:
www.tutima.com

Founded:
1927

Number of employees:
approx. 60

U.S. distributor:
Tutima USA, Inc.
P.O. Box 983
Torrance, CA 90508
1-TUTIMA-1927
info@tutimausa.com
www.tutima.com

Most important collections/price range:
Patria, Saxon One, M2, Grand Flieger,
Hommage / approx. $2,600 to $22,000

Tutima

The name Glashütte is synonymous with watches in Germany. The area, known also for precision engineering, already had quite a watchmaking industry going when World War I closed off markets, followed by the hyperinflation of the early twenties. To rebuild the local economy, a conglomerate was created to produce finished watches under the leadership of jurist Dr. Ernst Kurtz consisting of the movement manufacturer UROFA Glashütte AG and UFAG. The top watches were given the name Tutima, derived from the Latin *tutus*, meaning whole, sound. Among the brand's most famous timepieces was a pilot's watch which set standards in terms of aesthetics and functionality.

A few days before World War II ended, Kurtz left Glashütte and founded Uhrenfabrik Kurtz in southern Germany. A young businessman and former employee of Kurtz by the name of Dieter Delecate is credited with keeping the manufacturing facilities and the name Tutima going even as the company sailed through troubled waters. In founding Tutima Uhrenfabrik GmbH in Ganderkesee, this young, resolute entrepreneur prepared the company's strategy for the coming decades.

Delecate has had the joy of seeing Tutima return to its old home and vertically integrated operations, meaning it is once again a genuine *manufacture*. Under renowned designer Rolf Lang, it has developed an in-house minute repeater. In 2013, Tutima proudly announced a genuine made-in-Glashütte movement (at least 50 percent must be produced in the town), Caliber 617. With characteristic restraint, the brand has placed this fine piece of engineering inside the new Patria, which comes with a subsidiary second display or a second time zone. Another recent sign-off is a modern interpretation of a classic older pilot's watch for the Grand Flieger collection. The look is fresh, the hands longer, and the functionality outstanding.

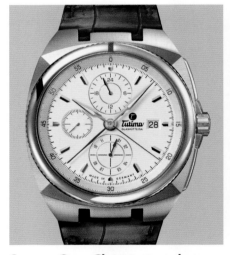

Saxon One Chronograph
Reference number: 6420-04
Movement: automatic, Tutima Caliber 521;
ø 30 mm, height 7.9 mm; 25 jewels; 28,800 vph;
sweep minute counter; 44-hour power reserve
Functions: hours, minutes, subsidiary seconds;
additional 24-hour display; chronograph; date
Case: stainless steel, ø 43 mm, height 15.7 mm;
bidirectional bezel with reference marker; sapphire
crystal; transparent case back; screw-in crown;
water-resistant to 20 atm
Band: reptile skin, folding clasp
Price: $6,700
Variations: stainless steel bracelet ($7,100)

Saxon One Chronograph LS
Reference number: 6422-01
Movement: automatic, Tutima Caliber 521;
ø 30 mm, height 7.9 mm; 25 jewels; 28,800 vph;
sweep minute counter; 44-hour power reserve
Functions: hours, minutes, subsidiary seconds;
additional 24-hour display; chronograph; date
Case: stainless steel, ø 43 mm, height 15.7 mm;
bidirectional bezel with 60-minute divisions,
reference marker; sapphire crystal; transparent case
back; screw-in crown; water-resistant to 20 atm
Band: stainless steel, folding clasp
Price: $7,100
Variations: reptile skin band ($6,700)

Saxon One Automatic
Reference number: 6120-03
Movement: automatic, Tutima Caliber 330;
ø 25.6 mm, height 5.05 mm; 25 jewels;
28,800 vph; 38-hour power reserve
Functions: hours, minutes, sweep seconds;
weekday, date
Case: stainless steel, ø 42 mm, height 13 mm;
bidirectional bezel with reference marker; sapphire
crystal; transparent case back; screw-in crown;
water-resistant to 20 atm
Band: reptile skin, folding clasp
Price: $3,800
Variations: stainless steel bracelet ($4,200)

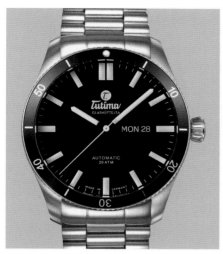

Grand Flieger Airport Automatic

Reference number: 6101-02
Movement: automatic, Tutima Caliber 330;
ø 25.6 mm, height 5.05 mm; 25 jewels;
28,800 vph; 38-hour power reserve
Functions: hours, minutes, sweep seconds;
weekday, date
Case: stainless steel, ø 43 mm, height 13 mm;
bidirectional bezel with luminous marker; sapphire
crystal; transparent case back; screw-in crown;
water-resistant to 20 atm
Band: stainless steel, folding clasp
Price: $3,200
Variations: leather strap ($2,800)

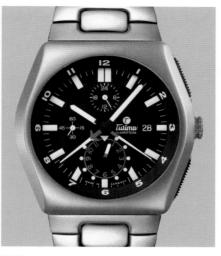

M2

Reference number: 6450-03
Movement: automatic, Tutima Caliber 521;
ø 30 mm, height 7.9 mm; 25 jewels; 28,800 vph;
sweep minute counter; 44-hour power reserve
Functions: hours, minutes, subsidiary seconds;
additional 24-hour display; chronograph; date
Case: titanium, ø 46 mm, height 15.5 mm; sapphire
crystal; screw-in crown; water-resistant to 30 atm
Band: titanium, folding clasp
Remarks: magnetic field protection from soft-iron
inner case
Price: $7,100
Variations: Kevlar strap ($6,500)

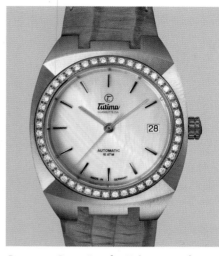

Saxon One Lady Diamonds

Reference number: 6701-02
Movement: automatic, Tutima Caliber 340;
ø 25.6 mm, height 3.6 mm; 25 jewels; 28,800 vph;
42-hour power reserve
Functions: hours, minutes, sweep seconds; date
Case: stainless steel, ø 36 mm, height 10.7 mm;
bezel set with 48 brilliant-cut diamonds; sapphire
crystal; screw-in crown; water-resistant to 10 atm
Band: reptile skin, folding clasp
Price: $6,700
Variations: stainless steel bracelet ($7,100)

Grand Flieger Classic Chronograph

Reference number: 6402-01
Movement: automatic, Tutima Caliber 320;
ø 30 mm, height 7.9 mm; 25 jewels; 28,800 vph;
44-hour power reserve; DIN-certified chronometer
Functions: hours, minutes, subsidiary seconds;
chronograph; date
Case: stainless steel, ø 43 mm, height 16 mm;
bidirectional bezel with reference marker; sapphire
crystal; transparent case back; screw-in crown;
water-resistant to 20 atm
Band: calf leather, folding clasp
Price: $5,700
Variations: stainless steel bracelet ($6,100)

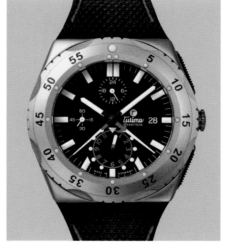

M2 Pioneer

Reference number: 6451-02
Movement: automatic, Tutima Caliber 521;
ø 30 mm, height 7.9 mm; 25 jewels; 28,800 vph;
sweep minute counter; 44-hour power reserve
Functions: hours, minutes, subsidiary seconds;
additional 24-hour display; chronograph; date
Case: titanium, ø 46.5 mm, height 16 mm;
bidirectional bezel with 60-degree division and
inserted luminescent capsules; sapphire crystal;
screw-in crown; water-resistant to 30 atm
Band: Kevlar, folding clasp
Remarks: magnetic field protection
Price: $6,900
Variations: titanium band with changing kit ($7,500)

Patria

Reference number: 6600-02
Movement: manually wound, Tutima Caliber 617;
ø 31 mm, height 4.78 mm; 20 jewels; 21,600 vph;
screw balance with weight screws and Breguet
spring; Glashütte three-quarter plate; winding
wheels with click; gold-plated, finely finished;
65-hour power reserve
Functions: hours, minutes, subsidiary seconds
Case: rose gold, ø 43 mm, height 11.2 mm;
sapphire crystal; transparent case back; water-
resistant to 5 atm
Band: reptile skin, buckle
Price: $19,900
Variations: Arabic numerals ($19,900)

Ulysse Nardin SA

3, rue du Jardin
CH-2400 Le Locle
Switzerland

Tel.:
+41-32-930-7400

Fax:
+41-32-930-7419

Website:
www.ulysse-nardin.ch

Founded:
1846

U.S. distributor:
Ulysse Nardin Inc.
7900 Glades Rd., Suite 200
Boca Raton, FL 33434
561-988-8600; 561-988-0123 (fax)
usa@ulysse-nardin.com

Most important collections:
Marine chronometers and diver's watches;
Dual Time (also ladies' watches);
complications (alarm clocks, perpetual
calendar, tourbillons, minute repeaters,
jacquemarts, astronomical watches)

Ulysse Nardin

At the beginning of the 1980s, following the infamous quartz crisis, Rolf Schnyder revived the venerable Ulysse Nardin brand, which once upon a time had a reputation for marine chronometers and precision watches. He had the luck to meet the multitalented Dr. Ludwig Oechslin, who realized Schnyder's vision of astronomical wristwatches in the Trilogy of Time. Overnight, Ulysse Nardin became a name to be reckoned with in the world of fine watchmaking. Oechslin developed a host of innovations for Ulysse Nardin, from intelligent calendar movements to escapement systems. He was the first to use silicon and synthetic diamonds and thus gave the entire industry a great deal of food for thought. Just about every Ulysse Nardin has become famous for some spectacular technical innovation, be it the Moonstruck with its stunning moon phase accuracy or the outlandish Freak series that more or less does away with the dial.

Schnyder died suddenly in 2011. His wife Chai Schnyder was named president of the board of directors, and Patrik Hoffmann was appointed CEO. The brand continued exploring new paths in horology, with a focus on building new movements while cutting back on new models. They developed a strategy of partnerships and acquisitions, notably of the enameler Donzé Cadrans SA, which gave rise to the Marine Chronometer Manufacture, powered by the Caliber UN-118. A new anchor escapement consisting of a suspended silicon frame holding the two blade-driven fork arms became the talk of Baselworld 2014.

All these moves made Ulysse Nardin a perfect prize for the French luxury group Kering. The deal was completed in 2014.

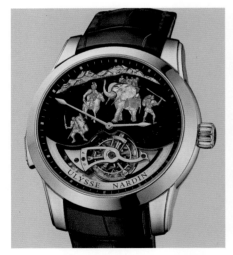

Hannibal Minute Repeater

Reference number: 789-00
Movement: manually wound, Caliber UN-78; 36 jewels; 18,000 vph; 1-minute tourbillon; hour, quarter hour, minute repeater with jacquemarts (automated figures); 70-hour power reserve
Functions: hours, minutes; minute repeater with jacquemarts
Case: platinum, ø 44 mm; sapphire crystal; transparent case back
Band: reptile skin, double folding clasp
Remarks: granite dial
Price: on request; limited to 30 pieces

Ulysse Anchor Tourbillon

Reference number: 1786-133
Movement: manually wound, Caliber UN-178; 29 jewels; 18,000 vph; 1-minute tourbillon; double spring barrel, Ulysse Nardin constant force escapement; 168-hour power reserve
Functions: hours, minutes; power reserve indicator
Case: rose gold, ø 44 mm; sapphire crystal; transparent case back
Band: reptile skin, buckle
Remarks: enamel dial
Price: $89,400; limited to 18 pieces
Variations: white gold ($93,600; limited to 18 pieces)

"Jazz" Minute Repeater

Reference number: 749-88
Movement: manually wound, Caliber UN-74; ø 27.6 mm, height 8.5 mm; 36 jewels; 28,800 vph; hour, quarter hour, minute repeater on 2 gongs with synchronous jacquemarts (automated figures)
Functions: hours, minutes; minute repeater with jacquemarts
Case: platinum, ø 42 mm, height 14 mm; sapphire crystal; transparent case back
Band: reptile skin, double folding clasp
Price: on request; limited to 18 pieces

Musical Watch "Stranger Vivaldi"

Reference number: 6902-125/VIV
Movement: automatic, Caliber UN-690; ø 37 mm, height 10.06 mm; 64 jewels; 28,800 vph; silicium escapement, pallet lever, hairspring; music box on dial with visible peg disc, 10 gongs
Functions: hours and minutes (off-center), subsidiary seconds; date; music box (plays melody hourly or on demand)
Case: rose gold, ø 45 mm; sapphire crystal; crown with integrated pusher
Band: reptile skin, double folding clasp
Price: $105,000; limited to 99 pieces

FreakLab

Reference number: 2100-138
Movement: manually wound, Caliber UN-210; ø 35 mm, 28 jewels; 28,800 vph; flying 1-hour tourbillon on orbital carousel, dual Ulysse silicon escapement and hairspring; components used as hands; 168-hour power reserve
Functions: hours, minutes; date
Case: white gold, ø 45 mm, height 13.5 mm; bidirectional bezel sets hands, winding by turning case back; sapphire crystal; transparent case back
Band: reptile skin, double folding clasp
Price: $95,000

Freak Blue Phantom

Reference number: 2080-115/03
Movement: manually wound, Caliber UN-208; ø 35 mm; 28 jewels; 28,800 vph; flying 1-minute tourbillon on orbital carousel; silicon escapement and hairspring; components used as hands; approx. 170-hour power reserve
Functions: hours, minutes, subsidiary seconds
Case: white gold, ø 45 mm, height 12.5 mm; bidirectional bezel sets hands, winding by turning case back; sapphire crystal; transparent case back
Band: reptile skin, double folding clasp
Price: $140,000
Variations: rose gold ($128,000; limited to 28 pieces)

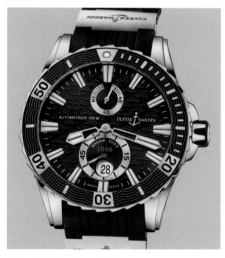

Maxi Marine Diver

Reference number: 266-10-3/93
Movement: automatic, Caliber UN-26; ø 25.6 mm, height 5.1 mm; 28 jewels; 28,800 vph; 42-hour power reserve
Functions: hours, minutes, subsidiary seconds; power reserve indicator; date
Case: rose gold, ø 44 mm, height 13 mm; unidirectional bezel with 60-minute divisions; sapphire crystal; screw-in crown; water-resistant to 30 atm
Band: rubber with rose gold elements, folding clasp
Price: $31,700
Variations: stainless steel ($8,500)

GMT Perpetual

Reference number: 329-10/92
Movement: automatic, Caliber UN-32; ø 31 mm, height 6.95 mm; 34 jewels; 28,800 vph; perpetual calendar mechanism crown-adjustable back and forth; COSC-certified chronometer
Functions: hours, minutes, subsidiary seconds; additional 24-hour display (2nd time zone); perpetual calendar with large date, weekday, month, year
Case: platinum, ø 43 mm, height 12.5 mm; sapphire crystal; transparent case back
Band: reptile skin, double folding clasp
Price: $69,500; limited to 250 pieces
Variations: rose gold ($52,500; limited to 250 pieces)

Classico "Kruzenshtern"

Reference number: 8156-111-2/KRUZ
Movement: automatic, Caliber UN-815; 28,800 vph; 42-hour power reserve; COSC-certified chronometer
Functions: hours, minutes, sweep seconds
Case: rose gold, ø 40 mm; sapphire crystal; transparent case back
Band: reptile skin, buckle
Remarks: hand-painted enamel dial
Price: $39,800; limited to 30 pieces
Variations: white gold ($42,900; limited to 30 pieces)

Dual Time Manufacture

Reference number: 3346-126LE/93
Movement: automatic, Caliber UN-334; 49 jewels; 28,800 vph; silicon escapement and hairspring
Functions: hours, minutes, subsidiary seconds; additional 24-hour display (2nd time zone); large date
Case: rose gold, ø 42 mm, height 13 mm; sapphire crystal; transparent case back
Band: reptile skin, double folding clasp
Price: $26,500; limited to 500 pieces
Variations: stainless steel ($9,800; limited to 1,846 pieces)

Dual Time Manufacture

Reference number: 3343-126/912
Movement: automatic, Caliber UN-334; 49 jewels; 28,800 vph; silicon escapement and hairspring
Functions: hours, minutes, subsidiary seconds; additional 24-hour display (2nd time zone); large date
Case: stainless steel, ø 42 mm, height 13 mm; sapphire crystal; transparent case back
Band: reptile skin, double folding clasp
Price: $9,800
Variations: rose gold ($26,500)

Marine Chronograph Manufacture Blue Baltics

Reference number: 1503-150LE-3RG/43-BALT-V2
Movement: automatic, Caliber UN-150; ø 31 mm, height 6.4 mm; 25 jewels; 28,800 vph; silicon escapement
Functions: hours, minutes, subsidiary seconds; chronograph; date
Case: stainless steel and titanium, ø 43 mm, height 15 mm; sapphire crystal; transparent case back; screw-in crown
Band: rubber with rose gold elements, folding clasp
Price: $19,700; limited to 250 pieces
Variations: rubber with titanium elements ($13,100)

Classico Small Second Manufacture

Reference number: 3206-136-2/33
Movement: automatic, Caliber UN-320; 28,800 vph; 42-hour power reserve; COSC-certified chronometer
Functions: hours, minutes, subsidiary seconds; date
Case: rose gold, ø 40 mm, height 9 mm; sapphire crystal; transparent case back
Band: reptile skin, buckle
Price: $14,500
Variations: eggshell dial ($14,500)

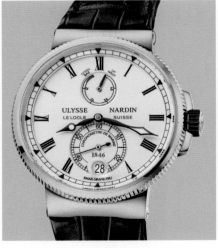

Marine Chronometer Manufacture

Reference number: 1186-126/E0
Movement: automatic, Caliber UN-118; ø 31.6 mm, height 6.45 mm; 50 jewels; 28,800 vph; silicon hairspring, diamond-coated silicon escapement (DiamOnSil); COSC-certified; 60-hour power reserve
Functions: hours, minutes, subsidiary seconds; power reserve indicator; date
Case: rose gold, ø 43 mm, height 13 mm; sapphire crystal; transparent case back; screw-in crown
Band: reptile skin, double folding clasp
Remarks: enamel dial
Price: $31,900; limited to 888 pieces
Variations: rubber band/rose gold elements ($33,300)

Marine Chronometer Manufacture

Reference number: 1185-126/45
Movement: automatic, Caliber UN-118; ø 31.6 mm, height 6.45 mm; 50 jewels; 28,800 vph; silicon hairspring, diamond-coated silicon escapement (DiamOnSil); COSC-certified; 60-hour power reserve
Functions: hours, minutes, subsidiary seconds; power reserve indicator; date
Case: stainless steel, ø 43 mm, height 13 mm; rose gold bezel; sapphire crystal; transparent back; screw-in crown
Band: reptile skin, double folding clasp
Price: $15,200
Variations: stainless steel bracelet ($23,400)

Maxi Marine Diver Black Sea

Reference number: 263-92LE-3C/923-RG
Movement: automatic, Caliber UN-26; ø 25.6 mm, height 5.1 mm; 28 jewels; 28,800 vph; 42-hour power reserve; COSC-certified chronometer
Functions: hours, minutes, subsidiary seconds; power reserve indicator; date
Case: stainless steel with rubber coating, ø 45.8 mm, height 14 mm; unidirectional rose gold bezel with 60-minute divisions, sapphire crystal; transparent case back; screw-in crown; water-resistant to 20 atm
Band: rubber with ceramic elements, folding clasp
Price: $13,500; limited to 1,846 pieces

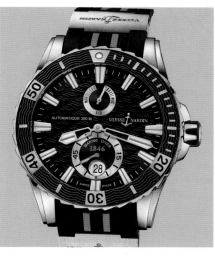

Marine Diver

Reference number: 263-10-3/952
Movement: automatic, Caliber UN-26; ø 25.6 mm, height 5.1 mm; 28 jewels; 28,800 vph; 42-hour power reserve
Functions: hours, minutes, subsidiary seconds; power reserve indicator; date
Case: stainless steel, ø 44 mm, height 13 mm; unidirectional bezel with 60-minute divisions, sapphire crystal; screw-in crown; water-resistant to 30 atm
Band: rubber with titanium elements, folding clasp
Price: $8,500
Variations: stainless steel bracelet ($9,700)

Marine Chronometer Manufacture

Reference number: 1183-122-3/42 V2
Movement: automatic, Caliber UN-118; ø 31.6 mm, height 6.45 mm; 50 jewels; 28,800 vph; silicon hairspring, diamond-coated silicon escapement (DiamOnSil); COSC-certified; 60-hour power reserve
Functions: hours, minutes, subsidiary seconds; power reserve indicator; date
Case: stainless steel/titanium, ø 45 mm, height 13 mm; sapphire crystal; transparent back; screw-in crown
Band: rubber/titanium elements, double folding clasp
Remarks: enamel dial
Price: $10,300
Variations: stainless steel bracelet ($11,300)

Caliber UN-334

Automatic; silicon escapement, single spring barrel, 48-hour power reserve
Functions: hours, minutes, subsidiary seconds; additional 24-hour display (2nd time zone); large date
Jewels: 49
Balance: variable inertia balance
Frequency: 28,800 vph
Balance spring: silicon
Shock protection: Incabloc
Remarks: patented quick adjustment for 2nd time zone; perlage on plate, bridges with concentric côtes de Genève ("côtes circulaires")

Caliber UN-118

Automatic; patented DiamOnSil escapement; single spring barrel, approx. 60-hour power reserve
Functions: hours, minutes, subsidiary seconds; date; power reserve indicator
Diameter: 31.6 mm
Height: 6.45 mm
Jewels: 50
Balance: silicon balance with variable inertia
Frequency: 28,800 vph
Balance spring: silicon
Shock protection: Incabloc
Remarks: perlage on plate, bridges with concentric côtes de Genève ("côtes circulaires")

Caliber UN-178

Manually wound; 1-minute tourbillon, Ulysse Nardin DiamOnSil anchor escapement (anchor turns without pivots between 2 blades) with new geometry; double spring barrel, 168-hour power reserve
Functions: hours, minutes; power reserve indicator
Diameter: 37 mm
Height: 6 mm
Jewels: 29
Balance: glucydur
Frequency: 18,000 vph
Balance spring: silicon

Urwerk SA
114, rue du Rhône
CH-1204 Geneva
Switzerland

Tel.:
+41-22-900-2027

Fax:
+41-22-900-2026

E-Mail:
info@urwerk.com

Website:
www.urwerk.com

Founded:
1995

Annual production:
150 watches

U.S. distributor:
Ildico Inc.
132 South Rodeo Drive, Fourth Floor
Beverly Hills, CA 90212
310-205-5555

Urwerk

Felix Baumgartner and designer Martin Frei count among the living legends of innovative horology. They founded their company Urwerk in 1995 with a name that is a play on the words *Uhrwerk*, for movement, and *Urwerk*, meaning a sort of primal mechanism. Their specialty is inventing surprising time indicators featuring digital numerals that rotate like satellites and display the time in a relatively linear depiction on a small "dial" at the front of the flattened case, which could almost—but not quite—be described as oval. Their inspiration goes back to the so-called night clock of the eighteenth-century Campanus brothers, but the realization is purely *2001: A Space Odyssey*.

Urwerk's debut was with the Harry Winston Opus 5. Later, they created the Black Cobra, which displays time using cylinders and other clever ways to recoup energy for driving rather heavy components. The Torpedo is another example of high-tech watchmaking, again based on the satellite system of revolving and turning hands. These pieces remind one of the frenetic engineering that has transformed the planet since the eighteenth century. And with each return to the drawing board, Baumgartner and Frei find new ways to explore what has now become an unmistakable form, using high-tech materials, like aluminum titanium nitride (AlTiN), or finding new functions for the owner to play with. Their Electro-Mechanical Control mechanism is a typically radical concept that shows beat deviations and allows the user to regulate the watch. The power comes from a microgenerator.

UR-105 TA

Movement: manually wound, UR 5.02, 52 jewels; 28,800 vph; aluminum revolving hour satellites with Geneva cross control; PEEK dial mask; winding with air stream decoupling and variable efficiency; 48-hour power reserve
Functions: hours (digital, rotating), minutes,
Case: titanium, 39.5 x 53 mm, height 16.8 mm; pink gold bezel; sapphire crystal; water-resistant to 3 atm
Band: reptile skin, buckle
Remarks: lever to regulate winding efficiency (on back)
Price: $72,000

UR-210S "Full Metal Jacket"

Movement: automatic, UR 7.10; 51 jewels; 28,800 vph; revolving hour cubes with retrograde minutes arc, winding system regulated by fluid dynamics decoupling/adjustable efficiency; 39-hour power reserve
Functions: hours (digital, rotating), minutes (retrograde); power reserve display; winding efficiency display
Case: stainless steel/titanium, 43.8 x 53.6 mm, height 17.8 mm; sapphire crystal; water-resistant to 3 atm
Band: stainless steel, folding clasp
Remarks: hour cubes travel over semicircular minute scale, at end of scale skeletonized minute hand jumps back/picks up next satellite
Price: $170,000

EMC Black

Movement: manually wound, UR EMC; 28,800 vph; integrated rate precision monitoring with optical sensor on escapement/comparison with referential oscillator (16,000,000 Hz) via pusher; adjustment screw on movement side; power from microgenerator with large collapsible winding handle on case side; 80-hour power reserve
Functions: hours/minutes (off-center), subsidiary seconds; power reserve display, rate precision display
Case: titanium with black DLC coating, 43 x 51 mm, height 15.8 mm; sapphire crystal; functional elements, rate tuning screw on back; water-resistant to 3 atm
Band: reptile skin, buckle
Price: $130,000

UTS Watches, Inc.
630 Quintana Road, Suite 194
Morro Bay, CA 93442

Tel.:
877-887-0123 or 805-528-9800

E-Mail:
info@utswatches.com

Website:
www.utswatches.com

Founded:
1999

Number of employees:
2

Annual production:
fewer than 500

Distribution:
direct sales only

Most important collections/price range:
sports and diver's watches, chronographs /
from $2,500 to $7,000

UTS

UTS, or "Uhren Technik Spinner," was the natural outgrowth of a company based in Munich and manufacturing CNC tools and machines for the watch industry. Nicolaus Spinner, a mechanical engineer and aficionado in his own right, learned the nitty-gritty of watchmaking by the age-old system of taking watches apart. From there to making robust diver's watches was just a short step. The collection has grown considerably since he started production in 1999. The watches are built mainly around ETA calibers. Some, like the new 4000M, feature a unique locking bezel using a stem, a bolt, and a ceramic ball bearing system invented by Spinner. Another specialty is the 6 mm sapphire crystal, which guarantees significant water resistance. Spinner's longtime friend and business partner, Stephen Newman, is the owner of the UTS trademark in the United States. He has not only worked on product development, but has also contributed his own design ideas and handles sales and marketing for the small brand. A new watch released in 2014, the 4000M Diver, boasts an extreme depth rating even without the need for a helium escape valve and is available in a GMT version. The collection is small, but UTS has a faithful following in Germany and the United States. The key for the fan club is a unique appearance coupled with mastery of the technology. These are pure muscle watches with no steroids.

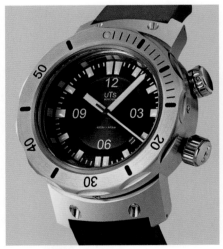

Diver 4000M

Movement: automatic, ETA Caliber 2824-2;
ø 25.6 mm, height 4.6 mm; 25 jewels; 28,800 vph;
42-hour power reserve
Functions: hours, minutes, sweep seconds; date
Case: stainless steel, ø 45 mm, height 17.5 mm;
bidirectional bezel with 60-minute scale; 6 mm
sapphire crystal, antireflective on back; screwed-
down case back; screw-in crown and buttons;
locking bezel; water-resistant to 400 atm
Band: stainless steel with diver's extension folding
clasp or rubber or leather strap
Price: $6,800

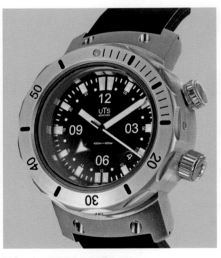

Diver 4000M GMT

Movement: automatic, ETA Caliber 2893-2;
ø 25.6 mm, height 4.6 mm; 25 jewels; 28,800 vph;
42-hour power reserve
Functions: hours, minutes, sweep seconds; date;
2nd time zone
Case: stainless steel, ø 45 mm, height 17.5 mm;
bidirectional bezel with 60-minute scale; 6 mm
sapphire crystal, antireflective on back; screwed-
down case back; screw-in crown and buttons;
locking bezel; water-resistant to 400 atm
Band: stainless steel with diver's extension folding
clasp or rubber or leather strap
Price: $6,800

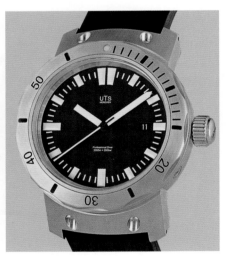

2000M

Movement: automatic, ETA Caliber 2824-2;
ø 25.6 mm, height 4.6 mm; 25 jewels; 28,800 vph;
42-hour power reserve
Functions: hours, minutes, sweep seconds; date
Case: stainless steel, ø 44 mm, height 16.5 mm;
unidirectional bezel with 60-minute scale; automatic
helium escape valve; sapphire crystal, antireflective
on back; screwed-down case back; screw-in crown
and buttons; water-resistant to 200 atm
Band: stainless steel with diver's extension folding
clasp, comes with rubber leather strap
Price: $3,950

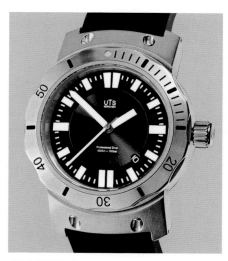

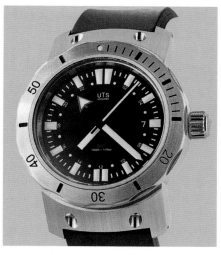

1000M V2

Movement: automatic, ETA Caliber 2824-2; ø 25.6 mm, height 4.6 mm; 25 jewels; 28,800 vph; 42-hour power reserve
Functions: hours, minutes, sweep seconds; date
Case: stainless steel, ø 43 mm, height 14 mm; unidirectional bezel with 60-minute scale; sapphire crystal, antireflective on back; screwed-down sapphire (optional) crystal case back; screw-in crown and buttons; water-resistant to 10 atm
Band: stainless steel with diver's extension folding clasp or rubber or leather strap
Price: $3,390

1000 GMT

Movement: automatic, ETA Caliber ETA 2893-2; ø 25.6 mm, height 4.1 mm; 21 jewels; 28,800 vph; 42-hour power reserve
Functions: hours, minutes, sweep seconds; 2nd time zone; date; quick set GMT hand
Case: stainless steel, ø 43 mm, height 14 mm; unidirectional bezel with 60-minute scale; sapphire crystal, antireflective on back; screwed-down case back with optional transparent back (sapphire crystal); screw-in crown and buttons; water-resistant to 100 atm
Band: stainless steel with diver's extension folding clasp or rubber or leather strap
Price: $3,750

Adventure Automatic

Movement: automatic, ETA Valgranges Caliber A07.111; ø 36.6 mm, height 7.9 mm; 24 jewels; 28,800 vph; 46-hour power reserve
Functions: hours, minutes, sweep seconds; date
Case: stainless steel, ø 46 mm, height 15.5 mm; screw-in crown; antireflective sapphire crystal; screwed-down sapphire crystal case back; water-resistant to 50 atm
Band: rubber, buckle
Price: $3,950
Variations: leather strap; stainless steel bracelet with folding clasp and diver's extension

Adventure Automatic GMT

Movement: automatic, ETA Valgranges Caliber A07.171; ø 36.6 mm, height 7.9 mm; 24 jewels; 28,800 vph; 46-hour power reserve
Functions: hours, minutes, sweep seconds; date; 2nd time zone
Case: stainless steel, ø 46 mm, height 15.5 mm; screw-in crown; antireflective sapphire crystal; screwed-down sapphire crystal case back; water-resistant to 50 atm
Band: rubber, buckle
Price: $4,550
Variations: leather strap; stainless steel bracelet with folding clasp and diver's extension

Chrono Diver

Movement: automatic, ETA Valjoux Caliber 7750; ø 30 mm, height 7.9 mm; 25 jewels; 28,800 vph; 45-hour power reserve
Functions: hours, minutes, subsidiary seconds; date; chronograph
Case: stainless steel, ø 46 mm, height 16.5 mm; unidirectional bezel with 60-minute scale; screw-in crown and buttons; antireflective sapphire crystal; screwed-down case back; water-resistant to 600 m
Band: stainless steel, folding clasp
Price: $4,550
Variations: leather strap

Adventure Manual Wind

Movement: manually wound, ETA Unitas Caliber 6497; ø 36.6 mm, height 5.4 mm; 18 jewels; 18,000 vph; 48-hour power reserve
Functions: hours, minutes, subsidiary seconds
Case: stainless steel, ø 46 mm, height 14 mm; screw-in crown; antireflective sapphire crystal; screwed-down sapphire crystal case back; water-resistant to 50 atm
Band: leather, buckle
Price: $3,400
Variations: rubber strap

Vacheron Constantin
Chemin du Tourbillon
CH-1228 Plan-les-Ouates
Switzerland

Tel.:
+41-22-930-2005

E-Mail:
info@vacheron-constantin.com

Website:
www.vacheron-constantin.com

Founded:
1755

Number of employees:
approx. 800

Annual production:
over 20,000 watches (estimated)

U.S. distributor:
Vacheron Constantin
Richemont North America
645 Fifth Avenue
New York, NY 10022
877-701-1755

Most important collections:
Harmony, Patrimony, Traditionnelle,
Historiques, Metiers d'Art, Malte, Overseas,
Quai de l'Ile

Vacheron Constantin

The origins of this oldest continuously operating watch *manufacture* can be traced back to 1755 when Jean-Marc Vacheron opened his workshop in Geneva. His highly complex watches were particularly appreciated by clients in Paris. The development of such an important outlet for horological works there had a lot to do with the emergence of a wealthy class around the powerful French court. The Revolution put an end to all the financial excesses of that market, however, and the Vacheron company suffered as well . . . until the arrival of marketing wizard François Constantin in 1819.

Fast-forward to the late twentieth century: The brand with the Maltese cross logo had evolved into a tradition-conscious keeper of *haute horlogerie* under the aegis, starting in the mid-1990s, of the Vendôme Luxury Group (today's Richemont SA). Gradually, it began creating collections that combine modern shapes with traditional patterns. The company has been expanding steadily. In 2013 it opened boutiques in the United States as well as China, and it has become a leading sponsor of the New York City Ballet.

Vacheron Constantin is one of the last luxury brands to have abandoned the traditional way of dividing up labor. Today, most of its basic movements are made in-house at the production facilities and headquarters in Plan-les-Ouates and the workshops in Le Brassus in Switzerland's Jura region, which were expanded in the summer of 2013. In 2015, Vacheron Constantin presented three new chronograph calibers that filled any remaining gaps in its portfolio.

Harmony Chronograph

Reference number: 5300S/000R-B055
Movement: manually wound, Vacheron Constantin Caliber 3300; ø 32.8 mm, height 6.7 mm; 35 jewels; 21,600 vph; crown pusher control; hand-engraved balance cock with anniversary decoration; 65-hour power reserve; Geneva Seal
Functions: hours, minutes, subsidiary seconds; power reserve indicator; chronograph
Case: rose gold, 42 x 52 mm, height 12.81 mm; sapphire crystal; transparent case back; water-resistant to 3 atm
Band: reptile skin, double folding clasp
Remarks: dial with pulsometer scale
Price: $69,000; limited to 260 pieces

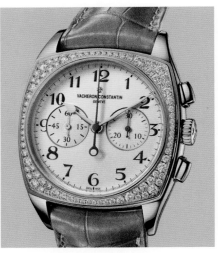

Harmony Chronograph Small Model

Reference number: 5005S/000R-B053
Movement: manually wound, Vacheron Constantin Caliber 1142; ø 27.5 mm, height 5.57 mm; 21 jewels; 21,600 vph; hand-engraved balance cock with anniversary decoration; 48-hour power reserve; Geneva Seal
Functions: hours, minutes, subsidiary seconds; chronograph
Case: rose gold, 37 x 46.6 mm, height 11.74 mm; 84 diamonds on bezel; sapphire crystal; transparent case back; water-resistant to 3 atm
Band: reptile skin, double folding clasp
Price: $65,000; limited to 260 pieces

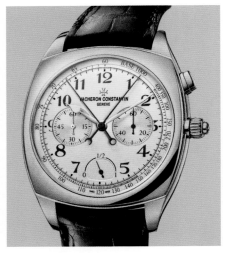

Harmony Chronograph Ultra-thin

Reference number: 5400S/000P-B057
Movement: automatic, Vacheron Constantin Caliber 3500; ø 33.4 mm, height 5.2 mm; 47 jewels; 21,600 vph; hubless peripheral rotor; crown pusher control; 51-hour power reserve; Geneva Seal
Functions: hours, minutes, subsidiary seconds; power reserve indicator; split-second chronograph
Case: platinum, 42 x 52 mm, height 8.4 mm; sapphire crystal; transparent case back; water-resistant to 3 atm
Band: reptile skin, double folding clasp
Price: $339,000; limited to 10 pieces

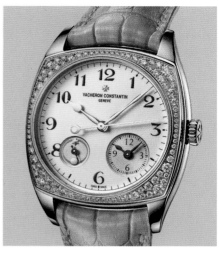

Harmony Tourbillon Chronograph

Reference number: 5100S/000P-B056
Movement: manually wound, Vacheron Constantin Caliber 3200; ø 32.8 mm, height 6.7 mm; 39 jewels; 18,000 vph; 1-minute tourbillon; crown pusher control; 65-hour power reserve; Geneva Seal
Functions: hours, minutes, subsidiary seconds (on tourbillon cage); power reserve indicator; chronograph
Case: platinum, 42 x 52 mm, height 12.81 mm; sapphire crystal; transparent case back; water-resistant to 3 atm
Band: reptile skin, double folding clasp
Price: $288,000; limited to 26 pieces

Harmony Dual Time

Reference number: 7810S/000R-B051
Movement: automatic, Vacheron Constantin Caliber 2460DT; ø 28 mm, height 5.4 mm; 27 jewels; 28,800 vph; gold rotor; 40-hour power reserve; Geneva Seal
Functions: hours, minutes, sweep seconds; additional 12-hour display (2nd time zone), day/night indicator
Case: rose gold, 40 x 49.3 mm, height 11.43 mm; sapphire crystal; transparent case back; water-resistant to 3 atm
Band: reptile skin, double folding clasp
Price: $40,000; limited to 625 pieces

Harmony Dual Time Small Model

Reference number: 7805S/000G-B052
Movement: automatic, Vacheron Constantin Caliber 2460DT; ø 28 mm, height 5.4 mm; 27 jewels; 28,800 vph; gold rotor; 40-hour power reserve; Geneva Seal
Functions: hours, minutes, sweep seconds; additional 12-hour display (2nd time zone), day/night indicator
Case: white gold, 37 x 46.6 mm, height 11.18 mm; 88 diamonds on bezel; sapphire crystal; transparent case back; water-resistant to 3 atm
Band: reptile skin, double folding clasp
Price: $46,500; limited to 500 pieces

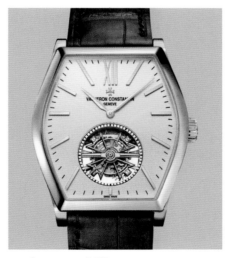

Malte Small Second

Reference number: 82230-000G-9962
Movement: manually wound, Caliber 4400 AS; ø 28.6 mm, height 2.8 mm; 21 jewels; 28,800 vph; Geneva Seal
Functions: hours, minutes, subsidiary seconds
Case: white gold, 36.7 x 47.61 mm, height 9.1 mm; sapphire crystal; water-resistant to 3 atm
Band: reptile skin, buckle
Price: $24,700
Variations: rose gold ($24,700)

Malte Tourbillon

Reference number: 30130/000R-9754.
Movement: manually wound, Caliber 2795; 27.37 x 29.3 mm, height 6.1 mm; 27 jewels; 18,000 vph; shaped with 1-minute tourbillon; 45-hour power reserve; Geneva Seal
Functions: hours, minutes, subsidiary seconds (on tourbillon cage)
Case: rose gold, 38 x 48.24 mm, height 12.73 mm; sapphire crystal; transparent case back; water-resistant to 3 atm
Band: reptile skin, folding clasp
Price: $159,000
Variations: platinum ($194,000)

Patrimony Traditionnelle 14 Days Tourbillon

Reference number: 89000/000R-9655
Movement: manually wound, Caliber 2260; ø 29.9 mm, height 6.8 mm; 31 jewels; 18,000 vph; 1-minute tourbillon; 336-hour power reserve; Geneva Seal
Functions: hours, minutes, subsidiary seconds (on tourbillon cage); power reserve indicator
Case: rose gold, ø 42 mm, height 12.2 mm; sapphire crystal; transparent case back; water-resistant to 3 atm
Band: reptile skin, folding clasp
Price: $296,000

Patrimony Traditionnelle Manual Winding

Reference number: 82172/000P-9811
Movement: manually wound, Caliber 4400;
ø 28.6 mm, height 2.8 mm; 21 jewels; 28,800 vph;
65-hour power reserve; Geneva Seal
Functions: hours, minutes, subsidiary seconds
Case: platinum, ø 38 mm, height 7.77 mm;
sapphire crystal; transparent case back; water-resistant to 3 atm
Band: reptile skin, buckle
Price: $32,500
Variations: white gold ($19,500); pink gold
($19,500)

Patrimony Traditionnelle Day Date with Power Reserve

Reference number: 85290/000P-9947
Movement: automatic, Vacheron Constantin Caliber
2475 SC; ø 26.2 mm, height 5.7 mm; 27 jewels;
28,800 vph; 40-hour power reserve; Geneva Seal
Functions: hours, minutes, sweep seconds; power
reserve indicator; weekday, date
Case: platinum, ø 39.5 mm, height 10.65 mm;
sapphire crystal; transparent case back; water-resistant to 3 atm
Band: reptile skin, buckle
Remarks: Excellence Platine collection
Price: $80,000

Traditional World Time

Reference number: 86060/000P-9979
Movement: automatic, Caliber 2460 WT;
ø 36.6 mm, height 7.55 mm; 27 jewels; 28,800 vph;
40-hour power reserve
Functions: hours, minutes, sweep seconds; world-time display with 37 time zones
Case: platinum, ø 42.5 mm, height 11.62 mm;
sapphire crystal; transparent case back; water-resistant to 3 atm
Band: reptile skin, folding clasp
Price: $90,500
Variations: rose gold ($48,000)

Patrimony

Reference number: 81180/000R-9159
Movement: manually wound, Caliber 1400;
ø 20.35 mm, height 2.6 mm; 20 jewels;
28,800 vph; 40-hour power reserve; Geneva Seal
Functions: hours, minutes
Case: rose gold, ø 40 mm, sapphire crystal;
transparent case back
Band: reptile skin, buckle
Price: $18,000
Variations: white gold ($18,000); yellow gold
($18,000)

Patrimony Date Automatic

Reference number: 85180/000R-9166
Movement: automatic, Caliber 2450 VC;
ø 26.2 mm, height 3.6 mm; 27 jewels; 28,800 vph;
40-hour power reserve; Geneva Seal
Functions: hours, minutes, sweep seconds; date
Case: rose gold, ø 40 mm, height 8.31 mm;
sapphire crystal; transparent case back; water-resistant to 3 atm
Band: reptile skin, buckle
Price: $25,600
Variations: white dial; white gold ($25,600)

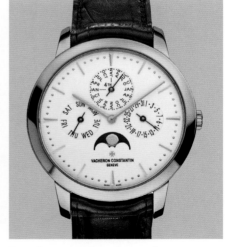

Patrimony Perpetual Calendar

Reference number: 43175/000R-9687
Movement: automatic, Caliber 1120 QP;
ø 29.6 mm, height 4.05 mm; 36 jewels;
19,800 vph; 40-hour power reserve; Geneva Seal
Functions: hours, minutes; perpetual calendar with
date, weekday, month, moon phase, leap year
Case: rose gold, ø 41 mm, height 8.9 mm; sapphire
crystal; transparent case back; water-resistant to
3 atm
Band: reptile skin, folding clasp
Price: $76,000

Patrimony Minute Repeater Caliber 1731

Reference number: 30110/000R/9793
Movement: manually wound, Caliber 1731; ø 32.8 mm, height 3.9 mm; 36 jewels; 21,600 vph; 65-hour power reserve; Geneva Seal
Functions: hours, minutes, subsidiary seconds; minute repeater
Case: rose gold, ø 41 mm, height 8.09 mm; sapphire crystal; transparent case back
Band: reptile skin, folding clasp with safety lock
Remarks: comes with "La Musique du Temps" resonance body
Price: $376,000

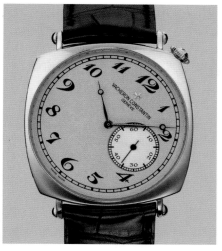

Historique American 1921

Reference number: 82035/000R-9359
Movement: manually wound, Caliber 4400; ø 28.5 mm, height 2.8 mm; 21 jewels; 28,800 vph; 65-hour power reserve; Geneva Seal
Functions: hours, minutes, subsidiary seconds
Case: rose gold, ø 40 mm, height 8 mm; sapphire crystal; transparent case back; water-resistant to 3 atm
Band: reptile skin, buckle
Remarks: modeled after 1921 vintage piece
Price: $34,000

Quai de l'Ile Retrograde Annual Calendar

Reference number: 86040/000R-I0P29
Movement: automatic, Caliber 2460 QRA; ø 26.2 mm, height 5.4 mm; 27 jewels; 28,800 vph; 40-hour power reserve; Geneva Seal
Functions: hours, minutes, subsidiary seconds; annual calendar with date, month, moon phase
Case: rose gold, 43 x 54 mm, height 13.5 mm; sapphire crystal; transparent case back; water-resistant to 3 atm
Band: reptile skin, folding clasp
Price: $65,000
Variations: many options for personalization

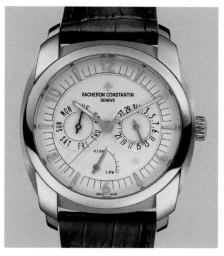

Quai de l'Ile Date and Weekday Display with Power Reserve

Reference number: 85050/000D-G9000
Movement: automatic, Caliber 2475 SC1; ø 26.2 mm, height 5.7 mm; 27 jewels; 28,800 vph; 40-hour power reserve; Geneva Seal
Functions: hours, minutes, sweep seconds; power reserve indicator; weekday, date
Case: palladium, 41 x 50.5 mm, height 12.9 mm; sapphire crystal; transparent case back; water-resistant to 3 atm
Band: reptile skin, folding clasp
Price: on request
Variations: many options for personalization

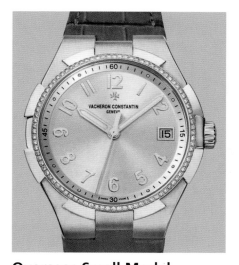

Overseas Small Model

Reference number: 47560/000R-9672
Movement: automatic, Caliber 1226 SC; ø 26.6 mm, height 6.6 mm; 36 jewels; 28,800 vph; 40-hour power reserve
Functions: hours, minutes, sweep seconds; date
Case: rose gold, ø 36 mm, 88 brilliant-cut diamonds on bezel; sapphire crystal; screw-in crown; water-resistant to 15 atm
Band: reptile skin, double folding clasp
Remarks: with rubber and reptile skin straps
Price: $30,800

Overseas Chronograph

Reference number: 49150/B01A-9097
Movement: automatic, Caliber 1137; ø 26 mm, height 6.6 mm; 37 jewels; 21,600 vph; 40-hour power reserve; Geneva Seal
Functions: hours, minutes, subsidiary seconds; chronograph; large date
Case: stainless steel, ø 42 mm, height 12.4 mm; sapphire crystal; screw-in crown; water-resistant to 15 atm
Band: stainless steel, double folding clasp
Price: $21,000
Variations: rose gold ($60,500)

Caliber 2755

Automatic; 1-minute tourbillon; single spring barrel, 55-hour power reserve
Functions: hours, minutes, subsidiary seconds; perpetual calendar with month, leap year, weekday, date; hour, quarter-hour, and minute repeater
Diameter: 33.3 mm
Height: 7.9 mm
Jewels: 40
Balance: glucydur
Frequency: 18,000 vph
Remarks: 602 components; Geneva Seal

Caliber 1731

Manually wound; single spring barrel, 65-hour power reserve
Functions: hours, minutes, subsidiary seconds; hour, quarter-hour, and minute repeater
Diameter: 32.8 mm
Height: 3.9 mm
Jewels: 36
Balance: glucydur
Frequency: 21,600 vph
Remarks: perlage on plate, beveled edges, bridges with côtes de Genève; Geneva Seal

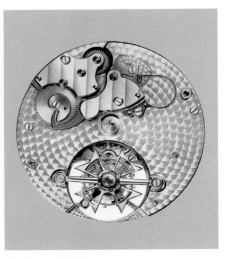

Caliber 2260

Manually wound; 1-minute tourbillon; single spring barrel, 336-hour power reserve; Geneva Seal
Functions: hours, minutes, subsidiary seconds (on tourbillon cage)
Diameter: 29.1 mm
Height: 6.8 mm
Jewels: 31
Balance: glucydur
Frequency: 18,000 vph

Caliber 1136 QP

Automatic; column wheel control of chronograph functions; single spring barrel, 40-hour power reserve
Functions: hours, minutes, subsidiary seconds; perpetual calendar with month, moon phase, leap year, weekday, date
Diameter: 28 mm
Height: 7.9 mm
Jewels: 38
Balance: glucydur
Frequency: 21,600 vph
Remarks: 228 components

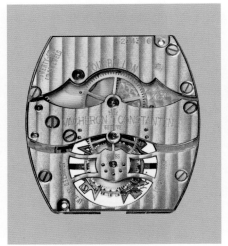

Caliber 2795

Automatic; 1-minute tourbillon; single spring barrel, 45-hour power reserve
Functions: hours, minutes, subsidiary seconds (on tourbillon cage)
Measurements: 27.37 x 29.3 mm
Height: 6.1 mm
Jewels: 27
Balance: glucydur
Frequency: 18,000 vph
Remarks: tonneau-shaped; Geneva Seal

Caliber 1003

Manually wound; single spring barrel, 31-hour power reserve
Functions: hours, minutes
Diameter: 21.1 mm
Height: 1.64 mm
Jewels: 18
Balance: glucydur
Frequency: 18,000 vph
Remarks: currently thinnest movement being produced; Geneva Seal

Caliber 4400SQ

Manually wound; single spring barrel, 65-hour power reserve
Functions: hours, minutes
Diameter: 28.6 mm
Height: 2.8 mm
Jewels: 21
Balance: glucydur
Frequency: 28,800 vph
Remarks: entirely skeletonized and engraved by hand; Geneva Seal

Caliber 3300

Manually wound; column wheel control of chronograph functions; horizontal clutch; single spring barrel; 65-hour power reserve; Geneva Seal
Functions: hours, minutes, subsidiary seconds; power reserve indicator; chronograph with crown pusher
Diameter: 32.8 mm
Height: 6.7 mm
Jewels: 35
Balance: glucydur
Frequency: 21,600 vph
Remarks: 252 components

Caliber 3200

Manually wound; 1-minute tourbillon; column wheel control of chronograph functions, horizontal clutch; single spring barrel, 65-hour power reserve; Geneva Seal
Functions: hours, minutes, subsidiary seconds (on tourbillon cage); power reserve indicator; chronograph with crown pusher
Diameter: 32.8 mm
Height: 6.7 mm
Jewels: 39
Balance: glucydur
Frequency: 18,000 vph
Remarks: 292 components

Caliber 3500

Automatic; 2 column wheels to control split seconds chronograph, horizontal clutch; hubless peripheral winding rotor with gold oscillating mass; ultrathin construction, single spring barrel, 51-hour power reserve; Geneva Seal
Functions: hours, minutes, subsidiary seconds; power reserve indicator; split seconds chronograph, with crown pusher
Diameter: 33.4 mm
Height: 5.2 mm
Jewels: 47
Balance: glucydur
Frequency: 21,600 vph
Remarks: 459 components

Caliber 2460 WT

Automatic; stop-second system; single spring barrel, 40-hour power reserve; Geneva Seal
Functions: hours, minutes, sweep seconds; additional 12-hour display (2nd time zone), day/night indicator
Diameter: 28 mm
Height: 5.4 mm
Jewels: 27
Balance: glucydur
Frequency: 28,800 vph
Remarks: gold rotor, 233 components

Caliber 2460 SCC

Automatic; stop-second system; single spring barrel, 43-hour power reserve
Functions: hours, minutes, sweep seconds
Diameter: 26.2 mm
Height: 3.6 mm
Jewels: 27
Balance: glucydur
Frequency: 28,800 vph
Remarks: perlage on plate, beveled edges, bridges with côtes de Genève; polished steel parts; gold rotor of "Chronomètre Royale" type, Geneva Seal; COSC-certified chronometer

Van Cleef & Arpels
2, rue du Quatre-Septembre
F-75002 Paris
France

Tel.:
+33-1-70-70-36-56

Website:
www.vancleefarpels.com

Founded:
1906

U.S. distributor:
1-877-VAN-CLEEF

Most important collections:
Cadenas, Charms, Pierre Arpels, Poetic
Complications

Van Cleef & Arpels

Surviving as a luxury concern requires a fine sense of how the market is segmented. Richemont only picks the cream of the crop. In 1999, while shopping around for more companies to add to its roster of high-end jewelers, the group struck on the idea of purchasing Van Cleef & Arpels. The venerable jewelry brand had a lot of name recognition, thanks in part to a host of internationally known customers, like Jacqueline Kennedy Onassis, whose two marriages each involved a Van Cleef & Arpels ring; Elizabeth Taylor; Farah Pahlavi, the queen of Iran; and Grace Kelly. It also had a reputation for the high quality of its workmanship. It was Van Cleef & Arpels that came up with the mystery setting using a special rail and cut totally hidden from the casual eye.

Van Cleef & Arpels was a family business that came to be when a young stone cutter, Alfred van Cleef, married Estelle Arpels in 1896, and ten years later opened a business on Place Vendôme in Paris with Estelle's brother Charles. More of Estelle's brothers joined the firm, which was soon booming and serving, quite literally, royalty.

Watches were always a part of the portfolio, as demonstrated by the 1930s Cadenas, which was rereleased in 2015 with a quartz movement. But after joining Richemont, Van Cleef now had the support of a very complete industrial portfolio that would allow it to make stunning movements that could bring dials to life. It was a collaboration with Jean-Marc Wiederrecht and Agenhor, however, that produced outstanding combinations of artistry in design and crafts, with horological excellence that made the watch-loving public take notice: the double retrograde Pont des Amoureux, showing a man and a woman meeting on a bridge, or the Pierre Arpels Heure d'ici & Heure d'ailleurs, a very restrained GMT featuring two apertures for the time zones and retrograde minutes.

Lady Arpels Pont des Amoureux

Reference number: VCARN9VI00
Movement: manually wound, JLC846 base with exclusive Agenhor retrograde module; 34 jewels; 30-hour power reserve
Functions: retrograde hours and minutes
Case: white gold, ø 38 mm, height 11.8 mm; white gold bezel with round diamonds; sculpted bridge; diamond on crown
Band: reptile skin; white gold buckle set with diamonds
Remarks: grisaille enamel dial; special complication shows meeting of couple on bridge at 12 o'clock
Price: $115,000
Variations: white gold bracelet with diamonds (price on request)

Pierre Arpels Heure d'ici & Heure d'ailleurs

Reference number: VCARO4II00
Movement: automatic, exclusive Agenhor caliber; 48-hour power reserve
Functions: double jumping hours and retrograde minute; dual time zone
Case: white gold, ø 42 mm, height 7.97 mm; white gold bezel; round diamond on crown; sapphire case back; water resistant up to 3 atm
Band: shiny black alligator strap; white gold hallmarked pin buckle
Remarks: white lacquer dial with piqué motif
Price: $40,900

Cadenas Sertie Bracelet Or

Reference number: VCARO4IL00
Movement: quartz movement
Functions: hours; minutes
Case: yellow gold, 26 x 14.5 mm; snow-set diamonds on bezel; water resistant up to 3 atm
Band: yellow gold snake chain with yellow gold clasp
Remarks: white mother-of-pearl dial
Price: $42,200
Variations: white gold with diamonds ($45,500)

Victorinox Swiss Army

This brand with the Swiss cross in its logo is a real child of the years of rapid industrial expansion in central Europe. Today, it is as much a symbol for Switzerland as cheese and chocolate are. In 1884, the brand was founded as the cutler to the Swiss army, and in the over 125 years of its existence, the practical and versatile officer's knife known as the Swiss Army Knife has become a legend, especially in what has grown to be its main market: the United States. The Victorinox concern, which is a family enterprise, owns a handful of divisions, though, whose products all epitomize the principle of functionality coupled with style.

Perfect quality, high reliability, and consistent functionality also characterize this brand's watches and its business practices as well. Faced with a massive recession, CEO Karl Elsener saw to it that redundant employees had alternative sources of income till after the storm, while he opened new markets and developed new products, such as a line of suitcases and perfumes.

Since the purchase of its American branch, Swiss Army Brands, Inc. in 2002, the Victorinox concern has gone by the name Victorinox Swiss Army and has successfully begun to transfer the proverbial versatility and robustness of the practical pocketknives to its affordable watch line. The evidence can be found in the Infantry, Airboss, and Alpnach watches, which have emerged over the past several years and established themselves in the market. The Chrono Classic cleverly converts the watch's hour and minute hands into a chronograph with 100ths of a second displayed in the large-date window.

Victorinox Swiss Army Watch S.A.
Chemin des Grillons 4
CH-2501 Biel/Bienne
Switzerland

Tel.:
+41-32-344-9933

Fax:
+41-32-344-9936

E-Mail:
info@victorinoxswissarmy.com

Website:
www.victorinoxswissarmy.com

Founded:
1884 / watches since 1989

Number of employees:
1,700

U.S. distributor:
Victorinox Swiss Army
7 Victoria Drive
Monroe, CT 06468
800-422-2706
www.swissarmy.com

Most important collections/price range:
Active, Classic, Professional / $325 to $3,695

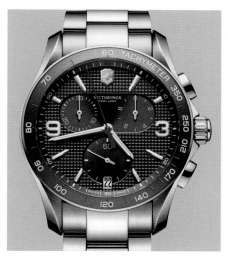

Chrono Classic

Reference number: 241656
Movement: quartz, ETA Caliber G10.211
Functions: hours, minutes, subsidiary seconds; chronograph; date
Case: stainless steel, ø 41 mm; sapphire crystal; water-resistant to 10 atm
Band: stainless steel, folding clasp
Price: $695

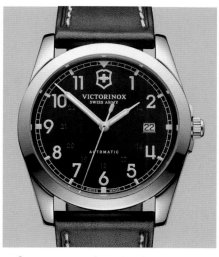

Infantry Mechanical

Reference number: 241646
Movement: automatic, ETA Caliber 2824-2; ø 25.6 mm; height 4.6 mm; 25 jewels; 28,800 vph; 38-hour power reserve
Functions: hours, minutes, sweep seconds; date
Case: stainless steel with golden PVD coating, ø 40 mm; sapphire crystal; water-resistant to 10 atm
Band: calf leather, buckle
Price: $750
Variations: quartz movement ($450)

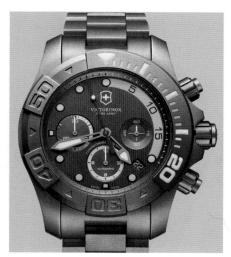

Dive Master 500

Reference number: 241660
Movement: automatic, ETA Caliber 2894-2; ø 28.6 mm; height 6.1 mm; 37 jewels; 28,800 vph; 42-hour power reserve
Functions: hours, minutes, subsidiary seconds; chronograph; date
Case: titanium, ø 43 mm; unidirectional bezel with 60-minute divisions, sapphire crystal; transparent case back; screw-in crown and pusher; water-resistant to 50 atm
Band: titanium, folding clasp
Remarks: limited to 500 pieces
Price: $3,295

Koliz Vostok Co. Ltd.

Naugarduko 41
LT-03227 Vilnius
Lithuania

Tel.:
+370-5-2106342

Fax:
+370-4-2130777

E-Mail:
info@vostok-europe.com

Website:
www.vostok-europe.com

Founded:
2003

Number of employees:
24

Annual production:
30,000 watches

U.S. distributor:
Vostok-Europe
Détente Watch Group
244 Upton Road, Suite 4
Colchester, CT 06415
877-486-7865
www.detentewatches.com

Most important collections/price range:
Anchar collection / starting at $759; Mriya /
starting at $649

Vostok-Europe

Vostok-Europe is a young brand with old roots. In 2014, it celebrated its tenth anniversary.

What started as a joint venture between the original Vostok company—a wholly separate entity—deep in the heart of Russia and a start-up in the newly minted European Union member nation of Lithuania has grown into something altogether different over the years. Originally, every Vostok model had a proprietary Russian engine, a 32-jewel automatic built by Vostok in Russia. Over the years, demand and the need for alternative complications expanded the portfolio of movements to include Swiss and Japanese ones. While the heritage of the eighty-year Russian watch industry is still evident in the inspirations and designs of Vostok-Europe, the watches built today have become favorites of extreme athletes the world over.

"Real people doing real things," is the mantra that Igor Zubovskij, managing director of the company, often repeats. "We don't use models to market our watches. Only real people test our watches in many different conditions."

That community of "real people" includes cross-country drivers on the Dakar Rally, one of the most famous aerobatic pilots in the world, a team of spelunkers who literally went to the bottom of the world in the Krubera Cave, and world free-diving champions. Much of the Vostok-Europe line is of professional dive quality. For illumination, some models incorporate tritium tube technology, which offers about twenty-five years of constant lighting. The Lunokhod 2, the current flagship of the brand, incorporates vertical tubes in a "candleholder" design for full 360-degree illumination.

The watches are assembled in Vilnius, Lithuania, and Zubvoskij still personally oversees quality control operations. The Mriya, named after the world's largest airplane, will be the first watch in the world to carry the new Seiko NE88 column wheel chronograph movement.

Mriya Chronograph Automatic

Reference number: NE88-5554238
Movement: automatic, Seiko Caliber NE88; ø 28 mm, height 7.6 mm; 34 jewels; 28,800 vph; column wheel control of chronograph functions; 45-hour power reserve
Functions: hours, minutes, subsidiary seconds; chronograph; date
Case: stainless steel with black PVD coating, ø 50 mm, height 17.7 mm; unidirectional bezel with 60-minute divisions, mineral crystal; screw-in crown; water-resistant to 20 atm
Band: calf leather, buckle
Remarks: includes additional silicon bracelet
Price: $2,585; limited to 500 pieces

GAZ 14 Automatic

Reference number: NH35A-5651137
Movement: automatic, Seiko Caliber NH35a; ø 26.6 mm, height 5.32 mm; 24 jewels; 21,600 vph; 45-hour power reserve
Functions: hours, minutes, sweep seconds; date
Case: stainless steel, ø 45 mm, height 15 mm; mineral crystal; water-resistant to 5 atm
Band: calf leather, buckle
Remarks: "Trigalight" constant tritium illumination
Price: $469

World Timer Automatic

Reference number: 2426-5604240
Movement: automatic, Vostok Caliber 2426; ø 24 mm, 32 jewels; 18,000 vph; blued screws; 31-hour power reserve
Functions: hours, minutes, sweep seconds; additional 24 hour display (2nd time zone)
Case: stainless steel with black PVD coating, ø 43 mm, height 13.8 mm; mineral crystal; transparent case back; water-resistant to 5 atm
Band: calf leather, buckle
Price: $499

Lunokhod 2 Automatic "Tritium Gaslight"

Reference number: NH35A-625210
Movement: automatic, Seiko Caliber NR35; ø 26.6 mm, height 5.32 mm; 24 jewels, 21,600 vph
Functions: hours, minutes, sweep seconds; date
Case: stainless steel, ø 49 mm, height 15.5 mm; unidirectional bezel with 60-minute divisions, mineral glass; water-resistant to 30 atm, helium release valve
Band: silicon, buckle
Remarks: with 2nd calf-leather band
Price: $899

Anchar "Tritium Gas Light"

Reference number: NH35/5105141
Movement: automatic, Seiko Caliber 35A; ø 27.4 mm, height 5.32 mm; 24 jewels; 21,600 vph; 45-hour power reserve
Functions: hours, minutes, sweep seconds; date
Case: stainless steel, ø 48 mm, height 15.5 mm; unidirectional bezel with 60-minute divisions, K1 mineral glass; screw-in crown; water-resistant to 30 atm
Band: rubber, buckle
Remarks: with calf-leather band
Price: $759

Expedition North Pole – 1

Reference number: 2432-5955192
Movement: automatic, Vostok Caliber 2432; ø 24 mm, height 4.14 mm; 32 jewels; 19,800 vph; 38-hour power reserve
Functions: hours, minutes, sweep seconds; date; 24 hour disc and day/night indicator
Case: stainless steel, ø 48 mm, height 18 mm; K1 mineral glass; transparent case back; water-resistant to 20 atm
Band: leather, buckle
Remarks: with calf-leather band
Price: $499

Big Z Lunokhod 2 "For the World's Strongest Man"

Reference number: NH35A/6205344
Movement: automatic, Seiko Caliber NR35; ø 26.6 mm, height 5.32 mm; 24 jewels, 21,600 vph
Functions: hours, minutes, sweep seconds; date
Case: stainless steel, ø 49 mm, height 15.5 mm; unidirectional bezel with 60-minute divisions, K1 mineral glass; water-resistant to 30 atm
Band: silicon, buckle
Remarks: with 2nd calf-leather band
Price: $1,179

Mriya Automatic Full Lume Dial

Reference number: NH35-5554234
Movement: automatic, Seiko Caliber NR35; ø 26.6 mm, height 5.32 mm; 24 jewels, 21,600 vph
Functions: hours, minutes, sweep seconds; date
Case: stainless steel, ø 50 mm, height 17.5 mm; unidirectional bezel with 60-minute divisions, K1 mineral glass; water-resistant to 20 atm
Band: silicon, buckle
Remarks: with 2nd calf-leather band
Price: $749

Anchar "Full Lume Dial"

Reference number: NH35-5104245
Movement: automatic, Seiko Caliber 35A; ø 27.4 mm, height 5.32 mm; 24 jewels; 21,600 vph; 45-hour power reserve
Functions: hours, minutes, sweep seconds; date
Case: stainless steel, ø 48 mm, height 15.5 mm; unidirectional bezel with 60-minute divisions, K1 mineral glass; screw-in crown; water-resistant to 30 atm
Band: rubber, buckle
Remarks: with calf-leather band
Price: $759

Gerhard D. Wempe KG

Steinstrasse 23
D-20095 Hamburg
Germany

Tel.:
+49-40-334-480

Fax:
+49-40-331-840

E-Mail:
info@wempe.de

Website:
www.wempe.de

Founded:
1878

Number of employees:
717 worldwide; 24 at Wempe Glashütte /SA

Annual production:
5,000 watches

U.S. distributor:
Wempe Timepieces
700 Fifth Avenue
New York, NY 10019
212-397-9000
www.wempe.com

Most important collections/price range:
Wempe Zeitmeister / approx. $1,000 to
$4,500; Wempe Chronometerwerke / approx.
$5,000 to $95,000

Wempe

Ever since 2005, the global jewelry chain Gerhard D. Wempe KG has been putting out watches under its own name again. It was probably inevitable: Gerhard D. Wempe, who founded the company in the late nineteenth century in Oldenburg, was himself a watchmaker. And in the 1930s, the company also owned the Hamburg chronometer works that made watches for seafarers and pilots.

Today, while Wempe remains formally in Hamburg, the manufacturing is in Glashütte—a natural, as the company has long entertained a close relationship with the Saxon hub of horology. The workshops have been set up in the former Urania observatory and a factory in the Altenburgerstrasse.

But this does mean that the coveted Swiss COSC seal of approval is not an option. So Wempe built its own chronometer testing site, which operates under the German Industrial Norm (DIN 8319), with official blessings from the Saxon and Thuringian offices for measurement and calibration and accreditation from the German Calibration Service.

The Zeitmeister collection meets all the requirements of the high art of watchmaking and, thanks to its accessible pricing, is attractive for budding collectors. All models are in the middle price range, which the luxury watch industry has long shunned. The models produced under the Wempe Chronometer logo (*Chronometerwerke*) are exclusive, the result of a partnership of ideas at the highest level, that is, with Nomos in Glashütte or with the Swiss workshop MHVJ.

Chronometerwerke Tonneau Tourbillon

Reference number: WG 740001
Movement: manually wound, Wempe Caliber CW 2; 22.6 x 32.6 mm, height 6.5 mm; 19 jewels; 21,600 vph; 1-minute tourbillon; Breguet balance spring; sunburst pattern on bridges; rhodium-plated; DIN-tested chronometer
Functions: hours, minutes, subsidiary seconds
Case: platinum, 40.9 x 51 mm, height 13.7 mm; sapphire crystal; transparent case back
Band: reptile skin, buckle
Remarks: limited to 25 pieces
Price: $87,575

Chronometerwerke Manually Wound Tonneau

Reference number: WG 040008
Movement: manually wound, Wempe Caliber CW 1; 22.6 x 32.6 mm, height 3.6 mm; 23 jewels; 21,600 vph; 80-hour power reserve; DIN-tested chronometer
Functions: hours, minutes, subsidiary seconds
Case: yellow gold, 37 x 45.6 mm, height 10.2 mm; sapphire crystal; transparent case back; water-resistant to 5 atm
Band: reptile skin, buckle
Price: $12,100
Variations: stainless steel ($6,350)

Chronometerwerke Power Reserve

Reference number: WG 080005
Movement: manually wound, Wempe Caliber CW 3; ø 32 mm, height 6.1 mm; 42 jewels; 28,800 vph; three-quarter plate, 3 screwed-in gold chatons, hand-engraved balance cock, Glashütte stopwork; 80-hour power reserve; DIN-tested chronometer
Functions: hours, minutes, subsidiary seconds; power reserve indicator
Case: yellow gold, ø 43 mm, height 12.5 mm; sapphire crystal; transparent case back; water-resistant to 3 atm
Band: reptile skin, buckle
Price: $19,950
Variations: stainless steel ($8,500)

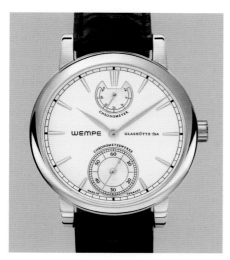

Chronometerwerke Power Reserve

Reference number: WG 080007
Movement: manually wound, Wempe Caliber CW 3; ø 32 mm, height 6.1 mm; 42 jewels; 28,800 vph; three-quarter plate, 3 screwed-in gold chatons, hand-engraved balance cock, Glashütte stopwork; 46-hour power reserve; DIN-tested chronometer
Functions: hours, minutes, subsidiary seconds; power reserve indicator
Case: stainless steel, ø 43 mm, height 12.5 mm; sapphire crystal, transparent case back; water-resistant to 3 atm
Band: reptile skin, buckle
Price: $8,500
Variations: yellow gold ($19,950)

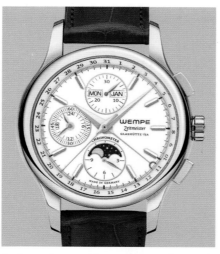

Zeitmeister Chronograph with Moon Phase and Complete Calendar

Reference number: WM 530001
Movement: automatic, ETA Caliber 7751; ø 30 mm, height 7.9 mm; 27 jewels; 28,800 vph; 48-hour power reserve; COSC-certified chronometer
Functions: hours, minutes, subsidiary seconds; added 24-hour display; chronograph; full calendar with date, weekday, month, moon phase
Case: stainless steel, ø 42 mm, height 14.71 mm; sapphire crystal; water-resistant to 5 atm
Band: reptile skin, folding clasp
Price: $4,975

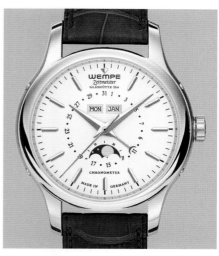

Zeitmeister Moon Phase with Complete Calendar

Reference number: WM 350001
Movement: automatic, ETA Caliber 2892 with module; ø 25.6 mm, height 5.35 mm; 21 jewels; 28,800 vph; 42-hour power reserve; DIN-tested chronometer
Functions: hours, minutes, sweep seconds; full calendar with date, weekday, month, moon phase
Case: stainless steel, ø 42 mm, height 14.1 mm; sapphire crystal
Band: reptile skin, folding clasp
Price: $3,580

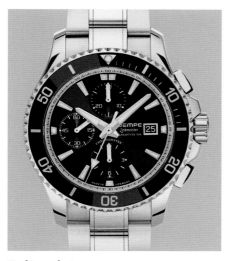

Zeitmeister Sport Diver's Chronograph

Reference number: WM 650009
Movement: automatic, Sellita Caliber SW500; ø 30 mm, height 7.9 mm; 25 jewels; 28,800 vph; 48-hour power reserve; DIN-tested chronometer
Functions: hours, minutes, subsidiary seconds; chronograph; date
Case: stainless steel, ø 45 mm, height 16.5 mm; unidirectional bezel with 60-minute divisions; sapphire crystal; screw-in crown; water-resistant to 30 atm
Band: stainless steel, folding clasp with safety lock and extension link
Price: $4,825

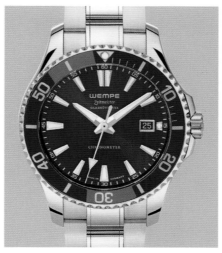

Zeitmeister Sport Diver's Automatic

Reference number: WM 650006
Movement: automatic, Sellita Caliber SW300; ø 25.6 mm, height 3.6 mm; 23 jewels; 28,800 vph; 42-hour power reserve; DIN-tested chronometer
Functions: hours, minutes, sweep seconds; date
Case: stainless steel, ø 42 mm, height 14.5 mm; unidirectional bezel with 60-minute divisions; sapphire crystal; screw-in crown; water-resistant to 30 atm
Band: stainless steel, folding clasp with safety lock and extension link
Price: $3,540

Zeitmeister Aviator Watch Chronograph XL

Reference number: WM 600005
Movement: automatic, ETA Caliber A07.211; ø 36.6 mm, height 7.9 mm; 25 jewels; 28,800 vph; 46-hour power reserve; DIN-tested chronometer
Functions: hours, minutes, subsidiary seconds; chronograph; date
Case: stainless steel, ø 45 mm, height 15.45 mm; sapphire crystal; water-resistant to 5 atm
Band: horse leather, folding clasp
Price: $3,580

Zeitwinkel Montres SA
Rue Pierre-Jolissaint 35
CH-2610 Saint-Imier
Switzerland

Tel.:
+41-32-940-17-71

Fax:
+41-32-940-17-81

E-Mail:
info@zeitwinkel.ch

Website:
www.zeitwinkel.ch

Founded:
2006

Annual production:
approx. 800 watches

U.S. distributor:
Tourneau
510 Madison Ave., New York, NY 10022
212-758-5830
Right Time
7110 E. County Line Rd., Highlands Ranch,
CO 80126
303-862-3900; 303-862-3905 (fax)

Most important collections/price range:
mechanical wristwatches / starting at around
$7,500

Zeitwinkel

Timeless, simple, and sustainable—attributes every watch manufacturer aspires to endow its creations with. Zeitwinkel (the name means "time angle") models hew tightly to this perspective: The simplest exemplar is a two-hand watch; the most complicated, the 273°, a three-hand watch with power reserve display and large date. The dials are completely flat and marked with the company's stylized "W." With cases designed by Jean-François Ruchonnet (TAG Heuer V4, Cabestan), the watches look fairly "German," which comes as no surprise, because Zeitwinkel's founders, Ivica Maksimovic and Peter Nikolaus, hail from there.

The most valuable part of the watches is their veritable *manufacture* movements, the likes of which are very rare in the business. The calibers were developed by Laurent Besse and his *artisans horlogers*, or watchmaking craftspeople. All components come courtesy of independent suppliers—Zeitwinkel balance wheels, pallets, escape wheels, and Straumann spirals, for example, are produced by Precision Engineering, a company associated with watch brand H. Moser & Cie. The latest 273° offers a smoked sapphire crystal dial that opens to reveal the model's caliber.

In keeping with the company's ideals, you won't find any alligator in Zeitwinkel watch bands. Choices here are exclusively rubber, calfskin, or calfskin with an alligator-like pattern. Gold cases were also once taboo for the brand, but thanks to a partnership with the Alliance for Responsible Mining, the watches now come in "fairmined" gold cases.

273° Saphir Fumé

Reference number: 273-4.S01-01-21
Movement: automatic, Caliber ZW0103;
ø 30.4 mm, height 8 mm; 49 jewels; 28,800 vph;
German silver three-quarter plate and bridges, côtes de Genève, beveled and polished screws and edges; perlage on dial side; 72-hour power reserve
Functions: hours, minutes, subsidiary seconds; power reserve indicator; large date
Case: stainless steel, ø 42.5 mm, height 13.8 mm; sapphire crystal; transparent case back; water-resistant to 5 atm
Band: calf leather, folding clasp
Remarks: smoky black sapphire crystal dial
Price: $14,450

273° Rose Gold

Reference number: 273-42-02.5N-21
Movement: automatic, Caliber ZW0103;
ø 30.4 mm, height 8 mm; 49 jewels; 28,800 vph;
German silver three-quarter plate and bridges, côtes de Genève, beveled and polished screws and edges; 72-hour power reserve
Functions: hours, minutes, subsidiary seconds; power reserve indicator; large date
Case: rose gold, ø 42.5 mm, height 13.8 mm; sapphire crystal; transparent case back; water-resistant to 5 atm
Band: calf leather, folding clasp
Price: on request

181° Galvano-black

Reference number: 181-21-01-21
Movement: automatic, Caliber ZW0102;
ø 30.4 mm, height 5.7 mm; 28 jewels; 28,800 vph;
German silver three-quarter plate and bridges, côtes de Genève, beveled and polished screws and edges; 72-hour power reserve
Functions: hours, minutes, subsidiary seconds; date
Case: stainless steel, ø 42.5 mm, height 11.7 mm; sapphire crystal; transparent case back; water-resistant to 5 atm
Band: calf leather, folding clasp
Price: $7,490
Variations: silver or blue dial; various bands

Zenith

The tall narrow building in Le Locle, with its closely spaced high windows to let in daylight, is a testimony to Zenith's history as a self-sufficient *manufacture* in the entrepreneurial spirit of the Industrial Revolution. The company, founded in 1865 by Georges Favre-Jacot as a small watch reassembly workshop, has produced and distributed every type of watch from the simple pocket watch to the most complicated calendar. But it remains primarily linked with the El Primero caliber, the first wristwatch chronograph movement boasting automatic winding and a frequency of 36,000 vph. Only a few watch manufacturers had risked such a high oscillation frequency—and none of them with such complexity as the integrated chronograph mechanism and bilaterally winding rotor of the El Primero.

That the movement even celebrated its fortieth anniversary, though, was thanks to the mechanical watch revival. After Zenith was sold to the LVMH Group in 1999, the label was fully dusted off and modernized perhaps a little too much. Eccentric creations catapulted the dutiful watchmaker's watchmaker into the world of *haute horlogerie*.

Also being dusted off for the firm's 150th anniversary in 2015 was the historic complex in Le Locle, which was put on UNESCO's World Heritage list in 2009. Over eighty different crafts are practiced here. New materials and new machines may be used, but the loyalty to tradition remains one of the chief hallmarks of the brand with the star. That is the course set by Jean-Frédéric Dufour during the recession, and it is one maintained by his 2014 successor Aldo Magada.

Zenith
LVMH Swiss Manufactures SA
34, rue des Billodes
CH-2400 Le Locle
Switzerland

Tel.:
+41-32-930-6262

Fax:
+41-32-930-6363

Website:
www.zenith-watches.com

Founded:
1865

Number of employees:
over 330 employees worldwide

U.S. distributor:
Zenith Watches
966 South Springfield Avenue
Springfield, NJ 07081
866-675-2079
contact.zenith@lvmhwatchjewelry.com

Most important collections/price range:
Academy / from $82,700; Elite / from $5,100; El Primero / from $6,900; Pilot / from $7,600; Star / from $5,800

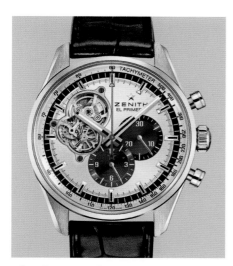

El Primero Chronomaster 1969

Reference number: 03.2040.4061/69.C496
Movement: automatic, Zenith Caliber 4061 "El Primero"; ø 30 mm, height 6.6 mm; 31 jewels; 36,000 vph; 50-hour power reserve
Functions: hours, minutes; chronograph
Case: stainless steel, ø 42 mm, height 14.05 mm; sapphire crystal; transparent case back; water-resistant to 10 atm
Band: reptile skin, folding clasp
Price: $9,800
Variations: rose gold ($21,600)

El Primero Chronomaster Power Reserve

Reference number: 03.2080.4021/01.C494
Movement: automatic, Zenith Caliber 4021 "El Primero"; ø 30 mm, height 7.85 mm; 39 jewels; 36,000 vph; partially skeletonized under regulator; 50-hour power reserve
Functions: hours, minutes; power reserve indicator; chronograph
Case: stainless steel, ø 42 mm, height 14.05 mm; sapphire crystal; transparent back; water-resistant to 10 atm
Band: reptile skin, folding clasp
Price: $9,800
Variations: black dial/stainless steel band ($10,300); rose gold/steel ($12,300); rose gold ($21,600)

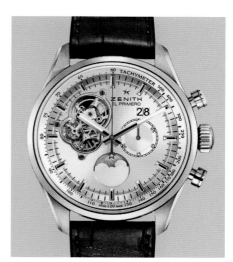

El Primero Chronomaster Open Grande Date

Reference number: 03.2160.4047/01.C713
Movement: automatic, Zenith Caliber 4047 "El Primero"; ø 30.5 mm, height 9.05 mm; 32 jewels; 36,000 vph; 50-hour power reserve
Functions: hours, minutes, subsidiary seconds; chronograph; large date; sun/moon phase displays (integrated day/night indication)
Case: stainless steel, ø 45 mm, height 15.6 mm; sapphire crystal; transparent back; water-resistant to 5 atm
Band: reptile skin, folding clasp
Price: $13,100
Variations: rose gold/steel with leather strap ($15,700) or bracelet ($18,300); rose gold ($28,500)

El Primero 36'000 vph

Reference number: 03.2040.400/69.C494
Movement: automatic, Zenith Caliber 400B "El Primero"; ø 30 mm, height 6.6 mm; 31 jewels; 36,000 vph; 50-hour power reserve
Functions: hours, minutes, subsidiary seconds; chronograph; date
Case: stainless steel, ø 42 mm, height 12.75 mm; sapphire crystal; transparent case back; water-resistant to 10 atm
Band: reptile skin, folding clasp
Price: $8,800
Variations: black or white dial ($9,000)

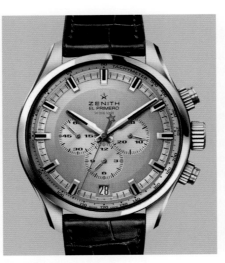

El Primero Sport

Reference number: 03.2280.400/01.C713
Movement: automatic, Zenith Caliber 400B "El Primero"; ø 30 mm, height 6.6 mm; 31 jewels; 36,000 vph; 50-hour power reserve
Functions: hours, minutes, subsidiary seconds; chronograph; date
Case: stainless steel, ø 45 mm, height 14.1 mm; sapphire crystal; transparent case back; water-resistant to 20 atm
Band: reptile skin, double folding clasp
Price: $11,000
Variations: stainless steel bracelet ($11,600)

Academy Georges Favre-Jacot

Reference number: 18.2210.4810/01.C713
Movement: manually wound, Zenith Caliber 4810 "El Primero"; ø 37 mm, height 5.9 mm; 30 jewels; 36,000 vph; fusée and chain winding; COSC-certified chronometer
Functions: hours, minutes, subsidiary seconds; power reserve indicator
Case: rose gold, ø 45 mm, height 14.1 mm; sapphire crystal; transparent case back; water-resistant to 3 atm
Band: reptile skin, double folding clasp
Price: $82,700
Variations: titanium ($76,100)

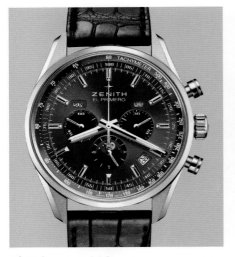

El Primero 410

Reference number: 03.2097.410/51.C700
Movement: automatic, Zenith Caliber 410 "El Primero"; ø 30 mm, height 7.7 mm; 31 jewels; 36,000 vph; 50-hour power reserve
Functions: hours, minutes, subsidiary seconds; chronograph; full calendar with date, weekday, month, moon phase
Case: stainless steel, ø 42 mm, height 12.75 mm; sapphire crystal; transparent case back; water-resistant to 5 atm
Band: reptile skin, folding clasp
Price: $11,700
Variations: silver dial ($11,200); rose gold ($22,100)

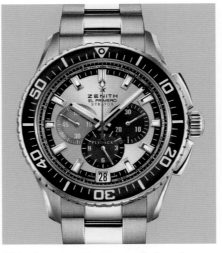

El Primero Stratos Flyback "Tribute to Felix Baumgartner"

Reference number: 03.2066.405/609.M2060
Movement: automatic, Zenith Caliber 405B "El Primero"; ø 30 mm, height 6.6 mm; 31 jewels; 36,000 vph; 50-hour power reserve
Functions: hours, minutes, subsidiary seconds; flyback chronograph; date
Case: stainless steel, ø 45 mm, height 14.1 mm; unidirectional bezel with 60-minute division; sapphire crystal; water-resistant to 10 atm
Band: stainless steel, double folding clasp
Price: $9,300
Variations: rubber strap ($8,500)

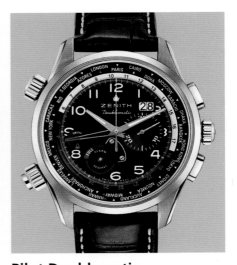

Pilot Doublematic

Reference number: 03.2400.4046/21.C721
Movement: automatic, Zenith Caliber 4046 "El Primero"; ø 30 mm, height 9.05 mm; 41 jewels; 36,000 vph; 50-hour power reserve
Functions: hours, minutes; world-time display (2nd time zone); alarm clock with display of functions/power reserve; chronograph; large date
Case: stainless steel, ø 45 mm, height 15.6 mm; crown rotates inner bezel with reference cities; sapphire crystal; transparent case back; water-resistant to 5 atm
Band: reptile skin, folding clasp
Price: $16,400
Variations: rose gold ($31,900)

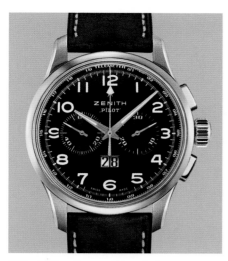

Pilot Big Date Special

Reference number: 03.2410.4010/21.C722
Movement: automatic, Zenith Caliber 4010 "El Primero"; ø 30 mm, height 7.65 mm; 31 jewels; 36,000 vph; 50-hour power reserve
Functions: hours, minutes, subsidiary seconds; chronograph; large date
Case: stainless steel, ø 42 mm, height 13.5 mm; sapphire crystal; transparent case back; water-resistant to 5 atm
Band: calf leather, double folding clasp
Price: $7,600
Variations: stainless steel Milanese mesh bracelet ($8,200)

Pilot Type 20 GMT

Reference number: 03.2430.693/21.C723
Movement: automatic, Zenith Caliber 693 "Elite"; ø 25.6 mm, height 3.94 mm; 26 jewels; 28,800 vph; 50-hour power reserve
Functions: hours, minutes, subsidiary seconds; additional 24-hour display (2nd time zone)
Case: stainless steel, ø 48 mm, height 15.8 mm; sapphire crystal; water-resistant to 10 atm
Band: calf leather, buckle
Price: $8,100

Pilot Type 20 Extra Special

Reference number: 29.2430.679/C753
Movement: automatic, Zenith Caliber 679 "Elite"; ø 25.6 mm, height 3.9 mm; 27 jewels; 28,800 vph; 50-hour power reserve
Functions: hours, minutes, sweep seconds
Case: bronze, ø 45 mm, height 14.2 mm; sapphire crystal; water-resistant to 10 atm
Band: calf leather, buckle
Price: $7,600

Elite 6150

Reference number: 03.2270.6150/01.C493
Movement: automatic, Zenith Caliber 6150 "Elite"; ø 30 mm, height 3.9 mm; 35 jewels; 28,800 vph; 100-hour power reserve
Functions: hours, minutes, sweep seconds
Case: stainless steel, ø 42 mm, height 9.45 mm; sapphire crystal; water-resistant to 5 atm
Band: reptile skin, folding clasp
Price: $8,300

Elite Moonphase

Reference number: 03.2143.691/01.C498
Movement: automatic, Zenith Caliber 691 "Elite"; ø 25.6 mm, height 5.67 mm; 27 jewels; 28,800 vph; 50-hour power reserve
Functions: hours, minutes, subsidiary seconds; large date, moon phase
Case: stainless steel, ø 40 mm, height 10.35 mm; sapphire crystal; transparent case back; water-resistant to 5 atm
Band: reptile skin, buckle
Price: $7,800
Variations: rose gold ($15,400)

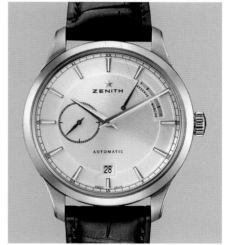

Elite Power Reserve

Reference number: 03.2122.685/01.C493
Movement: automatic, Zenith Caliber 685 "Elite"; ø 25.6 mm, height 4.67 mm; 38 jewels; 28,800 vph; 50-hour power reserve
Functions: hours, minutes, subsidiary seconds; power reserve indicator; date
Case: stainless steel, ø 40 mm, height 9.25 mm; sapphire crystal; transparent case back; water-resistant to 5 atm
Band: reptile skin, buckle
Price: $6,500
Variations: black dial ($6,500); rose gold ($14,100)

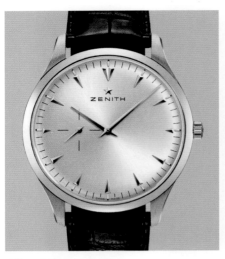

Elite Ultra Thin

Reference number: 03.2010.681/01.C493
Movement: automatic, Zenith Caliber 681 "Elite"; ø 25.6 mm, height 3.47 mm; 27 jewels; 28,800 vph
Functions: hours, minutes, subsidiary seconds
Case: stainless steel, ø 40 mm, height 8.3 mm; sapphire crystal; transparent case back; water-resistant to 5 atm
Band: reptile skin, buckle
Price: $5,300
Variations: black or white dial ($5,300); rose gold ($13,400); rose gold with rose gold bracelet ($25,400)

Montre d'Aeronef Type 20 Annual Calendar

Reference number: 03.2430.4054/21.C721
Movement: automatic, Zenith Caliber 4054 "El Primero"; ø 30 mm, height 8.3 mm; 29 jewels; 36,000 vph; 50-hour power reserve
Functions: hours, minutes, subsidiary seconds; chronograph; full calendar with date, weekday, month
Case: stainless steel, ø 48 mm, height 15.8 mm; sapphire crystal; water-resistant to 10 atm
Band: calf leather, buckle
Price: $11,300

Elite Central Second

Reference number: 03.2020.670/22.C498
Movement: automatic, Zenith Caliber 670 "Elite"; ø 25.6 mm, height 3.47 mm; 27 jewels; 28,800 vph; 50-hour power reserve
Functions: hours, minutes, sweep seconds; date
Case: stainless steel, ø 40 mm, height 8.15 mm; sapphire crystal; transparent case back; water-resistant to 5 atm
Band: reptile skin, folding clasp
Price: $5,800
Variations: silver dial ($5,800)

El Primero Synopsis

Reference number: 03_2170_4613_01_C713
Movement: automatic, Zenith Caliber 4613 "El Primero"; ø 30 mm, height 5.58 mm; 19 jewels, 36,000 vph; partially skeletonized under regulator; 50-hour power reserve
Functions: hours, minutes, subsidiary seconds
Case: stainless steel, ø 34 mm, height 11.7 mm; sapphire crystal; transparent case back; water-resistant to 10 atm
Band: reptile skin, double folding clasp
Price: $6,900
Variations: stainless steel bracelet ($7,500); silver or black dial with rhodium-plated hands/hour markers ($6,900); rose gold ($15,300)

Academy Christophe Colomb Hurricane

Reference number: 18_2212_8805_36_C713
Movement: manually wound, Zenith Caliber 8805 "El Primero"; ø 37 mm, height 5.85 mm; 53 jewels; 36,000 vph; gyroscopic automatically leveling escapement cage ("Gravity Control"), constant force with fusée and chain; 50-hour power reserve
Functions: hours and minutes (off-center), subsidiary seconds; power reserve indicator
Case: rose gold, ø 45 mm, height 14.35 mm; sapphire crystal; transparent case back; water-resistant to 3 atm
Band: reptile skin, double folding clasp
Price: $280,000; limited to 25 pieces

El Primero Stratos Open

Reference number: 75_2060_4061_21_R573
Movement: automatic, Zenith Caliber 4061 "El Primero"; ø 30 mm, height 6.6 mm; 31 jewels; 36,000 vph; côtes de Genève on rotor; 50-hour power reserve
Functions: hours, minutes, subsidiary seconds; chronograph
Case: stainless steel with black DLC coating, ø 45 mm, height 14.1 mm; unidirectional bezel with 60-minute divisions; sapphire crystal; transparent back; water-resistant to 10 atm
Band: rubber, textile covering, double folding clasp
Price: $9,100
Variations: rose gold ($22,600)

Caliber El Primero 410

Automatic; single spring barrel, 50-hour power reserve
Functions: hours, minutes, subsidiary seconds; chronograph; full calendar with date, weekday, month, moon phase
Diameter: 30 mm
Height: 6.6 mm
Jewels: 31
Balance: glucydur
Frequency: 36,000 vph
Balance spring: self-compensating flat spring
Shock protection: Kif

Caliber El Primero 4054

Automatic; single spring barrel, 50-hour power reserve
Functions: hours, minutes; chronograph; annual calendar with date, weekday, month
Diameter: 30 mm
Height: 8.3 mm
Jewels: 29
Balance: glucydur
Frequency: 36,000 vph
Balance spring: self-compensating flat spring
Shock protection: Kif

Caliber El Primero 4047

Automatic; single spring barrel, 50-hour power reserve
Functions: hours, minutes; chronograph; large date; display of sun and moon phases (integrated day/night indication)
Diameter: 30.5 mm
Height: 9.05 mm
Jewels: 41
Balance: glucydur
Frequency: 36,000 vph
Balance spring: self-compensating flat spring
Shock protection: Kif

Caliber El Primero 4057B

Automatic; single spring barrel, 50-hour power reserve
Functions: hours, minutes, subsidiary seconds; chronograph shows 1/10th of a second thanks to fast drive of chronograph hands (1 revolution every 10 seconds), totalizer for 6 revolutions; date
Diameter: 30.5 mm
Height: 6.6 mm
Jewels: 31
Balance: glucydur
Frequency: 36,000 vph
Balance spring: self-compensating flat spring
Shock protection: Kif

Caliber El Primero 400B

Automatic; single spring barrel, 50-hour power reserve
Functions: hours, minutes, subsidiary seconds; chronograph; date
Diameter: 30 mm
Height: 6.6 mm
Jewels: 31
Balance: glucydur
Frequency: 36,000 vph
Balance spring: self-compensating flat spring
Shock protection: Kif

Caliber Elite 681

Automatic; single spring barrel, 50-hour power reserve
Functions: hours, minutes, subsidiary seconds
Diameter: 25.6 mm
Height: 3.81 mm
Jewels: 27
Balance: glucydur
Frequency: 28,800 vph
Balance spring: self-compensating flat spring
Shock protection: Kif

Concepto

The Concepto Watch Factory, founded in 2006 in La Chaux-de-Fonds, is the successor to the family-run company Jaquet SA, which changed its name to La Joux-Perret a little while ago and then moved to a different location on the other side of the hub of watchmaking. In 2008, Valérien Jaquet, son of the company founder Pierre Jaquet, began systematically building up a modern movement and watch component factory on an empty floor of the building. Today, the Concepto Watch Factory employs eighty people in various departments, such as Development/Prototyping, Decoparts (partial manufacturing using lathes, machining, or wire erosion), Artisia (production of movements and complications in large series), as well as Optimo (escapements). In addition to the standard family of calibers, the C2000 (based on the Valjoux), and the vintage chronograph movement C7000 (the evolution of the Venus Caliber), the company's product portfolio includes various tourbillon movements (Caliber C8000) and several modules for adding onto ETA movements (Caliber C1000). A brand-new caliber series, the C3000, features a retrograde calendar and seconds, a power reserve indicator, and a chronograph. The C4000 chronograph caliber with automatic winding is currently in pre-series testing.

These movements are designed according to the requirements of about forty customers and at times heavily modified. Complicated movements are assembled entirely, while others are sold as kits for assembly by the watchmakers. Annual production is somewhere between 30,000 and 40,000 units, with additional hundreds of thousands of components made for contract manufacturing.

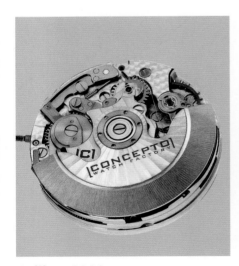

Caliber 2000

Automatic; column wheel control of chronograph functions; single spring barrel, 48-hour power reserve
Functions: hours, minutes, subsidiary seconds; chronograph; date
Diameter: 30.4 mm; **Height:** 8.4 mm
Jewels: 27
Balance: screw balance
Frequency: 28,800 vph
Balance spring: flat hairspring
Shock protection: Incabloc
Remarks: plate and bridges with perlage or côtes de Genève, polished steel parts and screw heads

Caliber 8000

Manually wound; 1-minute tourbillon; single spring barrel, 72-hour power reserve
Functions: hours, minutes
Diameter: 32.6 mm
Height: 5.7 mm
Jewels: 19
Balance: screw balance
Frequency: 21,600 vph
Balance spring: flat hairspring
Remarks: extensive personalization options for finishing, fittings, and functions

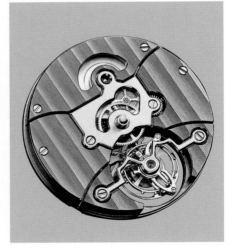

Caliber 8050

Automatic; 1-minute tourbillon; bidirectional off-center winding rotor; single spring barrel, 72-hour power reserve
Functions: hours, minutes
Diameter: 32.6 mm
Height: 7.9 mm
Jewels: 19
Balance: screw balance
Frequency: 21,600 vph
Balance spring: flat hairspring
Remarks: extensive personalization options for finishing, fittings, and functions

ETA

This Swatch Group movement manufacturer produces more than five million movements a year. And after the withdrawal of Richemont's Jaeger-LeCoultre as well as Swatch Group sisters Nouvelle Lémania and Frédéric Piguet from the business of selling movements on the free market, most watch brands can hardly help but beat down the door of this full service manufacturer.

ETA offers a broad spectrum of automatic movements in various dimensions with different functions, chronograph mechanisms in varying configurations, pocket watch classics (Calibers 6497 and 98), and manually wound calibers of days gone by (Calibers 1727 and 7001). This company truly offers everything that a manufacturer's heart could desire—not to mention the sheer variety of quartz technology from inexpensive three-hand mechanisms to highly complicated multifunctional movements and futuristic Etaquartz featuring autonomous energy creation using a rotor and generator.

The almost stereotypical accusation of ETA being "mass goods" is not justified, however, for it is a real art to manufacture filigreed micromechanical technology in consistently high quality, illustrated by the long lead times needed to develop new calibers. This is certainly one of the reasons why there have been very few movement factories in Europe that can compete with ETA, or that would want to. Since the success of Swatch—a pure ETA product—millions of Swiss francs have been invested in new development and manufacturing technologies. ETA today owns more than twenty production locales in Switzerland, France, Germany, Malaysia, and Thailand.

In 2002, ETA's management announced it would discontinue providing half-completed component kits for reassembly and/or embellishment to specialized workshops, and from 2010 only offer completely assembled and finished movements for sale. The Swiss Competition Commission, however, studied the issue, and a new deal was struck in 2013 phasing out sales to customers over a period of six years. ETA is already somewhat of a competitor to independent reassemblers such as Soprod, Sellita, La Joux-Perret, Dubois Dépraz, and others thanks to its diversification of available calibers, which has led the rest to counter by creating their own base movements.

Caliber A07.111 Valgranges

Automatic, ball bearing rotor, stop-seconds, power reserve 42 hours
Functions: hours, minutes, sweep seconds; quick-set date window at 3 o'clock
Diameter: 36.6 mm (16 3/4''')
Height: 7.9 mm
Jewels: 24
Frequency: 28,800 vph
Index system: Etachron with index correction
Related calibers: A07.161 (power reserve display)

Caliber A07.171 Valgranges

Automatic, ball bearing rotor, stop-seconds, power reserve 42 hours
Functions: hours, minutes, sweep seconds; separately settable 24-hour hand (2nd time zone); quick-set date window at 3 o'clock
Diameter: 36.6 mm (16 3/4''')
Height: 7.9 mm
Jewels: 24
Frequency: 28,800 vph
Index system: Etachron with index correction

Caliber A07.211 Valgranges

Automatic, ball bearing rotor, stop-seconds, power reserve 42 hours
Functions: hours, minutes, subsidiary seconds at 9 o'clock; chronograph (30-minute counter at 12 o'clock, 12-hour counter at 6 o'clock, sweep chronograph seconds); quick-set day and date window
Diameter: 36.6 mm (16 3/4''')
Height: 7.9 mm
Jewels: 25
Frequency: 28,800 vph
Index system: Etachron with index correction

Caliber 2660

Manually wound, power reserve 42 hours
Functions: hours, minutes, sweep seconds
Diameter: 17.2 mm (7 3/4''')
Height: 3.5 mm
Jewels: 17
Frequency: 28,800 vph
Fine adjustment system: Etachron

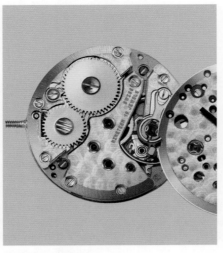

Caliber 1727

Manually wound, power reserve 50 hours
Functions: hours, minutes, subsidiary seconds at 6 o'clock
Diameter: 19.4 mm
Height: 3.5 mm
Jewels: 19
Frequency: 21,600 vph
Fine adjustment system: Etachron
Remarks: based on design of AS 1727

Caliber 7001

Manually wound, ultra-flat, power reserve 42 hours
Functions: hours, minutes, subsidiary seconds at 6 o'clock
Diameter: 23.3 mm (10 1/2''')
Height: 2.5 mm
Jewels: 17
Frequency: 21,600 vph

Caliber 2801-2

Manually wound, power reserve 42 hours
Functions: hours, minutes, sweep seconds
Diameter: 25.6 mm (11 1/2''')
Height: 3.35 mm
Jewels: 17
Frequency: 28,800 vph
Fine adjustment system: Etachron
Related caliber: 2804-2 (with date window and quick set)

Caliber 6497

Only a few watch fans know that ETA still manufactures 2 pure pocket watch movements. Caliber 6497 (the so-called Lépine version with subsidiary seconds extending from the winding stem) and Caliber 6498 (the so-called hunter with subsidiary seconds at a right angle to the winding stem) are available in 2 qualities: as 6497-1 and 6498-1 (rather sober, undecorated version); and 6497-2 and 6498-2 (with off-center striped decoration on bridges and cocks as well as beveled and striped crown and ratchet wheels). The photograph shows Lépine Caliber 6497-2.

Caliber 6498

Manually wound, power reserve 38 hours
Functions: hours, minutes, subsidiary seconds
Diameter: 36.6 mm (16 3/4''')
Height: 4.5 mm
Jewels: 17
Frequency: 21,600 vph
Fine adjustment system: ETACHRON with index
Remarks: the illustration shows a finely decorated hunter version like Nuremberg-based watchmaker Thomas Ninchritz uses

Caliber 2671

Automatic; ball bearing rotor, stop-seconds, power reserve 38 hours
Functions: hours, minutes, sweep seconds; quick-set date window at 3 o'clock
Diameter: 17.2 mm (7 3/4''')
Height: 4.8 mm
Jewels: 25
Frequency: 28,800 vph
Fine adjustment system: Etachron with index
Related caliber: 2678 (additional day window at 3 o'clock, height 5.35 mm)

Caliber 2681 (dial side)

Automatic; ball bearing rotor, stop-seconds, power reserve 38 hours
Functions: hours, minutes, sweep seconds; quick-set date and day window at 3 o'clock
Diameter: 19.4 mm (8 3/4''')
Height: 4.8 mm
Jewels: 25
Frequency: 28,800 vph
Fine adjustment system: Etachron with index
Related caliber: 2685 (sweep date hand and moon phase 6 o'clock)

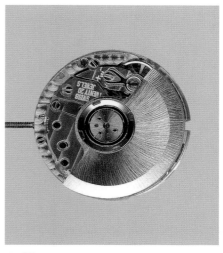

Caliber 2000

Automatic; ball bearing rotor, stop-seconds, power reserve 40 hours
Functions: hours, minutes, sweep seconds; quick-set date window at 3 o'clock
Diameter: 19.4 mm (8 3/4''')
Height: 3.6 mm
Jewels: 20
Frequency: 28,800 vph
Fine adjustment system: Etachron with index

Caliber 2004

Automatic; ball bearing rotor, stop-seconds, power reserve 40 hours
Functions: hours, minutes, sweep seconds; quick-set date window at 3 o'clock
Diameter: 23.3 mm (10 1/2''')
Height: 3.6 mm
Jewels: 20
Frequency: 28,800 vph
Fine adjustment system: Etachron with index

Caliber 2824-2

Automatic; ball bearing rotor, stop-seconds, power reserve 38 hours
Functions: hours, minutes, sweep seconds; quick-set date window at 3 o'clock
Diameter: 25.6 mm (11 1/2''')
Height: 4.6 mm
Jewels: 25
Frequency: 28,800 vph
Fine adjustment system: Etachron with index
Related calibers: 2836-2 (additional day window at 3 o'clock, height 5.05 mm); 2826-2 (with large date, height 6.2 mm)

Caliber 2834-2 (dial side)

Automatic; ball bearing rotor, stop-seconds, power reserve 38 hours
Functions: hours, minutes, sweep seconds; quick-set date window at 3 o'clock and day
Diameter: 29 mm (13''')
Height: 5.05 mm
Jewels: 25
Frequency: 28,800 vph
Fine adjustment system: Etachron with index

Caliber 2891-A9

Automatic (base caliber ETA 2892-A2); ball bearing rotor, stop-seconds, power reserve 42 hours
Functions: hours, minutes, sweep seconds; perpetual calendar (hand displays for date, day, and month), moon phase disk, leap year indication
Diameter: 25.6 mm (11 1/2''')
Height: 5.2 mm
Jewels: 21
Frequency: 28,800 vph
Fine adjustment system: Etachron with index
Related calibers: 2890-A9 (without second hand and stop-seconds)

Caliber 2892-A2

Automatic; ball bearing rotor, stop-seconds, power reserve 42 hours
Functions: hours, minutes, sweep seconds; quick-set date window at 3 o'clock
Diameter: 25.6 mm (11 1/2''')
Height: 3.6 mm
Jewels: 21
Frequency: 28,800 vph
Fine adjustment system: Etachron with index

Caliber 2893-1

Automatic; ball bearing rotor, stop-seconds, power reserve 42 hours
Functions: hours, minutes, sweep seconds; quick-set date window at 3 o'clock; world time display via central disk
Diameter: 25.6 mm (11 1/2''')
Height: 4.1 mm
Jewels: 21
Frequency: 28,800 vph
Fine adjustment system: Etachron with index
Related calibers: 2893-2 (24-hour hand; second time zone instead of world time disk); 2893-3 (only world time disk without date window)

Caliber 2895-1

Automatic; ball bearing rotor, stop-seconds, power reserve 42 hours
Functions: hours, minutes, subsidiary seconds at 6 o'clock; quick-set date window at 3 o'clock; world time display via central disk
Diameter: 25.6 mm (11 1/2''')
Height: 4.35 mm
Jewels: 30
Frequency: 28,800 vph
Fine adjustment system: Etachron with index

Caliber 2896 (dial side)

Automatic; ball bearing rotor, stop-seconds, power reserve 42 hours
Functions: hours, minutes, sweep seconds; power reserve display at 3 o'clock
Diameter: 25.6 mm (11 1/2''')
Height: 4.85 mm
Jewels: 21
Frequency: 28,800 vph
Fine adjustment system: Etachron with index

Caliber 2897

Automatic; ball bearing rotor, stop-seconds, power reserve 42 hours
Functions: hours, minutes, sweep seconds; power reserve display at 7 o'clock
Diameter: 25.6 mm (11 1/2''')
Height: 4.85 mm
Jewels: 21
Frequency: 28,800 vph
Fine adjustment system: Etachron with index

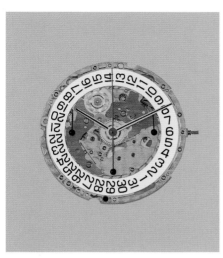

Caliber 2094

Automatic; ball bearing rotor, stop-seconds, power reserve 40 hours
Functions: hours, minutes, subsidiary seconds at 9 o'clock; chronograph (30-minute counter at 3 o'clock, 12-hour counter at 6 o'clock, sweep chronograph seconds); date window at 3 o'clock
Diameter: 23.3 mm (10 1/2''')
Height: 5.5 mm
Jewels: 33
Frequency: 28,800 vph
Fine adjustment system: Etachron with index

Caliber 2894-2

Automatic; ball bearing rotor, stop-seconds, power reserve 42 hours
Functions: hours, minutes, subsidiary seconds at 3 o'clock; chronograph (30-minute counter at 9 o'clock, 12-hour counter at 6 o'clock, sweep chronograph seconds); quick-set date window at 4 o'clock
Diameter: 28.6 mm (12 1/2''')
Height: 6.1 mm
Jewels: 37
Frequency: 28,800 vph
Fine adjustment system: Etachron with index
Related caliber: 2894 S2 (skeletonized)

Caliber 7750

Automatic; ball bearing rotor, stop-seconds, power reserve 42 hours
Functions: hours, minutes, subsidiary seconds at 9 o'clock; chronograph (30-minute counter at 12 o'clock, 12-hour counter at 6 o'clock, sweep chronograph seconds); quick-set date and day window at 3 o'clock
Diameter: 30 mm (13 1/4''')
Height: 7.9 mm
Jewels: 25
Frequency: 28,800 vph
Fine adjustment system: Etachron with index
Related caliber: 7753 (tricompax arrangement of counters)

Caliber 7751 (dial side)

Based on chronograph Caliber 7750, Caliber 7751 differs in having 24-hour hand, moon phase indication, sweep date hand, and windows for day and month placed prominently below the 12. All calendar functions, including moon phase, can be quick set.

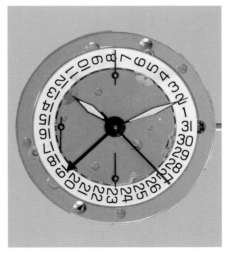

Caliber 7754 (dial side)

Automatic; ball bearing rotor, stop-seconds, power reserve 42 hours
Functions: hours, minutes, subsidiary seconds at 9 o'clock; chronograph (30-minute counter at 12 o'clock, 12-hour counter at 6 o'clock, sweep chronograph seconds); quick-set date window at 3 o'clock; settable sweep 24-hour hand (2nd time zone)
Diameter: 30 mm (13 1/4''')
Height: 7.9 mm
Jewels: 25
Frequency: 28,800 vph
Fine adjustment system: Etachron with index

Caliber 7765

Manually wound; stop-seconds, power reserve 42 hours
Functions: hours, minutes, subsidiary seconds at 9 o'clock; chronograph (30-minute counter at 12 o'clock, sweep chronograph seconds); quick-set date window at 3 o'clock; settable sweep 24-hour hand (2nd time zone)
Diameter: 30 mm (13 1/4''')
Height: 6.35 mm
Jewels: 17
Frequency: 28,800 vph
Fine adjustment system: Etachron with index
Related caliber: 7760 (with additional 12-hour counter at 6 o'clock and day window at 3)

Sellita

Sellita, founded in 1950 by Pierre Grandjean in La Chaux-de-Fonds, is one of the biggest reassemblers and embellishers in the mechanical watch industry. On average, Sellita embellishes and finishes about one million automatic and hand-wound movements annually—a figure that represents about 25 percent of Switzerland's mechanical movement production according to Miguel García, Sellita's president.

Reassembly can be defined as the assembly and regulation of components to make a functioning movement. This is the type of work that ETA loved to give to outside companies back in the day in order to concentrate on manufacturing complete quartz movements and individual components for them.

Reassembly workshops like Sellita refine and embellish components purchased from ETA according to their customers' wishes and can even successfully fulfill smaller orders made by the company's estimated 350 clients.

When ETA announced that it would only sell *ébauches* to companies outside the Swatch Group until the end of 2010, García, who has owned Sellita since 2003, reacted immediately, deciding that his company should develop its own products.

García planned and implemented a new line of movements based on the dimensions of the most popular ETA calibers, whose patents had expired. Having expanded within a new factory on the outskirts of La Chaux-de-Fonds with 3,500 square meters of space, Sellita offers a number of movements—such as SW 200, which corresponds in all of its important dimensions to ETA Caliber 2824, and Caliber SW 300, equivalent to ETA Caliber 2892.

Another expansion project began as a joint venture with Mühle Glashütte: Gurofa in Glashütte currently makes some components for Calibers SW 220 and 240.

Caliber SW 200

Mechanical lever movement with automatic winding, ball bearing rotor, stop-seconds, power reserve 38 hours

Functions: hours, minutes, sweep seconds, date window with quick-set function
Diameter: 25.6 mm (11 1/2'''); **Height:** 4.60 mm
Jewels: 26; **Frequency:** 28,800 vph
Fine adjustment system: eccentric screw
Balance: nickel-plated for standard movement, glucydur on request
Balance spring: Nivaflex II for standard movements, Nivaflex on request
Shock protection: Novodiac
Remarks: base plate and rotor with perlage

Caliber SW 220

Mechanical lever movement with automatic winding, ball bearing rotor, stop-seconds, power reserve 38 hours

Functions: hours, minutes, sweep seconds, day/date window with quick-set function
Diameter: 25.6 mm (11 1/2'''); **Height:** 5.05 mm
Jewels: 26; **Frequency:** 28,800 vph
Fine adjustment system: eccentric screw
Balance: nickel-plated for standard movement, glucydur on request
Balance spring: Nivaflex II for standard movements, Nivaflex on request
Shock protection: Novodiac
Remarks: base plate and rotor with perlage

Caliber SW 300

Mechanical lever movement with automatic winding, ball bearing rotor, stop-seconds, power reserve 42 hours

Functions: hours, minutes, sweep seconds, date window with quick-set function
Diameter: 25.6 mm (11 1/2'''); **Height:** 3.60 mm
Jewels: 25; **Frequency:** 28,800 vph
Fine adjustment system: eccentric screw
Balance: nickel-plated for standard movement, glucydur on request
Balance spring: Nivaflex II for standard movements, Nivaflex on request
Shock protection: Novodiac

Soprod

Soprod, at home in Reussilles, Switzerland, has made a name for itself in the era of the mechanical renaissance by reassembling mechanical movements from ETA *ébauches*. Now the company also manufactures interesting display and function modules that can be added to a standard ETA caliber. Power reserve displays, dial train modifications for subsidiary seconds and regulators, calendar modules, and many other variations have given numerous small watch brands the possibility of adding value to their collections with somewhat more exclusive dials, thus setting themselves apart from other manufacturers.

ETA's announcement of no longer offering individual components or *ébauche* kits for reassembly after 2010 has thus hit Soprod especially hard.

In 2005, this company was purchased by a group of Swiss investors—and so came into direct contact with SFT (quartz movements) and Indtec (micromechanics and component production) in Sion, which also belonged to the same concern and already had automatic and chronograph movements developed to the serial production stage. The Peace Mark Group, headquartered in Hong Kong, purchased all three companies in 2007 and began adding capacity, especially to the reassembly departments. At the same time, business with universally usable automatic calibers in the popular eleven-and-a-half-line format (such as ETA 2824 and 2892) is slated for expansion.

Surprisingly, at the end of 2008, the Festina Lotus Group, whose president also owns the H5 Group (Perrelet, Le Roy), formerly a minority shareholder, acquired Soprod's entire capital stock. Thus, Festina and the other companies belonging to that group have now also received a new platform base for Swiss-made mechanical watches. Soprod will continue to supply third-party brands.

 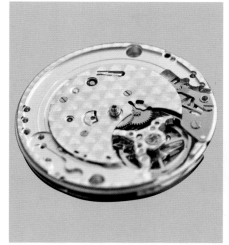 

Caliber A10

Mechanical with automatic winding, stop-seconds, regulated in 4 positions, power reserve 42 hours
Functions: hours, minutes, sweep seconds, date window with quick-set function
Diameter: 25.6 mm (11 1/2''')
Height: 3.60 mm
Jewels: 25
Frequency: 28,800 vph
Fine adjustment system: index system with pinion
Balance spring: flat hairspring
Shock protection: Incabloc
Remarks: base plate available with various fine finishings

Caliber A10 Visible Balance

Mechanical with automatic winding, stop-seconds, regulated in 4 positions, power reserve 42 hours
Functions: hours, minutes, sweep seconds
Diameter: 25.6 mm (11 1/2''')
Height: 3.60 mm
Jewels: 25
Frequency: 28,800 vph
Fine adjustment system: index system with pinion
Balance spring: flat hairspring
Shock protection: Incabloc
Remarks: cutaway in base plate to make balance visible, base plate available with various fine finishings

Caliber A10 Red Gold

Mechanical with automatic winding, stop-seconds, regulated in 4 positions, power reserve 42 hours
Functions: hours, minutes, sweep seconds, date window with quick-set function
Diameter: 25.6 mm (11 1/2''')
Height: 3.60 mm
Jewels: 25
Frequency: 28,800 vph
Fine adjustment system: index system with pinion
Balance spring: flat hairspring
Shock protection: Incabloc
Remarks: red gold, base plate available with perlage, côtes de Genève or côtes circulaire; bridges with côtes de Genève

SPEAKE-MARIN
A PASSION FOR WATCHMAKING

VELSHEDA
J-Class Collection

Single-hand time indication | Central 'topping tool' second wheel
Hand-finished automatic movement with 4-5 day power reserve
42mm Piccadilly case in stainless steel

For US retailers, visit
www.speake-marin.com

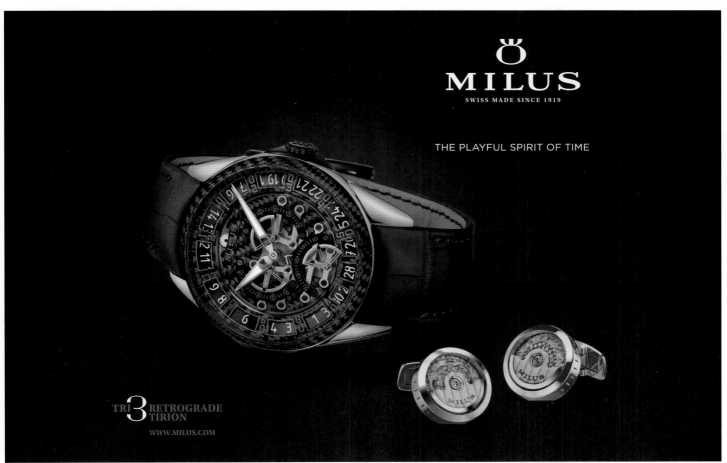

MILUS
SWISS MADE SINCE 1919

THE PLAYFUL SPIRIT OF TIME

3 TRI RETROGRADE
TIRION
WWW.MILUS.COM

MILUS INTERNATIONAL SA | CH-2502 BIEL-BIENNE | SWITZERLAND | TEL. +41 (0)32 344 39 39 | INFO@MILUS.COM

Watch Your Watch

Mechanical watches are not only by and large more expensive and complex than quartzes, they are also a little high-maintenance, as it were. The mechanism within does need servicing occasionally—perhaps a touch of oil and an adjustment. Worse yet, the complexity of all those wheels and pinions engaged in reproducing the galaxy means that a user will occasionally do something perfectly harmless like wind his or her watch up only to find everything grinding to a halt. Here are some tips for dealing with these mechanical beauties for new watch owners and reminders for the old hands.

1. DATE CHANGES

Do not change the date manually (via the crown or pusher) on any mechanical watch—whether manual wind or automatic—when the time indicated on the dial reads between 10 and 2 o'clock. Although some better watches are protected against this horological quirk, most mechanical watches with a date indicator are engaged in the process of automatically changing the date between the hours of 10 p.m. and 2 a.m. Intervening with a forced manual change while the automatic date shift is engaged can damage the movement. Of course, you can make the adjustment between 10 a.m. and 2 p.m. in most cases—but this is just not a good habit to get into. When in doubt, roll the time past 12 o'clock and look for an automatic date change before you set the time and date. The Ulysse Nardin brand is notable, among a very few others, for in-house mechanical movements immune to this effect.

2. CHRONOGRAPH USE

On a simple chronograph start and stop are almost always the same button. Normally located above the crown, the start/stop actuator can be pressed at will to initiate and end the interval timing. The reset button, normally below the crown, is only used for resetting the chronograph to zero, but only when the chronograph is stopped—never while engaged. Only a "flyback" chronograph allows safe resetting to zero while running. With the chronograph engaged, you simply hit the reset button and all the chronograph indicators (seconds, minutes, and hours) snap back to zero and the chronograph begins to accumulate the interval time once again. In the early days of air travel this was a valuable complication as pilots would reset their chronographs when taking on a new heading—without having to fumble about with a three-step procedure with gloved hands.

Nota bene: Don't actuate or reset your chronograph while your watch is submerged—even if you have one of those that are built for such usage, like Omega, IWC, and a few other brands. Feel free to hit the buttons before submersion and jump in and swim while they run; just don't push anything while in the water.

3. CHANGING TIME BACKWARD

Don't adjust the time on your watch in a counterclockwise direction—especially if the watch has calendar functions. A few watches can tolerate the abuse, but it's better to avoid the possibility of damage altogether. Change the dates as needed (remembering the 10 and 2 rule above).

4. SHOCKS

Almost all modern watches are equipped with some level of shock protection. Best practices for the Swiss brands allow for a three-foot fall onto a hard wood surface. But if your watch is running poorly—or even worse has stopped entirely after an impact—do not shake, wind, or bang it again to get it running; take it to an expert for service as you may do even more damage. Sports like tennis, squash, or golf can have a deleterious effect on your watch, including flattening the pivots, overbanking, or even bending or breaking a pivot.

5. OVERWINDING

Most modern watches are fitted with a mechanism that allows the mainspring to slide inside the barrel—or stops it completely once the spring is fully wound—for protection against overwinding. The best advice here is just don't force it. Over the years a winding crown may start to get "stickier" and more difficult to turn even when unwound. That's a sure sign it is due for service.

6. JACUZZI TEMPERATURE

Don't jump into the Jacuzzi—or even a steaming hot shower—with your watch on. Better-built watches with a deeper water-resistance rating typically have no problem with this scenario. However, take a 3 or 5 atm water-resistant watch into the Jacuzzi, and there's a chance the different rates of expansion and contraction of the metals and sapphire or mineral crystals may allow moisture into the case.

Bovet's barrier to pressing the wrong pusher.

Panerai makes sure you think before touching the crown.

Do it yourself at your own risk.

7. SCREW THAT CROWN DOWN (AND THOSE PUSHERS)!

Always check and double-check to ensure a watch fitted with a screwed-down crown is closed tightly. Screwed-down pushers for a chronograph—or any other functions—deserve the same attention. This one oversight has cost quite a few owners their watches. If a screwed-down crown is not secured, water will likely get into the case and start oxidizing the metal. In time, the problem can destroy the watch.

8. MAGNETISM

If your watch is acting up, running faster or slower, it may have become magnetized. This can happen if you leave your timepiece near a computer, cell phone, or some other electronic device. Many service points have a so-called degausser to take care of the problem. A number of brands also make watches with a soft iron core to deflect magnetic fields, though this might not work with the stronger ones.

9. TRIBOLOGY

Keeping a mechanical timepiece hidden away in a box for extended lengths of time is not the best way to care for it. Even if you don't wear a watch every day, it is a good idea to run your watch at regular intervals to keep its lubricating oils and greases viscous. Think about a can of house paint: Keep it stirred and it stays liquid almost indefinitely; leave it still for too long and a skin develops. On a smaller level the same thing can happen to the lubricants inside a mechanical watch.

10. SERVICE

Most mechanical watches call for a three- to five-year service cycle for cleaning, oiling, and maintenance. Some mechanical watches can run twice that long and have functioned within acceptable parameters, but if you're not going to have your watch serviced at regular intervals, you do take the chance of having timing issues. Always have your watch serviced by qualified watchmaker (see box), not at the kiosk in the local mall. The best you can expect there is a quick battery change.

Gary Girdvainis is the founder of Isochron Media Llc., publishers of WristWatch *and* AboutTime *magazines*

Glossary

ANNUAL CALENDAR

The automatic allowances for the different lengths of each month of a year in the calendar module of a watch. This type of watch usually shows the month and date, and sometimes the day of the week (like this one by Patek Philippe) and the phases of the moon.

ANTIMAGNETIC

Magnetic fields found in common everyday places affect mechanical movements, hence the use of anti- or non-magnetic components in the movement. Some companies encase movements in antimagnetic cores such as Sinn's Model 756, the Duograph, shown here.

ANTIREFLECTION

A film created by steaming the crystal to eliminate light reflection and improve legibility. Antireflection functions best when applied to both sides of the crystal, but because it scratches, some manufacturers prefer to have it only on the interior of the crystal. It is mainly used on synthetic sapphire crystals. Dubey & Schaldenbrand applies antireflection on both sides for all of the company's wristwatches such as this Aquadyn model.

AUTOMATIC WINDING

A rotating weight set into motion by moving the wrist winds the spring barrel via the gear train of a mechanical watch movement. Automatic winding was invented during the pocket watch era in 1770, but the breakthrough automatic winding movement via rotor began with the ball bearing Eterna-Matic in the late 1940s. Today we speak of unidirectional winding and bidirectionally winding rotors, depending on the type of gear train used. Shown is IWC's automatic Caliber 50611.

BALANCE

The beating heart of a mechanical watch movement is the balance. Fed by the energy of the mainspring, a tirelessly oscillating little wheel, just a few millimeters in diameter and possessing a spiral-shaped balance spring, sets the rhythm for the escape wheel and pallets with its vibration frequency. Today the balance is usually made of one piece of antimagnetic glucydur, an alloy that expands very little when exposed to heat.

BAR OR COCK

A metal plate fastened to the base plate at one point, leaving room for a gear wheel or pinion. The balance is usually attached to a bar called the balance cock. Glashütte tradition dictates that the balance cock be decoratively engraved by hand like this one by Glashütte Original.

BEVELING

To uniformly file down the sharp edges of a plate, bridge, or bar and give it a high polish. The process is also called *anglage*. Edges are usually beveled at a 45° angle. As the picture shows, this is painstaking work that needs the skilled hands and eyes of an experienced watchmaker or *angleur*.

BRIDGE

A metal plate fastened to the base plate at two points leaving room for a gear wheel or pinion. This vintage Favre-Leuba movement illustrates the point with three individual bridges.

CARBON FIBER

A very light, tough composite material, carbon fiber is composed of filaments comprised of several thousand seven-micron carbon fibers held together by resin. The arrangement of the filaments determines the quality of a component, making each unique. Carbon fiber is currently being used for dials, cases, and even movement components.

CALIBER

A term, similar to type or model, that refers to different watch movements. Pictured here is Heuer's Caliber 11, the legendary automatic chronograph caliber from 1969. This movement was a coproduction jointly researched and developed for four years by Heuer-Leonidas, Breitling, and Hamilton-Büren. Each company gave the movement a different name after serial production began.

CHAMPLEVÉ

A dial decoration technique, whereby the metal is engraved, filled with enamel, and baked as in this cockatoo on a Cartier Tortue, enhanced with mother-of-pearl slivers.

CERAMIC

An inorganic, nonmetallic material formed by the action of heat and practically unscratchable. Pioneered by Rado, ceramic is a high-tech material generally made from aluminum and zirconia oxide. Today, it is used generally for cases and bezels and now comes in many colors.

CHRONOGRAPH

From the Greek *chronos* (time) and *graphein* (to write). Originally a chronograph literally wrote, inscribing the time elapsed on a piece of paper with the help of a pencil attached kind of hand. Today this term is used for watches that show not only the time of day, but also certain time intervals via independent hands that may be started or stopped at will. Stopwatches differ from chronographs because they do not show the time of day. This exploded illustration shows the complexity of a Breitling chronograph.

CHRONOMETER

Literally, "measurer of time." As the term is used today, a chronometer denotes an especially accurate watch (one with a deviation of no more than 5 seconds a day for mechanical movements). Chronometers are usually supplied with an official certificate from an independent testing office such as the COSC. The largest producer of chronometers in 2008 was Rolex with 769,850 officially certified movements. Chopard came in sixth with more than 22,000 certified L.U.C mechanisms like the 4.96 in the Pro One model shown here.

COLUMN WHEEL

The component used to control chronograph functions within a true chronograph movement. The presence of a column wheel indicates that the chronograph is fully integrated into the movement. In the modern era, modules are generally used that are attached to a base caliber movement. This particular column wheel is made of blued steel.

CONSTANT FORCE MECHANISM

Sometimes called a constant force escapement, it isn't really: in most cases this mechanism is "simply" an initial tension spring. It is also known in English by part of its French name, the *remontoir*, which actually means "winding mechanism." This mechanism regulates and portions the energy that is passed on through the escapement, making the rate as even and precise as possible. Shown here is the constant force escapement from A. Lange & Söhne's Lange 31—a mechanism that gets as close to its name as possible.

COSC

The Contrôle Officiel Suisse de Chronomètrage, the official Swiss testing office for chronometers. The COSC is the world's largest issuer of so-called chronometer certificates, which are only otherwise given out individually by certain observatories (such as the one in Neuchâtel, Switzerland). For a fee, the COSC tests the rate of movements that have been adjusted by watchmakers. These are usually mechanical movements, but the office also tests some high-precision quartz movements. Those that meet the specifications for being a chronometer are awarded an official certificate as shown here.

CÔTES DE GENÈVE

Also called *vagues de Genève* and Geneva stripes. This is a traditional Swiss surface decoration comprising an even pattern of parallel stripes, applied to flat movement components with a quickly rotating plastic or wooden peg. Glashütte watchmakers have devised their own version of *côtes de Genève* that is applied at a slightly different angle called Glashütte ribbing.

CROWN

The crown is used to wind and set a watch. A few simple turns of the crown will get an automatic movement started, while a manually wound watch is completely wound by the crown. The crown is also used for the setting of various functions, almost always including at least the hours, minutes, seconds, and date. A screwed-down crown like the one on the TAG Heuer Aquagraph pictured here can be tightened to prevent water entering the case or any mishaps while performing extreme sports such as diving.

EQUATION OF TIME

The mean time that we use to keep track of the passing of the day (24 hours evenly divided into minutes and seconds) is not equal to true solar time. The equation of time is a complication devised to show the difference between the mean time shown on one's wristwatch and the time the sun dictates. The Équation Marchante by Blancpain very legibly indicates this difference via the golden sun-tipped hand that also rotates around the dial in a manner known to watch connoisseurs as *marchant*. Other wristwatch models such as the Boreas by Martin Braun display the difference on an extra scale on the dial.

ESCAPEMENT

The combination of the balance, balance spring, pallets, and escape wheel, a subgroup which divides the impulses coming from the spring barrel into small, accurately portioned doses. It guarantees that the gear train runs smoothly and efficiently. The pictured escapement is one newly invented by Parmigiani containing pallet stones of varying color, though they are generally red synthetic rubies. Here one of them is a colorless sapphire or corundum, the same geological material that ruby is made of.

FLINQUÉ

A dial decoration in which a guilloché design is given a coat of enamel, softening the pattern and creating special effects, as shown here on a unique Bovet.

GEAR TRAIN

A mechanical watch's gear train transmits energy from the mainspring to the escapement. The gear train comprises the minute wheel, the third wheel, the fourth wheel, and the escape wheel.

GLUCYDUR

Glucydur is a functional alloy of copper, beryllium, and iron that has been used to make balances in watches since the 1930s. Its hardness and stability allow watchmakers to use balances that were poised at the factory and no longer required adjustment screws.

INDEX

A regulating mechanism found on the balance cock and used by the watchmaker to adjust the movement's rate. The index changes the effective length of the balance spring, thus making it move more quickly or slowly. This is the standard index found on an ETA Valjoux 7750.

JEWEL

To minimize friction, the hardened steel tips of a movement's rotating gear wheels (called pinions) are lodged in synthetic rubies (fashioned as polished stones with a hole) and lubricated with a very thin layer of special oil. These synthetic rubies are produced in exactly the same way as sapphire crystal using the same material. During the pocket watch era, real rubies with hand-drilled holes were still used, but because of the high costs involved, they were only used in movements with especially quickly rotating gears. The jewel shown here on a bridge from A. Lange & Söhne's Double Split is additionally embedded in a gold chaton secured with three blued screws.

FLYBACK CHRONOGRAPH

A chronograph with a special dial train switch that makes the immediate reuse of the chronograph movement possible after resetting the hands. It was developed for special timekeeping duties such as those found in aviation, which require the measurement of time intervals in quick succession. A flyback may also be called a *retour en vol*. An elegant example of this type of chronograph is Corum's Classical Flyback Large Date shown here.

GUILLOCHÉ

A surface decoration usually applied to the dial and the rotor using a grooving tool with a sharp tip, such as a rose engine, to cut an even pattern onto a level surface. The exact adjustment of the tool for each new path is controlled by a device similar to a pantograph, and the movement of the tool can be controlled either manually or mechanically. Real *guillochis* (the correct term used by a master of guilloché) are very intricate and expensive to produce, which is why most dials decorated in this fashion are produced by stamping machines. Breguet is one of the very few companies to use real guilloché on every one of its dials.

LIGA

The word LIGA is actually a German acronym that stands for lithography (*Lithografie*), electroplating (*Galvanisierung*), and plastic molding (*Abformung*). It is a lithographic process exposed by UV or X-ray light that literally "grows" perfect micro components made of nickel, nickel-phosphorus, or 23.5-karat gold atom by atom in a plating bath. The components need no finishing or trimming after manufacture.

LUMINOUS SUBSTANCE

Tritium paint is a slightly radioactive substance that replaced radium as luminous coating for hands, numerals, and hour markers on watch dials. Watches bearing tritium must be marked as such, with the letter T on the dial near 6 o'clock. It has now for the most part been replaced by nonradioactive materials such as Superluminova. Traser technology (as seen on these Ball timepieces) uses tritium gas enclosed in tiny silicate glass tubes coated on the inside with a phosphorescing substance. The luminescence is constant and will hold around twenty-five years.

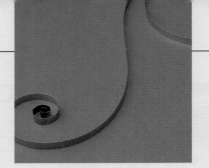

MAINSPRING

The mainspring, located in the spring barrel, stores energy when tensioned and passes it on to the escapement via the gear train as the tension relaxes. Today, mainsprings are generally made of Nivaflex, an alloy invented by Swiss engineer Max Straumann at the beginning of the 1950s. This alloy basically comprises iron, nickel, chrome, cobalt, and beryllium.

MINUTE REPEATER

A striking mechanism with hammers and gongs for acoustically signaling the hours, quarter hours, and minutes elapsed since noon or midnight. The wearer pushes a slide, which winds the spring. Normally a repeater uses two different gongs to signal hours (low tone), quarter hours (high and low tones in succession), and minutes (high tone). Some watches have three gongs, called a carillon. The Chronoswiss Répétition à Quarts is a prominent repeating introduction of recent years.

PERPETUAL CALENDAR

The calendar module for this type of timepiece automatically makes allowances for the different lengths of each month as well as leap years until the next secular year, which will occur in 2100. A perpetual calendar usually shows the date, month, and four-year cycle, and may show the day of the week and moon phase as well, as does this one introduced by George J von Burg at Baselworld 2005. Perpetual calendars need much skill to complete.

PERLAGE

Surface decoration comprising an even pattern of partially overlapping dots, applied with a quickly rotating plastic or wooden peg. (Here on the plates of Frédérique Constant's *manufacture* Caliber FC 910-1.)

PLATE

A metal platform having several tiers for the gear train. The base plate of a movement usually incorporates the dial and carries the bearings for the primary pinions of the "first floor" of a gear train. The gear wheels are made complete by tightly fitting screwed-in bridges and bars on the back side of the plate. A specialty of the so-called Glashütte school, as opposed to the Swiss school, is the reverse completion of a movement not via different bridges and bars, but rather with a three-quarter plate. Glashütte Original's Caliber 65 (shown) displays a beautifully decorated three-quarter plate.

POWER RESERVE DISPLAY

A mechanical watch contains only a certain amount of power reserve. A fully wound modern automatic watch usually possesses between 36 and 42 hours of energy before it needs to be wound again. The power reserve display keeps the wearer informed about how much energy his or her watch still has in reserve, a function that is especially practical on manually wound watches with several days of possible reserve. The Nomos Tangente Power Reserve pictured here represents an especially creative way to illustrate the state of the mainspring's tension. On some German watches the power reserve is also displayed with the words "auf" and "ab."

QUALITÉ FLEURIER

This certification of quality was established by Chopard, Parmigiani Fleurier, Vaucher, and Bovet Fleurier in 2004. Watches bearing the seal must fulfill five criteria, including COSC certification, passing several tests for robustness and precision, top-notch finishing, and being 100 percent Swiss made (except for the raw materials). The seal appears here on the dial of the Parmigiani Fleurier Tonda 39.

SAPPHIRE CRYSTAL

Synthetic sapphire crystal is known to gemologists as aluminum oxide (Al_2O_3) or corundum. It can be colorless (corundum), red (ruby), blue (sapphire), or green (emerald). It is virtually scratchproof; only a diamond is harder. The innovative Royal Blue Tourbillon by Ulysse Nardin pictured here not only features sapphire crystals on the front and back of the watch, but also actual plates made of both colorless and blue corundum within the movement.

PULSOMETER

A scale on the dial, flange, or bezel that, in conjunction with the second hand, may be used to measure a pulse rate. A pulsometer is always marked with a reference number—if it is marked with *gradué pour 15 pulsations*, for example, then the wearer counts fifteen pulse beats. At the last beat, the second hand will show what the pulse rate is in beats per minute on the pulsometer scale. The scale on Sinn's World Time Chronograph (shown) is marked simply with the German world *Puls* ("pulse"), but the function remains the same.

RETROGRADE DISPLAY

A retrograde display shows the time linearly instead of circularly. The hand continues along an arc until it reaches the end of its scale, at which precise moment it jumps back to the beginning instantaneously. This Nienaber model not only shows the minutes in retrograde form, it is also a regulator display.

ROTOR

The rotor is the component that keeps an automatic watch wound. The kinetic motion of this part, which contains a heavy metal weight around its outer edge, winds the mainspring. It can either wind unilaterally or bilaterally (to one or both sides) depending on the caliber. The rotor from this Temption timepiece belongs to an ETA Valjoux 7750.

SCREW BALANCE

Before the invention of the perfectly weighted balance using a smooth ring, balances were fitted with weighted screws to get the exact impetus desired. Today a screw balance is a subtle sign of quality in a movement due to its costly construction and assembly utilizing minuscule weighted screws.

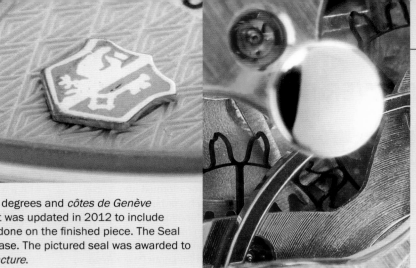

SEAL OF GENEVA

Since 1886 the official seal of this canton has been awarded to Genevan watch *manufactures* who must follow a defined set of high-quality criteria that include the following: polished jewel bed drillings, jewels with olive drillings, polished winding wheels, quality balances and balance springs, steel levers and springs with beveling of 45 degrees and *côtes de Genève* decoration, and polished stems and pinions. The list was updated in 2012 to include the entire watch and newer components. Testing is done on the finished piece. The Seal consists of two, one on the movement, one on the case. The pictured seal was awarded to Vacheron Constantin, a traditional Genevan *manufacture*.

SILICIUM/SILICON

Silicon is an element relatively new to mechanical watches. It is currently being used in the manufacture of precision escapements. Ulysse Nardin's Freak has lubrication-free silicon wheels, and Breguet has successfully used flat silicon balance springs.

SKELETONIZATION

The technique of cutting a movement's components down to their weight-bearing basic substance. This is generally done by hand in painstaking hours of microscopic work with a mini handheld saw, though machines can skeletonize parts to a certain degree, such as the version of the Valjoux 7750 that was created for Chronoswiss's Opus and Pathos models. This tourbillon created by Christophe Schaffo is additionally—and masterfully—hand-engraved.

SONNERIE

A variety of minute repeater that—like a tower clock—sounds the time not at the will of the wearer, but rather automatically (*en passant*) every hour (*petite sonnerie*) or quarter hour (*grande sonnerie*). Gérald Genta designed the most complicated sonnerie back in the early nineties. Shown is a recent model from the front and back.

SPLIT-SECONDS CHRONOGRAPH

Also known in the watch industry by its French name, the *rattrapante* (exploded view at left). A watch with two second hands, one of which can be blocked with a special dial train lever to indicate an intermediate time while the other continues to run. When released, the split-seconds hand jumps ahead to the position of the other second hand. The PTC by Porsche Design illustrates this nicely.

SPRING BARREL

The spring barrel contains the mainspring. It turns freely on an arbor, pulled along by the toothed wheel generally doubling as its lid. This wheel interacts with the first pinion of the movement's gear train. Some movements contain two or more spring barrels for added power reserve.

SWAN-NECK FINE ADJUSTMENT

A regulating instrument used by the watchmaker to adjust the movement's rate in place of an index. The swan neck is especially prevalent in fine Swiss and Glashütte watchmaking (here Lang & Heyne's Moritz model). Mühle Glashütte has varied the theme with its woodpecker's neck.

TACHYMETER

A scale on the dial, flange, or bezel of a chronograph that, in conjunction with the second hand, gives the speed of a moving object. A tachymeter takes a value determined in less than a minute and converts it into miles or kilometers per hour. For example, a wearer could measure the time it takes a car to pass between two mile markers on the highway. When the car passes the marker, the second hand will be pointing to the car's speed in miles per hour on the tachymetric scale.

TOURBILLON

A technical device invented by Abraham-Louis Breguet in 1801 to compensate for the influence of gravity on the balance of a pocket watch. The entire escapement is mounted on an epicyclic train in a "cage" and rotated completely on its axis over regular periods of time. This superb horological highlight is seen as a sign of technological know-how in the modern era. Harry Winston's Histoire de Tourbillon 4 is a spectacular example.

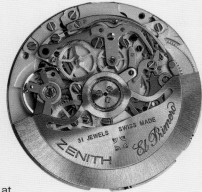

VIBRATION FREQUENCY (VPH)

The spring causes the balance to oscillate at a certain frequency measured in hertz (Hz) or vibrations per hour (vph). Most of today's wristwatches tick at 28,800 vph (4 Hz) or 21,600 vph (3 Hz). Less usual is 18,000 vph (2.5 Hz). Zenith's El Primero was the first serial movement to beat at 36,000 vph (5 Hz), and the Breguet Type XXII runs at 72,000 vph.

WATER RESISTANCE

Water resistance is an important feature of any timepiece and is usually measured in increments of one atmosphere (atm or bar, equal to 10 meters of water pressure) or meters and is often noted on the dial or case back. Watches resistant to 100 meters are best for swimming and snorkeling. Timepieces resistant to 200 meters are good for scuba diving. To deep-sea dive there are various professional timepieces available for use in depths of 200 meters or more. The Hydromax by Bell & Ross (shown) is water-resistant to a record 11,000 meters.

Copyright © 2015 HEEL Verlag GmbH, Königswinter, Germany

English-language translation copyright © 2015 Abbeville Press,
116 West 23rd Street, New York, NY 10011

Editor-in-chief: Peter Braun
Editor: Marton Radkai
Copy editor: Ashley Benning
Layout: Muser Medien GmbH
Composition: Kat Ran Press

For more information about advertising, please contact:
Gary Girdvainis
Isochron Media, LLC
25 Gay Bower Road, Monroe, CT 06468
203-485-6276, garygeorge@gmail.com

For more information about book sales, please contact:
Abbeville Press, 116 West 23rd Street, New York, NY 10011 or call 1-800-ARTBOOK.

ISBN 978-0-7892-1236-8

Eighteenth edition
10 9 8 7 6 5 4 3 2 1

Library of Congress Cataloging-in-Publication Data available upon request.

For bulk and premium sales and for text adoption procedures, write to Customer Service Manager,
Abbeville Press, 116 West 23rd Street, New York, NY 10011, or call 1-800-Artbook.

Visit Abbeville Press online at www.abbeville.com.

ISBN 978-0-7892-1236-8 U.S. $37.50

EAN

9 780789 212368   53750